# S DETROIT

## FROM JAZZ TO HIP-HOP AND BEYOND

Edited by M. L. Liebler
with a Foreword by Dave Marsh

A Painted Turtle book
Detroit, Michigan

© 2016 by Wayne State University Press, Detroit,
Michigan 48201. All rights reserved.
No part of this book may be reproduced
without formal permission.
Manufactured in the United States of America.

20  19  18  17  16        5  4  3  2  1

ISBN 978-0-8143-4122-3 (paperback)
ISBN 978-0-8143-4123-0 (ebook)

Library of Congress Cataloging Number:
2016940283

Designed and Typeset by Bryce Schimanski
Composed in Adobe Caslon Pro

Wayne State University Press
Leonard N. Simons Building
4809 Woodward Avenue
Detroit, Michigan 48201-1309

Visit us online at wsupress.wayne.edu

For Steve King and Joel Martin
who opened the door and invited me in

*and*

for Eddie Baranek
who carries the flame of music in Detroit forward

# CONTENTS

# CONTENTS

# FOREWORD

# Makin' Thunder

We were young and proud

We were makin' Thunderbirds

—Bob Seger

The ores came from West Virginia, Bolivia, Asia. The rubber from Africa, then Akron. The men who made the steel and aluminum were from Eastern Europe, China, Mexico, Tennessee, and Alabama, not to mention most of the places in between. Sometimes, the fathers of the men who assembled the finished parts were men whose own fathers (or grandfathers, or both) had done the same. Sometimes they were newly arrived from Lebanon, Oklahoma, Latvia, or Louisiana. Sometimes their families had come many generations past from Scotland or the west coast of Africa or Central America. Ships, trains, and trucks moved the raw materials, down from Lake Superior or across the Atlantic or up through Kentucky and Indiana, where many of the men who manned those vessels had their origins. Men from Canada and the Michigan thumb, Georgia, Greece, South Carolina, Traverse City, operated the trucks that took the finished cars all over the United States and, ultimately, all over the world. A significant number of "the men," which is how everyone referred to the workers, were women.

They were the richest working people in the history of the world, if they didn't get laid off or replaced by machinery, fall into the foundry furnace, punch a foreman, show up drunk (well, drunk enough), or have their fingers smashed or their legs broken by the machines or the line that crawled by, never quite slowly enough. They had, most of the time, not a damned

thing in common. But most of them shared a pride in the cars they produced, a love of how they looked and their speed, not to mention their sex appeal. Some grew so besotted that they went home and tinkered with their own vehicles, creating a whole culture of cruising cars. This hobby allowed them to pay the close attention to detail—from the motors to the paint—that the line prevented them from exercising, no matter how slowly it sped by. Even those who prayed every night that their kids would never have to work in a place "so loud it really hurt," as Bob Seger sang in "Makin' Thunderbirds," sometimes shared in this attitude. They were proud that autoworkers could come up with designs more beautiful, and far faster, than those of the company's big shots.

Detroit music shares a lot with the auto world. (Not that anyone who's made it in this scene was only in it for a paycheck.) The music comes with all sorts of personalities—and when I say "all sorts," I don't mean many or more than a few; I mean every one of them (that I know anything about) is neither a leader nor a follower. What's come out of the Motor City, on stage and on record, is nothing like the immediately recognizable musical signatures of New Orleans, Nashville, Memphis, or even Austin, or in certain periods Kansas City, San Francisco, and Hollywood. Detroit has an attitude, but it's not necessarily, as some have claimed, that the music is particularly aggressive (although the aggressive music is *truly* aggressive); or oriented to madmen; or even that most of those who've made their mark were working class, except in the very broadest sense. Even then, Berry Gordy's family members were very successful strivers, and Aretha Franklin's father was the best-known preacher in town, even to white people. But Stevie Wonder's talent was first discovered on the doorstep of a housing project, Eminem's mother was straight out of Eight Mile (the street if not the movie), and I could give you two dozen other examples, none of them obscure. It isn't where you come from, not here. It's where you wind up.

I have thought and written about this subject—Detroit music as a generality—for going on fifty years, and I still cannot find the place where Iggy Pop's scabrous screams unite with the cool elegance of Tommy Flanagan's jazz piano. Nor where Levi Stubbs's psychodrama on "Bernadette" intersects in any musical (or perhaps diagnostic) sense with Del Shannon's psychodrama on "Stranger in Town." I can explain the blackness of Mitch Ryder's soul-rock singing and the whiteness of the Funkadelic's funk-rock, insofar as illusions can be explained, but not what Bootsy Collins and Anita Baker share that is somehow distinctively Detroit. I can hear it, sure enough, but not articulate it in a way that might make sense to someone who never lived in Michigan's southern peninsula (from which, don't forget, Toledo was long ago stolen). And for that matter, I can't explain how any of this could have, even in its most mischievous prankster mode (that is, Insane Clown Posse), led to the national disgrace of Ted Nugent. But then I cannot exactly explain how it led to the never-simple glory of Aretha Franklin or even the contrasting greatness of Bob Seger, Marvin Gaye, and Marcus Belgrave. (Don't tell *me* that ain't a balanced equation, though.) I can comprehend Elvin Jones, Johnny Bee, Benny Benjamin, Pistol Allen, and Uriel Jones as stylists, but it's hard enough to tie together the three Motown drummers (which is why

there *were* three), let alone incorporate them all in an overarching thesis.

I know why Alice Cooper came and, pretty much, why Berry Gordy left about the same time. I do not think that this (or much of anything else except maybe 4/4 time) unites "Only Women Bleed" and "Lonely Teardrops." I can hear it, and probably you can, too. I could feel it in every foot of film in Eminem's *Eight Mile* and Paul Justman's *Standing in the Shadows of Motown*, just like I know it anew every time I play Nolan Strong and the Diablos' perfect doo-wop "The Wind" for a near stranger or whip out "Raw Power," "Devil with a Blue Dress," "Leaving Here," "Kick Out the Jams," "Toy Soldiers," and "Back and Forth" to explain the *real* history of rock 'n' roll.

The puzzle of my lifetime is a riddle: What the hell do John Lee Hooker, the MC5, Twinkie Clark, Gino Washington, Juan Atkins, Aaliyah, James Carter, Kid Rock, Bob Seeley, and the Romantics have in common?

All I really know is that the answer's not nothing.

If I were the only one who thought so, I'd surrender my James Jamerson fan club membership card. But I've talked about it with Smokey Robinson and Mitch Ryder, Stew Francke, Rob Tyner, Duke Fakir, Juan Atkins, and the Electrifying Mojo. They know—and not because everybody wrapped up in this thing dreamed the same dream, followed the same star, or even likes the same records.

In the passionate genealogy of Scott Morgan's "Detroit," which perfectly represents our singularity in community, there is a truth. (The song includes such immortal lines as "Jeep Holland, Holland Dozier Holland," "Tony Clark, Question Mark," and, my favorite, "Jimmy Ruffin and the Stooges," an act I'd like to see if not hear.) That truth boils down to one thing: to understand it all, you have to hear as much of it as you can fit into your ears, and once you do know, you don't need to *say* it. You need to do it.

Detroit audiences possess a notoriously ferocious avidity. They will rush the stage, with or without invitation, but only if what they're hearing is great. The first night the J. Geils Band played for us, at the Eastown Theatre, the house was less than half full, most of it congregated at the very rear of the room. It couldn't have taken sixteen bars to move every last one of us to the front, all the way up, kids (were we kids then?) leaning on the lip of the stage, never leaving until about fifteen years later when the band broke up. Half a century earlier, McKinney's Cotton Pickers, the first great jazz big band that didn't include Louis Armstrong (Don Redman, Todd Rhodes, Benny Carter, Doc Cheatham, James P. Johnson, and Rex Stewart), established a residency at the Greystone Ballroom on Woodward and stayed because the crowds got it and came back and, I believe, *fed* back their energy. I believe it because I've seen similar things happen for the MC5, the Faces, Procol Harum, Al Green, and too many more to count. Jazz and gospel audiences had similar reputations. You would not have wanted to receive the opposite response, which really did boil down to "kick out the jams or get off the stage," with no wimpy "brothers and sisters," either.

I have always believed (and it was the essence of *Creem* magazine in its early days that everybody bought into at least partway) that musicians came and stayed because we were a city imbued with rock 'n' roll because it was our only way to spit in the eye of those who abused it, at work or school or anywhere. (You better believe that this was, implicitly and explicitly, an attack on racism. That's why John Lee Hooker sings like he has a sharp blade between his

fingers, not just a pick. It's what made David Ruffin and Iggy Pop dangerous, to themselves and others. Anyone who thinks that rock was, even for the span of one bad 45 RPM record, "white" does not understand thing one about Detroit aesthetics.)

If I live to be ninety-nine and a half (this far in and I haven't mentioned *Wilson Pickett*?), I will go out still believing in that interaction between artist and audience, which amounts to a sudden leveling that can take your breath away or make it feel like the first time you ever drew a deep breath. From Pete Cavanaugh's Sherwood Forest club, just south of Flint, to the 3.2 beer joints just over the border in Toledo to the Motortown Revue at the Fox, Detroit rock 'n' roll represented a place large enough that *MOJO* calling it "the Metro" seemed not like an exaggeration but one step toward solving the riddle.

I have not lived in Detroit for a very, very long time except attitudinally. I owe a very large part of my very existence to Detroit music, which taught me in an instant that racism was a lie, that the truth was hard to dig out, that every betrayal could lead to an inspiration, and much more than can be summarized on a page. *You have to do it.*

But don't trace the tracks of *my* tears. We have all been very fortunate to be inspired, in the numberless idiosyncratic ways that bind us, by music at all, and this particular defiant, hard-edged, broken-hearted, passionately loving, uncompromising-to-a-fault form of it in all its guises. If we are both lucky and smart, we still are. The secret ingredients—which, for the good of the world, shouldn't stay a secret— occupy the rest of this book. It's an honor and a pleasure, and a risk and a pledge, to be here.

*Dave Marsh*

xiii

# INTRODUCTION

"Heaven was Detroit!" This a line from a faux letter sent to Detroit music journalist Dave Marsh from the legendary rock writer Lester Bangs in 1986. The slight problem was that Bangs had passed away four years earlier, so who actually wrote the letter is something of a mystery. Lester Bangs was one of the best-known and most iconic American rock writers of his generation (as portrayed in the film *Almost Famous*), and he cut his teeth right here in Detroit writing for *Creem* magazine. Bangs's letter to Marsh arrived from heaven on Lester's own "cloud stationery," and I swear it's true. I saw it for myself on the Internets.

In that infamous 1986 letter, "Lester" wrote, "You know that jive about 'if there's a rock 'n' roll heaven, they must have a hell of a band up there'?" Bangs went on to say, "It's a nightmare. The only musicians [here] in heaven are Jim Croce, Karen Carpenter, Cass Elliot, and Bobby Bloom singing 'Montego Bay' over and over." Bangs concludes his heaven-sent letter by writing, "Take it from me Dave. *Heaven was Detroit*, Michigan. Who woulda thunk it?"

"Heaven was Detroit." Is it really possible that a single place like the Motor City, a working-class, blue-collar, industrial-turned-postindustrial city, could have created such original, divine, unique American music for more than one hundred years from jazz to hip-hop and everything in between? Well, believe it! Detroit has done, and continues to do, just that.

In early twentieth-century Detroit, the sounds of American jazz first crept up Woodward out of Paradise Valley and up Hastings Street in Black Bottom where the great John Lee Hooker, fresh off a double shift on the line, and others played and recorded at Joe Von Battle's Record Store and Studio. The world was being given a cultural gift unmatched by any other city anywhere. These sounds of early Detroit would eventually move a little farther north to Fortune Records on Linwood and then over to Hitsville U.S.A. on West Grand Boulevard, in the shadows of the General Motors Building. It was at this location where an old house and a converted garage gave rise to the combination of blues and R&B that produced "the sound of young America." Berry Gordy took what was once called "race music" and played only on African American stations, and he reimagined it as a new innovative music, thus creating the Motown sound. This new style of soul music became the sound track to the civil rights movement and the Vietnam War and, in general, it attempted to answer the question "What's going on?" Gordy's vision boldly claimed this new style of music would bring all people together, and Hitsville U.S.A. did just that then, and it still does to this day.

However, it is also important to note that before Hitsville, the embryo of what came to be known as "soul music" (the Brits call it "Northern Soul") was formed in a run-down building located first at 11629 Linwood featuring a dirt-floor studio and a couple of microphones. (The company later moved to the Wayne State campus on Third Street.) As S. R. Boland points out in his essay here, Fortune Records had a raw, tough R&B sound with singers like

Andre Williams, Nathaniel Mayer, and the Falcons, all backed by a band led by the great Joe Weaver.

I think the role our city has played in creating the Detroit sound is based on the fact that the Motor City has always been a hard town to prosper and make it in. Everything here in the twentieth century depended upon industry, and especially the auto industry. The car business has always produced a feast-or-famine type of mentality. In this type of environment, what is here today will not likely be there tomorrow, and so forth. This helps artists to develop a certain type of art that can continually reinvent and reimagine itself. It is about survival on these mean streets. In this type of world, you have people with an attitude Eminem describes in his famous song from the film *8 Mile* titled "Lose Yourself":

> Look,
>
> If you had
>
> One shot
>
> Or one opportunity
>
> To seize everything you ever
>
> wanted
>
> In one moment
>
> Would you capture it
>
> Or just let it slip?

The innovating artists (of all types) in Detroit are those who "capture it" and do not "just let it slip" away. This attitude keeps Detroit musicians, song-writers, poets, and artists searching for the unique, the new, the original, and the different, which eventually becomes the new standard, and then we move on to another new concept or idea.

As the reader will see in this collection of essays, Detroit music is constantly changing, shifting, and reinventing itself. Just look at the genres touched upon in the table of contents: jazz, blues, R&B, soul, rock, Latin, folk, country, techno, experimental, alternative, and hip-hop. There are many artists here who combine many of these diverse styles into their own music.

So, Lester Bangs famously, allegedly wrote "Heaven was Detroit!" and lovers of Detroit music will certainly understand his point! Even if he didn't really say it, we think it. The depth and range of great popular music that has come out of our city for so many decades is staggering and, maybe just a little, unbelievable. One could speculate for a lifetime about how and why this has happened here in this alleged postindustrial wasteland. But really, the Motor City is the best incubator for the new. This is a place that struggles daily with unemployment, racism, a weak-to-nonexistent transportation system, crime, a flawed educational system. It's a slowly disappearing city with broken neighborhoods full of burnt-out streetlights, high weeds in way too many vacant lots, abandoned half-burned houses, and more. Still, the music, art, and poetry of Detroit rise like the mythical phoenix, and the city keeps on keepin' on, reinventing, reimagining, and reshaping all our tomorrows. Our history and the scars of our healing wounds show this world what the spirit of Detroit is really made of. We have been tested, and we continue to survive and create.

So, why did it happen here? That answer can be studied, but it really can be *felt*: between the jazz of Pepper Adams and Faruq Z. Bey, between the soul of Nathaniel Mayer and the Supremes, between the rock and wisdom of the MC5 and Rodriguez, between the beat of the York Brothers and Kid Rock, between the bass bottom of the Belleville Three and the poetry of Eminem, between the craftsmanship of Jack White and the Insane Clown Posse, and on and on it goes. What's next? For every artist written about in this collection, there are hundreds more that haven't yet moved across the cultural radar of Detroit, the country, or the world. But they are here (Tunde Olaniran, Flint Eastwood, Invincible, Jessica Care Moore, Monster Island, Planet D Nonet, Volebeats, et al.), and discerning listeners can find them without looking too hard.

This anthology is my effort to offer *some* perspective on our unique musical history in Detroit. The nearly fifty excellent and very talented writers whose writing appears in these pages were asked to shine a little light on Detroit's music history. I asked them if they could take us around the city, going from iconic locales like the Blue Bird Café on Detroit's west side to the Hideout on the east side to Uncle Russ's historic Grande to the '80s punk nostalgia of Wayne State's beloved Freezer Theater to Zoot's Café, a '90s favorite that featured Sleater-Kinney and many then unknowns, to Bookies, the Community Concert Series, and let's not forget Dally in the Alley where this editor first appeared with the Magic Poetry Band in the 1980s.

I wanted these writers to offer a meditation on the aspects of our Detroit music culture and history that inspired them. In this anthology of mostly original work, readers may not find *every single aspect*, every important band or quintessential Detroit artist, or every minute detail about Detroit music history, but I can definitely guarantee that readers will find enough good material on Detroit music and culture to keep them coming back again and again to this tome to discover and rediscover Motor City music.

Some of the topics here may jog your memory and make you hungry to hear some of that good music from those old-time, used-to-be days, while other essays will offer astonishing new insights as to "Why Detroit?" The hope is that readers will be able to make their own informed opinions on this phenomenon called Motor City music.

The time is now, or as the MC5 so exquisitely stated in their seminal song lyric "future now," for Detroit to fully embrace its deep, culturally rich, and diverse art forms, and to celebrate Lester Bangs's genius wisdom, alleged or authentic, when he said some thirty years ago, "Heaven was Detroit!" And it is indeed!

*Detroit, January 2016*

# 1 DETR

OIT JAZZ

Teddy Harris. © Leni Sinclair Collection.
Wendell Harrison. © Leni Sinclair Collection.

# A Top-Down Motown Bebop Pubescence
## Twelve Takes
*Al Young*

**1/**

For any instrument that rose to my ear, I'd mastered my deft air versions. Hand jive. Except for some re-al-life trumpet or piano now and again, I conducted my imaginary concert-listening sessions with creative gusto. Saxophones, trombone, French horn, oboe, harp, harpsichord, guitar, clarinet, flute, violin, bass, drums—I had it covered. All I had to do then was blow the dust off my sapphire or diamond stylus, set the needled tone arm down in the groove, and let the vinyl whirl.

**2/**

With the friendliest of crackles, universes floated, coating my brain and heart, kicking up sound all around. Talk about your big bang; music was the biggest. Invisible worlds ruled by vibration. While some of it I got, or kind of understood, the delicious mysteries that power most music and poetry electrify me yet. Like all adolescents, I daydreamed big time. A common fantasy had me performing the featured solo—the juicy part—to a special section reserved for wowing womanly girls I longed to woo.

**3/**

In London years later, before the advent of podcasts, two unforgettable BBC Radio interviews—Little Richard, then drummer Louis Hayes—hypnotized me completely and got me laughing so much I almost missed a flight. I'd known Louis since the seventh or eighth grade at Hutchins Intermediate School, Detroit, in the early 1950s. We played in the school band. Tuba-playing me sat way back there in the rhythm section with drum-playing Louis. "Lover" was a popular song for a self-taught pianist like me to torture people with. Whenever Mr. Kracje, our band teacher, wasn't hovering, I would pound out "Lover" on the unsupervised band-room keyboard. Hearing me, Louis Hayes would clutch a round-bottomed chair between his knees and redouble my offering with a conga-style Latin beat. We loved those Afro-Latin beats; the clave beat, the *guanguancó*. We loved Dizzy's "Manteca" and his version of the great Cuban *conguero* Chano Pozo's "Tin Tin Deo" as much as we loved Machito and Charlie Parker's *South of the Border* LP. You can probably retrieve Louis's exact words now. I just remember him telling the BBC interviewer something like: "And even if you played the harp, you couldn't come to Detroit and get away free. We had us a harpist named Dorothy Ashby. And if you didn't watch out, she might probably cut you." When Louis Hayes's percussionist cousin Finnroy Hayes and I made All-City Orchestra, we'd walk Saturday mornings all the way from our Hutchins neighborhood to rehearsals downtown at Cass Tech High. Five miles over, five miles back. But we didn't have to pack or lug our instruments. I remember how good it felt to blow the tuba parts that undergird and guide the blue nostalgia segment of Gershwin's "An American in Paris."

3

DETROIT JAZZ

## 4/

Among stuff pinned to the wallpaper of my east-side-facing attic room at Edison and Twelfth—before Twelfth Street became Rosa Parks Boulevard—images clipped from catalogs and magazines hung. Iconic live-fast-die-young relics from the era of E=MC$^2$ included images of Charlie Parker, Billie Holiday, Dylan Thomas, and James Dean. It was Marilyn Monroe and Emmett Till, it was Little Rock, Ray Charles, "I Like Ike," and, yikes, it was chart-topping Patti Paige asking, "How Much Is That Doggie in the Window?" It was Pat Boone, Little Richard, operatic pop star Mario Lanza (whose hit "Be My Love" Ornette Coleman quoted in early recordings). It was the Paradise Club (where Dizzy Gillespie hit on my mother in 1947), Flame Show Bar, Klein's Show Bar, Baker's Keyboard Lounge, and, later, the Cup of Socrates and the Minor Key. It was Elvis and Hula-Hoops and the panacean tonic sold as Hadacol. Elvis's manager, Colonel Parker, stood grinning behind all three money-makers. It was Ruth Brown, baby! It was "Mama, He Treats Your Daughter Mean." Earl Williams, my neighbor and classmate, a great, uncelebrated studio drummer, would later marry Ruth Brown's sister. Years later they had me to dinner at their big Brooklyn flat. It was witch-hunt inquisition time again. It was no time to be coming of age.

## 5/

As much as I'd like to brag otherwise, I wasn't old enough to get into the Blue Bird Inn, the West End, or any of the joints where Bird or Miles played. I was a kid. I could go, though, to World Stage Playhouse, a theater-in-the-round venue that rented out space to the New Music Society on Sunday afternoons and Monday nights for jazz performances. The ad hoc New Music Society decided to put out a journal, which took the form of a tabloid-sized newspaper. Somehow I, a junior at Central High, got wind and made it to the founding meeting held at the home of Harold and Jodi Neal, blocks away from me on Atkinson Street. *Idioms*—that's the name we settled on for the journal. By 1955, the word "idiom" rang hip to jazz ears. The staff decided I would contribute poetry, along with anything else I wished. Having edited and coedited newspapers since grade school, I didn't flinch. A lover of jazz and the realms to which jazz lifted me, I was glad to find my art-hungry, high school self so warmly received by elders. It was there, at Harold and Jodi Neal's modest home on Atkinson Street, that I met pianist Barry Harris, guitarist Kenny Burrell, Paul Chambers, and other illustrious and some valuable, lesser-known players (bassist-turned-chemist Ed Gunther, for instance, and drummer Rudy Tucich). At *Idioms* meetings, held Sunday afternoons at the Neals' home, I feasted on personal, spoken histories that flowed on tap or flushed. Private, up-close stories swirled: Sonny Stitt, Herb Jeffries, Donald Byrd, Doug Watkins, Elvin Jones, Thad Jones, Hank Jones, Bu Bu Taylor, Billy Mitchell, Dinah Washington, Frank Gant, Yusef Lateef, Charles McPherson, Lonnie Hillyer, Junior Cook, Betty Carter, Roy Brooks, Milt Jackson, Frank Rosolino (Jackson and Rosolino were Miller High grads), Tommy Flanagan, Pepper Adams, Curtis Fuller, and bassist Ernie Farrow. With his skinny half-sister Alice McCleod at piano and Earl on drums, Ernie's little trio gigged around greater Detroit and across the river in Canada. At Alice's insistence, Earl would bring me with my reel-to-reel 3M Wollensak tape recorder to their rehearsals.

I was doing make-believe radio shows and would announce their numbers on tape, then play them back up in my attic room, where WYSS (the YSS stood for Young Sound Studios), my imaginary radio station was housed. Leon Reynolds, my buddy and neighbor and schoolmate, whose madness matched mine, hosted a station, too. WLMR, he called it, after his full name of Leon McKinley Reynolds. We both had lucrative *Detroit News* and *Detroit Free Press* paper routes to support our record-buying and recording habits. Leon's much older brother John, a fully grown insurance salesman, played pretty good alto saxophone. *Birth of the Cool*, the landmark Miles Davis album, recorded in the late 1940s and kept in Capitol Records' vaults until the 1950s, had just come out on 78. John loved the smooth, inflectionless alto sound of Lee Konitz (he mispronounced the saxophonist's name, calling him Leo Ko-NITZ). "After Johnny Hodges, Benny Carter, Bird and Stitts," he told us, "Leo Ko-NITZ—that's my man." We were too respectful to correct him. You just didn't correct grown folks then. In fact, for fun, Leon and I would deliberately mispronounce Konitz's name. We were also too dumb and thoughtless to preserve all the music we taped. Tape wasn't cheap. We couldn't wait to erase our reels of tape to record over them something new. Who knew that Alice McLeod would first marry bop singer Kenny "Pancho" Hagood and then John Coltrane, then transform herself into Alice Coltrane? And the funny part is, Leon and I, still kids at Central High, had hung out with and looked up to Pancho Hagood. We'd heard him sing on records with Dizzy Gillespie, and we'd caught him with Buddy Hiles's big rehearsal band that gathered Saturday afternoons at the community center near Northern High. He'd turn up, too, at Mel's Record Shop on Twelfth Street.

I remember how Pancho liked to joke and kid. "Elect me," he cried out in the middle of a midtempo blues, "and I promise you a chicken in every pot—and some pot in every chicken."

## 6/

It was such a big picture. Like one of those jumbo-sized, artful jigsaw puzzles the child-me loved, this Detroit bebop chart still defied and resisted assemblage. How do you connect the music I heard coming out of tenor saxophonist/reed master Yusef Lateef with my rush to read British Muslim Marmaduke Pickthall's *The Glorious Koran*, an enduring English translation of the Qur'an? When I would see Yusef Lateef seated down front at the Thursday night Detroit Symphony concerts, to which we student musicians got tickets for fifty cents, he was always all dressed up. I watched Yusef jot stuff down with a pen in a musical-score notebook. What did I make of this? And what did I make of homeless vibraphonist Abe Woodley, who sometimes serenaded us Monday nights with Sigmund Romberg's "Softly, as in a Morning Sunrise"? Abe played the blues so lyrically at the World Stage Playhouse on Woodward in Highland Park I didn't know then that this soulful musician was scuffling. The term "soul" had just sailed into our musical lexicon, thanks to Ray Charles's impact. *Homeless* wasn't even in common use in the 1950s. Stories emerged. A classmate in my Central High homeroom, from my musical description, identified Woodley as the boyfriend of the cleaning woman his parents had hired. Jews had yet to flee altogether from Detroit's Northwest to the suburbs to Southfield. My schoolmate said of Abe Woodley: "He rides and sleeps all night on the DSR, the city bus, all night long, that's how Abe lives." I'd learned about people who slept in their cars summer nights at Belle Isle, but it would take decades for me to fit the pieces together, to connect the wee dots.

## 7/

Now we get down to drummers: Earl Williams, Roy Brooks, Frank Gant, and Louis Hayes; a pianist: Kirk Lightsey (a shoe salesman at the time); a bassist: Bob Friday; saxophonists: Leon Williams, Sonny Red Kyner, and Charles McPherson; a trumpeter: Lonnie Hilliard. The key to all this freewheeling association was Earl Williams, the drummer who lived a block from me on Edison Street. In the late 1940s, Paul Williams, Earl's never-home dad, had scored a colossal hit record. "The Hucklebuck" was a twelve-bar R&B hit whose melody coincided with Charlie Parker's history-making "Now's the Time." Jazz professors still argue about which came first. To "The Hucklebuck" we danced and sang:

> You do the hucklebuck
> Do the hucklebuck,
> And if you don't know how to
> do it,
> Boy, you outta luck.

Later, to Bird's "Now's the Time," we sang but didn't dance to Jon Hendricks's prescient lyric:

> You've heard it every way:
> A dog will have his day,
> But when it comes to wailing,
> Dogs ain't got a thing to say.

## 8/

Like ragtime, like Dixieland, like boogie-woogie, like swing, like big band, like bebop, like cool jazz, like progressive jazz, like hard bop, like loft jazz, like rock 'n' roll, like soul, like bubblegum, and like Motown—bebop outlives its label. Around the same time that I leapt into the recorded bebop legacy that I, at thirteen, felt I needed to absorb, West Coast jazz, a softened style of bop, reached Detroit. Gerry Mulligan, Chet Baker, Shorty Rogers and His Giants, Chico Hamilton, Art Pepper, Laurindo Almeida. By and by, Ornette Coleman, Sun Ra, and Cecil Taylor would swoop down and ease in. Meanwhile, I was wading and swimming in the ocean, rivers, and streams of Duke Ellington, Count Basie, Lester Young, Billie Holiday, Lionel Hampton, Jazz at the Philharmonic, Bud Powell, Thelonious Monk, Wardell Gray, Sonny Rollins, Nat King Cole, Erroll Garner, Ella Fitzgerald, Sarah Vaughan, Boyd Raeburn, George Handy, Lennie Tristano, Woody Herman, Oscar Peterson, George Shearing, Dave Brubeck, Stan Getz, Zoot Sims, Stan Kenton, June Christie, Max Roach and Clifford Brown, Horace Silver, Jimmy Smith, Teddy Charles, and Charles Mingus.

## 9/

Every time I watch *Standing in the Shadows of Motown* (2003) to hear how veteran jazz pianist Joe Hunter morphed into the prime keyboardist with the Funk Brothers, Motown's audible, just lately visible, hit-stirring backup band, I have to smile. While this brilliant, jazz-rooted rhythm section built a fire under singers like Marvin Gaye, the Supremes, Gladys Knight and the Pips, the Contours, Stevie Wonder, Junior Walker and the All-Stars, Martha and the Vandellas, Motown's stars sold more hit records than the Rolling Stones and the Beatles combined. The Funk Brothers went unsung; jazz, bumped into the shadows, lay largely unsung and undanced. From, say, 1915 to 1945, before it got bebopped or kidnapped (as lovers of traditional jazz or swing might put it), jazz had been America's pop music. You danced and socialized to it. It was in 1940s Detroit, probably at a Graystone gig with Bird, that Dizzy Gillespie looked out over the crowd from the ballroom stage and saw fans dancing to sprint-tempo numbers like the now-famous "Koko" and Bird's fiery approach to Ray Noble's "Cherokee" by way of bandleader Charlie Barnet. According to Diz, the ballroom dancers simply halved or quartered the beat. By the time I jumped ship and came ashore to Ann Arbor and college, jazz—a folk-like, social music—was edging in upon itself and turning inward. By then I was bopping through life to Horace Silver's "Señor Blues," John Lewis and his Modern Jazz Quartet's "Django," and Charles Mingus.

**10/**

The unsung hero, a staple in jazz lore, thrills the youthful heart. In *Bluff Your Way in Jazz*, authors Peter Clayton and Peter Gammond put it like this: "After a brief period of being underrated they find their distinctive tone, making recordings by which they will always be known in their twenties, get ambitious in their thirties, and in their forties start on the road to oblivion."

**11/**

Oblivion? What is oblivion? From what I recall, to the fifteen-year-old me the notion of oblivion dazzled. What better certainty of genius than its incomprehension, its denial, its obscurity? Bebop

paid and played tribute to adolescence, budding pubescence, so all-powerful because you didn't have to prove or demonstrate anything. Don't show, blow! Such thoughts brushed past me when I listened to my dad's thick 78s. No wonder they called them platters. Except for that little hole in the middle, you could wash and eat off of them. You could fling or sail them like Frisbees across parks and fields.

**12/**

And, oh, did we ever sail! From the jolt and thrill that bebop delivered, we heard stuff. I got the message. The squashed and squeezing bourgeois world must go. Squares had neither eyes nor ears for what was hip. Driven by its need to flatten the world into a shiny, dull habitation, square capitalist civilization cared nothing for life. Jazz did. Bebop outdid jazz. Where bebop ventured, late bebop adventured. Like late capitalism, late bebop serviced an urgent agenda. From World War II onward—as we locked up most of our Japanese Americans, locked up some Italian Americans and some German Americans— our State Department tapped into the power of America's jazz and popular music as propaganda. Democracy? This was the concept that radio host Willis Conover emphasized in his worldwide Voice of America broadcasts. How could a nation that's given the world such lovable Negro-inflected music and dance not stand for freedom for all? Eager but green, we fledgling bopsters of Detroit's 1950s and 1960s (vocal wizard Betty "Bebop" Carter, pianist Kenny Cox, trumpeter Marcus Belgrave) heard and peeped in Joe Henderson's blurred bleat-and-cry one wistful, unfinished wink.

# Bebop in Detroit
## Nights at the Blue Bird Inn
*Lars Bjorn and Jim Gallert*

In the jazz world, one sure sign of veneration is having tunes named for you. By that measure, Detroit's Blue Bird Inn has made it. At least two prominent Motor City jazz stars have honored the legendary jazz nightclub—their old stomping ground—with tune titles in recent years.

First there was trumpeter Thad Jones's composition "5021." It refers to the Blue Bird's address on Tireman, on the city's near west side. Then there's pianist Tommy Flanagan's "Beyond the Bluebird," the title track of his acclaimed 1990 recording with his former bandmate, guitarist Kenny Burrell. This CD is a virtual compilation of Blue Bird–related tunes.

Why has the Blue Bird come to be such a symbol of Detroit's contribution to modern jazz? Simply put, the Blue Bird Inn was the hippest modern-jazz nightspot during the city's bebop heyday. Almost every significant 1950s hard-bop veteran in the city either played or hung out there during its peak years.

What made the Blue Bird unique were the people who played, listened, and enjoyed themselves there. It was a neighborhood bar that welcomed jazz lovers. The late Detroit baritone saxophonist Pepper Adams once recalled its "great atmosphere": "Nothing phony about it in any way…no pretensions and great swinging music."

Musicians not only graced the bandstand, they were an important part of the audience. As bassist James "Beans" Richardson points out, "The majority of the people in there played an instrument, so, musicwise, they were very 'up,' you know. When there was a lousy record on the jukebox, even the bartenders would say, 'Get that record off!'"

Sometimes those musicians played unusual instruments. Donald "Martini" Martino played excellent bebop choruses on kazoo! All in all, as the *Michigan Chronicle* concluded, "In the late '40s the Blue Bird was a mecca for the goatee and beret, a sort of cave for the 'musically misunderstood' and a gallery for the set who talked rapidly in terms of 'atonal qualities, polyphonic melodies and counterpoint.'"

It all started in 1948 when the Blue Bird hired pianist Phil Hill and told him to assemble a house band specializing in the newest thing from New York City—bebop. There had been music at the Blue Bird Inn intermittently since the mid-'30s, but this was the first time that the new generation of beboppers was heard there. Hill hired vibraphonist Abe Woodley and drummer Art Mardigian (later shortened to Mardigan). Mardigan soon left Detroit to pursue national prominence, but his brief stay at the Blue Bird had a strong effect on someone who has since become one of the world's greatest drummers—Elvin Jones.

"I used to go to the club and listen to Wardell Gray and all these cats," Jones remembers. "Art

Mardigan was the drummer, and he was always very friendly and helpful to me. He used to ask me to sit in, but I would never do it. I thought it was presumptuous to sit in with these musicians, because to me, they were the greatest people I knew."

The real attraction of the Blue Bird for younger musicians was the freedom it offered them. They could play what they wanted to play.

"It had all the support a jazz club needed," Flanagan says. "Everyone who loved jazz in Detroit came. We were always able to play what we wanted to play, and the people liked what they heard." The *Michigan Chronicle* saw it that way, too, observing that "the musicians who take chorus after chorus on the bandstand are just about the most uninhibited, relaxed and frenetic bunch of men in the city."

The Blue Bird quickly developed a national reputation because of its completely up-to-date music policy. For nearly a decade, the Blue Bird featured the best modern-jazz artists in Detroit, most of whom went on to national prominence. The original Phil Hill combo in 1949 backed up tenorist Wardell Gray. The following year, they recorded a classic session for Prestige Records. A quartet with Flanagan and tenorist Frank Foster also appeared at the club in early 1950. Their sound was captured by dedicated jazz fan Porter Crutcher on portable recording equipment. Crutcher, a former U.S. Army radio technician, was a regular at the Blue Bird in 1949 and 1950; and he had the foresight to buy a Presto portable disk recorder and cut records there on several occasions.

Today Crutcher's "hobby" is the stuff of legend. An example: One night in late 1949, someone told him that bebop legend Charlie Parker had just walked into the club. Crutcher quickly drove four blocks to his home, grabbed his equipment, and hurried back to the Blue Bird.

"When I got back, I couldn't get in the place!" he recalls. "I was outside and so I took my microphone and passed it inside to somebody. . . . I caught the last part of 'Now's the Time.'" Crutcher also recorded Wardell Gray playing "Lester Leaps In" and "What Is This Thing Called Love" on another occasion.

Percussionist/drummer Jack Tian, then just out of high school, was working weekends with the Willie Anderson Quartet at the Bowl-O-Drome and spent weeknights at the Blue Bird during 1948 and 1949. Tian, a protégé of Art Mardigan, brought his bongos into the club one evening and sat in with the quartet. "The guys didn't chase me off the stand, so I came back the next night," he recalled. "I became an unofficial member of the band." Most weeks Tate Houston was the horn player, but often different guys, home from a road trip, would play for a one- or two-week stretch. Frank Foster, Billy Mitchell, and Wardell Gray all played there. Tian is present on the Gray acetates.

Tian got a real treat one night when he arrived at the club. "It was during intermission," he remembered. "The guys told me to go pick up Charlie Parker outside of Masonic Auditorium." Bird was in town with Jazz at the Philharmonic, and he came outside to meet Tian "with two absolutely gorgeous Jamaican women," said Jack, smiling broadly. "I took them to the club, and went back on stage with Art after intermission. It was a really small stage with room for maybe one or two horns. Bird played more than 'Now's the Time,' but I don't think he stayed more than one set. I didn't talk to Bird on the stand, I just played my instrument as usual. I drove them either to the airport or to a hotel afterward. I can't remember which."

The Hill house band was replaced in the early 1950s by the Billy Mitchell Quintet, which featured drummer Elvin Jones along with his brother, trumpeter Thad Jones. That group got recorded, too, but under much more ideal studio conditions. They waxed four titles for Detroit's Dee Gee records.

The Blue Bird was built on its extremely hip reputation, billing itself as "the west side's most beautiful and exclusive bar." It attracted a mainly black audience from both the immediate neighborhood and the city at large. Those who visited the place were first struck by its distinctive exterior—a pure-blue façade accented with a New York City–style awning that ran across the sidewalk and right up to the curb. It was just as attractive inside. The acoustics were excellent, and the small, understated, semicircular bandstand could hold a quintet with something close to comfort. The bandstand was moved from near the front to its present location at the rear of the club around 1957 by owner Clarence Eddins, who had taken over the club from the DuBois family four years earlier.

Besides its music policy, the Blue Bird became nationally known for its friendly but fierce jam sessions and its penchant for attracting visits from national stars when they were in town for concerts at larger venues.

The most celebrated Blue Bird visitor was Miles Davis. Miles came to Detroit for an extended stay in the latter half of 1953, when he was trying to kick his heroin habit. Eddins befriended him and gave him a job with the Mitchell band. Since Eddins and Davis were about the same size and build, Eddins shared his wardrobe with the trumpeter. Davis never forgot

his kindness, and even after he became a huge star, he always gave Eddins a great price for appearances by his group. Davis came as a solo musician in 1954 to play with the house band, and in the latter half of the decade his groups were frequent attractions.

Phil Hill's brother, Carl, the Blue Bird's doorman, remembers Miles vividly:

He was living in Sunny Wilson's hotel on Grand River and the (West Grand) Boulevard. . . . It was in the winter, and he walked from the hotel to the Blue Bird and the joint was packed; everybody was waiting for Miles Davis. So when he came in, he had on this grimy white shirt and a navy-blue sweater and Clarence told him to go home and put on a tie. . . . So Miles went outside and took a shoelace out of his shoe and tied it up under his shirt and said 'How do you like this, boss?' and went on the bandstand and played.

While Eddins extended many a kindness to musicians such as Miles, he could also be feisty and combative. One incident between Eddins and Sonny Stitt that involved a damaged saxophone and a shotgun actually led to the blacklisting of the club by the American Federation of Musicians. For a time, AFM members were not permitted to work at the Blue Bird.

Slowly, the club's attention to the local scene decreased. By the late 1950s, the Blue Bird was largely presenting touring national acts, many of whom were former Detroiters. The Blue Bird Inn's house band soon became a thing of the past. Meanwhile, the migration of many of Detroit's best players to New York City, where they affected big changes on the music's stylistic evolution, continued unabated. Those players who had spent so many nights blowing at the Blue Bird spread the club's name and legend far and wide.

The Blue Bird continued to present music in the 1960s. But in the early '70s, the live music stopped. By then, it was frequented by Eddins's pals from earlier days, and stories would be swapped, beers would be drunk, and heads would nod as memories of the good old days flowed freely. Eddins kept the place spotless and the piano tuned, but it wasn't often played in the later years. There were a few concerts featuring Blue Bird alumni like Tommy Flanagan, but times had changed. The neighborhood had changed, too, and it wasn't as safe as it once was. This, coupled with rising entertainment costs, ensured the Blue Bird would never resume its place as a prime music outlet.

Following Eddins's death in 1993, his widow, Mary, decided to resume the live music policy after decades of silence. There was a Sunday afternoon jam session (with complimentary buffet, no less) that ran for several months. But Mary's health was marginal, and those sessions ended. After her death in 2003, the Blue Bird Inn alternated live music with a DJ, but business was slow. It reverted to a neighborhood bar rich in history. Walking into the dim interior was like entering a time machine— the booths, 1950s outer-space style lights, and the compact bandstand were not of this world. The jukebox now had space for nonjazz artists and the bandstand held mixing equipment used by the DJ. But the many photographs on the walls—of Bird, Miles, and Stitt, among others—remained.

The building went on the auction block in 2008, and today much of the interior is damaged or has been removed. The bandstand was recently removed by the Detroit Sound Conservancy, a new organization devoted to preserving as much of Detroit's music history as possible. So today, only the exterior of the most important building in modern jazz history in Detroit remains. Fortunately, die-hard enthusiasts captured some of the sounds produced in the building in its heyday.

11

Donald Byrd. © Leni Sinclair Collection.

Pepper Adams. Photo courtesy of the
Pepper Adams Estate.

# The Donald Byrd–Pepper Adams Quintet
## Jazz in Detroit, 1958–61

*Gary Carner*

Although they seldom performed together in Detroit as teenagers, trumpeter Donald Byrd and baritone saxophonist Pepper Adams established an enduring musical partnership in their late twenties that coalesced a few years after both had moved to New York City. Their first New York gig was probably at the Cafe Bohemia in early February 1958. Later that month, they were paired as the front line for a Thelonious Monk studio recording, just as they began a residency at the Five Spot that lasted until June. Already in demand as a dynamic front-line duo, their four-month run (with Detroiters Doug Watkins and Elvin Jones) gave them the opportunity to launch the Byrd-Adams Quintet as a working group. Riverside Records recorded them live in April. Six months later, the band would record *Off to the Races*, its first of a series of recordings for Blue Note Records that cemented the band's place in jazz history.

Donald Byrd (born in 1932) was two years younger than Adams. Both did their military service, but Byrd had the fortune of being based close to New York City, which allowed him to meet musicians like Max Roach and John Lewis. Like Adams, he played the Blue Bird Inn, located at 5021 Tireman on Detroit's west side, with the house band, and it is very likely that they shared that stage at some point. Byrd's first recording as a leader was with the Blue Bird band in August 1955 (*First Flight*, originally on Transition records) but was actually recorded at the New World Stage. The band included Barry Harris and tenorist Yusef Lateef. By December 1955, Byrd had gotten his big break when he joined Art Blakey and the Jazz Messengers in New York.

In the summer of 1958, however, directly after the lengthy Five Spot engagement, Donald Byrd toured Europe with Watkins and Belgian tenor saxophonist Bobby Jaspar. Adams, for his part, accepted a six-week engagement with Benny Goodman. Again, in early 1959, the Byrd-Adams Quintet would be shelved in favor of Byrd and Adams's four-month commitment to the Thelonious Monk Big Band (culminating with the influential *Thelonious Monk Orchestra at Town Hall* date for Riverside). This on-again/off-again schedule would characterize the early history of the quintet, from mid-1958 well into 1960. Because steady work wasn't available for the group's first two and a half years as a unit, Byrd and Adams continued to take gigs as sidemen while also maintaining active careers as solo artists.

From 1958 to 1961, Byrd and Adams were busy indeed, working and recording in many settings. Besides their membership in Monk's orchestra in early 1959, Adams did two tours with Benny Goodman and another with Chet Baker before May 1959, when the Byrd-Adams Quintet recorded *Byrd in Hand*, their second date for Blue Note. By then, the quintet had already worked two weeks at New York's Village Vanguard. In October 1959, the band

13

was touring again, this time playing gigs in Toronto and Pittsburgh.

In the spring of 1960, the Byrd-Adams Quintet (including Bill Evans, Paul Chambers, and Philly Joe Jones) recorded three tunes for a stereophonic sampler project for Warwick Records. Before that, Byrd, without Adams, had worked his way from New York to San Francisco and back while Adams formed a short-lived quintet with tenor saxophonist J. R. Monterose. But by July 1960, the quintet's superb rhythm section of Duke Pearson, Laymon Jackson, and Lex Humphries had coalesced. And with Adams back in the group, the quintet began its incarnation as a steadily working ensemble. A three-month tour took the band to Cleveland, Chicago, Minneapolis, Dallas, Salt Lake City, Denver, Detroit, Kansas City, and Pittsburgh, then back to Chicago and Detroit before returning to New York in late October.

During the group's two-month stint in Chicago (that would extend into January 1961), pianist Herbie Hancock was hired to replace Duke Pearson. This was Hancock's first gig outside of Chicago with a touring band. Hancock moved from Chicago to New York to join the group.

Back in New York, the quintet recorded again for Warwick, then toured for most of the year before disbanding in October. In February and March 1961, the group gigged throughout the eastern United States and Canada, working at the New Showboat in Philadelphia, then Montreal and Toronto and back to the Bird House in Chicago before working in Indianapolis and Rochester, New York. Returning to New York in April, the group recorded two more dates for Blue Note (*Chant* and *The Cat Walk*) within a two-week period.

Looking back at the group's history, there seems to be a direct relationship between the amount of recordings the Byrd-Adams duo made and the frequency of quintet gigs. Stated another way, the more recordings Byrd-Adams made, the more they created demand for their quintet to be heard live in performance. Their first recording, *10 to 4 at the Five Spot*, released in mid-1958, was followed by the release of the quintet's first two Blue Note recordings in 1959, *Off to the Races* and *Byrd in Hand*. Those were followed in turn by a double LP recorded in November 1960 (*Live at the Half Note*) and five studio sessions (*Motor City Scene*, *Out of This World*, *Chant*, *The Cat Walk*, and *Royal Flush*) all recorded before October 1961. This upward arc of activity in the studios was equaled by their dense club-date calendar. Band itineraries, magazine articles, and advertisements in the jazz and lay press all demonstrate that 1960 and 1961 were, indeed, the glory days for the working quintet, when the band was performing regularly and functioning at its peak. This is the main reason why I find the quintet's cluster of six recordings made in less than a year's time to be their finest work. Working steadily for only a year also explains why the Donald Byrd–Pepper Adams Quintet remains to this day not nearly as well known as some of the other similarly constituted great small bands of its time, such as those led by Max Roach, Miles Davis, Art Blakey, Horace Silver, or Cannonball Adderley.

What other conclusions can we make about the quintet's three early recordings leading up to their great body of work done in late 1960 and 1961? First, it's clear that Byrd and Adams favored Detroit musicians in their group whenever possible. The live

1958 Riverside date, for example, was an all-Detroit group except for pianist Bobby Timmons, though I suspect they tried to hire Tommy Flanagan.

For their second and third dates—the quintet's first two for Blue Note—commercial pressures dictated that Byrd, as leader, feature some of the musicians in Blue Note's stable. It also necessitated expanding the front line to three horns. These all-star sessions would soon be phased out in favor of showcasing the working quintet. That's because the group started touring steadily in mid-1960, congealing as a unit, and attracting attention as a unique band with its own sound.

Two other things characterize the quintet's recordings: their inclusion of original compositions and the use of the ballad feature. Both Byrd and pianist Duke Pearson used these recording dates as opportunities to write original tunes and arrangements for a small group. The ballad feature—a convention of jazz performance, and something Byrd would've been asked to perform as a member of Art Blakey's band, à la trumpeter Clifford Brown—is something Byrd and Adams would always do in club dates and also on several of their recordings. They used ballads as solo features for either Byrd or Adams, typically undergirded by the rhythm section, and as a way to create variety within each set of music. Additionally, having one of the horn players drop out on a slow-tempo number was sensible in another way. It would by necessity abbreviate the duration of the tune and not unduly disrupt the set's momentum.

Taking the entire sweep of their work into consideration, it's clear to me that Byrd's exclusive recording contract with Blue Note catalyzed the Byrd-Adams Quintet. Their increasing popularity,

due to the wide distribution and overall excellence of their first two Blue Note recordings, also led to them eventually being picked up by the Shaw Agency, who booked tours for the group throughout North America.

Fortuitously, too, a brief lapse in Byrd's Blue Note contract allowed Byrd and Adams the opportunity to fit in two additional recording dates. One, *Out of This World* for Warwick, was for the working group. The other, *Motor City Scene* (under Adams's leadership for Bethlehem), was for sextet, with the addition of Detroiter Kenny Burrell on guitar.

For all their recordings, steady work on the road, and critical acclaim, the Shaw Agency's predilection for booking the quintet on very long road trips still spelled disaster for the band. Exhausting car rides (Minneapolis to Dallas, Salt Lake City, Denver, then Detroit, for example) were already booked by Shaw in October 1960. In July and August 1961, the group was back at it, driving from New York to Cleveland, then St. Louis, Kansas City, Chicago, and Detroit, leading up to *Royal Flush*, their last New York studio date, in September. In October, the band returned to St. Louis, then played Kansas City, where the club folded and the group wasn't paid. Years later, Adams cited transportation costs relative to what they were earning as the main reason for ending the four-year collaboration. But the Kansas City experience must have functioned as a telling metaphor and as an embodiment of the group's pent-up frustrations. It was the quintet's final gig.

Despite their all too brief time together, three outstanding recordings were made in the late 1950s and six superb dates were made in a ten-month stretch beginning on November 11, 1960, for the

Blue Note double LP *Live at the Half Note*. The *Half Note* date is the only quintet recording to have never gone out of print in the United States, some measure of its enduring value. From it, Duke Pearson's composition "Jeanine" is the quintet's only tune that has become a standard in the jazz repertoire. *Live at the Half Note* reveals the band at the height of its power and remains the best example of what the band sounded like at the time.

Just after the *Half Note* recording, the quintet, in a burst of activity, recorded four more dates in New York. First was the Bethlehem session, led by Adams, which returned to the favored all-Detroit formula (with Tommy Flanagan, Kenny Burrell, Paul Chambers, and Louis Hayes). A January date for Warwick, *Out of This World*, featured the working group, now with young Herbie Hancock on his very first record session, but with drummer Jimmy Cobb in place of Lex Humphries. In April and early May, the quintet's two Blue Note studio dates used other drummers entirely: Philly Joe Jones on *The Cat Walk*, because they couldn't locate Humphries, and Teddy Robinson on *Chant* because he was already touring with the band at the time. One final quintet date, *Royal Flush*, was done in September 1961. It's just as excellent as the others. It features Byrd, Adams, and Hancock, with bassist Butch Warren and drummer Billy Higgins.

Summing up the totality of the band's output, what is it about this group that made it unique? First and foremost, of course, the quintet featured two great instrumental stylists backed by a terrific, interactive, hard-swinging rhythm section. Their repertoire was fresh and compelling, comprised of a blend of unusual standards, interesting originals, and cleverly adapted tunes, such as an up-tempo version of "I'm an Old Cowhand" and Henry Mancini's "Theme from Mr. Lucky."

Sonically, trumpet with baritone sax is an exquisite pairing, even more aurally spread than the customary trumpet/tenor sax pairing of its time. A trumpet/baritone front line was still rather unusual in 1958, especially one playing this brand of intense post–Charlie Parker small-group jazz. But more than that, Byrd and Adams meshed so well because their styles were so complementary. Byrd, at root, was a very melodic, soulful, lyrical player who used nuance, space, and blues inflections in his solos. Adams did, too, though he was more of a rhapsodic player, who delighted in double-time playing and exhibiting other technical flourishes. Byrd, it could be said, was more of a "horizontal" soloist; Adams was more "vertical." What a perfect counterbalance! And when Byrd and Adams stated each tune's theme, their phrasing—often using impressive dynamics or provocative counterpoint lines—was always so beautifully rendered.

All told, during the four-year stretch that reached its apotheosis in 1960–61, the Donald Byrd–Pepper Adams Quintet recorded eleven dates—seven studio albums, one sampler, and three live LPs—assuring their place as one of the great jazz groups of its time. The band launched the career of Herbie Hancock, and it gave Byrd, Duke Pearson, and, to a lesser extent, Adams and Hancock a forum to write original compositions. Some of the tunes in their book ("Curro's," "Bird House," and "Jorgie's") immortalized jazz clubs. The quintet surely helped Adams's career, too. He was heard widely in clubs throughout North America, and the Blue Note dates in particular were well distributed in the United States and abroad during his lifetime.

## DISCOGRAPHY

With the exception of *Live at the Half Note*, all of the Donald Byrd–Pepper Adams Quintet's Blue Note recordings have been collected in a Mosaic Records box set. The records *10 to 4 at the 5 Spot* and *Motor City Scene* have been reissued on CD. *Out of This World* has been reissued on CD, too, but beware of cannibalized recordings from bootlegs that cut and paste some of the tunes almost beyond recognition. Most of the Quintet sessions were under Byrd's name because Blue Note's contract was with him. The dates on other labels fall under Pepper Adams's leadership or Adams-Byrd.

No film or videotape footage of the Byrd-Adams Quintet has been uncovered as yet, but a terrific clip from the 1958 Cannes Jazz Festival featuring the Bobby Jaspar–Donald Byrd Quintet is listed below. Each member of that rhythm section (Walter Davis Jr., Doug Watkins, and Arthur Taylor) recorded with the Byrd-Adams Quintet on Blue Note.

Pepper Adams, *Motor City Scene,* Bethlehem BCP-6056.

———, *10 to 4 at the 5 Spot*, Original Jazz Classics CD: OJCCD-031-2.

Pepper Adams–Donald Byrd, *Out of This World*, Fresh Sound CD: FSR-335.

Donald Byrd, *At the Half Note Cafe* (Vol. 1), Blue Note CD: CDP-7-46539-2.

———, *At the Half Note Cafe* (Vol. 2), Blue Note CD: CDP-7-46540-2.

Donald Byrd–Pepper Adams, *The Complete Blue Note Donald Byrd/Pepper Adams Studio Sessions*, Mosaic CD: CDBN-7-46540-2.

Bobby Jaspar–Donald Byrd, INA videotape (France): http://youtu.be/XEwuLs5hCRE.

Thelonious Monk, *Thelonious Monk Orchestra at Town Hall*, Original Jazz Classics CD: OJCCD-135-2.

## COMPOSITIONS

Who wrote all those great tunes for the Byrd-Adams Quintet? I always knew Donald Byrd wrote a bunch and Duke Pearson wrote a few. When I began assessing their repertoire, I was surprised to see the degree to which Byrd's writing dominated the amount of original material written for the band from 1958 to 1961. Thirty-three original compositions were written during that period. Of that, 70 percent of the oeuvre was written by Donald Byrd or (in the case of "Each Time I Think of You") co-written by Byrd and Duke Pearson.

Nine of the tunes were written by various pianists in the band: Walter Davis Jr., Duke Pearson, and Herbie Hancock. Pepper Adams wrote his two compositions for *Motor City Scene*, the 1960 Bethlehem date under his leadership. It seems doubtful that either of Adams's tunes was ever played by the quintet in club dates. Herbie Hancock's first recorded composition, "Requiem," can be heard on *Royal Flush*, the quintet's last studio date while still a touring band.

"Jeannine," written by Duke Pearson, was recorded by Cannonball Adderley about six months before the November 1960 *Live at the Half Note* date. Although not written for the Byrd-Adams Quintet, it's included below, albeit as an outlier, because Byrd-Adams helped make the tune part of the standard jazz repertoire. That's in part due to the fact that their seminal Blue Note recording never went out of print in the United States.

What about the rest of the book? Judging from the data, twenty-eight other tunes were either recorded or performed in clubs. A few of these tunes were standards, but most were tunes that few others performed. Even some of the standards were modified in creative ways, such as the ballad "That's All" and the novelty number "I'm an Old Cowhand," which were made into up-tempo flag-wavers. See the Byrd-Adams repertoire list below.

*Pepper Adams*

"Libeccio"

"Philson"

*Donald Byrd*

"6M's"

"Amen"

"Bird House"

"Cecile"

"Curro's"

"Devil Whip"

"Down Tempo"

"Great God"

"Here Am I"

"Hush"

"Jorgie's"

"Kimyas"

"Pure D. Funk"

"Shangri-La"

"Soulful Kiddy"

"Sudwest Funk"

"The Cat Walk"

"The Injuns"

"Off to the Races (The Long Two/Four)"

"When Your Love Has Gone"

"You're Next"

"Yourna"

*Donald Byrd–Duke Pearson*

"Each Time I Think of You"

*Walter Davis Jr.*

"Bronze Dance"

"Clarion Calls"

*Herbie Hancock*

"Requiem"

*Duke Pearson*

"Chant"

"Child's Play"

"Duke's Mixture"

"Hello Bright Sunflower"

"Jeannine"

"My Girl Shirl"

"Say You're Mine"

*Tunes Recorded and Performed by Byrd-Adams*

"A Portrait of Jennie" (J. Russel Robinson)

"Between the Devil and the Deep Blue Sea" (Harold Arlen)

"Bitty Ditty" (Thad Jones)

"Cute" (Neal Hefti)

"Day Dream" (Billy Strayhorn)

"Hastings Street Bounce" (traditional)

"I'm a Fool to Want You" (Jack Wolf–Joel
    Herron–Frank Sinatra)

"I'm an Old Cowhand" (Johnny Mercer)

"I Remember Clifford" (Benny Golson)

"It's a Beautiful Evening" (Raymond Rasch)

"Like Someone in Love" (Jimmy Van Heusen)

"Little Girl Blue" (Richard Rodgers)

"Lover Come Back to Me" (Richard Rodgers)

"Mr. Lucky" (Henry Mancini)

"One More for the Road" (Harold Arlen)

"Out of This World" (Harold Arlen)

"Paul's Pal" (Sonny Rollins)

"Sophisticated Lady" (Duke Ellington)

"Stardust" (Hoagy Carmichael)

"Stuffy" (Coleman Hawkins)

"That's All" (Bob Haymes–Alan Brandt)

"'Tis" (Thad Jones)

"Trio" (Errol Garner)

"When Sunny Gets Blue"
    (Marvin Fisher–Jack Segal)

"You're My Thrill" (Jay Gorney)

"Witchcraft" (Cy Coleman)

# Teddy Harris
## A Jazz Man in Motown
*Lars Bjorn and Jim Gallert*

Few Detroit musicians illustrate the link between jazz and Motown music better than Theodore Edward Harris Jr. (1934–2005). He boxed with Berry Gordy, sang with Jackie Wilson, and was a Motown road-band conductor/arranger. He was also the Supremes' music director for over a decade.

His jazz roots are deep, too. His father worked for decades as a bandleader, pianist, and organist. Harris was a central figure in Detroit's informal "jazz academy," and he exemplifies the "Detroit way"—older musicians helping younger musicians.

Detroit has been a premier jazz city for a long, long time. Our reputation grew in the turbulent 1940s when Bird was the word. We absorbed that language and made it our own. By the 1950s, Detroit's jazz talent pool overflowed, swamping Manhattan with Detroiters.

Our education system was second to none, instilling into youngsters the basics of playing their instrument and reading music. Equally important lessons happened after school, in musicians' homes, bands, and orchestras, where dedicated musicians with a knack for nurturing practice the "Detroit way." Those nurturing musicians essentially forfeited their chances for national exposure and recognition. A city's reputation is made by those musicians who leave; it is sustained by those who remain. Musicians who remain are special, and they form the backbone of our jazz community.

Louis Cabrera, Barry Harris, and Marcus Belgrave were among their number.

Teddy Harris was one of those special musicians.

Theodore Harris Jr. was born in Detroit on August 27, 1934, to Theodore Harris and Ruth Woody. Both parents came to Detroit from the South; they met at Miller High School. Their families lived on the east side of the city and moved to the North End after World War II.

Harris's grandfather played trombone, and he gave the instrument to Teddy's father as a wedding present. "My dad never could play it, so he took it to the pawn shop and traded it for a clarinet," said Harris. That clarinet became his first instrument. Harris Sr. played keyboards, and there was always a piano in his house. "Seems like from the time I could walk, I was always fooling around on the piano," mused Teddy Harris.

Teddy was attracted to the saxophone ("I have no idea why," he chuckled) and captivated by Duke Ellington, whose music he first heard at the age of nine. "My parents took me to the Paradise Theater to hear Duke's band," he recalled with a smile. "I knew then and there I wanted to be a musician."[1] Most musicians rely on a day job to get by, especially if they have a family to support, but Harris had an arsenal of talents to draw from.

"The only nonmusic job I recall Teddy having was a job at a [gas station]," his brother Don remembered. "We both worked there for a few years. . . . It was obvious to me that Teddy would be a musician."[2] Don, five years younger than Teddy, was a businessman who ended up managing musicians and bands, including Jackie Wilson and the Butterfield Blues Band. The brothers were similar in many ways—thoughtful, earnest, responsible, and confident. They comported themselves with dignity and class. Both were passionate about music.

Teddy Harris went to Northern High School. Like most Detroit high schools, it had a superb music program. Harris's teacher at Northern was Orvis Lawrence, "who played with Glenn Miller and the Dorsey Brothers," according to Harris. "I went to Northern the same time as Donald Byrd, Sonny Red, Tommy Flanagan. I studied saxophone."

Teddy was in neighborhood bands during his Northern years, including one group with legendary tenor saxophonist Stoney Nightengale. He developed on several fronts while at Northern—saxophone, piano, and arranging. For the latter, he got some help from fellow tenor man Frank Foster, then a presence on the Detroit scene.

"Frank Foster used to help me. . . . He was becoming a pretty astute arranger. He would come over to the school [Northern], we got out of school at two-thirty, he would get Donald Byrd, Sonny Red, and myself and Claude Black and take us to his house where he would teach us how to read his arrangements."

After graduating, Harris began playing in bands. He gained valuable experience from working with his father. "My dad was playing organ, I was playing tenor sax," he recalled. Harris Sr. led bands around town for many years, including a stay at the 606 Horseshoe Lounge in 1954, where he was billed as an "interpretive organ stylist."

"My daddy was one of the first organists in Detroit," Harris recalled. "His main instrument was piano, but he played nine different instruments, all of them well."

Harris and his pals used to drop by his dad's gigs, said trumpeter Felton Jones. "He had a gig at the Gay 90s on Woodward playing solo piano," Jones remembered. "Teddy played his tenor when we did that." All of Harris's early jobs (in the 1950s) were on tenor sax. According to bassist Robert Allen and Jones, Harris was a fine tenor man with a big, strong sound.[3] That's not surprising considering his respect and admiration for Yusef Lateef and Sonny Rollins.

According to Harris: "Yusef, I grew up on Yusef, he was really one of my favorite guys. When I played tenor sax, people used to tell me I sounded a lot like him. . . . He was a *real* influence on my playing." Sonny Rollins, then the dominant tenor voice on the jazz scene, was another favorite.[4] "Teddy used to always play 'Shadrack,' that was his favorite tune," said Felton.[5] "He loved Sonny." Jones and Harris played in a bebop quintet organized by Robert Allen in 1954, and they stayed together until Harris started working at Motown. Jones played trumpet, Harris was on tenor, Johnny Cleaver played drums, and the piano chair was pretty open. "We were all about Miles [Davis] and Sonny," Jones remembered. "One day [drummer] Louis Hayes brought Eddie Chambliss by, and Eddie had his horn [tenor sax] with him. After Teddy heard Eddie play, he switched over to piano, and Eddie played tenor," Jones laughed. "Eddie was even *more* like Sonny. Teddy couldn't touch him." Harris was a nimble instrumentalist, able to move from one instrument to another thanks to his talent and his schooling. Jones characterized Harris's playing as "two fingered" at first, but he improved quickly, and their band found steady work for dances and club gigs as far north as Flint.

During the 1960s, Mr. Kelly's, an east-side club, featured Sunday afternoon jazz sessions (Ed Love's Jazz Workshop), which attracted "all of the Detroit notables," according to drummer George Davidson, a longtime friend and associate of Harris's. "Any national guys who were playing in town would be there, along with guys like Kirk Lightsey, Freddie Waits, Bennie Maupin, and Teddy. Those sessions were real learning experiences for me." Harris led a quintet at Mr. Kelly's that backed up Sonny Rollins during a guest appearance in November 1962, shortly after Harris returned from the army. It is important to note that Harris had many gigs over the years, often two or three each week, so they were parallel, not serial.

Harris was drafted in August 1959. Much to Harris's chagrin, he ended up in a tank, not an orchestra. He tried several times to join the Seventh Army band, but he was good at his job and Harris's commanding officer didn't want to lose him. "Every time they would cut orders to send for me to be transferred to that band, my company commander would send back a notice they were short of personnel, and they needed me. I never did get into the army band!"

In the army, Teddy met Eddie Harris, who was in the band, and the two traded lessons. "He was playing the piano," Teddy remembered. "I was stationed in Germany by this time . . . in my little outfit, the musicians had no piano player. So I started playing the piano and studying. I got

a chance to study with a couple of German piano teachers. Eddie Harris and I became friends. . . . He started to tutor me on the piano, and I started tutoring him on the saxophone. He wound up being a saxophone player, and I play the piano most of the time." Harris's piano chops improved significantly.

Teddy was less a music theoretician and more a practitioner with an intuitive grasp of music theory. "I met a guy in the army with a master's in music who could not play [jazz]. I could play everything he talked about. Maybe I didn't know the terminology, but I could play it."

After his discharge, Teddy went straight to Paris, soaking up the rich Left Bank jazz scene and studying briefly with respected French pianist Nadia Boulanger.[6] Harris returned to the United States late in 1962, just in time to latch onto the Motown juggernaut.

Berry Gordy was a friend from high school. "We were both on boxing teams at Brewster Center," Harris said. Teddy was also tight with Jackie Wilson. "Jackie and I were like brothers," he recalled. "In fact, most people thought we were brothers. We used to sing in a little quartet. We used to sing in churches." Harris had backed up Wilson in a Gordy-produced single, "Reet Petite," which was a smash hit.[7] Harris worked in saxophonist Choker Campbell's orchestra, backing Gordy's vocal groups. He worked for Motown in the arranging department.

"I kept all of the road charts after the recording was done," he remembered. "My biggest job was on the road. When we went on the road with the Motown Revue . . . I could handle the girls pretty good . . . they liked that." After Diana Ross left Motown, Harris began working with the Supremes, arranging their music and occasionally going on road trips conducting the band. "When Gil Askey finally left, I took the reins," Teddy recalled. "Those girls had so many hit records. . . . I made them into three medleys so they could do a little bit of each." Harris worked with the Supremes well into the 1970s.

He was in demand and was seldom idle, working at clubs like Odum's Cave (Joe Henderson was in that band too, according to Teddy) and leading the house band at Dummy George's in the early 1980s.

Teddy Harris joined Aretha Franklin's trio in 1965. Hindal Butts played drums and James "Beans" Richardson played bass. George Davidson replaced Butts in Franklin's group, and Harris recalled that Davidson was "perfect for Aretha. He was a traditional bebop player, bluesy, safe. He gave her just what she needed."[8]

That meeting was the start of a long-lasting collaboration between Davidson and Harris. They played together in many bands, including the Paul Butterfield Blues Band from 1969 to 1971. Butterfield's band included Rod Hicks on bass and vocals. Hicks recommended Harris to Butterfield (rumors circulated that "Butter" unsuccessfully tried to snag ace jazz arranger Gil Evans), and Harris used the talented horn section (which included David Sanborn) to craft a unique sound, a mix of jazz, electrified blues, and rock 'n' roll.[9] Harris's playing and arranging captured the cultural *zeitgeist* of the late '60s.[10] Butterfield's band paralleled Miles Davis's "Bitches Brew" experiment, which also fused jazz with rock 'n' roll.

Teddy Harris was always aware of the wealth of fresh, young talent available in Detroit, and always tried make use of it. Harris knew the importance of a disciplined environment for neophyte musicians. He started his New Breed Be Bop Society Orchestra in 1983. Until Harris's death in 2005, it was a premier

Motor City jazz outlet. The New Breed was a solid mix of seasoned Detroit regulars and youngsters. Like his idol Duke Ellington, Harris got to hear his music immediately, but the real kick for him was helping young musicians find their voices. Sometimes after a performance, a beatific grin would slowly form on his face and his eyes would sparkle. That look was the reason Harris kept his band together, even if their only gigs were Tuesday night rehearsals.

Detroit saxophonist James Carter cycled through the New Breed while in high school. "I used to hang at Dummy George's with my colleagues," he recalled. "Teddy invited me to his rehearsals and recruited me. I played tenor. . . . He invited me to play 'Epistrophy' with his band, and I used his soprano sax. It was a Yamaha, and I got one after that, I liked his instrument."[11]

Saxophonist and teacher Ernie Rodgers kept his ears open for subs for Harris's big band, thus ensuring promising students spent time in jazz bands. Educators such as Rodgers and Ben Pruitt were the equivalent of minor-league managers, developing students through the Detroit "farm system." A trio comprising Harris, Davidson, and bassist Don Mayberry hosted the Wednesday jam sessions at Baker's Keyboard Lounge for years, ending only when Harris passed away.

One of Harris's finest bands worked at BoMac's Lounge ("Friendliest place in town," said their business card) in 1992. His group included saxophonist Phil Lasley, Roderick Hicks, and drummer Lawrence Williams, with trumpeter Dwight Adams occasionally added to form a classic bebop quintet.

Teddy played piano in that band, and for six months they were *burnin'* every weekend. A good drummer can push a band to new heights, and Williams did exactly that—some nights it sounded like Elvin Jones was in the house. Teddy kept his band, and his drummer, on time and in line with his choice chords and tempos and his discipline. Harris's "Passion Dance" was a highlight every night.

Teddy met the love of his life in the early 1960s. Martha Hall was a model; she was beautiful, classy, and married with three young daughters. The attraction between them was irresistible, and they finally got together and married in the early 1970s. "They got married in Las Vegas, while Teddy was touring with the Supremes," Karla Hall-Harris recalled. "Mary Wilson gave the reception." What did Karla think of her stepfather and his occupation? "I learned so much from Teddy. I was sixteen years old when they married, and Teddy kept an eye on the young men who wanted to go out with me . . . he had ways of letting me know who I should date." Harris's feelings for Martha made a deep impression on Karla. "I learned how a man is supposed to love a woman from Teddy," Karla said. "And I saw how much music meant to Teddy. It was his life, he was always at the piano, or practicing, or rehearsing."[12] Martha was a great partner, publicizing his gigs, encouraging him, helping with details. They were rarely apart, a power couple who moved easily around the universe of music. The bond between them was obvious, and long lasting.

After Martha passed in October 2000, Teddy lost some of his flair, but his music was always there. Harris had his Tuesday rehearsals and a steady diet of gigs, as well as his family's ever-present love and support. He worked until he couldn't make his gigs, then, when he went into Detroit's VA hospital, he worked there, playing for his fellow patients. He

passed on August 15, 2005, two weeks shy of his seventieth birthday. His funeral was stately and filled with warmth. The church was overflowing and the music was wonderful. Teddy meant a lot to many of us, and he is missed.

For fifty years, Teddy Harris contributed to Detroit's fertile music community as a musician, teacher, and bandleader. He worked in jazz clubs and Motown road bands, spreading Detroit's music message to the world. His big band was an incubator that allowed younger musicians like Dwight Adams, James Carter, and Geri Allen to gain valuable experience. Harris knew that young musicians had to receive an education—and practical experience— for jazz to survive and prosper.

Harris received many awards, including the Arts Midwest Award in 1993, and he toured with the Michigan Jazz Masters. The 2005 Detroit Jazz Festival was dedicated to Teddy, and it featured a reunion of his beloved New Breed Be Bop Society Orchestra, stocked with many of the musicians who played in it decades earlier.

Teddy Harris is a good example of a "pure" jazz musician adapting to and working for Motown Records. Detroit had many such musicians, and they contributed an important ingredient to Motown: improvisation. Jazz guys could always come up with a nifty riff or slick lick that propelled the music over the top and made it fill the performing space with that tingly sensation people love to feel. Teddy was one of our best musicians.

## NOTES

1. Ellington had a weeklong stand at the Paradise, February 11–17, 1944. This was Duke's first Midwest tour following his second Carnegie Hall

appearance in January; he likely featured parts of "Black, Brown, and Beige" in this concert.

2. Don Harris, interview by Gallert, July 14, 2013.

3. Hindal Butts, interview by Lars Bjorn, July 29, 1993. Harris worked in Butts's quartet in 1959; when Harris was drafted, his replacement was a young Joe Henderson.

4. John Coltrane didn't attract much attention until joining Davis in 1955.

5. "Shadrack" was recorded by Rollins for Prestige on December 17, 1951.

6. Boulanger (1887–1979) was a highly regarded pianist and pedagogue. Her pupils include Donald Byrd.

7. Discographies show this title as recorded in NYC, but it's possible the Detroit session was a demo disc. Teddy was adamant that the session took place in Detroit.

8. They appear on Franklin's *The Great American Songbook* collection on Columbia Records.

9. Hear them on *Keep on Movin'* and *The Paul Butterfield Blues Band Live!*

10. The Jazz Alliance of Michigan organized a Butterfield reunion, which featured Davidson, Hicks, and Harris, among others.

11. James Carter, conversation with Jim Gallert, July 10, 2013. Harris switched to soprano sax as his saxophone of choice in the 1960s and after that he rarely touched his tenor.

12. Karla Hall-Harris, interview with Jim Gallert, July 14, 2013.

Tribe. © Leni Sinclair Collection.

Phil Ranelin, 1975. © Leni Sinclair Collection.

# Rebirth of Tribe

*Larry Gabriel*

Ancestors call out with beats
To those with ears and soul
Gather my children and dance
To the sound of radical truth
Stories of pain and new hope
Dance the love laid before us
This is an organic message

A child of the tribe eventually
Becomes an elder, respected
Fusing the Diaspora of sounds
Into unity for those who know
That what we were then
And who we are now
Is like water flowing endlessly
Remixing in birth, death and rebirth

The dance of life, more beautiful
And more dangerous than fire
We groove in the cleansing heat
Moving mightily as one

## TRIBAL GROOVE: D-BOP ROOTS

Tribe was a labor of love, learning, and kindred spirits. Tribe was about cool grooves and creative music, but it was also about community, rebellion, and black self-determination.

Those were edgy days. The civil rights movement had passed its peak and black power brought a more assertive attitude to many African American enterprises—including jazz. An indefatigable curiosity gripped musicians of all stripes. The doors of creativity and experience were wide open, and funky soul-rock had entered the jazz pantheon along with the swing, bebop, postbop, and avant-garde of earlier years.

Detroit was an integral part of that jazz history, having served as a particularly fertile breeding ground for bebop. Pianist Barry Harris, saxophonist Yusef Lateef, guitarist Kenny Burrell, trumpeter Thad Jones, drummer Elvin Jones, and trumpeter Donald Byrd were among the Detroit jazz luminaries who went out and created a path for others to follow. And they did follow, going out, coming back, and going out again, mixing the local influences with those across the musical spectrum and the world.

Saxophonist Wendell Harrison was one Detroiter who headed out along the trail blazed by his forebears. In 1960, already a seasoned musician at eighteen, he split for New York, where he hooked up with the likes of Jack McDuff, Lloyd Price, Grant Green, Hank Crawford, Betty Carter, and Sun Ra. He lived in the lofts, which were gathering places for the musicians breaking free of their pasts and creating new sounds for the new age. They rebelled against the war in Vietnam, racial inequality, the capitalist system, and anything they perceived as getting in their way.

That was the decade when Miles Davis created a revolutionary, popular, and successful fusion of jazz and rock. Sun Ra also fused the genres mined by Davis, but Ra turned left at Saturn and spaced the music out, mixing electronic innovation with stretched-out bop, atonal harmonics, edgy modern dance, and fantasy-ridden poetry. Needless to say, few record labels were ready for the onslaught, and Ra had to hold his space-age big band together by touring and selling self-produced records at his exuberant, sensually overwhelming shows.

Harrison reveled in all of these sounds, particularly learning from the do-it-yourself attitude of Sun Ra. Unfortunately, he also picked up a drug habit in the hard environs of New York City. While on the road in California, he joined the Synanon rehab community to kick heroin. After more than two years there, during which time he recorded a critically acclaimed album with Esther Phillips, he headed back east in 1970. Wary of New York and its temptations, he stopped off in Detroit "just for a minute" to visit family and friends. It was a hell of a minute; Harrison still hasn't left the Motor City almost four decades later.

Harrison reconnected with friends, including pianist Harold McKinney, a longtime cultural warrior who chose to remain on the home front rather than wandering the country, and trumpeter Marcus Belgrave, who had settled in Detroit after years on the road with Ray Charles and others. They found a job for Harrison teaching music to young people at the nonprofit Metropolitan Arts Complex. He busied himself building a curriculum and composing choral and big band works.

"I was trying to stay busy as hell to keep from self-destructing," Harrison remembers.

He noticed that the once-vibrant club scene had disappeared along with the once-cohesive African American community that supported it. Black Bottom and Paradise Valley, the black neighborhood and its thriving business district, had been destroyed by urban renewal. Hastings Street, with its myriad jazz and blues clubs, was wiped out and replaced with I-75. Musicians no longer had the community outlets that kept them working and their music vibrant.

## REBELLION

When Motown Records officially closed its Detroit offices in 1972 and relocated virtually all operations to Los Angeles, it was the culmination of a years-long process. Detroit had lost one of the few beacons of its musical culture. A lot of musicians headed west to work in the Motown studios and back up the groups for their tours. But others were adamant about remaining. Trombonist Phil Ranelin and trumpeter Marcus Belgrave had moved to Detroit for session work at Motown Records. Harrison was familiar with both from his days on the road. He and Ranelin had met in Indianapolis while Harrison was touring with saxophonist Hank Crawford. He met Belgrave while living in New York. Neither of them wanted to leave Detroit.

"Phil and Marcus said, 'To hell with that, we're going on and doing our own thing.' We were tired of backing folks up anyway," Harrison recalls with a laugh.

One day during a band rehearsal at Metro Arts, Harrison and Ranelin chatted about the music scene. "We discovered that we shared some of the same dreams," says Ranelin. "We both had a burning desire to lead a band and perform and record our own original music. We were developing a sound."

Unfortunately, their free-ranging ideas didn't fit the formulas used by recording companies. Motown, Ranelin recalls, used a tight, almost paint-by-number approach. The black-owned label's musical assembly line hadn't allowed much room for quirky ideas, at least not the kind of quirkiness that jazz improvisers were drawn to.

What would come to be Tribe grew out of that discussion.

"The idea of Tribe was just an expression of what we felt about the music business," says Belgrave. "It was sort of like a rebellion. There was too much dictation going on; the company executives weren't jazz musicians. The musicians went underground to present their own music and cut out the record companies; it was a noble and historic thing that happened. Music gained a lot more freedom. Cats were doing what they really felt."

What they really felt was the synergy of their tremendous range of experiences. It was impossible to keep their inspirations inside a box. Harrison had worked with the roots blues of Big Maybelle, the pop of Marvin Gaye, and the avant-garde of Sun Ra. Ranelin had played beside Eddie Harris, Freddie Hubbard, and Pharoah Sanders. Harold McKinney was a product of the great Detroit piano lineage and had played with Kenny Burrell and John Coltrane. He'd toured with Wes Montgomery. Belgrave had cut his musical teeth playing with Clifford Brown, and worked with such luminaries as Charles Mingus, Max Roach, and McCoy Tyner. All of them had worked for Motown or with Motown artists. They had years of seasoning.

"You know, as jazz musicians you had to work with everybody," muses Harrison. "That kind of rounds you out. We wanted to do all the stuff that had been bottled up inside of us for many years, give ourselves a chance to put this stuff on wax. The nature of who we were as artists, we didn't have to talk about that. We respected each other's music. When people saw us together, they felt that this was the cream of the crop of the jazz community. Our reputation had been made already. That's what Tribe really was, a bunch of individuals coming together."

Their music was round, square, convex, and obtuse; any way you wanted to play it, these guys could take it there and back. Tapping that experience, Tribe began formally as a partnership between Harrison and Ranelin. Harrison's first wife, Pat, a graphic artist, worked on administration and promotion.

"We were trying to write, compose, trying to arrange for big band and orchestra, playing all kinds of styles of music," Harrison recalls. "The job was to find out who we were and put it down on a recording."

"Wendell came out of Synanon," Belgrave says. "He brought that feeling of self-producing, getting up off our knees and not waiting for the record company. He brought that kind of feeling. It seemed like we would get together every day. We all decided to record each other's music. All the money that we had went toward pressing and manufacturing the music. The concept of a tribal thing came from that. We weren't the only ones doing it. It was all over the country." Indeed, Strata-East in New York, the Black Arts Group in St. Louis, and the Association for the Advancement of Creative Musicians in Chicago were some of the more notable musicians' organizations that were springing up.

As Tribe coalesced, pianist Harold McKinney served as something of a mentor. Born in 1928, he was about ten years older than the other members of Tribe and he had the perspective of age.

"Harold would talk for hours about details," Harrison says. "He was great in terms of presentation being up to a certain standard. A lot of us didn't regard that as important as he did. Harold would correct us in terms of the way we spoke. He was like a big brother."

## MIND-EXCURSION MUSIC

In contrast to McKinney, the rest of the guys just wanted to get their musical ideas out there. The first big Tribe project was a 1971 show at the Detroit Institute of Arts called *An Evening with the Devil*, featuring suites composed by Harrison and Ranelin, in addition to poetry and dramatic presentations. From the beginning, Tribe showed a penchant for multigenre expression, breaking down the walls between the arts. It was spiritual and militant. Even the name of their collective, Tribe, spoke to the nascent Afrocentrism of the day. And they explored the burning social issues of the times.

Harrison's work, *An Evening with the Devil (Suite in 3 Movements)*, had parts titled "Mary Had an Abortion," "Where Am I," and "Angry Young Man." Those were obvious outgrowths of the contentious discussions the group had. Ranelin's piece *What Now? (Freedom Suite)* traveled the same path, with sections named "What We Need," "Angela's Dilemma," and "How Do We End All of This Madness."

The titles and the music were provocative. The entire concept was provocative. Those were the ideas progressive African Americans wrangled about in 1971. A few months after the DIA show, they recorded the music in a studio and released it as

*A Message from the Tribe*. Liner notes from the album discussed the Tribe concept:

The Tribe is an extension of the tribes in the villages of Africa, our mother country. In Africa everyone has a talent to display. There were no superstars, just people, and collectively all the people of the village played a vital role in shaping that culture. We see all the black communities within this country as villages and the tribes are the people residing within them. . . . Pure music must portray our way of life. . . . Our music is reflecting more so than ever before the stress, tension, and discord that is taking place within our communities along with the positive and harmonious things happening.

Well, that was on one version of the initial recording. Tribe put out three versions of *Message*. Originally, the suites were pressed as continuous music without pauses between sections. That made it all the more difficult to get radio play. They released *Message* again with different cover art and banding between the sections of Ranelin's suite; Harrison's suite was replaced by three other compositions by him, "Wife," "Merciful," and "Beneficent." After that, *Message* was released a third time with a third cover.

The original music ranged from the free jazz chaos of "Mary Had an Abortion" to the subdued soul of "What We Need." A postbop consciousness was evident throughout, with soulful, modal grooves and angular horn lines. Each piece was accompanied by poetry or vocals expanding on the themes in the titles. And everything pushed at the boundaries of what was possible.

"Everything I wrote had lyrics, and they were basically protest and black-struggle-oriented songs," Ranelin remembers. "I didn't deliberately set out to write those lyrics; they were inspired by the times. All of those songs had revolution written all over them. I couldn't separate the things that were taking place socially from what I was doing musically. As an artist, I don't think you can separate the two. In other words, I can't help myself, especially back then I couldn't."

Steve Holsey, columnist for the *Michigan Chronicle*, Detroit's black weekly, reviewed the album and wrote: "Theirs is not tranquilizing music, either. It's more like mind-excursion music. It swirls through the brain, enters the bloodstream and disturbs the senses. . . . The listener is jolted, transfixed and almost hypnotized."

But music was just the starting point. Having taken the enterprise into their own hands, Ranelin, Harrison, and the others had to learn about management, recording, publishing, distribution, and publicity. They became students of all aspects of the music business. The Harrisons handled most of that work. And it was noticed internationally, with a spurt of interest and sales first in Poland, at the time still part of the Soviet bloc. Requests to license the earliest Tribe recordings followed from labels in Japan and the United Kingdom.

"The shit was out of control, everybody wanted some attention." Wendell laughs. "I was sitting there on the phone every day trying to push it around the country, taking orders. Those records made a pretty good splash in terms of sales. I sold to Jim Grey out of Washington, and he would ship stuff to Poland and Russia and everywhere. Rick Ballard Imports was selling mostly in Asia, on the Pacific Rim. They were astonished that black folks were doing that, talking about black consciousness from a jazz perspective. Music Unlimited was distributing out of Chicago, and Black Fire Productions and Records out of Washington, DC."

## MEDIA MELD

In Detroit, Tribe rented halls for performances, primarily at the DIA and the University of Detroit, and sold advertising for program books. Author Herb Boyd, then teaching black history at Wayne State University, noted the advertising base and convinced Tribe to add some topical stories to create *Tribe* magazine. The articles followed the lead of the edgy music. The first magazine came out in November 1972. It had a story on abortion, which was being argued in the United States Supreme Court at the time in the *Roe v. Wade* case. The *Tribe* piece compared the 1972 arguments on the legal rights of unborn babies with those justifying slavery in 1857. The same issue of the magazine included articles on black studies at WSU, artist and nightclub profiles, poetry, and announcements of community events.

It also included a Ranelin-penned philosophical commentary about the music scene, which said: "The time for musicians to organize and stick together is now. We have to be independent individuals. Speaking for myself, I have the kind of personality that calls for nothing but independence. I cannot and will not be ruled by anyone."

The glossy-cover magazine grew to as many as forty-eight pages and continued to take thoughtful, provocative, and revolutionary stances on local, national, and international events. The stories became more sophisticated: a historical perspective on black Republicans, examinations of Coleman A. Young (Detroit's first black mayor, elected in 1973), school busing, black liberation, black colleges in crisis, unions, African politics, the Vietnam War, and even WGPR, the nation's first black-owned television station (licensed to the black masons in Detroit during the Nixon administration). There were also artist profiles; record, film, and book reviews; fashion spreads; and even fiction.

Tribe expressed itself through various media, with music, publicity, graphic arts, and print arms serving the cause. There were other groups in Detroit working toward similar cultural goals, notably the Strata record label and concert gallery founded by pianist Kenny Cox and trumpeter Charles Moore (both of whom also worked with Tribe). But while Strata went for a more traditional business model (Cox worked at selling stock in the enterprise), Tribe was a wide-open, go-for-it collective that shot from the hip.

*An Evening with the Devil* reappeared as the title track of a Wendell Harrison release on the Tribe label in 1973. The album also had a couple of additional compositions ("Consciousness" and "Rebirth") and poetry delivered by the Black Messengers, Oba and Vajava, performing in the same vein as the better-known Last Poets. The cover art was a rendering of Wendell's astrological chart with a drawing of a bent-over, naked man holding the scales of justice balancing a skull and a leg. Though he was bent over, his penis was visible; it was a very unusual record cover, particularly for the times. The graphic was about power, street justice, and the different realities lived by black and white America.

Tribe was on a roll. Harrison and his first wife, Pat, lived in the large home his grandfather, a doctor

who moved up from Texas, had bought in an upscale neighborhood. The house was Tribe central, with a recording studio in the basement, offices on the second floor, and telephones in every room.

## STRETCHIN' OUT

In 1974, Belgrave's *Gemini II* was the next album released on the Tribe label. The year before, driven by a laudatory statement from Charles Mingus, a *DownBeat* magazine poll had named Belgrave a "Talent Deserving Wider Recognition." Shortly after, he'd taken a vacation to the Bahamas and hung out with musicians there.

"I saw musicians in the Bahamas who were in the studio all the time," he reminisces. "They had a natural affinity toward the freedom of music. They were freer than we were. They were doing their own style of music and the tourist thing. That motivated me to get my record out."

*Gemini II* opened with "Space Odyssey," a futuristic excursion that started with a spacey synthesizer lift-off and theremin-like tones from the musical saw contributed by "drumist" Roy Brooks. The music swung through dense avant-garde, postbop, electric fusion, and soul while always staying true to Belgrave's vision.

At the same time, Belgrave had been working with McKinney in the group Creative Profile. That sophisticated ensemble became the basis of the next Tribe release.

"We'd be playing and people would start dancing," says Belgrave. "We didn't look at it as dance music, but it ignited something in people."

McKinney's *Voices and Rhythms of the Creative Profile* stretched the music in another direction with three drummer/percussionists driving the deeply

African-rooted music and choral voices evocative of a soulful opera. Harold was himself an accomplished vocalist, as was his singer-wife, Gwen, who led the chorale; the vocals gave *Voices* a surprising sophistication in light of earlier Tribe recordings. As much as Tribe was a revolutionary response to the time, McKinney's approach took the response to a profoundly spiritual place. *Voices* broke with Tribe's drive to record only original compositions by including imaginative covers of Eddie Harris's "Freedom Jazz Dance" and Herbie Hancock's "Dolphin Dance."

Ranelin followed with *The Time is Now*, and indeed it was Tribe's time. Along with *Gemini* and *Voices*, *The Time is Now* marked three LP releases from Tribe in 1974, its most prolific year. It was also the time of heavy rhythms. Every one of Tribe's releases that year used multiple drummers. Up to that point, every Tribe recording had included miscellaneous percussion from the assembled musicians, but the 1974 recordings featured dedicated rhythmists such as Ike Daney, Roy Brooks, Lorenzo Brown, Billy Turner, and Ron Jackson. For the first time, Ranelin seemed at a loss for words: *Time* was his first all-instrumental release, no poetry, no singing.

The independent-music spirit was catching hold across the United States. Strata-East Records turned heads in 1974 with Gil Scott-Heron's *Winter in America*, featuring its dance-floor cut "The Bottle." Scott-Heron's effort caused a lot of record distributors to see the possibilities in music coming from small black labels across the country. Tribe dealt with as many as thirty distributors during its heyday from 1972 to 1977. Wendell found himself spending about 75 percent of his time managing Tribe while playing music fell to the wayside. At times, he toyed with the nearly unthinkable idea of giving up saxophone playing to focus on administrating the business.

At the same time, all of the Tribe mainstays were working their regular musical avenues. Ranelin was doing studio sessions. McKinney kept on with his work performing (often with his brother Ray on bass) and educating another generation of musicians, notably his daughter, drummer Gayelynn, and his nephew, pianist Carlos. Belgrave was still in demand and often headed out on the road with Detroit-based drummer J. C. Heard, a veteran of the swing era and Jazz at the Philharmonic. While in New York, Belgrave ran into drummer Doug Hammond.

Hammond, who grew up in Florida, had moved to Detroit in 1965 as a warm-up before heading for the Big Apple. He played with Smokey Robinson and the Miracles but turned down Motown session work because he found the pay scale insultingly low. He worked with various blues and jazz bands around town. Before leaving Detroit in 1970, he crossed musical paths with most of the Tribesmen, particularly while with the Detroit Creative Musicians Association. DCMA presaged some of the creative approaches that Tribe later developed, such as putting theater and poetry into the mix with music. When Belgrave saw Hammond in New York, the drummer said he had an album with keyboardist David Durrah recorded and almost ready to go. Strata-East had planned to release it, but some internal problems had shelved the project. Belgrave suggested Hammond take it to Tribe.

The Hammond-Durrah album, *Reflections in the Sea of Nurnen*, came out in 1975. Compared to the music Tribe had formerly released, *Nurnen* was understated, yet melodic to the max. There were R&B currents, such as "Wake Up Brothers," with self-reflective lyrics like, "Who's to blame, that the brothers are running a game on each other. . . . We are dying for crumbs and cars, our family starves," delivered by Hammond in a soulful, grooving tone. The haunting "Moves," also recorded by Charles Mingus, featured acoustic violin gently navigating the melody.

"My Tribe experience was good as far as the record production and promotion," Hammond says. "Then David and I came from New York to promote the recording, and that was it. I was never really involved in Tribe's music. I was only on the label. I actually have a different style of music. I like Tribe's music, but it did not influence my musical direction. I like and liked that my musical direction is a complement and shows the differences on the Tribe label. It's good that labels have a variety of directions."

Shortly after, Durrah released a single with "Venus Flytrap," a blowout jam with the power to stand with the electric fusion of Miles Davis, and "Kai," a moody dreamscape prescient of the coming electronica aesthetic.

Ranelin, the most prolific Tribesman, recorded and released *Vibes from the Tribe* in 1976. He apparently dusted off his pen for this outing. He wrote lyrics for Wendell's composition "Wife," which had appeared on the second version of *Message from the Tribe*. And while Tribe regulars Harrison and drummer George Davidson formed the nucleus of the crew, a wide assortment of the Motor City gang showed up on various tracks, including Ralphe Armstrong (who would later play with Mahavishnu

Orchestra and Frank Zappa) and members of the group Griot Galaxy. Ranelin says:

> It turns out this album, years later, kind of defined who I was, and also was an important element in the sound that was associated with Tribe. All of the tracks on the album were done in one take. The song "Vibes from the Tribe" was recorded at the Strata Gallery by Charles Moore, and some of the people associated with Strata were on that track, in particular Kenny Cox and Ron English. Bud Spangler helped produce it. I had everything written out, but when we recorded it I wanted to do some sort of sound effect kind of things with Marcus, and I wanted George Davidson not to immediately start playing that beat but to meld into it. Ironically enough that's the part that most of the younger generation gets into. . . . I had been writing a lot of lyrics and poetry during that period and had written lyrics on a couple of Wendell's tunes. I wanted to record my vocal version of "Wife." I basically used Wendell's original arrangement and just added the lyric.

The same recording session also produced Harrison's single "Farewell to the Welfare," which was so megafunky it sounded like it belonged on the soundtrack to *Shaft*.

"That was the sound of the time," Harrison smiles. "The groove changes every ten years or so, but that was the sound for those days."

The last LP to come out on the Tribe label, in 1976, was *Mixed Bag's First Album*, made by a group of seasoned local cats, but none of them—Ron Brooks, Eddie Russ, Jerry Glassel, Dave Koether, Larry Nozero, Dan Spencer—were Tribe insiders. This was a tight group of musicians who were mostly bandleaders in their own right. Their music was truly a mixed bag of Latin, and straight-ahead and fusion jazz, with a tinge of funk. In the true Tribe tradition, all of the pieces were composed by band members. But it was an album on the Tribe label, not truly a Tribe group.

## DIASPORA

Tribe was a furiously creative force in Detroit when it came together. But after several years and some nine albums (counting the multiple versions of *Message*), the flame had begun to dim. The collective had served its purpose; the musicians had put their music and their ideas out there at a time when there was a dearth of creative outlets. They made their statement, but nobody was making a living off Tribe. In 1977, after session work in Detroit dried up for Ranelin, he made the move to Los Angeles. Belgrave was on the road, and in and out of the country, on a regular basis. Harrison and McKinney started working as a piano and saxophone duo. The Tribe was dispersing.

"When Phil left, it took out a big element," Belgrave says. "Phil had a lot of songs. That was the real Tribe sound. The other stuff, Harold did his own thing with *Voices*. My thing was *Gemini*; it was closer to Tribe's thing than Harold's."

Poet, political activist, and music impresario John Sinclair had put together some Tribe shows in nearby Ann Arbor and a small tour. Before that, Sinclair had been a main mover in the Ann Arbor Blues and Jazz Festivals. In Detroit, he had been involved in the Jazz Workshop. He got together with Harrison to set up Harrison's new organization, Rebirth, as a nonprofit to support tours and produce albums.

"Getting Rebirth together changed everything," Harrison says. "My second wife, Pam, got it organized. Rebirth was producing some of the same content and the same cats, but it was a different label. We started bringing some more cats in doing straight-ahead stuff, more national cats like Leon Thomas, Eddie Harris, and Woody Shaw. With the grants, we could pay people up front. We re-recorded and retitled some of the Tribe stuff with a different hook and fresher grooves. The groove that we did in the 1970s wouldn't work in the 1980s. Traditional stuff stays the same, but the commercial stuff changes."

*Tribe* magazine was never revived, but Rebirth eventually began doing radio broadcasts with WDET-FM, public radio in Detroit. They also got some shows on rotation on public access cable television. As society changed, so did the musicians. Today, you can find all the Tribe participants on the Internet.

The big change for Harrison in the 1980s was getting into the clarinet again. He started playing it when a tour with Lou Rawls called for the difficult reed instrument. Then, one day in Cleveland, his car was stolen with his soprano saxophone in it. He made do with the clarinet on the job. The audience loved it, and Harrison began exploring the clarinet as a modern instrument, even writing new material and putting together a clarinet ensemble, Mama's Lickin' Stick, to perform the work. In the new decade, Harrison had again re-created his music with new challenges.

Starting in 1990, Arts Midwest, an arts-support organization partnered with the National

Endowment for the Arts and nine midwestern states, began honoring "Jazz Masters." It shouldn't be a surprise that by 1993 five of the twelve midwestern artists so designated were Detroiters, and four of them—Harrison, Belgrave, McKinney, and Roy Brooks—had worked with Tribe.

"The Jazz Masters gave us status," says Belgrave. "We definitely knew that part of the reason we were honored was because of what we did with Tribe."

In 1995, the Michigan Jazz Masters, along with sometimes Tribe rhythmists George Davidson on drums and bassist Don Mayberry, were assembled as a group. The only member with no Tribe background was Jazz Master pianist-saxophonist Teddy Harris Jr. The group played a series of concerts around the state, then, with support from Arts America, a government cultural exchange agency, they toured through Ivory Coast, Senegal, Tunisia, Egypt, Turkey, Jordan, and Syria. However, the group was focused on more traditional fare, covering music by composers such as Eddie Harris and Horace Silver; and even when the band played original compositions, it gave them a more mainstream interpretation than on a Tribe outing.

But Tribe had not been forgotten. Even during the MJM tour, Harrison took phone calls from Ranelin about labels interested in Tribe works. Eventually, every one of their records was licensed for distribution around the world on labels such as P-Vine in Japan, Soul Jazz in the UK, Scorpio Music in New Jersey, Ubiquity in San Francisco, Enja in Germany and Tropic in Detroit.

"I was out there taking care of all kinds of international business," Harrison says. "We're selling as much now as we did in the 1970s. Only it's not as much work. Instead of having to distribute it, we give them a master and get so much up front and royalties every six months or a year."

In 1996, Britain's Universal Sound released *Message from the Tribe*, an anthology of cuts from various Tribe releases. The package included a booklet with reprints of some of the stories and images from *Tribe* magazine. Even some of the advertising was reprinted. It's amusing to see ads for the local whole wheat bakery and a collision shop nestled in with those from Ford Motor Company and McDonald's.

## A NEW DAY

And there's still life to be found in this Detroit movement from the 1970s. Pioneering techno DJ and Grammy-nominated producer Carl Craig has long been weaving a jazz thread through the fabric of his music, with the mid-'90s Innerzone Orchestra and via his work as a coproducer on 2003's creatively daring the *Detroit Experiment*, which brought together jazz, Motown, hip-hop, and electronic musicians. Belgrave worked on the project along with stellar jazz musicians such as Bennie Maupin, Geri Allen, Regina Carter, Allan Barnes, and Francisco Mora. Belgrave's "Space Odyssey," from his *Gemini II* Tribe release, was included on the *Detroit Experiment*, and Belgrave continued to perform with Craig at concert dates.

In 2007, Belgrave couldn't make a date with Craig in Paris due to teaching commitments at Oberlin College. He suggested Harrison as a replacement. The reedman brought his clarinet and wowed Craig and the audience with his nonstop, balls-out blowing.

"I knew that Wendell would fit right in with that stuff," Belgrave says.

Harrison fit in so well that Craig dubbed his clarinet the "Charmer." The concert was recorded and released as an EP called *Paris Live*. The Paris concert was the seed that sprouted into a full-blown Tribe revival. Around 2002, Craig gathered Harrison, Ranelin, Belgrave, and Hammond—McKinney passed away in 2001—together in the studio to record new material and remakes of some of their classic works.

"It was my first time in the studio with Tribe," Hammond enthuses. "I loved it. I've never worked with someone like Carl, who does this electronic music. I've never done overdubs, always did everything live. I'm basically all acoustic. With Carl, what's really interesting to me is his respect for the acoustic area. The openness and the respect were reassuring."

Musicians old and young came together on the sessions. Guitarist John Arnold; drummers Karriem Riggins and Gayelynn McKinney (Harold's daughter); bassists Ralphe Armstrong, Damon Warmack, and Pathe Jassi; keyboardists Kelvin Sholar, Amp Fiddler, and Pamela Wise; and vocalist Joan Belgrave were all in the mix for this great revival of Tribe.

"I didn't know how it was going to work," Harrison says. "We hadn't played together in thirty years. But it felt like old times because of the reaction we got from people. Carl Craig brings a central focus to Tribe as a producer. We never had that kind of help. We were dealing with Tribe as an umbrella, but we had all our different projects. Carl's got more of a personal interest in Tribe as an entity."

The single "Livin' in a New Day," written by Ranelin, is the first release from those sessions. Ranelin explains:

That was also inspired by the times, and I wrote that in 2003. I looked around and everybody was doing things differently. Things had changed with all this new technology, computers, and email. There are a lot of positives, but the negatives were just as intense. So, for me, I had to relearn how to survive. But see, the Bush government was lying to us about everything and playing dirty tricks and making people afraid to protest. It was really upsetting me. The oil people were doing a number on us, and you had all these unnecessary wars going on. This makes the people you encounter on the street warlike. It seemed like everything had sped up too much and that we needed to slow down some and, instead of promoting death, promote life and love and peace and happiness.

Another single, a regrooved "Vibes from the Tribe," was also released in 2008. And the group played New York's JVC Festival, along with some of the younger crew, receiving critical acclaim and creating anticipation for the new project. Once a small seed germinating in Detroit, today Tribe is welcomed by the world. It is indeed a new day.

37

John Sinclair and Charles Moore.
© Leni Sinclair Collection.

Bill Harris.
© Leni Sinclair
Collection.

# Strata Records

*John Sinclair*

In the fall of 1964, cornetist Charles Moore; photographer Magdalene Arndt; artists Larry Weiner, Howard Weingarden, and Ellen Phelan; poets George Tysh, Robin Eichele, Jim Semark, and myself; and several of our friends in the neighborhood around Wayne State University founded an artists' collective called the Detroit Artists Workshop.

The Artists Workshop served as an important meeting ground for resident artists, like musicians Charles Moore and saxophonist Larry Nozero, with outstate natives like Lyman Woodard from the Flint area, John Dana from Mt. Pleasant, and Ron English and Danny Spencer from Lansing.

Charles Moore had formed a cooperative ensemble called the Detroit Contemporary 5 with Nozero, Dana, English, and Spencer that performed on Sunday afternoons at the Artists Workshop and soon began to appear on the WSU campus and at college venues in other parts of Michigan.

In the creative cauldron that was the Detroit Artists Workshop, we learned to develop cooperative ensembles and cross-cultural collectives, manage our own gallery and performance facility, produce our own concerts and cultural events, design and print our own books and magazines, publicize our products and productions, and keep our creative activity firmly rooted in the immediate community. It was the DIY ethic in action.

Another prominent Detroit contemporary musician was pianist and composer Kenny Cox, a member of a cooperative quintet with trombonist George Bohanon, tenor saxophonist Ronnie Fields, bassist Will Austin, and drummer Bert Myrick. Cox teamed up with Charles Moore to form the Contemporary Jazz Quintet and, subsequently, the Strata Corporation.

"First of all, Strata was a group," Charles Moore explained to Cary Loren in a 2004 interview.

It was a five-piece group called the Contemporary Jazz Quintet. The group formed when Kenny Cox came off the road with jazz singer Etta Jones and took a gig with Danny Spencer and Ron Brooks at the Town Bar in Ann Arbor. Joe Henderson's brother Leon, a tenor saxophonist, and I used to commute up there from Detroit to play with these guys.

It was going so well sitting in with them, we thought why not put a group together. This was in 1967. We started rehearsing every day, and we did a d.b.a. as a partnership—a collective: a five-way, equal-split partnership.

The CJQ achieved local and regional jazz success through the excellence of its performances and gained recognition on the national scene when a leading jazz label, Blue Note Records, signed the Contemporary Jazz Quintet to a recording contract and issued a pair of well-reviewed albums.

"Then we started to produce concerts, and we rented the small auditorium in the Detroit Institute of Arts," Charles Moore remembers. "We started the Synergy concert series for a couple of years. WDET was in on that, and Bud Spangler would produce and record the concerts."

Cox and Moore were involved in public radio station WDET-FM, where Spangler was employed as a staff producer. Guitarist Ron English, a close friend of Spangler's at Michigan State University, was working around Detroit with Lyman Woodard and others. The four of them bonded around the concept of an artist-controlled production and recording collective through which the artists themselves could deal with all the exigencies of the music business that affected their lives and professional careers.

Cox brought to the new collective a finely honed business sense and professional experience in banking and the construction industry, while Moore was deeply rooted in cultural activism, collective action, and the community arts. Charles Moore recalls:

So we decided to get incorporated. Kenny Cox pulled in another partner, Harold Gardner, who was working for Ford Motor Credit, because we were going to go public with this. We rented a space on Michigan Avenue, a small warehouse, built a stage, got it fixed up, and called it Strata.

The name Strata came from a musicologist by the name of Joseph Schillinger [who] talked about layers of sound. He gives you endless variations of everything, including orchestration, theory, form, all layers of sound—that we call the strata thing. That's his terminology.

At some point we switched from Michigan Avenue and got into George Kalamo-

to's photography studio at 46 Selden, just west of Woodward, which held about two hundred people, and we decided to have a concert/gallery. It just kept going. We broadcasted every concert live to WDET on the phone lines. Bud Spangler taped everything, he took care of that. That enabled us to make deals with the musicians and start a collection of high-quality recordings.

The core group was aided and abetted by key associates Barbara Cox, Krista English, and a few others, and they began to build an organization that could attack the problems they faced as artists and entrepreneurs.

The collective developed the Strata Corporation, establishing several operative divisions—most notably the Strata Gallery, Strata Productions, Strata Records, and Hot Man record distribution—and a nonprofit affiliate, the Allied Artists Association, headed by Ron English.

Thus, Strata helped keep creative music in the forefront of Detroit's artistic community for a period of almost ten years and played a seminal role in the artists' self-determination movement in modern music. As Charles Moore told Cary Loren:

At some point when we had this studio space, John Sinclair made a deal to get the portable recording studio that had been used by John Lennon and Yoko Ono and belonged to producers Steve Gebhardt and Bob Fries from Cincinnati. They were the recordists for Joko Productions. They didn't have much call for the truck after they split from Joko Productions, and Sinclair

convinced them to let his outfit in Ann Arbor use the truck for recording the Ann Arbor Blues and Jazz Festival in 1973.

After the festival ended, the truck was housed in a warehouse in Ann Arbor for a few months, where Sinclair did some production work with the mobile studio, and then we talked to John: "What are you gonna do with that?" Because it was just sitting there. "Let us borrow the truck."

So he said, "If you maintain it, you can borrow it." We had to punch a hole in the back of our building big enough to get the truck through. But it was the perfect thing, because the truck fit inside the building and you could run cable and record. So Strata became a recording studio. It was a full sixteen-track studio, and now instead of just recording live, we were recording with the truck.

We were making recordings by everybody in Detroit: Larry Nozero, Ursula Walker, Ron English, Lyman Woodard, David Durrah, and Ron Brooks—with Larry Nozero, Danny Spencer, Gary Schunk, Dave Koether, and Jerry Glassel—had a group called Mixed Bag. With our own money, we released three or four records, including *Saturday Night Special*, with a group named Sphere.

There was also a live recording by Kenny Cox and George Bohanon released under the name of the drummer, Bert Myrick, and a new album by CJQ that followed up on its two Blue Note releases.

Early in 1975, this writer decided to return to Detroit after seven years in Ann Arbor and

approached the Strata principals to suggest that I would like to join forces with them, trading work on Strata Records for office space in their building. I established my own desk in the Strata building, and there I assisted in the development of Strata Records and carried on the artists' management and production business that I had established in Ann Arbor as Rainbow Productions.

I served as album coordinator and publicist for the Strata project centered on Lyman Woodard, which produced the well-received album called *Saturday Night Special*. I also oversaw the design and annotation of several projected Strata Records releases, including albums by Ron English, Kenny Cox, Larry Nozero, the CJQ, and others. These had been recorded and produced at the Strata complex, and I developed a marketing plan to coordinate these new releases with Strata's existing products by the CJQ, Sphere, the Bert Myrick Quintet, and a Chicago-based artist called Maulawi. Charles Moore explains:

> So, with this kind of stuff, we thought we needed to get some kind of venture capital in here. We worked out a business plan in order to come up with something real and practical. It turned out that we were trying to raise half a million dollars using Kalamoto's property, the truck, and all the recordings we had stored for collateral, and we needed the money to expand.
>
> We went to the Small Business Association, and they said, "In order to get an SBA loan, you need to get the regular banks to turn you down." That ain't a difficult thing to do in Detroit. So we went

to the banks and they all said, "Screw you guys—you're all a bunch of crazies." So we went back to the SBA and they took the loan package.

Then we assembled a coherent package of our music and Sinclair took it to New York to present to Clive Davis at Arista Records while Kenny Cox and I took it to California to present to Herb Alpert at A&M Records and to the people who were running ABC Records.

And at that point: *the wall.* The financing was gone. We're trying to sell our catalog. Then we get a call from the SBA minority-business people: They're gonna turn the package down. So we just had to abandon it. That was 1976, to be exact, when we decided to put the corporation to sleep.

We had the manufacturing and distribution lined up, but we couldn't supply the product. You have to spend cold cash to be able to provide the distributors with product, and then they'll carry you. But we just couldn't afford to get the production up, and we had to throw in the towel.

But in terms of the large-scale manufacturing of records on an independent label, we were the first. We know that for sure.

At the same time in Detroit came the Tribe collective, a musicians' cooperative organized by saxophonist Wendell Harrison and Harold McKinney in 1972. By the next year, Tribe Records was issuing albums by Harrison, McKinney, Marcus Belgrave, Phil Ranelin, Doug Hammond and David Durrah, and Mixed Bag, followed by a periodical titled *Tribe*, and

a production company that presented the members of the collective in concert.

In New York City, pianist-composer Stanley Cowell, who had played with trumpeter Charles Moore in the Detroit Contemporary 4 in 1965–66, partnered with trumpeter-composer Charles Tolliver to form Strata-East Records and released over sixty albums in the 1970s, including recordings by Tolliver, Cowell, Pharoah Sanders, Clifford Jordan, M'Boom with Max Roach and Roy Brooks, Billy Harper, and Gil Scott-Heron, whose 1974 album *Winter in America* was the label's biggest seller.

"Kenny Cox and Charles Moore came to New York with their papers for Strata Corporation and convinced us to form a corporation," recalls Cowell, who says he and Tolliver were so inspired by Strata that they began to work on plans for a similar operation in New York:

Strata-East, Inc. would be part of a larger artist-controlled concept. As we saw the potential for our catalog to expand more rapidly, we decided to form Strata-East Records, Inc.

The notoriety that began to follow upon our releases caught the attention of other independent black artists and producers who had tapes and wanted LPs pressed and distributed.

The artist-producers signed a contract with Strata-East Records, furnished the recorded material, and paid for the initial cost of fabrication. Strata-East Records then sold the LPs via our distributors. The artists/producers received the lion's share of the profits, as Strata-East Records only took a minor percentage after costs.

Over the years since, the seminal contributions of the artist-owned record companies Strata and Tribe spawned a vast movement of self-produced recordings, independent album releases, and grassroots distribution by jazz artists and musicians of every description all over the world.

Forty years later, following the virtual demise of the commercial record business as we knew it, the approach pioneered by Strata Records in Detroit has become the basic way of life for creative musicians today.

Roy Brooks with Clarence Edins. © Leni Sinclair Collection.

# Roy Brooks
## Detroit Downbeat
*Bill Harris*

To appreciate and understand Roy Brooks, listen for his message when he speaks and works. Schooled by the bebop drummers who stretched beyond merely keeping time, Brooks has progressed even further, adding his own verbal and performing vocabulary.

"I am a drumist," he says. "That's like a pianist or bassist. . . . The word 'drumist' is a name that implies I am a drummer and I am a percussionist."

Drumist Brooks resides in Detroit, where he was born fifty-odd years ago. He attended Northwestern High School at a time when music education was not only available in public schools but extremely high quality. "But his biggest school was the back door of the Blue Bird," remembers baritone saxophonist Thomas "Beans" Bowles, one of the many professional Detroit jazz musicians responsible for the musical foundation on which the Motown phenomenon was based. Though only a high school student, Brooks was serious about playing music, a commitment that sent him to hang out by the back door of the Blue Bird Inn and other nightspots regularly to hear what he could. Tommy Flanagan, Barry Harris, Thad and Elvin Jones, Billy Mitchell, and Phil Hill were just some of the musicians Brooks absorbed in the company of his friend and young musical peer, saxophonist Charles McPherson. They were too young to enter the bars legally, but that did not deter Brooks from sneaking in occasionally to sit in for a tune at the invitation of

senior musicians who were impressed by his prodigy. Beans Bowles was one such elder. "I remember Beans coming to my house and asking my mother if I could play in his band," Brooks recalls. "I was twenty then, and I was going to Detroit Institute of Technology (on an athletic scholarship), but I still wasn't old enough to be in a bar."

With his mother's consent, he joined the band, which sent him on tour to Las Vegas playing backup for the Four Tops. That was in February 1959. Seven months later, he moved to New York to replace drummer Louis Hayes in Horace Silver's band.

"He moved from the Four Tops to Horace Silver, and from there he never looked back," Bowles recalls. From such fast and heady beginnings, Brooks went on to join the groups of Yusef Lateef, Charles Mingus, Pharaoh Sanders, and James Moody, eventually fronting his own ensembles during his sixteen years in New York (1959–75).

There are messages in the names of various groups led by Brooks. He is instructive in this and other regards: MUSIC (Musicians United to Save Indigenous Culture); the Artistic Truth, one of his New York groups, which at various times featured Detroiters trumpeter Marcus Belgrave, pianist Geri Allen, and bassist Bob Hurst, as well as New York names Olu Dara, Hamiet Bluiett, George Coleman, and the late Woody Shaw and Eddie Jefferson. It was during the New York years that he began his ongoing association with Max Roach and cofounded

M'Boom, an all-percussion orchestra now in its twenty-first year. Roy is "one of the leading lights" of the group and the "greatest drummer here in Detroit," Roach says of Brooks.

"Roy started teaching after he came back from Max," Beans Bowles continues, "and has been teaching ever since." His method of instruction parallels the African tradition in which an elder musician gathers fledglings around him and nurtures them in the ways of music and the world. It was done for Brooks; he now does it for others.

*Edutainment* is a term used by Brooks to explain his approach to teaching, which combines entertainment and education, a technique that works for students and laymen alike. "It's ancient," Brooks says. "The student can't help but learn."

As a performer, he is as adept at accompaniment as he is at soloing. In the blink of an eye, he can change from a thunderous, rock-steady tom-tom barrage with the intensity of a 1950s auto-factory stamping plant, to rapid-fire trap drum press rolls, dance-slashing like machine-gun tracers, to brushes on cymbal patterns with the delicacy of a butterfly's flight and the subtlety of a Japanese floral arrangement.

The Aboriginal Orchestra is Brooks's percussion choir, a huge and exciting ensemble with representation from the entire percussion family and then some. In concert at Hart Plaza in Detroit, the orchestra of more than twenty musicians and a tap dancer uses a 4/4 backbeat to charge a crowd of ten thousand, inspiring their participation and rhythmic hand clapping.

Brooks, a big man in a tuxedo and blue-black silk skullcap that Thelonious Monk would envy, makes his way deliberately through the maze of instruments and musicians to center stage. Under his arm, he carries a handsaw. Is he some beatific, sartorially splendid carpenter making a house call? The crowd knows better. In anticipation they shout their encouragement, "Play the saw, Roy. Play the saw!"

Brooks adjusts the mic to waist height. The 4/4 groove continues, building through repetition. "Roy Brooks!" they chant, clapping in unison. Like a blues blacksmith, with the saw handle locked between his knees, Brooks begins whacking the business end of the implement with a mallet. The saw sings: "When I lost my ba-by . . ." Brooks, getting tremolo by bending the instrument/implement like a serrated steel snake with his left hand, does a languorous lateral body movement from pelvis to knees. The notes are extended until they vibrate. "I almost lost my mind" eases into "I'm so lonely I could die."

"Play the saw, baby. Play the saw!"

Brooks ends his solo by gripping the handle firmly and shaking it with the ferocity of a shaggy dog emerging from a swim. A warbling steel crescendo explodes with the force and sound of a southern gale across a sharecropper's tin-roof shack.

"Play the saw, Roy!"

The years of serious work, exploration, and mastery have not obscured his sense of the dramatic. A performance by this landmark innovator is big fun—edutainment. Oblivious to the applause and the many musicians staring at him for direction, Brooks strikes a pizza-sized gong, with short, powerful strokes, and then disappears into the wings, applause still ringing.

M'Jumbe is his Swahili name. It means "Messenger."

# Musician Interrupted
## Faruq Z. Bey

*W. Kim Heron*

He'd gone to see saxophonists John Coltrane and Pharaoh Sanders the year before at a place on Dexter called the Drome Lounge, and their wail was like nothing he'd ever experienced before: magnificent, powerful, polyrhythmic, polytonal, polychromatic, emotional, form-shattering—the purest music he'd ever experienced before or since.

And when the word went out that Coltrane had died on a Monday in July—or gotten so heavy he'd fallen off the planet, as some wags would have it—it was only fitting to call for a memorial party. A dozen or so fans worshipfully played records and made music through Saturday night at the cramped apartment on Chicago Boulevard where he lived with his wife. Around daybreak came the sound of cars speeding away from Lord knew what, and being reckless guys, they went to check out the commotion and soon found themselves at the epicenter of the brewing Detroit rebellion of 1967. It was a revelation: "The people who were rioting in the street, they moved like one mind. It was almost like a hive of insect moves. It was like a wave; it just moved, but that whole episode put me in a frame of mind of thinking about our position here as a 'subculture,' and how to deal with that. And since music was always an interest of mine and seeing how our music defined itself and our relationship to the greater environment as well."

Faruq Z. Bey with members of his band Griot Galaxy.
© Leni Sinclair Collection.

The issues all seemed intertwined.

A couple days later, with the riot still raging, he became the owner of his first saxophone, a Martin tenor, for the unusually low price of eighty dollars.

Asked whether, in the parlance of the time, the saxophone had been "liberated," he laughs dryly. "I got it during the riot," he says more than once.

Asked whether this all seemed prophetic—Coltrane dying, the memorial, the riot, the saxophone—his eyes widen as if it's obvious. He laughs again. "It was significant, I'll put it that way."

Life seemed to take on a new seriousness. "Before that, I was just floating and having fun doing what was expected of me by the culture at large and the tradition and yadda yadda," he says.

Within a few years, Jesse Davis would have new names. He would become Malik Z. Bey, then Faruq Z. Bey. His marriage would dissolve, as would two more during the '70s. He'd become part of an artistic, spiritualist, pan-African political milieu; he'd eventually become a sort of poster boy for that set. He'd read his poetry to rapt listeners, pontificate on the meaning of life and culture, play in more bands and jams than anyone can be expected to keep track of. He'd impress a lot of folks as brilliant and charismatic; he'd attract talent like a magnet. He'd garner a rep as a ladies' man. He'd live wildly, nearly die, watch much of what he'd worked for unravel, and slowly recover.

At sixty-one, six foot four, lean, and with a slow gait and a slight stoop, Faruq looks like a human question mark when he bends forward.

He can be alternately comically terse and loquacious. To talk to him is to realize how his own premeditated take on things is wrung from his own questioning. A word as simple as "hey" in a conversation can lead to a digression on its origins. Back in the '80s, his friend, the writer and magazine editor Kofi Natambu, interviewed him for hours and published pages of the transcript, which looped through Faruq's thoughts on the origin of the word *jazz* ("It's obviously an Arabic word") to his hopes as an artist ("to communicate some positive forces in the environment") to the quandaries of the musical life ("placed on some kind of pedestal . . . and on the other hand starve to death").

Talking over coffee at a suburban Borders store, he takes a listener on a similarly wide-ranging conversational trip. He talks about his youth growing up in Detroit's Conant Gardens neighborhood, the eldest of five children of a city bus driver and his stay-at-home wife who would find their artistic and wayward son increasingly hard to comprehend. Neighborhood role models included Eddie Floyd, then of the doo-wop group the Falcons, who would later have the hit "Knock on Wood."

Faruq talks about being one of those insatiably curious kids who stayed up after bedtime, hid in the closet, and read with a flashlight. He started writing poetry at thirteen. He fell under the influence of beboppers as a teen and studied string bass at school. (Jazz educator James Tatum was one of his teachers.) At various times, he wanted to be an auto designer, a physicist, or a scholar instead of a jazz bassist; it all depended on the position of the moon, he says. He had a relatively uneventful air force stint, had a daughter with one woman and married another, worked factory jobs, studied existentialism at community college—all in the time leading up to the riot, which ignited when he was twenty-five.

And he talks and talks about music and language, and music as language, and how those relate to society. Here is some of what he has to say about jazz:

In jazz—quote-unquote—the model is text (which is the melody or the construct, you dig, the tune, if you will) and commentary (which is the improvisatory thing). Now you've got people at different ends of the spectrum. You've got people who are really concerned with text, so their improvisatory comment sounds more and more textual.

They follow or allow rules that are more and more locked down and concrete, which is leading away from the intent of the whole thing. On the other hand, you've got people who do away with text entirely. How are you gonna talk about something when there's nothing to talk about? You're just out there babbling, in other words.

He often talks about the meaning of intervals in language, both musical and verbal. Most African languages, for instance, use tone to convey meaning. Even in largely atonal English, the interval—or note-to-note leap—called a flatted fifth describes the rising tone of the typical question. The meanings of these intervals in language and music fascinate Faruq to no end. He'd like to develop a universal catalog of languages "to find which intervals persist in their meaning about the planet." And his music is informed by a long study of modes and scales, which are ways of stacking intervals. *The Sound of Music*'s song "Do-Re-Mi" ("Doe, a deer, a female deer . . .") traces the familiar major scale, also known as the Ionian mode. Any five consecutive black keys on a piano comprise one of the pentatonic scales. The variations and combinations are limitless.

Faruq recalls that the writer Amiri Baraka once said that, in essence, a language is a logic. "It is a logic you speak," Faruq continues. "And when you get into what they call music, now you get into a different language. And with a different logic, you deal with different syllogistic principles and different conclusions."

This language-equals-logic equation is long out of fashion among academic linguists, but not to Faruq. As on many subjects, he's worked through his sources to his own conclusions with an evident rigor.

That's one reason why so many of his friends and acquaintances describe him in similar terms. "One of the most brilliant men I've ever met in my life," says one. "Frankly, I thought he was a genius," says another of their first encounter.

"A lot of people don't know the depth of his intellect and his studies," says the poet and editor of this anthology, M. L. Liebler, a collaborator since the mid-'80s who has also published Faruq's poetry and his music-theory book.

"He has this really intense understanding of surrealism and history because he's reading all the time," adds Liebler. (Faruq names as his favorite poets T. S. Eliot and the Negritude writers Léopold Senghor and Aimé Césaire.)

"An incident comes to mind," says Liebler. "Not too long ago, we were playing up north in Petoskey. We're sitting in the van, and he's sitting there with some sort of super-duper science calculator, like the ones the brainy kids use in calculus or something. He's reading a book on Egyptian mathematics, and he's doing all these math figures and writing musical notes down in another book." Liebler pauses, hard-pressed to quite convey his awe at this scene.

For all the destruction of the riots—forty-three dead and $45 million in property damage—for all the dread that shook liberals and conservatives, there were plenty of blacks (often young, but not always) who felt the slogan "Burn, baby, burn" to be a metaphoric match lighting their imaginations.

"It was postriot Detroit. It was all wide open," says Sadiq Bey—sometimes known instead as Sadiq Muhammad, sometimes as just Sadiq—now a performer and writer in New York City. "We were brand-new people. Whatever we wanted to be, we could be. We were making jewelry, making art,

49

performing. It was a renaissance. Everybody was a renaissance man. It was incredible."

In the scene from which Sadiq and Faruq emerged, you could shed your old lifestyles and even your old names. The two worked together for more than a decade.

"There was an intense period of intellectual fervor, if you will," says Faruq, who talks of studying religion with members of the Moorish Science Temple (a sort of forerunner to the Nation of Islam) who had adopted the name Bey; he later studied Islam. "Things just kind of grew from that. But then that's the way I remember it. Other people might remember it totally differently."

Sadiq recalls being with Faruq at a jam session of poetry and music at a private residence around '68. In a sense, that jam went on for years.

"It was such an incredible connection that we just decided to live together as a commune sort of thing. It just grew from that. Guys brought their girlfriends in and people started having kids, and it was just this huge family, and we all decided to be Beys," he says.

There were a half dozen or more Bey families in the informal cooperative, Faruq says.

Several self-appointed Beys—chiefly Faruq, Sadiq, and Jalil—became known as the Bey Brothers as they performed poetry and music together at places like the old Concept East Theater, a hotbed for new, politicized voices in black theater.

"They'd be around black nationalist things and events and institutions," recalls Geoffrey Jacques, a poet, former WDET-FM jazz host, and now a New York–based writer and teacher. "And even then they were sort of the kings of the musicians—for relatively younger musicians in their twenties. They always had this aura of mystery about them."

The Bey Brothers gave way to the First African Primal Rhythm Arkestra, playing what Sadiq described as "basically free improv." But some members of that group moved on. "I sort of left and moved on and got married and had a family, and everybody sort of split up," says Sadiq.

"Then it was Faruq's idea to bring this group back together," says Sadiq, "and he named it Griot Galaxy." And rather than total improvisation, Faruq wanted to bring composition and structure to bear. Meanwhile, he had been working on his saxophone chops, primarily on his own, but he'd also sought out guidance from sympathetic older musicians like Leon Henderson (brother of the famous Joe Henderson).

If—and this is a big if—Griot Galaxy had been part of Ken Burns's nineteen-hour, ten-part documentary *Jazz*, the group would have been jammed into the couple of dismissive minutes that covered the avant-garde that flourished between Coltrane's death in 1967 and the back-to-tradition revival that Wynton Marsalis heralded fifteen years later. Bands and musicians like the Art Ensemble of Chicago and Sun Ra challenged preconceptions about what jazz should be; in turn, they were accused of alienating the jazz audience—especially the African American audience—and driving the music into obscurity. Or so goes one version of jazz history. Those were the bands that influenced Griot. And like so many bands in the avant-garde, the members of Griot wore their sense of history on their musical sleeves and later on their faces. (For the record, Faruq detests the term *avant-garde*, citing its military roots, a designation for advancing troops doomed to take the highest casualties.)

In traditional West African societies, the griot—pronounced "gree-oh"—is a praise singer, historian, and preserver of culture. In Alex Haley's epic *Roots*, it's a village griot who confirms the story of Haley's ancestor's capture generations earlier.

So much for the past. According to Faruq, the *galaxy* part of his group's name signified that "we were the griots of the galaxy period . . . our quadrant anyway."

But one former member jokingly suggested that it might as well have referred to the dozens of musicians who fell in and out of the ranks over the ten years or so that followed the group's formation in 1972.

A key stretch in the group's development came with a mid-'70s residency at Cobb's Corner on Cass at Willis. In this pregentrification period in the Corridor, Griot helped make Cobb's the epicenter of jazz in Detroit. It was about the third edition of Griot Galaxy by Faruq's count, the first with the chance to grow week to week with a steady gig.

One member of the band remembers that when they started there, Cobb's was rough and fistfights were common. But it became the focal point for bands led by funky organist Lyman Woodard and trumpeter Marcus Belgrave. Griot found its own crowd, practically a cult at the beginning, as Kofi Natambu recalls.

"They had a small, highly energetic, and very supportive group of people who loved what they were doing . . . a lot of artists, painters, a lot of poets, a lot of writers were interested in the band," says Natambu, now based in Oakland, California, and author of a recent Malcolm X biography. As Natambu puts it, the followers were drawn to "the visionary aspect of what Griot Galaxy was doing," not to mention their charisma and theatricality. And with eight or more musicians crowded on the stage,

it was quite a sight and a glorious sound. (And when they'd leave the club for a concert gig, they'd add dancers and such to magnify the spectacle.)

Patrice Williams (then known as Kafi Patrice Nassoma), who played flute and harp with the band, recalls the company of such musicians as pianist Ken Thomas and clarinetist-saxophonist Elreta "Duchess" Dodds. Then there was drummer Tariq, who could play the exact accents to complement the actions around him. "He could finish all my thoughts," Williams says.

Free jazz was an influence, Sadiq says, but the band worked from compositions—mostly Faruq's—and used "all sorts of visual cues and musical cues" to move the music along. On the best nights, the interactions seemed telepathic. Music like that, Sadiq explains, "is an act of worship."

One night in Ann Arbor, the band played between sets by the Art Ensemble of Chicago. Some members say the band held its own in following the AEC—in itself a considerable achievement. Others, like Sadiq, say they kicked AEC's ass for the first set with a "pinnacle performance" embracing poetry and drama along with the music. (On the other hand, all the band members interviewed for this piece agreed the AEC reclaimed top-dog billing later that night. Their second set, says Faruq, had an undeniable message: "That was nice, kids; this is how it's really done.")

"It was just truly spontaneous, energetic expression," says Williams of the group. Offstage it was a musical community, she adds, "willing and brave to try something new." She and others recall "rehearsals" where not a note would be played—there'd be philosophical discussions instead. At listening sessions, members would play records of everything from Andean pan pipes to the clattering rhythmic voices of a hundred-plus-member Balinese chorus in what's known as "The Monkey Chant." "We were exposing ourselves to everything," she says.

But there were, eventually, tensions within the group, musical and personal, conflicting pursuits. Sadiq left to lead an edgy reggae band, Aziz, which included Faruq. Guitarist Spencer Barefield left to concentrate on his Creative Arts Collective, which presented more than one hundred concerts at the Detroit Institute of Arts, presented the Griot circle, and fostered collaborations with out-of-towners such as Anthony Braxton and the Art Ensemble's Roscoe Mitchell.

Williams says that when she and Dodds were eased out, she felt that maybe they had been exploited for the novelty of having women in a jazz band; yet she credits Faruq for at least having given her and Dodds that much exposure.

But the shifts also involved a vision that Faruq and the other remaining members had for the band. "There were too many variables when the group was big," says Faruq. As a composer, the smaller group meant he could better "manipulate the forces."

Drummer Tani Tabbal is blunt. He says the members were becoming impressed with their cultural stardom. Meanwhile, the fans didn't know what they were missing: "The stuff was not turning out right, and Jaribu [bassist Jaribu Shahid] and I used to come home and listen to the stuff [on tape] and it used to just drive us crazy. We couldn't stand it."

And they didn't. From Tabbal's perspective, the contraction amounted to "a little power play."

The downsizing ushered in the ultimate phase of Griot, featuring Faruq—now the sole Bey in the lineup and the eldest member by a decade—with four relatively late additions. There was Pontiac saxophonist Tony Holland. There was saxophonist David McMurray, the rare musician who can play for the avant-garde set and record with pop acts as big as the Rolling Stones. The backbone was the team of Tabbal and Shahid, who locked as tightly as any bassist and drummer in recent decades of jazz.

Both had played with that mystical showman of jazz, Sun Ra. A big band leader with an affection, at different stages in his career, for Egyptian-style regalia and silver lamé space suits, "Sunny" played music as intriguing as it was wide ranging. Tabbal, originally from Chicago, had furthermore played extensively with a former Sun Ra sideman named Phil Cohran. Though barely a footnote in most jazz books—and virtually unrecorded outside of Ra's band—the Chicago cornetist is a visionary giant to Tabbal.

Through the influences of Ra and Cohran, Jaribu and Tabbal augmented Faruq's interest in modes and in the myriad ways of grouping musical beats into meters. Ideas that had long been part of Griot Galaxy were being refined and pushed toward their limits.

Through the '60s, most jazz, like most pop even to this day, flowed in a familiar four beats to a bar—tap your foot, 1-2-3-4, 1-2-3-4. There had been jazz waltzes at three beats to the bar (1-2-3, 1-2-3), and Dave Brubeck made "Take Five" a hit with five beats to the bar in the '50s. But odd meters became pervasive in jazz starting in the '60s. Griot made metric juggling acts—layering these different meters and shifting from meter to meter—as dizzily compelling as anyone before or since.

Faruq, says Tabbal, "would sit there and write continuously"; he remained the group's chief composer, even though all of the members made contributions. But the execution was a group affair.

"Faruq would say, 'I want the drums in seven and the bass in five,' and we just said, 'Cool,' and we did it," says Shahid. "Stuff would be like swirling, swirling, swirling," says Holland, describing the effect and the challenges of Griot's music.

They played long sections that explored spaces with no discernible beat at all, sometimes softly, sometimes with almost volcanic eruptions in what Geoffrey Jacques calls "ecstatic energy space." But the prototypical Griot sound, more than anything else, was one of these odd-meter excursions that still rocked the house.

They augmented the more pointed music with a more defined stage presence. Faruq's poetry stayed. But now they donned silver face paint and called themselves a "science fiction" band.

Members of the Art Ensemble of Chicago wore African-style face paints to evoke performances as rituals. It was the ultimate statement of their "Great Black Music," linking the most "far out" extrapolations to bop, swing, blues, field hollers—all the way back to the music of the African motherland.

But in industrial Detroit, Griot's face paint was metallic. This was ritual, yes, but as Faruq puts it, it was also "a response to a more modern environment speaking about androids and robots and that sort of thing."

Less frequently a bar band now, this edition of Griot Galaxy drove audiences wild at Hart Plaza during such events as the African World Festival and what in the early '80s was the Montreux-Detroit International Jazz Festival.

Without an actual manager, the band's business dealings were always ad hoc—creating a tension between Faruq's laid-back approach and Tabbal and Shahid's feeling that the band should be more aggressive about getting beyond Detroit. Yet, there was a feeling among the fans that the rest of the music world had to catch on to what Detroiters knew.

At one point, band fan and friend Ron DeCorte figured he'd be part of that process. He frequently followed the band lugging a sixty-five-pound Crown SX 800 reel-to-reel tape recorder. Other times, he took them into the studio, including for the 1981 release *Kins*, on his own Black and White label. He pressed two thousand copies to little avail. Shortly after, he was laid up in a motorcycle accident; during his convalescence, fifteen hundred or so of those copies were hauled from storage at a relative's house and set out with the trash.

With or without a release, Griot's reputation continued to build. Tabbal and Shahid (plus Barefield) toured Europe as the rhythm section for the Art Ensemble of Chicago's Roscoe Mitchell. That led, in the spring of '84, to an Austria-Germany tour and live recordings for both Griot (minus McMurray, who didn't have a passport) and the trio of Holland, Tabbal, and Barefield. Things were looking up that fall.

Then, as Tabbal puts it, "Faruq fell on his head."

Faruq was a striking figure in the run-up to the crash, the African-style garb now replaced with biker's leather, his dreadlocks having grown into a leonine mane cascading well past the shoulders of his tall frame. The sensitive, emotional guy that many attest to was at least superficially masked by the image of a mystery-man badass. He was a regular

53

at the Cass Corridor watering hole Alvin's, drinking, playing in reggae bands, talking it up, dancing. There are women from those days who talk about their long-lasting, soulful relations with Faruq; graffiti in Alvin's upstairs women's bathroom celebrated his quick magnetism and sexual prowess.

Natambu dedicated a poem to his "friend and brother" Faruq and titled it "We Think We Know You or the Roving Enigma Blues." One section reads:

> But what is it that we know?
> That the shining grey
> mask you seem to wear is an
> affirmation of our fears? That
> the melodies you ponder and
> furtively reveal are cultural
> readymades for us to wear then
> discard when the houselights
> come on?
> Is this our history you sing as
> your grinning groupies
> crawl in for the delicious kill?
> What about the painters
> who buy you too much beer
> as we finger that aching
> saxophone
> sweating between sets in the
> corner?

Faruq himself talks vaguely about that chapter—Griot on the verge of wider success—as "a rough period for me socially and artistically and every other way . . . there was just a lot of confusion." He describes it as a time of "bad habits," and asked if he

means drugs, he answers, "All that stuff that didn't have to do with the music itself."

One friend suggests that deep down, Faruq was afraid of success, or of possible disappointment. Another friend suggests that something like the accident was inevitable and could have been worse.

Faruq doesn't remember the accident itself. He'd left Alvin's with a young woman riding on the back of his souped-up Yamaha 750 Triple.

"Somebody told me it had something to do with some railroad tracks," he says, "but the fact of the matter was a bad mix of alcohol and motorcycles."

His rider was uninjured. Faruq was in a coma at Receiving Hospital for more than two weeks while a circus swirled around him.

A piece of thinly veiled fiction by Sadiq, "Excerpts from the Jesse Davis Medical Fund," captures his version of events. (It was published in a long out-of-print anthology edited by Natambu and titled *Nostalgia for the Present: An Anthology of Writings from Detroit*.)

In the story, the accident is reported in "the dailies and the rags," conferring star status on the musician. Friends, lovers, and blood relatives crowd the waiting room and vie for access to the comatose patient; at times they nearly come to blows over "who was who" in his life.

Sadiq, the narrator—here called Coodeek—tells one friend that the accident is a sign: "I mean, we're all abusing our bodies to the hilt." The friend has to agree.

"I saw Jesse sprawled on the roller bed," Sadiq/Coodeek observes at one point. "His dreadlocks scattered like black yarn over the pillow. There was a majestic, regal quality about him. He jerked and struggled a little, almost like he knew we were there. . . . He had every imaginable tube and needle in his body. A fucking Frankenstein Monster sniffing the flowers of death. A 6' 4," 185 lb. black grass eater reduced to a sleeping menace. A menace to our love for him."

The story invokes the Egyptian myth of Osiris in which a god is betrayed and dismembered but ultimately regains his wholeness. And the story suggests Faruq eventually does, too. But in real life, the reconstitution dragged on for years.

Even as Faruq worked through rehabilitation for a closed head injury and eventually returned to music, the band disintegrated. Among the personal conflicts and dramas was a clash over whether Faruq was up to the demands of the music—and whether there could be a Griot Galaxy without Faruq.

After some Faruq-less gigs, the band went on hiatus for a couple of years. When Faruq rejoined, there were problems.

"He wasn't quite there yet," says McMurray. Tabbal says Faruq's drinking problems complicated his recovery and return to playing.

Adds McMurray: "It was just going into turmoil because this was basically Faruq's group, but the keeper of the music was Jaribu—always. And he would keep everything going because he was organized; a lot of that music might have gotten destroyed, but he guarded it . . . and because of him the music still exists, the written music."

Tabbal and Shahid also said they felt obligated to register the name Griot Galaxy—and themselves as owners—to safeguard it. Eventually the group resumed playing without Faruq—sometimes with the up-and-coming Detroit saxophonist James Carter in his stead.

For the group's final Detroit gig, in March 1991 at the DIA, a couple of picketers protested that the group was being hijacked; the behind-the-scenes conflict was embarrassingly out in the open.

The band played as Griot Galaxy just once after that—at a festival in Holland with a lineup featuring Carter, according to Tabbal. When Carter's career subsequently took off—he was lauded by some critics as the most important voice of his generation—Tabbal and Shahid worked with him for years. Detroit listeners couldn't help but think of the Griot connection when Carter's band sizzled.

And what does Faruq say about the last days of Griot?

He pauses when asked if he felt betrayed, then turns philosophical: "I was very uncomfortable with it, but what it came down to was everybody has a different view of what the thing is, especially something as complex as that band at that time because that wasn't a popular recording band . . . or even your traditional jazz band. That was a very different social and cultural experiment. Everybody has a different view. The reality of their different views manifested themselves. Yeah, I was disappointed, but that was because of the view of the band that I had that didn't match with everybody else in the band."

A little later, he consigns Griot Galaxy to the great flux—all "playing environments" are "just transitory states, part of the changing same."

Faruq's personal recovery was arduous. He left the hospital with his left side paralyzed, uncertain whether he'd ever play again. Asked how he made it, he laughs and says:

Poorly, not well at all, but I did what was necessary. I did jobs. I did day jobs. I availed

55

myself of whatever benefits were, you know, and that kind of thing . . .

After that period of the accident and all that, I went underground and woodshed-ded for a few years. I kept a low profile to try to regroup. . . . Then I started coming out here and there doing a few things.

He sought help for his chemical dependencies: "The accident and events that happened after let me see I was actually operating in a mental fog and I had to come out of that and get to a clear mind again."

But for Faruq, the lessons of the accident and its aftermath go beyond avoiding booze and bikes, or the volatile dynamics of great bands, or kicking bad habits. There was something he grasped in the coma that he's still trying to come to grips with, let alone explain: "I came away with another knowledge, another knowing about this condition we call life, so I can understand things now that I didn't understand before about my personal reality and about my social reality, about my cultural and political reality, the reality of my collective past. All of that I see differently now."

When the group disbanded, DeCorte lost track of Faruq and the other Griots.

At his home in Toledo, his fifty hours or so of old tapes "just sat for years and years and years. I listened to them from time to time, but that was it. They were for my own private use."

About a year ago, on a whim, he searched the Internet to see whether any of those rare copies of the *Kins* disc were being sold as collectibles. It was still the only full-length Griot record aside from the '84 tour record, *Opus Krampus*, which had been released to rave reviews on the Sound Aspects label.

DeCorte found bootleg *Kins* tapes being sold in Europe, but none of the rare vinyl. And he stumbled onto something much more important, references to a new record, *19 Moons* on the Entropy Stereo label, by Faruq Z. Bey in collaboration with a group called the Northwoods Improvisers.

Through email, DeCorte got in touch with Entropy's Mike Khoury, one of those label owners who has carved out a niche on the far margins of the industry, where the music is fascinating and the market is small. Khoury has released material from some of the leading lights in improvisational music—including England's Derek Bailey and Australia's Jon Rose—and boosted the visibility of the Northwoods group, whose members were musical mentors during Khoury's youth in Mt. Pleasant.

Shortly after that email, Khoury and Faruq trekked to Toledo to listen to DeCorte's tape cache. They zeroed in on a performance that cap-tured the group in peak form. Faruq's poetry is missing, but the nearly ninety minutes of music, recently released as *Live at the D.I.A. 1983*, include everything else that made the group distinctive. The music draws on the roots of jazz and on the sounds of the New York and Chicago-St. Louis avant-gardes—and offers something specific to Detroit in the '80s.

There are compositions from Bey, Tabbal, and Shahid; two cover versions of Sun Ra pieces; and an explosive interlude with guest drummers—Sadiq and Fahali Igbo—joining Tabbal. At times, collages of instrumental sounds float as if in search of a larger picture to attach themselves to—and finally coalesce in dramatic shapes and structures.

The key performance may be Faruq's "Fosters," a crowd-pleasing paean to a down-home Detroit eatery that sustained him when a marriage had gone kaput and his culinary skills were nil. It starts off with a braying horn line—a sort of allusion to blues so old they creak—works into hum-along midtempo stomp, then raises the tension and ante each time it circles back to the theme.

"I feel I missed a lot when I listen to this music," says Khoury, who moved to the Detroit area after Griot Galaxy had passed from gigdom to local-legend status. "I can't believe the levels they reached. You hear people just going crazy in the audience. It was a special time for some special music."

You'll get no dissent from the five Griot members on the disc. Some of them hadn't spoken in years, but all readily signed on to the idea of putting this music out. In fact, they all say that they'd consider—if not welcome—performing together again.

The time may be oddly ripe for this record and any hoopla it generates. The jazz avant-garde never had a commercial heyday, yet the interest endures. Sun Ra, for instance, is by some measures more popular now—consider the number of records commercially available, a biography, a book-length discography, an ongoing Internet listserv—than when he was alive a decade ago. Faruq and, even more so, Griot as a whole certainly have a link to all of that.

Faruq joined the Northwoods Improvisers at Xhedos Café in Ferndale to celebrate the release of the live Griot disc and *Ashirai Pattern*, their follow-up to *19 Moons*. Their two sets captivated a standing-room-only crowd.

"Sun Ra-tastic!" a twenty-one-year-old hooted after one tune, a cover of Sun Ra's "Shadow World." He would have been all of a year old when Faruq and Griot Galaxy recorded that same piece at the DIA.

"It ought to be a book," Natambu says, waxing about Griot Galaxy and "that particular cultural matrix."

There are certainly enough personalities to chart. Natambu is now working on a book of essays to be titled *A Brand-New Bag* to examine "the centrality of black artists in America as a cultural force from 1955 to 1975."

The former Griot flutist and harpist Williams is a librarian for the *Detroit Free Press*.

Another band member from that period, reed player Dodds, writes Christian tracts, the most recent being "Is God a Chauvinist?" which had a nice display at local Borders stores.

Any number of the '70s members remains active musically. At least one seems to be MIA; one became a lawyer.

Of the Griot Galaxy quintet heard on the record, McMurray remains in demand for recording sessions and touring and puts out his own records in a commercial-jazz vein. Holland works locally with jazz groups and with a steel drum band whose leader, Hugh Borde, had been discovered by Liberace.

Tabbal lives in Woodstock, New York, where he has rebounded after the removal of a benign brain tumor a year and a half ago. He plays in the dance department of Bard College and tours with David "Fathead" Newman, among others.

Shahid lives in Long Beach, New Jersey, and can still be seen occasionally playing around Detroit. In 2015, he was a special guest with R. J. Spangler's Planet D Nonet and he still tours with saxophonist David Murray and other name musicians.

Of the original Bey Brothers, the poet Jalil moved to Florida where he battled hypertension and related ailments and passed away some years ago. Sadiq is busy in New York; among his recent projects is a libretto for a radically reconfigured *Othello* in which Shakespeare's Moor becomes Sadiq's "mean fuck" opium addict. He's hoping it will be performed in the future at the Vienna Biennale, an ultraprestigious international art gathering.

Over the phone, Sadiq talks frankly about drug addiction, alcoholism, and getting clean. He says his experiences in Detroit made him the person that he is: "If it wasn't for my spiritual growth with those people, I would probably be sleeping in Central Park right now."

And Faruq, during the long interview for this article, talks about his many projects, a sort of personal renaissance he's entered during the last couple of years. He has a band, Speaking in Tongues, and an all-reeds ensemble, the Conspiracy Winds. Besides the Northwoods collaborations, other projects include working with Liebler's Magic Poetry Band and in a trio with Liebler and the blues musician (and former WDET-FM host) Robert Jones. He's working on a new book of poetry, revising a music-theory book. The list goes on.

But after all that, Faruq also reminisces about his daughter—he concedes he's never been as close to her as he would have liked—and her three children. One day, Faruq had an epiphany, seeing the eldest of that trio, a boy now seven years old, move with the same body language as Faruq and Faruq's now-deceased dad before him. "I guess that blew me away. I sat there just staring. I was just in awe, like, wow," he says.

The lesson being that "as much as I tried to forge an iconoclastic persona, I guess I'm a regular guy after all, I'm not Superman of the mind and spirit. I'm just a regular guy."

Later, being driven back to Faruq's home in a tattered stretch of Detroit's east side, this interviewer puts on an advance copy of the DIA release. The three Griot horns shout a theme, and Faruq identifies it as "Shadow World."

"One of Sunny's tunes," he adds, as in Sun Ra.

"Boo-wah-du-ooh," he sings along with the cascading melody, the text, as he'd put it. Then he falls silent.

After the theme, a tenor saxophone solo begins torrentially.

"Who is that?" asks the interviewer.

"Oh, that's me," he says and smiles his half smile. "Commentary," he explains, translating his fevered notes and overtones. "What is that? What do you mean?"

Then he falls silent.

## POSTSCRIPT

On the first Tuesday in June 2012, about 250 mourners gathered at Detroit's Muslim Mosque and Community Center to pay last respects to Faruq Z. Bey, who had died the previous Saturday, the first of the month.

He was seventy years old and had been in ill health for many years, his oxygen tank and emphysema constant companions. But so had been music, it seemed. In the previous decade, among other associations, he'd led several groups, published a book of poetry and music theory, recorded and performed endless shows with Liebler and the Reverend Robert B. Jones as The Detroit Legacy Project, and released numerous solo CDs and band CDs and DVDs with The Northwood

Improvisors. Griot Galaxy released two discs in its heyday; years later, the DIA live disc made for a third. With The Northwood Improvisers and others, he made more than a dozen discs in the 2000s. And with The Northwood Improvisers he'd at last played New York.

At the time of his death, he was slated to play as part of an annual Detroit event of recent years: the Don Was Detroit All-Star Revue at the Concert of Colors. His work was to be highlighted in an exhibition of Afro-futurism at the Museum of Contemporary Art Detroit. The nomenclature of critical discourse finally had a category for him, finally had caught up.

In Detroit, musicians, artists, and folks who just felt his work knew that a giant had passed on. In an online comment thread at *Metro Times*, where the above piece originally appeared, some of them shared the loss.

The painter Gilda Snowden (she, too, has now departed) recalled how he counseled her on getting with the dreadlock hairstyle (another way Faruq had been a pioneer in Detroit). His advice had been "be natural, don't force it, let it flow." He was also giving her, she later realized, "a template for the creation of art."

The jazz historian Jim Gallert recalled how any conversation with Faruq "raised my intellectual level." The poet M. L. Liebler recalled him as a hero who became a friend; poet Melba Boyd wrote of his impact on the creative community: "We are who we are because he was who he was."

Mike Johnston, The Northwood Improvisers' bassist, and Bey bandmate, explained that when invited to try something new musically, Faruq typically responded: "I ain't scared."

At the mosque there were remembrances of Faruq the artist and philosopher and friend who had knocked folks for a loop and raised them up, touched them spiritually as well as musically. The performance poet and artist Ann Holdreith recounted that Faruq had told her of his youthful dreams of being an automotive designer—a quintessential Motor City aspiration—"until I heard Coltrane and it ruined me."

For many of those from the music-art scene who knew him, or thought they knew about him, there was at least one revelation on this island of the Arabic East risen in Detroit. Most of us knew that Faruq studied Islam, even devoutly, but not of his stature in orthodox Islam in Detroit going back to the early '70s.

Just as the First African Primal Rhythm Arkestra and the Bey family were the roots of the Griot Galaxy story, we learned from the official obituary that they also led to the genesis of Masjid As Salaam, with Faruq and Imam Muhammad Jalil Bey among the handful of founders noted by name.

So the narrative arcs of two communities were converging as we joined the Islamic service on the carpeted floor—men here, women there.

And then the service was over. But not the echoes of the man.

59

# 2 DETR

OIT BLUES

Alberta Adams. © Leni Sinclair Collection.

# Alberta, Alberta

## The Alberta Adams Story

*R. J. Spangler*

I first saw Alberta Adams in 1979 in a live blues revue my friend Ron Alpern produced. It was part of a series at what some folks call Lakewood Park, along the Detroit River where it meets Lake St. Clair. The official name of the place is Alfred Brush Ford Park. Those early concerts in the late 1970s were incredibly well attended. Playing in that series with our band Kuumba and, later, joining the Sun Messengers on that same stage for their official unveiling were important gigs in my fledgling career.

Rick Steiger was my musical partner back then, and we still chuckle about hearing Alberta calling out from the stage for Ron, calling him Al Pern! I remember that Detroit blues revue had Chicago Pete on bass and singing some extremely deep blues. This was not like the later suburban-blues boom with guitar players and their Strats and cowboy hats. Pete *delivered* the low-down blues, and it was highly entertaining!

Chicago Pete, Alberta, and the others in this wonderful revue were purveyors of real, black, urban blues, for an urban audience, delivered with an almost mystical edge. Many folks in attendance, both black and white, were locals who would walk to the concerts.

Alberta Adams was born in 1917, orphaned as a child by her alcoholic mother, and raised by relatives that had too many mouths to feed. She later found her mom and cared for her until she passed. She was and still is that kind of person.

She got started in show business as a teen, first as a dancer, then as a singer. By the 1940s, Alberta was a solo dancer in a revue in which Kitty Stevenson was the featured blues singer. Back then, clubs like the Flame Show Bar, the Club 666, and the Club Congo all had house bands, chorus lines, shake dancers, ballad singers, blues singers, and more. These were big productions. The auto plants were humming around the clock. People had a few bucks to spend, and clubs were full. There was work for musicians and entertainers.

One night, Kitty took sick and Alberta asked if she could fill her spot. The owner asked her, "What do you do?" She told him that she knew two tunes, "Hey! Ba-Ba-Re-Bop" by Lionel Hampton and another blues song. He let her try out. She did her bit that night, and that was her start as a blues diva.

Later she toured with another singer named Chubby Newsome, and they called themselves the Bluesettes. They toured with the Tiny Bradshaw Orchestra. Alberta would go on the road to work with Louis Jordan, Eddie "Cleanhead" Vinson, and T-Bone Walker. One night at the Flame Show Bar, she was discovered by Dave Clark, an A&R man for Chess Records in Chicago. She signed to that legendary label and made a handful of great records. Later, she recorded a single for the Thelma label, named after Thelma Gordy, Berry Gordy's sister, and part of the Motown family.

Alberta was quite active through the 1960s but eventually took a day job at a nursing home to provide for her son, James Drayton, and her daughter, Barbara Jean. She still worked weekends with various pickup bands until the time we became a team.

In 1994, I was chairman of the Detroit Blues Society and the bandleader/drummer for Johnnie Bassett and the Blues Insurgents. Johnnie had been Pete's guitarist in the 1980s and was just establishing himself as a front man on the Detroit blues scene. Johnnie started as a sideman with Joe Weaver and the Blue Notes, recording for the Fortune and DeLuxe labels in the mid-'50s. He went on to play with many famous Detroit blues artists, like John Lee Hooker and Eddie "Guitar" Burns.

In June 1994, Detroit Blues Society president George Seedorff and I were involved with producing a blues festival back at Lakewood Park. We had many of the top Detroit blues artists booked, including Alberta, along with Johnnie, Eddie Burns, Willie D. Warren, and Harmonica Shah. It was a glorious day of Motor City blues; the excellent Garfield Blues Band backed Willie D. and Alberta. Famous Coachman was representing Alberta at the time. He was a DJ at WDET-FM, and owner of an east side record store. (A chapter could—and should—be written about Famous!)

Alberta had seen how well things were going for Johnnie, and asked me to manage her as well. Up to this point, I'd been a percussionist and bandleader, and I was starting a new chapter as drummer and manager for Johnnie. I hadn't thought about expanding beyond managing him. I had a lot on my plate already with booking, managing, drumming, and running a busy band.

I'd had local success framing Johnnie as a veteran from his days at Fortune and DeLuxe. Now, here comes Alberta, who had recorded for Chess, the big daddy of postwar blues labels. Interestingly enough, Johnnie had recorded sides at Fortune that had James Drayton, Alberta's only son, singing baritone. I was poised to shepherd Johnnie well beyond Michigan. Should I do the same for Alberta? Why not?

Alberta was an engaging singer with her own way of phrasing the blues, a solid pro who knew how to work an audience, and just plain wonderful to be around. I asked about Famous, and she said not to worry about him, so I said I'd manage her.

After recording a live CD for Johnnie on Mike Boulan's No Cover imprint, I had secured deals for Johnnie with Savant in New York City, Black Magic in the Netherlands, and Cannonball in Minnesota. Cannonball's boss, Ron Levy, a real blues-music veteran and a great guy, was doing a series he called Blues Across America, which featured top regional blues acts. When he came to the Detroit scene, he had Johnnie and also the Butler Twins. He wanted a third act and asked if I could suggest a woman. I mentioned Alberta, and that was the start of her comeback.

As I was quite busy with Johnnie at the time, I booked Alberta's gigs and arranged for friends of mine to back her up when I couldn't. Often, that job fell to guitarists Doug Deming and Gary Meisner. Gary was a real veteran player, having worked extensively with Chicago Pete and Eddie Burns. Doug was young, hungry, and ready to hit the road. I sent them down to Florida and other areas. Alberta loved Doug and his guys. Later, Alberta, Doug, his bassist Dale Jennings, and I would do short trips to New York City; Philadelphia; Hartford, Connecticut; and Springfield, Massachusetts.

Ever hear the joke about how to piss off a musician? Give him a gig. Cats often complain in this business, but not Alberta. She liked to travel, she liked to perform, she was happy to be there at all times. She called us her "band boys," and we were proud to be called that. She could sit in the van for long drives, arrive at the show, take the stage, and command the audience. Then, she could head back to the motel, sleep, wake up, and do it all again.

Our first national tour came after Johnnie and I had parted company professionally. Alberta and I played festivals and clubs across Canada, ending up in Vancouver. I had some guys from Johnnie's band with us; my dear pal Keith Kaminski on sax, Pat Prouty on bass, and my old friend Al Hill on keys, guitar, and vocals (he opened the show before Alberta came on). We were a damn good band. Keith is now with Bob Seger; both Al and Pat went with Bettye LeVette. Al is still her bandleader.

We ended up doing many tours like that: Detroit to Vancouver, to San Francisco, to Los Angeles, with stops in Iowa, Minnesota, and South Dakota. We toured Canada from Victoria to Halifax; we went to Buffalo and across Pennsylvania. We covered the South: Memphis, Nashville, Charleston, Charlotte, Mobile, and Atlanta, then throughout Florida, including Key West. We had great relationships with clubs that had us back repeatedly in all those cities. People loved Alberta. We visited thirty states and eight Canadian provinces over the next fifteen or so years.

One friend we made was a former Detroiter who calls himself Kenny Millions. His given name was Keshavon Maslak, and he had been a well-regarded avant-garde sax player in New York, which meant that he was also a cab driver. He was a graduate of Cass Tech and studied classical sax at the University

of Michigan. Kenny had quite a discography of recordings under his name; I owned a number of his titles. He saw things changing in New York and wanted none of it. After visiting his mom in Hollywood, Florida, he opened a combination Japanese restaurant/music venue. He had married a woman that he'd met on a tour of Japan, and she was quite a chef. She ran the back of the house, he ran the front, and they called it Sushi Blues.

Hollywood, Florida, is well-known to Jewish Americans, including the Maslak family. I remember a menorah painted in the window of his restaurant to signify Jewish ownership, which was common among businesses up and down the street.

I had an agent in Tallahassee who booked us throughout the state, but on one tour, we had an open date. I scoured the Internet and came upon Sushi Blues. After clicking on their website, I noticed Kenny right away and remembered those avant-garde jazz LPs that I'd bought in the late 1970s. It was the same dude. So I sent him an email and played the Detroit card right away, saying, "Hey, hook a brother up from back home, I dug your records." He responded right away and we had a date. Kenny brought us back many times and always blew his horn with us. Later, I returned the favor by bringing him to play with my swing band; we even recorded him with us and put out a CD. Kenny is still a bad cat. And he loved having Alberta at his club.

By 1999, Johnnie Bassett had been nominated for a W. C. Handy Award (now called the Blues Music Awards), the top award in our business. The award ceremony is held annually in Memphis. At the time, we recorded for Cannonball, and they had us on a label showcase at the New Daisy Theater on Beale Street. Elvis Presley and Jerry Lee Lewis had performed on that stage. Alberta was also on Cannonball and so she came down as well.

This really was Alberta's coming-out party. We did our thing with Johnnie to a great reception, but when Alberta joined us, it was like the paparazzi had shown up for a star-studded Hollywood event! Photographers lit up the already bright stage! She was a blues legend who hadn't been on the national stage in decades. The true blues aficionados and scholars had figured they'd never see her in person!

Alberta went on to be nominated a number of times for Best Blues Singer at the Handy Awards, and I was even nominated once, for Best Drummer in 2003. Going to Memphis every year got to be a thing for us. She reconnected with her old friend Ruth Brown a number of times, and we met other blues royalty, as well as celebrities like Steven Seagal.

I eventually put together RJ's Rhythm Rockers to back Alberta as we traveled across the continent, and to work local gigs. Some guys came and went, like our bassist Tim Marks, who now lives in Nashville and records with Taylor Swift. Other bassists included Ben Luttermoser and Mike Marshall, a true blues veteran and fellow east sider. Mike backed up Koko Taylor in the 1970s when she performed in Detroit. Mike was always making sure Alberta was OK. He's that kind of guy.

Our keyboardists were Martin Simmons and then Shawn McDonald. Both sang quite well, which was important as we had a mini blues revue, modeled in our own modest way on the gigs that Alberta had done in the old days on Hastings Street. Shawn went on to tour the world with the Larry McCray Band.

Sometimes we took sax player Joe Piccolo with us. Joe is a rousing front man, and he also kept us all entertained on long drives. He now lives in Edmonton, Alberta, where he is busy playing his horn and entertaining the folks.

We really only had one guitar player in that band, Paul Carey, my buddy since Boy Scouts. Paul plays with great passion and always brought the house down with his strong solos on slow blues. Alberta loves him and all the "band boys." Today Paul leads his own band around town.

On one West Coast tour, Ben and I took turns driving with Alberta in the backseat. After a late start in Whistler, British Columbia, we made it to Coeur d'Alene, Idaho, with two long days of driving ahead of us. The next morning, Alberta overheard us discussing taking turns driving and not stopping at a motel that night. She said, "Go ahead," quite enthusiastically. We drove straight to Detroit, more than two thousand miles. After a few weeks out, she was ready to get home, and another night in a motel held no interest for her. Road dogs call that "dead-heading." Not many octogenarians can do it, or would want to.

I learned much from Alberta over the years. She always kept a cool head, even in tough situations. She had my back at all times and is the most loyal person I know. People interview her about her life, and she can't talk enough about me.

Like all great artists, she has her own way of phrasing the blues. She is an original and a great Detroiter, and has the awards from the city council to prove it. She was honored in Paradise Valley Park while still alive and able to enjoy it. To me, she is the best, and I love her.

# John Lee Hooker and Joe Von Battle
## No Magic, Just Men
*Marsha Music*

I was interviewed in 2001 by a young man who was writing about Detroit blues. As he researched this seminal music of the city, his work increasingly focused on my late father, Joe Von Battle. From the mid-'40s until 1967, my father recorded dozens of blues and gospel artists, most in the recording studio in the back of his record store, Joe's Record Shop, and on location in churches and clubs.

He recorded Little Sonny, Johnnie Bassett, Sonny Boy Williamson II, the Meditation Singers (with Della Reese), the Violinaires, Bro. Will

John Lee Hooker. © Leni Sinclair Collection.

Hairston, and the list goes on and on; artists famous and artists unknown except in the arcane world of blues-record collectors.

Joe Von Battle was the sole producer of the over seventy-five albums of sermons and songs by the legendary Reverend C. L. Franklin, the "Man with the Million-Dollar Voice." He was the first to record the million-dollar voice of Franklin's daughter, Aretha, and produced her earliest gospel records, which she recorded at the age of fourteen.

He also produced records by John Lee Hooker (at first, at the now-iconic United Sound Studios in Detroit), but that wasn't a singular achievement because Hooker recorded with just about anyone who would put his voice on tape. He even recorded under other names, like John Lee Booker. Nevertheless, he and my father were good friends, and John Lee Hooker hung around Daddy's store and back-room studio, and sometimes slept on the couch in the back of the shop for days at a time.

One day in 1959, a photographer, Jacques Demetre, and a writer, Marcel Chauvard, came to the United States from France; they were writing a book about the blues, and they stopped in three cities—Chicago, New York, and Detroit. When they got here, they went straight to Joe's Record Shop, as they had heard that it was the place for the blues.

When they arrived, my elder brother, Joe Jr., was there; when my father got there, he picked up the phone and called his friend Aaron Willis, a.k.a. Little Sonny, and told him that there was a man from France that had come to take pictures. My father made another call, too, and soon, John Lee Hooker came from around the corner of Mack onto Hastings Street. Joe Jr. says that the French photographer almost fainted—he was so astonished and delighted to see the already legendary bluesman come into view.

Demetre snapped John Lee Hooker in front of the record shop, and eventually the photo he took became an iconic album cover; John Lee, dapper in slacks and a white shirt, posed with his guitar on the sidewalk in the same spot where my father, mother, and her sisters always stood for photos back in the day. The camera faces north, up Hastings Street; the spire of St. Josaphat on Canfield Street is in the background on the left. Hastings is long gone, most of it is a freeway service road now, but that church is still there, one of the few remaining structures adjacent to Hastings Street from back in those days.

Several amazing blues photographs came from that shoot, including one of Little Sonny in the same spot. As of this writing, in 2015, Demetre is still alive in France—a nonagenarian—and remembers his long-ago visit very well; my brother, approaching eighty, recounts it like it was yesterday.

So, back to the young writer who was interviewing me in 2001—he had decided to travel from Michigan to California to interview Mr. Hooker, who had, by then, become a very old man. As he prepared for this trip, I gave him a copy of an old photo to take with him; it was of John Lee and my father hanging out at a bar in Detroit, back in the day.

As the writer prepared to leave for San Francisco, we were both aware of Mr. Hooker's advanced age. We understood the import of this San Francisco trip—we had a sense, unspoken, that this young writer might be one of the last to have an audience with this great blues man, that John Lee Hooker might not have many more interviews to give.

I asked the young writer to relay my familial greetings to Mr. Hooker, and I bid him farewell. He visited San Francisco, Mr. Hooker's adopted home, for about a week. Upon his return, he told me that Mr. Hooker was very frail but remembered many things, and that he had great memories of my father, long ago on Hastings Street. He remembered well the great times they used to have at Joe's Record Shop, and he asked about Joe Jr. and my three elder sisters, whom he had known quite well.

Before he left, I had cautioned the young man not to fall into a common trap when writing: too often Hooker and other black blues artists are deified and made into mystical, mythical figures—hoodoo men, all.

Years before my friend's San Francisco visit, Mr. Hooker was performing at a Detroit riverfront venue called Chene Park, and I went backstage afterward to say hello. There he sat holding court postconcert; frail as a wisp underneath his trademark fedora, surrounded by dozens of adoring white kids at his feet.

They sat raptly—blissfully even—listening to him as if he were an oracle (while calling him by his first two names, as if he were their age), though I'm sure that they could barely understand his cryptic, whiskeyed, slightly impedimented Delta speech that was so familiar to me. (It had never ceased to amuse my late mother that Mr. Hooker—who strung words together in sometimes incomprehensible Southern non sequiturs—was oft regarded as a magus, a shaman, a voodoo man.)

I couldn't help but envision that they had walked right past many similarly aged, wizened old black men on the streets—maybe on the way to that very concert—who had been totally invisible to them, mere background shadows of the urban experience, if not on that day, on any other day in Detroit.

The elevation of these bluesmen in this way, even if well-meaning, can be dehumanizing, separating them from their existence as real men like other real men, enduring the challenges of survival; attributing their genius to uncommon magical powers, and not the profound strength and wisdom of that generation of black men.

He was not a sorcerer, nor a magus. It was not magic that allowed him to continue despite great obstacles. He was not mystically protected from the pressure cooker of life in segregation, on urban streets, in factories, and around the robber barons of the music business.

To turn him into a mystical figure is to deny his essential humanness; it is to make him somehow exempt from the particular indignities and powerlessness that black men of his generation experienced. He was not exempt, he was not magical—he was a man.

Hooker drew from the same deep reservoir of pain and strength as did all other black men of his time who lived lives beset with unspeakable humiliations and extraordinary troubles and challenges. Yet they persevered with courage, intelligence, and savvy, and gained the admiration and respect of their communities. Some, like John Lee Hooker, gained the notice of the world.

Now, that is not to say that a divine power was not at work in and around him all of his many decades, catapulting him to stardom as the northern, urban voice of the Delta blues.

For there was surely such a power—I'll call it God, and so, I think, would he—that put people like my father and many more into his life who understood his talent and put others there who looked out for him in his old age. But there was nothing magic about him, really.

No, he was just a man, like other black men on the streets of the city; a man with a guitar, a tapping foot, and the tales about life that all old black men have. Perhaps this made him more a man than those who worshiped him as godlike; perhaps it is the reason they worship him so.

Mr. Hooker died only days after the San Francisco interview. His memories of my father were the last that he would share. Maybe he and Daddy are having another Johnny Walker Red in that blues joint in the sky, like they were doing in that photo that I have that was taken so long ago—when he was not magical, but just a man.

# Searching for the Son
## Delta Blues Legend Son House in Detroit
*Rev. Robert B. Jones Sr.*

I grew up in Detroit with a grandmother who loved all kinds of music. She loved gospel, and when she cranked up the old Magnavox console you could hear the sounds of Rev. James Cleveland, or the Soul Stirrers, or the Harmonizing Four all over the house. She also loved R&B and soul music. But perhaps more than any style, she loved the blues. I grew up listening to the likes of Sonny Terry and Brownie McGhee, Sam "Lightnin" Hopkins, B. B. King, and Slim Harpo. Somewhere along the line, I came to love blues as well. When I went to college at Wayne State University in the mid-'70s I found myself looking through bins of old records and re-releases, searching for my own tastes in blues. While I was in college, I got a job at Wayne State's public radio station, WDET-FM.

Working at WDET gave me access to its music library. That vast and eclectic mix of shows required a vast and eclectic collection of music to sustain them. In what was a relatively small room, on the fifteenth floor of the School Center Building where WDET was housed, was an astonishing record collection. Almost every known style of recorded music was represented there—classical (American and European), jazz (Dixieland, bebop, avante-garde, modern), blues (urban and country), country and western, bluegrass, R&B, Native American, Hispanic, Indian, Asian, African—it was all there. Every chance that I got, I would go explore that library. While I was interested in many kinds of

Son House. © Stanley Livingston.

music, the music that fascinated me the most was blues. If I asked nicely, and if I promised to take care of them and return them promptly, I was able to take some of these recordings home or to make tapes for my own use. This is the place where I first met Son House.

In those days, before the coming of compact discs, each of the artists the radio station played would be represented by albums, LPs, which would be filed neatly and in alphabetical order. In the middle of the *H*s sat an album titled *Son House, Father of the Delta Blues*. I think that part of what drew me to this album was the striking cover photo of a man wearing a Mississippi string tie and holding an ancient and battered National resonator guitar. This man looked like he could sing the blues, and you knew that his guitar could play the blues. You knew by just looking at it.

There is a hierarchy of bluesmen. In those days before records, compact discs, and easily accessible recordings, blues was spread by sound and reputation. Every region had its own sound. Bluesmen from Texas would often try to model themselves after the likes of Blind Lemon Jefferson. East Coast pickers would sound like Rev. Gary Davis or Blind Blake. In Mississippi, though, that model was Son House. In fact, young McKinley Morganfield, the man the world would later know by the name Muddy Waters, recalled going to a juke joint for three weeks straight just to see and learn from the great Son House. Muddy was once quoted as saying, "It was Son House who influenced me to play. Son House . . . was the best. Whenever I heard he was gonna play somewhere, I followed after him. . . . I learned to play with the bottleneck by watching him for about a year."[1] Likewise, a young Robert Johnson would

follow House around from roadhouse to juke joint, just waiting for House to take a break so that he could grab his guitar and try to make the music that he had just heard.

Then, a second generation of musicians, like John Nicholas, John Mooney, Alan Wilson, Stefan Grossman, and Rory Block, kept House's music going. By the time House was "rediscovered" by the likes of Dick Waterman, his promoter and agent, in the 1960s, Son had forgotten how to play many of his own legendary songs. Fortunately, a young musician who would make a name for himself in a group called Canned Heat had so studied and learned House's style and repertoire that he was able to teach House how to play his own material. Now, a third generation, including the likes of Jack White, Eric Clapton, Cassandra Wilson, and even Chuck D of Public Enemy continue to keep House's music alive, whether by direct or indirect influence. Son House was one of those "blues bosses" whose influence transcends generations and even musical styles.

Eddie James House Jr. was born on March 21, 1902, in Riverton, Mississippi. Named after his father, Eddie quickly acquired the nickname "Son," to distinguish him from his father. Throughout his life, a conflict tore at Son. He'd felt a strong draw to the ministry. In fact, he started preaching at the age of sixteen, and like most southern preachers in the '20s and '30s, he preached against the blues. Much like the reputation that follows much of hip-hop music today, there was a reputation that followed blues music. Where blues was played there was dancing and whiskey drinking, violence, and adultery. Son House was quoted in an interview with Studs Terkel explaining how he came to acquire his skill with a slide, or bottleneck, his specialty and trademark:

I was around thirty. Something around along in there, because I belonged to a church called Alley Chapel. I was good and in my thirties.

I didn't like guitar when I first heard it. Oh gee, I couldn't stand a guy playing guitar. See I's churchy then, you know, but he was playing so good with the bottleneck. I didn't want the people to see me watching. All them 'round him, you know, together, and it sounded so good to me that I eased up behind him and peeped over his shoulder, you know, it sounded so good. I didn't want them to know I was watching see, see, 'cause I's so churchy. So I said, "Well, I believe I'll try this thing." But he had a medicine bottle you know. I tried it with a medicine bottle. I cut my hands a couple of times. I said, "I'm going to study up another plan for this thing." So I studied up the plans what I got now.

I had done started playing with those bottlenecks well, Charley [Patton] could never use them and neither could Willie Brown. Nary a one of them couldn't use them. Because if you just take the bottleneck, just like you take your naked finger, you know, and chord like that, well that bottleneck ain't gonna do nothing. It sound like the devil. You got to keep your hand moving. And they never could get that hand so they could play.[2]

Son House had a unique and slashing style dripping with emotion and power. He played and sang every song with the intensity of a man on fire. He was a man that learned early on how powerful an image could be. He wrote his own verses, and he used them to convey emotions like grief, loneliness, frustration, and pain in a way that few singers in the history of American music could match. In his song "Death Letter Blues," House sings from the perspective of a grieving husband:

> I woke up this morning, about
> the break of day,
> I was hugging on the pillow
> where she used to lay.
> Hush! I thought I heard her
> call my name,
> She didn't call so loud, but
> Lord, so nice and plain.

Another thing that set Son House apart from many other singers of his generation was the kind of guitar that he played. Son House played a National steel guitar. These guitars were the predecessors of the electric guitar. They were invented by a trio of brothers named Dopyera who had emigrated from Czechoslovakia and set up shop in California in the 1920s. They had come with a vision of building resonator instruments; instead of building an instrument that produced sound from vibrations of the top, these instruments used a vibrating aluminum cone to amplify the sound. This made for a guitar that was loud, and the fact that these guitars and mandolins were made of metal (sheet steel or German silver) made them tough, flashy, and modern looking. Another musical advantage of these guitars was that notes lasted for a long time, a quality called "sustain." The Dopyera brothers had thought that their new guitars would be popular among jazz guitarists trying to be heard in the midst of trumpets and saxophones.

However, the fact that these guitars had such a long sustain really worked against their popularity among jazz guitarists. Jazz demanded guitars that were loud but that had a quick decay. Archtop guitars dominated the jazz scene. The musicians that really fell in love with these peculiar guitars were blues and country players. A National Duolian (a basic steel-bodied model) sold new for thirty-two dollars, still a significant amount in the middle of the Depression, but they were the rage for traveling musicians who needed the volume and sustain that these guitars were known for. These guitars became the stuff of musical legend. Musicians just called the National guitars *steels*. But just as Nationals were cutting-edge instruments of the 1920s and 1930s, by the 1940s they were essentially obsolete. The electric guitar had replaced resonators from New York to California, but in the nonelectrified South of Mississippi, Nationals were still popular. So when Son House was persuaded to start playing again in the 1960s, he requested a National guitar, an instrument that had been obsolete for twenty years everywhere else.

Son House had made his first recordings in Grafton, Wisconsin, in 1930, when he was joined by fellow singers and guitarists, including the greatest musicians in the Mississippi Delta: Charley Patton, Willie Brown, and an otherwise unknown female pianist named Louise Johnson. On this occasion, House recorded ten sides, most of which survive. His career as a recording artist was interrupted by a prison sentence for a homicide that took place at a violent party in the Delta. By 1941, however, House was free again. This time he was recorded by Alan Lomax for the Library of Congress. Then, Son House disappeared again. Around 1952, with the death of his guitar-playing partner, Willie Brown, and with

the popularity of electric blues, Son House sold his guitar, gave up music, and moved to Rochester, New York, finding work as a railroad porter. Then, in the 1960s, House was discovered yet again. This time, House would become part of a resurgent interest in country-blues and folk music in the early '60s. He would record a number of albums, but probably none more influential than the Columbia recording *Father of Folk Blues*. This was the album that would capture my imagination in WDET's library, almost thirty years after its release. In the 1960s, House would play festivals to worldwide acclaim, eventually coming to settle in Detroit.

So it was that around 1985 I came to hear rumors that Son House was not only alive but still living in Detroit. In fact, I ran into a friend by the name of John Cohen who told me that he knew Son House. Later I saw a published photograph of Son House playing at the Ann Arbor Blues and Jazz Festival. In that photograph, a man is placing a National guitar in Son's lap, and that man was John Cohen. Over the next couple of years, I ran into John from time to time, and each time he offered to introduce me to House. I, however, hesitated. I have never been big on hero worship. I didn't want to meet Son House just to say that I had met him, I wanted to meet Son House so that I could learn from him. So, I continued to practice his music and the music that he had influenced, and I promised myself that one day, I would take John up on his offer.

When we meet our heroes, a strange thing often happens. We discover that the image that we have been chasing is often radically different from the person that we associate with it. I remember hearing a story from a young trumpeter who had idolized jazz great Miles Davis. When he got a chance to meet the great man, the experience fell flat. When the artist, now a great musician himself, extended his hand toward his hero, Davis pushed past him, saying, "Get outta my face, Motherfucker." That didn't happen when I finally got to "meet" Son House, but the experience was just as anticlimactic.

The years had not been great to the blues great. Time, alcoholism, and senility had all taken their toll. By the time I got around to finding Son House, he was a patient at the New Light Nursing Home on West Chicago Boulevard in Detroit. I have visited many nursing homes since that day, but the mixed odors of hospital disinfectant and urine were nearly stifling. I went to the front desk and was sent into Son's room. There he was, the great man, slumped in a patient's chair with a restraint around his waist. He was wearing a clean white shirt, and embroidered on the front was *E House*. In fact, on the front of his pants were the same letters, *E House*. Now I know why this was: in every nursing home, things get lost and stolen, and the only thing that keeps things from walking is clear labeling. I suspect that every article of clothing he had bore the same label. Like I said, he was slumped in his chair, and my best efforts at rousing him only resulted in a series of incoherent mumbles. Eventually, out of respect and frustration, I just turned and left. That was in the summer of 1987. In October 1988, Son House would pass away from complications of Alzheimer's disease. As strange as it might seem, it was at his death that my search for Son House really started.

At the time of his passing, I was myself a professional blues musician. I was also the producer and host of a radio show on WDET called *Blues from the Lowlands*. As a result, I was known as one of the few people who was perhaps qualified to talk about Son House and his legacy as a musician. So, upon finding out that Son House would be laid out at the House of Johnson Funeral Home, I attended his wake. I was struck by a thought that hit me like a thunderbolt: Here I was, looking at a casket that held the body of the father of folk blues, the man who had taught Robert Johnson and Muddy Waters, a man who had helped to shape American music and, strangely, none of his loved ones knew it! I mentioned to one of House's relatives that I was there to honor one of the greatest bluesmen who ever lived. He looked at me quizzically and said, "Uh really, well I heard that Uncle Eddie had made some records or something, but I don't know much about it."

The funeral was held at the Mayflower Baptist Church, and even though there were some blues luminaries in attendance, including Son's longtime manager, Dick Waterman, the overall tenor of the service was the same as it had been at the House of Johnson. I was asked to make a few remarks at the funeral, as was Dick Waterman. We both said essentially the same thing, that we were honored to be at the homegoing of a man who had changed American music forever. Again, we got the same blank stares. That is when I got it. I realized that a man could be a legend in one place and just a man in another.

After the funeral, Son was interred at the Mt. Hazel Cemetery in Detroit, but his legend demanded that he have a gravestone worthy of his accomplishments. Along with Rich, the late Maureen Delgrosso, Eric Glatz, and several other blues lovers, I had helped to organize the Detroit

Country and Classic Blues Society (now shortened to the Detroit Blues Society). The society decided that, since Son House's body was buried in Detroit, it was only proper for the society to raise money to purchase a proper gravestone. So began a series of benefits, with each benefit generating a new design. At one point before I jumped off of the gravestone train, the intended design included a life-sized depiction of the bluesman, sitting on a bench with a dove landing on the headstock of his guitar. Strangely enough, no one had bothered to check with the Mt. Hazel Cemetery. It turned out that they had no tolerance for such an elaborate mess. Ultimately, the society ended up placing a very dignified stone that reads, "EDDIE JAMES SON HOUSE, JR, March 21, 1902–October 19, 1988" in bold type. In addition, there is an embedded photo of House holding his battered National guitar. On the front of the stone, written in a cursive font, are the words, "Go away Blues, go away and leave poor me alone." These words are taken from one of Son's own songs, "Death Letter Blues," where he sings, "Blues leave me alone, I ain't had no lovin' since my gal been gone." The Detroit Blues Society continues to place markers on the unmarked graves of blues luminaries. While I am proud to be associated with their efforts, I am amazed at how willing people are to honor the dead, rather than to support or help the living.

I found out, later on, that Son's wife, Evie, was known to hide his guitar and his heavy brass slide from him because Son playing guitar meant Son drinking. I learned that promoters had discovered that if they couldn't keep Son House away from the bottle, they were in for a disastrous performance. During one of his last major performances at the Ann Arbor Blues and Jazz Festival, Son had gotten so drunk that all he could do was apologize profusely to his audience that he could "do better."

In fact, there is a film from the Newport Folk Festival that shows a drunken Son House harassing the great Howlin' Wolf during one of Wolf's performances. Frustrated by Son's loud and rambling commentary during his performance, Wolf actually stops, points to House, and says, "Look, you had a chance with your life and you ain't done nothing with it . . . you don't love nothin' but your whiskey."[3]

Not only did Son have to deal with chronic alcoholism, he also dealt with inner conflict that sought to rip him apart. Men and women of House's generation had been taught that sacred and secular music could not coexist in one person. House would often say, "I was brought up in church, and I didn't believe in the blues. . . . I play the blues and I play church songs too! But you can't take God and the devil along together. 'Cause them two fellas they don't get along so long so well together . . . you got to follow one or the other. You can't hold God in one hand and the devil in the other. You gotta turn one of 'em aloose."[4] Son often seemed torn by his love for the church and his love for the blues. House had not experienced blues as a style of folk music or as a cultural by-product; for Son House, the blues was a music that he had experienced in all-night, whiskey-soaked Mississippi juke joints. For House, the blues was the soundtrack of a life that had led to at least one homicide, a stint in Parchman Prison in Mississippi, and multiple failed relationships. But more importantly, the blues were in direct conflict with his own religious beliefs. As assuredly as he felt called to preach, he felt a call to the blues. He just couldn't reconcile a life that included both.

I continue to search for Son House and the countless others just like him. The Internet, YouTube, and recently produced DVDs continue to give insight into the complexity of his persona. Sometimes, you see a man of great dignity bringing with him a legacy of blues that stretched back toward slavery and even before. At other times, you see a mercurial man-child, looking like a deer caught in headlights. I have come to realize that all of these men are Son House, and yet, none of these is Son House. These are images of a man, recorded at different times and from different perspectives.

Artists are not their images. In over thirty years of performing, research, and radio, I have come to realize how treacherous it can be when your life is in conflict with your art. When you are present for your audience, you are often absent for your family. Can you be the "father of the blues" and still be Uncle Eddie? Of course you can, but you have to be grounded in something that is deeper than your publicity. Who knows how many Son Houses there are in Detroit? I think of great artists that I have known who have made their homes in Detroit and yet whose artistic contributions are largely unrecognized. There was a one-man band named Buddy Folks who had one of the funkiest sounds in the 1970s blues scene, but his self-effacing personality and his fear of flying kept him anchored as a virtual music unknown. One of the greatest blues singers I've ever known was a woman named Juanita McCray. The first time I met her, she was a loud, sexy, and self-assured woman wearing a tight leopard-skin-print wrap dress that fully captured my seventeen-year-old imagination. The last time I saw Juanita, she was an aging, still

beautiful, but sickly looking grandmother, battling heart trouble and swollen legs. Even though Juanita could dominate a stage and had a voice that was both sensual and powerful, when she passed away it was with such little recognition that I have not been able to find even an obituary or any details about her life. I once met a musician who had played in Hank Williams's band. He was skilled on guitar, mandolin, banjo, and fiddle. His name was Birt C. Boles, and he had gone blind and lived quietly with his wife in Dearborn, Michigan. Then there were the Butler Twins, natives of Florence, Alabama. Before their passing, within a year of each other, they had begun to acquire a modicum of fame and recognition. Curtis and Clarence Butler had learned to play blues from their father, "Butch" Butler. Butch was apparently the best player in and around Florence. Clarence and Curtis were greatly accomplished on guitar and harmonica. Very few musicians could match Clarence's harmonica tone or Curtis's old-style guitar accompaniment. However, those who knew them knew that they lived together in a small and musty apartment over the Attic Bar, in Hamtramck, sitting together on a broken-down couch reminiscing about better days.

Perhaps the ultimate lesson that comes from searching for Son House is the acknowledgment that Son had a genius. To have a genius is to have a gift from God. However, there is a difference between having a genius and being one. Before Descartes, when people talked about "having a genius," the belief was that inspiration followed an artist around and when the "genius" came upon him he had to be prepared to express the thing that was coming through him. Your responsibility as an artist was to be open to your genius and to hone the skills necessary to express the gift you had been given. After Descartes, though, the thought was that the artist *was* the genius. This puts the onus on the artist to produce, and to become the image. Detroit is filled with people of genius. Searching for Son House has taught me a lot of things, but perhaps the most important thing that I've learned is that genius is not really that rare. However, the recognition of it comes with a cost. Genius can bless you or it can kill you. Son House had a great genius, but he could never live up to his own image. No one can.

## NOTES

1. *Devil Got My Woman: Blues at Newport 1966*, Vestapol 13049, liner notes, 22.
2. *Delta Blues Guitar*, Stefan Grossman, Oak Publications, 1969, 37.
3. *Devil Got My Woman: Blues at Newport 1966*, Vestapol 13049.
4. *Masters of the Country Blues*, Yazoo 500, 1991.

Johnnie Bassett. © Leni Sinclair Collection.

# Johnnie Bassett
## Cadillac Bluesman from the Motor City

*John Sinclair*

The blues has always been a big part of life in the Motor City, but it's been a long time since Detroit's musically fertile blues community has seen one of its own citizens go on to national and international success. Not since Little Sonny landed a contract with Stax Records and issued a series of excellent albums on the Enterprise label in the 1970s, in fact, has a Motor City bluesman raised much of a ruckus in the blues industry.

The scene changed with the reemergence of veteran Detroit bluesmen like Johnny "Yard Dog" Jones, winner of a Handy Award for Best New Blues Performer in 1997 on the strength of his debut CD, *Ain't Gonna Worry*, and the Butler Twins, Curtis and Clarence, who made two fine recordings for the British JSP label. Cannonball Records spotlighted the Detroit scene in Ron Levy's *Blues Across America* series and in 1998 issued what is, almost incredibly, the first album ever by venerable Detroit blueswoman Alberta Adams.

But some of the biggest noise ever made from the Motor City was by Johnnie Bassett, a soulful, jazz-inspired guitarist and singer who commenced a new life as a featured artist after toiling since the early '50s behind virtually every singer and front man to grace the city's gritty blues bars and nightclubs.

Johnnie Bassett's singing and playing—perfectly backed by his splendid ensemble, the Blues Insurgents, led by drummer R. J. Spangler—propelled him into the center of the modern blues scene with a series of albums recorded over ten years

and a busy touring schedule that took the band from coast to coast and across the Atlantic several times.

Discovered by Spangler at a Montreux-Detroit International Jazz Festival performance as a member of organist Ben Baber's band, Johnnie recorded his debut album live on the same spot in 1995 for a small Detroit company, No Cover Records.

An energetic tour de force through a program of blues standards arranged to showcase Bassett's mellow blues recitations and driving jump-blues swingers backed by pianist Bill Heid and a six-piece horn section, this recording led to the band's first European tour and the opportunity to record for Holland-based Black Magic Records.

By the time the Blues Insurgents entered the studio in May 1996 to make *I Gave My Life to the Blues,* an album of original material by Bassett, Heid, Martin Gross, organist Chris Codish, and his father, Bob Codish, the band had jelled into a tight, completely sympathetic blues unit seriously dedicated to realizing the full potential of Bassett's considerable talents.

By that time, Johnnie himself had grown fully into the frontman role, displaying new confidence and strength as a guitarist and singing with power and conviction in every setting.

Back in the States, Bill Heid landed Johnnie a one-off recording deal with Fedora Records and contributed an entire program of tailor-made originals to *Bassett Hound,* a relaxed excursion with the Bill Heid Trio into the mellower and jazzier sides of Johnnie's musical personality.

R. J. Spangler, then acting as manager and agent for the band, parlayed these two excellent releases into gigs around the United States, a return trip to Europe, and a recording contract with Cannonball Records.

Introduced by producer Ron Levy with four selections on his *Blues Across America: The Detroit Scene* compilation for Cannonball, the Blues Insurgents thrust themselves into the forefront of the blues world with their current release, *Cadillac Blues*, and have completed a second album with Levy to be released in 2016. Bassett and the band also support Johnnie's old friend Alberta Adams on her new Cannonball release.

*Cadillac Blues*, recorded at Willie Mitchell's studio in Memphis, demonstrated Johnnie Bassett's utter freshness and vitality as a contemporary bluesman. His own compositions, "That's Fair Play" and the memorable blues ballad "Memories of Your Perfume," shared the limelight with original tunes by a bevy of modern-day Detroit songwriters, including Chris and Bob Codish, drummers Leonard King and Ron Pangborn, and organist Tim Brockett.

The Blues Insurgents was a well-seasoned musical organization powered by Codish's Hammond B-3 organ (including foot-pedal bass) and highlighted by the horns of saxophonist Keith Kaminiski and trumpeter Dwight Adams. The band provides the perfect setting for Bassett's tasty guitar and singular vocal stylings.

The title track of *Cadillac Blues*, a typically tongue-in-cheek Bob Codish composition, nicely sums up Johnnie's status: "I've still got the blues, but I've got them in my Cadillac." Johnnie Bassett

came a long way to get behind the wheel of Detroit's classiest vehicle, but he was riding in style, and the open road had just begun to stretch out in front of him for the first time in the almost fifty years since his brother bought him a guitar for his sixteenth birthday in 1951.

I eventually caught up with Bassett and the Blues Insurgents at the Blues Estafette in Utrecht, Holland, where I spent a pleasant Sunday afternoon in one late November afternoon talking with Johnnie and R. J. Spangler in the comfortable confines of their Dutch hotel.

*John Sinclair*: Let's go to the basics of where and when you entered the planet Earth.

*Johnnie Bassett*: I was born October 9, 1935. That was sixty-three years ago now, in a little town down in Florida called Marianna. That's in the panhandle. We had a successful business there: my dad was a bootlegger. Very successful—successful enough for us to open a restaurant and run it.

*John Sinclair*: Was that a dry area? Except for your father?

*Johnnie Bassett*: Yeah, it was then. They knew that he was making corn whiskey, you know, and they enjoyed it because he had the best in the county. So everybody bought from him, including the sheriff, you know. And periodically they would give him chase, to let everybody know that they were on the job. But they never caught him.

*R. J. Spangler*: He was a mechanic, and they had a souped-up car . . .

*Johnnie Bassett*: With a horn that played "Mary Had a Little Lamb." Yeah. So we left—my dad left Florida in the late 1940s and moved to Michigan, then sent for the family after he got his job in place. So we moved up to Michigan in '47, and been there ever since. I was eleven at that time.

It was a good time to get to Detroit. It was a fun time, you know. People still left their doors unlocked and stuff. Everybody was workin', and neighbors cared about each other, and everybody looked out for everybody's kids and stuff like that, you know. A lot of old Southern traditions was still—because there was a lot of Southern families there in the neighborhood that I was living in at the time when I first went to Detroit.

I grew up in Ferndale, and I had both—the good of both worlds, because I lived in Ferndale about two years, and then I moved on the Detroit side. So I had friends on both sides of Eight Mile Road. I grew up there on Bethelon, right off Eight Mile, right there behind Uncle Tom's Cabin.

Oh, man, that was a great place. All the jazz musicians, all the top names in jazz would come to Uncle Tom's, man. We used to sit out in the parking lot, on top of the cars, man, and listen to the music when I was a kid. You could hear the music in the summertime, you know, they had the doors open.

I heard people like the Count Basie [Orchestra], and so many guys would come through, because they had big names come through there at least once a month. Oh yeah, all the swingin' guys—Billy Eckstine's band, I heard him when I was twelve years old. Al Hibbler, I heard him sing there, you know, when I was twelve.

I remember all those guys, because he used to hire the kids and they would go around and put up the posters on the telephone poles, and I was one of the kids that used to have to go around and put up all the posters up and down Eight Mile Road, you know, to advertise who was the next coming attraction. It was great, man. We'd sit out on the parking lot there and hear all these people sing and bands play, and it was great.

*John Sinclair*: Did you get to meet the cats?

*Johnnie Bassett*: No, I didn't meet any of 'em when I was a kid, but we were allowed to stay out until ten-thirty at night and catch the first show. The guy that owned the club, Doc Washington—I think that was his name, everybody called him Doc—when I moved on the Detroit side, that's where he lived.

He lived on Cherrylawn between Norfolk and Pembroke, I remember, and I was one of the good kids, so he hired me and my buddy—one of my friends who lived across the street from me—he hired us to wash his car, and keep his lawn mowed, and that type of stuff, and clean up around his house, keep his yard clean, and hey—I've been a hustler for a long time, man, made good money, you know.

That was a good gig, man. Because we were good kids. We didn't steal or nothin' like that—good kids around the neighborhood. And the two of us had a little business goin'—we would go around and, once we got that job and everybody knew we did a good job, and then we got other jobs from that, you know? Cutting lawns, and cleaning up garages, and—oh, man, cleanin' up businesses.

*John Sinclair*: Did you have brothers and sisters?

*Johnnie Bassett*: Four sisters and one brother. And it's three of us left out of that: two sisters and my brother and myself. So it's four of us. Mom and Dad has passed away, and my two older sisters. I got a

81

slew of nephews and nieces still left, and I have two kids and four grandkids myself. They live in Seattle, which I did for five years, after my service days—I was stationed out at Fort Lewis, Washington. After I got out in 1960, I just decided to hang around out there, because the money was good, you know, I was making good and playing and I enjoyed it and that's where I stayed.

*John Sinclair*: So when did you start playing?

*Johnnie Bassett*: I started playin' about 1951, but not professionally. I just started foolin' around with the box. Before then I had fiddled around with it, because my older sister played the church songs, and we would sit around and we would sing the church songs. She had an old guitar that she would lay on her lap and fram the chords, and when I was in eighth grade I would come home from school and I'd go get that guitar and fram it and, you know, play around with it.

After we left Florida I went to grade school there in Ferndale. Then I went to Carver, George Washington Carver, and Higginbotham, on the Detroit side. Then I went to Condon, which is on [Grand] Boulevard and Buchanan, on the west side, and I went to Northwestern High School, on the Boulevard and Grand River. That's where I met Joe Weaver. I met Joe before then, but he went to Northwestern, too. I got into playing music the more and more I was around it. In school, I started in the ninth grade playing clarinet.

*John Sinclair*: Northwestern had a pretty strong music program then.

*Johnnie Bassett*: Oh, very good, very good music program.

*John Sinclair*: Who came out of there? Roy Brooks and . . .

*R. J. Spangler*: He worked with Joe Weaver and the Blue Notes, at the Basin Street over in Delray, for a year.

*Johnnie Bassett*: OK, well, my sister was a waitress there in Delray—Louise, she was a waitress out there at the West End Hotel for a long time. Those guys used to have that session out there every weekend. It started at two o'clock in the morning and it'd go from two to seven a.m. Kenny Burrell, Tommy Flanagan, Paul Chambers, Yusef Lateef, all the guys used to come through that was playin' down at the Flame [Show Bar], and the Rouge Lounge, used to come out to the sessions.

You know, I went through that, and I started playin' in high school, I played alto sax and clarinet, and got interested in music. But the guitar was the thing, though. I liked playin' with that, because it was light, easy to carry. At that particular time I had a little Kay guitar that my brother bought me in a pawnshop for my birthday, in 1951.

*John Sinclair*: Would you have to carry your own amplifier?

*Johnnie Bassett*: Yeah, I had a little amplifier with a little eight-inch speaker in it. I don't know if you ever saw that picture of me in the magazines? That's the one. I heard Joe Weaver playing an old upright piano at his girlfriend's house down the street from where I was living. I was going to Condon Junior High when I first heard Joe, my last year in junior high, matter of fact, when I first heard him in the summer after school was out and everything.

I was going to the cleaners, which was down the street—long blocks, really long blocks between Buchanan and Hancock—long blocks, oh—and I was going to the cleaners and I heard Joe playing. So, you know, all this playing, and stompin' on the floor—boy, he would stomp his feet, you know—so I stood there and listened for a while and then I went on back home. And a couple days later, I was going back to get the clothes from the cleaners, you know, and I heard him again. I said, man, geez, this cat's good. You know? What I heard. So, I didn't meet him, but I heard him.

So about two months later, we moved from off of Buchanan—we bought a house over on Herbert, which was basically the same neighborhood but down near Warren and a couple of blocks over from where we were living. I had been living on Bangor, between Buchanan and Hancock, and we moved on Herbert, which was three streets over and two long blocks down. It was still in the neighborhood, so we still used the cleaners around on Hancock and Bangor.

So I went to that cleaners again—this was sometime after I got my guitar, for my birthday—and I heard Joe playing over there, and I said, "Let me go see who this is," you know, because there was people all on the porch, and everybody havin' a good time, and he's in there just bangin' away.

So I stood there, and they told me to come up on the porch, you know, and I went up on the porch, and oddly enough, the young lady that lived there, we had met already. Incidentally, Joe and the young lady ended up gettin' married—she was his first wife, Ruth Tyler.

And I went in, and there's Joe. I had seen him around the neighborhood, but I didn't know it was him. I didn't know he played, you know. I saw him practically every day, but it never dawned on me that it was him. But sure enough it was Joe.

I said, "Man, hey," I said, "You play piano?" "Yeah!" I said, "Man, you sure do sound good. You mind if I play with you?" He said, "What you play?" I said, "Guitar a little bit." He said, "Where is it?" I said, "At home." He said, "Go get it."

Man, I ran back home and got my box, and I come back and plugged it in, and we had the biggest jam session. Man, we had folks comin', you know, dancin' all over the porch and stuff. And that's how I got started.

And we got a drummer out of high school, who played in the band, and we started doin' amateur shows right in high school. Three-piece group, without a bass player or anything, just the three of us. Calvin Andrews, a very good drummer. And we won our first amateur show, at the Arcadia Theatre, over on West Warren and Junction.

All of the theaters all over the city was having amateur shows, because this one guy was doing that—Frank Brown—he was a big promoter. He brought in all the big-name shows around the city of Detroit, OK?

He was a big promoter of concerts, and he'd bring in all the big names. And he was hooked up with all the theater owners, and doin' the talent thing. It was a good thing, too, because it gave the kids something to do during the summertime other than, you know, hang out in the parks and whatever.

We would go and do these amateur shows all over the city, and whatever we played, we would win in our category. They had the musical categories—instrumental category, singers, vocal, and female singer category, single instrument, whatever. And we would win, and we kept winning, and kept winning, every weekend we went to the theaters all over the city.

We'd go east side to west side, and, you know, down on Hastings, they had a little theater down there, and we'd win that one. There was a little theater right there around the corner from where I used to live, on Buchanan and the Boulevard there, the theater there, they'd turn that into a bowling alley after a while. But we played there, too.

Then we picked up a saxophone player from one of the amateur shows, who was doing a Big Jay McNeely–type thing, kickin' up his heels and blowin' this one note. Jesse Ulmer, we called him Jesse "Mad Lad" Ulmer—he got that name from doin' flips and stuff—blowin' his horn. He won that day from being a solo act.

And so we got hold of Jesse and asked him if he wanted to play with the group. He said, "Yeah, man," so we started rehearsin' and playin' with the saxophone.

We'd rehearse over to Joe's girlfriend's house, and it was quite funny, you know, because when I met Joe, we didn't know a hell of a lot about music or playin', but I was listening to blues since I was a kid, you know, and I had a lot of knowledge about it.

I could play in about five keys when I met Joe, and Joe could only play in one. Joe played only on the black keys, in E, man, Joe played in E—everything on the black keys. I'd say, "Whatta you got against the white keys, man? Don't you play those, too?"

He said, "No, man." [*laughs*]

So we rehearsed every weekend, man. When we had some time, I'd get together with him and go over some tunes and stuff like that. And he was interested enough to want to do that, and we would take records and put on the record player and go note for note, man, and play, and pick 'em out. Amos Milburn and Willie Mabon, and stuff like that, you know.

*R. J. Spangler*: Johnnie's dad was friends with Big Bill Broonzy and . . .

*Johnnie Bassett*: Yeah, and Tampa Red. Back when I was a kid, they'd spend a lot of time at my grandmother's house every summer. My grandmother would have this big fish fry, you know, once a year, and all the guys like that would come through. We had a big record collection, and when I was a teenager, goin' to that intermediate school on Eight Mile, we used to pick up, on a good night, in the summer especially, we would hear records being played on the radio all the way from Nashville—WLAC—Gene Nobles, John R. We would order all our records from Randy's Record Shop in Gallatin, Tennessee. When I was twelve and thirteen, fourteen years old, you know, I had paper routes and everything, so I had my own money and I could buy my records, man. When they came out, I'd have my own money to pay for 'em.

So Joe and I hooked up, you know, in high school, and we did the amateur show thing until, after winning so many, we went in one night and the guy told us, said, "You guys can't play tonight." He says, "If you wanna play," he says, "what I'll do, I'll just hire you to back up everybody that don't have their own accompaniment, so you'll make a few more bucks." So we said, "OK, that'll work."

*R. J. Spangler*: Who were the singers you were backing up?

*Johnnie Bassett*: The first singer we backed up that didn't have accompaniment was winning first place all over in the male vocalist [category], [it] was Little Willie John. He was great, too. Willie would sing anywhere he could get a chance to sing, man—he'd sing on the corners, on the playground, stuff like that.

Willie and me grew up in the same neighborhood. He was just four blocks over. I lived on Northlawn between Chippewa and Pembroke, and he lived on Greenlawn between Chippewa and Pembroke. He lived on the east side later, but they was from the west side—from the Eight Mile Road district. Then they moved over on Canton.

So we backed up all sorts of people—Johnny Mae Matthews had a thing going, and Laura Lee, and—oh man, there was so many. Hank Ballard and those guys—you know, I didn't play with those guys until I was in professional things, some years later. We played professionally in 1953, that's when I first started a nightclub gig. It was a place called Basin Street, right down in Delray, two blocks from the West End. It used to be called the Black and Tan, because that's what it was in that area at that time: the black and tan.

*R. J. Spangler*: You and Joe were telling me a wild story last night.

*Johnnie Bassett*: Oh, yeah. Well, there was a crowd of people in the club. We had built up our popularity around town from the amateur shows, and playin' house parties and stuff like that, and we were in this club, and it was a line out around the building to get in. The place was already full, and people were waitin' to get in to see us, and there was a young couple that just had gotten married, and this guy was pushin' and shovin' at the door tryin' to get in—it was only two dollars to get in—and this guy stepped on somebody's shoes, and the guy got in a confrontation with him—they say he apologized and all like that—but he got in a confrontation with the guy, shovin' and pushin' and carryin' on, and the guy stabbed him and he died—right there at the door, man. We were in there playin' and didn't know nothin' about it until the next night. It happened on a Friday, and, you know, we didn't even know it until the next night. Didn't even know it, the place was so crowded.

*R. J. Spangler*: Lines around! You must've been huge.

*Johnnie Bassett*: Yeah, and it was like that for a long time. Back then, people were goin' to nightclubs, they were supporting live music.

*R. J. Spangler*: How many guys in that group, Johnnie? There was Mad Lad and you, and was there a bass player?

*Johnnie Bassett*: No, that's when Joe was using an Organa, with the bass thing. That was before we had the bass player. So Joe bought an Organa for the piano, old upright piano—that was the only thing you could use it on.

*R. J. Spangler*: So it was a quartet. You had Roy Brooks on drums?

*Johnnie Bassett*: Yeah, I had Roy playin' drums. We had some good drummers, boy. Paul Humphrey played drums with us, Roy Brooks, and Louis Hayes. These guys went on to bigger and better things. And Paul Williams's son, Earl Williams, played drums with us.

Paul "Hucklebuck" Williams. George Davidson was in the studio with us on some of those Fortune things.

We had a good time comin' up through the music thing. I went in the service and left the group in 1958. I played with Joe and the group until I went in the service, and that's when I left.

They carried on for a while, but when I got out of the service, I didn't come back to Detroit until 1965. I came back off and on to visit, but I always went back to Seattle because I was playin' out there with several groups.

*John Sinclair*: Between '53 and '58, did you start recording then?

*R. J. Spangler*: Oh yeah. Before Fortune, I was on DeLuxe. We had a tune called "1540 Special" and "J.B. Boogie." On DeLuxe. We recorded that in Joe's Record Shop on Hastings. That's where I met John Lee Hooker the first time. Yeah, Joe Von Battle's record shop. Because his son and I were in high school together, Joe Battle Jr. Yeah, we had classes together. It was great, you know. He hooked us up with his dad, matter of fact. And Jesse's father knew the old man, Joe Battle Sr. Jesse Ulmer's father knew him, because Jesse's dad owned a restaurant down the street, two blocks away, in Paradise Valley. And that's where we used to go after our rehearsals— we'd always go to the restaurant and eat.

So we recorded that "1540 Special"—at a rehearsal. We wasn't planning on recording anything, but he always had the microphones and the tapes going, and that's what happened. When we heard that thing again it was out on the street. What he would do, he would allow us to come in and rehearse. He'd say, "Well, when the studio's not being used, you guys can come in and rehearse any time you get ready, you know, after school." And fine, we'd go over there, and he'd have the microphones and everything set up, and we didn't know they were on. He'd have the tapes rollin', and he'd splice stuff together, and put stuff together, and "1540 Special" was a result of that. Joe Weaver and the Blue Notes.

[1540 Brewster Avenue—the address of King Records in Cincinnati.]

*Johnnie Bassett*: That's right. That was on DeLuxe, which was a subsidiary of King, and that's what happened. And it was a big seller. "1540" was a big seller, man. And we didn't get nothin' for it. He did, you know, but I think we got fifty dollars out of it— apiece. You know. And we didn't get compensated for the writers' parts—we didn't know anything about all that stuff, so we got ripped off a lot of times.

Then we got with Fortune. Going down the street— we were all over in the area, on Linwood, right across from Central High School. We had been playing ball over there, and we were coming down the street and we heard this quartet singing inside. And Joe said, "Hey, man," says, "somethin' goin' on in here. Let's check it out."

So we go in there and who do we hear but Andre Williams. It's guys in there doo-woppin' and singin', and we went in and started listenin', and then they wanted to know who we were and everything, so the introductions were made. We told him we had a band and, "What? You guys play?" "Yeah!"

Fortune Records, that was Jack Brown and his wife, Devora. Yeah, Jack was somethin', man. They were very nice people, they were very nice, but they didn't know a lot about the business, you know. They were very enthusiastic about—"You guys play? Come on, hey, you can come and play here." You know. You got a group.

So we ended up comin' back there and rehearsin' those guys, you know, no charts or music or nobody had written any music out or anything like that, just words on paper. And they would sing and say, "Listen to this, man, listen to this." And they'd sing and say, "What can you put with this? Put somethin' with this." And we'd put the music to it, and that's the way it came out. You know, creative minds together.

*R. J. Spangler*: You backed them up on their first recordings? "Goin' Down to Tiajuana" and "Pulling Time"?

*Johnnie Bassett*: Yeah, we did practically all of it. And then there was Nathaniel Mayer, he came in and did some things, and Nolan Strong and the Diablos—"The Wind," "Mind Over Matter"—and then there was another group, the Royal Jokers, "You Tickle Me, Baby." They were great groups, I mean, those guys are, you know, they are the ones that really made Fortune Records—Nolan Strong, Little Eddie Hurt, and the Five Dollars, all those guys, they made the label.

It was a great time around the city. Music was all over town, man, everybody was playin' on every corner. We had bars on every corner that had live music, you know. I played with John Lee Hooker when I was still in high school. I played with John Lee for about, oh, a little over a month, down in Black Bottom, in a storefront bar. They didn't have anybody but a piano player and a drummer and me and John Lee.

I played with Eddie Burns during that same time, after that, and Eddie Kirkland, I played with Little Sonny, you know, played with Mr. Bo—practically everybody that was anybody during that time, that needed a guitar player, heard about me through bein' in Joe Weaver and the Blue Notes, and when I wasn't playin' with the group, somebody would hire me to play, so I was always busy playin' somewhere.

*R. J. Spangler*: Johnnie played over at the Good Time Bar with Washboard Willie.

*Johnnie Bassett*: Yeah, on Buchanan and Lawton. Pete McCluskey's, McKinley and Buchanan, Bucket of Blood, they used to call that place. Oh, man. Wow.

*R. J. Spangler*: You playcd a couple years with Mr. Bo and the Blues Boys.

*Johnnie Bassett*: I played with Bo three years, and a couple of years with Little Sonny, down at the Apex, and the Bamboo Lounge. The Bamboo was on Brush and Gratiot, and the Calumet was down on Twelfth Street, and then there was another bar, the Webbwood Inn [at Woodward and Webb]. I played with Joe Weaver and everybody else down at the Webbwood—the Four Tops used to play there.

I played at the Angel Bar, over on Linwood and Euclid, and I forget the name of that other club down there where the Temptations used to play before they were the Temptations. I played behind them. They were called the Primes, and matter of fact, I'm the one that told 'em that, hey, you guys oughta be called Temptations, the way those girls are actin' out there. We was in the dressing room at the time, the dressing room was downstairs in the basement, you know, little old dressing room where we always hung out down there, drinkin' wine and talkin' shit.

We had a good time with those guys. Plus we made the Miracles' first four records, in Esther Gordy's living room, in the early '60s, "Found a Job" and those things. That was on Motown—no, on Tamla, that was Berry Gordy's first label.

But anyway, it was a great time, man. The music scene back then when we was kids was a lot of fun. Wasn't anybody makin' a great deal of money, you know, but it was a lot of fun and everybody enjoyed it. We were all kids, and it was like one big family, man. These guys, when we would get together on the shows, like when Frank Brown hired us to back up—he had a rhythm and blues versus jazz tour-type thing, and it came to the Paradise Theatre, and we backed up Joe Turner, Big Maybelle, Arthur Prysock and Red Prysock, and Bobby "Mumbles" Lewis.

*R. J. Spangler*: Johnnie recorded with him on "Tossin' and Turnin'," not the one on Beltone but an earlier version; it might've been on Chess.

*Johnnie Bassett*: Yeah, it might've been Chess. But, you know, the music scene back then, the musicians didn't go behind and undercut somebody to get a job. Everybody was tryin' to work and everybody was one big family, and when you left this club, it was an understanding that they would hire the group that come in behind you at the same money, you know, because we were all local cats tryin' to make it.

It was just a lot of fun, man, jam sessions all the time. I mean, every time you wasn't workin', somebody would be havin' a jam session somewhere. It was a good thing for the guys to keep playin', you know, and keep their interest. Every day it was someplace.

*R. J. Spangler*: Johnnie played house parties with, what was his name, Stanstill?

*Johnnie Bassett*: Rudolph Stanfield, yeah. That was before Joe Weaver. Rudolph and I, we took my old guitar, man, the first weekend my brother bought it for me, and went and played a house party and made, shoot, fifteen bucks, in tips, plus free chicken sandwiches, fish dinners, and stuff like that.

*R. J. Spangler*: When you were with the Blue Notes, did you ever go out on any tours?

*Johnnie Bassett*: We did a couple. We backed Faye Adams when she had "Shake a Hand," and we did a little thing with Lowell Fulson in Richmond, Indiana. I used to go every weekend and play down in Columbus, Ohio. That's where I met Roland Kirk, Rahsaan Roland Kirk, down in Columbus, Ohio. He was playin' in one of the bars like we were playin', where you'd go behind the bar and the bandstand was up behind the bar, you know, and, boy, they'd get you up there—a nightmare gig, man. You'd be up there with all these horns.

*R. J. Spangler*: Did you ever play that farm down there in Toledo?

*Johnnie Bassett*: Castle Farms! Yeah, we played there. We came from Kentucky to come to Castle Farms. We had played a VFW hall up in, I think, Richmond, Kentucky, yeah, something like that, and we came back from Kentucky to Castle Farms.

Our big thing at that time, though, was "Honky Tonk," our big instrumental thing. Everybody wanted to hear that, and I taught it to Joe, because I heard it on the radio and went home and then picked it out note for note, and then I went to the record store and bought the record when it came out—I had to wait for it to come in—and then played it for him.

I played along with it and he said, "Man, how you do that?" I said, "The way you gonna do it." He said, "But that's the organ, man!" I said, "Hey, if you do the bass line, the rest is simple."

So I showed him the bass line, and he finally got the bass line with his left hand. And then I had to make Jesse listen to the horn line and, you know, we studied that record, man, for about three days, and after that—that's all people would want to hear.

We'd play "Honky Tonk" at the beginning of the night, and at the end, you know, in the clubs, and that was it. That was the big thing. Once people found out we could play "Honky Tonk," oh, man, we had more jobs than we could handle [laughter]. Because we was the only band that could play it. We were the only band around town that could play "Honky Tonk" almost like the record, with a piano. Not too many organs around then.

There was a lot of great stuff happened at Fortune Records, man. Mack Rice went through there for a while and helped the guys out, with material and stuff, and helped coordinate the groups. We went to high school together, man. Mack was always a good writer, good lyric writer.

There was a lot of other little groups around that came through that never got any recognition, because the guys wasn't interested enough to stay together. They'd do some stuff and then, you know, their girlfriends would bind 'em up or whatever, and they wouldn't stay in music.

But the leader thing was—I was always a sideman in most all the organizations. When I came back in '65, I had my own organ group, you know, and I played

around the city for a long time. Clarence Price was my organ player—he was a blind organist.

Then I had Benny Baber, he was another organist that I used. And I played with Rudy Robinson and the Hungry Five, I played with Sonny Allen—he's another organ player—and Andy Martin. He was just seventeen when I met him, playin' with Mr. Bo.

*R. J. Spangler*: Were you always listening to jazz as well?

*Johnnie Bassett*: Both, yeah. Yeah. From an early age. I always liked the big bands—that was all there was.

*R. J. Spangler*: He got to play with Dinah Washington one weekend.

*Johnnie Bassett*: Yeah, at the Frolic Showbar in Detroit, down on John R, down the street from the Flame. I played at the Frolic after it moved over on John Lodge, too. Don Davis used to be over there. Don and I are good friends, too. We go back a ways. We used to play together, off and on. But he just wasn't interested enough in playing—his thing was in the studio.

He tried to sell me his guitar at the Paradise one time—no, at the Graystone Ballroom once. This was in '55, and I just had bought my Gibson and I said, man, I just got a guitar. He had a Guild, with all those buttons on it and everything, and it frustrated him because he couldn't get the sound he wanted out of it.

He said, "Man, why don't you buy this one?" And I said, "Man, why didn't you see me two weeks ago? Where were you two weeks ago before I bought this one? I just got this, I'm makin' payments on this thing." So he held on to it for a while. I don't know what he ever did with that guitar, but it was a good guitar. Beautiful. It had more buttons than I wanted—I didn't want it, either, you know, I didn't know what to do with all those damn things. I never saw one after that, either. Of course he went to Memphis and he got with Stax and everything, and the rest is history.

*John Sinclair*: So you were in Seattle for the early sixties?

*Johnnie Bassett*: Yeah, '60 to '65, with the Gil Ray combo. We hooked up—he was in the service, he was a sergeant and he had a group and he was in special service. I worked with him until I got out of the service. I met him when I first got to Fort Lewis. That's where we met.

*John Sinclair*: I was just in Detroit to help celebrate the fourth anniversary of Johnnie Bassett and the Blues Insurgents at the Music Menu Cafe. How did you guys hook up?

*R. J. Spangler*: I saw Johnnie playing one year at the Montreux-Detroit Jazz Festival, it must've been 1991, and it was with Ben Baber's organ group. Ben was gonna die of cancer that year, and he had one more shot at Montreux, so a lot of cats who were interested in organ groups came out to see him.

He says, "I'm gonna feature the bluesman in my group." And Johnnie gets out of the back row and he comes up and stands there and plays this slow T-Bone Walker kind of thing, B. B. King, funky blues, and I loved it. I knew [Detroit jazz scholar Jim] Gallert was a pretty good friend of Ben Baber's, so I asked him for Ben's number. And that's it.

We hooked up and we made that tape with [keyboardist Bill] Heid. See, Heid was a great Fortune-o-phile, being from Pittsburgh, so I used

Bill with Johnnie and he was knocked out and said, "Let's do some stuff." The tape came before the band, really, and then Bill left, so [organist Chris] Codish came into the group to play organ with us full time about five years ago.

This group's been together basically about five years in this incarnation, and we had a solid year or two ahead of that with Scott Peterson on sax and Bill [Heid]. But Bill was always taking off to go to Japan for six months at a time, so Chris came in.

We wanted to build this group up to do something, because we thought we had the potential to go somewhere with it. Mike Boulan bought a tape that I'd gotten from the Montreux-Detroit Jazz Festival, and he put it out on the No Cover label, and that enabled us to tour Europe for the first time in 1996.

*John Sinclair*: That's the part that's remarkable to me—after all these years you guys were the first ones to really emerge out of Detroit and blaze a trail.

*R. J. Spangler*: Yeah, since Little Sonny made his records in the '60s, we're the next group to come along—it's been so long since someone came out of Detroit. There was a big dry spell. We still meet people on the road that ask me how Eddie Burns is, you know, or Little Sonny, around the world, because they were really the last people from Detroit to make a dent out here. What's his name, he's been gone for so long—Eddie Kirkland—he's barely a Detroiter, I guess, although I hear he's spending time there again lately.

So we made the record on No Cover, and we came over here, and while we were here, we made a record for the Black Magic label, and with that record we were able to acquire agents over here, and they've really got us going over here now. We come a couple times, two or three times a year now, and . . .

*Johnnie Bassett:* This is my fourth trip to Europe with the group, and this is building and building. They want us back over here again, and hopefully we can do it equally as well the next time we come over, you know. It's hard work, but it's fun, you know, and it's a living. [*laughs*]

I'm hoping to play the North Sea Jazz Festival next year, and I haven't played the King Biscuit Blues Festival yet, and when I make those two then I'll be satisfied.

## EDITOR'S NOTE

The great Johnnie Bassett, known on the Detroit Music Scene as "The Gentleman," unfortunately passed away on August 4, 2012, at St. John's Hospital in Grosse Pointe Farms after battling cancer. He was seventy-six. He had visited my Wayne State University class a few times, where he told tales and played blues for my students. He was a real Detroit gem that will be missed much and loved forever. Bassett released his final album, *I Can Make That Happen*, before his death in 2012 as a follow-up to his acclaimed 2009 release *The Gentleman Is Back*.

# Motor City Blues through the Ages

*John Sinclair*

Except for a couple of raggedy blocks straggling south from East Grand Boulevard, Detroit's Hastings Street is gone now. The Motor City's major African American entertainment thoroughfare was gouged out in the late 1950s to make way for the Walter P. Chrysler Freeway, a federally subsidized fast track laid down to facilitate the flight of the city's white population to the northeastern suburbs of Hazel Park, Warren, Ferndale, Royal Oak, Madison Heights, and points north.

But for twenty years before that, Hastings Street swung all the way from Paradise Valley downtown for fifty or sixty blocks north. The legend of Hastings Street was perhaps best told in a 1948 recording by the Detroit Count, a rough barrelhouse pianist who immortalized that pulsating scene by enumerating the many theaters, lounges, bars, and rude nightspots that thrived along the length of the stroll in his two-part 78 RPM single on JVB Records titled "Hastings Street Opera."

Then there was the man they called the Mayor of Hastings Street, a dapper, diminutive gentleman named Sunnie Wilson who painted a vivid portrait of Detroit in the '30s, '40s, and '50s in his 1997 autobiography, *Toast of the Town*, written with John Cohassey and published by Wayne State University Press. Wilson was an intimate of the great Joe Louis and the popular proprietor of nightclubs, restaurants, and hotels serving African American citizens in the racially segregated east-side neighborhood between Woodward Avenue and Hastings Street. He saw and heard it all, and his account is a valuable addition to the small body of literature that examines the city's history.

In its prime years, Hastings Street throbbed with music, from the elemental blues of John Lee Hooker, Eddie Kirkland, Eddie Burns, Boogie Woogie Red, and Washboard Willie and His Super Suds of Rhythm to the swinging jazz of the Teddy Wilson Trio (with drummer J. C. Heard), Maurice King and His Wolverines (with vocalist LaVerne "Bea" Baker), Paul "Hucklebuck" Williams, T. J. Fowler, Todd Rhodes and His Toddlers, and the Mathew Rucker Orchestra.

Jazz stars like Charlie Parker, Billie Holiday, Count Basie, Duke Ellington, Billy Eckstine, and Cootie Williams played the Forest Club or the Flame Show Bar as well as the Paradise Theatre on Woodward Avenue, sharing the stage with rhythm and blues recording stars like Dinah Washington, Wynonie Harris, Amos Milburn, B. B. King, and T-Bone Walker. Sonny Boy Williamson even spent a few months in Detroit in the early '50s, playing with Calvin Frazier and Baby Boy Warren and providing inspiration to a young Aaron Willis, who gained national recognition some fifteen years later as Little Sonny, "New King of the Blues Harmonica."

As Hastings Street began to disappear, a whole new generation of singers and musicians who grew up in or around the immediate vicinity emerged to extend its influence across the world, from Jackie

Wilson, Andre Williams, Little Willie John, and Hank Ballard and the Midnighters in the '50s to the Motown Records stars who put Detroit on the map in the '60s: the Supremes, the Temptations, the Four Tops, Smokey Robinson and the Miracles. Aretha Franklin's father, the Reverend C. L. Franklin, pastored the New Bethel Baptist Church on Hastings, where his sermons were recorded by Joe Von Battle and leased to Chess Records in Chicago. Aretha's first recordings were made there when she was fourteen years old, and Joe's Hastings Street record store and JVB imprint were also home to bluesmen ranging from One-String Sam, Detroit Count, and Will Hairston to fledgling guitarist Johnnie Bassett, one of the leaders of Detroit's blues renaissance of the 1990s.

After Hastings Street disappeared, the Motor City blues scene dwindled to a handful of bars in rough neighborhoods where stalwarts like Little Sonny, Washboard Willie, Boogie Woogie Red, and Little Mack Collins and the Partymakers continued to entertain their friends and patrons, well outside the mainstream of modern entertainment. In the early '70s, Little Sonny had a shot at blues stardom via several fine albums for Stax Records' Enterprise imprint; a wild collection of Motor City blues artists was spotlighted at the 1973 Ann Arbor Blues and Jazz Festival; and bluesman Bobo Jenkins and DJ/entrepeneur Famous Coachman established a series of free Detroit blues festivals, a Detroit Blues Society, and a weekly blues radio program on WDET-FM, but these were at best shots in the darkness of American life in the '70s.

More than a decade would elapse before a new crop of Detroit bluesmen would emerge from the gloom of the city's postindustrial landscape. The advent of the 1990s brought to light well-seasoned veterans like Eddie Burns, Louis "Mr. Bo" Collins, and Sir Mack Rice, whose music was documented by a fledgling little record label in Toledo called Blue Suit Records. Another intrepid local label, Blues Factory Records, issued intriguing albums featuring previously unrecorded Motor City bluesmen like the Butler Twins, Willie D. Warren, Harmonica Shah, Uncle Jessie White, and Johnny "Yard Dog" Jones (who went on to make an excellent CD, *Ain't Gonna Worry*, for Chicago's Earwig label and won the city's first Handy Award in the process).

Now, guitarist Johnnie Bassett, who got his start on Hastings Street, is issuing albums on a variety of labels and touring the world to wide acclaim. The late blues vocalists Alberta Adams and Joe Weaver, fellow Hastings Street survivors, followed closely in Johnnie's footsteps, and blues from Detroit have begun to be heard wherever music lovers congregate.

One of the most hopeful documents of the turn-of-the-century Motor City blues scene was by John Rockwood and Bob Seeman of Blue Suit Records, which continues to lead the way in providing an outlet for what's happening today. *Hastings Street Grease: Detroit Blues is Alive, Volume One* presented music by eight vital modern bluesmen with deep roots in the Hastings Street era, including Eddie Kirkland, Piano Fats, Eddie Burns, Willie D. Warren, Harmonica Shah, Emanuel Young, and Leon Horner. On "Hastings Street Revisited (Part 1)" Detroit Piano Fats shares his memories of the old stomping grounds with Harmonica Shah, and Kirkland looks back in sorrow on "I Walk down Hastings Street."

Yet the raw energy and drive of the Detroit blues remain intact throughout, as fresh and exciting as ever, almost as if the musicians had come straight to the recording studio from their gigs at some of the little joints on Hastings. There's nothing of nostalgia here—nothing of the hokey kind of tribute album ambience that's so popular with the big-label blues producers of today. This is the low-down Detroit blues at its most elemental, and it's as precise and effective as a JVB 78.

Now, Blue Suit brings forth *Detroit Blues Is Alive, Volume 2*, a second generous helping of modern-day Motor City sounds gathered from the same relaxed, sympathetic sessions that produced the first *Hastings Street Grease* collection. Piano Fats takes Harmonica Shah way back in the day on "Hastings Street Revisited (Part 2)" and goes "Strolling through Paradise Valley," the downtown entertainment mecca from which the music spread north along Hastings.

Emanuel Young and Leon Horner pay tribute to Detroit blues giant John Lee Hooker with "I'm in the Mood" and "Boogie Chillen," respectively, while Harmonica Shah salutes Jimmy Reed on "Have Mercy, Mr. Reed" and contributes the chilling Motor City anthem "Bring Me My Shotgun." Willie D. Warren adds a new dimension to the Memphis Slim favorite simply by pointing out that "Everyday We Have the Blues" and then reveals "What Goes On in the Dark" with a special dedication to Shah.

Eddie Kirkland, the Hastings Street bluesman who began his career fifty years ago backing up John Lee Hooker, continues his contemporary resurgence with a pair of strong tracks in "Going Back to the Backwoods" and the ominous "There's Got to Be Some Changes Made." Eddie Burns is in typically

fine form on a live treatment of "When I Get Drunk." The dynamic Griswold brothers, Art and Roman, of Toledo, Ohio, romp and stomp on a great live cut titled "Daddy, Daddy," and the venerable Uncle Jessie White's distinctive approach is nicely showcased on the classic "Bad Luck Is Falling."

Hastings Street may have been laid to rest forty years ago, but its sound and spirit live on in the performances recorded here and in the music of the Detroit bluesmen who have managed to survive the cruel vicissitudes of time and social deterioration to keep on moving forward, all the way into the twenty-first century. That's definitely something Detroit can be proud of, and it's all right here on this compact disc. Put on your bibs and tuckers, ladies and g's, and dig into these musical ham hocks and chitlins cooked to funky perfection with plenty of that old-time Hastings Street grease.

# 3 EARLY D

# ETROIT SOUL

## THE PRE-MOTOWN SOUNDS

# Fortune Records for Truly Great Music

*S. R. Boland*

I t was the "shoulda, woulda, coulda" of Detroit record companies. It should have achieved the iconic status of a Chess Records, or a Specialty, or a King—but it didn't. It would have had better success if it had secured national distribution—but it didn't. And it could have had that distribution, and sold millions upon millions of records, if only the owners had had more foresight and vision—but they didn't.

The contender in question is Fortune Records, Detroit's influential independent label of the '50s and '60s. At its worst, Fortune's approach to recording was amateurish and clichéd. At its best—

which was often—Fortune made records that were raw, immediate, and compelling. The Fortune sound hit you in your face with its originality. For decades, fans of Detroit music have been able to easily identify a Fortune production by a particularly earthy, primitive, focused tone that seemed to leap out of the grooves of the record and into the ears of the listener. Although accidental, the limitations of Fortune's crude studio and basic equipment created a powerful mix like no other label had.

Fortune Records, 2002. © Leni Sinclair Collection.

Cub Koda, noted music historian and member of rock band Brownsville Station, once remarked: "Fortune Records is the great secret record company in the history of Detroit rock 'n' roll. They're the missing piece in the Detroit rock 'n' roll historical equation. Any discussion . . . without mentioning them is totally inaccurate and incomplete."

Fortune was started in the fall of 1946 with a $3,000 investment by Jack and Dorothy "Devora" Brown, a white Jewish couple. Jack was an accountant by trade, and Devora was an accomplished pianist and songwriter from Cleveland; they met in the mid-'40s. Having started a music publishing company with Devora's brother—Trianon Publications—to manage Devora's songwriting talents, the Browns launched Fortune as a recording arm of their enterprise.

Jack jokingly told Devora that they'd make a fortune off her songs when casting about for a name for the record label—and with a couple of different breaks or decisions, they might have made that fortune. In the long run, Fortune's revenue probably did put food on the Brown family table—there were children, Janice and Sheldon, to provide for—but not much more than that.

Jack Brown was a friendly, likable man. He developed connections all over town and would personally make calls on disc jockeys and distributors to hawk his new recordings. With his wife nearby, he would often poll customers on which side of a current Fortune single they preferred. After the customer passed judgment, Jack's dismayed exclamation would usually be, "See, Devora, I told you—we're pushing the wrong side!"

Devora Brown wrote many of the songs recorded by the artists, especially in the early days, and engineered most of the recording sessions. Devora's songwriting often focused on the exotic: spiritualism, magic lamps, gypsies, crystal balls, the Orient, and Latino culture. She has been characterized as a well-meaning but naïve woman who viewed her roster of artists as her children.

Fortune was but one of many independent (nonmajor) Detroit-based labels in that era; others were JVB (owned by black record-store proprietor Joe Von Battle); Von (again, owned by Von Battle); Sensation (run by Bernie Besman and John Kaplan); Staff; and Prize. However, Fortune would have the biggest impact of any Detroit indie until the rise of Motown Records.

Generally speaking, rock 'n' roll was birthed by the four groups that mainstream, middle-class America didn't want (or at least didn't want to acknowledge): blacks, hillbillies, Italian Americans, and Jews. The artists of the genre usually came from the first three groups; the independent label owners usually belonged to the last category. In Detroit in the '50s, Fortune's artists and owners pretty much followed that same paradigm.

What made Fortune different from a typical New York or Los Angeles indie was that the label was very much an amateur operation. The Browns ran it almost as a hobby, a cottage industry, with a paternalistic approach to its artists. Often, Devora Brown would bring homemade soup or sandwiches into the studio for the artists to eat during a break.

But the Browns also had a limited outlook, were fiercely protective of their assets, and were fearful—some would say paranoid—of being ripped off.

And so, those same artists eating Devora's chicken soup in the studio would receive no overtime pay, and little or nothing in royalties from the record company. The conventional thinking of the time was that the artists would make their money mostly from shows and personal appearances, booked as a result of the popularity of their records.

The US postwar record industry was innovative, especially among the smaller independent labels. For example, Sam Phillips at Sun Records in Memphis would try unorthodox equipment and mixing board settings to get "the sound." Other studios would rig up giant echo tanks, or put baffles in front of microphones to muffle the vocalist's volume. But the Browns took it all a step further. They seemed to actually encourage instrumental cacophony, odd vocalizing, weird songwriting, and unorthodox recording concepts, unintentionally establishing an atmosphere on Fortune's records that would rank as one of the most identifiable and eccentric ever.

By the mid-'60s, Fortune's primitive production values led to its decline in the face of slicker competition from Motown and other new Detroit soul labels; but in the '50s and early '60s, Fortune's "line up the mics, roll the tape, and let it rip" approach gave the recordings honesty and immediacy (if not a "tinny" quality, a comment often made about Fortune's singles).

Moreover, Fortune had no national distribution network and chose to promote records via local radio airplay (yes, often involving a little payola), with ads in trade papers like *Billboard* and *Cash Box*, at record shops, and by word of mouth. Fortune's artists would also sell their own releases at personal appearances and shows.

When Fortune began to record popular music, the operation became a microcosm of what was going on musically across America in the nation's various ethnic communities. Detroit had a sizable black population, so Fortune recorded blues and rhythm and blues. Detroit had a burgeoning community of white immigrants from the South and Appalachia, so Fortune recorded hillbilly music. And Fortune recorded straight pop, as well as gospel and polka music, to cater to other demographics. Fortune even released a few albums of gypsy music. But after about 1955, rock 'n' roll—the new name for rhythm and blues—became the dominant sound, and Fortune began to orient its production to the growing numbers of young people who wanted blues-based music with a heavy beat. Fortune became a champion of Detroit R&B—in solo-artist and group ("doo-wop") varieties.

Fortune's labels were adorned with the Fortune logo in a distinctive font, accompanied by a graphic of a lute. Across the top was the slogan "For Truly Great Music." The label color on most of the early releases was maroon, but Fortune also used purple, royal blue, dark blue, orange, pink, aqua, red, and yellow (among others) for its labels during its thirty-plus years of existence. Record collectors have long been frustrated by Fortune's record-catalog numbering system: some numbers were skipped; records were released out of sequence; and three or four different numbering series were usually running concurrently.

The 100 series—begun in '46—was originally the main pop series but became (as numbers advanced into the 180s, 190s, and 200s) a niche grouping, mostly featuring country or rockabilly. The 500 series started out with jazz and group rhythm and blues in 1953–54 but ended up being the main series by the early '60s, with mainstream pop/rock'n'roll added. The 800 series started in 1950 with the gospel classic "Death Comes Knocking" by the National Harmonizers but typically featured hardcore blues and lowdown R&B. The 1300–1400 series was gospel. There were polka records in a 400 series. However, Nathaniel Mayer records numbered in the 400s were not really Fortune releases at all but issues leased to United Artists Records (in UA's sequence), with a Fortune banner/logo on them.

Yet, even within each series, there were genre exceptions; and of course, with Fortune being Fortune, chaos abounded. Many records were assigned alternate B sides during a pressing run in order to promote a new song, and occasionally some Fortune issues had the labels swapped to the wrong sides, to generate maximum confusion. Some record numbers were duplicated. For example, catalog number 538 was used twice, once for the Earthquakes' "This Is Really Real"/"Crazy Bop" and again for Dr. Ross's "I'd Rather Be an Old Woman's Baby Than Be a Young Girl's Slave"/"Sugar Mama."

For record collectors today, the Fortune disc at the apogee of hair-tearing insanity was Fortune 839, put out in late '57 and early '58. It's believed that at least three separate pairings were used by the Browns for that one, which was an Andre Williams record. One combination saw "The Greasy Chicken" backed with "Come on, Baby"; another completely different pressing of Fortune 839 featured the bizarre "Pass the Biscuits Please" with the irresistible "Don't Touch," which included Gino Parks. Some labels carried Parks's original name, Gino Purifoy; and sometimes, that release was denoted as Fortune 839X. In another variation, "Pass the Biscuits Please" was occasionally printed

as "Please Pass the Biscuits." And, according to some documentation, it seems that there was also a version of 839 that combined "The Greasy Chicken" with "Pass the Biscuits Please" for the ultimate food-themed party record.

The label's first single in late 1946, Fortune 101, was a 78 RPM pop record (there would be no 45 RPM releases until the early '50s), "Jane (Sweet as Summer Rain)"/"Texas Tess Down Texas Way" by Russ Titus with the Artie Fields Orchestra. It sold well locally, and Fortune was off and running. Many of the early releases were country oriented. In 1949, Fortune re-released the original 1939 hit version of "Hamtramck Mama" by the York Brothers, and the record sold well all over again, doing big business in local jukeboxes. Other standout early country recordings on Fortune included "Dirty Boogie" by pianist Roy Hall and "The Tattooed Lady" by Skeets McDonald. The label's first big regional hit came in late '52 and early '53: "Jealous Love" by the Davis Sisters (Betty Jack Davis and Mary Frances Penick, who became Skeeter Davis). Fortune recorded a treasure trove of great hillbilly music in its early years, by artists like Earl and Joyce Songer, Eddie Jackson, Johnnie White, Farris Wilder, May Hawks, Boots Gilbert, and Chief Redbird.

Fortune was at first operated out of the Browns' home but soon took up offices in two consecutive locations on the northern stretch of Twelfth Street, near Elmhurst. By autumn 1950, the couple had moved their operation into a rented storefront at 11629 Linwood across from Central High School. Fortune's first studio of its own was a room at the Linwood location. Earlier Fortune releases were often recorded at United Sound Systems on Second Avenue, which was (and is) a professional-grade studio. Pre-Linwood, the Browns also used recording facilities at Vogue in Detroit and in Toledo, Ohio, at Sweeny Sound Engineering. In 1953, Fortune acquired a one-track Ampex 350 reel-to-reel tape deck, which would be used to record all the label's masters well into the '60s.

In the fall of 1956, the Browns relocated Fortune Records to its most famous address, 3942 Third Avenue, near Selden in the Cass Corridor, south of the Wayne State University campus. Third Avenue was a seedy area then, and it would get even more sketchy in the '60s and '70s.

The building at 3942 Third was relatively new—only six years old—at the time the Browns bought it. They added a large, hand-painted sign above the door and front window, proclaiming Fortune Records, Trianon Publications, and Hi-Q (and later, Strate-8). Hi-Q and Strate-8 were Fortune's main subsidiary labels; Hi-Q was started about 1956, and Strate-8 followed in '59. (Earlier occasional subsidiaries included Rendezvous and Renown.) A Fortune Records neon sign hung in the front window, where the latest releases were displayed along with various posters and photos of artists.

There was a record shop in the front, which was open to the public, but Jack Brown later ran his one-stop wholesale record operation (the Hi-Q Record Mart, originally located at 3137 Woodward) from that area, too. In the back, through a narrow hallway, was the legendary eighteen-by-forty-foot studio. The studio on Third was more crude than the one that had been in the Linwood storefront.

By rights, it should have been a terrible place to record in—it was a garage-like affair with a small control booth with a window, a homemade mixing board, a few mics, and a piano (which, it's said, was often out of tune). For sound deadening, there were sheets hanging from overhead, along with egg cartons glued to the walls. To top it off, part of the studio floor was dirt in the early years. Often, the Browns recorded at "hot" levels to get more sound to tumble out of the grooves—to make louder records. A common Fortune gimmick was to add a little (or a lot of) mixing-board echo.

Beginning in about 1955, Joe Weaver and the Blue Note Orchestra (sometimes billed as the Blue Note Band) were used as the backup group on so many Fortune recordings that they essentially became the label's house band. Joe Weaver was the leader and piano player; Johnnie Bassett, later a blues star in his own right, was the group's guitarist. Weaver had a regional hit with "Baby I Love You So" in 1956 with the Don Juans (the Five Dollars) on backing vocals and followed that one up with "Looka Here Pretty Baby" the following year. Weaver would later relate how the released, lo-fi version of "Baby I Love You So" was just supposed to be a rehearsal, and that he was kicking a box under his piano to provide a beat.

Three acts epitomized the Fortune sound and contributed the most to the label's success: Nolan Strong and the Diablos, Andre Williams, and Nathaniel Mayer.

But without question, Fortune's franchise act was the Diablos, signed to a contract in late 1953. The group had been formed back in 1950 when the members were attending Central High School.

The group's sound featured the soaring, otherworldly tenor of lead singer Nolan Strong (born January 22, 1934, in Scottsboro, Alabama). Original members also included Juan Gutierriez, tenor; Willie Hunter, baritone; Quentin Eubanks, bass; and Bob "Chico" Edwards on guitar. Nolan

Strong's brother, Jimmy, joined the group later in 1954, replacing Gutierriez; and George Scott would supplant Eubanks. The group's name is believed to have come from a book, *El Nino Diablo* (The Little Devil), that Nolan Strong was reading for a high school book report.

Nolan Strong, like every other R&B tenor of his day, was profoundly influenced by Clyde McPhatter (of the Dominoes and the Drifters); and Strong, in turn, profoundly influenced a young Smokey Robinson, who made a point of attending Diablos shows.

The Diablos ventured into the Linwood studio to audition for Fortune in late 1953, and while Jack Brown thought that Nolan Strong's voice might be a bit too high, Devora felt that the same quality would set him apart from other singers. The Diablos were signed.

For their first record, the group was given a Latin-styled Devora Brown tune, "Adios My Desert Love," and it sold well locally. But the group became famous for their eerie-harmony ballad, "The Wind." The guys wrote "The Wind" while they were taking a drive on Belle Isle, and the recording was supervised by Flame Show Bar bandleader Maurice King. A solid regional hit in 1954, it was re-released in 1960 and went through several pressings. (A New York group, the Jesters, covered the song in 1960, and since that time a debate has raged among doo-wop fans over which version is better.)

In 1955, the Diablos' bluesy "The Way You Dog Me Around" made number 12 on the *Cash Box* R&B chart. Other topnotch songs were recorded during '55 too: the bouncy "Route 16," the rockin' "Do You Remember What You Did," and the autobiographical "Daddy Rockin' Strong." As for other early Diablos recordings, "Jump, Shake, and Move" features some scorching Bob Edwards guitar work; "You Are" shows off some midtempo harmony; and "Try Me One More Time" is relentless, fast doo-wop. Young J. W. "Jay" Johnson joined the group in late '56 and would prove to be the group's longest-serving bass singer.

By that time, the Diablos were playing gigs all over Detroit (venues like the Madison Ballroom, the Flame Show Bar, and the 509 Club) and touring nationally. The Diablos would headline at the Apollo Theatre in New York, the Uptown in Philadelphia, the Howard in Washington, DC, the Regal in Chicago, and the Orchid Room in Kansas City.

Nolan Strong's suave looks and star quality made him a natural magnet for female fans, but he was drafted into the army at the end of 1956. After he returned to lead the group again in 1958, things had changed. Strong, formerly a straight arrow, had picked up the habits of drinking and pill-popping while in the military. He grew increasingly unreliable even as the Browns continued to promote him and cater to him.

While Nolan Strong was away in the Army, lead duties had been taken over by baritone Willie Hunter. One Diablos single was put out with Hunter on lead vocal: "Harriet"/"Come Home Little Girl." But the magic just wasn't there without Strong's sky-high tenor.

Even before Nolan Strong's stint in the military, the other members of the Diablos were being marginalized by Fortune; but the balance of power really began to shift after 1958. Devora Brown saw Strong as Fortune Records' top talent and star attraction: billing on the record labels went from "The Diablos featuring Nolan Strong" to "Nolan Strong and the Diablos" to simply "Nolan Strong."

Devora Brown was certainly very fond of Nolan and had come to view him almost as a son. Strong was invited to dinner many times at the Brown home.

The inequities didn't end with how the group was (or wasn't) listed on the record label. The group members weren't seeing much in the way of royalties, period; but Nolan's share of any payout was always greater.

The romping "My Heart Will Always Belong to You" (with fantastic Bob Edwards guitar fills) was a stellar effort for the group in '58, and '59 started off with another good fast one, "Goodbye Matilda." However, the group's next record would prove to be an all-time favorite with Diablos fans. "If I (Could Be with You Tonight)" had an appealing midtempo doo-wop groove, and it would even be reissued a few years later by Fortune as "If I, Oh I" for a second go-round.

Perhaps the best showcase for Nolan Strong's outstanding voice was 1960's "Since You're Gone," a recording that straddles the line between R&B group ballad and pop/lounge fare—complete with a jazzy piano break. Strong is perfect on the song, and it should have been a hit.

The group's last big record, "Mind over Matter," reached number 1 on the local Detroit radio surveys in 1962 (making only number 82 nationally on *Cash Box*), but it was put out as a Nolan Strong solo record despite the undeniable presence of the Diablos' background vocals.

"Mind over Matter," written by Devora Brown, has been called a Detroit classic. The record jells because Strong's superb vocals float over a churning rock 'n' roll mix that includes memorable riffs by Chuck Chittenden, a white guitarist. (Did Keith Richards get the idea for the Rolling Stones' "Start Me Up" lick from Chittenden's playing?) Drummer Charles "Butch" Vaden (who made other records for Fortune under his own name) propels everything along with an infectious beat.

It was such a great record that Motown's Berry Gordy decided he had to try to capitalize on it. He took his group, the Temptations, into the studio and renamed them the Pirates for a cover of "Mind over Matter" on his Mel-o-Dy subsidiary. The cover version bombed; the public wanted only the Nolan Strong original.

It was about the time of "Mind over Matter" that Gordy asked Strong to join his burgeoning Motown empire. Strong met with Gordy but refused to defect; his loyalty to the Brown family outweighed all future possibilities of greater success. Besides, Gordy wouldn't offer any money to Strong up front to jump his Fortune contract, although he did offer legal defense if the Browns decided to sue. It was a moot point, though—Strong was staying with Fortune. There are stories of earlier offers from Gordy to buy the contract of the entire Diablos group as well.

There were some listenable records to follow "Mind over Matter": "I Really Love You," "Everything They Said Came True," "(Yeah, Baby) It's Because of You," and a fine Nathaniel Mayer song, "Real True Love." The last Nolan Strong single was a truly bizarre one: "Ali Coochie"/"(You're Not Good Looking but) You're Presentable," released in 1966. By that time, the core Diablos group had disbanded; an offshoot group called the Velvet Angels (Jay Johnson, Willie Hunter, Cy Iverson, and Bobby Calhoun, with some guest vocals from Nolan Strong) had made some impromptu a cappella recordings in 1964, and some of them were released on 45s. Nevertheless, the Velvet Angels episode was short-lived.

By the late '60s, Nolan Strong recordings had tapered off and the singer was on a downhill spiral with alcohol. Not much is known about the last years of his life. Strong died all too young, at age forty-three, on February 21, 1977. Strong's legacy is championed today by Jay Johnson, who heads up Nolan Strong's Diablos. The current iteration of the group makes selected appearances, often on the East Coast.

Another important chapter in the Fortune story was written by Andre Williams, a flamboyant showman who could sing a little and entertain a lot. Zephire Andre Williams was born November 1, 1936, in Bessemer, Alabama, and his mother died when he was six. He wound up dividing the rest of his childhood between his steelworker father in Chicago and his sharecropper grandparents in Alabama. The sounds of Hank Williams's records were an early musical memory. Later, truancy would become an issue when the long hours of young Williams's job at Cadillac Bob's steak house would infringe on his sleep and make him miss school. His job was just down the street from the famous 708 Club, a blues joint, and so Williams was exposed to many well-known blues and R&B musicians. Of all the stars at the time, Williams was most impressed with Cab Calloway. At fifteen, Williams decided to go into the navy by using falsified papers with his older brother's name on them, but eventually he was discovered and drummed out of the military.

At just seventeen years old, he attracted attention after coming into Detroit and winning multiple talent contests at the Warfield Theatre on Hastings Street. The Warfield's manager alerted Devora Brown to Williams's charisma. He had started singing with a Detroit vocal group, the Five Dollars (originally known as the Del-Torros). Williams's connection to the Five Dollars was through the lead singer, Little Eddie Hurt, to whom he was related by marriage.

After a brief audition with Vee-Jay Records in Chicago, the Five Dollars, whose members had already written some original songs, signed with Fortune; and Williams also signed as a solo artist. The Five Dollars would be known as the Don Juans when they sang background on Williams's solo records and for other Fortune solo acts.

Williams soon became the Five Dollars' main draw because of his irreverent, bold manner and his wild stage antics, which included leaps from theater balconies. He was a natural leader and stayed with the Five Dollars into 1956.

Williams's first few records under his own name were billed as by Andre Williams and the Don Juans, and there were some gems: "Down to Tia Juana," "Mozelle," "Pulling Time." But with his mediocre vocal range, Williams knew he could never be a pure singing talent. "You see, I had realized that I was not a Clyde McPhatter, I was not a Nolan Strong," Williams said. "And the guys that were selling records were high tenors, and I knew that if I didn't come up with something, I was gonna fall through the f—in' tomb. I had to come up with a f—in' gimmick." Williams set out to make unique, entertaining records that told a story.

His initial offering in that vein was a dance number called "Bacon Fat," billed as by Andre Williams and His New Group and released in November 1956. The New Group included a teenage J. W. "Jay" Johnson, who was soon to take over as the Diablos' bass singer; and also Gino Parks (real surname, Purifoy), a fine tenor with an emotional, fiery style who made the impeccable "Last Night I Cried" for Fortune and dynamic singles like "That's No Lie" and "For This I Thank You" for Motown. The New Group was rounded out by Bobby Calhoun and Steve Gaston.

"Bacon Fat," also known as "Didlee Didlee Womp Womp," was one of the last important Fortune recordings made at the Linwood studio. It features a protorap (talking in rhythm) over a sleazy, sax-dominated arrangement. Williams claims that he wrote the song while eating a bacon sandwich on a road trip to a show in Memphis and noticing cotton pickers near the railroad tracks (Jay Johnson, however, remembers the composition as more of a group effort). When presented with the song in the studio, Devora Brown didn't like the idea of spoken lyrics, but WJLB DJ "Frantic" Ernie Durham, present at the session, urged her to give the song a chance and record it.

"Bacon Fat" took off in Detroit in late '56 and reached number 9 on the national *Billboard* R&B charts in early 1957 after the recording was leased to Epic, a Columbia subsidiary. It was Fortune's biggest success to date.

After "Bacon Fat," Epic was interested in promoting Williams and issuing more singles by him, but Fortune quickly squelched that idea. The Browns balked at sharing more profits off Williams with Epic; they felt that they had been shortchanged in the lease deal. Fortune had received only $500 for the master lease arrangement and $2,000 in royalties for a record that had made the national R&B Top 10.

Williams followed "Bacon Fat" with "Jail Bait," an outrageous and funny morality play on the perils of messing with underage girls:

It's a rough temptation
But a common invitation
And a good association
But a quick elimination
That will take you out of
circulation . . .
Yes, I'm talking about that younger
generation . . .
So take my advice, fellas
For goodness' sake
fifteen . . . sixteen. . . seventeen . . .
that's . . . jail bait

"Jail Bait" was recorded with a big-band orchestra, lending extra oomph to the dramatic lyrics. More Andre Williams singles followed with a food motif, notably the aforementioned "Pass the Biscuits Please" and "The Greasy Chicken." Other solid offerings were pure rock 'n' roll: "Don't Touch," and "Movin'."

Williams left Fortune in 1960 and would go on to work with Berry Gordy at Motown for a couple of years. He then took hold in Chicago for a time as a writer, arranger, producer, and artist. He's well known for writing the much-covered "Shake a Tail Feather" for the Five Du-Tones and "Twine Time" for Alvin Cash. In later years, he worked with Ike Turner, got addicted to cocaine, and spent some time virtually homeless on the streets. He eventually pulled himself out of his hole in the mid-'90s and made some new albums, and he's still touring today to appreciative audiences.

Fortune's biggest hit and closest shot to national success came not with the polished Nolan Strong or with the raunchy hustler Andre Williams but with the impassioned vocals of a teenage east-sider, Nathaniel Mayer. Mayer, born on February 10, 1944, had first ridden his bicycle over to hang around the Fortune studio at age twelve and finally signed with the label in 1959, after going through two managers, Gwen Gordy (Berry's sister) and the quintessential Detroit record man, Harry Balk.

Balk worked with Mayer for a short time, grooming him for success. But Mayer was impatient. After seeing a novelty song he'd written, "Silly Milly," get recorded by another act (the Devotions, whose record was released on the MGM subsidiary, Cub, in 1958), Mayer rode his bike back over to Fortune and cast his fate with Jack and Devora Brown.

Mayer's first record was "My Last Dance with You," a title previously used by Andre Williams, but the two songs are nothing alike. Mayer's record had a recitation in the middle and the ballad's production was reverb drenched. The flip was "My Little Darling," a faster offering that featured a flute solo and a sound not unlike a Marv Johnson record. (Mayer would later cite Johnson as one of his main influences, along with Sam Cooke and James Brown.) The record was released in 1960 and sales were limited. But Mayer wasn't done.

Not long after turning eighteen, Mayer wrote and recorded the Detroit anthem "Village of Love" in the early spring of 1962. Was it derivative? Hell, yes—it had the ubiquitous I-vi-IV-V chord progression and turned-around lyrics cribbed from Ray Charles's "What'd I Say":

> Tell your ma
> Tell your pa
> We're going back
> To Arkansas

To top it off, the repeated "hey, hey" was a shout-out to Jackie Wilson's "Lonely Teardrops."

No matter. Mayer was singing for his life on "Village of Love"—he wanted a hit, and he got one.

The record, by Nathaniel Mayer and His Fabulous Twilights, took off regionally in the spring, and Fortune made a deal with Art Talmadge of United Artists Records for national distribution. After Fortune leased the master to UA, the record (now pressed up with a yellow nonlogo Fortune label and a UA catalog number, 449) made number 16 on the *Billboard* R&B chart. It also made number 22 on the *Billboard* Hot 100 pop chart. However, it made a huge impact in the big-city markets, reaching number 8 on a Los Angeles radio survey, number 6 in New York City, number 2 in Chicago, and, of course, number 1 in Detroit.

"Village of Love" had a *sound* that was irresistible. From the booming "Why don't you come" bass intro, to the strident urgency of Mayer's lead vocals, to the jet-propelled handclaps, to the soulful guitar lead by Willie "Flukey" Fleming, the record was two minutes of pure greasy goodness. The eighteen-year-old kid from the east side had created a masterpiece. He dropped out of Eastern High School to concentrate on music.

Soon, he got a call from Dick Clark's office and was invited to appear on *American Bandstand*; Mayer was the only Fortune artist to ever perform on the popular TV show. A tour with the top hit makers of the day ensued; he went on the road with Mary Wells, Clyde McPhatter, LaVern Baker, the Vibrations, Maxine Brown, and the Marcels. He played a string of theaters that included the Apollo in New York and the Howard in Washington, DC. Mayer was especially floored by the acrobatics of

107

the Vibrations ("The Watusi"), whom he called the most impressive act he'd ever seen. "Village of Love" was covered by the Halos ("Nag") and by Dee Dee Sharp on an album, but Mayer's rendition remained the definitive version.

For a follow-up to "Village of Love," Devora Brown came to Mayer with the aforementioned "Mind over Matter." Mayer thought the song was too pop-sounding for his style, so he suggested that the song be given to Nolan Strong. After Strong recorded the song with the Diablos, Mayer saw "Mind over Matter" become a big regional hit—with Mayer's own band on Strong's record! Perhaps Mayer made the wrong call.

The next Nathaniel Mayer release turned out to be a stomper called "Leave Me Alone." It was also leased to UA by Fortune, but it failed to chart nationally (although it sold well in the Detroit area). Perhaps its success was stalled because the flip side of the record, "Hurting Love"—a haunting ballad that featured an ethereal harmony part sung by Nolan Strong—was initially promoted instead. But "Leave Me Alone" is one of the Fortune label's most primitive rockers—a profound mix of R&B and garage-rock styles, it was way ahead of its time when issued in July 1962. "Leave Me Alone" showcased Mayer's backing band well, in particular the savage slashing of guitarist Chuck Chittenden and the pounding beat of drummer Butch Vaden. In true Detroit rock 'n' soul fashion, Mayer's band members were white. The Fabulous Twilights were Mayer's background singers, and personnel varied from record to record.

After the flop of "Leave Me Alone"/"Hurting Love," Fortune decided to promote its own records. The Browns did some math and felt they were severely shortchanged on revenue from the sales of

"Village of Love." UA finally paid the Browns for the sales of 180,000 records on "Village," but the Browns felt—and justifiably so—that the record had sold in much higher numbers. In fact, it's believed that "Village of Love" might have sold close to a million copies.

Meanwhile, Art Talmadge of United Artists tried to buy Mayer's contract from Fortune, but no dice. Mayer himself wanted to go with UA, but he was locked in to the label at 3942 Third. As time went on, his Fortune contract became more frustrating. The second big hit never came. At one point, Berry Gordy talked to Mayer about leading Motown's Contours, but that came to naught; Mayer liked being a solo artist and didn't want to become part of a group.

However, there were some other great moments on Fortune wax for Mayer: "Well, I've Got News for You" was a Devora Brown song that became a listenable record near the end of '62 (the flip was the explosive "Mr. Santa Claus"); and "I Had a Dream," from 1963, is Mayer at his best: raw, pounding, and danceable. "I'm Not Gonna Cry" is a gut-wrenching ballad right out of the James Brown book.

There were misses, too: "Work It Out" was basically a thin rehash of "Village of Love"; "Going Back to the Village of Love" was an attempt to revive the success of Mayer's big hit, but the sound is limp and the recorded-live-at-a-party atmosphere sounds fake (which it was). "Don't Come Back" and the return-to-doo-wop "A Place I Know" were good songs, but Fortune recorded them superdistorted—the tape deck's level meter must have slammed all the way into the red during the session. By that time, the listening public expected better production values (such as Motown's); but Fortune, with its crude equipment, could only compensate by taping at hotter levels.

In 1966, Mayer was doing a stint at the Detroit House of Correction (usually referred to as DeHoCo) for being along on a joy ride in a stolen car; he decided to write a song about being incarcerated and got his friend Timmy Shaw ("Gonna Send You Back to Georgia"), also detained, to help him. The result was the funk-laden "(I Want) Love and Affection (Not the House of Correction)," with a plot line that used the old Robins hit "Riot in Cell Block Number 9" as a springboard. Paired with the soulful "From Now On," "Love and Affection" sold very well in Detroit, and Mayer would later call it his "underground hit." The chorus is infectious; it's nearly impossible to not sing along!

Mayer's sound was becoming more like James Brown's, and his stage show also reflected Brown's influence. Beginning in the late '60s, Mayer fronted a revue with his own band, the Detroit Sounds, along with some dancers. The revue often also featured Motor City stalwarts like Jimmy Ruffin, Spyder Turner, Emanuel Laskey, J. J. Barnes, Gino Washington, and "Sweet" James Epps. Mayer kept the revue going for about ten years.

But gradually, Mayer disappeared from the mainstream music scene, playing only occasionally at small cabarets in Detroit neighborhoods. Then, in 2002, Norton Records put out a previously unreleased side, "I Don't Want No Bald Headed Woman Telling Me What to Do" (produced by Gino Washington, recorded in 1968). With the help of some promoters and young, eager musicians, Mayer staged a comeback of sorts. All of a sudden, he was touring again, playing bigger venues and festivals, and astounding audiences

with his energy (even if his voice had become raspy and rough). Mayer released two new, well-received albums, *I Just Want to Be Held* and *Why Don't You Give It to Me*, before a series of strokes cut him down. He died on November 1, 2008, after months of hospitalization.

Even without Andre Williams, the previously mentioned Five Dollars were one of Fortune's premier acts. Originally, the group was called the Shamrocks and then the Del-Torros. Little Eddie Hurt was the lead/high tenor; the other members were tenors Lonnie Heard and Richard Lawrence, baritone James Drayton, and bass Charles Evans. All were teenagers at the time the group was signed to Fortune in 1955 except Drayton, who was about twenty.

The group had picked up a manager, Sandy St. Amour, who was a florist by trade but who had become a fan after hearing them sing at a club. St. Amour began working with the Five Dollars, rehearsing them and trying to get them gigs. Their first Fortune release was "Doctor Baby"/"Harmony of Love."

Devora Brown invented an alter-ego name for the group—the Don Juans—to be used when they were backing Fortune's solo artists. And even though Andre Williams was supposed to be part of the group, Williams's releases were billed as by Andre Williams and the Don Juans. Sometimes, the group would even perform in public as both the Five Dollars and the Don Juans (in different outfits). The second identity didn't sit too well with the group, and they began to feel neglected by Fortune and dominated by Williams.

In early 1956, Fortune released the Five Dollars' "So Strange," which is . . . strange. With no lyrics

109

(reminiscent of "Harmony of Love") and a boogie-driven melody line, the record is mesmerizing.

Williams left the group to go solo about the same time the group lost its manager. After that time, the Five Dollars assumed a more minor role in the Fortune stable but still managed to put out some gems under the group name, like "I Will Wait," "Hard Working Mama," "You Fool," and the later "My Baby-O." Some members of the Dollars complained later that their released records were often only intended to be rehearsals but that Devora Brown put them out anyway.

Another key Fortune group was the Earthquakes, whose leader, Armond Abney, made solo records as Armond Adams and was also billed as Arlando King on some sides. The Earthquakes were mostly known for their moving ballads, like "Darling Be Mine," the stunning "This Is Really Real," and the heart-wringing "Look What You've Done." Abney, with his strident, emotional delivery, had real talent—and the Earthquakes made some noise (and sold some records) for a while. Up-tempo sides like "Bashful Guy," and especially "Crazy Bop," showed that the group could have some fun and rock with the best of them.

The legendary bluesman John Lee Hooker—who first moved to Detroit in 1943—would come and go at Fortune over the years, making many recordings and not caring if he was under contract to another label at the time. In fact, Jack Brown claimed to have made some of the very first recordings on Hooker, driving him down to Sweeny Sound Engineering in Toledo in 1948 and waxing "609 Boogie" and "Miss Sadie Mae (Curl My Baby's Hair)." Hooker would often hang out at Fortune and cut a few songs when in Detroit. Most Fortune

releases by "The Hook" were during the late '50s and early '60s, notably "Crazy 'Bout That Walk."

A lot of bluesmen made stops at Fortune, and one of the best was Dr. Ross, "the Harmonica Boss." One of his most acclaimed sides, "Cat Squirrel," was cut in the studio on Third Avenue. Another blues/R&B great to record at Fortune was Eddie Kirkland (sometimes billed as Eddie Kirk), who played with John Lee Hooker for a long time and was supremely talented in his own right.

Many Fortune releases were made as custom pressings; the artist was not under contract, and so he or she paid for the studio time, the engineering, and the pressed records. Often, custom jobs were not given as much care in engineering as in the recordings by artists that Fortune had under contract. Still, it was a valuable service that Fortune provided, because anyone could walk in and make a record for a reasonable price. Such custom records were usually sold by the artists at live performances.

One enduring Detroit rockabilly act who actually began his career with a Fortune custom pressing was Johnny Powers (born John Leon Joseph Pavlik on May 25, 1938). Powers had been performing country music before hearing Jack Scott's "Baby She's Gone," which swayed him toward rock 'n' roll.

Still without a stage name at the time, he walked into the building on Third Avenue in 1957 and paid the grand sum of one hundred dollars to make a record with his band, the Rockets. Recording two sides, "Honey Let's Go (to a Rock and Roll Show)" and "Your Love," under the direction of Devora Brown, he was teamed with a black vocal group that "might have been the Diablos." The definite influence of Scott's "Baby She's Gone" can be heard in the structure of the A side.

Devora Brown told the singer that his real name wouldn't work on a record label and that he'd need a new identity as a performer. She noticed that he was eating a Power House candy bar and told him, "That's it, your new recording name is Johnny Powers." Ultimately, Powers's signature tune would become "Long Blond Hair, Rose Red Lips," released on Fox Records in 1958.

Jack and Devora Brown were involved in an auto accident in 1973, which left Jack severely crippled; he died in April 1980. Janice, their daughter, had begun to take a more active role in the label, modernizing operations, but she succumbed to cancer in 1981. Devora and son Sheldon continued to run the label and put out reissues until the mid-'90s, when the building on Third Avenue was vacated (after some break-ins that saw stacks of record stock and a Fortune wall clock stolen) and sold.

The Fortune building on Third Avenue is long gone, having been demolished at the end of October 2001 despite a last-ditch effort by local preservationists to save it. (A fire in the late '90s had gutted the structure and left it roofless.) The older Fortune location on Linwood is just a vacant lot now, too.

The whereabouts of the master tapes are unknown, but it's believed that Jack and Devora's son, Sheldon (also known as Don), has stored them somewhere. Although nearly all of Fortune's released output has been available through bootleg records and CDs for years (with varying degrees of quality), it's certain that there are some incredible performances on tape that were never released. Devora Brown was notorious for rolling the tape on everything, from rough rehearsals to fully orchestrated sessions.

At times over the years, Sheldon Brown attempted to sell the master tapes to larger record labels that would produce proper reissues, but nothing ever came of his efforts. Today, the Fortune catalog, still under Sheldon Brown's control, is administered by the Westwood Music Group in Florida.

## ESSENTIAL LISTENING: FORTUNE RECORDS

"The Tattooed Lady"—Skeets McDonald

"Dirty Boogie"—Roy Hall and his Cohutta Mountain Boys

"Jealous Love"—The Davis Sisters

"Steel Wool"—Chuck Hatfield and the Treble-Aires

"Death Comes Knocking"—The National Harmonizers

"Soft, Sweet, and Really Fine"—The Five Dukes of Rhythm

"Rose of Tangier"—The Four Kings

"The Wind"—The Diablos featuring Nolan Strong

"Do You Remember What You Did"—The Diablos featuring Nolan Strong

"The Way You Dog Me Around"—The Diablos featuring Nolan Strong

"My Heart Will Always Belong to You"—Nolan Strong and the Diablos

"If I (Could Be with You Tonight)"—Nolan Strong and the Diablos

"Since You're Gone"—Nolan Strong and the Diablos

"Mind over Matter"—Nolan Strong

"Going Down to Tia Juana"—Andre Williams and the Don Juans

"Mozelle"—Andre Williams and the Don Juans

"Bacon Fat"—Andre Williams and His New Group

"Jail Bait"—Andre Williams

"Don't Touch"—Andre Williams and Gino Parks

"Doctor Baby"—The Five Dollars

"So Strange"—The Five Dollars

"Last Night I Cried"—Gino Parks and the Hi-Fidelities

"Village of Love"—Nathaniel Mayer and His Fabulous Twilights

"Leave Me Alone"—Nathaniel Mayer and His Fabulous Twilights

"I Had a Dream"—Nathaniel Mayer

"(I Want) Love and Affection (Not the House of Correction)"—Nathaniel Mayer

"Gonna Get Me a Satellite"—Little Ernest Tucker

"Cat Squirrel"—Dr. Ross

"I Must Have Done Somebody Wrong"—Eddie Kirkland

"This Is Really Real"—The Earthquakes

"Baby I Love You So"—Joe Weaver and the Blue Note Orchestra

"You Ain't No Good for Me"—Jimmy Lee

"Honey Let's Go (to a Rock and Roll Show)"—Johnny Powers

"Rock the Universe"—Dell Vaughn

"Rock and Roll Grandpap"—Don Rader

"Drunk Driver's Coming"—Richard Brothers

"September in the Rain"—The Royal Jokers

"I Don't Like You That Much"—The Royal Jokers

"I'm Laughing at You"—The Gardenias

"Listen to the Rain"—The Delteens

"(Why Don't You) Love Me"—The Delteens

"Harem Girl"—Butch Vaden

"I Won't Be Your Fool"—Melvin Davis

"Valley of Tears"—The Destinations

"Your Star"—Gene and the Jeanettes

"Love, Boy"—Tony Valla and the Alamos

# Nathaniel Mayer in the Twenty-First Century

*Matthew Smith*

Nathaniel Mayer's house on Detroit's east side, on Burns Street between I-94 and Van Dyke, was an oasis of seminormalcy in the middle of a war zone. Most of the houses on his street looked like they'd been blown up. The remaining houses were mostly crack houses. Nathaniel's place was a nice, old house that made you feel comfortable enough to forget you were living in the twenty-first century. The house looked like it hadn't changed much since 1960, which is about the time Nate's musical career began.

One night Nate's bass player and I were at the house celebrating Nate's birthday, hanging out and watching a video of Nate singing his 1962 hit "Village of Love" on a TV special. When it was time for us to leave, Nate's family and friends suddenly seemed very concerned that we might not make it to our car alive, even though it was parked directly in front of the house. Nate stepped onto the front porch, looked up and down the street, and declared, "They'll be alright. Everybody knows they're with Nay-Dog."

Nathaniel Mayer had lived a hard life on the streets of Detroit, and was still living it that way, even though he was getting some recognition lately. Nathaniel stopped making records in 1968. His life was intertwined with many of the ups and downs of the city he lived in. He didn't like to talk about the riots in the '60s, and he didn't want to talk about the assassination of Dr. Martin Luther King, and he didn't want to talk about anything that happened in the '70s. We didn't talk much about the '80s or '90s,

either. Nate had fond memories of the Detroit he knew, which had begun to disintegrate sometime in the '60s, and had gotten worse and worse every day, like a nuclear bomb going off in slow motion. He would often talk about how nice his neighborhood used to be. Nate had recently started making records and playing concerts again, and he had become a living, breathing reminder of a world that seemed to have been destroyed. The way he talked, the way he dressed, and especially the way he sang, all made you

Nathaniel Mayer at the Millenium Theatre, 2002.
© Leni Sinclair Collection.

feel like you'd stepped into a time machine when you were in his presence.

I had noticed, over the years, that when you mentioned Nathaniel Mayer's name to people in Detroit, you'd get a variety of reactions. The rock 'n' roll fans and musicians who discovered him after hearing the Detroit Cobras' version of "Village of Love" considered him a superstar. The record collectors already knew about him and some of them claimed he'd invented funk when he cut "From Now On" in 1966.

Mention him to some of the old-timers from Detroit's doo-wop and soul scene, and it was a whole different thing. Some people loved him. Some people were just plain freaked out by him. Some maintained that he had blown out his voice. When you'd talk to them about his comeback, they'd react with surprise and look at you like you were crazy. Nathaniel's long history of drug and alcohol problems was not a secret. It was also not a secret that Nathaniel had been associated with the Errol Flynns street gang. He was a soul singer who had developed a reputation as a wild performer, who was equally wild offstage. In many ways, he had more in common with Iggy Pop than he did with most of his R&B peers.

On a purely musical level, Nathaniel Mayer was a powerhouse, an all-around talented guy with amazing energy who could write great lyrics and possessed a distinctive vocal style. And he really knew how to build a groove. Even in his last days, when he could barely walk, let alone dance, he was still able to hypnotize his audiences in a strange way that had more in common with Fela Kuti's African grooves than with the Motown sound.

Nate's music could be wild, crazy, and over the top, but it was always accessible. His voice reflected

the fact that he truly and completely worshipped James Brown, but he had also learned some musical secrets hanging out with Nolan Strong back in the '50s, and Nolan Strong was one of the greatest singers ever. When Nate started performing again in the twenty-first century, his voice was damaged and ravaged from too much drinking, smoking, and onstage screaming. His speaking voice was like a cross between Redd Foxx and Miles Davis. He would occasionally leave messages on my answering machine in a familiar growl that was totally incomprehensible. Still, whenever he got in front of a microphone, he would employ breathing techniques that he presumably learned from Nolan Strong, and he could project the sound in a way that was astonishing. And his range was quite high. He told me that one of his favorite records was "Every Breath I Take" by Gene Pitney, and whenever I hear that record, I laugh at all those little vocal inflections that Nate was probably obsessed with and had practiced to perfection.

One day, driving around listening to the radio, I heard a voice that I thought was Nate's, belting out a song I'd never heard before. It turned out to be "Contract on Love" by Nate's old pal Stevie Wonder. It's a great record, with Stevie singing pretty much exactly like Nate. Recorded in 1962 for Motown, it seems to be an homage to one of Stevie's musical heroes.

I heard Nate tell an interviewer that Berry Gordy wanted to sign him to Motown. Nate decided to stay with the tiny Fortune Records label instead, and he considered this to be the worst mistake he had ever made in his life.

After decades of hearing the same Motown songs played over and over on the radio, defining the narrative of Detroit's soul music history, Nate was actually surprised when people started rediscovering all his records on the Fortune label. He told me, "At the time, I thought those records were OK. Not great, just OK. Now everybody's telling me I was ahead of my time. I don't know." But he loved those records. He was one musician who loved listening to his own records. The old stuff and the new stuff. We would be on tour, driving in the van listening to the drummer's iPod full of obscure soul records, most of which Nate knew many historical details about, and Nate would inevitably say, "I think it's time to hear some Nathaniel Mayer." He would be dancing in the backseat, singing along.

One time he told me, "I don't see anything wrong with what I'm doing. I'm just trying to make people happy." It seemed that some people around him had disapproved of his musical career. Maybe they thought he should have been a gospel singer instead. One time I tried to put a Hammond organ overdub on a tune we were recording. He immediately jumped up and shouted, "Get that organ off of my record! It sounds like I'm in church!" He sang in church when he was a kid. He was still a kid when he recorded his first record, "My Last Dance with You," in 1961. His one nationwide hit, "Village of Love," must have been received as a fit of quasi-pagan blasphemy to the straightlaced churchgoing folks in his life at that time.

"Village of Love" refers to the Village, a Detroit venue where Nate played and hung out. It was there that Nate met and gave encouragement to a band called Billy Lee and the Rivieras, who became Mitch Ryder and the Detroit Wheels. Nate really liked those guys. It was not unusual to hear Nate in the studio telling the musicians, "I want it tough . . . like Mitch Ryder and the Detroit Wheels."

There was a rumor that when Nate appeared on *American Bandstand* singing "Village of Love," he told Dick Clark to fuck off. No way of confirming or disproving this rumor, but it's a rumor worth repeating, since it's a part of Nate's story whether it's true or not.

One time I dropped by the house on Burns Street in the daytime. Nate and I were standing by my car listening to tracks from his upcoming album. A kid from the neighborhood walked by and paused to listen to the music.

> Kid: "Hey, is that you?"
> Nate: "Yeah."
> Kid: "Man, you sound like Mick Jagger!"

I gave Nate a cassette of the songs, so he could listen to them in his car. A couple of days later, he left a message on my answering machine: "Matt. Call me. Police took the damn car . . . but the tape was in the car. You gotta get me a new tape." I've heard various accounts of how the cops took the car with the tape, but one thing everyone agrees on is that they told Nate, "You can either go to jail, or we can take the car," to which Nate happily replied "Take the car!" I dropped off the new tape early one morning around nine a.m., and there was a guy across the street yelling through a door about wanting to kill someone named Carlos.

Soon Nate lost the house. Some sort of foreclosure crisis mishap. Nate found a high-rise apartment on Chene and Lafayette that was pretty safe, except for the occasional gunfights between drug dealers a block away.

Around this time, Nate was really having trouble walking. He had injured one of his knees, and it wasn't getting better. Still, he was determined to play the upcoming gigs that had been booked in Europe. He told me, "I'm gonna do those shows if I have to crawl on that stage!" Nathaniel practically had to crawl off the plane after the long flight from Detroit to Paris. A wheelchair had arrived for some CEO-type guy, who became outraged and astonished as the pilot took the man's wheelchair away and gave it to Nate. As we approached customs, with Nate's wheelchair pushed by a pretty French girl, and his unsavory-looking backing musicians stumbling half-asleep behind him, we were whisked past customs as if we were U.N. ambassadors. The European audiences loved Nate, but it would be his last tour.

Back in Detroit, at a rehearsal, we spontaneously started playing the opening riff to "My Girl" by the Temptations. Nate jumped in and crooned a stunning, soulful version of that song—a version to be heard only by his backing band in a cramped Hamtramck kitchen. Nate then asked if Shorty Long was still around. Dave, the drummer, reminded him that Shorty Long had died over forty years ago. Nate said, "Oh yeah, that's right." On an earlier occasion, Nate had told us all about Shorty's death, and Nate had a good memory for details, so it was obvious that something was wrong. By the time we headed to Las Vegas to play our next gig, Nate was having trouble remembering certain songs. When we returned to Detroit, he agreed to go see a doctor. A couple of days later, he had a stroke. He spent the next year in hospitals and nursing homes, fighting for his life. His brothers and his sister and other friends and family members continually visited him to give him encouragement, but every improvement in his health was followed by some other medical problem, and this cycle just went on and on.

The last time I visited him was just before the 2008 election. He couldn't talk, so he just listened to me telling him about how America was about to elect a black president. He occasionally smiled and looked interested, but though his eyes were alert, there was this peaceful look on his face that I hadn't seen before. He was done fighting. In his last days, his sister had managed to talk to him about the religious issues that seemed unresolved in his life. Only able to nod his head, Nate apparently was able to resolve some of those things.

Nathaniel Mayer's funeral was attended by a huge crowd of musicians, friends, and relatives. The three religious dignitaries who presided over the service looked uneasy, like they'd been asked to do a funeral for Count Dracula. Like somebody radioactive was in that coffin. Like they expected Nay-Dog to jump out of the coffin at any minute, screaming, "I want love and affection, not the house of correction!" They took turns telling everybody that none of Nate's accomplishments on Earth meant anything, that there were spiritual matters of much greater importance. These guys were not Nathaniel Mayer fans. They didn't know about the joy that Nathaniel Mayer brought to everyone who ever heard his music, saw him on a stage, or even met the guy for a few brief moments. I got the impression that they would've cut him some slack if only he'd recorded for Motown.

# Back in Detroit City with Andre Williams

*Matthew Smith*

The phone rang.

"Andre Williams is looking for you. He wants to work with the guys who were working with Nathaniel Mayer. Here's his number." I call Andre. Andre immediately says, "What kind of record do you think I ought to make?" Without hesitating, I blurted out, "Well, Mick Jagger's been trying to sound like you for a long time now. Maybe you ought to do something with a Stones kind of feel." Andre's deep baritone, or bass voice, or whatever it actually is, quickly replied, "We will have to pay close attention to what the Rolling Stones have done."

I'd met Andre in 1997, when he was in Detroit recording the album that would launch his comeback, *Silky*. At that time, I knew some of his songs from the '50s, but all I really knew about him was that the Gories liked him. I didn't have any idea that I was in the presence of a major figure in music history, one of the guys who helped invent rock 'n' roll, as well as a few other genres.

I was in the studio, recording an album called *Michigan Babylon* with Hollywood legend Kim Fowley, when I was told that Andre Williams had arrived in Detroit and was writing songs with the guys from the Gories. Kim Fowley had a gig coming up at the Magic Stick that week, so he invited Andre to perform onstage with him. Kim, of course, knew exactly who Andre was: "Isn't he Mr. Rib-Eye?" Mr. Rhythm actually, although he did make a record called "Rib Tips." Andre showed up and performed "Let Me Put It in," which he had just written with Mick Collins and Dan Kroha. Andre looked great and sounded great. He was dressed like someone who had just stepped out of a time machine from the 1940s. Perhaps he'd had a few drinks and done a few drugs throughout the years, but his magnetism and talent were obviously intact. It must have been the first time anyone in Detroit had seen Andre Williams on a stage in at least thirty years. Suddenly, Andre found himself connected to a new generation of rock 'n' roll fans and musicians.

After a week of recording and other rock 'n' roll madness with Mr. Fowley, I got a phone call from Mick Collins requesting that I play guitar on a country and western song that Andre wanted to record. They were recording an album in the same studio where I'd been producing Kim Fowley, Ghetto Recorders. It was a new studio built into what appeared to be a former slaughterhouse located above a 1920s movie palace. You would walk up an abnormally long staircase, built as a kind of secret passageway, into an expansive apartment that used to belong to some fugitive or drug kingpin or something, and through another corridor into a kitchen sent through a time warp from the 1970s, and then beyond that into a large room with concrete walls that was now a recording studio. The studio room looked like the Warhol factory after a burglary. Stuff strewn everywhere. A refreshingly chaotic environment where nobody bothered with "getting sounds" or any of that other useless stuff that generally happens in studios where making records is an endlessly expensive and frustrating process. The engineer, Jim Diamond, was probably the last guy in music history to actually be trained in the engineering secrets of the '50s and '60s. He still edited tape with a razor blade, and the tape machines looked like props from an old *Twilight Zone* episode. The technology in this place was being put to use in a way that was hermetic and surreal, compared to the way other recording studios in the '90s were doing things.

Andre was dressed appropriately for the hot and totally uncomfortable Detroit summer weather, in a short-sleeved shirt and shorts. He was squinting through reading glasses at a bunch of scrawled lyric sheets. Right away, Andre started to tell me how, back when he was working in the cotton fields of the south and listening to Hank Snow on the radio, he'd always wanted to sing a country and western song. I started to play a cowboy chord progression on the guitar, and suddenly we were recording, and all the musicians joined in, playing this nice midtempo country riff. Andre opened his mouth and repeated *exactly* the conversation we'd just had, which was now the lyric to "Country and Western Song," the only song on the album suitable for airplay, it turns out. What happened, apparently, was that the record company asked for a "raw" recording, meaning they weren't looking for the production values of Duran Duran or Pink Floyd's *Dark Side of the Moon*. The audio fidelity of an old John Lee Hooker recording was more to their taste. Andre, being a contemporary of Redd Foxx and Rudy Ray Moore, thought that "raw" meant they were demanding X-rated lyrics on every song. In any case, the resulting album, *Silky*, was deemed unsuitable for Top 40 radio. In fact, it's a

crazy, demented-sounding record, built around the musical chemistry between Andre and producer Mick Collins. After the country and western song was in the can, I was asked to play organ, piano, and electric piano on a bunch of the other songs. I played a distorted electric piano on "Bring Me Back My Car Unstripped," while a bunch of people smashed a bunch of large auto parts that had been dragged into the studio. I watched Andre argue for a half hour with a woman who was offended by the lyrics to "Pussy Stank," before she finally stopped telling him to f— off long enough to join the chorus of backup singers shouting, "Pussy stank, but so do marijuana." I played an organ overdub on another song where all the instruments were out of tune with each other *and* the organ. I mentioned this to Mick, and he told me not to worry about it and just keep playing. As it turns out, a room full of out-of-tune instruments can sound really great with the right musicians.

Flashback to forty years earlier, when Andre, ejected from the navy for enlisting under his older brother's name, had managed to avoid prison time and ended up in Detroit. He was broke and found himself entering a talent show at a theater, desperate to win twenty-five dollars. He won the twenty-five dollars and drifted into the heart of the Detroit doo-wop scene, singing with the Five Dollars and recording for Fortune Records. His solo record "Bacon Fat" became a R&B crossover hit in 1956, followed by "Jail Bait." These records are notable for, among other things, introducing a kind of casual attitude of juvenile delinquency into pop culture. John Fogerty and Elvis Presley expressed their appreciation for Andre's work directly to him, and Keith Richards said that these records had made a huge impression on him. Keith Richards expressed his gratitude for Andre in Rolling Stones liner notes from 2003. There's also a strange, modern feel to the music on these records. The music seems simple, not a lot of chords, not too busy. But there's a rhythmic precision and subtlety going on that functions like some kind of Dionysian or voodoo energy current. It is more like the Stooges, Parliament, or Funkadelic than, say, Louis Jordan. And this was in the '50s.

Andre produced tons of records in the '60s, mostly in Detroit and Chicago, and every one of these records bears the unmistakable stamp of Andre Williams's style, attitude, and personality. He introduced Berry Gordy to some important music business connections in the early days, which led to Andre being hired as a staff producer at Motown. Andre worked with Mary Wells, the Contours, and many others, but it turned out that Andre's musical vision was in conflict with Gordy's. This led to Andre being hired and fired by Gordy numerous times. Andre also wrote the R&B standard "Shake a Tail Feather." He would eventually make countless great soul records with everyone from George Clinton to Ike and Tina Turner.

Sometime in the '70s, Andre got lost in a haze of booze and drugs. He made some records during that time, but he had really faded into near-total obscurity. During this difficult period, he spent a lot of time stoned, wandering the streets of Chicago. His reappearance in Detroit in the late '90s turned out to be the beginning of the comeback he'd been waiting for.

Andre toured the world throughout the next decade, making numerous records with young rock musicians. Though Andre was a pioneer of R&B and soul music, it was the rock 'n' rollers who

became fascinated with him and resurrected his career. However, with his new career came a total immersion in the rock 'n' roll lifestyle, which led to a nonstop party going on wherever he was recording or playing a gig. It also led to frequent visits to hospitals, as the unbelievable amounts of drugs and alcohol he was ingesting had started to really take a toll on his physical well-being.

So when I called Andre on the phone in 2009, he was making a serious effort to kick the booze and drugs. He told me, "I'm living in a halfway house on the south side of Chicago. I've been sober for six months, but I think I better stay here for a few more months, just to be sure."

Andre and I produced his first drug- and alcohol-free record, titled, "That's All I Need," in the summer of 2009. It had been over ten years since *Silky*. He arrived by train, dressed in a phosphorescent, metallic-looking, dark-blue suit, looking like some kind of space-age hologram of Cab Calloway. This time, we recorded in a living room in Hamtramck, not far from the old Motown studio, in a house with very similar architecture to the Hitsville U.S.A. building. Andre was overflowing with musical ideas and lyrics. One of Andre's methods in the studio is to make the musicians play a groove over and over again until he hears the thing he's looking for. And when it hits, he knows it, and we'll start recording. Andre will usually sing the lead vocal right there, live with the band. In his seventies at this time, he was still more energetic than anyone around him. The only time anyone noticed he wasn't a teenager was when he'd get irritable because you had kept him up past his bedtime, which is usually nine p.m. when he's not performing onstage. In terms of instrumentation, this turned out to be Andre's

Stones album after all. I only suggested we make a Stones-style record because it was our first phone call and I had to say something at that moment. On another day, I might have said Quicksilver Messenger Service. But as Andre and I were eating breakfast one morning, Andre told me that he knew Mick Jagger. He said Mick used to hang out with him back when Andre was working for Ike Turner. He told me that "when Mick Jagger sings slow songs, he writes words. When he's singing fast songs, he's just making stuff up."

A few months later, I asked Andre what it was like being sober in the studio for the first time. He said, "It was traumatic. It was like somebody shot me out in space and I woke up on Pluto."

The following year, clearly wanting to return to Pluto, Andre came back to Detroit to make another record. This was going to be his folk album.

*Hoods and Shades* was recorded live with acoustic instruments, and a few overdubs were added later. These sessions were primarily focused on the chemistry between Andre and Motown session guitarist Dennis Coffey. The two of them had worked together on countless records back in the '60s, and to watch them building grooves and developing ideas together was a rare experience of seeing two masters at work. At one point during the recording, our Australian drummer Jim White asked Andre what his favorite kind of music is. Andre replied, "Country music." Then Andre talked about how he used to hang out with Billie Holiday, Count Basie, and Duke Ellington back in the '50s. I thought to myself that the only way to make an authentic rock 'n' roll record these days is to find a guy in his seventies who had hung out with Billie Holiday. Try it with a bunch of twenty-first-century teenagers and it's not so easy.

Another year passed, and I called Andre to tell him that someone had offered to give us a few thousand bucks to make another album. Andre said, "I need that money *right now*. Tell him to send it right away." Ultimately, we had just enough money to record an album down at Ghetto Recorders, as long as we did it in two days. We attempted to do just that, and came close to finishing it up the second day, when the session had to be canceled due to an emergency one of the musicians had to deal with. The next day, Andre returned to Chicago. When I returned to the studio a few days later to finish it up, I noticed that we had worked so intensely and quickly on these songs that we were basically in a trance throughout the sessions. I barely remembered writing and recording the songs. I did recall the writing process for the song "Blame it on Obama." It consisted of me trying out various chord progressions, asking Andre how it sounded, and Andre slamming his hands down on mine while I played, yelling "No, no, no, no, no!" He sounded kind of like that vocal instructor in the music lesson scene in *Citizen Kane*. After a while, I finally came up with something that he liked. Come to think of it, he did the same thing back when I was playing organ on *Silky*, and I think that situation was a very important moment for me. I'm certain that it made me a better keyboard player, even if the result sounds like someone wearing mittens trying to play like Ray Charles. Anyway, listening back to these latest sessions, I felt like I was hearing it all for the first time. The unfinished record sounded really good, but it wasn't easy to get back into the Andre trance without Andre actually being there dancing, shouting, singing the individual parts to the musicians, and basically conducting the whole scene in a shamanic frenzy. I tinkered with the remaining overdubs and mixes until the album *Life* emerged. These sessions reminded me that working fast is always more interesting than working slowly and meticulously. Andre works fast, and he writes spontaneously. He's got an unusual working method that's been working for him for over half a century.

Just as soon as *Life* hit the record shops, Andre suffered a stroke. He was unable to move or talk for several weeks. The doctors said they didn't think he was going to bounce back like he had after his previous hospital ordeals. But bounce back he did, and before long he was swearing at the doctors and nurses and walking around again. After months of physical therapy, he was ready to record again. He loves recording. So he came back to Detroit to cut some more tracks. I picked him up at the train station, not the abandoned one but the little Amtrak station on Woodward Avenue near Grand Boulevard, right down the street from Motown. Andre arrived dressed in one of his fabulous suits, walking quickly through the station, completely agile, looking healthy, with no sign of a stroke in his speech. He is getting close to eighty years old, so he's got to be careful, but he doesn't like to slow down. His intellect and his musical imagination are moving so fast that everyone else can barely keep up with him.

MATTHEW SMITH

# Jack Scott
## Detroit's Unsung Rock 'n' Roll Pioneer

*S. R. Boland*

ntense. Sincere. Energetic. A little dangerous. That's the image of Jack Scott, the first rock 'n' roll star to be popularly identified with the city of Detroit. Scott, born Giovanni Dominico Scafone Jr. on January 24, 1936, grew up a Hank Williams acolyte but later infused the Detroit rock 'n' roll attitude into his shows and records. He was a dominant force on the radio and on pop music charts from 1958 through 1961, placing nineteen songs in the *Billboard* magazine Hot 100. Unlike many rock 'n' roll and pop music stars of his era, Jack Scott wrote the vast majority of his own hit songs.

Scott was born in Windsor, Ontario, and lived there until he was ten. His father then moved the large Scafone family to the blue-collar Detroit suburb of Hazel Park, and it was there that young John (as he was then known) honed his singing and guitar skills. He loved classic hillbilly music and formed his own country band as a teenager, performing top tunes of the day. It was a disc jockey on WEXL radio, Jack Ihrie, who—after watching the young singer perform at his high school—suggested that he change his stage name to the easier-to-pronounce (and less ethnic-sounding) Jack Scott.

Scott was like many up-and-coming young musicians in the mid-'50s—he was profoundly affected by the sound and charisma of Elvis Presley. Although Hank Williams remained his idol, Scott embraced rock 'n' roll after Presley's explosion onto the music scene in 1956. Scott—who had been

putting on his own shows at Bill's Barn near Utica—began to include current up-tempo rock numbers into his performances, along with country songs. He also started to write his own compositions. Jack Scott performances at another local venue, the Dance Ranch, became very popular with Detroit-area teens.

By that time, Scott's band included his cousin Dominic Scafone on drums, Stan Getz (a local boy, not the famous jazz saxophonist) on string bass, and Dave Rohelier on lead guitar. Rohelier's searing guitar licks are prominent on Scott's first two singles, recorded during 1957 at United Sound Systems, then considered the best studio in Detroit.

Scott's first manager was Carl Thom, owner of the Harmony House record store (later to become a well-known local chain) in Hazel Park, and Thom was successful in placing two original songs cut at United Sound with the ABC-Paramount label. The first single was "Baby She's Gone," backed with "You Can Bet Your Bottom Dollar." The latter was a country love song; the former was a pounding rocker. "I wrote 'Baby She's Gone' very quickly," says Scott. "I would get inspired and the lyrics would just come." The band worked out the arrangement on the spot in the studio, and Scott's vocal delivery on "Baby She's Gone" was obviously influenced by Elvis.

"I was riding in my car, listening to the radio," Scott remembers, "and Mickey Shorr, the disc jockey, came on and announced a new song by Jack Scott. He played my record three times in a row!" Understandably, Scott was thrilled.

"Baby She's Gone" was a very good regional seller but failed to make an impact nationally. Scott went back into the studio, but the follow-up record, "Two-Timin' Woman"/"I Need Your Love" wrote a similar story later in '57. Due to reshuffling at ABC-Paramount, Scott found himself without a record label, but he returned to the United Sound studio in early spring 1958 to lay down two more tracks.

Now it was ace picker Al Allen on lead guitar instead of Rohelier (who was unavailable for the session), and teenager George Katsakis of the Royaltones (soon to hit pay dirt with the instrumental "Poor Boy") was added on honking tenor sax. The final touch was the addition of the Canadian vocal group, the Chantones, on background harmonies. Scott wanted a backup group comparable to Presley's Jordanaires—and the Chantones, although they had a less polished style, filled the bill. The Chantones' bass singer, Roy Lesperance, gave Scott's recordings a bottom-heavy vocal sound similar to that on R&B or gospel group records.

In the session, Scott paired a storming rock 'n' roll song, "Greaseball"—about a friend who always seemed to land in jail—with "My True Love," a heartfelt ballad with a recitation in the middle. Scott played the new recordings for a music distributor that he'd been working with, but to the singer's dismay, the distributor declined to promote the songs. Specifically, the recitation in "My True Love" was singled out as passé, and Scott was told that prison songs were out.

However, a representative from Southern Music in New York, Lucky Carle, had been present at the meeting and had liked what he'd heard. The rep thought he could find a label that would be interested in the songs. He took the acetates to the popular WKMH disc jockey Robin Seymour, who agreed that the tunes were good. Ultimately, the recordings made their way to Joe Carlton, owner of the newly formed Carlton label in New York.

Carlton wanted to release the master tapes as a new Jack Scott single, but there was concern that "Greaseball" could be construed as a slur against Latinos. Scott maintained that *greaseball* was considered a cool nickname but agreed to write alternate lyrics and re-record the song.

Back at United Sound Systems, Scott took a bathroom break and noticed "Leroy Was Here" scrawled nearby on the wall. Seizing the inspiration, he returned to the studio, declared that "Leroy" was the new title, and the musicians proceeded to lay down the track.

Carlton Records heavily promoted the new record; ads in trade papers shouted, "Leroy's Broken Loose!" with jailhouse artwork. Indeed, sales of "Leroy" took off during the spring of '58 and the song would eventually reach number 25 on the *Billboard* Hot 100 (doing even better on the Best Sellers in Stores chart). But the real breakout came when a Carlton promo man decided to encourage DJs to flip over the 45 and play the B side, "My True Love." By mid-July, "My True Love" eclipsed "Leroy" in popularity, and Jack Scott had a double-sided hit on his hands. In fact, the record would be certified gold, with more than one million copies in sales, and "My True Love" would climb all the way to number 3 (in August) on the *Billboard* Hot 100. The song even made the Top 10 on the US R&B chart and Top 10 in the UK.

123

Scott's Italian American good looks and muscular physique soon made him a rock 'n' roll heartthrob to young female fans. It didn't hurt that he began to appear on Dick Clark's *American Bandstand* TV show, lip-synching his hits to screaming audiences. Yet Scott, with his serious outlook, projected a more mature presence than teen idols like Fabian or Ricky Nelson.

"With Your Love," a fine ballad with an unusual chord change, was the follow-up to "My True Love" in autumn 1958. The recording hit number 28 in *Billboard*. The flip was "Geraldine," a fast song that repeated the cool chick's name a total of 102 times, and interspersed a wailing Katsakis sax break and a tasty Al Allen guitar solo between verses. "Geraldine" made the lower reaches of the pop charts.

Scott was performing extensively as well as making records. He took his trademark Gibson SJ-200 acoustic guitar on national tours that included the likes of Dion and the Belmonts, Buddy Holly, and Jerry Lee Lewis, and he forged friendships with many of his fellow artists. He particularly enjoyed the company of Dion, Lewis, and, later, Mark Dinning (of "Teen Angel" fame) and Bobby Vee.

But just as his career was starting to soar, he was shot down with a draft notice from Uncle Sam. In response, he wrote and recorded "Goodbye Baby," a farewell to his girl, and the recording was released in the late fall of 1958. It was a repetitive record with a compelling, almost hypnotic effect, due to Scott's rich baritone vocal and the Chantones' popping counterpoint. It was also a smash, peaking at number 8 on the *Billboard* pop chart in early '59. The B side of "Goodbye Baby" was "Save My Soul," a rousing gospel number appropriate for a tent revival show. "Save My Soul" only charted at number 73, but the

recording shows off Scott's vocal talents and flair for the dramatic. Scott had now logged three double-sided hit records in a row. Later, "Goodbye Baby" would be featured in the Barry Levinson movie *Diner*, and the song would be listed in the book *The Heart of Rock & Soul: The 1001 Greatest Singles Ever Made* by music critic Dave Marsh (at number 835).

Scott had no choice but to report for basic training, and he served at Fort Knox, Kentucky, from January to May 1959, eventually being allowed an early honorable discharge under medical circumstances for a chronic ulcer. Meanwhile, the Carlton label put out the next Jack Scott release, albeit without the benefit of any live performances to support it.

"I Never Felt Like This" appeared in record stores in March 1959, and it's one of Scott's best efforts—a minor-key uptempo song, with clever lyrics ("I stood there petrified and I got 'lectrified / when she pressed her lips to mine"). Nevertheless, it only reached number 78 on the Hot 100.

It was the following record, the vaguely menacing, take-me-as-I-am "The Way I Walk," that cemented Scott's brooding, tough-guy persona. He originally intended the song to fill out an album he was working on, and he hadn't completed it lyrically. To fill in the gaps where the lyrics would be, the Chantones repeated "de-oo-wee, oo-wee, oo-wee, oo-wee, oo-wah, yep-yep-yep" in those spots. Scott figured he could dub in more vocals later on, once he finished writing it. To his surprise, Carlton went ahead and released "The Way I Walk" on a 45 as it was.

It worked. "The Way I Walk" is one of those accidental gems that turned out to be a classic, and today it's one of Scott's best-known songs, famously covered later on by Robert Gordon (whose rendition appeared in the Oliver Stone film *Natural Born Killers*) and also by the Cramps. In the summer of 1959, Scott's version reached number 35 on the *Billboard* pop chart and heralded his return from the army. "The Way I Walk" features another great Al Allen guitar lead and a rowdy sax solo by George Katsakis. The B side, "Midgie," was a stomper written by Scott about a girl who was even more racy than Geraldine.

That fall, Scott put out the self-penned "There Comes a Time," a wistful, midtempo, country-tinged song of heartbreak and one of his most interesting recordings. It rose only to number 71 and was the last of his Carlton singles. Although his first album, *Jack Scott*, had been released and was successful, his days at Carlton were numbered. Maneuverings behind his back resulted in Scott's management severing ties with Joe Carlton.

After cutting a new song, "What in the World's Come Over You," for Carlton, the singer was told that he was being moved to a new label, Top Rank, with headquarters in England and offices in New York. Scott was advised that he would now record in New York, not Detroit. Contractually, he had no choice in the matter. What's more, he was told he would have to wax a new version of "What in the World's Come Over You" for Top Rank, and he did so near the end of 1959. The original Carlton version has never surfaced.

"What in the World's Come Over You" is the pinnacle of Scott's songwriting, with one of the best rhyming lyric lines ever in a pop ballad ("Every night, I reminisce / dreaming of your tender kiss-es"). He wrote it in his car, driving, while he was having a quarrel with his girlfriend. As for the recording, it's a top-notch production with a typically superb lead vocal and perfect backups by the Chantones. No wonder, then, that it went to number 5 on the *Billboard* pop chart in early '60 (also, amazingly, to number 7 R&B) and was certified gold. Over the years, it's been covered by many artists; it has become Scott's signature tune. The flip side, "Baby, Baby," was a rollicking hand-clapper.

There is footage of Scott performing (lip-synching) "What in the World's Come Over You" on Dick Clark's *Saturday Night Beech-Nut Show*; Scott was also a headliner on Clark's Caravan of Stars bus tours. However, he was never enthusiastic about the grueling schedule of rock 'n' roll touring, which took him away from his family and girlfriend for weeks at a time. In fact, relations with Dick Clark went cold for a while after he once abruptly got off the bus in the middle of a Caravan of Stars tour to make his way home to Detroit for a few days.

Even though Scott wasn't under contract to Joe Carlton any more, Carlton still had a few unreleased Jack Scott recordings "in the can," and they would come out on a subsidiary label, Guaranteed, during 1960. There would also be a second album, *What Am I Living For*, on the Carlton label. Neither of the two Guaranteed singles were hits, but one of them, "Go Wild Little Sadie," is one of Scott's most primal rockers.

Scott found himself very ill during the recording of his *I Remember Hank Williams* album, a tribute to his hero. He was also working on "Burning Bridges," a countrified ballad (authored by Walter Scott, a British songwriter) that was to be his next single. Because he was sweating through a high fever, the session was cut short after a preliminary run-through of "Bridges." Some time after returning home to Detroit, Scott was astonished to find out that Top Rank had actually okayed the vocals he'd done on "Burning Bridges" while he was sick and had released the song. It turned out to be Scott's biggest hit ever, reaching number 3 on *Billboard*'s pop chart and number 5 R&B. Strangely, the song did not get on the country chart—in fact, none of Scott's records during his high-water years did. But the 45 was another double-sider, with the bouncy flip side, "Oh Little One," making it to number 35. Al Allen's guitar was once again front and center on the B side.

So, in 1960, the future never looked brighter for Jack Scott. He seemed to be on a roll; he was charting big hits, making personal appearances, and his "What in the World's Come Over You" LP was out. A gospel album recorded with the Chantones, *The Spirit Moves Me*, would appear later in the year. But the music business is fickle, and "Burning Bridges" would be Scott's last big hit. Later recordings for Top Rank in 1960 and 1961—notably "It Only Happened Yesterday," "Patsy" (written by Clyde Otis, a collaborator on Brook Benton's records), "Is There Something on Your Mind," and the charmingly primitive "Found a Woman" ("I told Ma/Ma told Pa/Pa said, uh-hmm, found a woman")—sold only moderately well.

Then came another upheaval in Scott's career: EMI/Capitol Records bought out Top Rank and all its assets. Suddenly, Scott belonged to one of the biggest majors, and Capitol was happy to have such a proven hit maker.

The A sides of Scott's first three Capitol singles were all authored by Jack himself. The first of the three was "A Little Feeling (Called Love)." It managed to scrape the bottom of the Hot 100. His next attempt was "My Dream Come True," and it did slightly better, peaking at number 83. The flip was another interesting uptempo Scott composition, "Strange Desire." Then came "Steps 1 and 2," which also fizzled. The record-buying public's tastes had changed fast, and Jack Scott wasn't hot anymore.

There were more listenable singles during 1962: "Cry, Cry, Cry" (paired with the sly "Grizzly Bear"), "You Only See What You Wanna See," and "If Only" (how could that one not be a hit?). Yet the well was dry. Scott's Capitol contract was to expire in '63, and the label released a couple more singles before it released Scott.

Berry Gordy of Motown Records stepped up and approached Jack about a new contract. Gordy admired Scott and would later say, "Jack Scott started it all for Detroit." At the time, Gordy had decided to use his Mel-o-Dy subsidiary label to release country records and must have believed that Scott, with his country-influenced style, would be a good fit there. Both Dorsey Burnette and Bruce Channel, fairly big names, would end up recording on Mel-o-Dy in 1964. But Scott never saw himself as a straight country artist, and he was not comfortable with the idea of being under the Motown banner, either.

Besides, he had an offer from someone else he respected very much—guitar legend Chet Atkins. Atkins, who headed RCA Victor's operations in Nashville, proposed that Scott join RCA's Groove subsidiary. But Scott soon found his efforts swamped by the Beatles and the rest of the British Invasion. For a while, it became difficult for any American act to get a big hit.

Five singles were released on Groove; three were released on the parent label, RCA. Standouts from the period include "I Knew You First," "What a Wonderful Night Out," "Wiggle on Out," the quirky "Flakey John," and Scott's 1963 Christmas single about his girl's affair with Santa Claus, "There's Trouble Brewin'" (first cut back in '58 with a different arrangement).

Scott bounced from one label to another from the mid-'60s through the mid-'70s: ABC-Paramount, Jubilee, GRT, and Dot. At Dot, he would finally squeak into the country charts with "You're Just Getting Better" in 1974.

Scott has never stopped performing; today, he performs some local dates but mainly plays larger venues out of town and in Europe. He's stayed in good physical condition and his musical prowess remains sharp. His shows continue to wow audiences, and he takes time afterward to meet fans.

Numerous musicians down through the decades have cited him as an influence. Yet, to most of the public, he's relatively obscure compared to artists of his era like Eddie Cochran, Gene Vincent, and Ritchie Valens (and Scott outcharted and outsold each of those three). And despite his impact, accomplishments, and fame in his era, Jack Scott has never been seriously considered for the Rock and Roll Hall of Fame. It is generally accepted that the Rock and Roll Hall of Fame nominating and induction process is largely a political one, and Scott has always stayed out of those kinds of politics. He is, however, a member of the Rockabilly Hall of Fame, the Michigan Rock and Roll Legends Hall of Fame, and the Canadian Songwriters Hall of Fame.

Jack Scott is rock 'n' roll's unsung pioneer, and he belongs to Detroit.

Artie Fields. Photo courtesy of Joel Martin.

# Two Detroit Music Icons and Two Classic Theaters
## Artie Fields and Harry Balk
*Joel Martin*

In 1973 I was a sixteen-year-old kid from Oak Park, and I had just managed to score an internship as an apprentice at Artie Fields Productions in Detroit. This was my entree into a business and profession that I would become immersed in and forever identified with for the rest of my life. My career all started with Artie Fields, and that eventually would lead me to a friendship with the great Harry Balk.

At the time I started interning for Mr. Fields, he was already a giant in the music jingle business, producing over ten thousand spots for the biggest ad agencies in the country, and he already had a track record of musical success that spanned from leading the Fortune Records Orchestra to producing recordings by the MC5, Gladys Knight, the Ohio Players, the Detroit Emeralds, and more. Artie Fields's success as a major Detroit music producer started in 1967 when he purchased an old movie house called the Alhambra Theatre. The old theater, located on Woodward at Kenilworth Street in the Boston-Edison neighborhood, was originally built as a state-of-the-art movie house in 1914, but the Alhambra is most remembered nowadays for being the place that got dancers grooving as a notable recording studio from 1967 into the 1970s.

Artie turned the aging theater into a unique recording studio in 1967. Fields had the lobby of the old theater divvied up into smaller rooms. Oddly, the control room was on a different side of the building from the recording studio. The auditorium was used for storage and as an echo chamber for recordings. Far and away, the best-known album recorded at the studio was the MC5's *High Time*, which had the old movie joint rocking in September and October 1970. Gladys Knight's "Midnight Train to Georgia" was laid down by Fields in the old Alhambra, as were a number of albums by Westbound Records acts, including the Ohio Players, the Detroit Emeralds, and the Fantastic Four.

Fields also ran his own record label, Top Dog Records, out of the old theater, and he produced all of the label's singles. Among the Top Dog artists were Joe Towns (a well-known R&B singer who had a major hit with "Together We Can Make Such Sweet Music"), the Camel Drivers (a great Detroit Merseybeat-sounding rock and R&B group with several hits, most memorably "Sunday Morning 6 O'Clock" and Sonny Bono's "It's Gonna Rain"), and local hit makers Don Rondo and Kris Peterson. Previous to his recording success, Artie had led an orchestra for Fortune Records in the late 1950s and wrote songs for Don Rondo, Spanky Wilson, and others. He also penned the classic song "Go Get'Em, Tigers" in 1967 for Detroit's baseball team and such beloved commercial jingles as "Where the Rubber Meets the Road" for Firestone tires; "Let's Go Kroger-ing" for the supermarket chain; and General Motors' "Mark of Excellence," among others.

The studio used the Funk Brothers as frequent players for Artie's jingle-production work (which

129

paid way better than Berry Gordy's Motown sessions). The Alhambra Theatre studio was also a place where the Detroit Symphony players made great money working on union gigs that brought residual income. The studio inside the old theater continued to pump out recordings through the 1970s. The theater was later converted into a church and sat empty until 2007 when it was razed. Artie Fields passed away at the age of eighty-seven in 2009, but he remains a spiritual presence in Detroit's music history.

Another important legend who was a key part of Detroit's rich music history is the great producer and Motown A&R man Harry Balk. I had known of Harry's many contributions to Detroit music for years before I met him in the fall of 2012. At the age of eighty-six, Harry decided to move back to Detroit after forty years of living the California dream. My sister-in-law Suzy managed the senior citizens home that he "retired" to, and she asked me if I "ever heard of a guy named Harry Balk," a new resident who said he used to be in the record business. "Really? *The* Harry Balk?" I was amazed! "Son of a bitch! Harry Balk is living near my home!" Harry's reputation as a producer was already legendary by the time I started working in Artie Fields's studio as a sixteen-year-old intern in 1973, so I needed to finally meet the man behind the legend. I did, and we have become very good friends.

When Harry started his career, the record game back in the '50s and '60s was wide open, and it seemed like anyone could take a chance on an act with a record that sounded like it could be a hit. Find a crazy but talented artist, record the song in a couple of days, press it up and take it to the local station. Back then, having a DJ friend at CKLW might mean that you could get enough spins and cause enough of a listener demand that you might end up either with a record deal or selling the record to a distributor in New York that could break the record nationally. Sensations were made overnight, and a hit record could generate a windfall of cash for the artist and the managers. Rags to riches. And like the lottery, once you get the taste of cashing in a winner, you are hooked.

Harry Balk was the pure image of the classic record guy: a cigar-chomping, physically imposing figure full of swagger and conviction. He could have easily passed as a movie gangster (or the real thing), if he was just going for the effect. But no, he *was* the real thing, something out of a Damon Runyon novel, or the main character from an Elmore Leonard Detroit tale.

Harry was born in 1924 in Detroit, and by the time he was eighteen years old, he was managing his uncle Sol's Krim Theatre. The Krim opened in 1941 as an ultramodern movie theater on Woodward in Highland Park. To boost business, Harry decided to hold weekly talent contests. While hosting these contests, he soon discovered a sixteen-year-old baby crooner that would electrify audiences week after week, winning every talent contest he competed in. Harry would be the first to sign R&B and rock 'n' roll legend Little Willie John (widely acknowledged as the pioneer of Detroit soul/R&B). It would be the first of many unbelievable bets Harry made throughout his career.

Harry Balk would spend the majority of his life betting on the next big thing; the hit around the corner that could let you live large and keep you going until the next big fix. Quick, crazy money that came and went faster than you could spend it. Sex, drugs, and rock 'n' roll way before anybody had ever heard of the phrase.

Amazingly, his first smash as a producer was with a new fresh-faced teen rocker from Coopersville, Michigan, just outside Grand Rapids, by the name of Charles Weedon Westover. Harry would rename him Del Shannon and sign him. Harry produced Del's first smash hit, "Runaway," arguably the classic original "garage" rock record from the early days of American rock 'n' roll. Fresh off the success of Del Shannon, Harry would form his first record company, Twirl, with his business partner Irv Michanek. Together, Harry and Irv had a solid stable of hit-making artists that included Johnny and the Hurricanes, the Royaltones (featuring a young Dennis Coffey), and others. In 1965, Harry and Irv parted ways, and Harry sold his share of Twirl to Irv, who then moved the label to New York City.

Harry formed a new label, Impact Records, and a new publishing company called Gomba, and took in John Rhys as a junior partner, scoring a Top 10 hit in "Oh How Happy" by the Shades of Blue. He retained some of the artists, like the Volumes, elements of the Royaltones, Mickey Denton, and Patti Jerome, while discovering new talent. One of the artists he discovered in the early days of Impact was a young Latino fellow by the name of Sixto Rodriguez. Harry signed a young Rodriguez to a five-year songwriting contract in 1966, and in August of 1967 he produced his first single, "I'll Slip Away"/"You'd Like to Admit It" (Impact 1031), released as by Rod Riguez.

He later started Inferno Records, but in 1969, Harry would close Impact Records after receiving an offer he couldn't refuse from Motown's Berry Gordy. Gordy hired Harry as the first white Jewish head of A&R at Motown, allowing him to start the Rare Earth record label and to sign acts that would never have considered Motown as a home. Harry signed bands like Rare Earth, the Sunday Funnies, and others. One of Harry's major contributions to popular American music was his effort for Motown to release Marvin Gaye's single "What's Going On" despite Berry Gordy's protests. Harry succeeded, and the rest is history.

In 1972, after Motown operations left Detroit, Harry, with his wife, Patti Jerome, followed Berry and the label west to stake a claim in Los Angeles. By the mid-'70s, Motown, along with the changing culture in the record business, was no longer a place for the lone gambler placing bets on talent and hits. Motown had changed; it had become corporate, tangled up in and run by committees.

Balk and Fields, two visionary music producers and hustlers from Detroit, were quickly becoming relics of a bygone era. Gone. But because I know Harry Balk and worked for and knew Artie Fields, they will never be forgotten. I will always be ready to testify to their history and their extremely important and essential contributions to American music history and, more important, to Detroit's music history. This awestruck author can attest to a place out of time when a gambler with instinct, moxie, and talent could achieve anything in the record business. I personally learned many lessons working with Artie and Harry. Artie Fields and Harry Balk are Detroit treasures, and their contributions will live on forever in American music history.

# Nine Times out of Ten
## The Clix Records Story
*Michael Hurtt*

uried next to I-75 in Troy, Michigan, just south of the Big Beaver Road exit, they sit, surrounded by strip malls, corporate high-rises, and recently constructed apartment complexes: a smattering of old farmhouses—some still heated by oil furnaces and kerosene heaters—on a two-block stretch of dirt and gravel road accessible only through an abutting parking lot.

One has the eerie feeling that this rural enclave, standing in stark opposition to its overly developed surroundings, won't be here long. But even after the last old homestead has been mercilessly uprooted and the final skyscraper is finished—indeed, after even *that skyscraper* meets its bitter end—one aspect of Troy's countrified past will remain: its status as the hometown of Clix Records, a tiny operation that captured the sounds of Detroit's teeming Appalachian population—as well as the occasional teenage rock 'n' roll combo—like no other did.

"It was out in the sticks back then," says Hugh Friar, whose Clix debut, "I Can't Stay Mad at You," helps frame the tale of one of the most elusive, seamless, and sought-after imprints in all of early rock 'n' roll. The Clix Records story is one that's as unique as it is varied. With less than twenty releases, it's an aural snapshot that runs the gamut from primitive bluegrass boppers to raunchy garage instrumentals, all spiked with a heavy dose of striking, homemade originality.

Friar's guitarist, Jimmy Kirkland, may be best known for his infectious 1958 Fox/Teen Life rockers "Come on Baby" and "I Wonder If You Wonder," as well as the high-octane leads on Johnny Powers's "Rock Rock" and "Long Blonde Hair, Rose Red Lips," but he cut his teeth in Friar's band, the Virginia Vagabonds. After they polished their stage show with a uniquely nonderivative style, Clix founder John Henson caught the Vagabonds in a honky-tonk and invited them to record for his fledgling label. The studio was a bedroom in his house, recalls Friar:

> You know that shaky guitar lead on "I Can't Stay Mad at You"? Jim Kirkland and Dave Morgan played twin leads on that song, and Jim had a Voice of Music tape recorder he hooked his guitar into to get the sound. Not bragging or anything, but we had quite a following back then, and Jim was a very fine musician. We must have recorded that song three or four times, and would you believe they released the wrong take?

Nevertheless, serendipity was smiling on Friar that day: Kirkland's echo-drenched solo practically explodes from the speakers—as does his lead on the flip, "Empty Arms," and both sides of Friar's follow-up disc—capturing a time when country and rock 'n' roll were colliding head-on. Like labelmates Ford Nix, Swanee Caldwell, and Palford Brady,

Friar and his band stood at a musical crossroads, sounding as if they could jump any which way at any given moment.

Then there was Jimmy Lee, whose weirdly ethereal falsetto framed his Clix release, "She's Gone"/"Baby, Baby, Baby." Forecasting the genre-busting future of the imprint, Lee struck a mood both sophisticated and primal, his earthy vocals backed by modern jazz piano runs, jumping horns, jiving backing vocals, and—not to get too uptown—a primal electric guitar.

With just one other foray into rock 'n' roll—the haunting hill-jack blues "You Ain't No Good for Me," which he waxed for Fortune in 1956—Lee returned to his given name of Jimmy Williams for a fruitful career in bluegrass gospel and the ministry, but not before introducing a few of his acquaintances to Henson's bare-bones recording company. "I knew Jimmy and he got me involved with Clix," says bluegrass banjo player Ford Nix. "We recorded right in John's living room, had a big old fire goin', and you could hear that thing a-clickin' on the record! But it didn't do much damage to the song. He just had a little tape recorder, but they didn't cut it right; we didn't have the right band with us. We called 'em the Moonshiners, they was just a bunch of old boys from up here that helped me do that. I even played the guitar on that song 'cause I couldn't find a guitar picker!"

One spin of Nix's phenomenal debut, "Ain't No Sign I Wouldn't If I Could"/"Nine Times out of Ten," proves that *not* having the right band may have been what made the songs so magical.

"That was a part of it," Nix concedes with a smile.

Like Detroit's aforementioned Fortune label, where Friar, Lee, and Nix also recorded, a current of anything-goes electricity reverberated throughout the entire Clix discography. Alabama native Ray Taylor, for instance, specialized in a kind of blues-tinged bluegrass on tunes like "Clocking My Card" and "I'll Never Let You Worry My Mind Anymore," both of which feature superb banjo playing from Nix. But when it came time to wax his future cult classics, "My Hamtramck Baby" and "Connie Lou," Taylor dispensed with any semblance of a formal string band, stripping the proceedings down to the rawest core: as his teenage son Dolphus bashed away at a primitive drum kit, guitarist Chuck Reeves wrenched gnarled leads from his instrument. Over it all, Taylor strummed powerhouse rhythm in time with his hollering vocals.

While Lee, Nix, and Taylor were blurring the lines between bluegrass and rock 'n' roll, the dyed-in-the-wool style of Gene Stump and Bill Swain stuck closer to the source with the excellent "Stream of Love" and its Latin-tinged follow-up, "Rosalita," echoing both the archaic tradition and adventurous originality of much small-label bluegrass of the time. Then there was Curly Dan Holcomb, whose superb "I Flubbed My Dub"/"You'll Be the One to Cry" helped jump-start one of the most prolific and fascinating careers in midwestern country music, as well as the emerging Motor City bluegrass scene. Holcomb's record, which featured legend-in-the-making Bill Napier on mandolin, even made it back down south, where it sparked the imagination of at least one future Detroit bluegrass musician. "I heard 'I Flubbed My Dub' on a jukebox in a pool hall in Campton, Kentucky," recalls mandolin-master Nolan Faulkner. "I never thought I'd ever meet Curly Dan; then I came to Michigan."

Following Faulkner's arrival in 1959, the two became labelmates at Happy Hearts Records, another local recording outpost that would release Holcomb's biggest hit, "South on 23," in 1961. With his wife, Wilma Ann, now slapping the bass, they billed themselves Curly Dan, Wilma Ann and the Danville Mountain Boys. "South on 23" struck a deep chord with a growing element of the Detroit demographic: the displaced white southerner. Celebrating a return home via the "Hillbilly Highway" that had brought so many Appalachians to Detroit for work, the song was so popular that the group recorded variations of it on five different labels. Their strikingly original songs, which perfectly encapsulated the melancholy alienation felt by so many country folks adapting to life in a strange, new city, soon spread to labels such as Fortune, Dearborn, Old Homestead, and their own Danville imprint, defining Detroit bluegrass in a way that no other group would.

When Holcomb waxed his last record, the echoes of his Clix debut could still be heard, but this was hardly true of his labelmates Swanee Caldwell and Palford Brady, both of whom recorded their earliest efforts for Clix. Caldwell's double-sided masterpiece, "Thrill Happy"/"Mixed Up Heart," was the high point of his career, as were the fine rural rockers "L-O-V-E" and its follow-up "More Lovin'" (which was released on the Clix subsidiary Conteste) for Brady. The fact that the performances were unvarnished and underproduced lent a certain energy to them that was severely lacking on later outings for bigger labels such as King. Perhaps, according to Clix session drummer Patrick Bergin, it wasn't entirely intended to be that way:

The thing is, when Jack Scott became popular, every hillbilly in Michigan decided they wanted to be the next Jack Scott. And most of 'em didn't have musicians, they just had a guitar and a song. So what Clix did, they'd give 'em a certain amount of recording time. The artist would pay 'em a hot $400 up front and they would get a bunch of copies of the record, they would get the mastering done—which was basically just flat recording—and then they'd get the studio time and the musicians, all that would be a part of it. They'd have the things pressed in Owosso and they would get however many copies of their record and they themselves would go out and try to cut a deal with somebody. They'd either try to get 'em into stores—which a lot of 'em did, that's what Palford did, he'd take 'em around himself and drop them off at record stores—other guys would have a little bit more promotional sense and they'd go out to radio stations and so forth and try to get the thing played so another label would pick it up. The idea would be to use that as the genesis for a major label or a bigger label to pick it up and then actually do another recording session. There wasn't supposed to be a major release; they were supposed to redo them. But of course, a lot of them didn't get redone, they would just lease the master to somebody and they would put it out.

Palford tried hard. I mean, every time he'd put one of those records out he would hit the road and he'd go to these various places; he'd go to radio stations, he'd go to record stores. He used to come to Walter's Music Store in Lapeer, that's how I knew him. My band, the Invictas, were quite popular in Michigan back in the day and were interested in doing some recording. Marge, who manned the desk at Walter's, knew, of course, that I played in this band, and she introduced me to Palford. We never put out any records of our own but we backed up everybody else. We did a whole bunch of recording sessions in one form or another; some of us would play on some, some of us would play on others, but usually the core guys would go out, we could cut some demos on weekends and make a bunch of money. Well, a bunch of money in those days.

Brady introduced Bergin to local producer Howard Walker, who owned Drifter Records. He also happened to be a friend of Henson's, as Bergin remembers:

We did a bunch of sessions at Clix. It was in a house—most of the studios back then in Detroit were in houses. To me, one house looks a lot like another house so I have an awful lot of trouble trying to remember. For years and years, I thought that I had recorded at Motown, and as it turns out I've never even been in the place. But it was a house so I looked at it, and thought, Oh yeah, that looks right. Well, there was like five or six other places like that and Clix was one of them. It was at 500 Trombley in Troy.
The bottom line was we got $15.75 for those sessions, they were called dub ses-

sions. And you're supposed to get an hour of recording time out of those dub sessions. Well, all of our guys could read music, they could sight read. And most of the guys we were backing couldn't write music, they'd have a guitar and they'd know some chords and hell, we could knock that sucker off in fifteen minutes. So we would do a bunch of those; there might be three or four of those guys. Well, you know, $15.75 an hour back then in today's money is a hundred and something dollars an hour! So for a fourteen-year-old like I was, that was quite a lot of money. They'd give us a call and say, 'We've got three sessions on Sunday.' And we'd go down. If you had the chops—and by that I don't mean particularly great technical skills but in the case of a drummer like myself, if you were a good backbeat drummer, a good pocket drummer, and you had good time—that's what they needed. And there weren't too many of us that did, it was pretty interesting how many of these guys couldn't really do recording sessions.

Meanwhile, over at Royal Oak's Kimball High School, the Flamethrowers were beginning to stir up a greasy, vibrato-damaged racket that could have only come from witnessing one too many performances by Detroit's brutally raw instrumental rock 'n' roll squadrons of the time. And there were plenty to choose from, confirms guitarist Bruce Stratton:

We saw a lot of bands back then. We were pretty mobile by the time we were starting out, so if there was a band within driving distance, we would go out and see what we could pick up; see what we could steal. The best band that ever came out of Detroit, bar none, was the Royaltones. They were our heroes. I don't remember where I first saw them and the only reason I don't remember is because I saw them as often as possible whenever they were playing. Besides the Royaltones, we were big fans of Danny Zella and the Zell Rocks and the Thunder Rocks.

Rounded out by Ron Bergman on guitar and Fritz Larose on drums, the Flamethrowers were fittingly named. Their sound was, simply put, scorching, recalls Stratton:

> Fritz was a marching band drummer. He played in the school band, he had a snare drum and that was about it. Ron and I played through one twelve-inch amplifier, and depending on how long the dance was, we played some versions of "Rumble" and "Honky Tonk" that went on forever! After about six months, we'd learned so many records, I just told the guys, "*We* need to make a record," not knowing that you really couldn't do anything like that. We'd come up with two songs, "Suzette" and "The Knights' Caper," and we thought they were pretty good. "Suzette" was a gambit to impress three girls up the street, all of whom I'd dated, all of whom were named Susan, and all of whom thought that "Suzette" was about them. "The Knights' Caper" was named after the Kimball High School Knights. We figured if nobody liked

the record, at least the high school would appreciate it.

> Back then, if you had a rock 'n' roll band, you didn't know that you couldn't just *walk in* and make a record someplace. So, not knowing any better, I looked in the phone book and found Clix Records in Troy, Michigan. Troy was next to Royal Oak so we had enough gas money to get there. We went over there to see John Henson and we told him about our band. He didn't seem too impressed. He said, "Well, we're basically a country label, we've put some things out that bordered on rock 'n' roll"—probably meaning some of the rockabilly experiments—"but you can come out on Saturday and I'll listen to you."

> Teenagers being teenagers, we figured we'd go down there and blow him away. Well, he was very, very nice but probably wasn't sure what he was listening to and sort of dismissed us out of hand. We went home feeling kind of rejected. I had been home a couple of days when John called me. It turned out that he had a teenager in the family—I think it was a teenage girl. She'd listened to us and really liked it. So he said, "Well, we're really a country label, but we'll go ahead and put out one record on you and see how it does." So we went out there on a Saturday morning and it was a pretty involved thing. His recording studio was quaint by today's standards, but he had it set up pretty well. He had the recording equipment in a separate room and the studio in his den.

Henson, whose experience recording instrumental rock'n'roll had thus far been limited to the mysterious, R&B-flavored Stan "D"'s Rockets, engineered the Flamethrowers to raunchy perfection.

"Link Wray was one of my guitar heroes," continues Stratton. "And on the Clix record, I wanted a combination of Link Wray and the Royaltones." Needless to say, Stratton more than succeeded. Fritz set the stage for "The Knights' Caper" with inventive cymbal work that punctuated driving six-string antics, then downshifted to some serious jungle rhythm, while "Suzette" defied its sweet title with a sinister Wray vibe, climaxing with a final, stinging treble note that hung in the air at the song's end like a musical exclamation point.

Released in the fall of 1960, "Suzette" and "The Knights' Caper" took their rightful place alongside similarly crude Detroit anthems like the Emanons' "Stomper," Danny Zella's "Wicked Ruby," the Thunder Rocks' "Warpath" and "What's the Word," and the Egyptians' "Party Stomp," all of which were unleashed during the particularly potent years of 1959 and 1960.

Inspired by the release of their 45, Stratton and Bergman upgraded both their equipment and their lineup in short order: "Fritz was basically a marching band drummer and didn't have a full set of traps, so we went looking for a drummer. We ran into Lowery Day, and he just blew our socks off. And at the same time that we found Lowery we found Paul, the bass player, and he just really rounded out the group."

The only thing left to do was cut another record. They went to see Henson.

"We went back to Clix," says Stratton, "and he recorded us again on 'Intensity' and 'Whippy Wow,' and by then you can tell we were a much, much better band. But he wouldn't put it out. He said, 'Guys, I'll be glad to give you your sessions, but I can't put out another record right now; I'm not putting out any records right now.' I think he was strapped for cash at the time, and, you know, this was a labor of love for him. He never had a huge seller."

The Flamethrowers took their tape to Falcon Recording, a primitive setup located on Crooks Road in Royal Oak that specialized in pressing acetates and the occasional run of 45s. It was run out of a garage, Stratton recalls. "I remember the guy had one press in there. And it took forever for him to get his shit together! There was a Bel-Mar Cleaners in Royal Oak near Kimball High School, and we didn't have a name for our label. We weren't going to put Flamethrower Records on there because we knew that was a dead giveaway that this was not a big-time record label. But I remembered Bel-Mar Cleaners and liked the name, so we put 'Bel-Mar presents . . . the Flamethrowers.'"

Despite turning down the opportunity to release the second Flamethrowers single, Henson's next release was another pair of down-and-dirty guitar instrumentals, "Zaragoza" and "Track Number Seven," by some mystery group that no one knew named Johnny Guitar and his Rhythmaires. They may not have been the band of Henson's choice, as their presence on his Conteste subsidiary seems to suggest, but their sound was nearly as memorable as anything else in his catalog. Henson had started Conteste in 1961, distributing flyers advertising a talent contest, wherein contestants were asked to send in the name of an artist, band, or group they thought merited attention. If their nomination resulted in a recording contract, contestants were then asked to guess the amount of records sold by their nominee before a certain date. Prizes were to be paid in royalties to the contestant as well as the band, although it's doubtful that anyone made a penny from the proceedings. If it sounds complicated, it was; one can only speculate that Henson may have thought that playing the musical lottery might help him score that elusive hit, or at the very least sell some records. Neither of these things happened, and after only one other known single—the aforementioned "More Lovin'" by Clix veteran Palford Brady—Conteste, along with the entire Clix operation, seems to have ground to a halt.

Henson then disappeared from music entirely, surfacing during the '70s with a short-lived label, True Tone, that was named after his old Clix publishing company. At some point during that decade, Ray Taylor approached him and asked him to repress both of his 45s. Henson obliged, and that was seemingly the last anyone saw or heard of him. "He came into my store wanting to sell me those repressings of the Ray Taylor records," says Detroit record store owner Cappy Wortman. "And from what he told me at the time, he was operating out of a motel on Eight Mile Road." He handed Wortman a True Tone business card and vanished.

Somehow, these circumstances seem appropriate. So many musical stories begin and end in marginal places. Fortunately, when that story is one of a record label, it's shared with the world, even if many of its mysteries remain embedded in the grooves. Clix records rarely got airplay, recalls Nix, with the exception of WEXL in Royal Oak, which seems to have played every one of them. But like so much Detroit music, their undiluted honesty makes them invaluable.

"People need to know about all this," says Ford Nix, "because that was the backbone of our country, the kind of music we played."

Special thanks to Keith Cady, Craig Maki, and Loney Charles.

# MOTOWN

## THE SOUND OF YOUNG AMERICA

# The Story of Hitsville
## Motown Days

*Gary Graff*

Oh, we have a very swinging company

Working hard from day to day . . .

Our main purpose is to please the world

With songs the DJs love to play

Nowhere will you find more unity

Than at Hitsville USA

— Smokey Robinson, "The Motown Company Song"

It was called Hitsville U.S.A. for good reason. The company that Berry Gordy Jr. started with an $800 loan from his family did indeed please the world. The largest black-owned company of its time produced fifty-three number 1 singles on the *Billboard* Hot 100 and another 138 that topped various other charts. It was a success story of massive proportions, showcasing artistry that helped unite a racially divided country and establishing itself as a symbol and a cultural icon whose impact remains an inspiration around the world.

Berry Gordy Jr. had a dream and the tenacity to make it happen, as well as an ear for talent. He gave the world Smokey Robinson and the Miracles, Diana Ross and the Supremes, the Four Tops, the Temptations, Martha (Reeves) and the Vandellas, Marvin Gaye, and Stevie Wonder. Even Motown's "second tier"—Mary Wells, the Contours, Kim Weston, the Marvelettes, Rare Earth—was as formidable as other labels' A lists, and Motown was also a key stopping point for the Isley Brothers, Gladys Knight and the Pips, and even a fledgling Meat Loaf.

There was a wealth of talent behind the scenes, too, on West Grand Boulevard and, later, Woodward Avenue at I-75: writers and producers such as the Holland-Dozier-Holland juggernaut, Barrett Strong, Mickey Stevenson, Norman Whitfield, and more, and of course the ferocious Funk Brothers, musicians drawn from Detroit's jazz and soul clubs who made Studio A one of the most prolific sound laboratories in the world.

Gordy famously, or infamously, moved Motown's headquarters to Los Angeles in 1972, where the company's hit-making ways continued with the Jackson 5; the Commodores; Stevie Wonder with his string of Grammy Awards; and Diana Ross, with her early film triumphs. Rick James and Lionel Richie, along with Wonder, kept things afloat during the '80s, but the company began to fade, even though its catalog remains a marketer's dream.

There are a lot of ways to tell the Motown story, but nobody tells it quite like those who were there. So, let's put on some Tempts and Tops and let the Motown family offer a look inside the magic . . .

*Berry Gordy Jr. (Motown founder)*: Detroit has always been extremely close to me. That's where my roots are, where I got my feeling, my upbringing. I've always thought of it as kind of a country town, where the people are so wonderful. When I was growing up, you could get food in Detroit from any family, if you were hungry. The place was full of those *town* kind of people. So that's what that Motown name means—warmness. When people hear it today, they feel warm if you mention the word Motown. In all the different countries around the world that know Motown, there's something warm about it, and that's something I was very interested in. That's the legacy of Motown, and that's what I felt about Detroit.

*Kim Weston (Motown singer)*: Detroit has always been a mecca of music. One of my schoolteachers was Mr. George Shirley, who was the first black tenor in the Metropolitan Opera. The background here in music has always been rich.

*Berry Gordy*: It was really one idea. My talent was looking at people and finding that magic, or talent—I thought everybody had it—and showing them how to bring it out. I was pretty cocky. I thought I could make a star out of anybody.

*Smokey Robinson (Motown songwriter, producer, and executive)*: People ask me many times, they say, "Why were there so many talented people in Detroit?" I guarantee you that all over the world, in every little township, every little village, every little city, every big city, there is an abundant amount of talent. But the difference in Detroit was that we did have Berry Gordy. We had a man there who had a vision, who had a dream, and he had whatever fortitude and whatever it took to make a thing like that happen.

*Claudette Robinson (The Miracles)*: Berry had a dream, many years before we met him, of having a record company and producing artists and writing songs. His first ventures were writing songs for Jackie

Wilson. When we auditioned for Jackie Wilson's manager, we saw this gentleman walking around, and that gentleman turned out to be Berry Gordy, who was very interested in our group and most especially Smokey, because he had this little spiral notebook of about a hundred songs.

*Berry Gordy*: When I heard Smokey first sing was when I was a writer for Jackie Wilson. I had no company. I was just a writer, and I was in an office, writing a song for Jackie, and Smokey and [the Miracles] came in to audition for Jackie Wilson's manager, and I just happened to be sitting there. And after they sang three or four songs, they were rejected, and I just thought they were just the cutest, the greatest, the most inspired.

*Claudette Robinson*: Many people were not aware that the Miracles were the very first group ever to sign a contract for Berry Gordy and Motown Records. We were the only group that was around at the time with Berry. The only other artist at the time was Eddie Holland. We're talking about 1957.

*Berry Gordy*: They were dejected, and they were walking out. . . . I left after them and talked to them in the hallway and told them how great they are. And when they found out I was Berry Gordy, Smokey had been studying Jackie Wilson, and I was a big star to him, and so I felt like I was somebody special. It was important for me to play the act of being more important.

*Claudette Robinson*: In the early days, Berry was like his own distributor, basically, taking the records around to the disc jockeys to get them played. He also had to pawn his suits so he could get money for recording sessions for us.

143

*Berry Gordy*: The distributors sold a lot of records, but there were other companies and they would have to pay everybody, so they'd pay the hottest company. . . . So we would have to wait until after they paid the hot companies and, when our money was due, they would either be close to bankruptcy or not paying us, and we would take what we could get and hope for another hit record. And when we got another hit record, we'd go in and demand the money, and if they could afford to pay us, they would.

*Esther Edwards (Berry Gordy's sister)*: Eight hundred dollars was a lot of money. I kept asking him, "How are you going to pay it back? You don't have a job." He had quit his good job, eighty-five dollars a week, at the Ford Motor [Company] factory, on the assembly line. He had three children. My sister Gwen told him she knew he could write songs, and that she was going to pay his child support for a year to give him a chance to get going.

*Berry Gordy*: It was tough, but I was pretty strong and firm and I sold my heart out. I had a record I wanted to make with Marv Johnson, "Come to Me." We had this family loan thing where everybody put in ten dollars a month, so part of it was my money, anyway, but they had never let anybody borrow anything from that before, and they felt if I borrowed anything it would open up the floodgates and everybody would use the savings club. But I pitched my thing. I said, "I need this thousand dollars," and I said, "I'm gonna be rich, I'm gonna be famous, and I'm gonna be the greatest thing in the world!" And they said, "Yes, but you've been a failure in anything you've ever done in your life!" But I had two sisters, Gwen and Anna, that were really in my corner. They said, "Give him the money. Give him the money!" And finally my

mother looked at my father, and they looked at each other, and they felt so sorry for me that they said, "We won't give you $1,000, but we will give you $800. But you've got to sign this IOU and sign your life away." So they made me promise whatever, and that was it. I made the record "Come to Me," and the rest is history.

*Otis Williams (The Temptations)*: Here comes a city that's noted for making primarily cars, and out of that, here comes this entity such as Motown, with Berry at the head and all the talented people that were under Berry's guidance. I can only think that it was God's will wanting Motown to become the entity it has become.

*Martha Reeves (Martha and the Vandellas)*: Mary Wells had written a song and taken it to Berry Gordy, and Berry said, "You're a good singer. Sing it as opposed to just being the writer." And he discovered her when she was fourteen years old.

*Kim Weston*: I was singing in church one day and a guy asked me if I was interested in doing some demos for a writer who happened to be the cousin of Eddie and Brian Holland. Eddie was at the demo session; they didn't like the guy's material, but they liked my voice so they recommended that I come to Motown.

*Levi Stubbs (The Four Tops)*: We had been singing for a little while together but never knew success as far as records were concerned. It was a real treat for us to see this kind of camaraderie and love at this record company, hardworking people who were finally having the chance to show their wares.

*Martha Reeves*: Berry was smart. He and Mickey Stevenson, my boss, went all 'round Detroit and signed the best of the jazz musicians and the best of the talent. Amateur shows were a big thing in Detroit. . . . When Hastings, the street that was torn down for urban renewal, had movie houses on it, that's where we auditioned. I knew nearly all the artists on an amateur level that Motown sort of corralled to 2648 West Grand Boulevard.

*Berry Gordy*: When "Please Mr. Postman" came, that was our first number 1 record. It was what we called a clean-up record. And then after that, we had trouble getting money from that, so something else happened along the way. If we had any one year when we didn't make a big profit, we would have gone out of business, because we were going from record to record during that period.

*Martha Reeves*: When I met him, [Gordy] was a young man, not much older than us. He always looked like he had a dream in the back of his eyes. But he always had a plan; all we had to do was what he told us, just cooperate. He had in his mind a show business that none of us even knew about.

*Levi Stubbs*: He was the right person at the right time for a lot of people. He was a genius as far as songs were concerned. He had that gift, and it was very subtle, 'cause that's a very frustrating position to be in, to try to get the best out of everybody, and a lot of times they never knew themselves what they had. I think he's a genius in that respect.

*Esther Edwards*: Berry had the skill to make strong men out of boys. He could also do the same for the girl singers. He was kind of a father figure—not that much older than the artists, but so many of them were from one-parent or no-parent homes. Smokey was eighteen and his mother had died when he was ten, and he was raised by a sister who had eleven children.

*Claudette Robinson*: Berry was the head, like a father, and we were like the children. It was very easy to follow him, his direction and guidance and whatever, 'cause he wanted to become successful just as the artists wanted to become successful.

*Otis Williams*: There are a lot of people who don't know that he's a very funny, humorous person. During the times when we were really seeing each other quite often, Berry would get into these bits of telling about his exploits of being a prizefighter and situations and things that he had gone through during his life, and as he's telling them, he's acting them out, and his eyes are bugging out and the whole mannerisms. I would just stand there and say, "Man, you are a funny, funny person."

*Berry Gordy*: I decided to call it Motor City [Records] first, because Detroit was called the Motor City, of course. And I thought "city" was a little too cold, because I always felt like Detroit has been a warm town. It was a factory town, and everybody kinda liked everybody else, so it had this warmness to it. So I decided rather than Motor City, I would take Motor *Town*, and then I contracted it to just Motown. And I named it Hitsville because I knew that hits were going to be made there, and I wanted to get a hip name. And those days, "ville" was the cool thing to say, so I said, "OK, we're gonna call this Hitsville because that is where hits are gonna be made."

*Kim Weston*: It was kind of like the assembly line at Ford or something. I would say that there was a production system used at Motown. It was my understanding that Berry worked at one of the factories, so he may have had that in mind with the process he was using.

*Martha Reeves*: There were people breaking down the doors of Motown in its early days, because Berry had the goods.

*Diana Ross (The Supremes)*: I was a very close friend of Smokey's niece, and I used to listen to Smokey rehearse in the basement. And then Smokey was the one who helped us get our first audition at Motown. And Berry just happened to be passing through, and he stopped and said, "Would you sing that song again?" I think we were doing "There Goes My Baby" or "Night Time is the Right Time," and we were busy really trying to sell it. We were really singing our hearts out.

*Berry Gordy*: Diana's voice was not the greatest; she had sort of a little nasally sound. But . . . she was so inspired with it, and so I wasn't crazy about the song, but I thought she was . . . very good. I asked them what grade they were in, and she said she was in twelfth grade, and they wanted to start singing right then. And I said, "No, go to school. Get your education. When you graduate, come back and see me." And that's what happened. They came back.

*Diana Ross*: So I came back and I was his secretary during the summer.

*Berry Gordy*: And yes, she was very enthusiastic about being a singer. She would just really work at it. She was willing to pay the price. She said she was a great secretary, and would I give her a job. And I did. I think she lasted about three weeks.

*Diana Ross*: Of the first nine records we had out, we didn't have any hits. And Berry kind of stayed

with us. And with every one of the artists, he kind of stuck with them through when it was difficult, when we were learning.

*Mary Wilson (The Supremes)*: I kinda coined the phrase "The No-Hit Supremes" because I knew everyone was talking behind our backs. We were the first girl group at Motown; of course, the Marvelettes came along and they got their hit record, "Please Mr. Postman." Of course, Martha and the Vandellas came along, the Velvelettes, all kinds of girl groups. Everyone had gotten a hit record and we were still waiting. We were kind of anxious, our parents were threatening they were going to send us to college. I wasn't the spokesperson, but I kind of spoke up and I told Eddie Holland, "Eddie, our parents are gonna send us to college if we don't get a hit record! We've got to prove that we can do this, or we've got to get real jobs!"

*Claudette Robinson*: I remember how long it took the Supremes to get a hit. I mean, time after time after time—it just wasn't happening for them. I think when they finally got a hit, everybody was really happy for them. I know I was.

*Mary Wilson*: When [Holland-Dozier-Holland] brought us these songs, "Baby Love," "Where Did Our Love Go" and all, we didn't like them at all. I love them now, but at the time we were really a group that did harmony and we considered ourselves very, very good. So these songs, especially "Where Did Our Love Go," it was so simple. It had no harmony. Florence [Ballard] and I were singing unison, which we thought was so beneath us. All we had to sing was "baby baby, ooh baby baby." And Eddie laughed at me and said, "Just trust me. These songs are gonna be hits," and you know how right he was about that.

*Martha Reeves*: Our first experience of traveling [with the Motortown Revue], it was rough. We were all from meager means. We went on the road with a twelve-piece band, ten acts, and a Trailways bus. It broke down whenever it felt like it. On one occasion, we were in the hills of Kentucky, and the bus brakes went out and the driver was driving furiously, and we didn't know why. When we got to the foot of the hill and the bus came to a stop, he let out a big sigh. And we asked why, what's wrong with him? He explained to us that the brakes had gone out several miles back and it was a blessing that we could stop.

*Claudette Robinson*: For our first professional date at the Apollo Theater, we made $750 for the week, and that was for all five of us plus our guitar player, and with that we had to buy our meals, we had to join the union, we had to pay for cleaning and our hotel bill and manage to get to the Apollo from Detroit. Even when things didn't cost as much, that still was not a lot of money for all those people. We drove, and we stayed at the Theresa Hotel across the street from the Apollo. And when we came home, we actually had nothing left.

*Rick James (Motown session musician and solo artist)*: You walk into this little house on West Grand Boulevard, and it didn't give the ambience or presence that you were in a capitol of some major corporation. You would never know—other than the people standing around are Marvin Gaye, the Isley Brothers, Stevie Wonder, or somebody—that you're even in a studio of insurmountable fame and joy. Inside it was like a family atmosphere; everybody talked to each other. Everybody kicked around, everybody joked, everybody laughed.

*Esther Edwards*: Ours was a close-knit family that helped each other to do what they were trying to do. Everybody that joined the company kind of became like a part of the family.

*Raynoma Gordy Singleton (Gordy's second wife)*: Motown was built on faith and trust and loyalty. It was a family.

*Otis Williams*: You knew that here we are at a company that had a very different, special kind of vibe going for it—so much so that when the company closed at six o'clock, me and a few others would be there cleaning the floors, emptying the ashtrays in the trash cans, and getting ready for the next day for people to come back and work. Now, in most cases, you don't find artists doing something like that. But it was such a fun, loving place and with a family-oriented kind of feel, you just went beyond the call of being an artist. You wanted to do whatever you could to make Motown become what it's become now.

*Smokey Robinson*: Hitsville was a unique place, because that's where we hung out. When we came off of a fifty-one-nighter tour and you'd be dead tired, rather than going home to get some rest . . . everybody went there, because we knew that everybody was going to be there. We hung out there because it was a wonderful place to be.

*Martha Reeves*: The juices were flowing. The energy was new and fresh. "Mickey's Monkey" was recorded on the spur of the moment; Smokey came up with this idea and came up to the lobby where everyone was sitting and hanging around. He said, "Come on everybody, let's make a record!" When we got into the studio, he said, "All right! Is everybody ready?" It became part of the record. It was not supposed to be on there; the record was supposed to start with "lum-di-lum-di-aye." But because of the energy and the sound, it was kept on.

*Otis Williams*: The only real Miracle on that was Smokey. They couldn't find the other Miracles, I guess, so myself and some of the Vandellas and whoever else was around. . . . We were pulling for anybody that was connected with Motown as artists and producers. The producer or songwriter would say, "Hey, we need somebody to clap their hands" or "We need some foot stompers," and we would go in there and do it. Like on "Try It, Baby," that's the Temptations behind Marvin Gaye. You would do whatever it would take to help people make it, as well as to help yourself make it.

*Levi Stubbs*: There was never a rivalry [with the Temptations]. That was for show, I guess, but there was never a rivalry. We were the best of friends. We were always genuinely pleased when they got a number 1 record.

*Diana Ross*: We were doing something that we loved. We probably at that time didn't have to be paid. We just wanted to sing and wanted to make music.

*Rick James*: [The Funk Brothers, Motown's session musicians] were the greatest overall players of a sound that existed, moreso than the Beatles or anyone else. The Beatles were great as four guys who played together and just had an overall sound, but the Funk Brothers, the Motown musicians, stand beyond anybody as far as the music that they did and the sound that they created. They were all real wonderful guys; there was never any ego with any of them. They always had much love and admiration for one another.

*Kim Weston*: The producers were young people, too. It wasn't like you were walking into an establishment that had been in existence for a long time. A lot of things were trial and error; they tried it, and if this didn't work, they tried something else until they got something right.

*Rick James*: Once you went into the studio, into that back room, it was all business. Ah, really, it wasn't. It would take a minute 'cause the musicians would come into the session, and they'd all be laughing or joking about the night before or whatever, and you'd have to calm them down. I remember James Jamerson, who was the bass player for the Funk Brothers, he told me how to scream at the guys. . . . These were the main session men, and I remember he made me scream at the top of my lungs, telling them to "shut the fuck up and let's do this session!" I was scared shitless . . . but they all got quiet.

*Berry Gordy*: It was hard work. It was fierce competition. But it was a lot of hugging and kissing and stuff. It was just a time and place where it was all about the music. We had fierce competition and fierce love, and even though people would compete in those meetings, the competitors would work on each other's records. It was the strangest thing. It was competing, but they had love, and Norman Whitfield would work on a Marvin Gaye session, and Marvin Gaye would play drums on a Supremes session, even though he had his records coming up against theirs. So it was unique. It's hard to duplicate that feeling in any company.

*Esther Edwards*: They saw it as competition, but it was not competition because everybody supported everybody else. When one artist got a hit, everybody was so happy. They would help each other—"Hey man, that tune you just mixed, there's a bad note in there. Check that out." It was that kind of spirit.

*Berry Gordy*: When songs came out of there, we knew they would be hits because we had these Friday meetings where we would argue over them. We'd have these long, hard-fought, debated sessions. But when we released the record out of that meeting, we knew it was a great record because everybody voted on it. We were pioneers, and no one knew it would be successful. And when they found out it was, then that's when the competition got very, very heavy.

*Eddie Holland (Motown songwriter and producer)*: Berry, being the songwriter and record producer he was, set a certain standard, and I think everybody was aware of this standard and was reaching for that. He believed in the song having a good idea and a melody that was catchy, and putting those things together is what caused the songs to be as effective as they were.

*Mickey Stevenson (Motown songwriter, producer, and executive)*: It was a feeling of creating something that we felt could be different and unique. With that in mind it was the *art* of doing it, the feeling of doing it. Berry would listen to [the songs] all the way down, man. He'd turn his chair around and listen all the way through. And everyone would be on pins and needles, waiting to hear what he thought—and what other people would have to say.

*Berry Gordy*: I *was* in charge, but I made logic the boss, so people could argue with me, and if they had a more credible, more logical [argument] than me, they would be able to win. They would ask my opinion, and I usually didn't give 'em the major

thumbs-up that other people did, but I wasn't nearly as negative as some of the other people.

*Leon Ware (Motown songwriter)*: Berry pitted talented people against each other. The challenge was you didn't even bring your song in unless you were really sure about it, 'cause the people you were up against would walk in with some really brilliant work. What you did there had to be excellent.

*Eddie Holland*: We would bring in kids off the street. We would bring them in and say, "Listen to this music. What do you guys think is best?"

*Mickey Stevenson*: We'd end up with two great songs, sometimes three. We'd pick out the one to go out, and then we'd have other songs ready to go, so we never ran out of [hits].

*Eddie Holland*: I just wanted to know, "Was it a hit record?" If you could get a record in the Top 10, that's wonderful, really. That's a big hit. If it went gold, that was the ultimate. Number 1 was more of a prideful thing, I guess. It was always nice to think you had the most-loved record this week. But next week, somebody else would be number 1, and the week after that somebody else . . . So you can't get too wrapped up in that number 1 thing, at least I didn't. I just wanted the hit.

*Berry Gordy*: "My Cherie Amour" by Stevie Wonder, that was on the B side of a record called "I Don't Know Why I Love You," and we promoted it like mad. The few people who bought the record, they turned it over and played "My Cherie Amour" and started calling the radio stations trying to get them to play it. After a month or so we started promoting ["My Cherie Amour"], and it became an international smash.

*Stevie Wonder (Motown singer)*: I was only like nine years old when it started. . . . And me having the wish, you know, that I could be a singer and being as fascinated by that sound that came out of a radio, how all that could happen. And obviously, within a matter of two years after that, I had the pleasure of meeting some of those great people that I never imagined that I would. So that was a great, a great thing.

*Levi Stubbs*: Holland-Dozier-Holland, when they wrote a song, they would call us in, get a key on it, and let us take a shot at it. It wouldn't take but a few moments for them to get it together, because they could communicate with the musicians. We'd be recording with the musicians at the same time, in some cases, and in some cases we'd do it to a track. It all depended on how much time there was.

*Berry Gordy*: There was so much love when we made that music, and there was so much creativity, and there was so much realness. And that's why the music had the magic. It wasn't because we thought we were going to be something or even at some point realized that we were [something].

*Diana Ross*: [Gordy] not only made it so that we could sing our songs, and he wasn't just about making the record and making the money, but he taught us—or they put together a group of people that taught us.

*Maxine Powell (Motown etiquette instructor)*: I taught young artists the life skills they needed to succeed. I taught class, style, and refinement. I told them they were being taught to stand before kings and queens at Buckingham Palace and the White House, and they did.

*Martha Reeves*: The good thing about Motown is the fact we were groomed. We had music theory. We had choreography by Cholly Atkins. And Mrs. Powell definitely made a difference in all the ladies' lives; she worked with some of the guys, too, but the finishing course she gave us allowed us to go anywhere in the world and be accepted.

*Smokey Robinson*: Mrs. Powell was the one who groomed us. She was such an integral and important part of what we did. It didn't matter how many hits you had or how well you were known around the world, two days a week at Artists Development— that was mandatory. She was so important to what we were trying to do in developing our artists.

*Rick James*: Marvin [Gaye] was telling me how they wanted him to go to that shit. I think he did go once or twice. He was saying it's the most ridiculous thing in the world.

*Diana Ross*: Even today, if I think about how I'm sitting. . . . Miss Powell taught us how to sit those legs in the right way when you're sitting in front of people.

*Duke Fakir (The Four Tops)*: She was one of the great moving parts of Motown. She was still teaching me [in 2013, before her death]; I saw her during the summer and asked her, "Ms. Powell, how old are you?" and she said to me, "Boy, did your mother not teach you anything? You don't ask a lady her age!"

*Rick James*: In essence, it was a good thing. There's nothing wrong with learning a little etiquette . . . how to walk right if you slump or how to order wines and eat right. Those kinds of things all proved beneficial for all those people who went, 'cause a lot of these guys just came out of the ghettos, and they were drinking apple Ripple and Thunderbird, Cold Duck.

So when they went to that school, they learned about Dom Perignon and lobster and crème brûlée and all that kind of shit.

*Lionel Richie*: I just felt like I was joining Motown University, and what a great, tough university it was to go to. The competition and the instructors were off the Richter scale, if you consider competing against Marvin Gaye or competing against Stevie Wonder, and of course Berry had a wonderful way of pitting you against each other.

*Martha Reeves*: We were as active in the civil rights movement as any other organization. The difference is we didn't picket or march and parade. We got onstage and sang our music, and everybody fell in love.

*Berry Gordy*: [W]e had the trials and tribulations of change, the racial tensions, the marches, and they were all doing it to Motown music—both sides. And that just thrills me.

*Smokey Robinson*: Diana Ross and the Supremes opened a lot of doors for the rest of us. They were almost like the entertainment guinea pigs. Berry saw something in them that, honestly, the rest of us didn't have. So he opened a lot of doors with them.

*Tito Jackson (The Jackson 5)*: Our biggest dream when we lived in Gary, Indiana, was to be on Motown. We were listening to Smokey and the Temptations and the Tops and Little Stevie Wonder. We wanted to be like them. That was our dream, to be like those guys and be with Motown as the company that would make you stars.

*Jackie Jackson (The Jackson 5)*: We performed at Berry Gordy's house, for his birthday party. That was pretty much an audition. We pulled up in this van and saw him in his backyard, which was like a golf course. He called us to come over toward him; he told us, "If you get this ball in this hole, I'll give you one hundred dollars." That was a lot of money for us back then. He had a bowling alley downstairs and pinball machines and indoor swimming pool, and I was very, very nervous 'cause all my brothers were running around bowling and playing and doing all the things like that and I was worried they weren't taking it seriously. I was like, "We got this big show to do," and I knew the Temptations were going to be there, the Four Tops, Smokey Robinson, Diana Ross. . . .We had to sing their songs in front of their faces. That was scary, man.

*Martha Reeves*: Anybody gets ticked off when they don't understand things. We had the best of the show business world because of the instruction. But you have to pay when you go to college. There is a tuition. I feel that those that are angry do not understand that they had no money when they went to Motown, and that the creative forces there did generate capital. However, it was Berry Gordy's capital.

*Levi Stubbs*: If they were bitter, it was their fault, 'cause Berry had said things to them like, "Don't spend your money so fast. Take your time. Let this money accumulate. You're not a millionaire just because you had a hit record." When a person that's been poor all their lives all of a sudden has an opportunity to buy a car, a home, whatever, they tend to want to do it right then and there. They spend more money than they have . . . and they feel like they have to blame somebody when what they should do is blame themselves.

151

*Joe Billingslea (The Contours)*: Berry Gordy told us, "You don't need the diamonds, the Cadillacs. Save your money."

*Berry Gordy*: I never liked the spotlight, never liked getting in front of the cameras to defend anything. And I was too busy moving forward to answer anything. Sometimes I think it was wise, and other times I think it might have been a mistake to not stop some of that stuff. But if I had, if I had taken the time to do that instead of working on the music, maybe Motown wouldn't have grown the way it did. But the truth only wins if you can afford to fight for it; otherwise people will rewrite history. And so many people tried to do that on [Motown], but because of the loyalty of the artists and my determination to fight for the truth, we finally came over the hump of that.

*Lionel Richie (Motown singer)*: The interesting thing about being a part of Motown is when you signed the contract, you automatically thought you had won, with no record yet. Just the fact you passed the big test, you thought you must be something special because they wanted to sign you to Motown.

*Berry Gordy*: They came up with all kinds of reasons why black kids came up with all this stuff and had all this success, and therefore we had all kinds of rumors throughout the country and the world about our successes. They didn't want to think that it was just the incredible talent of all these great people who come out of Detroit—the Supremes, Diana Ross, Marvin Gaye, Stevie Wonder, Gladys Knight and the Pips, and Smokey and the Miracles and Rick James, and then the unsung people like the Funk Brothers [Motown's studio musicians]

and everybody who worked in the offices. It was teamwork and a team effort, and I'm so grateful to those people that followed me.

*Esther Edwards*: I really don't think that Berry Gordy would have ever moved if he had known how important we were in Detroit. We had over 450 staff employees at one time when we were there, but there was no chamber of commerce, no city people, mayors, or anybody recognizing that.

*Berry Gordy*: We would have been better off with the record thing if we had stayed in Detroit. There have been times when I felt it was stupid to come out here and get into something, even though we had successful movies like *Mahogany* and *Lady Sings the Blues*. I wanted to be in the movie business and to do things out here and that was it. It was growth. So we gained the movie thing, but the record thing didn't go as well.

*Martha Reeves*: There was a big outburst of tempers when the company moved. That hurt me 'cause I had a new little baby, an infant son. But that didn't stop me, because I had instructions, the things I was taught at Motown.

*Dennis Edwards (The Temptations)*: It was a big mistake. We all should have stayed in Detroit. Mr. Gordy had aspirations of doing the movie business, and [Los Angeles] was the place to be. But our roots were there in Detroit. There was a camaraderie there. We didn't get that family atmosphere [in LA]. I think it would have made the city [of Detroit] better, too. We left a little bit of a void there.

*Berry Gordy*: We were pioneers, and no one knew it would be successful. And when they found out it was, then that's when the competition got very, very heavy. And many other things happened in the '60s and '70s that have changed the whole system. The whole system changed.

*Rick James*: The Motown sound, by this particular time in the '70s, 1977 or so, had basically died. It hadn't died, but it was definitely calling for respiratory assistance. The Commodores and Stevie Wonder were the only original things that were coming out of Motown at that time, when I came on the scene. I was probably one of the last ones to hold it up. After me, it was all gone.

*Lionel Richie*: I was not in Motown Detroit. I was in Motown LA, but I caught the last remnants of what the old Motown was. When I walked in the door, there was the Temptations in the hall, Marvin Gaye in the hall, Diana Ross was in the halls. The Four Tops were still there. The Temptations were still there. It still felt like the Motown I grew up with.

*Jackie Jackson*: That was a whole 'nother world, Los Angeles. Going out there, seeing palm trees and the nice, warm weather, people living in the hills and driving down Sunset Boulevard and seeing the Rolls-Royces and Ferraris. . . . It was like you were in heaven somewhere. It was a dream come true. And to be with Motown in Los Angeles and working with Berry Gordy and all the top producers and writers, we learned so much about writing a song and producing a record. Motown was like a family, even out there; they didn't just record you, they taught you so many things.

*Smokey Robinson*: Even when I wasn't a Motown artist . . . I feel like any artist that's ever been connected to Motown, who became popular there: no matter where you go or what you do, people always associate you with Motown.

*Rick James*: It had its day, man. There was a day for Motown. There comes a time when music changes around you, and what happened with Motown was everybody wasn't able to make the change. When Sly and the Family Stone started to happen and Jimi [Hendrix] and the independent black thing and the "hey, we don't have to wear the same suit" thing started . . . the whole industry changed for black R&B performers. Motown just couldn't fit that genre anymore. They were trying to relive the '60s, and consequently it fell.

*Otis Williams*: With any company, be it Motown or General Motors or IBM, you have fluctuation points. You go up and down. Motown is no different than all the other corporations that have gone through changes. Motown has done that and is still around, even though I must say Motown today is not the Motown I'm really well acquainted with from the '60s and early '70s.

*Berry Gordy*: I listen to all of it. I was in the car . . . and heard "Let's Get It On" by Marvin Gaye. I was amazed at how great it sounded.

*Rick James*: Berry will always be a genius. My take on him now is that he's enjoying life, but his eyes and his hands, contrary to popular belief, are still on Motown. I'll always believe that. That's like his child, and you never let your child go.

*Berry Gordy*: You have to remember each one brings back such memories to me. I remember, sitting at Motown 25, I would hear a song and I would be looking at the person singing it and see them in the past. When I'm listening to songs now, I get double enjoyment.

*Martha Reeves*: I imagine that God came along and sprinkled some blessings over 2648 West Grand Boulevard, because of the way everyone joined together and united and made a loving music that will last forever.

*Otis Williams*: Motown's music stands head and shoulders above some of the best. You go to the movies, you see trailers, and you hear some Motown music. You turn on the television, and you hear some Motown music on commercials. I've been in elevators and the Muzak is Motown music. It's like there's no escaping the Motown music. I'm very proud that I came along at that point in time and was part of something that will no doubt be going on when we're all dead and gone.

*Diana Ross*: I travel a lot . . . and the music is so very *now*. It's still right here and right in the moment. And, you know, I'd like to be able to look back another forty years and say the kids are still liking the music, because it's real, it's genuine.

*Berry Gordy*: It's just a unique situation, and I'm the major recipient of that now because I can look back and . . . it's a different kind of enjoyment. I enjoyed making the records. I enjoyed dealing with the people. I enjoyed directing and hanging out and . . . now I can look at it a different way and say, "OK, we did it. We really did it."

*Rick James*: The bottom line is that for forty years, Motown stood tall among every record company and it gave more joy than any record company I can think of. It damn sure raised me, and it damn sure raised you.

*Berry Gordy*: One thing about the people who are with Motown, they cannot *not* love each other. Like

any family, we get mad, we get happy, we get this and that, but that love will always stay. So even though I was in a lawsuit for thirty years with Holland-Dozier-Holland because they left the company and believed some of the stuff people were saying and they felt maybe they were cheated. . . . Well, after thirty years of depositions and all that, we all came together and they said, "Hey, we love you so much," and I said, "I love you guys." We had this misunderstanding and we had to thrash it out, and, even though it took a long time, they are my biggest supporters and I am theirs. And many of these people are my best friends today—Smokey is my very best friend, you know? To look back and find those same people I spent all that time and did all that work with talking about me and understanding me and loving me as much as they do, my goodness. Who wouldn't be thrilled with that? That's what I did it all for—to be loved.

Beans Bowles. © Leni Sinclair Collection.

# For Beans

### Written on the Occasion of the Funeral Service for Dr. Thomas "Beans" Bowles Sr., February 5, 2000, at Central United Methodist Church

*Bill Harris*

James Carter, with his tarnished
baritone, began blowing "Nature Boy."
He chanted the melody and soloed for
a couple choruses, but soon, as became
evident throughout
the day, no one in this place, on this
day had to carry the burden alone.
Don
Mayberry, on bass, began with a toll-
like, single note throbbing, as Carter
eased into
his journey from the bottom of the
horn,
meditating,
and somewhere some way we were
into
"Amazing Grace,"
coming, at that moment from two
directions at once,
    " . . . how sweet the sound . . ."
Carter gathering himself, his wits, and
wisdom:
a whisper growing through a growl, to
a honk.
And we in the congregation smiled,

nodded our heads, discreetly waved
our hands,
looked up, looked down, as he
continued, playing his horn, climbing
in register and intensity and emotion,
combining blues and gospel, and
mother wit, telling the
church,
    "My mama done tole me, when I
      was in knee pants . . ."
And we talk back to him. "You go'n'
wake Beans up!" somebody warned.
    "There was a boy, a very
      strange, enchanting boy."
The man in the first pew put his arm
around Harold, and Bean's oldest son
laid his
head on the man's shoulder and took
his hand, as Carter maneuvered back
down to
the horn's bottom again, like
approaching thunder rolling across the
high places and
the low, the hills and the valleys,
or across the centuries,

157

like the thundering hoof beats of
fiery-eyed steeds swinging down the
sweet chariot,
and stirring the night creatures,
causing heads to rise, eyes to widen,
ears to perk, and notes from before
language to
echo in their throats;
making owls hoot, canines howl,
felines scratch the door,
and grown men turn on the light,
as Carter, with circular breathing,
sustained the swirling, whirling
tension,
and Mayberry
Boomed,
Boomed,
Boomed,
Boomed like the breaking hearts of
each and all of us Beans blessed with
the
cleansing ablution of
his music,
and his manner,
and his love,
and we leapt to our feet, applauding
the seeming nearing end of the tune.

But young Carter,
knowing,
in that way a healer, age old, or new
ordained,

knows,
knew
we weren't quite ready to release, or be
released,
not with the weight of the burden
Beans and we had to bare
and bear,
so, Carter, proving to us, we could
stand more than we thought—
a lesson learned a thousand times a
day in this America,
but too easily forgotten.
Carter continued to blow as he began
to bow and straighten,
back and forth, calling,
as he bowed and straightened,
saying farewell,
and he bowed and straightened
preaching, honking, trilling, testifying
to and for us,
putting us in even closer connection
with ourselves
and Beans
and all the music makers we have
smiled with, and nodded to,
and waved at,
and egged on in other communal
moments and settings
sacred and secular,
and back and forth, Carter bowed and
straightened,
blowing

"...and then one day he
       passed our way..."
back and forth, bowing and
straightening,
       "...how sweet the tune that
       saved a wretch like me..."
holding us,
uniting us
in the moment,
in that moment of accord and
correspondence and harmony,
bowed and straightened,
a human metronome. Time made
flesh.
To and fro, and his horn moans and
wails, Catalonian,
Pentecostal, its sound, and its
intention breaking
with the relentless timelessness of
tides in the patient tenacity,
breaking against us as if at the seawall
of our resistance
and subsides to gather and rush and
wane. To
and fro. Wave upon wave.
       "Amazing grace, how sweet..."
till the wall was worn away to a wash
of sand, and
we were one,
and were ready
one and all,
to be released,

one and all,
and to release,
one and all,
and in our unity
acknowledge
and grant
and consent and concede
and profess and allow
that Beans had been a privilege and a
blessing,
and a reward and an opportunity and
a bonus and a bounty,
and we,
one and all
acknowledged
as we in our unity
had to,
acknowledged
that it was time,

time to bow and straighten and
witness
that another
good brother
was going home.

# Half a Mile from Heaven
## The Love Songs of Motown
*Herb Jordan*

etroit in the 1960s was an unlikely stage for a production that featured some of the most inspirational love songs ever written. It may seem equally unlikely that most of those songs were written by young black men. Default notions of romance are an awkward overlay to the reality of this city of steel and sweat, Joe Louis, and Jimmy Hoffa. Rough? Tanks that rolled off Detroit's assembly lines and onto Europe's beaches as liberators returned home twenty years later to quell urban rebellion. But there was no simple way to quiet the musical movement that was surging in the basements and on the street corners of Detroit's black neighborhoods.

The city vibrated. Every block had a band, it seemed, and on summer nights young men harmonized under the streetlights. Mixed in with homegrown versions of hits by Ben E. King and the Moonglows were original songs penned by the neighborhood tunesmith. Sunday morning you had to arrive early to get a seat at church. Overcome with the spirit, preachers resorted to singing their sermons. At New Bethel Baptist Church, you didn't mind standing for two hours if you could hear the Franklin sisters—Aretha, Carolyn, and Erma—sing "How I Got Over."

But there was a new sound. As word spread through the neighborhood, teenagers scrambled, with high-top shoes and bicycles, to the parking lot of the Bi-Lo Supermarket where on a makeshift stage twelve-year-old Stevie Wonder performed

"Fingertips." Before long, record store clerks were inundated with customers describing, and sometimes attempting to sing, a few bars of the sound they heard on their transistor radios.

These were the 1960s, and poverty, segregation, Vietnam, and nuclear gamesmanship convened in a funnel cloud that threatened to rip through the fabric of America. But with the innocence of a first kiss, the poets of Motown conjured up a black Camelot and took America "up the ladder to the roof" for a view of heaven. From rooftops to blue-lit basements they danced, black and white, fast and slow, as young men testified that they would "find that girl if [they] had to hitchhike 'round the world," and women replied, "ain't no mountain high enough to keep me from getting to you." Boys in the hood—long typecast as the least productive, most destructive element of society—wrote knowingly and elegantly of life and love. The young women dazzled with a mix of soul and social graces, grace they maintained even when on southern highways gunshots were directed at the Motown tour bus.

The thought of white teenagers falling under the spell of black music mobilized the guardians of white culture. Everyone knew the invisible perimeter that insulated white America would soon be irreparably breached. The usual operatives took measures to thwart it. Music was on the front lines of the battle. In retrospect, the last-gasp efforts at interdiction seem comical. A now infamous poster that circulated throughout the South warned white parents not to allow their children to listen to Negro music, lest they end up *with* one, on the dance floor or otherwise.

As great as Motown's records were, the company's executives knew the power of live performance. The Motown Revue featured almost the entire roster of artists and a live stage band. The artists were confronted for the first time with overt segregation when the caravan rolled into southern towns. Neighborhoods in Detroit were neatly divided along racial lines, but in the South the lines were often drawn with firearms. What was taken for granted in northern cities could be a perilous undertaking in the South. Bobby Rogers of the Miracles recalls that a gas station owner confronted him with a gun after he used a white restroom. White and black teenagers were typically assigned to opposite sides of auditoriums in southern venues. But on many occasions the police were powerless to enforce the separation as the teenagers, in their own version of a freedom march, just stepped to the beat.

In the mid-'50s, television sponsors squirmed at the thought of having their products associated with Nat King Cole's variety show; in the absence of commercial support, the show quickly vanished from the air. But by the early 1960s, families gathered on Sunday evenings to watch Ed Sullivan introduce the latest Motown sensation. Disc jockeys thought nothing of sandwiching a Rolling Stones track between hits by Martha and the Vandellas and the Four Tops. The seeds of this social revolution were scattered on the winds of radio and television airwaves. While activists preached and lawyers agitated, Motown crept into white homes, southern and suburban, through Radio Free America. Once

the Marvin Gaye poster went up, there was no turning back. White girls swooned over Marvin as had their mothers for Frank Sinatra. Even in the heartland, white boys earnestly attempted Motown dance routines and, for a moment, imagined that they were black.

The specter that this music might incite race mixing was rivaled only by the fear of images of *black* romance. The myth ran deep that among blacks love was characterized more by physical urges than by the complex universe of emotion that transcends motor response. Thomas Jefferson could have been a Hollywood studio executive when he dismissed sentiment among blacks as "less felt and sooner forgotten." If you didn't see *Porgy and Bess*, *Carmen Jones*, or *Paris Blues*, you might have missed Hollywood's entire pre-Motown output of film portrayals of black romance. In the age before videotape, DVDs, and cable, most people, black and white, had never seen affection expressed between blacks in film or on television. While major studios ignored black love affairs, the Motown songwriters understood the poetry of Everyman. These songs explored romance's jagged landscape—infatuation, discovery, love's grip, love lost. They told of brokenhearted men and wrote of women who know "how sweet it is."

A sign over the door of the house on Detroit's West Grand Boulevard read HITSVILLE U.S.A., a slick slogan worthy of the other major presence a half mile down the boulevard, General Motors. Motown's eagerness to market its own assembly line obscured for some what really went on inside that house. Close observers watched the parade of odd-shaped instrument cases that concealed everything from bongos to bassoons, and the procession of young men with skinny ties, cropped hair, and satchels stuffed with staff paper. They were the ones who knew the secret language of song. It *was* a production line but one that dispensed magic. Names such as Ivy Jo Hunter, Sylvia Moy, Hank Cosby, and Clarence Paul were scarcely noticed by a public in love with the flourish of sequined stars. The songwriters, invisible architects of the Motown sound, assembled the substance of everyday into songs that were at once sophisticated and earthy, personal and universal. In many ways, it was the Great American Songbook of the second half of the century.

Fans may have believed that Diana Ross wrote "You Can't Hurry Love." She *was* convincing. The truth is, before a song reached the artist a songwriter or two had labored over the turn of a phrase, reshaping it until its internal rhythm and contours fit the music like counterpoint. Not long after the spark of an idea had blossomed into a song, it was thrust into the glare of the Hitsville proving ground. Each song had to run the gauntlet of rival songwriters, producers, and the man who started it all: Mr. Gordy, who himself had written a string of hits. Berry Gordy instinctively knew that great music is built from the song up. Songs were placed on trial, and any facet, from the euphony of the words to chord structure, was fair game. Morris Broadnax, who, with a teenage Stevie Wonder and Clarence Paul, wrote the masterwork "Until You Come Back to Me," recalls that "new songs were worked on between Tuesday and Thursday, and on Friday all the songwriters presented their best material to the staff. There was so much great music that you hoped that yours was one of the few chosen on Monday." Collaboration and competition sharpened the writing. Smokey Robinson, Holland-Dozier-Holland, Ashford and

Simpson, Strong and Whitfield, and Stevie Wonder would arrive on Fridays and place their latest in the hands of musicians James Jamerson, Benny Benjamin, Robert White, and Earl Van Dyke—the Funk Brothers. Cutting sessions—jazz musicians' venerable device for raising the creative bar—found a home in the basement of Hitsville. It was hand-to-hand musical combat, and whoever was left standing made a record.

Love has long been a staple in the American song tradition. Black songwriters have always created the template for jazz and blues, and W. C. Handy and Duke Ellington knew their way around a love song. But beginning in the 1930s, black artists often looked to Jewish songwriters for a seemingly endless string of pop hits. Cole Porter, Irving Berlin, and George and Ira Gershwin lined the pages of the American songbook with interpretations by the great black singers. The combination was potent. Imagine American song in the absence of Ella Fitzgerald and Louis Armstrong's "Cheek to Cheek" duet or Sarah Vaughan's "April in Paris." This brilliant symbiosis continued in the late '50s and early '60s as black popular artists turned to writers such as Jerry Leiber and Mike Stoller, and Carole King and Gerry Goffin for songs like "Stand by Me" and "Will You Love Me Tomorrow." But Motown—from the musicians and singers to the producers and songwriters—was a community project. While everyone was invited to the party, this music was a product of the tough public housing projects and Detroit's strong black middle-class neighborhoods of neatly cropped lawns, family dinners, and traditions that went back generations. The accumulated musical knowledge of neighborhood masters was summoned. The call went out to poets, arrangers, practitioners of jazz and gospel, and the classically trained to form what writer and producer Clay McMurray describes as a Noah's ark of talent. The studio was said to have been open twenty-four hours a day, seven days a week.

In the 1960s, the times they were a-changin'. Songwriters drew their inspiration from issues of the day. Artists believed in the power of music, that they could change the world with a song. The '60s manifesto assured us that "Blowin' in the Wind" and "We Shall Overcome" could end the war and make the walls of segregation "come tumblin' down." Singer-songwriters chronicled the unfolding social drama, and when they spoke of love it was in the most personal way. Detached, formulaic love songs now seemed anemic, as Bob Dylan and the Beatles redefined the subject matter of popular music. For a love song to grab hold of this generation, something different was required.

The Motown writers responded with songs that transformed the prosaic into the poetic. The girl down the block became a goddess, and the path to her heart, an epic journey. From "Bernadette":

> And when I speak of you, I see
> envy in other men's eyes,
> And I'm well aware of what's on
> their minds.
> They pretend to be my friend,
> when all the time
> They long to persuade you from
> my side.
> They'd give the world and all they
> own
> For just one moment we have
> known.

The Motown roster of artists was packed with female vocalists. Men wrote for Mary Wells, the Supremes, the Marvelettes, Martha and the Vandellas, and every other woman on the label. Sylvia Moy's early compositions—"I Was Made to Love Her," "It Takes Two," "My Cherie Amour"—did much to establish a standard of idealized romance. To write effectively for female vocalists, the male songwriters were forced to immerse themselves in a woman's point of view. Women wait for, agonize over, and celebrate love when it finally arrives. The male songwriters rejected Pavlovian swagger; like Marco Polo bearing gifts from a strange land, they delivered to the male vocalists the textures of romance. Gone was the supposed indifference to the joy and pain of love. These writers discovered love as a force of nature, a celestial presence around which pride, reputation, and the grab bag of male defense mechanisms simply orbited. But this was no weak, victim-of-love routine. The men sang songs infused with unmistakable ardor and palpable virility and with the sort of strength that flows from the yin and yang of love. "Ain't Too Proud to Beg" laments, "I know you want to leave me," and then stiffens, "but I *refuse* to let you go." Marvin implored, "Let's get it on," but assured, "I won't push you, baby." When the men expressed overblown confidence, it was as a foil for the failure to win the love of a woman. "Can't Get Next to You": "I can live forever if I so desire . . . I can make the grayest sky blue . . . But I can't get next to you."

These were strong men who understood the power of love and women's power in love. Grown men dropped to their knees onstage and wished it would rain. It was this willingness to pierce the façade of male invulnerability that endeared

163

Motown to anyone who had a heart. Smokey:

> So, take a good look at my face.
> You'll see my smile looks out of place.
> If you look closer, it's easy to trace
> The tracks of my tears.

When it happened, love was strong, supportive, and reciprocal. Lyricist Nick Ashford, as sung by Marvin Gaye to Tammi Terrell:

> Like an eagle protects his nest,
> For you I'll do my best,
> Stand by you like a tree
> And dare anybody to try and
> move me.

The best of Motown navigates the narrow passage between sophisticated linguistic expression and popular tastes; one obscure metaphor too many, and the audience vanishes. Popular music, by definition, speaks the common tongue. But an overdose of cliché guarantees a song will not survive beyond the moment. Like Billy Strayhorn and Lorenz Hart, the writers of Motown knew that a well-timed intelligent phrase was the soul of cool. It was sexy as hell. It playcd both in the housing projects and in Peoria:

> I did you wrong.
> My heart went out to play.
> But in the game I lost you.
> What a price to pay.

This was soul music, sensual and sweet and unafraid to display its affection publicly. Much of it may have been created in the midst of the bare-knuckle brawl that was, and is, urban life, but the music transcended bitterness in favor of life-affirming dignity. Barrett Strong, who cowrote, among others, "Just My Imagination" and "I Heard It through the Grapevine," cites "real life" as his inspiration: "Most of us came from homes where there was a sense of family and optimism." There was always the whispering sage. Mama said, "You can't hurry love" and "You better shop around." The songs were girded by an African American ethic of grace in romance: Beauty's only skin deep. Wait patiently for the real thing.

America was enchanted. The Supremes graced the cover of *Time* magazine. When the Motown tours went international, European teenagers, who had learned English by singing along with the records, enthusiastically delivered background vocals from the audience. Musical artists from every quarter spoke of Motown with admiration bordering on reverence. The Beatles, Laura Nyro, and James Taylor, master songwriters themselves, recorded Motown songs. Bob Dylan spoke of Smokey Robinson as "the greatest living American poet." Singer-songwriter Jackson Browne compared the songs to the era's engineering marvels produced in Detroit's auto plants. The best Motown songs *are* masterpieces of design. Like Oscar Hammerstein and Cole Porter, these songwriters could tell a story in Technicolor. You were given a private tour of the "seven rooms of gloom," invited to "walk the land of broken dreams," huddle "in the shadows of love," or were shown "a green oasis where there's only sand." The songs were often Greek drama in miniature; you understood what a mess the singer was in, but you also knew he caused it. Hubris was inevitably followed by some humbling comeuppance. Men who thought they had a woman dangling on a string were beaten to the punch and dismissed. Hunters were captured by the game.

In the 1950s, three chords ruled pop music, but these writers served up a Crayola box of harmonic colors. Songs such as "For Once in My Life," "Reflections," and "You're All I Need to Get By" displayed a broad harmonic vocabulary without an air of pretension—like the guy who can walk into a barbershop, use words like *pedantic*, and still be one of the fellas. Products of the Detroit public schools' then-legendary music program and neighborhood joints that still featured live jazz, the Motown songwriters knew song structure from way back. They could back cycle, dangle a plagal cadence, modulate, and flash a little chromaticism without breaking a sweat. When only two chords were needed to get the job done, they could weld C-sharp and F-sharp together so tightly they flowed with the inevitability of night into day. It sounded as if they were the first to discover a simple triad. The Motown songwriters instinctively understood the irreducible principle of writing anything: have something to say, say it, and stop. These writers delivered concise points of view, equal parts declarative and metaphorical: the average length of a Motown hit song between 1963 and 1968 is less than three minutes. The ghetto Zen masters set out the rules of love from the practical to the ethereal as if under the watchful eye of the haiku police. You were advised to ignore friends' advice if love hung in the balance, reassured that pretty girls were a dime a dozen, and emboldened that with a true heart you could still win the girl even if you didn't have a dime.

The musicians, not technically composers, contributed themes that became inseparable from the songs themselves. They echoed the lyrics with uncanny wordless precision. James Jamerson strung together bass lines of Morse code; you could hear Mama's relentless "Love don't come easy / it's a game of give and take." William "Benny" Benjamin introduced tunes with signature drum lines you couldn't imagine the song without. Even the baritone saxophone, a Snuffleupagus of an instrument, sounded hip. These musicians could have gotten people up on the dance floor with a chorus of tubas.

Through the funk, innocence percolated to the surface with birdlike girl singers and the nimble percussion of pizzicato. There were finger snaps against a backdrop of symphony strings. This was music full with anticipation. The days had faded when bluesmen painted the Delta with hard times and hellhounds. These were the '60s. There was talk of living where you wanted, getting jobs because you were qualified, and looking a white man in the eye without risking your life. Mr. Gordy *owned* the record company. Integration was one thing, freedom was another. When in 1964, Sam Cooke sang "Change Is Gonna Come" on the *Tonight Show*, it sounded like the words of a prophet.

As early as the mid-'50s, the nation's vast educational resources had begun to trickle into previously neglected neighborhoods. Smokey Robinson traces his interest in language and composition to the Young Writers' Club, an afterschool workshop convened by Ms. Harris, a visionary elementary school teacher. By the 1960s, a belief and investment in the untapped resources of marginalized Americans was becoming an article of faith. Programs from Leonard Bernstein's Young

People's Concerts to Head Start recognized that by denying opportunity to these communities the nation had robbed itself of untold contributions in science, art, and culture. The concept of a Great Society gained currency. On the neighborhood level, the Detroit public schools taught music theory, composition, and performance as if they mattered. The pace of social change was accelerated in the 1960s. What had been incremental and generational now arrived in clusters. In January of 1963, as Motown began to dominate the pop charts, a sixteen-year-old André Watts, substituting for an ailing Glenn Gould, walked onto the stage at Lincoln Center and delivered, note perfect, Liszt's E-flat Concerto. In 1964, as Motown's grip on the charts tightened, a fresh-faced Cassius Clay thanked America to refer to him henceforth as Muhammad Ali. Berry Gordy brought composers, lyricists, singers, and musicians together with his own defiant gospel of optimism and a belief that with opportunity and a forum for expression there were no limits to what could be accomplished. Their music was part flower-pushing-through-cracks in the concrete and part root shattering it.

The fleeting age of innocence and hope gave way to summers of discontent, and in an act of collective self-immolation black neighborhoods from Watts to Detroit were consumed in flame. A series of events conspired to dismantle the delicate, cautiously entertained aspirations. The descent was punctuated by the assassination of the messengers of change: Malcolm X, John and Robert Kennedy, and Medgar Evers. With the election of Richard Nixon by a silent majority that dismissed social programs as the product of a bleeding heart, reality fell far short of the vision. Hope withered. But for a time the sense of optimism in music held fast. Then, on a spring morning in 1968, word came from Memphis that Martin Luther King Jr. had been shot. The blues were back. As in the old Ellington hook, black America struggled to keep the song from going out of its heart. Within black songwriting, the battle had begun between romance and rump shaking. Defeatism is anathema to art. After what happened to Martin, it seemed that only a fool could believe.

Within months of the King assassination, the Temptations' "Cloud Nine" stripped the veneer of hope and exposed a reality that could be tolerated only through a cloud of marijuana smoke. This moment was more about raw reality than idealized love. From "Ball of Confusion" to "Papa Was a Rollin' Stone" and "Run Away Child (Running Wild)," the promise of a black Camelot settled into sullen defiance. When it came to love, male vulnerability was no longer an option. In "Uptight (Everything's Alright)," Stevie Wonder once bragged that he was the apple of his girl's eye, even though the only shirt he owned was hangin' on his back. Soon a caricature of masculinity would dominate black music. Why contemplate the way to a woman's heart when you could dazzle her with *your* jewelry, a block-long car, and a wad of cash? In the coming decades, music education was phased out of many of the public schools. Those with talent learned to use turntables to scratch out a new beat. Seduced by the illusion of props, a new generation of writers confused bluster with strength, and manhood with an impenetrable heart. Smokey Robinson wrote of love for a woman as "a rosebud blooming in the warmth of the summer sun." But as the African American tradition of romance faded from the music, a woman was more likely to be reduced to her anatomical components.

Still, the legacy of discipline and creative inspiration that defined the early days of Motown is manifest on Marvin Gaye's *What's Going On* and in a series of albums by Stevie Wonder culminating in *Songs in the Key of Life*. The teenage apostles of boy-girl love became standard-bearers of a spiritual, universal love. For them, soul music had evolved into music of the soul. Their lyrics have become sacred text: "War is not the answer, for only love can conquer hate," "Love's in need of love today." As did John Lennon with "Imagine" and John Coltrane with *A Love Supreme*, they looked beyond the personal and dreamed.

A Stevie Wonder lyric lamented that love had taken flight "and then a half a mile from heaven" dropped him back to this cold world. Motown's songs of romance ascended with the promise of change and faded with the onset of cynicism. In the process, the music was itself transformative, inspiring a community defined not by geography, class, or race but by a sense of common experience. The gospel of change that ignited the love affair in black music may have diminished, but for an incandescent moment, Motown celebrated life and love.

# Waiting for Smokey Robinson

*Melba Joyce Boyd*

" Are you sure he's coming?"

"Yeah," my cousin Hayward said with clear conviction.

"How do you know that? Just 'cause you saw him the other day doesn't mean he's gonna show up today," I contested.

We were sitting on the sidewalk of Belmont Street, directly across from the home of Smokey Robinson. It had only been about fifteen minutes, but it felt like forever, and I was bored waiting for the famous Motown artist to appear. Besides, it was summertime in Detroit—hot, humid—and

Hayward, who was seven years old and four years my junior, was notorious for engaging in mischievous pranks. My sister Sandy and I were beginning to suspect that this was another one of his tricks.

Usually when we visited my Aunt Odessa's house, I would nestle next to my older cousin, Bertha Dean, who was twenty-one, and certainly the smartest person in the world—at least the smartest grown-up who would allow me to tag along. As her loyal subject, I was inadvertently in training to become as outspoken as she. After all, we had a special bond. After my grandmother asked my

Smokey Robinson, 1976. © Leni Sinclair Collection.

168

parents to name me "Melba," Bertha Dean offered my middle name, "Joyce."

But earlier that week, she had suffered a sickle cell anemia crisis and was rushed to the hospital for blood transfusions to arrest the violent eruption of white blood cells attacking the red ones. It was like a war raging throughout her entire body. In another year, I would turn twelve and be old enough to visit her in the hospital. I could not have imagined the extremity of the pain. The family enjoined her suffering, and with a laying-on-of-hands prayed for divine intervention. My first visit was the last attack, and she died later that night.

I later came to believe these crises brought her in close proximity to God and, hence, closer to what was true. Bertha Dean never fell for bullshit images on television, especially invented stereotypes of Negroes, nor did she tolerate the internalized stupidity that came out of the mouths of her peers. "Negroes" is what we called ourselves then, because that's what our parents said we were, and because that's what the NAACP had proclaimed as the appropriate name for us at the time. It was 1961.

Bertha Dean later confirmed that Smokey Robinson and his wife, Bernadette, did indeed live in the two-story, two-family brick house down the block. She had seen him on two occasions—once getting into a car, and again in the neighborhood drugstore around the corner on Oakland Avenue. He was seated on a stool at the soda fountain's burgundy, linoleum-covered counter. She had also seen the famous preacher Prophet Jones there. He was another neighborhood celebrity who lived around the block on Arden Park Boulevard in a tacky, red-white-and-blue mansion. There was a huge white star painted above the front door between two large windows—a display of patriotism during the height of the civil rights movement. But Bertha thought his house looked ridiculous, as did his neighbors who shook their heads in disapproval whenever it intruded into view.

Prophet Jones was known more for encoding the "winning number" in his sermons than for his theological prowess. His faithful flock would decipher digits from scripture and verse and later place bets in the "numbers" gambling enterprise to supplement factory paychecks or more modest incomes (and to fill offering plates).

Needless to say, Bertha did not think much of or about Prophet Jones or his religious practices, but she did think that Smokey Robinson and the Miracles were impressive and talented. She played "Shop Around," their first number 1 hit record, and "Everybody's Got to Pay Some Dues" while my sister and I tried to learn the latest teenage dance. Anyway, since she liked Smokey and the Miracles, so did I. Whenever we visited Belmont Street, Sandy and I would wait for Smokey in sun or shade, playing a game of jacks to bide our time.

Upon further investigation, we discovered that Smokey Robinson wasn't the only popular star from this neighborhood. Before she moved into the Brewster Projects, Diana Ross also lived on Detroit's North End. Smokey met Aretha Franklin when she was only three years old through his friend, and her brother, Cecil. Their father, the Reverend C. L. Franklin, who was probably the antithesis of Prophet Jones, supported the civil rights movement and was known for raising funds for Dr. King's Southern Christian Leadership Conference. The Franklins lived in a mansion on Boston Boulevard, two streets from Belmont. While hanging out in the Franklin home with Cecil, Smokey surmised that he "might actually hear the great Clara Ward herself singing in the kitchen" (Smokey Robinson, *Smokey: Inside My Life*, McGraw Hill, 1989, 30). Smokey's mother also sang gospel music in her church choir, and like most black musicians of this era, gospel songs directly impacted Smokey's musical education.

But Smokey did not show up that day, or any other Saturday we held vigil to catch a glimpse of this elusive star, whose lyrics flowed from our radios, filling homes and neighborhoods, blending into the daily sounds of life as naturally as rain or air. Smokey's lyrics highlighted the 45s spinning on our record players, echoes emanating from our high-fidelity stereos while we memorized the words to "The Tracks of My Tears" and harmonized with the voices of the Temptations singing "My Girl." We were determined to master the entire discography of Motown hits, as they were endemic to our heritage, our Detroit style.

## FROM SELMA TO DETROIT

Smokey Robinson's father left Selma, Alabama, and headed to Detroit in a hurry after a violent confrontation with a white man. My father left Selma under more amiable circumstances—to attend college. After he graduated from Tuskegee Institute, he married my mother, and they relocated to Detroit. Smokey and I have roots in the same southern town, and our musical interests and orientations are quite similar. Smokey relays a story of his first performance onstage when he was only three years old. When I was three years of age, I performed in my first ballet recital at the YWCA, where my mother taught swimming.

Growing up in Detroit during the boom period after World War II accorded cultural diversity and educational opportunities that were limited for most blacks in Alabama. Smokey sang in the glee club in elementary school. Likewise, I sang in the glee club and played clarinet in the band at Boynton Elementary School. In his memoir, Smokey recounts how his English teachers encouraged him to write poetry and rhymes.

I still loved school. And teachers like Mrs. Harris made me love it even more. She was this wonderful old white woman with silver gray hair who started the Young Writers' Club. She encouraged us to create little stories, poems and sketches, and man, she'd be displaying some of my work nearly every week in the hallway, even my drawings. I had a Big Ten notebook where I would also be jotting down songs. Mrs. Harris was one of the first to make me see the value of writing.

I was writing and also singing. From the start I was also singing. From the start those two activities were hooked up on my heart. Words rhymed easily in my imagination, and I tried to sing with good articulation.

My musical education started in the fifth grade. (Robinson, 47)

Smokey even formed a quartet, and then another group in junior high, with Cecil [Franklin], Michael Fitzgerald, and Floyd Birch.

While the Detroit Public School District honed his skills and opportunities to perform, African American culture shaped his musical core and nurtured his talents. Smokey says in his autobiography that his musical roots can be traced "to a single source: Sarah Vaughan. . . . Long before I found rock 'n' roll, Sarah was part of my household. I adored her. I idolized her. I found her sound—her perfect enunciation, her lavish phrasing—soothing and sensuous."

Sarah Vaughan was my mother's favorite singer, and I grew up with a deep appreciation and reverence for her voice, as well as for the broad spectrum of jazz greats—Duke Ellington, Billy Strayhorn, Miles Davis, Max Roach, Billy Eckstine, Ella Fitzgerald, and the list goes on. Jazz was the musical score of my childhood that directly, emphatically, deliberately, and by osmosis provided the fundamentals and the sonic schematics for my engagement with all music then and thereafter.

In the '50s, the decade of rock 'n' roll, Smokey was "raised by the dazzling din of doo-wop," and he memorized "the background blends" of Harvey and the Moonglows (Robinson, 51). In addition to national figures, such as Sam Cooke and Frankie Lymon, Smokey admired Jackie Wilson, a Detroit legend, who "could sing high, low and every which-a-way; with his smooth moves and natural polish, he could out dance Fred Astaire" (Robinson, 51). In this same stride, Smokey organized his first singing group, the Five Chimes, while he was still a student at Northern High School (1955–57).

His next group was the Matadors: "Ronnie White, who introduced Smokey to modern jazz; Pete Moore, who 'idolized the gamers'—the pimps and the pool sharks"; and Bobby Rogers, who was a "playboy"; and Claudette Rogers, Bobby's sister, who was their "best dancer." Smokey fell in love with her at first sight (Robinson, 69). After a failed audition to be the opening act for Jackie Wilson,

Berry Gordy, who wrote songs for Wilson, was so impressed with Smokey's songs and the group, he offered to manage them. But Gordy renamed them the Miracles because he thought the Matadors "sounded jive."

## SMOKEY ROBINSON AND MOTOWN

While Berry Gordy recognized Smokey's writing talent, he also identified and told Smokey what his earliest songs lacked: "Your lyrics rhyme up real good, man, but songs are more than rhymes. Songs need a beginning, a middle and end. Like a story" (Robinson, 66). The Smokey Robinson–Berry Gordy relationship grew beyond management into a partnership in songwriting as well as a critical component in the development and success of Motown Records. Robinson not only wrote and performed Motown's first number 1 hit record, "Shop Around," he became a vice president, discovered new talent, and wrote an arsenal of hit songs for the company. It was stated in Smokey's autobiography that:

> Of the some four thousand tunes written or cowritten by Smokey, over three hundred of them were recorded and became prominent in the annals of popular music. In addition to the Miracles and the Temptations, the other Motown groups and solo artists who recorded his songs include: Mary Wells, the Marvelettes, Marvin Gaye, the Four Tops, Martha and the Vandellas, the Isley Brothers, the Contours, and the Supremes. (Robinson, 273)

I came of age during the Motown era, and I was attracted to and fascinated by Motown lyrics. When my siblings and I began to buy records, Motown dominated our rhythm and blues collection. I was not only interested in the performers as stars but also attentive to the songwriters—Smokey Robinson, Sylvia Moy, Holland-Dozier-Holland, Marvin Gaye, and, our contemporary, Stevie Wonder. Smokey wrote the lyrics for "The Way You Do the Things You Do," the Temptations' first big hit. He also wrote "It's Growing," "Since I Lost My Baby," "Get Ready," and "My Girl," which he composed especially for David Ruffin's voice, and it blew up the charts (Robinson, 128–29). In the mid-to-late 1960s, the tempting Temptations became our favorite group—David Ruffin, Eddie Kendricks, Paul Williams, Otis Williams, and Melvin Franklin.

There were four of us, so we were only short one singer, and since no one could imitate Melvin's deep bass, we had to be satisfied with four-part harmony. We wore the grooves off of the album *The Temptations Sing Smokey*, memorizing the words and practicing the steps in their routines as we performed in the secrecy of the basement of our home, where we had full control of the stereo. Although I sang lead on the songs Smokey wrote for Eddie Kendricks, I realized the limitations of my voice, and thought of myself as a "doo-wop girl," a back-up singer, an essential component for a complex and rich sound that cushions the lead singer's execution, accentuating the sensuality and key aspects of a song's theme.

We couldn't wait until the Motown Revue opened at the Fox Theatre downtown. For $1.50, we could go to the matinee and vicariously join their routines by moving our hands and feet while standing in the audience. We sang with Smokey Robinson and the Miracles, the Temptations, Marvin Gaye, Tammi Terrell, Stevie Wonder, the Supremes, Mary Wells, and the Four Tops to the amazing live band—the Funk Brothers. Except the girls in the audience shrieked so loudly for David Ruffin and Smokey, I can't truthfully say I actually heard their voices above the piercing shrills drowning out the performances.

When the British Invasion hit the United States, John Lennon and Paul McCartney praised Smokey Robinson's songwriting skills. Smokey met the Beatles in London in 1964, and they had already recorded "You Really Got a Hold on Me." Likewise, Mick Jagger and the Rolling Stones recorded "My Girl," and as a tribute to Robinson, George Harrison featured the song "Pure Smokey" on his *Thirty Three & 1/3* album. Divas Dionne Warwick and Aretha Franklin also recorded songs by Smokey.

As Motown fans and Detroiters, we appreciated this recognition because for decades many white American performers exploited black music and became stars, while the recordings of black musicians were relegated to the Jim Crow category of "race music." These artists were rarely acknowledged as innovators and entertainers. In the early 1960s, black music was rarely played on mainstream radio stations in Detroit. For the most part, we listened to Motown songs on our transistor radios from sunup to sundown on WCHB, Detroit's first black-owned station. The exception was the Canadian radio station CKLW in Windsor, Ontario, broadcasting just across the Detroit River and the US border.

Motown's universal appeal was its multicultural complexity, which generated an international flavor. As an aspiring musician, I admired and was excited about the unique music emanating out of Hitsville. My fellow band members and I would try to play the tunes by ear because we did not have access to the sheet music. We were trained to play symphonic music, and even scolded by our white high school music teacher whenever we broke out into jazz or rhythm and blues. But that didn't stop us as we applied our classical training to our cultural orientation, attempting to play Motown compositions that, more often than not, were beyond our fledgling abilities. After all, the convergence of jazz, blues, rock 'n' roll, and elements of classical music created Motown's unique sound. However, there was a significant difference between a collection of inexperienced music students and a band that made magic in the Snakepit, Hitsville's recording studio on West Grand Boulevard. The Funk Brothers possessed an unprecedented synthesis of complexity and range, and Smokey aptly describes them as a critical component of Motown's identity:

> Sweeping string arrangements by Paul Riser; incredibly gritty grooves ground out by one of the funkiest rhythm sections in human history—pianist Earl Van Dyke, bassist James Jamerson, drummer Benny Benjamin, guitarists Robert White, Eddie Wilson, and Joe Messina; killer charts by cats like Hank Cosby and Gil Askey; and striking sound singers like Diana and David and Mary and Martha. It was this and more.
>
> The Motown sound was a miracle. It spoke for—it was born from—a special time and place: Detroit, Michigan, in the sixties. It was the combination of an astonishing range of talents, politics and personalities, people who were naïve, happy, hungry for money, looking to be loved and accepted, dying to compete, burning with ambition, blazing with talent—first raw, then refined and finally irresistible. It was black music too damn good—too accessible, too danceable, too romantic, too real—not to be loved by everyone (Robinson, 137).

## LITERARY INFLUENCE

Unlike Smokey and many poets, I did not start writing poetry as a child, nor did I envision myself as a writer. But like most writers, I did grow up reading more than many of my playmates. Before I entered kindergarten, my father taught me how to read. Bookcases were a part of the decor of our home; reading was a part of our lifestyle. But as a teenager, listening attentively to Smokey's lyrics, playing the records over and over and writing down his words had an impact on my vocabulary and poetics. The language was subtly crafted not only to appeal to the sensuousness of the sounds but also to convey and finesse the imagery, rich with metaphors and similes interlaced to tell stories that capture the imagination. I could see the design in the words and feel the emotional value of the compositions. Consequently, I began to understand the meaning of poetic techniques discussed in my English textbooks, even in poems less engaging, less artful, and not as aesthetically interesting or as pleasing as Smokey's lyrics.

Certainly, when I began to write poetry in university it was the consequence of growing up in a literate and literary environment, but I am convinced that I also retrieved the poetics of Motown's vocabulary and its dense reservoir of sounds to create a unique voice. I was not consciously aware that I was doing this at the time, but in his review of my book of poetry, *The Inventory of Black Roses,*

MELBA JOYCE BOYD

in *The Black Scholar: Journal of Black Studies and Research* Lorenzo Thomas wrote about me: "Her voice is strikingly her own—Motown mellow and resonant" (50).

Motown music influenced many Detroit writers. The playwright Ron Milner incorporated Smokey's music into his play *Theme for Linda*, and these were the lines that impressed me as a graduate student of literature and language. I was aware of the influence, emulation, and incorporation of black music into black literature, but it was the first time I encountered music from my generation and my hometown in a major literary work. When Milner passed in 2004, I wrote a tribute poem, "Stage Black," in his honor. The opening stanza contains an allusion to Smokey's literary influence on Milner, and likewise on me:

I first met

you inside a play,

peering inside

the mind

of the character

Linda lamenting

with Smokey's

romantic croon—

"more love,

more love"—

a scene scripted

to a Motown tune.

I Second That Emotion

Bob Dylan once called Smokey Robinson "America's greatest living poet." I suppose Dylan arrived at this conclusion after realizing the power of Smokey's poetics. Reconstructing human experiences with words to convey meaning beyond language requires entrance into an artistic zone, a spiritual space that connects your thoughts and feelings with humans you've never known and may never meet. It is a nearly impossible task, albeit a wonderful pursuit. Smokey Robinson achieved that quest with distinction, repeatedly reaching millions of people around the planet, touching us in myriad ways and at unanticipated moments.

On a hot summer evening in August 1976, I was covering the Detroit Kools Jazz Festival as a freelance writer for the *Detroit Sun* newspaper (previously the *Ann Arbor Sun*) and Smokey Robinson was on the program. Unlike my Motown Review experiences at the Fox Theatre, where I was buried in a sea of screaming fans, this time I had a press pass.

I was backstage, in the left wing. Smokey was in clear view. His voice filled the space, surrounding me without the dissonance of audience response. I listened intently to the songs—some oldies but goodies and some more recent tunes from his 1976 release, *Smokey's Family Robinson*. His voice was clear and strong; and, despite the perils and challenges of an entertainer's lifestyle, he looked vibrant and even younger than his thirty-six years.

Armed with notepad, a 35 mm Minolta camera, and a telephoto lens, I wrote down my impressions and snapped several photos of him, the backup singers, and the band. I surmised that after his performance, if I stood firmly in position, he would have to pass right by me.

So, I waited with the clear conviction of Hayward and the confidence of Bertha Dean. I knew I would meet Smokey Robinson that night.

Midway through the performance, Smokey introduced the band and the backup singers. Time seemed to stop, when he announced: "Melba Joyce."

I thought I was hearing things, because he couldn't be calling me. Then, a young woman onstage smiled and tilted her head in Smokey's direction in response. If he would have said, "Melba," I might have hesitated, but even that would have caught my attention because my first name is unusual. I often have to repeat it, and make reference to Melba toast or peach Melba for people to recognize it. But he said my first and my middle name.

After the last song, Smokey waved at the audience and walked directly toward me. As he approached, he said, "Hello," and offered a cursory, "How ya doing?"

"Fine," I said with a smile. But my focus was on Melba Joyce, who was exiting the stage, a few steps behind Smokey. I rushed past him and greeted her.

"I must introduce myself." She stopped, smiling all the while. "My name is Melba Joyce Boyd."

"Really!" She was equally surprised. Of course, she was not from Detroit and was living and working in New York. She was featured on Smokey's new album as "on vocals." A few years later, I smiled while thinking about our chance encounter when I saw her (our) name listed as producer for a concert advertised in the Sunday *New York Times*.

"You won't believe this," she said. "I almost married a man with the last name Boyd," she exclaimed, which took our fates to another level of irony. I was waiting to meet Smokey, but I was actually waiting to meet Melba Joyce, the doo-wop girl. I couldn't wait to tell Sandy and Hayward.

175

Flo Ballard. Photo courtesy of Peter Benjaminson.

# Flo Ballard
## The Love Supreme
*Peter Benjaminson*

Florence Glenda Ballard, who died in 1975, was the founding member of the Supremes, the most successful female singing group in history. An international singing star by age twenty-one, she performed with the other two original Supremes, Mary Wilson and Diana Ross, before and during their glory years, 1964–67. Of the fourteen records they recorded during those years, five in a row and ten altogether rose to number 1 on the pop charts. In 1965 and 1966, five of the nine singles they recorded hit number 1.

Only the Beatles, the world's other top group at that time, would exceed the Supremes' record, but to maintain their status, the lads from Liverpool had to duke it out with the young women from Motown month after month. While the Fab Four's "Can't Buy Me Love," "Love Me Do," "A Hard Day's Night," and "Penny Lane" climbed the charts to number 1, pop perfections such as "Where Did Our Love Go?" "Baby Love," "Stop! In the Name of Love," and "You Keep Me Hangin' On" were right there alongside them.

The trio of singers Florence Ballard brought together was indisputably the most popular group the famed Motown Record Company ever produced. As late as 2006, a drawing of Ballard, Ross, and Wilson—the original Supremes—graced the cover of the Motown History Museum brochure. A banner commemorating "Stop! In the Name of Love" hung on the Detroit museum itself, a memorial to one of Motown's most popular songs.

The Supremes may have made seamless music together, but its members were not at all alike. In the beginning, at least, Flo was the spunky, funny one. Something of a comedienne onstage, she was, said Marvin Gaye, "a beautiful person—loving and warm. . . . She was down to earth, she loved to laugh and everyone loved her." Ex-boyfriend Roger Pearson called her "a great lady, a very proud person, and a person with a lot of dignity. I never heard her say one unkind word about anyone else." Flo's friend and the widow of Motown producer Hank Cosby, Pat Cosby, said, "Flo always greeted me with a smile, and that smile represented who she was."

Flo Ballard had auburn hair and such light skin that her friends called her Blondie. Beautiful, tall, and statuesque, she was never, during her performing years, as heavy as the wonderfully talented women who portrayed her in the Broadway and movie versions of *Dreamgirls.*

Mary Wilson was actually the quiet one. Serious and responsible, she was determined to survive, and if possible prosper, in what she correctly perceived to be an environment filled with traps and pitfalls.

Diana Ross was a skilled, hardworking, very slender, and attractive woman who was, by nearly all accounts, the most determined of the Supremes. Blessed with talent and drive, she was resolved not just to be successful but to be magnificently successful.

There is little disagreement that Florence Ballard had the strongest and most soulful voice of the three

Supremes. She could have competed seriously with fellow Detroiter Aretha Franklin, who sang for Atlantic Records. Flo's voice was deep and powerful but had sadness in it, too. "Flo was caught between poverty and opulence," said Pearson. "She was only two years out of the projects and into a whole new reality of opulence when she became a star." It was perhaps this in-between status that allowed Flo to sing both melancholy and cheerful songs with tremendous passion and believability.

Milton Jenkins, the manager of the Primes, who later became the Temptations, was looking around for some young female singers. Flo's sister Maxine told Jenkins that Flo could really sing. Jenkins wanted to hear Flo, so in early 1959 he invited her over to his residential hotel, which was not too far from the Brewster Projects, to sing for him and two of the Primes, Eddie Kendricks and Paul Williams.

Maxine took Flo over there, and as Flo said simply, "I stood there and sang one of the songs from the '50s." But there was much more to it than that. Flo knew instinctively that this was an important moment. If Jenkins rejected her and found other girls for his group, or if he abandoned the whole idea of a girl group, her career might be over forever.

Flo rose to the challenge. What Jenkins saw and heard that day was what people in the music business call "the real deal." As a witness to one of Flo's early performances told author J. Randy Taraborrelli, "She gave it her all, hitting the high notes, holding them with perfect pitch, selling the song . . . giving the total entertainer's package." Jenkins was impressed. He immediately asked her if she knew any other young women who could sing. "I said, 'No,'" Flo remembered, "then 'Yeah, I know a girl that can sing: Mary, Mary Wilson.'" Jenkins

asked Flo to bring Mary back with her. If Mary sang as well as Flo did, Jenkins said, the two would be the nucleus of a new singing group.

Mary remembers Flo running up to her in a school hallway, out of breath, and telling her about this astounding offer. According to Mary, while Flo panted out the details, she gripped Mary's arm very tightly, so tightly it almost hurt. There was no suspenseful period of consideration. As soon as Mary heard the word "singing," she said yes.

When Flo and Mary returned to Jenkins's apartment, Paul Williams was the only one there. Williams asked them if they knew any songs, Flo began singing "Night Time Is the Right Time," and Mary joined in. Williams liked what he heard, and the Primettes were born.

Thus, Florence Ballard founded the Primettes, later renamed the Supremes. Flo would call the creation of the world's most successful female singing group the major achievement of her life, and in the beginning, she was indeed its undisputed leader. She was older than Mary and Diana and sang with a full, warm, gospel-tinged voice that was stronger than theirs. "It was Flo's voice that put us over," Mary said.

Before any more songs were pressed or released, Motown execs decided that Primettes wouldn't cut it as the group's name—it was too 1950s. The young women themselves were asked to choose a new name from among the many ideas typed out on a sheet of paper, including the Darleens, the Sweet Ps, the Melodees, the Royaltones, and the Jewelettes. Part of the urgency for changing the name was that Gordy now wanted the girls to sign contracts with Motown, and he wanted a group that would keep its moniker, rather than change its name after signing, thereby consigning thousands of dollars of publicity to the ash heap.

The women were given an hour to choose the group's new name. Flo chose the Supremes and insisted on it despite opposition from Diana. "I gave us the name 'Supremes,'" Flo said proudly. She saw it as a link with the name Primettes, which means pretty much the same thing. "Diana said, 'No, it sounds like a man's group.' But I bet she's glad to this day that the group was named the Supremes," Flo said.

The Supremes started as girlhood friends, worked their way to the top as hardworking young women, and gained international fame as talented, glamorous superstars. Along the way, their friendship was sorely tested, and the struggle for each woman's position within the group became increasingly bitter. Flo was allowed to do the lead on "Buttered Popcorn" and on the Sam Cooke hit "Ain't That Good News." On *The Ed Sullivan Show*, Flo and Diana performed "You Keep Me Hangin' On" almost as a duet, with Flo's strong voice filling out and underscoring every word sung by Diana. Flo's voice can also be heard in all its glory in the two other recorded Supremes songs in which she was featured as the lead, "Hey Baby" and "Heavenly Father." One Detroit critic had commented, "The group has two lead singers, and only one is being featured." Otis Williams of the Temptations wrote that Flo's voice "had a real depth of feeling and a strong churchy sound. When Flo opened her mouth to sing, you sat up in your chair."

But as the Supremes' star rose, Florence began to feel her role diminish. In February 1963, when the group was recording a country and western album on which Florence had been given the lead on one of the tunes, according to Flo, Diana broke off the recording, walked into the control room, and told the producers that she was the lead singer for all the songs. "Mary and I heard it through the earphones, and neither one of us could believe it," Flo said. "We had started out as children—that's what we were, fourteen or fifteen—and I felt that because of our relationship, because we were as close as I thought we were, the lead should have been spread around, as in, 'You do this, and I'll do that.' But it wasn't. Diane wanted the complete lead, the complete control of the group."

And Diana kept getting what she wanted. Flo was originally slated to sing the lead on "The House of the Rising Sun" on the Supremes album *A Bit of Liverpool*, but that was taken from her. She and Diana had shared the lead on the song "Manhattan," meant for *The Supremes Sing Rodgers & Hart*, but the song was cut from the album and not released until 1986, ten years after Flo's death. When Flo did the "Silent Night" lead for a Christmas album, the recorded track was mysteriously "messed up," in Flo's words, and not released for many years.

Flo's last remaining lead, in "People (Who Need People)," was taken from her in one of several dramatic ways—depending on whom you believe—in the summer of 1965. The lead on "People" was tailor-made for Florence's soulful sound and not at all suited to Diana's voice, and at first the women were very democratic about it; Flo was assigned the lead at the beginning of the song, and Diana took the lead in the middle of the tune. Florence even thought that the "People" lead should be spread around among all three singers. There was a recent precedent for this—when the group had recorded a country album, each woman had sung a verse of the lead on one song, Willie Nelson's "It Makes No Difference Now." As Flo later said, "It's a heavy load to get up there and do two shows a night, with the

179

lead on every song. But Diane wanted to be the lead singer on every song."

And Berry Gordy agreed that she should be. According to Nelson George, author of *Where Did Our Love Go?*, the Motown head dismissed Flo's aspirations as a lead performer at a rehearsal at a Detroit nightclub, the Roostertail, in front of most of the Motown brass. Flo was allegedly only four bars into "People" when Gordy told her to stop. "Let Diana do the song," Gordy said. Flo flinched visibly and began crying, according to George.

According to Mary Wilson's account, however, the Copa was the site of a less dramatic scene. Wilson wrote that Harvey Fuqua, a Motown employee in charge of the company's Artist Development Department, merely "announced" that Flo would no longer perform "People." Many wondered about the announcement, since Flo had performed the tune on opening night at the Copa and, even though she had just recovered from the flu, sounded terrific. "A couple of nights later, however, Diane was singing it," Wilson wrote. According to Wilson, "We all suspected that Berry had taken the song from Flo, but Flo was thoroughly convinced of it, and she was crushed. How much more of the spotlight did Diane need? From that moment on, Flo regarded what was in fact the highest achievement of her career as a disaster. She was sad and moody, and I could see the three of us being torn apart."

Wilson wrote that Flo's response was to get defensive, and "understandably so. A talented singer and the founder of the group, Flo felt that her professional existence was being threatened."

All Flo would say in 1975 was, "They stopped me from singing the lead on 'People.' They said the show was too long or something."

With that, the battle for lead singer was effectively over, and Ross had won.

Flo fought against her diminishing role in the group she had founded by speaking up on behalf of what she perceived to be group interests. "In between [nightclub acts], if we came home," Flo said, "we'd be doing recording. We never really had that much of a vacation. I believe that sometimes we were overworked, 'cause we worked practically the whole year without a break. And if we did come to Detroit, we were working because we were still recording, which is a job, too. I objected—me—and Berry Gordy said I was the one who would always sit down, always think. I'm always thinking. I'm the type of person if I can't think, then something is wrong. So we were in New York one time, and he said, 'You girls are off for ten days, but I don't think I'll let you have a vacation, because Florence talks too much.'"

Flo's underlying aim had been to reassert some of her leadership of the group, but Gordy's reaction did not exactly buttress her position or even make her popular with her sidekicks.

Flo also fought back in other, counterproductive ways. Right or wrong, she believed that her founding and early domination of the group, along with her talent, should have made her the Supremes' permanent leader and she should have the enduring right to sing the lead on at least some songs. When leadership was denied her, she sometimes became sullen and angry. Generally happy, playful, and funny, she could also display a quick temper and sometimes responded to what she interpreted as insults, or attempts to limit her freedom, by challenging the offender verbally or even physically. It has been alleged that on one occasion she threw a drink in Gordy's face, which, if true, certainly would have made her situation worse.

Soon Flo discovered another outlet for her anger and frustration: comedy. "I said, 'If I can't sing "People" anymore, I'll start doing some comedy.' It just dropped out of the sky. Growing up, I used to jump around and kid around and this and that, but I never knew I had comedy potential."

Following a Motown script of onstage banter, Diana had started referring to Flo, onstage behind her, as "the fat one." One night Flo retorted—deep-voiced, sotto voce, and unscripted—"Honey, fat is where it's at." Laughter engulfed the crowd, and Sammy Davis Jr., who was in the audience, jumped straight into the air out of his seat and began applauding wildly, as did Harry Belafonte. Flo had neither planned this event nor anticipated the audience reaction, and her boldness frightened her.

"I was shocked. I was looking around and saying to myself, 'What did I do? Where did I get the nerve to interrupt the act?' I didn't even know I was that funny. It just came out of my mouth, out of nowhere. I was just ad-libbing on stage. Berry Gordy came backstage after the performance and told me, 'You stole the show.' And I said to myself, 'Uh-oh, stole the show' and worried even more."

After her worry subsided, however, she began planning her guerrilla attacks in advance. "One song had a line, 'Gold won't bring you happiness.' And I'd say, 'Wait a minute, honey. Give me some of that gold, and I'll do my own shopping.'" Another version of this dialogue emerged when Diana would sing, "You may be rich; you may possess the world and all its gold, but gold won't bring you happiness when you're growing old," and Flo would respond, "Now wait a minute, honey; I'm not so sure about that."

Flo was stretching when she called this comedy. It may have struck the audience as wildly amusing, but in reality Flo was clearly protesting being shunted to the sidelines by calling attention to herself.

"After a while," Flo recalled, "I knew exactly what to say and how to say it. I would wait until the audience had stopped applauding and then deliver another line. And that started them off again."

"I'm a strong believer in God, and I don't know where the words came from or what happened, but it just happened, and that was it. Whenever I saw a spot where I could get it in, then I would get it in. . . . Berry Gordy liked what I was doing, because he would come backstage to try to perfect my comedy, 'Say it this way; say it that way.' But I had to say it my way. . . . Saying it my way kept it coming across."

At the Coconut Grove, where the group performed for a doctor's convention, "Diane would say, 'At the end is Florence Ballard. She's the quiet one.' I would be way back from the mic. And I would say, 'That's what you think.'" The audience laughed loudly.

The issue of Flo's weight and the varying reactions it engendered had already appeared in joke form in the Supremes' stage patter. Under the thin veneer of humor, the women played out their very real personal conflicts in front of audiences that dimly understood what was happening.

Soon, however, Gordy began teasing Flo about something besides her weight. "He'd say, 'Florence, you drink too much,'" according to Flo. Her initial reaction was, "In other words, I guess I was supposed to say I was an alcoholic, from drinking two or three beers [a day]."

181

MOTOWN

Flo acknowledged that the Supremes drank casually in nightclubs, even when they were performing. "That was not unusual," she said. "Mary, Diane, all of us had drinks before we went onstage, or any time we felt like it." But she was also aware that she was sinking into depression as it became increasingly obvious to her than an effort was under way to eject her from the group, noting, "To be depressed and to drink with depression can cause a whole bunch of turmoil, especially when you are actually angered, as I was toward Berry, and I just began to lose all respect for him."

Flo's anger at Gordy and his effort to push her out of the group she had founded caused her to push her drinking, and her aggressive behavior, to a new level. Mary Wilson wrote, "Diane and I could drink without suffering any ill effects, but Flo's tolerance for alcohol was almost nil. After just one beer, she would be unsteady; any more than that and she was clearly intoxicated."

On Flo's last night performing as a Supreme, she recalled, "At this particular incident at the Flamingo in Las Vegas, I had me a few drinks. . . . And they kept calling me fat so much until I went on stage and I poked my stomach out as far as I could." Alcohol had undoubtedly clouded Flo's judgment, and this time, it would seem, she'd gone too far, giving Gordy the excuse he'd been looking for to cut her out of the group.

[Gordy] called me up the next morning and he said, "You're fired." And I said, "I'm what?" And he said, "You're fired." I said, "I'm not." And he said, "Well, you're not going on stage tonight.'" I said, "Yes, I am; who's going to stop me?" He said, "I will. I'll

182

have you thrown off if you go on." So it went on and on and on. I told him, "I'm going onstage, and that's the end of that," and hung up. And then his sister, Gwen Gordy, called and said, "I guess you know that my brother can't make you leave the group, because you have a contract." So it went on and on and on until finally I said to myself, "Oh, well, what the hell, I'll be miserable as hell out here anyways as long as he's around, so I just might as well leave." So I left. They had Cindy Birdsong already there. I don't know how long she had been there, but they had her there, and I flew on back to Detroit.

With that, what *Variety* had referred to as the "superb distinctive blend" of Ballard, Wilson, and Ross was over. Florence Ballard was twenty-four years old.

Although to some extent Flo may have brought on the expulsion herself, the effect it had on her was crushing. Being kicked out of the Supremes "stole her spirit and stole her energy," Roger Pearson said. "Flo felt something important had been stolen from her." Millions of Supremes fans believe there was something magical about the Supremes that the breakup ended forever. "Their three personalities formed a fourth, the Supremes," Pearson said. Florence's later decline, he insisted, was due to her inability to handle the impact of this betrayal, not an inability to handle fame.

Flo's expulsion from the Supremes in the summer of 1967 was immediately followed by the renaming of the group Diana Ross and the Supremes. Diane had won the biggest victory of her career.

# Mary Wells, "My Guy," and the Queen of Motown

*Peter Benjaminson*

Years before Diana Ross, Mary Wells was the first Motown superstar, the internationally popular songstress who sang the megahit "My Guy." Her songs crossed the color line and reached huge white (and black) audiences in America and England consistently, repeatedly, and seemingly miraculously.

Wells achieved star status with her very first song, which she wrote herself, without any musical training, and sold directly to Motown. It soon became a hit, as did almost every one of the succeeding songs she recorded for Motown and many of the songs she recorded for other companies. She set the tone for the many female Motown vocalists that came after her, showing them what they could do and how popular they could become. At the height of her career, she was the biggest-selling female soloist in the world.

Wells hit number 45 on the popular music chart and number 8 on the rhythm and blues chart with her first recorded song. Most of the succeeding songs she recorded for Motown did as well or better. She was the first artist on the Motown label to have a Top 10 and number 1 single, and she was the first to record an album for that label. And her departure from Motown gave the world its first sign that all was not sweetness and light at America's first major black-owned music company.

But Mary Wells was much more than a singer with an alluring voice. Without her irrepressible fighting spirit, along with a belief in her own talent that bordered on arrogance and sometimes inadvertently hurt her, she would never have progressed as far as she did. She also had to overcome a personal history that was extraordinarily tumultuous even by music world standards.

Raised by a stepfather she never felt close to and who sometimes abused her mother, Mary Wells spent most of her adult life searching for a man she could count on. She had a series of affairs and marital attachments with men, some of whom were famous, who in the end never seemed to be able to deliver the kind of safety she was looking for.

Mary Wells. Photo courtesy of Peter Benjaminson.

183

Many of Mary's romantic entanglements were worthy of a daytime soap opera. In 1964, she hid in fear in a hotel bathroom as her first husband shot her business manager in the head. Later, she accomplished the relatively rare feat of marrying two brothers, one after the other—both of them from the well-known Womack music family—and having children with both.

While all this was going on, Mary, who spent much of her post-Motown life on the road, scratching out a living as a touring artist, managed to survive several dangerous illnesses and endure at least two spectacular auto accidents, complete with shouted prayers to God and flying animals. By her own account, she was kidnapped by crazed fans during a road trip and driven halfway across America. She also tried to manage an extensive career while being a drug user.

Wells also fought a drawn-out and courageous battle with throat cancer, in some ways the most frightening disease that could strike a singer who made her living, especially in her later years, by her voice alone, rather than from hit records and royalties. In the gutsiest performance of her life, she refused to lose hope, and spent precious time near the end of her life in an anti-cancer crusade that included testimony to the US Congress about the need to continue to fund research aimed at curing cancer.

Having been brought up a religious young lady and virtually an only child, the teenage Mary was used to talking to God. So, she said, "I went into my closet, my secret closet" and asked God to help her write a song for star vocalist Jackie Wilson. The song "Bye Bye Baby" came into her mind, and she wrote it down. "Mary was a very mystical woman

and a spiritual little soul," Curtis Womack, her third husband, said years later.

Mary's "secret closet" contained not only her source of spiritual guidance but her ability to do things without a man, a talent she exercised only rarely during her life. But by writing this song herself, she pole-vaulted herself immediately into a different and a better universe than the one in which she had grown up. She did this on other occasions as well, and the results were always good.

Looking for a way to get the song to Wilson, she remembered that Robert Bateman of the Satin-Tones had told her to keep asking for membership in his singing group. She also realized that she had been friendly with a girl Bateman wanted to date, so she offered to introduce the girl to Bateman if he would arrange for her to sing the song she had written for Motown Records president Berry Gordy.

Mary wasn't aiming the song at Motown, however. She knew that Wilson recorded for Brunswick Records, not the struggling young Motown. Instead, she wanted to get the attention of Gordy, who had written nine hit singles for Wilson, including "To Be Loved," "I Love You So," "I'll Be Satisfied," and, in 1958, "Lonely Teardrops," which had hit number 1 on the rhythm and blues (black) charts and, very significantly, number 7 on the popular music (white) charts.

What Mary didn't realize was that because of a change of executives at Brunswick and a dispute over royalties, Gordy no longer wrote anything for Brunswick or Wilson. If any song she brought to Gordy was going to be recorded, Motown Records would do it.

After composing and memorizing the song she created (she couldn't read or write music and never wrote it down), Mary sang it for Bateman. He said he liked it, and he told her he'd get her a chance to let Gordy hear it. Her chance finally came when, directed by Bateman, she caught up with Gordy at the Twenty Grand, Detroit's hottest nightclub.

Gordy, busy directing a performance by vocalist Marv Johnson on one side of the club, and on his way to do the same thing for the Miracles on the other side, literally walked away when Mary started talking, saying he was too busy to listen to her sales pitch. Mary followed him down the hallway almost in lockstep, begging for an appointment so she could present him with the song she had written. Finally, annoyed, Gordy turned around and told her to "sing it right now." Mary immediately sang "Bye Bye Baby" a cappella on the spot.

What Gordy saw was a young, doe-eyed black girl from the Detroit ghetto, who, author J. Randy Taraborrelli noted, favored Dynel "House of Beauty" wigs and tight gowns that fanned out at the knees. Her enormous eyes and the Lauren Hutton–like gap between her two front teeth enchanted Gordy and would enchant many others. At seventeen, Mary was physically mature, with an attractive voice and appearance.

The voice Gordy heard was later described by one critic as "a unique contrasting blend of intimacy and assertion, a softness and a forcefulness all rolled into one."

She impressed Gordy so much—he later called her "a soulful-sounding chick"—that when she showed up at Motown at his request the next day, he told her she would record her song herself. Wells was so excited she whooped loudly and jumped around the office. She later said, "I just had wanted to be in the record business. I didn't think I could

ever be an artist." Gordy signed her as a Motown recording artist that day, July 8, 1960. (The legal age for signing contracts in Michigan was eighteen, so Mary brought her mother along to cosign the contract and make it legal.)

Several people have described Mary as shy and winsome, which was the way she often acted. But by singing a song a capella to a man she'd never met, she showed she was anything but shy. Vocalist Martha Reeves, who performed often with Mary both at Motown and later in life, insisted that, far from being bashful, "Mary was so confident that her very first song had a hit factor that she represented herself, and approached Gordy unafraid. She stood for all the courage and perseverance that any female should need to enter into show business and take a place in it." Mary's basic personality didn't change. A few years before her death, an English journalist described her as "attractive, friendly, and direct." Throughout her life, she went straight after any goal she wanted and did not stop until she had achieved it.

Like her voice, however, her personality harbored numerous contradictory elements, which added to her legend over time. She was sometimes shrewd but often broke, deeply religious but often sinful, and on many occasions aggressive and vulnerable simultaneously. But she did not stop being energetic until she lay dying.

By going along with Gordy and recording her first song on the Motown label, Mary became the first artist ever recorded on that label, which would become one of the most famous labels in pop music history. After two more hits by Mary on Motown, Gordy transferred most of his other promising artists, including the Supremes and Steve Wonder, from Tamla to Motown.

Mary recorded "Bye Bye Baby" as a raw R&B "shouter" in the style of Big Mama Thornton, Ruth Brown, and LaVern Baker. It was recorded on the A side of the record. She also sang the song "Please Forgive Me," which was placed on the B side.

At the recording session for "Bye Bye Baby," which was also Wells's first recording session ever, Gordy required her to do twenty-two takes of the tune before selecting the one he found acceptable.

Reviewers noted that while Mary's voice in subsequent songs was smooth and alluring, her voice on "Bye Bye Baby" could be described as a "gutsy gospel growl." Mary said that was because she had to sing the song twenty-two times. She didn't like repeating the song so many times in a row, and her growl wasn't the only indication of that exasperation: she ended the song with three banshee-like wails, a performance she never repeated on any other record.

The twenty-two repetitions of "Bye Bye Baby" were necessary, according to Mary, because at the time Motown had only a one-track recording system. On a one-track system, the background singers, the backup band, and the vocalist had to record simultaneously. Often, if the lead singer or any background singer or musician made a mistake, the whole taping was ruined, and everyone had to go back and start again. (Mary didn't mention it, but having to do as many as twenty-two takes might also have been a result of her inexperience, as well as the inexperience of some of the other performers and engineers who were working for the young company.)

Some years later, each component of a record was recorded on a separate track, which meant that one person's mistake didn't require a retake by all. In fact, multitrack taping forever severed the connections among the people making the record.

They didn't have to record together, in the same town, at the same time, or, for that matter, in the same era. Big-time groups would dash into town between tours to record their parts of future hits on top of background tracks already recorded and waiting for them.

Released in December 1960, Mary's "Bye Bye Baby" reached number 8 on the rhythm and blues charts early in 1961 and crossed over to a respectable number 45 on the pop charts. It stayed on the charts for three months. Especially in those days, for a black female singer to record a tune that landed this high on the pop chart and stayed on it for this long was unusual and encouraging. With the success of this record, Mary became Motown's first successful female solo singer.

The record also ended her career as a Motown songwriter. After its success, Gordy and his executives decided that in comparison to Mary's raw but effective songwriting skills, her voice, appearance, and singing ability were her biggest assets.

The music business is notorious for forcing the actual writer of a song to divide the songwriting credit with others, often including the owner of the company that records it. This leads to a diversion of some of the royalties from the writer to the owner. Gordy was not immune to this temptation. But in this instance, he let Mary keep all the writing credit for her first record. Mary's longtime friend Randy Russi credits this to Gordy's desperate search at the time for a successful female solo artist for his new company and his feeling that Mary would be the one. As Randy put it, Gordy, filled with gratitude, "was straight up and did Mary right" in this instance. Martha Reeves, who knew Mary when both she and Mary were young, noted that Gordy, by signing

Mary to Motown and then treating her right on royalties on her first song, "became a father figure to her" and thus a very important person in Mary's life.

Mary's instant success startled Detroit. "You heard 'Bye Bye Baby' at least six or seven times a day on [Detroit-area radio stations] WCHB, CKLW, and WXYZ," Martha Reeves told Susan Whitall, the author of *Women of Motown*.

Mary's continued rise in spite of the growth of the girl group phenomenon was vastly aided by the fact that, shocked at the failure of her third record, Gordy soon appointed his best friend, songwriter Smokey Robinson, to replace William "Mickey" Stevenson as her producer. He made the right choice. Wells and Robinson became Motown's first successful teaming of a songwriter/producer and an artist. The songs Mary sang under Smokey's direction were the classics she will always be remembered for.

While Gordy and Stevenson had encouraged Mary to belt out her first three songs in a low-down blues-and-gospel style, Robinson recognized Mary's true artistic asset: the girlish, sensuous, and vulnerable quality of her voice. Stevenson noted years later that "she had an innocent sound, almost a childlike innocence. It wasn't a great voice, but it was such an innocent voice, you were drawn into her sincerity. She had not been tainted." As author Nelson George put it, Mary, under Smokey's direction, sang "sweetly, coolly, and straightforwardly, sticking close to the melody line."

Adding to the appeal of Mary's music, her innocent voice contrasted sharply with the sometimes sensuous, sometimes suggestive lyrics that were written for her. As a result, in contrast to the deluge of louder, more playful, more adolescent-sounding girl group records flooding the market,

Mary sang her next few hits with the flavor of a knowing, worldly veteran of love.

Robinson built on this quality in Mary's voice by encouraging her to sing in a higher register with a sincere pop style in which only a touch of suffering and sadness could be heard. She followed his directions, then added her own smooth, knowing coyness, like a layer of delicious frosting, right on top.

Underlying the entire structure was a calypso beat. Robinson, a big fan of vocalist Harry Belafonte's calypso tunes, purposefully added this beat, which he called "an island-flavored bongo bop," to almost all the songs he wrote for Mary.

In 1962, her first record with Robinson, "The One Who Really Loves You" backed with "I'm Gonna Stay," rose to number 2 on the R&B charts and number 8 on the pop charts, appealing equally and massively to both black and white audiences and making Mary Motown's most consistent hit maker. Mary marveled at its success: "I didn't think 'The One Who Really Loves You' was going to be a Top 10 hit, because I was so used to people giving me records where I belted out songs," she said.

"Mary became my pet project," Robinson said. "Shy and eager to please the producer, she'd done a wonderful job on the first recording. I liked writing for her voice and experimenting with her sound."

Robinson told another interviewer that Mary "was a completely devoted artist. I'd teach her these songs at the piano. . . . As I went over the phrasing patterns she paid strict attention." He added that "she was always excited about the songs."

In "The One Who Really Loves You," Mary sounded soft, devoted, and delicately emotional, a plus for her and for her recordings. By singing demurely, she stayed much closer to herself at her best than she had when she had imitated big-voiced ghetto mamas on her pre–Smokey Robinson recordings. And as Mary noted, "If you're singing something soft with soul, you're going to sing it with feeling."

When Mary and Robinson worked together on a song he had written for her, Robinson worked closely with Mary but allowed her a great deal of freedom, she told interviewer Steve Bergsman. "He would play and sing it, then I would record the melody . . . in my head," she said. "I would get as close as I could to singing the basic melody, then I would emphasize certain points on certain phrases to make the picture of the song." Wells said that although Robinson "wanted me to put more of myself into each song," she sought feedback from him on "whether I was singing it closer to his dream, the way he wanted it." He would respond with advice aimed at particular passages, like, "Sing it like it really hurts you, Mary." According to Bateman, "Motown was a writer-producer-oriented company. You sang the record the way the producer told you to sing it."

From a different viewpoint, as Claudette Robinson later commented, "Mary had become Smokey's female counterpart." Bateman put it more dramatically. "When I had the radio turned down low," he said, "I'd say to myself, 'That's Smokey,' but when I turned it up, it would be Mary."

But Mary insisted that "once I got into the song, and put my life into it, what's natural would come out of me." Sometimes what was natural came out of her mouth on an extended basis. When she was recording "The One Who Really Loves You," she was singing over a prerecorded background track that kept running after Mary ran out of scripted words. A natural trouper, she just started ad-libbing, and the words stayed in the song.

Mary's best friend, Maye Hampton James-Holler, said the word among Motown producers was that it was simple to work with Mary and to convince her to sing a song the way the producers wanted her to. "Mary would hear a song one time and then she could record it," Maye said. "They didn't have to take the time to tell her, 'Hit this note and this note.' She'd just go in there and Smokey would sit there, singing it, just laying down the chords, and she would learn it right away."

Robinson told one interviewer, "Mary was motivated. She'd stay in the studio forever, never complaining or resisting a single suggestion." Another Motown insider described Mary in the studio as "pliant."

Mary described herself in essentially the same way. "Whenever I'm working with somebody, rather than pull against something that we're trying to make happen, I work with them to make it happen," she said. "If I think the person is getting upset, then I won't get upset."

Her next song, "You Beat Me to the Punch" (also released in 1962), sounded very much like "The One Who Really Loves You," but on this tune, Mary's haunting vocal was aided not only by the male vocal group the Love-Tones, which had backed her on "The One Who Really Loves You," but by bongos and vibes as well.

Critic David Ritz noted that "You Beat Me to the Punch," in which a boy and girl meet and then break up, "goes from ecstasy to agony in two minutes and forty seconds." It became a number 1 R&B hit and a number 9 pop single. With this record, Mary, whose tunes were now consistently played on white radio stations, became a gigantic Motown star.

"You Beat Me to the Punch" was backed with "Old Love (Let's Try It Again)," an early effort by Motown's songwriting team of Edward Holland, his brother Brian Holland, and Lamont Dozier. The team was known as Holland-Dozier-Holland.

Robinson and Wells pushed the boundaries of record-biz acceptability during that same year when Wells recorded the then semiscandalous song "Two Lovers." In this tune, she projected no shame, but plenty of vulnerability, over loving two men at the same time. She managed the amazing feat of sounding innocent and scandalous simultaneously. Although the song had a surprise ending, revealing that her two lovers were the two personalities of one man, many of her male fans disregarded the ending and concentrated on the theme. Dennis Bowles, son of Motown musician "Dr. Beans" Bowles, said in his book, *Dr. Beans Bowles*, that "when Dad played 'Two Lovers,' I was in love for the first time in my life. I used to fantasize, in a kid's way, of myself being the other lover." He was not alone.

In contrast to this common fantasy, Robinson said his motivation for writing the song was that his wife, Claudette, had the power to make him feel very sad or very happy with just one word or action.

This song, backed with "Operator," was Mary's second consecutive number 1 R&B hit and hit number 7 on the pop charts. In fact, 1962 was her annus mirabilis: in that one year, three of her records had risen into the pop chart's Top 10, a rare achievement.

Robinson and Wells, sensing they were on the roll of their lives, marshaled their best talents for a maximum effort.

Robinson wrote the music and lyrics for Mary's next song, which he called, "My Guy." A rare upbeat and jaunty song about love and loyalty, its tune is light and catchy. And the lyrics tower above some of the crass and misogynist lyrics by others who tackled the same subject over the years.

The lyrics also contained numerous Robinson touches best described as "where polite language meets the street," including such lines as "You best be believing I won't be deceiving my guy." (Similarly, on another record, Mary noted, "What love has joined together, can nobody take it apart.")

Mary's delivery was sweet and jaunty, sophisticated and assured. Author David Ritz, referring to both the lyrics and Mary's delivery, memorably called it "a fluttering study in fidelity."

Although the song's wording has come to be a symbol of what critics praised as the "spellbinding simplicity" of early Motown, it was also boosted into semi-immortality by the way Mary sang it, an addition at the beginning by the Motown house band, and a twist that Mary inserted at the end.

On the day of its recording, according to the book *Standing in the Shadows of Motown*, by "Dr. Licks" (Allan Slutsky) and James Jamerson, the Motown studio musicians had been working all day and, with only a half hour left in the session, had become bogged down in the intro section to "My Guy." As time and patience ran out, trombonist George Bohanon turned to studio bandleader and keyboardist Earl Van Dyke and pointed out that the melody from the song "Canadian Sunset" fit right over the chord changes of the "My Guy" intro. Van Dyke not only took Bohanon up on his implied suggestion but added the left hand from Eddie Heywood's "Begin

189

the Beguine." (The "Canadian Sunset" beginning is easily recognizable in "My Guy," once someone tells you about it; otherwise, it just sounds like a great intro to a great recording.)

"We were doing anything to get the hell out of that studio," Van Dyke said. "We knew that the producers didn't know nothin' 'bout no 'Canadian Sunset' or 'Begin the Beguine.' We figured the song would wind up in the trash can anyway." Van Dyke was usually right with such predictions. This time he was way wrong.

Now came Mary's part. As soon as Robinson had played the song on the piano for Mary, she had told herself, "I love this song. I hope it's a Top 10. It's a completely beautiful melody." She decided that she loved it so much that she "had to put something real cute on the end. And I thought about Mae West."

Wells, backed by the Andantes, recorded the ending the way Mae would have sung it were she trying to entice a lover upstairs with a sexy musical stutter. "I was really joking," Mary said. But the producers said, "Keep it going, keep it going." She kept it going:

> There's not a man-n t-day [*Mary*
> *stuttered*]
> Who could take me away
> From my guy.
> (Tell me more!) [*from the*
> *Andantes*]
> There's not a man-n t-day, [*she*
> *stuttered again*]
> Who could take me away,
> From my guy.

Released March 13, 1964, backed with "Oh Little Boy (Look What You've Done to Me)," in which Mary's pleading tones were amply demonstrated, "My Guy" became Mary's first number 1 pop chart single. Not only did it become Mary's signature song, it made her the nation's most popular singer.

The song caught on so fast with whites that Curtis Womack was briefly troubled. Himself a musician trying to cross the race barrier, Womack hadn't met Mary yet but remembers thinking, "This song ain't like 'Bye Bye Baby' and it ain't like 'You Beat Me to the Punch.' It sounded just like something Patti Page [a white singer] or one of them ladies would be singing, and I thought it wasn't going to go with black people like it did. But it *did*. It went with everybody."

"My Guy" has remained stuck in the minds of millions over the years, even more so than other pop hits. Motown sales chief Barney Ales was quoted in 1992 as saying that "no one age thirty through age fifty doesn't know the words to 'My Guy.'" For once, he was exaggerating only slightly.

"My Guy" remains a favorite backup tune in Hollywood movies and TV commercials to this day. It also remains the music to which thousands of people continue to fall in love. In 2010, one music business expert said that not twenty-four hours go by without "My Guy" being played on some radio station somewhere in the world.

The *Indianapolis Post-Tribune* noted without exaggeration in 1989 that the song had become part of American culture. "It doesn't die," Wells said.

# An Elegant Equation
## Changing World, Changing Motown
*Herb Jordan*

In 1967 it was clear that nothing would be as it was. The '60s were in full swing. Televised reports of war in Vietnam and the Middle East and the emergence of China as a nuclear power gave distant events an unsettling immediacy. The fragile façade of domestic tranquility cultivated in the 1950s dissolved into public protests for equality, against the war, and to save the planet. The image of heavyweight champion Floyd Patterson, the archetypical genial gladiator, had been supplanted by that of a defiant Muhammad Ali, a black Muslim who was stripped of his title for refusing induction into the military. In 1967, a dozen cities burned as black Americans demanded change. In Detroit, city police and the National Guard engaged in armed combat with rioters and ordinary citizens. And the band played on.

Some have described Motown as creating a production line whose records reflected the system more than the sensibilities of individual artists and writers. It has also been suggested that Motown's public image was an anomaly in an era with a revolutionary narrative. The truth is, Motown presented a point of view in music and image that was an elegant and indispensable component of a decade of change.

By 1967, the Motown record-making machine was fully engaged. What started as an intermittent smattering of hit singles had become a torrent. The irresistible charm of early Motown was still conspicuous, but the songwriting and production techniques had been sharpened by a process whose sole purpose was to make each record better than the last. When they weren't making records, the people at Motown carefully listened to everything from the Beatles to James Brown. With insight and instinct from years of nonstop record making, the old-guard songwriters and producers created the polished pop masterworks of 1967. Rather than merely formulaic, songs like "Bernadette," "Love is Here and Now You're Gone," and "You're My Everything" are testaments to the songwriters' and artists' sense of the art and architecture of a hit. On Gladys Knight's version of "I Heard It through the Grapevine," Norman Whitfield and Barrett Strong conjured up a mix of heartbreak and Sunday morning, and the Funk Brothers delivered an instrumental shout as joyous as any in popular music. Smokey Robinson, who had been known to turn a phrase, made words pirouette on "The Love I Saw in You Was Just a Mirage."

Still, Berry Gordy's drive to expand musical boundaries was insatiable. Nicholas Ashford and Valerie Simpson were invited to join the songwriting-production corps and brought a blend of freshness and familiarity to the music. Before moving to Detroit, Ashford and Simpson had written a number 1 hit for Ray Charles and honed their duet chops writing for Chuck Jackson and Maxine Brown. Ashford and Simpson had a subtle but palpable impact as the Motown sound

191

continued to evolve. On "Your Precious Love," instead of a driving beat, they employed finger pops and space to create tension and patience, but with a sense of urgency; the song is a perfect palette for Marvin Gaye and Tammi Terrell's splashes of color. With muted pizzicato, rim shots, and a bass that crept in on cat's feet, the opening measures of "Ain't No Mountain High Enough" articulate not the teenage anxiety of "Please Mr. Postman" but the anticipation that precedes a great love. The song unfolds as a portrait of mature devotion.

Motown had reached a creative summit, and its public image was picture-perfect. Early on, Maxine Powell had been engaged to instruct the artists on matters of presentation, from speech and posture to etiquette and attire. By 1967, Motown was both a sound and a stylistic point of view. The Motown finishing school drew from a tradition within the black community that most white Americans never knew existed. It taught the elegance of Ellington, updated for a mass audience. Media from *Time* magazine to *The Ed Sullivan Show* provided the glass enclosure to display the young men and women as a new vision of black America. It was a high-wire act best accomplished by not looking at the fire below.

The carefully cultivated public image belied the trouble at Hitsville. In the spring of 1967, Berry Gordy renamed the Supremes, by executive fiat, Diana Ross and the Supremes. Soon it would be the Supremes minus Florence Ballard. David Ruffin made a failed attempt to have the Temptations recast with him as the leader. By midyear, Holland-Dozier-Holland, dissatisfied that their compensation did not mirror their contribution, stopped writing. During a performance in Virginia, Tammi collapsed in Marvin's arms and three years later died of a

brain tumor. Mickey Stevenson, Kim Weston, and Clarence Paul departed as MCA and Motown's other rivals raided the staff in an attempt to buy the Motown sound. The musical challenges of 1967 were both intriguing and daunting. The technology of record making was changing, and seismic social and political events called into question the relevancy of the kind of music Motown made famous.

With few exceptions, black artists had traditionally been pop music's ventriloquists. In the 1950s, listeners heard and saw Elvis Presley, Jerry Lee Lewis, and Peggy Lee. But Otis Blackwell penned "All Shook Up," "Don't Be Cruel," "Great Balls of Fire," and "Fever." Pat Boone's covers of Little Richard and Fats Domino records were intended to provide middle America with a domesticated version of rhythm and blues. The startling contrast between the original and the facsimile only made the case for the vitality of black music and may have helped its modest infiltration of pop radio. With an image that rivaled Hollywood and a string of hit singles, Motown ushered in an era of fully integrated pop playlists. By 1967, a hit could come from anywhere. Aretha Franklin's "Respect," the Monkees' "I'm a Believer," Bobby Gentry's "Ode to Billie Joe," and Jackie Wilson's "Higher and Higher" all peacefully coexisted on AM radio. The *Billboard* charts of best-selling singles and albums were a kaleidoscope of musical styles and an industry in transition.

The singles charts were dominated by short, hook-driven pop songs, but FM radio became a venue for experimentation and innovation, featuring long-playing concept albums. The Beatles' *Sgt. Pepper's Lonely Hearts Club Band* and Jimi Hendrix's *Are You Experienced?* helped to open a more personal avenue for musical expression. From the beginning, music had been composition and performance. Starting with the earliest records, the art of production was essentially a matter of capturing the performance with the highest sonic fidelity. The development of new recording techniques and synthesized sound transformed record production from a technical necessity to an important element of the creative process. Hendrix's and the Beatles' albums featured improvised solos and production that manipulated the natural sounds of acoustic instruments to create sounds never before heard by the human ear. Led by James Brown's breakthrough "Cold Sweat," rhythm and blues delved deeper into funk and was largely unaffected by the new sound. On "Reflections," Holland-Dozier-Holland took rhythm and blues on an excursion into this evolving world.

"Reflections" should have been a disaster. The concept of passing off a miniature suite with synthesized extraterrestrial sound effects and symphonic interludes featuring a choir of flutes as a three-minute AM radio pop/R&B song is mind-boggling. Considering that the production was designed as background for the very orthodox Supremes, the record seems more likely to have ended up in the vaults than on the radio. Instead of sounding like an arranged marriage, well intentioned but awkward, we hear James Jamerson build bridges that make the song's contrasting sections flow one to another with a sense of inevitably. Diana seemed determined to demonstrate why it should be Diana Ross and the Supremes. The writers didn't abandon the hook. They used it as a centering axis around which the experimentation revolved. In the end, "Reflections" demonstrates that form and formula needn't stifle; in the hands of a master, a system is merely a tool.

In 1967's Summer of Love, an alienated generation tuned out the party line and set off to make the world in their image. In June, they turned to the power of global media with the *Our World* broadcast that featured the Beatles' "All You Need is Love." Detroit's musical scene was diverse and vibrant. Joni Mitchell relocated from Canada to Detroit, where she filled clubs with quiet introspection that challenged the audience to listen and reflect. Style and substance across the musical landscape reflected the volatile social and political climate. Hendrix merged music and theater at the Monterey Pop Festival, where he smashed amplifiers and set his guitar ablaze.

In 1967, Motown artists sang songs of love as if oblivious to the historical turbulence of their time. But Detroit is a city of contradiction. Its history of chronic race-based economic disparity is countered by the existence of strong black neighborhoods anchored by intact families and men with jobs. Sylvia Moy's composition "I Was Made to Love Her" provides a glimpse of life in the black middle-class neighborhoods. She recalls, "There was a sense of community. People looked out for each other and maintained beautiful homes. In the summer, we had block parties where everyone showed up to eat, listen to music, and dance." With the rise of a stable black workforce, black-owned businesses thrived.

There were retail shopping districts with bakeries, bookstores, and restaurants. Black-owned media offered its take on the news and served as a voice for the community. Black radio stations and the *Michigan Chronicle* were the first option for music and news in many neighborhoods. The Broadside Press, a black-owned publishing house, featured the works of poets and writers who celebrated black culture and chronicled the struggle for equality.

Teenagers may have enjoyed the innocent fun of a block party on a summer's afternoon, but at night Detroit earned its standing as a city where you could party until the sun came up—or the cops came down. Black Detroit played as hard as it worked.

In the 1920s, bluesman Blind Blake, who had never been to Detroit, sang of Hastings Street's reputation in the South as a nightlife mecca. Hastings Street was at the heart of the black entertainment district known as Paradise Valley. As Blake told it, down on Hastings Street, "They're doin' the boogie. Doin' it very woogie." Twenty years later, John Lee Hooker moved to Detroit from Mississippi to find they were still at it. In "Boogie Chillun," Hooker sings, "When I first came to town, people. I was walkin' down Hastings Street. Yes people, they was havin' a ball." For decades, Hastings Street reigned as the place to be, until, in a wave of "urban renewal," they paved Paradise Valley and put up a freeway.

By 1967, it was Twelfth Street that upheld the tradition of the blind pig, an illegal afterhours joint where one could gamble, drink, and mingle with both the workers and captains of the underground economy. On July 23, 1967, the police raided a blind pig on Twelfth Street and arrested people who were celebrating the return from Vietnam of two neighborhood men. Witnesses testified that violence erupted when police kicked and beat several of the partiers. The malignant mix of police brutality and underlying anger ignited widespread rioting. Many thought the neighborhood prophecies of a revolution had come to pass. When the riots ended, seven thousand had been arrested and forty-three Detroiters were dead.

Many of the once-vibrant neighborhoods were devastated. Rioters burned businesses, black owned and white owned. The forces that were sent to protect the citizens often contributed to the disorder. Police vandalized and firebombed Vaughn's Book Store, a location known for hosting forums on black culture. Motown was spared physically, but the symbiosis between the record company and Detroit was now fragile. The studio, which had remained open continuously for its entire existence, closed during the six-day melee. Afterward, Motown reopened, and on the surface things returned to normal, but the company's departure from Detroit had become inevitable.

The riots blindsided Motown, which had continued to make records that portrayed the idyllic side of black life. At the Fox Theatre, Martha and the Vandellas' performance was interrupted when the group was informed that the city was burning. Urban legend has it that "Dancing in the Street" was Motown's metaphorical shout-out to rioters. But the lack of a bona fide protest song is more likely the reason observers imputed a revolutionary subtext to what was perhaps the ultimate Motown party song, recorded years before the riots. With the assassination of Martin Luther King in 1968 and escalation of the war, songs like the Temptations' "Ball of Confusion" and Edwin Starr's "War" became a regular part of the Motown repertoire and reflected the sensibilities of another side of black Detroit.

Detroit had a long history of radical activism born out of the labor and civil rights movements. The Nation of Islam was founded in Detroit, and the Black Panthers had a sizable following in the community. A radical faction of autoworkers formed an organization called DRUM to protest oppressive conditions and the limited opportunity for advancement by blacks in the auto plants. The relationship between blacks and whites in general was not as adversarial as that between the black community and the police. There were genuine efforts in the black and white communities to effect social change. But there was growing anger in response to the police department's militaristic interactions with black Detroit. Detroit's first black mayor, Coleman Young, later described the police of that era as "an occupying force." Given the city's activist history and challenging racial climate, one might have expected Detroit to give birth to a genre of black protest music.

While prior to 1967 the music rarely touched on political themes, Berry Gordy was acutely aware of the social and political revolution. In 1963, Motown released a recording of Martin Luther King's speech at Detroit's Great March to Freedom. Referring to the march on Washington, Gordy stated that "the Negro Revolt of 1963 will take its place historically with the American Revolution."

Rather than mix politics and music, Gordy elected to cast Motown as a symbol of progress. Motown's existence and success did, in fact, make a powerful statement. The small black-owned enterprise headquartered in a modest house on Detroit's west side consistently outperformed record companies funded by the vast resources of corporate giants. And it did so with aplomb. Berry Gordy has an exquisite sense of the power of imagery. Motown's role, in Gordy's view, was cultural and social: to put on public display a vision of black excellence. The songs were vignettes of a side of black life that white America had never known, and the corporate story was a template for black America's participation in the economic mainstream.

Berry Gordy understood that a disciplined system allowed creative talent to flourish and that, in the theater of racial politics, social change has many agents. He was determined for Motown to deliver a consummate performance on both fronts. It was a delicate balance, an elegant equation in a world of unpredictable and often catastrophic change.

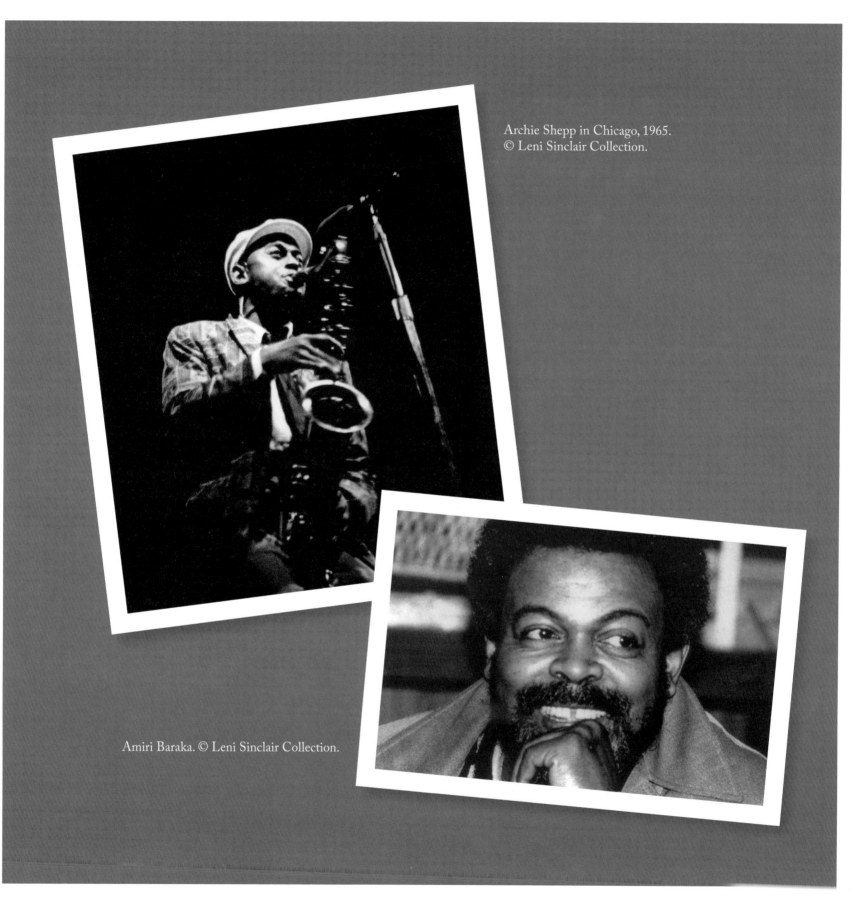

Archie Shepp in Chicago, 1965.
© Leni Sinclair Collection.

Amiri Baraka. © Leni Sinclair Collection.

# The Revolution Will Be Recorded
## Black Forum Records: Detroit Rarity of the Revolution

*Pat Thomas*

Even among diehard collectors of Motown's vast output, Motown's subsidiary Black Forum label remains obscure. It is overlooked in most Motown biographies, and no Black Forum recordings have ever been included in any Motown label anthology.

Even the thirty-song double-CD released by Motown in 2007 titled *Power to the People: Civil Rights Anthems and Political Soul 1968–1975* does not include Black Forum artists or mention the label in the booklet's overview of Motown during the black power era. And yet, the cover features a clenched-fist salute, and there's a photograph of Huey Newton and Bobby Seale inside the jewel case. There's also a sticker telling us that this CD includes "30 Militant Soul Anthems." OK then, where are selections from Elaine Brown of the Black Panther Party or poet/activist Amiri Baraka? Both had released albums of songs (rather than speeches) on Black Forum during the period covered on the compilation.

The label released eight albums between 1970 and 1973, including a speech denouncing the Vietnam War by Martin Luther King, a very heated address on race relations by Stokely Carmichael, and interviews with black soldiers fighting in Vietnam conducted by a *Time* magazine correspondent. There was also a narrative by writers Langston Hughes and Margaret Danner; an LP of poetry including Amiri Baraka, members of the Last Poets, and Stanley Crouch; and songs featuring Amiri Baraka as a vocalist backed by free jazz musicians. The final two

releases were Ossie Davis and Bill Cosby speaking in front of the first Congressional Black Caucus and the aforementioned singer-songwriter LP by renowned Black Panther Elaine Brown.

When I realized that Motown boss Gordy had authorized the Black Forum label and allowed the Temptations (among others) to release political songs well before Marvin Gaye's *What's Going On*, I wondered why the double standard? I thought about Gordy's reluctance to release Marvin Gaye's sociopolitical messages. In June 2008, I posed the question to Miller London, a Motown employee for three decades beginning in the '60s. London felt that Gordy was afraid of damaging Marvin's incredible mass following; he didn't want to mess with a winning formula. OK, fair enough, but I wondered why Gordy initiated Black Forum in the first place, and who ran it for him? Miller cited the civil rights movement in general as the label's inspiration and named Ewart Abner as one of the in-house forces behind it. (Abner passed away in 1998.)

In his 2002 book *Motown: Music, Money, Sex, and Power*, Gerald Posner suggests several factors that may have led to the start of Black Forum. During the late 1960s, black radio disc jockeys around Detroit who had always been supportive of the label began to feel that Gordy was more interested in currying favor with white DJs as Motown's singles increasingly gained attention outside the African American community with each passing year. This eventually led to a temporary boycott of Motown releases by Detroit-area black DJs.

Meanwhile, internationally successful acts like the Supremes were getting asked questions about their stand on the Vietnam War and the black power movement while touring England, and the artists didn't how to respond. There were letters from African American fans to Motown suggesting that the Supremes should wear their hair natural (Afro-style), which Gordy resisted, worried it could make the popular female trio look too radical for white America. While Gordy himself had remained nonpolitical throughout much of the 1960s, he had released an album of speeches by Martin Luther King titled *Free at Last* on the Gordy imprint in June 1968. He also supported the NAACP, one of the country's oldest civil rights organizations, founded in 1909 by W. E. B. DuBois. But times were changing with new, more outspoken black-rights coalitions gaining in popularity, and some young blacks began to criticize Motown for sounding too white.

The assassination of Martin Luther King on April 4, 1968, was a wake-up call for Gordy to make accommodations and embrace the black power movement. Sometime after that tragic event, Gordy brought together three employees—Ewart Abner, Junius Griffin, and George Schiffer—to organize the Black Forum label and oversee its output.

Before coming to work for Motown in the spring of 1967, Ewart Abner had been one of the partners in the Vee-Jay label, best known as the first American company to release records by the Beatles before Capitol Records stepped in. It's important to note that through Vee-Jay, Abner released the Impressions' first nationally distributed single, "For Your Precious Love," in the summer of 1958. In 1975, Abner became Stevie Wonder's manager, an arrangement that lasted a decade. During his long career, Abner was passionate about black pride as an advocate of minority education, a founding member of the Black Music Association, a member of the NAACP and the Urban League, and the organizer of two civil rights era marches on Washington. Abner helped infuse Motown with his beliefs and was a logical choice to be one of the driving forces behind Black Forum.

Also joining Motown in 1967 was Junius Griffin, who'd been the first African American reporter for the New York desk of the Associated Press during the early 1960s. In 1965, the Southern Christian Leadership Conference asked him to write speeches for Martin Luther King, which he did until joining Motown's publicity department two years later. He remained at Motown until the early 1980s and at end of that decade was public relations advisor to the Martin Luther King Jr. Center for Nonviolent Social Change in Atlanta. According to an interview in the February 12, 2004, issue of the *Los Angeles Times* with actor Max Julien, who starred in the 1973 blaxploitation movie *The Mack*, Griffin is credited with coining the term *blaxploitation* when in 1972 he complained in *Variety* about negative images of African Americans in the just-released film *Superfly*. Griffin's comments about the emerging cinematic genre apparently didn't stop there. In an editorial published by the *New York Times* on December 17, 1972, Griffin stated that "these films are taking our money while feeding us a forced diet of violence, murder, drugs, and rape. Such films are the cancer of 'Blaxploitation' gnawing away at the moral fiber of our community."

The third person behind Black Forum was George Schiffer, a white liberal who'd been Gordy's copyright lawyer since the early days of Motown. He worked for Motown from 1959 to 1975 and served as lead attorney for the Congress of Racial Equality (CORE) in New York City during the 1960s. Although CORE is usually mentioned in context with the civil rights era and the Deep South, it originated in Chicago during 1942, inspired by Gandhi's theories on organizing people through nonviolent protest campaigns. The "freedom rides" began in May 1961, guided by CORE director James Farmer. Freedom riders boarded Greyhound buses and traveled throughout the South in protest of segregation laws. As the 1960s progressed, the organization debated internally on which direction to take. Farmer resigned in 1966 in support of nonviolence and was replaced by Floyd McKissick, who led CORE in a black nationalist direction.

The first three Black Forum albums included the following mission statement on the back cover: "Black Forum is a medium for the presentation of ideas and voices of the worldwide struggle of Black people to create a new era. Black Forum also serves to provide authentic materials for use in schools and colleges and for the home study of Black history and culture. Black Forum is a permanent record of the sound of struggle and the sound of the new era."

## THE BLACK FORUM LABEL DISCOGRAPHY

Dr. Martin Luther King—*Why I Oppose the War in Vietnam* (LP)

Stokely Carmichael—*Free Huey* (LP)

Langston Hughes and Margaret Danner—*Writers of the Revolution* (LP)

Various Artists—*Guess Who's Coming Home: Black Fighting Men Recorded Live in Vietnam*

Ossie Davis and Bill Cosby—*Ossie Davis and Bill Cosby Address the Congressional Black Caucus* (LP)

Various Artists—*Black Spirits: Festival of New Black Poets in America* (LP)

Imamu Amiri Baraka—*It's Nation Time* (LP)

Elaine Brown—*Elaine Brown* (LP)

Elaine Brown—"No Time"/"Until We're Free" (7-inch single)

Sadly, Elaine's album marked the end of Black Forum, which certainly had nothing to do with her. It was inevitable that this sociopolitical detour of the Motown pop empire wouldn't last long. While each of the Black Forum releases are remarkable in their own right, none of them was destined for mass appeal. Also, by 1973, the black power movement that had inspired the label was fragmenting and winding down. Ultimately, like most things in life, it comes down to money. Black Forum records couldn't sell in the quantities that Motown had become accustomed to via hit makers like the Supremes, the Temptations, and the Jackson 5.

Although the label released only a handful of recordings during its existence, apparently their original intentions were more ambitious. An April 3, 1971, article in the *Philadelphia Tribune* outlined an impressive release schedule including two albums scheduled for later that year: *Black Unity* by James Baldwin and a selection of poetry read by Ted Joans titled *The Good Colored Man*. Additionally, they announced forthcoming releases by a diverse set of African Americans: Eldridge Cleaver; SNNC cofounder and congressman Julian Bond; Richard Gordon Hatcher and Kenneth Gibson (the mayors of Gary, Indiana, and Newark, New Jersey); Andrew Young (a key aide to MLK throughout the 1960s and a prominent politician in the following two decades); director of the NAACP Roy Wilkins. They also planned for a posthumous release from Whitney Young, head of the National Urban League from 1961 until his death just a few weeks before the *Philadelphia Tribune* article. None of these recordings were ever released.

Given the label's nonexistent legacy, one can't help but feel that the records simply never reached their intended audience in the first place. As I wound up my interview with former Motown executive Miller London, I asked if he had any final comments about Black Forum. He replied, "The main problem was that Motown's network of regional record distributors simply didn't want to stock the albums. The distributors were of course hungry for the next Motown pop album, but getting them behind these political releases was difficult."

Ultimately, he said, it was only the black-owned companies such as United Record Distributors in Chicago that got behind the Black Forum label. It's an age-old problem: if records aren't in stores, people can't buy them.

None of the Black Forum albums have ever been issued on CD, so while I was writing *Listen, Whitey!: The Sights and Sounds of Black Power 1965–1975* for Fantagraphics Books, I compiled an accompanying soundtrack CD (with the same title) for Light in the Attic Records. For the first time, three Black Forum recordings were reissued: an excerpt from Stokely Carmichael's "Free Huey" speech, the Elaine Brown song "Until We're Free" and, from

the *It's Nation Time* LP, Amiri Baraka's "Who Will Survive America."

After the *Listen, Whitey!* book and CD were released in 2012, there was distinct shift in the interviews that Berry Gordy did after that. He began mentioning the Black Forum label for the first time ever. Gordy's desire to reclaim that legacy was further confirmed in 2014, when I visited the Motown Museum in Detroit and saw a half-dozen Black Forum albums on display. They hadn't been there in previous decades.

# Excerpt from *What's Going On: Marvin Gaye and the Last Days of the Motown Sound*

*Ben Edmonds*

June 28, 1990. In the cruel light of day, Tiger Stadium looks as beat up and run down as the dilapidated Detroit neighborhood it sits in. But tonight, with an overflow crowd well above the official estimate of fifty thousand, there is an electric buzz of anticipation in the air that threatens to levitate the old ballpark. Aretha Franklin, Stevie Wonder, and Frankie Beverly will perform, but this is not a concert, and they are no more than supporting players.

A sleek town car glides across the field to the stage, and the throng erupts at the sight of its passenger, a dignified black man with graying hair. When Nelson Mandela approaches the microphone, the rowdy crowd falls silent. He is touring America to celebrate his freedom after more than a quarter century in prison, and few stops on his itinerary are as important as Detroit. In the city that serves, for better and worse, as the symbol of African American urban empowerment, Mandela's words carry the weight of the world. "When we were in prison," he says, "we appreciated and avidly listened to the sound of Detroit, Motor Town. On reaching Detroit, I recalled some of the words of the song sung by Marvin Gaye: 'Brother, brother, there's far too many of you dying. Mother, mother, there's far too many of you crying.'"

At this moment, maybe the stadium is levitating. The crowd knows every inflection of each of the words by heart. They were written here in Detroit, sung and recorded here, and now they belong to the world.

1969: Renaldo "Obie" Benson of the Four Tops had never been a particularly prolific songwriter, but something began to percolate during a tour stop in San Francisco that coincided with violent skirmishes between protesters and Berkeley police over a disused urban lot called People's Park. "They had the Haight-Ashbury then," he recalls. "All the kids up there with the long hair and everything. The

Marvin Gaye, 1976. © Leni Sinclair Collection.

police was beatin' on them, but they weren't bothering anybody. I saw this, and started wondering what the fuck was going on. What is happening here? One question leads to another. Why are they sending kids so far away from their families overseas? Why are they attacking their own children in the streets here?" With the help of lyricist Al Cleveland, who worked frequently with Smokey Robinson, Benson began shaping a song that addressed these issues.

The Four Tops, however, weren't interested in it. "My partners told me it was a protest song. I said, 'No, man, it's a love song, about love and understanding. I'm not protesting, I want to know what's going on.' But they never really understood what was happening." When the group toured England, Benson thought he'd stumbled onto an interesting match. "We were doing a TV show, *Top of the Pops* or one of those, and I tried to give it to this girl. This famous folksinger played a guitar. What's her name? I went into her dressing room, picked up her guitar, and played this song. I had some words, but they weren't the finished lyrics yet. She seemed interested, but somehow we got separated and I never got to finish presenting it to her. What was her name?"

Fate had in mind someone other than Joan Baez to deliver the unfinished "What's Going On."

"Marvin was the perfect artist for it," he says. "Marvin already felt like this. He was a rebel, and a real spiritual guy. The first time he sang it, I was playing guitar and he was playing piano, and it was so beautiful. I finally put it to him like this: 'I'll give you a percentage of the tune if you sing it, but if you do it on anybody else, you can't have none of it.' His wife told him, 'Marvin, this is a perfect song for you.' I'll love Anna forever for making him see the truth of that."

Benson readily concedes that Gaye put the finishing touches to the song: "He added lyrics, and he added some spice to the melody. He fine-tuned the tune, in other words. He added different colors to it. He added some things that were more ghetto, more natural, which made it seem more like a story than a song. He made it visual. When you heard that song, you could see the people and feel the hurt and pain. We measured him for the suit and he tailored the hell out of it."

The Motown assembly line was ready to provide plenty of assistance. The company, set up by Berry Gordy in 1959 with an $800 loan, had a stable of stars—Gaye, Smokey Robinson, Mary Wells, the Four Tops, the Temptations, Martha and the Vandellas, the Supremes, Little Stevie Wonder— and had grown into a multimillion-dollar business. And the studio at the Hitsville building on West Grand Boulevard ran twenty-four hours a day with three shifts of engineers. "We used to call it 'going to work at the factory,'" recalls keyboard player Johnny Griffith.

Something essential was added at each successive stage of the assembly line. To writer/ producer Richard Morris, for example, it was the sound of a beat-up old piano: "Downstairs in the basement of Hitsville was where the producers and songwriters had, like, a common room. All of us used to sit around a piano and take turns playing our material. We'd listen to each other's songs, criticize them, trade chords, helping one another develop them without any of the ugly competition that came in later. That's why Motown records had such a continuity of sound. It was there even before it got to the studio musicians, because it all came from that one piano."

The studio musicians who called themselves the Funk Brothers have belatedly begun to receive some recognition. Their primary asset as a band was the remarkable empathy they developed, due in large part to their shared roots in modern jazz.

Gaye brought two members into the Funk Brothers fold. Bongo Brown had been Gaye's valet before his percussion virtuosity earned him a permanent studio spot. And it was Gaye who introduced Jack Ashford into the brotherhood. "We met in Boston," Ashford says. "He stopped into a club where I was appearing with a jazz organ group led by Johnny 'Hammond' Smith. He was impressed with my vibes playing and had one of his people ask if I'd be interested in joining his road band. He was standing right there, but I had no idea who he was and said, 'Never heard of him.' That was the jazz attitude of the time; we were all trying to be cooler than Miles Davis." Still, they exchanged phone numbers. A couple of months later, he was persuaded to join Gaye's band on vibes, tambourine, and Latin percussion.

"I quickly found out about his strong appreciation of jazz," says Ashford. "Marvin made it very clear that he did not want to be singing 'Hitch Hike' and those things. That wasn't who he was. He liked to sing Nat King Cole songs. On the tour—at least in the beginning—there was a segment of the show where they'd put a stool out for him, and I'd push the vibes up and come behind him while he sang 'Unforgettable' and a couple of other standards. That segment got dropped fast because, though he sang those songs very well, he was putting his audience to sleep. Marvin would say, 'Man, I sure wish they'd accept it. That's what I really want to do.' I said, 'I understand that, but we need to get paid, too. Where

do you think I am? I'm used to playing "Boplicity" and "Round Midnight," and now I'm sitting up here behind you while you sing this shit that you hate.'"

Ashford needn't have worried. Once they got back to Detroit and he was introduced to the crew in the Snakepit, the main Hitsville studio, he never went on the road again. He was a Funk Brother, and he became integral to the rhythmic thrust of the band. "He was probably the world's greatest percussion player," says fellow percussionist Jack Brokensha. "He's a huge guy, with hands like big legs of lamb. On tambourine he was amazing; he could sound like a whole rhythm section. A lot of the feel of the tracks was down to the originality of his tambourine and James Jamerson's bass."

The man in line to arrange Gaye's next session was David Van DePitte, one of only four regulars on the Motown staff. "They must have had seventy-five producers, at least 150 songwriters, and God only knows how many artists," Van DePitte says, shaking his head at the scale of the enterprise. "And us four arrangers were responsible for cranking out all the music that came out of there. We did so much music that it was nuts; we were all going crazy, working nonstop. As long as you could keep your eyes open and a pencil in your hand, you were writing. There was a point when I must have been doing two— maybe two and a half—albums' worth of material a week. *A week.*"

Prodded by the song Obie Benson had dropped in his lap, Marvin began to broaden his vision of what his own next project would be. His younger brother Frankie had survived a three-year tour of duty in Vietnam. Like so many vets "back in the world," Frankie was haunted by what he'd seen and done. His sacrifice for his country was rewarded with disdain, disrespect, and unemployment. When he could find work, it was as a dishwasher or a doorman.

"Me and Marvin used to play G.I. Joe all the time as kids," Frankie told me in a soft voice that eerily recalls his older brother's:

We played all the shoot-'em-up games of children. Cowboys and Indians, cops and robbers, all that stuff. He was a better cowboy, but I was a pretty good Indian. Like a lot of people, Vietnam didn't become real until somebody close to him was touched by it. I wrote him a few letters, but it wasn't till I got back that it really hit him that I had been over there. "Wow, man, you were in the war." Then he wanted to know everything. I cried a lot during our talks. War is hell, believe me. The value of life is unbelievably low. Nothing you've ever experienced can prepare you for the terror. And the blood; all my memories of that time are swimming in blood. This horrified Marvin, but what moved him most was the image of children eating out of garbage cans. That was hard for him to get past. It's a sight that I don't think anybody wants to see: people—children—trying to live off what you throw away. Our garbage cans were always clean. When I saw that, I always tried to leave some food on my plate so that they would have something to eat. A lot of other GIs did the same. After my brother heard me, and saw my tears, he began to understand.

He said, "Damn, Frankie, what can I do?" I let him know that he could fight in so many other ways, especially through his

music. We were taught by my mother and father not to say things that produce bad images. But it was difficult for Marvin, because in his business bad images are a very salable commodity. Our parents taught us a lot of love. There was no hate; you couldn't even say the word. And you do not ever hurt another person. So it's strange that Lucifer should come into our house and do what he did.

His voice trails off. It was Frankie who rushed to the family home that horrible April afternoon in 1984 to find his brother Marvin dead of multiple gunshot wounds and the weapon in the hands of their father. Frankie Gaye is haunted by that day, and always will be. "Other people grieve and then get over it," he explains. "But every time I turn on the radio and hear Marvin's voice, the wound reopens and it all comes back." (Marvin Gaye Sr., a failed Pentecostal preacher, had beaten his son as a child and was jealous of his success as an adult. Marvin Jr. gave his father the gun that killed him.)

In the song Benson and Al Cleveland had presented him with, Gaye found a way to channel his sorrow for Tammi Terrell, his singing partner who had died of a brain tumor, his empathy for his brother's plight, and his own professional frustration into an artistic statement addressing the social and spiritual anguish he saw sweeping the real world, the one that existed outside of Motown. The shootings of Martin Luther King and Bobby Kennedy had hit him hard. The violence in the streets of Detroit in 1967, in Chicago during the Democratic National Convention of 1968, and at Kent State University in 1970 seemed like eruptions of insanity. Seeing a man walk on the moon when there was economic desperation within two miles of his own home was surreal and depressing. What the hell was going on?

The singer's expanding awareness had begun to strike terror in the hearts of his label's press liaisons. As part of the Motown finishing process, its stars were taught to offer bland, inoffensive pleasantries in interviews. Despite his publicists' strict admonitions not to talk about anything controversial, Marvin would show up for interviews carrying well-thumbed copies of books by Malcolm X and Carlos Castaneda. As he said later, "In 1969 or 1970, I began to reevaluate my whole concept of what I wanted my music to say. I was very much affected by letters my brother was sending me from Vietnam, as well as the social situation here at home. I realized that I had to put my own fantasies behind me if I wanted to write songs that would reach the souls of people. I wanted them to take a look at what was happening in the world."

"Take a look" is a key concept when discussing Gaye. The singer was hardly an activist in the traditional sense. He wouldn't have been found at a love-in or on the picket line. When smoke from burning homes and businesses in Detroit's infamous 1967 race riot scented the air in his upscale neighborhood, Marvin was watching the action unfold on TV. The collision of these images of horror and injustice with the sense of righteousness that had been instilled in (or beaten into) him as a child produced an activism of the imagination that, when it found the proper musical context, would move untold millions of people. This new song that had fallen from heaven was just the creative jump-start he needed.

Marvin Gaye was so energized by his work on "What's Going On" that he tracked down Berry Gordy to give him the good news personally. "I remember being in the Bahamas trying to relax and take a vacation," Gordy told a TV interviewer. "He called and said, 'Look, I've got to release this album. I've got these songs, it's great.' When he told me they were protest songs, I said, 'Marvin, why do you want to ruin your career? Why do you want to put out a song about the Vietnam War, police brutality, and all of these things? You've got all these great love songs. You're the hottest artist, the sex symbol of the '60s and '70s.'"

Motown was a black-and-tan Camelot. Outside its candy-striped walls, cultural revolution had been raging for years, but inside the Hitsville fortress the tried-and-true Motown sound was still serenading teenagers in a malt shop America that no longer existed. While rioting raged in the streets of Detroit in July 1967, Gordy was in Las Vegas at the Flamingo Hotel with Diana Ross and the Supremes. He was horrified to hear that "Dancing in the Street" had become the theme song for the insurrection.

To further disassociate himself from his tidy Motown image, the singer drastically altered his appearance. Like John Lennon and Jim Morrison, he grew a beard and dispensed with image-conscious fashion in favor of funkier attire. When people looked at Gaye, he wanted them to see someone they'd never seen before. And with his next single, he was determined to make damned sure that they heard something they'd never heard before.

"As I began to get a handle on what he wanted," the arranger Van DePitte says, "my first thought was that it was never gonna fly . . . I told Marvin I didn't think we were gonna get away with it. 'I don't care, man, I'm gonna do what I'm gonna do,' he said. After that, we both got into a kind of 'the hell with the company' mode. Whatever happened, happened."

Van DePitte says that Gaye wanted to stay away from anything resembling a standard Motown beat. The arranger brought in veteran big band drummer Chet Forest and augmented his sound with a phalanx of percussionists: Jack Ashford on tambourine, Eddie Brown on bongos and congas, Earl Derouen on congas, and Jack Brokensha on vibes and assorted percussive toys. To complete the unusual feeling, the artist/producer was down in the Snakepit playing piano and leading the rhythm section himself. For his first self-produced single, Gaye was leaving nothing to chance.

However, two of the record's signature features happened almost entirely by chance. The lovely alto sax figure that opens the record, which Van DePitte has heard at least eight musicians claim credit for, was the work of Eli Fontaine. Or, more accurately, it was his warm-up. When Fontaine had played enough to feel comfortable, he signaled that he was ready for a take. Marvin told him to go home; they already had what they needed. The confused saxophonist tried to explain that he had just been goofing around. "Well," Marvin replied, "you goof exquisitely. Thank you."

And the record's most imitated stylistic feature, Marvin's multilayered lead vocal, was not part of the original blueprint. "That double lead voice was a mistake on my part," admits engineer Ken Sands. "Marvin had cut two lead vocals, and wanted me to prepare a tape with the rhythm track up the middle and each of his vocals on separate tracks so he could compare them. Once, I played that two-track mix on a mono machine and he heard both voices at the same time by accident." This unintentional duet was not only kept, it became a creative strategy that was expanded and applied throughout the subsequent

album and in the rest of Marvin Gaye's career, becoming a hallmark of his vocal style.

The backgrounds were the work of amateurs, a gaggle of buddies that included two members of the Detroit Lions football team, Lem Barney and Mel Farr. Their parts weren't so much sung as chanted, then they were blended with the percussion-heavy track to create a tribal feel that was in part a nod to the long-haired, pot-puffing hippie tribe with which Gaye identified (albeit from a safe distance). In the break, these vocalists broke down into hip party chatter, while Gates (as Marvin was known to his friends, derived from Gayeskey, the nickname given to him by one of the Motown chiefs) "sang" through the solo space that would normally have been filled by a saxophone. During the chatter in the fade, there is a long, sustained intake of breath that sounds suspiciously like unlawful substances being ingested.

Jack Ashford recalls:

They had a room off to the side of the studio that had originally been designed to give the horns separation. Jack Brokensha and I had our percussion stuff set up in there, but for some reason all the guys who smoked grass used to do it in there. There was so much smoke in there that you couldn't see across the room. Jack and I didn't smoke, but I know I got high just breathing the air. Marvin chain-smoked reefer, and he made no attempt to hide it. He floated around with a joint in his mouth, going from guy to guy checking the parts. He was everywhere; you could tell he was really excited. When we started playing this stuff, it was really different, and I don't think it was just the air that I was breathing. There were things happening that other producers would never have even tried.

The record chugged along on a relaxed groove that in anybody else's hands might have degenerated into MOR, yet it became the most avant-garde hit Motown ever had. It begins with one of the most recognizable sax intros in all of pop, but the hook is never repeated, nor does the saxophone reappear. The primal pulse of chanting and percussion is countered by the refinement of Van DePitte's orchestration. The chatter of happy voices imparts a party-time flavor to a song that is deadly serious. The lyric expresses extreme hurt and anger, yet the song never gives in to either.

His handling of the entreaty "Picket lines and picket signs / Don't punish me with brutality" is so rhythmically nuanced that the harshness of the images melts before the simple dignity of the request. His solution to the death and desperation that surrounded him—"War is not the answer / For only love can conquer hate"—sounded hopelessly naïve to disillusioned hippies left holding bouquets of dead flowers in the aftermath of the massacre that took place at Kent State University only two weeks before Gaye commenced this recording. What Gaye offered was a faith through which all could be reconciled. "What's Going On" was a record on which absolutely nothing could have worked, but everything did. For once, the singer's conflicts and contradictions worked to his musical advantage.

It took multiple mixes to nail it down, but Marvin was ecstatic. He'd succeeded in creating something that was unlike anything else churned out by the Motown machine. Perhaps as important, "What's

Going On" was as different from "I Heard It through the Grapevine" as that song had been from run-of-the-mill Motown three years earlier. The band knew it, too. These supremely gifted musicians—veterans who'd played head arrangements with the likes of Charlie Parker, Dizzy Gillespie, Sonny Stitt, and Yusef Lateef—often looked down their noses at the pop music Motown hired them to roll out. Not on June 1, 1970. When bassist James Jamerson got home from work that night, he told his wife he had just cut a classic.

Imagine Marvin Gaye's reaction, then, when Berry Gordy refused to release "What's Going On," reportedly calling it "the worst thing I've ever heard in my life."

Marvin immediately issued an ultimatum of his own: until Berry Gordy and his quality-control cabal came to their senses and released "What's Going On," the singer would record nothing more for the company.

The three most important Marvin Gaye records to this point—"Grapevine," "Baby I'm for Real," and now "What's Going On"—had all been turned down by quality control, and three times the company's hand had to be forced to get them released. Pure coincidence? Not likely. It leads one to the more probable conclusion that greater forces than the department were at work here. At Motown, there was only one force greater than quality control.

Gaye's relationship with Berry Gordy had peaks and valleys. He had no trouble exploiting his proximity to the throne—he was married to Gordy's sister, Anna—when it suited his purposes, but he also didn't hesitate to butt heads with his powerful brother-in-law. Veteran Motown producer Hank Cosby says that one of his first memories of

Marvin Gaye was witnessing the young singer in a fistfight with Gordy. The pair were going at it out on the front lawn of Hitsville. "It was raining and they were slipping all over the place," recalls Cosby with a chuckle. "It was actually funny, more comical than anything. Marvin was real skinny, a ninety-pound weakling, but he was a mouthy guy. Berry's attitude with the young people was, 'I made you a star. I've done everything for you. I'm taking you there, so you be quiet and listen to me.' But Marvin wouldn't take orders from anybody."

This fight was the perfect metaphor for their relationship. Gordy, a former professional boxer, could have taken stringbean Gaye apart without breaking a sweat. Gaye, for his part, was probably convinced he could take the boss. Gordy, meanwhile, regarded his headstrong star with a mixture of affection and annoyance. Elaine Jesmer, Gaye's West Coast publicist, recalls: "It was one of those things between men that women don't get. A guy thing, where it was like they had their dicks in their hands and were having some kind of pissing contest. Marvin was not the sort to ever give up, so you just knew it was gonna be a war of wills forever."

Marvin's relationship with Anna Gordy Gaye was even more combustible. Road manager Joe Schaffner spent a lot of time around the couple:

In the beginning there was a lot of love. Anna was supportive, but always very jealous, too. Being older, she was experienced enough to know how it was out on the road. There were always a lot of ladies around, and these girls hounded Marvin.

Marvin loved the attention, but he got accused of doing a lot of things he never did. Basically, he didn't do anything on the road. He had plenty of lust in his heart, but he didn't act on it. In those days, a pornographic magazine would keep him happy after a show. In all the years I was out with him, there was one time—and only one time—that he slipped. He loved his wife. They'd talk on the phone for hours almost every night. Course, this was also Anna's way of checking up on him. Because he loved her, he was capable of great jealousy, too. He was convinced she was messing around, which she very well may have been. They started to provoke each other to do these crazy things.

Eventually, Marvin and Anna's marriage become troubled, which left Marvin crushed and devastated. He sincerely wanted to save the marriage, but ultimately it was not in the cards. In 1975, Anna filed for divorce. The divorce process was extremely contentious and lasted two years. Part of the final settlement was that Marvin would offer a portion of his royalties to his ex-wife from a forthcoming album to be named later. That album, *Here, My Dear*, was his sad, pain-filled farewell to Anna. Eventually, they settled their differences and remained friends until Marvin's early death at the age of forty-four on April 1, 1984, when he was shot in a fit of anger by his father in Los Angeles, California.

# The Motortown Revues

## An Edited Excerpt from *The Story of Motown*

*Peter Benjaminson*

Motown was starting to roll forward. Among its hits recorded in 1960 and 1961 were "Money" by Barrett Strong, "Please Mr. Postman" by the Marvelettes, and "Shop Around" by the Miracles. "Shop" reached number 2 on the charts, becoming the company's first Top 10 hit. But real success in the music industry cannot be based on recordings alone, for tunes become really popular only when the performers who record them go on tour.

But touring is expensive, and Motown had very little money. When early Motown acts toured, they couldn't afford airplanes or hotel rooms. Often they'd travel by Greyhound and wash up in the bus depot before the show, then return to the depot for the bus back to Detroit after the show.

When it became necessary, in the early 1960s, to send many Motown acts on tour to exploit the growing popularity of the company's records, Berry Gordy realized that sending each act on its own tour would be financial suicide. So he decided to send them all on the same tour at the same time.

There was another reason for sending the acts out together. The big talent agencies that arranged concert tours in the early 1960s didn't want to deal with black acts at all, certainly not one at a time. But when Motown put all its acts together, the package involved so much potential profit that even the most prejudiced agents were willing to book the Motown acts into clubs and theaters. No other record company—certainly no white record company—has ever found it necessary to send its acts on tour together.

Motown's massive touring groups were known as Motortown or Motown Revues, and they were massive. The 1962 Revue included forty-five performers riding in a bus and five cars. "It was too many people and too many miles and showed a lack of experience putting all those people out there," the Motown executive who managed that tour says. But the Motortown Revues introduced a lot of Motown acts to a lot of fans.

And what an introduction. As Michael Thomas wrote in *Rolling Stone*, "There'd be the bongos and Little Stevie Wonder would come on and open it and then it would go on nonstop with the Marvelettes and the Contours, who had 'Do You Love Me?' and Mary Wells and the Temptations and all the others and it would wind up with Smokey Robinson and the Miracles. He'd do that showstopper where he'd get down on one knee and then right flat on the floor, singing 'a little bit softer now . . . a little bit softer now' right down to where he was hardly whispering—and then he'd start to crank it up, 'a little bit louder now . . . a little bit louder now . . .' until he was back up jumping and pumping full steam and the roof would fall in."

The revues served another function: eliminating the acts that couldn't cut it and illuminating the superstars in the group. In this sense, the revues operated very much like farm teams in baseball.

209

Sometimes the touring artists weren't as well prepared for the revues as they might have been, in spite of Motown's training programs. Occasionally, performers would have only a day or two to learn a whole new act. Or they'd have to wear hand-me-down costumes that were too tight and came apart at embarrassing moments. But for the performers who were high-school dropouts or recent graduates living in Detroit when they joined Motown, traveling around America, even by bus, was tremendously exciting. For those Motown performers who'd literally never been beyond the Detroit city limits, a trip to a city like New York was a truly amazing experience.

But Gordy went farther east than New York. For years, white English groups had been covering and re-recording black music for the English market. Gordy had a hunch that English buyers would be interested in the real thing if they were exposed to it. So after Motown had established itself, but before English groups began to invade this country, Gordy sent the Motown Revues on an invasion of England. He spearheaded the attack himself, flying to England on the first Motortown Revue plane, along with his parents, his sisters, Stevie Wonder, the Four Tops, and the Supremes.

Although Gordy was optimistic about Motown's chances of success in England, the company's English contacts weren't encouraging. English record retailers, for instance, told Motown executives that there were too many tambourines on the company's records and that English record buyers didn't like tambourines.

There was another problem: The established English radio stations looked down their noses at black records and often refused to play them. But pitching and rolling in the icy waters just outside British territorial limits were modern-day "pirate ships," seaborne radio stations broadcasting illegally into England. The pirates, scorned by the establishment, were determined to show their power by making hits out of records the legal stations wouldn't even play. So Motown sent its records directly to these ships.

But after some initial successes, Motown's English offensive faltered. In an uncharacteristically halfhearted move, which he repeated in other countries, Gordy licensed an English record company to sell Motown records in England rather than establish a division there. The licensee tried to sell the Motown sound as a sound before Motown's artists had been heard widely enough to make their sound popular in England. (In the United States, the artists were sold as artists and the Motown sound's popularity arose from their success.)

Motown switched from one licensee to another, looking for the right approach. Although the Supremes were successful at first, appearing on fourteen London television shows on an early tour of the country, some of the early Motown Revues played to half-empty houses everywhere in England except London and Manchester.

Meanwhile, back in the United States, the touring Motown performers were having problems of their own. They were, after all, black people touring the country before the civil rights movement had had much effect. (Federal civil rights legislation wasn't passed until 1964.) This caused occasional problems even in the North. Motown employee Al Abrams often accompanied Smokey Robinson and the other Miracles on tour. Abrams and the group usually stayed together in the same hotel. On one tour, though, when the group was performing in Chicago,

Abrams arrived late and took a room by himself in a Hyde Park hotel. Robinson dropped over to talk to him. After Robinson left, the hotel manager called Abrams and told him he'd have to leave the hotel because it was against the rules to have black visitors.

In the South, the Motown performers were barnstorming through a largely segregated area at a time when civil rights leaders were still working to have equal rights for blacks made law, when civil rights marchers were being met with police dogs and fire hoses, and when troops were needed to force the admission of black students to southern universities.

The Motown performers tried to determine far in advance what hotels would house them and what restaurants would feed them. But their day might start with a visit to a restaurant where they would be refused service unless they lined up at the back door to buy take-out food. While waiting in line, they would be able to see whites being served at tables up front. Later in the day, they might try to use the restroom at a white-owned service station and be turned away by a shotgun-toting attendant. When they arrived at the theater where they were scheduled to perform, their audience might include both blacks and whites, but blacks could sit only in the balcony, and the restrooms were segregated by race as well. After the show, if they tried to check into a decent hotel, they might be refused rooms and end up in a flophouse. On one occasion, bullets were fired at the Motown Revue bus (although no one was hurt and no one ever found out who fired the shots.)

Nevertheless, especially in the North, the Motown Revues often attracted large, integrated, and peaceful crowds. "We were the only whites there," said Nancy Van Goethem, who attended one show in Detroit, "but there was no fear in us. Maybe we were naïve girls from the suburbs, but there was such a feeling of camaraderie and togetherness. Everyone would be on their feet, moving their bodies as much as they could, dancing in front of their seats."

The Motown Revues were eventually disbanded, but only because individual Motown artists had become so well-known they could draw large crowds when touring on their own.

Racial discrimination, even in public accommodations, didn't fade that quickly. In December 1970, Marty Beck of the William Morris Agency wrote Wayne Weisbart of Motown that the Supremes shouldn't stay at a large Oregon motel run by a major chain "as this particular motel is not receptive whatsoever to black people. I was informed that this motel gave the Tempts considerable problems when they stayed there as well as the Fifth Dimension."

Racial discrimination in the entertainment industry continued to exist as well. "It's not the public but the executives that are backward," says an unnamed former Motown executive. "The public is much more willing to accept something that makes sense than an executive is. Even now, television people will tell you mid-America won't accept a black artist. Their attitudes haven't changed, their words haven't changed. They shouldn't be thinking about the performers as black performers at all."

Discrimination wasn't the only problem faced by touring Motown entertainers. Exhaustion was another. Touring, together or separately, meant a lot of time on the road for a lot of artists, especially when each tour might consist of thirty to forty-five consecutive one-night appearances connected by long bus rides.

On their first individual tour, Martha Reeves and the Vandellas performed every night for seventy nights. Marvin Gaye remembered going to thirty-six cities in forty days. Some Motown performers were on the road eleven months a year.

Some Motown artists spent most of their time touring and recording. Diana Ross said the Supremes worked so much they didn't have a chance to spend any money. A visitor at Ross's Detroit home concluded that Ross had never cooked on the stove or even sat down in the kitchen, so rarely was she home.

Lust was another problem for touring Motown acts. When one male Motown vocalist was scheduled to perform at a concert in Gary, Indiana, Gordy sent Abrams to accompany the singer and make sure he returned to Motown as soon as the concert was over. Unfortunately for Abrams, the singer met a woman at the concert with whom he wanted to stay a while. When Abrams tried to get him to forget her and return to Detroit, the singer slugged him. Stunned, Abrams called Gordy, then went back to his hotel. A couple of hours later, the singer came in and apologized profusely. The two of them then took the bus back to Detroit. Gordy, furious, screamed at the singer for hours, berating him for staying with the woman and for striking Abrams.

One Motown all-male group actively recruited sexual partners. When one member of this group would spot an attractive woman in the audience at a performance, he would send the group's road manager over to the woman to tell her, "One of the guys would like to meet you. He finds you very attractive." Occasionally, the woman would put him in his place. "I came for the show," she might say. "I'm not interested in them personally." Or, if luck

was with the group, she might whisper excitedly, "I'm with this guy right now, but give me the name of the hotel and I'll be over there later."

The road manager didn't like this part of his job. "As a procurer, I felt like ten cents," he said. Often, he'd pretend he was needed elsewhere in the theater when the group sent him into the audience to solicit.

Sometimes the pursuit of sex nearly caused violence. A female security guard from a Baltimore theater accompanied one well-known male Motown singer to his motel room after a performance. The female guard's boyfriend and fellow guard drove up a few minutes later and started pounding on the singer's door, yelling, "Better let that bitch out or I'll kill you!" The woman snuck out the back window of the singer's room, wearing only a towel, and ran over and banged on the road manager's back window. "You can't come in here!" he yelled, but she insisted. The window, on louvers, only opened halfway and her hips got stuck. The road manager literally had to drag her into his room. But when the police arrived, in answer to the motel manager's complaints, the woman wasn't found in the singer's room and the incident was resolved.

Illicit sex may have been more of a problem for non-Motown groups, though. Motown performers and employees often toured together, attended each other's performances, and married each other: Gordy's sister Anna married Marvin Gaye; a second Gordy sister and Motown employee, Gwendolyn, married Motown producer Harvey Fuqua; a third Gordy sister and Motown employee, Loucye, married Motown performer Jermaine Jackson; Motown producer Mickey Stevenson married Motown vocalist Kim Weston; Stevie Wonder married Motown performer Syreeta Wright; Mary

Wilson of the Supremes married Pedro Ferrer, the group's manager; a Marvelette married a Contour; the Miracles all married fellow Motown performers; and many other intracompany weddings and liaisons took place.

And sometimes it wasn't sex that was the problem but alcohol. When a Motown group toured by plane, the first thing they'd be asked as they strapped themselves in was, "What can I get you to drink?" One of the group was likely to answer, "Since it's morning, I'll have something nourishing. How about a Bloody Mary or a Coffee Royale?" When they arrived at the theater, their dressing rooms would be fully stocked with booze. Club personnel would mix everyone his or her favorite drink without being asked.

Motown's problems had become those of success and popularity rather than those of poverty and bigotry. The company, and all of its performers, had indeed arrived!

PETER BENJAMINSON

Aretha Franklin, 1976. © Leni Sinclair Collection.

# Detroit, My Detroit

*Susan Whitall*

"How do you feel about never leaving Detroit?"

The question is sometimes friendly; at other times, it's weighted with a slight sneer.

Oh, right. I've been chained to a rusty Impala parked on Woodward Avenue for decades, while my friends jet back and forth from California to the pleasure domes of Brixton and Berlin.

"Never left," of course, is inaccurate. I'd already made one gut-wrenching move at the age of ten, when my engineer father got a better offer in the automotive industry and we moved from Philadelphia to Detroit. I missed four years of Detroit rock 'n' roll frenzy when I was in East Lansing, reading poetry by the banks of the Red Cedar from age seventeen to twenty. And I spent the better part of a year in 1974 on a Michigan State exchange program at the University of London, then lived with a family in Paris to polish my French.

How could I leave Detroit, anyway, when a world-class rock magazine was almost literally in my backyard? Even my troubled 1964 MG Midget, more like an enhanced motorcycle, could convey me from my parents' house to *Creem*'s shag-carpeted office at 187 South Woodward. And when I found myself interacting with the pop stars I'd followed since youth, particularly the soul and R&B stars— well, who could leave a town where you're invited to Aretha's Christmas party?

After I discovered *Creem* in an unmarked office in the Birmingham Theater building in 1975, I was invited to a few of their slumtastic functions. While

the guys encouraged me, it was resident rock chick Jaan Uhelszki who took me aside and said she had actual work for me. A few months later, I suggested to *Creem* publisher Barry Kramer that he should hire me full-time. I didn't know his quick yes came about in part because of Jaan's lobbying.

Barry was not typical of the time, in hiring so many women, as you can tell from a quick glance at the staffbox of *Rolling Stone* or any other rock magazine of the era. He was nudged along a bit by Dave Marsh and Lester Bangs, who demanded that Jaan be given equal footing with them. In theory and intent, *Creem* operated between the coasts as a sort of utopian women-friendly hippie paradise. The women of *Creem* had to fight some important and a few ridiculous battles, but at least we were there to do it.

Before my platform wedges slid into the door at *Creem*, there were many women; Robbie Cruger, Georgia Christgau, Jaan, and let's not forget Connie Kramer, advertising director and Barry's wife, an important feminine presence in the office. Before *Creem*, there was Gloria Stavers, editor of *16*, which was the best use of a quarter I knew of in 1965. Stavers was the original and ultimate rock-chick editor, spiritual muse to all who followed.

Soon after I was hired at *Creem*, by chance I found myself living a soul fan's dream. If there weren't several living witnesses, I might have thought I dreamed it.

Rod Stewart and the Faces were playing Cobo Hall, and I was going with Lester Bangs and Eric "Air-Wreck" Genheimer, *Creem*'s mailboy and soon-to-be assistant editor.

After the show, we were swept backstage along with Lester. Rod Stewart was off by the catering table, nibbling cheese and whispering with girlfriend Britt Eklund, but we found the band more fun anyway. "Want to go to a party at David Ruffin's house?" Do we?

The Faces had, of course, brilliantly covered the Temptations' "(I Know) I'm Losing You," and whenever they were in town, Ruffin would join them onstage to do the song. This time, he was also hosting a party at his Detroit home for Rod and the band. Well, the band was going, anyway.

"Bobby will ride with you and show you how to get there," Ron Wood told Lester. Bobby—that would be Bobby Womack, the suave soul star mentored by Sam Cooke and the composer of "It's All Over Now," which we of course knew best by the Rolling Stones. Bobby was also a self-taught, effortlessly funky studio guitarist, doing sessions for years out of Memphis. Bobby had played on so many soul classics. Lately, he was the good-time buddy and tour muse of the Faces. He was always in the thick of things backstage, circulating and making everybody laugh. He'd make you laugh, or die trying.

In case I didn't catch the significance of our navigator's identity, Lester elbowed me. "Bobby Womack is coming with us." Outwardly, Lester acted cool, as if we did things like this every night.

At Woody's signal, we piled into Eric's black Chevy van, Bobby riding shotgun in the front. Bobby grew up in Cleveland, but he had relatives here, and he knew Detroit. As we drove from Cobo through

Detroit neighborhoods, he barked out orders, telling Eric to turn left, turn right, turn left, so by the time we got to what I recall was a handsome brick two-story Tudor house, I had no idea where we were. The house was lit up like an airport runway, and people could be seen in the windows laughing and drinking. It was the height of urban sophistication, and here we came, clothed in standard-issue 1975 rock-kid jeans and T-shirts.

Ruffin answered our knock on the door and invited us in. There he was, one of the famously tall Temptations, thin and rangy, the guy whose rough, emotional baritone singing "My Girl" was coming out of every radio in Detroit when I was growing up.

Once inside, I could see we were in trouble. We were artfully scruffy, and that extended to the boys' manners.

Eric and I retreated to a sofa, but as soon as Eric set his beer down on a side table, a woman hustled over and slid a coaster underneath his bottle. Yes, we were heathens.

But that was nothing compared to Lester's situation. Glancing over toward the dining area/kitchen, we were horrified to see that he was not only dancing with Ruffin's redheaded date, he was *dirty*-dancing with her, hands all over the place, throwing in little grind action now and then. I burrowed into the sofa.

Why couldn't it have been Tammi Terrell he was dancing with? Tammi would have socked him and ended that nonsense.

How much time passed, I don't know, but at some point the partygoers had dispersed, and we were in a back room, singing while Ron Wood and Bobby played guitar. By that time, I was relaxed enough that my Presbyterian alto was blending with Ruffin's and Bobby's voices in song. It was a long way from the Hallelujah chorus on Easter morning in Birmingham, but somehow, I didn't faint dead away.

What almost did make me pass out were some of the words Lester was singing. He was doing a beat poet/rap/singing thing. I would need therapy to remember the words, then I would need even more extensive therapy to forget them. Eric remembers the N-word being in play. Maybe he was trying to push air into the word, play with it and obliterate its power.

This was the era of Richard Pryor, after all. One major difference: He was black.

Lester liked to think he was down with the brothers, because he loved black music so much, and thought he had a pass to talk like that. Most people could sense his good heart. It's possible Ruffin was like that. He was laughing—that I remember. I don't know. I read about Ruffin's troubles later on with drugs with much sorrow.

Some years later, I was circulating at one of Aretha's parties—she'd rented out the Somerset Mall (now Collection) in Troy—and there at a table enjoying the Duke Ellington Orchestra (Mercer conducting) was Bobby Womack. Bobby and Aretha were good friends and he was invited to most of her parties.

So there he was, "The Poet," sunglasses and charm in full effect. He was sitting at a table packed with women, each one hanging on every word. I sat nearby, not wanting to presume, but Bobby spotted me. "Come on over here, baby, don't sit by yourself!" he said.

Flattered by Bobby's attention, I pulled up a chair, despite disapproving side-eye from his admirers.

"Bobby," I said at one point, "you don't remember me, do you?"

"What do you mean?"

"We met once before. We were at a party at David Ruffin's house."

He gave me a long, appraising look—friendly, but with a bit of a smirk. Later, during a lull in the party, he said, "So what are you doing these days, baby?"

"Same thing I was doing when we met," I said. "I'm a writer—for the *Detroit News*. I was with *Creem*, the rock magazine, then. We were backstage with the Faces, remember?"

"Oh, boy," Bobby said. He laughed. "When you told me we met at David Ruffin's house, I thought . . . I thought you were a good-time girl!"

Ah, a good-time girl. Was that veteran musician lingo for someone who liked a party but wasn't quite a professional? Not that I don't like a good time every now and then.

When I told Aretha that Bobby Womack thought I was a good-time girl because he met me at David Ruffin's house, she laughed. When you make the Queen of Soul laugh, it's a pretty good day.

Basking in the warmth of Aretha's goodwill—say, if she happens to speak your name from the stage of a suburban amphitheater—is a wonderful thing. Provoking her wrath is like being in trouble with the toughest mom on your block. You need to run.

I first saw Aretha up close at an Arista Records party when I was still at *Creem*. I was surprised that she was shorter than me, although very curvaceous in a tube top. It seemed that voice and persona should need more avoirdupois than five foot two, but as you soon find out, she doesn't need height.

I had been in a swoon over her music from the first time I heard her Atlantic sides in the '60s. No matter where I am in the world, the sound of her earthy, spiritual voice takes me immediately back to Detroit.

I saw her regal side up close in 2003, in a back room of the Little Rock Baptist Church on Woodward. Luther Vandross was in the throes of his last illness, and Aretha was holding a prayer vigil for her friend.

I never pass up an opportunity to see Aretha sing in church. She's usually dressed in a modest, churchy suit and—buoyed by the familiar setting, with no need to entertain with ballet dancers and hoopla—she abandons herself to the moment.

The pressure is off, because others are singing and playing for much of the service. When moved, she stands up and sings, and you are transported.

She was so moved at Luther's service. She sang "Amazing Grace," and I haven't heard anyone top it.

In a pew set aside for press, a woman came and sat herself next to me where a *Free Press* reporter had been sitting. She introduced herself as a writer for a celebrity weekly. "That seat is occupied," I advised. We don't often hold seats for competitors, but her sense of entitlement was irritating. She moved, shooting me a look.

I saw Mary Wilson of the Supremes chatting with the Four Tops' Duke Fakir, so I went over and talked to them for a while. When I returned, the writer demanded, "Who is that woman you were talking to?" I smiled and gave her my best Gomer Pyle, "Who, me?" expression.

After the prayers and singing, although we'd been promised a press moment with Aretha, everybody had to leave to hit their deadlines except

for me and the weekly writer. We were told Aretha would be ready for us after she ate dinner.

Once her repast was done, we were summoned. The other writer pushed ahead of me and took the best spot directly in front of Aretha, who was seated by a table, nibbling at the remains of her fried chicken dinner.

Before any hellos were uttered, my nemesis was peppering Aretha with questions, as if it was a press conference.

Oh, you are done.

As the writer chattered, Aretha sat, impassive and serene. When there was a break in the torrent of words, Aretha turned almost completely around, showing the writer her back. "Miss Whitall," she said with that unmistakable lilt. When Aretha says your name with that pillowy voice, it is said, once and for all.

"Hi, Aretha."

"I just read something of yours," Aretha continued, taking her time. "What was it? Hmm. Let me think. Oh yes, it was about Sam Cooke. I enjoyed that."

The writer, seething, might as well have been in a UFW hall in the Upper Peninsula. She could have been a body laid out for viewing, as much interaction as she was going to have with Aretha.

After a few pleasantries, I asked Aretha my questions. My competition silently scribbled down the answers. She lived to see another day.

# 5 DETRO
# THE

# IT ROCKS

## '60s

**KICK OUT THE JAMS**

# DKT/MC5
## The Truest Possible Testimonial
*John Sinclair*

t's been more than ten years since Wayne Kramer, Michael Davis, and Dennis Thompson took the stage together in Detroit at Rob Tyner's memorial concert at the State Theatre, and more than thirty years since they lurched their way through their final performance as members of the MC5 at the Grande Ballroom on New Year's Eve 1972.

Thirty years is a long time in anyone's life, especially when most of those years are spent mired in frustration, poverty, and despair. But once in a while a small miracle occurs, and all of a sudden everything is right back on the beam and the future opens up on a brand-new note and everybody who's managed to survive is right back on center stage where they belong. So, when Davis, Kramer, and Thompson return to Detroit "in celebration of the MC5" at the Majestic Theatre on June 10, the disaster years will melt away and they'll begin to enjoy a new day in the sun, bringing the noise from the glory years and illuminating the dismal present with the power of the music created by the MC5. It's an amazing thing, but when you hear it and see it, you'll know what all the shouting was about.

MC5 singer Rob Tyner and guitarist Fred "Sonic" Smith have left us, of course, and it's difficult to imagine the 5's music absent them. But the essence of the MC5 was in its songs and the high-energy methodology the band developed to deliver

them, and those are the core elements brought back to life by the DKT/MC5 celebration band. (DKT stands for Davis, Kramer, and Thompson.)

"We've gone to great lengths with all the promoters to make it clear that it's not an MC5 reunion," Kramer says. "It would be wrong to call it that, because Fred Smith and Rob Tyner have passed on. They can no longer be with us, but we're still here, and these shows are a celebration of the music of the

The MC5. © Leni Sinclair Collection.

MC5 and the work of Fred Smith and Rob Tyner. It would be an insult to their memory and to the fans to pretend that this is an MC5 reunion."

While it's impossible for anyone to take their place, Royal Oak native Marshall Crenshaw will fill in on second guitar, and singers Mark Arm (formerly of Mudhoney) and Evan Dando (formerly of the Lemonheads) will share the lead vocal duties. But it's Davis, Kramer, and Thompson who know how it's supposed to go, and they haven't lost a step since the days of yore. Kicking out the jams is still the order of the day, and they'll be up there doing it without reservation.

"I don't feel like we're from the deep, dark past," Davis says with a chuckle. "What we're bringing to the stage is just as urgent and relevant as it ever was, and not out of step with 2004. We might've recorded this stuff last year—and, in fact, we did!"

"The MC5 was hard-chargin' and *all out*. There *were* no reservations," Kramer reminds us. "The MC5 was visceral—all sweat and muscle and the whole concept of high energy. It's a real thing. It's not just a theory. It's a way of life and a way to play music. It's wonderful to share it."

Yet the spirit of celebration is tempered by a simmering conflict. The Detroit show and the band's subsequent world tour are unfolding in the midst of a protracted battle over distribution of *MC5: A True Testimonial*, a critically acclaimed documentary about the band. Lawyers are involved. In the interest of full disclosure, as we say in the journalism racket, a *caveat* is in order. While this writer may be seen wearing several hats during the unfolding of the MC5 story, I'm here today principally as a professional journalist attempting to negotiate the twists and turns of a fascinating tale and tell it the best I can.

I first met the MC5 in August 1966, the day after I was released from the Detroit House of Corrections after a six-month sentence for possession of marijuana. They played at the Artists Workshop party celebrating my release. I saw them perform at the Michigan State Fair a month later, and I was there when they played at the opening of the legendary Grande Ballroom in October. I loved their music, missed few opportunities to hear them play, and gradually became close friends with Robin Tyner, the band's lead singer and chief theorist. A year after I met them, I would also become the band's manager.

Somehow, over the years, a popular myth, evolved by a succession of reactionary rock journalists, came to hold that the MC5 had been a bunch of innocent suburban rock boys who were corrupted, bamboozled, and manipulated by their left-wing radical manager (that would be me) into fronting for his bankrupt revolutionary politics. But the fact is that Tyner was himself a radical firebrand and a charismatic frontman who sang fervent pleas from the stage urging people to rise against the government and to reject the constraints and constrictions of mainstream culture and its "human being lawnmower" of a system.

Let me put it as simply as I can: I was probably even more deeply influenced by Tyner's thought and practice than he was by my own, and—with the possible exception of Thompson—so was the rest of the band. Tyner was our leader in thought and action, plain and simple.

I was a poet, music journalist, underground newspaper writer, and director of the Detroit Artists Workshop when I met the MC5. Tyner and I found that we shared a common outlook on what was wrong with our country. Our views matured and developed as a result of what was happening in the world we lived in, and we grew into radicalism together.

For the next year, I attended virtually every performance by the band and spent many long nights scheming with Tyner over endless joints and periodic acid trips, attempting to find a way to make some kind of positive change in the world around us. By September 1967, I had somehow assumed the duties of full-time manager of the MC5—not by contract or oral agreement, but almost by osmosis—and by the fall of '68, I had secured for them a recording contract with Elektra Records.

We cut the first MC5 album live at the Grande Ballroom on October 30 and 31, 1968, dates declared by the oracle Ramus—Jesse Crawford, the 5's road manager and stage MC—as the beginning of the first year of Zenta. The next day, we announced the "formation" of the White Panther Party (WPP) as an organization of fiercely resistant white youths committed to the principles and practice of the Black Panther Party for Self-Defense. The founding members of the WPP included this writer, Pun Plamondon, Crawford, Tyner, Kramer, Smith, Davis, and Thompson.

I served as the band's manager until Crawford, Bob "Righteous" Rudnick, and myself were abruptly and summarily discharged in mid-June 1969. Others had convinced the band members that ideological advocacy would impede possible commercial success, and they went for the old-time okey-doke with a greedy passion. A month later, I was convicted in Detroit Recorder's Court of possessing two joints of marijuana and sentenced to nine and a half to ten years in prison.

I spent the next twenty-nine months in Marquette and Jackson prisons before I was released on appeal bond in December 1971. My conviction was overturned on appeal by the Michigan Supreme Court in March 1972, and the state's marijuana laws were declared unconstitutional on several of the grounds raised in my appeal.

By the time I was released from prison late in 1971, the MC5 was well along its protracted slide from the musical and commercial peaks the band had reached in 1970 to its painful and ignominious demise in the final minutes of 1972.

A succession of ineffectual managers and two failed albums for Atlantic Records—exacerbated by the destructive drug habits several members of the band developed—led inexorably to the utter disintegration of the once-mighty ensemble from the Motor City, and the MC5 was soon consigned to the dustbin of rock 'n' roll history.

But, oh, in its heyday the MC5 was truly a wondrous thing to behold, and above and beyond everything else was the power and beauty of an MC5 performance. Holding nothing back, the 5 pounded and pulsated with unbelievable energy and incredible stagecraft.

Though the MC5 itself had little commercial impact, millions upon untold millions of dollars have been made since by reducing and narrowcasting the musical concepts, maniacal stage antics, defiant attitude, and blazing guitaristics perfected by Kramer and Smith and their brothers in the MC5 between 1965 and 1972. The MC5's go-for-the-throat audio onslaught and over-the-top theatrics—though utterly stripped of their social context and creative intelligence—live on in the legions of heavy-metal huffers who've repackaged the sound and fury of the 5 and gleefully sold it to successive generations of rebellious teenagers without a cause. The band's reckless advocacy of recreational drug use and its all-out, gob-of-spit-in-the-face-of-god-and-art defiance of authority and social convention likewise inspired the punk rock movement and whatever has succeeded it. But the 5's focus on musical invention, rhythmic thrust, and social change was replaced by the embrace of a musically inept, socially sleazy pseudo-anarchism lacking comparable intelligence or emotive force.

The MC5 also pioneered in combining jazz and rock to make a new musical form infused with unbridled energy and improvisational freedom, equating the imaginative explorations conducted by John Coltrane, Archie Shepp, Pharoah Sanders, Cecil Taylor, and Sun Ra with their own irrepressible urge to take the music to a higher level of emotional and intellective registration. But their music bears little relation to the lame brand of "fusion jazz" that rose to popularity in the wake of the 5's demise.

Even the MC5's fearless commitment to radical social causes and their incessant fund-raising for community organizations, political prisoners, victims of the dope police, and other outcasts helped create the template for socially conscious popular musicians who would allow their art to be utilized to raise millions of dollars for worthy recipients who were otherwise without hope or support.

But all that is now just so much water under the bridge. There has been no MC5 for more than thirty years, and there will never be another time like that—or another MC5 to illuminate it.

What remains is the music made by the MC5, and the way they played it. To celebrate the MC5 in 2004 by applying the principles of kinetic engagement with the music to its performance makes a beautiful tribute to what the Motor City 5 was all about.

For years, the idea of an MC5 reunion has been a particularly abhorrent concept. The band was indelibly stamped with the heat of the moment of its time, and it seemed ludicrous to think that its members could shake off all the negativism and distrust that led to its disintegration.

When Kramer, Davis, Thompson, and Smith got together in 1991 to honor Rob Tyner, however, the music they made together was anything but ludicrous—the surviving members hit hard and deep, their fabled attack still fully intact. But no one seemed to have any intention to make it more than a one-time thing, and even if they had, there were no market forces that would make a reunion tour economically feasible.

So the MC5 survivors went their separate ways again: Kramer back to Nashville, where he was working as a finish carpenter and cabinetmaker; Davis to his ranch in Arizona and his musical assignments with a series of hard-edged young southwestern rock bands; and Thompson to his home in suburban Detroit and his duties in the workaday world, from which he would emerge from time to time to essay various attempts at making music in public again. Kramer, in fact, had pretty much given up on the music scene after spending the late 1970s and early '80s trying to revive his career. Released from federal prison after serving almost three years on a cocaine conviction, he settled in New York City and did some lightweight touring with a band called Kramer's Creamers, formed Gang War with guitarist Johnny Thunders, toured and recorded with Detroit's all-star Was (Not Was) revue, then devoted several years to developing an underground gangster-rock musical, *The Last Words of Dutch Schultz*, with lyricist Mick Farren and a dedicated cast of musicians, singers, and actors.

Kramer found paying work outside the music world as a carpenter and showcased *Dutch Schultz* at a succession of small venues in the city on the side, but his efforts met with little success. So he finally packed it in and moved all the way south to Key West, where his musical opportunities were severely limited to the occasional bar-band gig. This situation proved so unsatisfying that he decided to abandon his quest for meaningful musical expression and concentrate on his woodworking skills.

But the reunion with his former bandmates in Detroit made Kramer start thinking about playing music again, and he got his chance when the owner of a Nashville recording studio where he was installing some cabinetry realized who this contractor really was and offered to trade him studio time in exchange for some additional carpentry work. Kramer recruited a rhythm section and cut some tunes, then took the tapes to Los Angeles in a bid to get them released. Bret Gurewitz at Epitaph Records, a member of the band Bad Religion, confessed that Kramer was one of his musical heroes and offered him a multiple-record deal with a cash advance sufficient to cover his living costs while he recut the tunes with a supporting cast drawn from the ranks of other Epitaph acts.

Kramer decided to resettle in Los Angeles to try to make the most of this unexpected opportunity, which resulted in four albums for Epitaph and the resumption of touring, in support of their release. The label's promotional efforts and the concomitant growth of the World Wide Web spawned consid-

erable new interest in Kramer and his history with the MC5, but Epitaph was unable to garner enough radio play or adequate sales to advance his career, and Kramer soon found himself back at square one without a record contract.

In the middle of all this commotion, Kramer was called back to the Motor City to mourn the untimely demise of his old comrade-in-arms, Fred Smith, who died in 1994. In recovery from years of drug and alcohol abuse, Kramer was moved to attempt to make things right with remaining MC5 bandmates Michael Davis and Dennis Thompson. There was a lot of unpleasant history to overcome, but it became increasingly important to Kramer that they put the past behind them and celebrate—while there was still time—the positive things they had done together.

Then another minor miracle took place: A team of first-time moviemakers from Chicago contacted Kramer, Davis, and Thompson about making a feature film that would document the story of the MC5. Operating as Future/Now Films, director David Thomas and producer Laurel Legler struck deals with Davis and Thompson with respect to their participation in the project. The filmmakers would form a company with the surviving MC5 members and representatives of the estates of Tyner and Smith, providing for any net profits the film made to be split among the members of the company.

Future/Now envisioned Kramer as the film's central on-screen informant and interpreter of the MC5 story, while Kramer also saw himself as music supervisor for the film and producer of the soundtrack album. Kramer and his manager, Margaret Saadi, were organizing their own production company, MuscleTone Records, and wanted to secure the right to produce and release the soundtrack on their label. In return, Kramer would cooperate fully with the film production, perform as directed in several shoots for the film, and personally instruct his music publisher, Warner/Chappell, to provide to Future/Now a gratis license for the use of his compositions in the movie.

Kramer and Saadi worked closely with Future/Now for the next four years as the film went into production, the producers sought financing and distribution, and the MC5 story slowly unfolded itself onto film.

"We became so involved in the creation of this film," Saadi says, "because we thought it was a great story which needed to be told and because we had an agreement that there was a job for Wayne."

Saadi and Kramer introduced Future/Now to Warner/Chappell; helped set up filmed interviews with Jon Landau, Danny Fields, and this writer; and vouched for the fledgling film production company with potential lenders and distributors. Completed in 2002, *MC5: A True Testimonial* follows the rise and fall of the MC5 from its origins as a teenage band in Lincoln Park to its phenomenal local success as the kingpin of the Detroit rock 'n' roll scene, its daring appearance as the only band to show up during the 1968 Democratic convention to play at the Festival of Life in Chicago, its emergence as a touring act with a Top 30 album on Elektra, its unique experience as cofounders and propagandists for the White Panther Party, its defection from the WPP and ensuing pursuit of conventional success in the music industry, its failure to gain popular acceptance or significant record sales, and its messy disintegration and dissolution in 1972.

David Thomas turns in a fine job in his directorial debut, marshalling the many disparate elements of the MC5 story into a coherent, well-paced exposition of the band's explosive impact and denouement. Most impressive is his deft editing of the archival performance footage—shot *sans* sound in the '60s with 16 mm Bolex and Super 8 cameras by Leni Sinclair (full disclosure: this writer's ex-wife)—to recorded performances of such MC5 staples as "Kick Out the Jams," "Looking at You," "High School," and "Shakin' Street." The performance footage, most of it previously unseen, is tightly interwoven with intimate interviews, government surveillance film shot at the Festival of Life, still photographs and images of the musicians from childhood to the present, and a powerful soundtrack pulsating with the triumphal yet underacknowledged music of the MC5.

*MC5: A True Testimonial* had its international premiere in November 2002 at the International Documentary Film Festival in Amsterdam. The film was then shown at the Raindance Film Festival in London, the Goteborg Film Festival in Sweden, and the Toronto International Film Festival, drawing enthusiastic audiences and widespread critical acclaim.

Going into 2003, everything seemed to be clicking right along. A new round of screenings would include the San Francisco International Film Festival, Tribeca Film Festival in New York City, and the Melbourne International Film Festival in Australia; and the filmmakers turned their focus to landing a DVD deal and signing with an agency to arrange commercial theatrical screenings for the movie.

But that's exactly when the shit hit the proverbial fan. Kramer had been a little edgy since 2001, when Future/Now screened a twenty-minute sequence from *A True Testimonial* that had been edited and soundtracked by director Thomas without Kramer's participation. More important, there was the matter of the absence of a written agreement between the parties with respect to Kramer's services. Also undocumented was Kramer's purported share in the ownership of the film and how he would be compensated for services rendered to the project.

In 2000, Future/Now had incorporated an entity called Zenta LLC (a name they lifted from its originators without permission) to own the film and distribute the net proceeds among its members, who were to include the investors as well as the three living bandmates; Tyner's widow, Becky Derminer; and the estate of Fred Smith. Membership in the corporation was contingent upon its members signing the Zenta LLC operating agreement, including an attached "publicity release," a waiver that delivered all appropriate rights to the corporation for its use in commercial exploitation of the completed film.

All the pertinent parties signed on except Kramer, whose deal was somewhat more complex. He and Future/Now had exchanged contract drafts without resolving their respective issues, and Kramer was particularly adamant in his rejection of a stipulation that would have granted the filmmakers "the absolute and irrevocable right" to use Kramer's name and likeness "for any purpose whatsoever, including but not limited to" the film.

"They want to own everything about me forever," Kramer has written.

Kramer signed and returned the Zenta LLC operating agreement in June 2002, but not the attached publicity release. Instead, he says, he submitted language of his own that granted the use of his name and likeness "in connection with the promotion, distribution, and exhibition of the Film." Kramer also sought written confirmation that MuscleTone Records would have the "exclusive right to produce, manufacture, promote, and distribute audio products as the Film's soundtrack," reserving for MuscleTone final approval of the musical program, packaging, and promotion of the album.

Though still not accepted into membership by Zenta LLC, Kramer joined his bandmates in August 2002 in approving the issuance by their publisher, Warner/Chappel Music, of a gratis one-year music license that allowed Future/Now to screen the film at festivals in order to attract distributors.

"We didn't want to stand in their way," Kramer writes on his website. "We wanted them to sell their movie. We hoped that they would do the right thing."

While Kramer and Saadi tried to resolve their differences with Future/Now so *A True Testimonial* could achieve commercial release, another thorny rights issue emerged from an entirely unanticipated direction. In Europe, Levi Strauss had issued an MC5 T-shirt in its vintage clothing collection and announced a complete line of casual shirts, jackets, and other apparel that would "celebrate the revolutionary spirit" of the MC5 with designs using the band's logo and the likenesses of its members. Levi Strauss had licensed MC5 designs from artist Gary Grimshaw and photos of the band from Leni Sinclair, then secured (to their satisfaction) the rights to the MC5 name, logo, and likeness through the agency of Rob Tyner's widow, Becky Derminer. The whole deal cost Levi's a trifling amount (less than five figures), and the textile manufacturer suddenly seemed to be the proud and fully licensed "owners" of the MC5 legacy.

Shocked by this new development, Kramer and Saadi thought first of a lawsuit, but decided on a course that could turn the situation to the advantage of the band while avoiding a court battle. When they contacted the Levi Strauss office in London, they had a bold plan in hand, and they found themselves talking to people at Slice, the company's public relations firm, who were more than a little receptive.

MuscleTone's concept was simple: Since Levi's was "celebrating" the MC5, why not stage a musical celebration at a London venue that would bring Kramer, Davis, and Thompson together with an array of sympathetic guest musicians and singers for an intimate, one-time, invitation-only concert—and film and record the event for release as a DVD. They would call it *A Celebration of the MC5*, and Levi's would foot the bills as part of the promotion for the MC5 vintage clothing line.

Slice's Alec Samways signed on to the project and became co-executive producer of the *Celebration* documentary with Saadi. As the plans for the project began to take shape, MuscleTone invited Future/Now Films to participate in the projected four-camera shoot, help with production of the film and DVD release, and also to screen *MC5: A True Testimonial* at the concert, scheduled to take place in March 2003 at the 100 Club.

But Future/Now, still operating without a signed agreement with Kramer, refused to participate and rejected Levi's invitation to show its film at the London concert. From this point on, they seem to have regarded Kramer and Saadi—and, by extension, Davis and Thompson, both very much a part of the

London project—as adversaries. The whole Future/Now project began to steer a very perilous course.

There is a certain cruel irony at work here: Three men in their fifties who had been bitterly estranged for twenty years are reunited in a creative context to make a film about their long-defunct band and the incredible music they made together. They begin to heal their wounds and build a new basis of artistic cooperation and trust by working together on the movie. They get cut out of what might have been a major licensing deal with Levi's yet manage to emerge smelling like roses, the heroes of a hot-ticket London concert celebrating their music that will be documented for release on DVD. But the people who brought them back together to make *A True Testimonial* now seem to regard them as some sort of Frankenstein's monster that's grown out of control, pitting the *movie* of the MC5 against the *lives* of the surviving band members.

So the two projects centered on the history and music of the MC5 rolled ahead on separate tracks. *A Celebration of the MC5* was staged under Levi's sponsorship to wild acclaim. Davis, Kramer, and Thompson brought the 5's music back to life in a series of rehearsals and then went onstage for the concert, joined by guest rockers Lemmy Kilmister of Motorhead, Nicke Royale of the Hellacopters, Ian Astbury of the Cult, Dave Vanian of the Damned, and singer Kate O'Brien, plus former Detroiters Dr. Charles Moore on trumpet and Ralph "Buzzy" Jones on tenor saxophone.

The set list for the show included MC5 favorites "Lookin' at You," "Gotta Keep Moving," "Skunk (Sonically Speaking)," "Rocket Reducer No. 62," "Tonight," "High School," and, of course, "Kick Out the Jams." The sound was hot and fresh, the stage remained in frenetic motion, and the crowd went crazy. The British music press responded with equal fervor.

"After all, the MC5 created the blueprint for all that's cool in modern rock 'n' roll," *New Musical Express* enthused. "They rip the 100 Club to shreds with a force-50 gale of everything you love about rock 'n' roll."

"You only get to see so many truly legendary gigs," *MOJO* magazine summed up, "and tonight was definitely one."

The concert's success also inspired the production of a thirty-minute MC5 documentary hosted by *MOJO*'s Andrew Male and Zane Lowe of BBC Radio 1 that was focused on the 100 Club show. Once the program aired on UK Channel 4, MuscleTone licensed the production for inclusion in *Sonic Revolution: A Celebration of the MC5*, the DVD that documents the concert with sixty scintillating minutes of performance footage. By the end of 2003, MuscleTone had fully cleared all the music for the *Celebration* DVD and licensed it to Image Entertainment and its affiliates for worldwide release on July 6, 2004. To make things even rosier, concert promoters all over the world, excited by the reports from London, had begun to agitate for the chance to hear and present *A Celebration of the MC5* on their own stages.

Before they knew it, Kramer and Saadi had cobbled together a string of dates that would take the show all over North America, Australia, Japan, and Europe this summer. Detroit is the second stop.

Meanwhile, *A True Testimonial* was careening along on a contradictory course: Future/Now had parlayed the film's enthusiastic reception by festival audiences and film critics into a deal with Avatar to book the movie into commercial theaters and a DVD distribution agreement with Private Music, a division of BMG. But Future/Now still had not concluded a working arrangement with Kramer for the right to use his name and likeness or his compositions.

Future/Now's limited license to exhibit the film at festivals expired at the end of the summer of 2003, and Warner/Chappell informed the company that the publishing house would not be able to grant them synchronization rights to the MC5 compositions until the filmmakers had worked out their issues with Kramer. A screening scheduled for October 30 at the Detroit Institute of Arts— the film's first ticketed theatrical exhibition—was allowed to proceed under a special dispensation from Warner/Chappell, but final clearance would be withheld pending Kramer's authorization to proceed. Despite this serious setback, Future/Now closed its deal with Private Music and accepted an advance, apparently maintaining that its licensing problems would be resolved by the projected release date, which had been set for May 6, 2004.

On the theatrical front, Avatar was arranging commercial bookings for the film in New York City, Chicago, San Francisco, New Orleans, Detroit, Ann Arbor, and other cities for the spring and summer of 2004.

Evidently convinced that Kramer would not cooperate, Future/Now and Becky Derminer teamed up to file a motion in Los Angeles on February 27, 2004, to reopen Kramer's Chapter 7 bankruptcy case from 1999. Future/Now claimed that Kramer had "entered into several agreements [in 1996 that] gave FN Films personality rights, and entitled and authorized FN Films to use all music and recordings in which [Kramer] held an interest." Future/Now claimed further that "under the agreements FN Films paid all of [Kramer's] expenses in connection with various shoots and interviews, and agreed to give [Kramer] . . . membership interests in [Zenta LLC]."

Yet eight years after all these deals purportedly were struck, no written agreement had been executed, and Kramer filed papers with the bankruptcy court denying that he had any income coming from *MC5: A True Testimonial*.

"Future/Now Films and their attorneys have asserted for many years now that there is no agreement," Kramer states in his filing with the court. "I have since been denied membership in Zenta LLC because I have refused to give my story away for no compensation whatsoever. There is no income stream for me related to their film."

Producer Laurel Legler, whose nine-year film project languishes in limbo, counters: "I disagree with everything that comes out of Wayne Kramer's mouth, because he doesn't tell the truth. We never reneged on agreements with Wayne Kramer. We tried to give him everything he wanted."

An equally exasperated Kramer says: "They have as yet made no concrete offer to solve their problem. We have lots of solutions for their problem, but it's not up to us to fix it. And I find it amusing that their story keeps changing. They can't keep their lies straight.

"No one's more disappointed than I am. I worked hard on that movie, and I always anticipated that they would do what we had agreed upon."

Kramer was furious about the court action, which he considered an attempt to pressure him into signing over the rights to his music, his image, and his personal story, so he decided to bring the

torturous negotiations to an end. In court papers, Kramer contended that the motion had been filed in an "attempt to scare, harass, and intimidate Mr. Kramer . . . [but] Mr. Kramer will not support the Film Project."

A week later, Davis and Thompson declared their solidarity with Kramer by means of a letter from their attorney, Jay W. MacIntosh, to Future/Now. Dated March 4, 2004, MacIntosh's letter says: "Please be advised that my clients Michael Davis and Dennis Tomich (p.k.a. Dennis Thompson) do not support the release of, licensing of, screening of, and/or sale of the film *MC5: A True Testimonial* until all issues have been resolved between the film company and MC5 band member and songwriter Wayne Kramer, and documentation of such has been provided to my office.

"Please note that this statement supersedes any statements previously made by myself or anyone else on behalf of Mr. Davis and/or Mr. Tomich. Any failure to recognize this shall be considered willful misrepresentation."

The next day, Kramer attorney Edward Saadi (Margaret's brother) wrote to Future/Now's lawyer to say that Kramer would do nothing "to assist Future/Now in its effort to obtain [the] license" from Warner/Chappell. He demanded that Future/Now "immediately and permanently" refrain from using Kramer's image and pay Kramer any money already generated from merchandising, box-office receipts, and other sources.

Warner/Chappell followed with a cease-and-desist letter barring further distribution of the film and mandating the cancellation of current and future commercial screenings. Private Music had distributed advance copies of the *True Testimonial*

DVD for media review, but the company was forced to announce that the film's release had been delayed.

Thompson says he believes Future/Now "made some errors in judgment. They essentially were showing a film without a license." He hopes all the wrangling can be resolved.

"We're all getting a little tired of hearing about it. Once it gets to the lawyers, who knows what's going to happen?" Thompson says, adding, "I don't wish [Future/Now] any ill will whatsoever, but I support Wayne Kramer. Wayne and I have come a long way toward making amendments to ourselves as human beings. This is about the music and the band. Future/Now is not MC5. We can create that spirit onstage. It's always this political cloud following us. There's always this black hole."

Rob Tyner's widow, Becky Derminer, is confident that *A True Testimonial* will eventually see theatrical and DVD release. "The film is a beautiful piece of art," she says. "This movie's going to come out. It's too beautiful to be hidden in a closet." Derminer says she won't be attending the show at the Majestic.

So there it sits, a vehicle disabled and fuming on the shoulder of the road while another wheels its way to the starting line with a full tank of gas and a precision crew at the controls. Of course, MC5 fans the world over hope that *A True Testimonial* will eventually hit the screen and the DVD racks, but those of us in the Motor City and the other stops on the DKT/MC5 tour won't have to wait any longer to see how Wayne Kramer, Michael Davis, Dennis Thompson, and their friends are celebrating the legacy of the MC5 onstage.

"It's great to get back together with Wayne and Michael and to be able to do this, and be able to bring this music to people who have never been able to hear it," Thompson says. "The bottom line is, we've got a world tour coming up. We had great rehearsals out in LA. We rehearsed some thirty-five-odd songs, so we'll be capable of playing any and all of the MC5 songs going all the way back to the beginning. This is about growth. This is about the MC5 attitude, the MC5 energy and spirit in 2004. This is not really the MC5. It's really a celebration of the MC5's music. If anyone is capable of playing this stuff, it's Wayne, Michael, and me."

Kramer concludes: "It's like uncorking some kind of nuclear device or something. This shit rocks *hard*, and we're having big fun doing this. It's one of those times when you can say that it doesn't get any better."

# Robin Tyner
## Early Days/Final Days
*Rebecca "Tyner" Derminer*

When first presented with the idea to write a narrative of my life with the MC5, I was very honored but also intimidated. Over the years, there have been so many articles, interviews, and interpretations, as well as different histories and events depending upon who was telling the story and how it related to their own personal agenda. How could I capture and share with others my experiences and how it felt to be involved in such a special time that had so many aspects of hopefulness,

Rob Tyner. © Leni Sinclair Collection.

dreams, visions, despair, disappointments, success, conflict, and darkness?

One of the very first thoughts that flooded my mind in thinking about this was one of synchronicity, the idea of meaningful events that seem to occur and/or exist at the same time. My dearest friend Donna and I were attending Wayne State University, and in the fall of 1964, we very bravely moved into an apartment near the WSU campus. One early evening, walking home from the bus that dropped me off a block away from our apartment after working at a mall, I was approached by a tall young man, with dark, short hair. He was dressed in black, wearing Beatle boots, and spoke with an English accent. He was inquiring as to the location of the party. I immediately responded that the party that night was at the apartment of Neil and Sandy in the basement of our building, and I left with my boyfriend at the time. Later that night, after I returned home, Donna told me that she discovered that the young man was not really English, but he seemed nice enough so she invited him to the party we were having the next week. That young man, Bob Derminer, continued to visit us and beguile us with stories and drawings and ideas beyond what we had ever imagined. We became close and committed, and fell into a place that was the beginning of a very deep and intense relationship that developed into love a few months later. What if that bus had been a few minutes earlier or what if it had been a few minutes later? Fate?

Rob was born Robert Wayne Derminer to a young teenage couple who separated soon after his birth. Rob and his mom moved in with his maternal grandmother, who completely adored him, and step-grandfather in an inner-city area located, ironically, not far from the Motown studios on West Grand Boulevard. His early days were spent in a diverse neighborhood where he embraced the music and rhythm of the streets along with his surrounding neighborhood. Around the age of four, a young man (whom Rob later learned was his dad) began showing up at his home and brought him a cowboy suit in order to gain his favor. It really didn't work, because he resented the intrusion into his idyllic life. Soon after, his parents reconciled, and later a younger brother was born.

When Rob was about ten years old, his family moved into a new, small bungalow in Lincoln Park, Michigan, for a better life as his dad fulfilled his dream of moving out of the city. Rob hated it, but found solace in his fantasy life as a caveman in a nearby park where he spent most of the time in his youth while not in school.

Rob fancied himself a greaser in high school and often sought out like-minded fellows, hanging out at the White Castle or down by the railroad tracks drinking beer. It was during this time that Rob met Gary Grimshaw, a fellow artist and rebel, and they became lifelong friends. They spent hours in Rob's basement building model cars. We later joked that they were probably getting high on the glue. They listened to jazz, read Jack Kerouac and science fiction, created art, and fancied themselves Beatniks. Because they were too young to drive, they somehow managed to have one of their mothers drive them to the Minor Key, a Detroit

jazz club where they saw the likes of John Coltrane and Cannonball Adderley. Rob always dreamed of attending art school, and his grandmother promised to help him. Unfortunately, she passed away and his step-grandfather remarried; helping Rob attend art school was out of the question. After high school, Rob began working at a warehouse and lurking around the Wayne State University campus near where his friend Gary Grimshaw had lived.

Through his younger brother, Rob was familiar with Wayne Kambes (who later changed his name to Kramer) and Fred Smith and became interested in their band. This led to him joining them as a bass player. However, he could not play the bass and he was soon fired. After several months, they asked him to come back, this time as a roadie. He refused but somehow managed to return a short time later as the lead singer. In the meantime, Pat Burrows began playing bass and Bob Gasper played drums, and the MC5 began playing local bars specializing in cover tunes of the day. They won several battle of the bands competitions and soon graduated to playing record hops sponsored by local radio stations. They wore matching fake-suede black shirts and were on their way to stardom! One of their first managers—after Wayne's mother, a Lincoln Park friend they coerced into helping them buy equipment, and a few others chosen primarily to help them promote their careers—was Ann Marston, an associate of the DJ Swinging Sweeney. Ann competed in the 1960 Miss America contest representing Michigan, and with her archery skills she won the talent competition but not the crown. She was helpful in getting exposure and gigs; however, her ability to achieve the next level of success in the Detroit area was limited, and soon she became less involved.

I met Rob soon after he was fired from the band. Donna and I were attending Wayne State University, and Rob was working. He lived with his family in Lincoln Park, but he began spending a lot of time with us. Our building was filled with students, derelicts, and welfare recipients. Across the hall was a couple who had just arrived from New York. Steve was a community organizer and his partner, Sandy, made sure you knew she was the coolest chick on earth. She had Liz Taylor Cleopatra eyes and black hair teased about six inches high and formed into flames. She spoke in a husky voice, and every other word was either *man* or *cool*. She told us she knew Bob Dylan, and we were very impressed. Two art students lived down the hall, one of whom was Michael Davis, and another art student, Jim, lived next door. Several political activists were also in our building. We stayed up late smoking cigarettes, drinking beer, experimenting with marijuana, and tackling all the issues of the day. We joined committees to end the war in Vietnam and promote civil rights. We were living the bohemian lifestyle we had created in our minds. We had fun.

Rob enjoyed being in the band and playing around town several times a month, and the group began to gain some recognition. Rehearsals were held in Wayne's mother's basement in northwest Detroit. Rob had changed his last name to Tyner after McCoy Tyner, a jazz pianist who played with John Coltrane. Everyone butchered the pronunciation of Derminer, and the name Tyner also honored his admiration for McCoy Tyner's work. Rob was an excellent writer, as well as an outstanding cartoonist, and he began writing songs. He was very pleased with himself the night he wrote the song "Looking at You" while stacking boxes on high shelving in the warehouse. However, Rob didn't quite fit the image his bandmates had for someone fronting the band. His hair was too curly, he was overweight, too intellectual, and how could they attract girls when he had a girlfriend? In an effort to please, he began using various products and processes on his hair in order to make it straight. That effort was not very successful since it broke his hair and burned his scalp. So we began setting his hair on large rollers, resulting in a bubble-like Beatles bowl style. The only problem with this was that when he performed and got sweaty, his hair would creep to the top of his face, become frizzy, and look ridiculous. He lost weight, too, but he continued in the role of my boyfriend.

Around this time, maybe the middle of 1965 or so, Steve and Sandy separated. Sandy looked around at her available options and chose Michael Davis to replace Steve, and they soon married. They moved to a nearby duplex and began using heroin. One late night, early in 1966, Rob and I were driving home and found Michael Davis walking down the street crying. He explained that Sandy had just returned from New York with her new friend, and Michael would have to leave since there was no place for him to sleep. We brought Michael home and he stayed with us for a while. He soon met other members of the band and would sometimes go to their gigs.

It was time for us to move; our space was too small. We all moved in February 1966 into the duplex formerly occupied by Sandy and her friends, who were on their way to Florida. Rob officially moved in, which angered his father, who had "worked and slaved his whole life to move his family out of the city and now you go back right where you came from." His father eventually came to terms with Rob's choices and in later years bragged about his

235

successes. We did not know we were under police surveillance until they confronted Donna and me one night, demanding to know the whereabouts of the former occupants. We were sort of freaked out that they had our names and knew all about us. Little did we know, at the same time we were being questioned, Michael and Rob had taken Owsley sugar-cube LSD, looked out the window, seen the police, and had a joint meltdown. That was the first time Rob had taken a hallucinogen, and it was a terrifying, never-ending ordeal for him, with all the predictable monsters, demons, and thoughts of dying. While Rob enjoyed the sacrament, he did not indulge in hard drugs.

The band continued to play and achieve a level of success, but there appeared to be discord about the band's future direction, which culminated in Bob Gasper and Pat Burrows leaving. Wayne thought it would be a great idea for Michael Davis to play bass with them because he was so handsome he would certainly attract the girls. It didn't matter that Michael couldn't play bass; he played a little acoustic guitar, and Wayne would teach him how to play the bass. Dennis Tomich, later known as Dennis Thompson, began playing drums with the group. Wayne knew Dennis from Lincoln Park, and he had played in various bands.

One day, folks from the government of the city of Detroit came to our house and told us we had to move since WSU classrooms were going to be built in that area. (They never were, and now that area is home to public housing.) Saul Alinsky, a well-known community organizer from Chicago, came to Detroit to help us fight the relocation battle to no avail. The city gave us $200 to relocate and we used the money to go camping in Canada. While we enjoyed our

"vacation," that was certainly meager compensation for others who had to leave their lifelong homes. We moved, just the two of us, into an apartment on the Wayne State University campus, with Donna moving downstairs. Our neighbor sold marijuana and was constantly knocking on our door telling us the big bust was coming down, get rid of everything! He was soon proven right, and there were several busts one night, including one with John Sinclair.

Rob and John Sinclair developed a friendship and spent long hours analyzing and debating various aspects of music and events of the day. The other band members began spending more time in the area and cultivating opportunities for recognition. Wayne, Fred, and Dennis moved in downstairs from us, and Michael was living with an alleged witch about a block away. During the summer of 1967, we watched army tanks rolling down our street with guns pointed at our building. We saw fires and smelled smoke everywhere. The Motor City was burning. John Sinclair and the Detroit Artists Workshop folks fared much worse. The Detroit police took advantage of the situation and intensified their harassment of John. The band discarded their uniform-style costumes and began designing their own clothes. Wayne modeled his choices on the Beatles' Nehru jackets; Rob became very Edwardian, with flaring jackets and ruffles; and Fred explored fringed, almost cowboy outfits. Rob, Wayne, and Fred's girlfriends crafted the clothes, and Dennis and Michael (without regular girlfriends) sort of had the leftovers when we could squeeze in the time to attend to their sartorial needs.

Soon, John became more involved with the band and became their manager even though they were deemed unmanageable. The band connected with

Russ Gibb and soon began playing at the Grande Ballroom. It was decided that the whole band would move into the building formerly occupied by the Detroit Artists Workshop and use the downstairs storefront as a rehearsal space. Rob and I gave up our jobs and supporting ourselves and began to rely upon band earnings. However, John, as the manager, collected all the money, paid our bills, and gave us a grocery and laundry allowance. Without any direct money, Wayne's girlfriend, Chris, and Fred's girlfriend, Sigrid, and I began sewing clothes for other people in order to have a little money for expenses like gas for our cars, cigarettes, occasional ice cream cones, material for clothes, etc. That arrangement continued until the band began working on their second album and moved from the Ann Arbor commune to a place in the woods in the spring of 1969.

Rob has been described by many as the soul and visionary of the band. He continued writing songs and reaching out for higher things in his life. He stopped straightening his hair and allowed it to grow into a beautiful halo that surrounded his face. He danced his ass off onstage and sang from deep inside his very being. He embraced Native American spirituality and found truth, beauty, and grace from the universe. Rob's sensitive nature made him an easy target for criticism from his bandmates regarding anything that did not go right, whether real or imagined. He was often subjected to group therapy sessions conducted by his bandmates, which essentially amounted to personal attacks and bullying. While becoming more introspective, he found a voice in the words of his songs and grew confident of his own abilities and talent. Songs such as "American Ruse" and "Human Being

Lawnmower" addressed political issues of the day. Others, like "Come Together" or "Let Me Try," embodied romance and lust. Some, like "High School" and "Rocket Reducer No. 62," for example, were just fun. "Starship" reflects elements of jazz and science fiction. Rob ultimately embraced his freedom, courage, strength, and persona with the words he crafted for the most famous of the MC5 songs, "Kick Out the Jams," declaring to anyone who would listen, "Let me be who I am."

Rob infused the band with dreams, inspiration, and visions that went far beyond the boundaries of the universe. It was a time when all things seemed possible. Time as we knew it mutated and became reality. It was a time of magic, when minutes were like years. All of us were lost in a maze of experiences during an explosive time on the planet. Music was everywhere, whether on the radio, the turntable, the streets, or streaming from rehearsal studios or a stage. Music was the flame that lit our lives.

Now, it is Rob's turn to reflect on his time with the MC5. Rob met his dear friend Howard Thompson in England when he was invited to write a piece on punk rock for the *New Musical Express*. When Howard joined Elektra records in New York, he was determined to re-release the MC5's first album and invited Rob to write the liner notes. These are Rob's words, written in 1991 for the re-release:

Brothers and Sisters . . .

If your eyes are scanning these words right now, you must have a spark of interest for a time long vanished. The cultural circumstances surrounding the creation of this music will never again occur. This

REBECCA "TYNER" DERMINER

237

shining disk that you now possess has, encoded in its whirling vortex, a moment of history frozen forever. This is a window through time, and you can unlock the fabled Grande Ballroom gates. Uncle Russ will take your ticket. Now, step through the kaleidoscope into a magic night in Motor City Rock and Roll.

Gaze deeply into the prismatic colors of this compact disk like a crystal ball and let the vision envelope your senses in mystic sound. Let yourself step back to a time when muscle cars ruled the Detroit streets and Motown battled psychedelics for the airwaves. It was a time when everything was everything. A time of girls without bras and sex without rules. Bands from all over the world came to Detroit to play in the arena of the Grande. Close your eyes and you shall hear earth-shattering sound waves and see panoramic light beams. Can you smell the fragrance of patchouli incense and strawberry cigarette papers?

This music is old enough to buy beer in any state in the union, so why is it important that it's being re-released by Elektra today?

Because, this album of songs is a microcosm of the times that spawned it. It was an idealistic attempt to make something more significant than the mere product that dominated the charts. This record has within it the vision and the violence of a turbulent time in America. This music expresses the frustration and future shock of the soul of the '60s. This is a portrayal of the struggle to create a world that was destined never

to be. An impossibly beautiful dream that was doomed by the nation's descent into the disco inferno of the '70s.

We were punk before punk. We were new wave, before new wave. We were metal, before metal. We were even "MC" before Hammer. Depending on your perspective, we were the electro-mechanical climax of the age, or some sort of a cruel counterculture hoax. We were considered killer, righteous, high-energy dudes who could pitch a whang dang doodle all night long. People concluded that we were:

No exalted talent.

The revolutionary hype.

John Sinclair's primary political tool.

Like 13 year olds on a meth power trip.

Intolerant to our British betters, and

Definitely born under a bad sign.

Some saw us as valiant rebels, cheerfully thumbing our noses at parental authority. Others saw us as a symptom of a sick society. We were hassled by the pigs and pushed around by both the media and the revolution. But the bullets bounced right off, and through sheer determination, we survived more death blows than any other band in history.

Return with me now to Halloween night, 1968. It is the New Year of the revolutionary Zenta calendar. Producer Jac Holtzman and engineer Bruce Botnick are ready at the recording console. John Sinclair and Danny Fields prepare for the musical onslaught. The prophet of Zenta, Brother J. C. Crawford readies himself to make the opening statement and invocation. Wayne Kramer and Fred Smith tune their atom-smasher guitars, resplendent in sequins and spangles. Drummer Dennis Thompson and Bassist Michael Davis prepare themselves for the manic experience to come. I can feel the anticipatory excitement building within me as I listen to the mounting noise of the waiting crowd. The moment approaches. This is the night we've been working for all our lives, when the MC5 will unleash sonic fury and devastate the cosmos with megabursts of thunder.

Come dance beside me in the snake pit of wires on the Grande's stage while the cataclysm explodes like a missile strike all around us. Watch the light show roll and flare, swirling all over the walls and ceiling, clashing off the mirror ball in a billion shards of glare. Feel the excitement of the crowd as they let the sound wash over them like a gigantic tidal wave, wiping out the last shreds of civilization and leaving them in a state of sweaty, primal oneness. See Grande girls with Day-glo face paint swirl under the black light, phosphorescing in the music's roar. Watch get-down Detroit dudes and their mini-skirted foxes do the tribal stomp, twirling as if it's the last night of the Universe.

Grande Days

If I had a time machine
I'd take you back with me
To the heyday of the Grande,
and
All the wonders there to see.
The walls ablaze with colors
Smell the incense in the air
Hear the music's sound and fury
When the English bands were
there.
In the psychedelic ballroom
As the light show whirled about,
and
All the people freaking freely
While the jams were kicking out.
Grande days, Grande days
I had some wild nights
Back in my Grande days.
You were there at the Grande,
I remember you
You had hair down past your
shoulders, and
You wore rainbow-colored shoes.
You were there with a chick in a
miniskirt,
They called her "Sister Mystery,"
and
One of us was blasted, and
It wasn't her or me.
Cause you spoke to me in Day-glo
words, and

239

You swore it was true
That you could hear the colors,
and
You could see the music too.
Alone at night in the Ballroom,
I heard a mournful, eerie call,
As though a tortured soul was
sobbing
Deep inside the walls.
Of my memories of the Grande,
This one disturbs me most,
I didn't believe the place was
haunted
'Till I heard the Grande ghost.
Now the Ballroom stands empty
Nobody ever comes to play.
They took out the PA system, and
Put the light show away.
But, if the Grande could talk
What stories she would tell,
Of when the music rolled and
thundered
Like fireworks from Hell,
Of the violence in the parking lot,
and
The craziness backstage
When the Detroit scene exploded,
and
The Grande was the latest rage.
Grande days, Grande days,
I had some wild nights
Back in my Grande days.

We rode the roads together and it was a brutally hard slog. We fought the fights and suffered the slings and arrows and still we won our share of victories in the great battles of the bands.

A lot of things have changed since the recording of this album. Some things are changed forever. But, if we could speak to you now, from the unity we once knew, I think we'd say . . .

People of tomorrow
From the deep past
We salute you!
Thunder in the night forever!

# Amboy Duke

*Gary Graff*

Revenge can be a powerful motivator.

And it's certainly why the Amboy Dukes came into existence and took us on a "Journey to the Center of the Mind"—and beyond.

The Dukes were the unintended result of an adolescent trauma for guitarist Ted Nugent, who in 1964 was a happy Detroit boy, soaking up the early Motown and British Invasion sounds and playing his guitar in a band called the Lords. Then, his world was upended; his father, a former army drill sergeant, was moving the family to Chicago after receiving a promotion from Uddeholm Steel, and Nugent learned the hard way that "my little hobby of rock 'n' roll didn't matter."

Not surprisingly, this did not sit well with the future Motor City Madman, who had been taught by his father to pursue what he wanted with unbridled passion. "I was going to pursue my musical dream with a vengeance, and God help anybody who got in my way," he recalls. "I wasn't going to let [moving away] compromise that at all."

Ultimately, however, the move may have been fortuitous. Almost as soon as he set foot in the Windy City, Nugent made his way to the Cellar, where the Shadows of Knight were kicking out their particular brand of jams. It was that night that Nugent met two fellow musicians—guitarist Gary Hicks, who was training horses by day, and Bob Leonard, who was singing on cruise ships— with whom he would form the Amboy Dukes, appropriating the name of a popular Detroit outfit that had featured highly regarded guitarists George Cole and John Finley.

"By that fall we were kicking the Shadows of Knight's ass," Nugent says, reveling in the memory. "I brought every Detroit spirit, every Detroit attitude and just gave the middle finger to Chicago. They didn't know what faster and louder meant; when those bands played cover songs, they played them just like the record. When we played cover songs we gutted them. People in Chicago didn't know what the fuck kind of noise we were making. 'What is he doing with that guitar?!' We were scaring people."

Conquering Chicago was not Nugent's goal, however; as soon as he graduated from high school in June 1967, he brought the Dukes back to Detroit and plugged them into a rock 'n' roll scene that was far more sophisticated than when he'd left three years before. Mitch Ryder and the Detroit Wheels had already rolled through, and riding in their wake were the likes of the Bob Seger System, the Stooges, the MC5, the SRC, the Rationals, the Frost, and many others.

"There was an intensification even I wasn't prepared for when I returned," Nugent acknowledges. "When I got back and watched the MC5, I was not quite prepared for that."

But—big surprise—Nugent wasn't intimidated by it, either. Recognizing that he needed to fortify the troops to do battle in his hometown, Nugent gradually replaced the Chicagoans, homesick and frustrated by the group's meager earnings anyway, with take-no-prisoners Detroit boys. John Brake (who changed his stage name to Drake when it was misspelled on the Dukes' first album) had sung in the Lords. Guitarist Steve Farmer was in a group called the Gang. Drummer Dave Palmer, bassist Bill White, and keyboardist Rick Lober rounded out the Dukes' first Detroit lineup.

Living in a house in the Detroit suburb of Livonia and playing "just enough shows to keep us in cereal and bread, keep the van running, and the speakers working with some degree," according to Nugent, the young Dukes were always either doing shows or rehearsing in the basement. "We would do twelve-, fifteen-, sixteen-hour jam sessions," Nugent remembers, "play at outrageous volumes, playing outrageous stuff. We were a bunch of young kids jamming on spontaneous music."

Drake recalls, "Our rehearsal schedule ran five days a week, eight hours a day—at least. That's what held it together. The band just stayed tight all the time."

Attention came quickly, mostly due to the band's high-octane delivery and Nugent's inherent sense of showmanship; eschewing the tie-dyed conventions of the time, he would appear onstage in Native American headdresses and in loincloths, adding the image of the hunter-savage to the Dukes' already potent and loud sonic concoction. And the Dukes' peers approved. Notes the MC5's Wayne Kramer, "They were good representatives of what was going on in Detroit in terms of bands trying to put on a show and trying to entertain people and bring the influences of R&B and what was happening at Motown and the influences of the first wave of the British Invasion." And in his liner notes for the celebrated *Nuggets* collection, Mike Stax wrote that

the Dukes' brash, toothy attack "for better or for worse pointed the direction for countless groups as the '60s drew to a close."

This lineup of the Dukes had one shining moment—its 1967 cover of Them's "Baby Please Don't Go" for producer Bob Shad's Mainstream Records, which had established its reputation with the first album for Big Brother and the Holding Company, which featured another burgeoning talent in singer Janis Joplin. "We were the first ones to get signed out of the [Detroit] scene," Nugent says, "not because we had better songs, but because of the hell we were raising."

He was raising hell within the band, too. Adamant about keeping the standards high, White and Lober were out, replaced by Greg Arama and Andy Solomon. Now the notoriously critical Nugent began to feel some degree of satisfaction. "We were all . . . nothing short of virtuosos, head and shoulders above musicians in rock 'n' roll back then," he says.

The group was still divided when it came to drugs, however. Nugent was staunchly against them, raised strictly to neither drink nor get high; he got his kicks—and subject matter for songs such as "Dr. Slingshot," "Good Natured Emma," and "Loaded for Beer"—in the woods, where he hunted and communed with nature. His bandmates, however, were more typical denizens of the psychedelic era.

"Everybody was doing opium and heroin and hashish—and they were just a wreck," Nugent laments. "I saw pop art and Peter Max. I saw all the LSD-relative stuff in the marketing of the day. But I didn't understand any of it, 'cause I never hallucinated. But I could twist a phrase with the best of them." The irony, of course, is that the Dukes' biggest hit, "Journey to the Center of the Mind"—a

Top 20 single in 1968—was something of a drug anthem. But Nugent contends to this day that he never gleaned that particular meaning from fellow guitarist Farmer's lyrics.

"I didn't have the faintest idea," he maintains. "I didn't know what those [opium] pipes were on the album cover, either. I thought, 'Journey to the center of the mind, yeah, it's good to be reflective, to journey inside yourself, to think before acting.' That still makes sense to me, actually, although for Steve Farmer it was more of an 'LSD will open the mind to the many colors of the rainbow.' If you look at the lyrics, it reflects either of those philosophies, really."

Drake recalls fairly innocent musical beginnings for the song, however. "We were hanging around the [band] house, eating and watching TV. Ted said, 'Y'know what? I bet you I can play the next commercial that comes on TV.' But it wasn't a commercial that came on; it was *Bonanza*. He picked up his guitar and played the theme song, and that's where ['Journey to the Center of the Mind'] started." It's a thought that would likely knock Ben Cartwright right off his horse.

The Dukes' journey became rockier as time went on, however. A combination of playing three hundred nights a year—which Nugent calls "the road destructo-derby of the spirit"—and the other members' escalating drug habits led to more lineup changes; thirteen members in all made their way through the group over the course of nearly twelve years and six albums. The Dukes also label-hopped from their abysmal Mainstream deal to Polydor and finally Frank Zappa's DiscReel imprint, where the group was billed as Ted Nugent's Amboy Dukes, reflecting the gunslinger reputation he was earning via a series of guitar duels with the MC5's Kramer,

Iron Butterfly's Mike Pinera, and Mahogany Rush's Frank Marino. It also marked the arrival of bassist Rob De Lagrange, who would remain with Nugent through his glory years of the mid- and late '70s.

The Dukes were a dead issue by 1975, when Nugent embarked on his solo career. In his wake, the group's legacy has been sadly relegated to "Journey to the Center of the Mind" and "Baby Please Don't Go," which savvier fans know is entirely unacceptable. Nugent, of course, went on to gold and platinum success as a solo artist and equal notoriety as a hunter and a conservative commentator and personality. The Dukes did, however, put a sweet note on their legacy when Nugent, Drake, Farmer, Lober, Solomon, and Bill White regrouped at the eighteenth Annual Detroit Music Awards in 2009 to receive a Distinguished Achievement Award and play together for the first time in nearly twenty-five years. With Johnny "Bee" Badanjek of the Detroit Wheels and the Rockets on drums, the group played "Journey to the Center of the Mind," "Baby Please Don't Go," and Mitch Ryder's "Jenny Take a Ride," defiantly proving, as Nugent told the audience that night, "Everyone knows that the Amboy Dukes are the ultimate garage band on planet Earth!"

243

# The Story of Detroit's Third Power Band

*Willy Wilson*

The Third Power were one of the best power trios I ever saw at the Grande Ballroom. . . . I just wish I could remember the Grande Ballroom!

—Tom Skinner

We had the reputation that we could make our amps sound ten times louder than they actually were.

—Jem Targal

Like a meteor shooting across the horizon, the Third Power lit up the Detroit music scene with a ferocious roar like no other group before them. Like all meteors, they burned brightly for just a short while, leaving only one 45 and one full-length album but a lasting legacy.

## BEGINNINGS

The Third Power was born at Oakland Community College in 1965 in a study class, when a student named Jem Targal started talking music with a

!!! *THIRD POWER* !!! @ "THE DETROIT LIBRARY STEPS" CONCERT

Photo by Jem Targal.

teacher's assistant named Drew Abbott. Originally, Jem was a violinist and Drew was a drummer. "Drew said that I'd make a good bass player because of my violin playing," remarked Jem. Both Jem and Drew decided to ditch their respective instruments, and, with guitars (matching turquoise Silvertones) in hand, they started jamming and writing songs with the intent of putting together a band. Said Jem: "Drew was basically learning the guitar and I was just learning the bass, so it worked out well. We actually built our own equipment. We came into some money, so we went out and bought six fifteen-inch JBL Lance speakers, and built these cabinets that you could have dropped out of an airplane and they'd still be fine. We also built our own Heathkit amps as well. I think we won our first battle of the bands because our equipment looked so cool and was so loud!"

When asked about the set list from the band's early days, Jem said:

> We started playing the standard covers of the era, but at the same time we were writing our own stuff. We'd be playing teen dances and frat parties trying to find the right balance of working our original tunes into the sets. Our biggest problem at the time was finding a drummer. We couldn't find the right guy. We had a drummer who couldn't even nail the breaks in "Mustang Sally." It was really embarrassing. Drew knew of someone that was just starting to get back into playing after an injury. A really good jazz drummer named Jim Craig. As soon as we jammed with him, Drew and I knew instantly Jim was the guy for us. After that, the biggest problem was trying to find gigs.

We really did have a lot of fun playing those early gigs. One of our first real gigs was at the Crow's Nest East with the MC5. We were still doing things like "Hey Joe," "Midnight Hour," "Time Won't Let Me," and "Route 66," as well as Young Rascals stuff and a few originals. We also played an early gig with the Rationals at a club called Mothers (in East Tawas, Michigan). We were in a parade during the day, so we painted flowers on Drew Abbott's 1951 Plymouth. When it was time for the gig, the Rationals were a bit snooty to us, so we ended up doing a version of "Respect," which was their big hit at the time. But after that we became pretty good friends with Scott Morgan and the guys.

Originally, we had this fifteen-year-old kid named Allen Licari booking us. Our big break came at a place called the Psychedelic Midway at Royal Oak Kimball High School. Our set was so loud that the police officers from the neighboring city of Clawson (which was five miles away) came by and shut down the gig. Lloyd Edwards, who saw the show, approached us about becoming our manager. Lloyd soon partnered with Bill Baron and formed a record label (Baron Records), which led to our first single, "We, You and I" and "Snow." It was a great time for the band as we started getting bigger and better gigs. We were also getting really creative. It seemed like every practice we had a new tune ready to go. Drew or I would come in with an idea and we would flesh out the song from there.

The Third Power sounded different from other rock trios of the time such as

Cream or the Jimi Hendrix Experience. The music tended to be more melodic and layered and didn't focus on one musician but on the band as a whole. "I remember when Drew brought copies of *Fresh Cream* and *Are You Experienced* to our practices," said Jem. "We were blown away. It was cool to see power trios that had the same energy as us. We were all like, 'Hey, we can do this! We can do this on our own terms!'"

## THE POWER FARM

Like a lot of the bands of the era, the Third Power moved into a communal home to create. Jem recalled:

It was an old farmhouse in Farmington. We had a ton of space, eighty acres with half of it being woods. We went in and picked out our rooms, as it was a really big farmhouse, with five or six bedrooms. We built a studio in the basement. We put up some of the Eastown Theater's old curtains in the room. They hung from the ceiling and circled the room. The floor was made up of carpeted swatches, so it looked like a checkerboard. We also had one of the old Eastown spotlights as well. It was so much fun working on tunes at the house. Someone would come to practice with an idea and we would just flesh it out. "Like Me Love Me" was born out of jamming that way.

The Power farm was also more than just a communal home. "We used to have great parties," Jem said laughingly:

246

Pretty much once a month, usually on a Saturday night after a gig. We had lots of bands and people all the time. We had huge outdoor parties, too. Hundreds of people showed up, even motorcycle gangs, like the Outlaws. But they were pretty cool. We also had a "pink cake party" for one of our roadies, Chuck Ziemba, who was going on tour with the Frijid Pink. A friend of ours, Psychedelic Mary, loaded the frosting on the cake with some mind-altering goodies. Photographer [and former Grande Ballroom manager] Tom Wright set up an Indian village back in the woods, complete with tepees. Somehow we found our way out to a big bonfire that they had started. After that, we ended up out in a field trying to talk to birds. It was lots of fun. The music scene in Detroit back then was like one big family. Bob Seger and a who's who of Detroit area musicians used to come by the farm to jam and hang out. Visitors like Tim Buckley, Bert Jansch, Carmine Appice, and a ton of others all dropped by to hang out, too. Rod Stewart and the Faces came by as well, and it was at one of our parties that Ron Wood met our roadie Roydan Magee (a.k.a. Chuch). Chuch ended up with The Faces and then the Rolling Stones, becoming their crew chief for over thirty years before he passed away.

## VANGUARD

Detroit was a very creative rock 'n' roll city in the late 1960s and early 1970s. The MC5, the Rationals, SRC, the Stooges, Frijid Pink, the Amboy Dukes, Catfish, and Savage Grace were all signed to major labels. Vanguard Records was a little late to the party, but with the success of the Frost (featuring Dick Wagner), they were looking to expand their Detroit rock 'n' roll roster. Says Jem: "Sam Charters saw us at the Detroit Rock Revival show at the Michigan State Fairgrounds." Sam Charters recalled, "I was in Detroit scouting groups, and they were one of the bands in a big afternoon outdoor concert festival—I think it was in a baseball park? What I really liked about them was their freshness and their openness to the big crowd. They just seemed to be enjoying themselves and they were very solid musically."

Jem:

Our manager Lloyd said Sam wanted to talk to us. We really didn't know that much about him at that time. We actually had a choice between Vanguard and Columbia. But we didn't really explore the Columbia connection as much as we should have. We really felt comfortable with Sam. The band on the whole thought that with Vanguard being a smaller label, they would actually try harder to push the band. Which, of course, didn't happen, but the Frost did OK with the label. Vanguard also kind of dropped the ball on the artwork as well. We all thought that the images on the back cover should have been the images on the front cover. We really enjoyed working with Sam on the record. He played the piano part on "Passed By." He told us that it was his favorite among the musical pieces that he had ever played on.

Sam Charters:

I played the keyboards on a lot of albums, since it was so much easier for me to just do it, rather than look around for somebody who could learn the arrangement and who would have to get paid. I was comfortable in the studio with them, partly because I had already learned how to work with the Detroit sound in working with the Frost. We didn't have all the technical difficulties that I had had to deal with when first working with the new power guitars and drums. We also got along because I respected their musicianship. It was such a busy time for me at Vanguard; we did so many recordings. I still remember the album with Jem, Drew, and Jim as a satisfying creative moment. I knew we didn't have an obvious single on the album, so I was working for an album concept in the studio. I tried to focus it upon what each of them had to offer in the musical mix.

## THE BREAKUP

The beginning of the end for the Third Power happened the way it did for a lot of great bands. A mixture of nonstop touring, a lack of record sales, and no label support all led to cracks within the group:

Drew and I [Jem] would have our differences at practice. It put Jim in a difficult spot. That's where a lot of the hard feelings came from. The final straw pretty much came while were performing with Grand Funk Railroad in New Orleans. Drew had a blowup with our roadie Chuch. That put everybody in a weird mood. We went down to Florida and did some shows with Quicksilver Messenger Service, but Jim quit soon afterward. Drew and I soldiered on for a while with a new drummer, Mike Richette. We were doing a lot of fusion stuff; it was awesome. Unfortunately, when we got back to Detroit, the Grande and the Eastown theaters were pretty much done. The only gigs around town were bar gigs. Which really didn't appeal to me. I just felt like it was time for me to do something else. But to this day, I still believe if we had been able to hold on and work things out, we would have really made it over the hump. I felt that our music and lyrics had really matured.

After the breakup, Drew, Jim, and Jem got on with their lives. Drew achieved great success as Bob Seger's right-hand man in the Silver Bullet Band. Jim moved out to California and settled in Los Angeles, where he is a successful building contractor. Jem went on to work in the automotive industry designing cars (he recently retired). He continued with his musical endeavors as well, releasing a solo album, *Luckey Guy*, in 1976. Jem also created the mind-blowing cartoon character called Jungle Bird. You can check out the adventures of the Jungle Bird at junglebird.com.

## REUNION

In October 2006, the Third Power put aside their differences and got together for a very special reunion show at the Royal Oak Music Theater to celebrate their fortieth anniversary. Sharing the bill with the Crazy World of Arthur Brown, Canned

Heat, and Big Brother and the Holding Company, the Third Power showed they had lost none of their chops. They came out and blew away the crowd (including yours truly), as well as the other bands. I was amazed to see how powerful a live act they still were after all these years away from each other. The old tunes sounded fresh, and they whipped out a stunning version of "Little Drummer Boy." For one special night, everything came together, full circle for the band. It was great to see the power of three working as one again.

# Bob Seger

## The Early Years

*Gary Graff*

ob Seger clearly recalls the first inkling that music might be his life's pursuit—as we'd expect from the guy who sings that rock 'n' roll never forgets.

"My dad made a big deal when I was, like, four years old about the fact that I sang, 'I'm Looking over a Four-Leaf Clover' in the back of his '49 Buick," Seger remembers. "He just went nuts over that. I think that was maybe the very first inclination for me."

Sixty-six years later, that's proven to be a sage revelation. Seger has carved out a four-decades-plus recording career in which he's sold more than 50 million albums and launched enduring hits such as "Ramblin' Gamblin' Man," "Night Moves," "Turn the Page," "Hollywood Nights," "Against the Wind," and "Like a Rock." "Old Time Rock and Roll," meanwhile, from 1978, is not only the number 1 jukebox selection of all time but has virtually replaced Creedence Clearwater Revival's "Proud Mary" as the celebratory anthem for weddings, bar mitzvahs, and similar occasions.

Moreover, Seger—a 2006 Rock and Roll Hall of Fame inductee and a 2012 Songwriters Hall of Fame arrival—is largely responsible for creating a model for, and voice of, the midwestern singer-songwriter, a different breed of rock 'n' roll animal than its East and West Coast counterparts. Seger and those who

Bob Seger at Pine Knob, 1976. © Leni Sinclair Collection.

followed drew the same kind of inspiration from Hank Williams, Woody Guthrie, and Bob Dylan but applied their own regional aesthetic to it—creating a more narrative form built on earthy parables about maintaining everyday ideals amid all manner of adversity and temptation. No plaintive troubadours, these folk, Seger and company also showed you could deliver these contemplative paeans with the same kind of furious energy that you'd use to sing about cars and girls.

"Bob Seger's music [is] thoughtful and badass, all in one measure," says John Mellencamp. "I learned to respect Bob for . . . playing by his rules and staying honest to who he is and where he comes from. I am proud to be part of his brood."

In his work, Seger celebrates the nobility of the "Beautiful Loser" and the workers on the assembly lines "Makin' Thunderbirds," as well as the metaphorical struggle of running "Against the Wind." The subject of his "Hollywood Nights" grapples with a double-edged sword as he lives life in too fast of a lane, while the exuberant freedoms of his "Ramblin' Gamblin' Man" and "Travelin' Man" are not as unfettered as they initially seem but rather tempered by a desire for more dependable relationships. And the warm nostalgia of "Night Moves," "Main Street," and "Brave Strangers" reveals the wisdom of remembering, but not necessarily wallowing in, the past in a pursuit to make sure "The Fire Inside" still burns hot.

Seger is not the first of rock's songwriters to espouse these values—nor are they the exclusive property of the heartland. But he's filled the songs on his studio albums with a richly interwoven set of place and beliefs that surely speak to a life spent, excepting a couple years in Los Angeles, soaking up inspiration from the Detroit environs where he still lives.

"I don't think it was really a choice; it was where I lived and where I felt comfortable," Seger explains. "By being in Detroit, I can keep things in perspective and just work as much as I can but also have a life outside of it where I'm grounded and where people put me in my place. Everybody there treats me just like a guy and not a rock star, and that's good. It's a more calm and grounded atmosphere to work in."

Seger's earliest influences came from his parents. His father, Stewart, was an autoworker who played a variety of instruments—clarinet being his best—and on weekends performed with bands in the Ann Arbor area. Seger describes his mother, Charlotte, as a serious music lover: "You name a song, and [she'll] tell you not only the singer but the writer and when it was recorded. She was like a music encyclopedia."

Seger's father gave him his start around age nine, teaching him some chords on the bass ukulele, which led the fledgling musician to learn songs by Elvis Presley, Buddy Holly, and Little Richard that he heard on his transistor radio late at night via stations such as WLAC-AM out of Nashville. Music remained important in the house even after Seger's father left the family when Bob was ten, sending them into poverty. Seger was able to live what he calls "a totally free-spirited life" while his mother and older brother, George, worked, but his contribution to the family was musical even before it became his livelihood.

"I brought the music back into the family," explains Seger, who worked short-term for automakers Ford and General Motors before he began making more money playing in clubs. "I always sat there and played ukulele and sang . . .

and kind of quelled all the anger and disturbance because of the fact that my father left."

Few around him thought ill of Seger's musical dreams; in fact, he notes, "All my friends when I was growing up and going through junior high and high school, they would always envy me. They would say, 'You know exactly what you want to do; you want to be a musician.' There was never any doubt."

Seger was a fixture on the Ann Arbor and Detroit club scenes by the early '60s, where he met future Eagle Glenn Frey (who sang backup on "Ramblin' Gamblin' Man") and cut his teeth in Doug Brown and the Omens. Pete Stanger, a guitar player he worked with, provided Seger's entrée into songwriting.

"He wrote a song and it was called 'Jackie the Thief,'" Seger recalls. "There was this really hot girl named Jackie Cobb, and he wrote it about her and had a big crush on her, and when he wrote it I said, 'That sounds like a good idea. I'll write, too . . .' The first one I wrote was called 'The Lonely One.' It's actually not bad for a first song."

It wasn't long before songwriting became his favorite musical thing to do and what he considered his primary occupation. He explains:

I've always thought of myself in that same sort of school of someone like [Bob] Dylan. I've always had an affinity for people like him and Tom Waits, Joni Mitchell, Paul Simon, Billy Joel . . . people who wrote solo. But at the same time I not only write but I help produce and I go on the road and I'm a bandleader—a lot of different hats.

But I still consider myself mainly a writer, and I've always felt great respect for those people because I know how hard it is to write solo. So being in that [Songwriters] Hall of Fame is very special to me.

Seger launched his solo career during the mid-'60s, hooking up with teen club operator Ed "Punch" Andrews, a former member of Seger's band the Decibels who became his manager and coproducer. Seger's regional acclaim—if everyone who says they saw him perform at their school really did, he could have retired by the time he was old enough to vote—helped sell more than 50,000 copies of his first single, a knock-off of Them's "Gloria" called "East Side Story." He kept his local-hero status intact with "Persecution Smith" and the primal "Heavy Music," while 1968's "Ramblin' Gamblin' Man" gave Seger his first visit into the *Billboard* Top 20.

The fallow period that followed has become the stuff of legend. Seger toured hard and kept recording, but nothing seemed to click. He tried different band configurations and changed labels; he even contemplated quitting music and going to college after recording his 1969 album, *Noah*. The Michigan fan base was always there; the rest of the world, however, was oblivious.

Seger never doubted himself, however. "In that seven-year period . . . even though we were playing, like 250 nights a year, I could tell I had something because the audiences wanted me back, and we killed every night," Seger says. "So I knew I had something." In hindsight, however, Seger is willing to guess that the music just wasn't good enough.

"I played too many nights," he says, "and I really didn't have enough time to write."

That changed in the mid-'70s, when he (or, as he tells it, Andrews) christened his Silver Bullet Band

251

and polished his craft for albums such as *Seven* and especially *Beautiful Loser*, a more carefully crafted and diverse set of material that provided a clear bridge to greater fortunes that followed. "Glenn Frey . . . heard the *Beautiful Loser* stuff and said, 'This is great, Bob. You're on your way. You've got it now; you're a songwriter,'" Seger says.

The songwriter quickly became a superstar. The definitive 1976 concert document, *Live Bullet*, became his first platinum album. *Night Moves*—with its Top 5 title track about a teenage love affair ("My first broken heart!" he says)—took Seger into the multiplatinum realm in 1976, where he stayed for his next four albums. For 1980's *Against the Wind*, he acknowledges, "We wanted to really have a number 1 album; that's what we went for." And he got it, spending six weeks atop the *Billboard* chart.

The past two decades have found Seger on a different sort of path, however. He's put together three studio albums and a variety of compilations. And while some of his writing has taken on more detailed, cinematic qualities, Seger will tell you his greatest satisfactions have happened away from music, in his twenty-one years of marriage to third wife Nita and in being a father to son Cole and daughter Samantha.

Not surprisingly, the man who was abandoned by his own father is driven to give his children "what I didn't feel when I was a kid, which is a great sense of affection and stability. It's just nice to focus on trying to do a good job." He's also taken time to become a championship sailor on the Great Lakes.

But the creative fire still burns inside, from fresh tracks for *Greatest Hits Vol. 2* and *Ultimate Hits: Rock and Roll Never Forgets* to rediscovered material for 2009's *Early Seger Vol. 1* to 2014's *Ride Out*, his first set of all-new material in eight years. "I think I'm writing a little simpler, a little more direct and a little more out front," Seger says. "I think I'm just coming into my own kind of groove. You just want to get up there and sing, y'know?"

He made some noises about packing it in as he approached seventy in May of 2015. "I just don't want to overstay my welcome," he explains. But even if that were the case, Seger says he imagines still writing, for and with others, and somehow keeping his hand in music.

"You think about how old I thought I was when I was writing 'Rock and Roll Never Forgets'—'Sweet sixteen turned thirty-one!'" he says with a laugh. "But back then, the career arc for most people in entertainment was three good years, five tops, and you were gone. I mean, who'd ever thought we'd be seeing McCartney at sixty or seventy on stage? Jagger? Nobody. And here I am—still. It's just . . . interesting. But really gratifying."

# Seger Unsettled

John G. Rodwan Jr.

When "Old Time Rock and Roll" came on the radio in the back of the bike shop, one repairman jokingly asked the others, "OK, who's the Bob Seger fan?" I'd previously witnessed a similar scene in a bar. When Seger started playing, someone wondered who'd made the laughably unhip jukebox selection. The song title precisely fits the musician's work. He set out not to reinvent his genre but to glory in its power to affect listeners and in its legacy leading up to the 1970s, the period of his most muscular work. The bard of deracination, who had his first major hit with "Ramblin' Gamblin' Man," ended up with an undeserved but unshakable reputation as the quintessential midwesterner. Other performers also evoke certain periods or become associated with particular regions without being looked down upon by those who carefully calibrate their likes and dislikes to some exclusive index of coolness, but digging Seger especially confers no cachet among the in-crowd.

Growing up in Detroit, I heard Bob Seger all the time. I didn't own any of his albums then; I didn't need to. He was a fixture on local radio. It wasn't until I moved away from Michigan that I learned how closely he was identified with the state. Say "Seger" or "Silver Bullet Band" anywhere else, and chances are those who know the names will immediately think of the middle part of the United States.

Tom Weschler, Seger's tour manager and photographer in the late 1960s and early 1970s,

resists this tendency to limit his former employer's scope and the extent of his impact. He pronounces Seger "one of American music's greatest artists." In *Travelin' Man*, a collection of his pictures and short snatches of recollections assembled with journalist Gary Graff, Weschler also calls Seger "an American music icon."

Other admirers simultaneously say Seger should be better appreciated and insist on regarding him principally as a local hero. In his foreword to Weschler and Graff's book, John Mellencamp labels Seger's work Midwest rock. In his afterword, Kid Rock calls it heartland music. In his introduction, Graff use both regional descriptors. Even with his insistence on Seger's national importance, Weschler's numerous snapshots of Seger backstage with local Detroit radio personalities (not always clearly identified as such) and onstage at area venues tend to confirm the easy identification of Seger with the place where he was born. (Mellencamp praises him for his dedication to the region.)

Seger, a Grammy Award–winning Rock and Roll Hall of Fame inductee whose albums sold millions of copies, hardly languishes as an unknown outside the Rust Belt. While having a song intimately associated with Tom Cruise dancing around in his underwear probably wouldn't be most musicians' preferred fate, *Risky Business*'s use of "Old Time Rock and Roll" graphically illustrates the distance Seger traveled from the shopping mall openings and universities he played (and Weschler

253

documented) early on. The 1983 film put the 1977 song on the *Billboard* Hot 100 chart for a second time. The firsthand episodes mentioned above also suggest Seger's impact far from the Great Lakes: the bicycle store playing classic-rock radio was on the West Coast, the pub on the East Coast.

Ironically, many of Seger's best songs involve escaping the geography listeners insist he embodies. For their collaboration, Weschler and Graff borrow an appropriate Seger title. Another song, "Roll Me Away," may mention Mackinaw City but imagines fleeing from too-familiar confines. Seger recorded it in California, the setting for "Hollywood Nights," which does involve a midwesterner too far from home, but he's unsure he can ever return to it. Seger says people he met in Hollywood inspired "Still the Same." California comes up again in "The Fire Down Below," which also mentions cities in Illinois, Nevada, and New York—but not Michigan. "Turn the Page" (which Metallica covers on *Garage, Inc.*) is another road song, and "Katmandu" dreams of getting far from the USA (where no one loves him anyway). "Makin' Thunderbirds," about building cars, may suggest a strong connection to the place where that used to happen, but singing about automobiles hardly sets Seger apart from innumerable peers who sing about wanting to speed somewhere else.

Perhaps the impulse to go elsewhere could be considered a fundamentally midwestern theme. I know I felt it. (My solution to the dilemma in "Roll Me Away" of whether to go east or west: both, sequentially.) Slashing his tires and leaving him stranded in the center states strips the singer's song of its essence, depletes his story's drama, and deprives the urge he articulates of its force. Besides, if it were a regional phenomenon, what does one

do with Bruce "Born to Run" Springsteen, next to whom Seger stands looking starstruck in one of Weschler's photos?

Other Seger tracks have nothing at all to do with specific sites. "Night Moves," about "tryin' to lose the awkward teenage blues," could be set anyplace. He recorded "Old Time Rock and Roll" about a musical state of mind, at Alabama's Muscle Shoals Sound Studios, where Aretha Franklin, the Staple Singers, Bobby Womack, Percy Sledge, and Wilson Pickett also made music. Seger made several other hit songs there, including "Mainstreet," which he does claim is about Ann Arbor, Michigan, where he grew up, but which really deals with lonesomeness and longing and also could take place anywhere.

In addition to telling stories of journeys, Seger creates characters. "Beautiful Loser," an ode to resignation, describes an honorable mediocrity. The persona of "Still the Same" tires of gamblers and hustlers. In "We've Got Tonight" a man tries to talk a stranger into a one-night stand. And what serious guitar slinger wouldn't have songs about women both desirable ("Her Strut") and duplicitous ("Sunspot Baby")?

Given Seger's commitment to narrative and character, as well as those Hollywood nights, it's no surprise that his music has figured in many movies (before and after *Risky Business*), some of which may have damaged his reputation. His songs appear on the soundtracks for films like *FM* (1978), *Urban Cowboy* (1980), *Teachers* (1984), *Mask* (1985), and *About Last Night* (1986). "Against the Wind," a tribute to perseverance, found itself in *Forrest Gump* (1994); "Roll Me Away" landed in *Armageddon* (1998). During the 1980s, he started making lousy music specifically for lousy movies. "Shakedown"—

written for *Beverly Hills Cop II* (1987) with sadly representative lyrics like "Breakdown, takedown, you're busted"—features a Synclavier, an electronic apparatus that emits sounds as euphonious as its name. The use of "Like a Rock," a celebration of endurance, in pickup truck commercials won him no acolytes in the cult of artistic purity.

The limp sell-out tag doesn't easily adhere to Seger. Mellencamp lauds him for his rigorous individualism, but he is someone who wanted to reach a large audience (no crime) and did whatever it took to do so. "We wanted to really have a number 1 album," he said of *Against the Wind* (1980). "That's what we went for." Possibly, he alienated sensitive subscribers to romantic notions of authenticity by appearing to compromise his artistic integrity and aiming to cash in. More likely, instead of standing steadfast with the Motown-meets-Muscle-Shoals-with-memories-of-the-Mississippi-Delta sound he'd forged, he sought to change with the times but ended up with something that didn't really suit him. He may have sung about being old-fashioned while still young, but nothing signals being out of touch like straining to seem up-to-date. This may have prompted his return to his familiar style on *Face the Promise* (2006), which resembles the earlier work but suggests an imitation of it rather than a triumphant return to a still-nourishing creative source.

If *Travelin' Man* doesn't convincingly elevate Seger from the provincial level or rehabilitate his image, that's because it has more modest goals. It doesn't try to rescue him from his midcareer misfires, which it basically ignores. It doesn't argue that *Face the Promise* is the artistic equal to *Seven* (1974), *Beautiful Loser* (1975), *Live Bullet* (1976), *Night Moves* (1976), or *Stranger in Town* (1978), relegating

it instead to the discography (and Kid Rock's reference to the thrill of working with Seger on one of his tracks). "*Travelin' Man* was not conceived as a full-scale, tell-all Seger biography," Graff explains. Instead, it's Weschler's story, told mainly through his camera lens. Yet the photographer stopped working for Seger before the name-making records came out, though he did subsequently shoot the occasional show or work on an album cover. Unremarkable in appearance, Seger is not the most likely candidate for a coffee table book, and Weschler can only mention events that might have yielded something more entertaining than standard concert and dressing-room shots. He refers to Bob Seger and the Silver Bullet Band opening for Kiss in 1975: "Nobody expected them to do that well on tour with a band that was so comic book oriented in their look but played their music like the real deal." Anyone hoping for documentation of the sweaty, long-haired, almost-stereotypical-biker-looking dude backstage while the high-heeled kabuki rockers apply their makeup will be disappointed. Weschler calls his years with the singer-songwriter as "fabled among Seger fans," but Graff calls the same period—following some early success in the 1960s but before the Seger hit-making assembly line started running full speed in the mid-'70s—a "fallow period that has become the stuff of legend." If Weschler envisioned capturing the rise of a rock star, he picked an unfortunate time to pursue "other endeavors." He left before the headliners stepped into the lights.

In one of his last essays, John Updike concedes that "the early works remain the ones I am best known by, and the ones to which my later works are unfavorably compared." He considers himself fortunate, however, in more than one way. "A writer's fan base, unlike that of a rock star, is postadolescent and relatively tolerant of time's scars," he observes. Still, his situation and Seger's might not be all that different. For one, Seger, unlike the musician Updike has in mind, never became "that skinny old man (Mick Jagger) [who] kept taking his shirt off and jumping around." (With his short gray hair, his well-padded paunch, and stodgy square glasses, the fifty-nine-year-old Seger at the 2004 Hall of Fame ceremony looks like he could be one of the Rolling Stones' stage technicians or, perhaps, one of Updike's golfing buddies.) More significantly, there's the fine, finished work. "An aging writer," says Updike, "has the not insignificant satisfaction of a shelf of books behind him that, as they wait for their ideal readers to discover them, will outlast him for a while." The same could be said for Seger, who wrote and recorded at least a dozen and a half sturdy musical stories that will, I believe, long continue to find and please listeners.

Perhaps even among those who don't want to admit it. I suspect that some who want to laugh at Seger secretly enjoy his stuff. After I confessed to liking him, others in a Brooklyn bar grudgingly allowed that he made some solid rock 'n' roll. Seger recorded his most well-known songs before the kids fixing bicycles in Portland were born, but they could all identify his work. And not one of them changed the station.

# The Rationals

*Scott Morgan*

Steve Correll had called me and asked me to play something over the phone. I knew two songs, so I played those into the mouthpiece. We had a band. We tried to back up Bob Seger, but everyone knew it would end up two different groups. Too much talent. We knew he worked at Wild's Men's Wear, so we went there and introduced ourselves. He invited us to join him and Tom Ralston, Ann Arbor's version of Mitch Mitchell. Bob was into Bobby Jameson and how he was such a big star he got a ticker-tape parade down Broadway. His eye was on the prize and he had the chops to pull it off. We got a gig inspired by local instrumental gods

the Renegades to play on a flatbed truck in front of Kline's Department Store. We played at Forsythe and some parties, but after "Apache" we started running out of ideas. Steve's parents sent him to military school, so while he was gone I recruited Terry Trabandt and Bill Figg. When Steve came back, it was a four piece. His brother called us the Rationals so we stuck with it.

Steve was left-handed, so he just turned a right-handed guitar upside down and played it with the strings still strung right-handed. It made for some wicked inversions that were impossible to copy for a right-hander. His father was a trumpet

The Rationals. © Leni Sinclair Collection.

player and his mother a music teacher, so he had the right background. His mom and mine had grown up together south of Ann Arbor, and their families were both German and ran farm implement stores. Looking back through my mom's history, I found out the Germans were the best farmers and followed the "walnut trail" from New York and Pennsylvania to Canada and eventually Michigan. Walnut trees grew in limestone soil, which made for the best farmland. Steve was born shortly before me at the same hospital, so finding him was the beginning of my band career.

We met an older guy named Bob Pretzfelder, who had a whole set of drums. He died in an auto accident after Steve left for military school. My guitar teacher had shown me Terry Trabandt's junior high photo and suggested I get in touch with him about working together, so I did, and we started jamming. That's when I met Bill Figg. He had a set of drums, so he, Terry, and I started jamming. When Steve came home, we talked Terry into playing bass, and now we had a four-piece band.

We made some tapes with local DJs Ted Heuzel and Don "Z" Zemanski. We knew we would have to sing and write songs like the Beatles so we made some pathetic attempts at Liverpudlian, Scouse-accented material. Looking back, it was pretty stupid when you realize the Beatles loved American music. We needed a manager, so we talked Jeep into it. That was really the beginning of our success. He put up with our amateur music for one single, "Gave My Love"/"Look What You're Doing (to Me Baby)," in 1965. Then he introduced us to soul. Taking his advice was the best move we ever made. There is something about soul music that makes people feel

good, particularly girls, which we could get behind immediately.

We covered Eddie Holland's "Leaving Here," which Holland-Dozier-Holland had written for Jackie Wilson. Everyone thought it was a hit. Even Iggy, who worked at Discount Records and hid all the copies. Deon Jackson played B3 organ and bongos on it, and I played harmonica with Steve on my Rickenbacker twelve-string on "Respect." It wasn't a hit for anyone. When we covered Otis Redding's "Respect" as a B side to the surefire "Leaving Here," the DJs promptly flipped it over to the B side in favor of "Respect." I had only heard Otis on "Fa Fa Fa," but when I heard him do "Respect," I heard the future.

We followed that with our own "Feelin' Lost" with Bob Seger producing and Iggy on bass drum. The flip side was Deon Jackson's "Little Girls Cry." Also not a hit.

But the next one was.

We had moved to a bigger house on Seventh Street, and my grandmother Bena had given me a Mercury Monterrey. I was in high school, and when I came back from vacation everything had changed. "Respect" was Top 5 in Detroit in 1966. After the show at Cobo Hall, we thought we had made it to the tippity top. Then we were shuffled off to play a basement hall gig, waving goodbye to ? and the Mysterians, who had "96 Tears" out at the time. Very deflating. We could grow our hair long at school now, and the goon squad wouldn't cut it. Our fan club was all girls, and they backed us all the way. All of a sudden we had arrived. We could play in Florida, New York, Philadelphia, Chicago, Cleveland, and points in between. This could be good. This could be real good. Then came Jeff

Barry and Ellie Greenwich's "Hold On Baby" with Bob Seger on high harmony and another crack at "Leaving Here" and nothing. Fortunately, that was not the end, just a bump in the road.

Our record company went out of business, and everyone connected to it was left high and dry, including Bob and ? and the Mysterians. That's when, in 1968, we discovered the Goffin-King song "I Need You." They knew how to write songs. Gerry's lyrics could see the woman's point of view, and Carole's music was beautiful. All you had to do was give it a convincing performance, and that's what we did. One song and we were back.

There was only one big problem. We were recording singles, but the market now wanted albums. We had been working with AM stations CKLW, WKNR, and WXYZ. CKLW, the "Big 8," even had a TV show hosted by Robin Seymour called *Swingin' Time*. Robin and Grande Ballroom manager Larry Feldmann took over our management. It was also regional, so the playlist in Detroit wouldn't be the same as New York, Miami, New Orleans, Chicago, or Los Angeles. That all changed when the format went to frequency modulation or FM radio. That fifty thousand watts now only went fifty miles, and the format was the same in every market. We creatively were forced to write whole albums now that would have national interest. The first song we came up with was "Guitar Army," which was as left-hand lethal as Steve Correll and as right-hand insistent as my lyrics. I dreamed that up as a group of guys walking around with guitars and amplifiers strapped to their backs.

In this transition period from AM to FM, even the fans didn't know which way to turn. Bob's band and Grand Funk guffawed when we did a joint interview, and I was asked what station I liked. My idea of a good answer was "none of them."

Since no one could understand going from "I Need You" to "Guitar Army," we went back to what we knew: Etta James, Dr. John, Robert Parker, the Knight Brothers, and soul music. We even tried our hand at "Handbags and Gladrags," which Rod Stewart liked, and the Spector version of "Zip-A-Dee Doo-Dah." Rod's version of "Handbags" came out at the same time as ours, and we found ourselves playing the two versions back to back on his radio promo tour. He was really nice to us and invited us to his hotel to bring him a copy of our album. He showed us a nice Gibson acoustic he had bought and offered us a drink. He told us he liked Steve's guitar part. We were on the cusp of corporate control in the business and had no clue how to handle the situation. Our producer put in the segues from "Ha Ha" between the tracks as an artistic touch. At the time it seemed to baffle everyone, but it was a rare touch. The album did OK, but it was no earth-shaker and we were squabbling with no clear direction. It ended unceremoniously at the Embassy Hotel Lounge in Windsor. There was only one way out. We broke up the band.

We had rung up five years of live shows and recordings. We had traveled from New York to Florida and the Midwest. We had recorded all of that time. In 2010, Alec Palau from Ace/Big Beat Records decided to compile our recorded history for a package release. It starts with our vinyl fan-club album, which included our first demos, our first two singles, and an unreleased "Smokestack Lightning" from Jeep Holland's A Square Records. That track was coupled with the Animals' "Inside Looking Out." "Smokestack" goes back to Charley Patton and

Howlin' Wolf when they worked together at Stovall Plantation. Also included is a version of the Kinks' "I Need You." The second vinyl album, *Out on the Floor*, includes our third single along with outtakes and album demo tracks "Temptation Bout to Get Me," "Sunset" (a Ron Asheton Favorite), and "Ha Ha." The rest of the record includes Rex Garvin's title track, Sam and Dave's "Said I Wasn't Gonna Tell Nobody" and "You Got It Made," Eddie Floyd's "Knock on Wood," Little Richard's "Poor Dog," the Esquires' "Listen to Me," and a commercial we made called "Turn On." The CDs included all the singles and B sides like our "Sing/Out in The Streets" and Albert King's "Not Like It Is," the Crewe album, and Little Johnny Taylor's "Part Time Love."

The band had dwindled down to Terry Trabandt and me. We tried to put together something like the Rationals with my brother David on drums and "Tex" Gabriel on guitar. We had a fanciful name, Guardian Angel, and we went to work, after a few false starts and experiments. David had been in a band called the Children, and Tex had played a bit with Mitch Ryder when he was forming Detroit. Jeep had done everything for us—management, booking, clothing, direction, and whatever else we needed. He had gotten us to the top in Detroit, but we left him for another manager, Larry Feldmann. I don't think the switch was for the best for anyone. Larry got us an album deal with Bob Crewe, but he left after it was released. Even famous local CKLW radio DJ and *Swingin' Time* television host Robin Seymour tried to manage us, but the band was becoming obsolete. Now, we were completely on our own. Big changes were happening in the world, and we would have to change with it. Tex left for New York and joined Elephant's Memory. Soon they

would be John Lennon's band. Jeff Jones had helped me through physics in high school, and I thought he would be a good guitar player for us. Soon we were being managed by Pete Andrews, who had guided SRC to success and become a music promoter.

John Sinclair had gone from managing MC5 to prison in the infamous "ten for two" bust. Everyone wanted him out. The entire Detroit music community was opposed to the Vietnam War, racism, and every other right-wing idea we butted heads with, and we were all for human rights. When I heard soul music, I didn't hear racism. I heard music, and I liked it. On Sinclair's release, he teamed up with Pete to form Rainbow Productions. First order of business: Guardian Angel; the Rockets with Jim McCarty and Johnny "Bee" Badanjek; and the band Detroit, soon to include Steve Gaines, who would become a guitarist with Lynyrd Skynyrd. They started covering all aspects of the bands' careers and decided to put on a huge blues and jazz festival.

Al Jacquez joined the band, and we added Tim McCoy on keyboard. We did some studio recording and released Johnny Taylor's "Hijackin' Love" backed with Jeremy and the Satyrs' "First Time Saw You Baby." It set a perplexing trend. A band that only released one single in several years, but something would follow that would portend the future. We recorded a live show on John Lennon's Butterfly Mobile Unit at the festival site, Otis Spann Field. The mobile studio had been used to record the Ten for Two concert and would later be used to record *Ladies and Gentlemen: The Rolling Stones*. Somehow we had turned one single into an eighteen-track album titled *Into Lightnin'*.

The later Easy Action release would include Don Covay's "Things Get Better," lifted from Delaney and

Bonnie; Wilbert Harrison's "Let's Work Together"; my song "Cool Breeze"; and Little Milton's "Feel So Bad." Two more studio tracks, "Take a Look" and "Soulmover," would loom large in my next band. The live album included Don Covay's "See Saw," lifted from Aretha; and the Allman Brothers' "Leave My Blues at Home"; Loman Pauling's "Tell the Truth"; Charles Wright's "Your Love Means Everything to Me"; and the Staple Singers' "Heavy Makes You Happy." We worked up a version of Candi Staton's "Sweet Feeling" that seems to have disappeared.

The album marks several momentous events. It is also the third Easy Action release, following the Sonic's Rendezvous Band's six-disc box set, and my three-disc retrospective, *Three Chords and a Cloud of Dust*. The band wouldn't last. Two years and it was over, but there was something coming. The studio version of *Lightnin'* was remixed with more guitars, including Fred "Sonic" Smith solos on "Take a Look" and "Soulmover." Mike Davis plays percussion. This marked the first time Fred and I recorded one of my songs together. We had worked together on the intro to the MC5's "Skunk" from the *High Time* album, which was recorded at Artie Fields's studio, where the Rationals had recorded their album. My brother, Dr. David Morgan; Terry Trabandt; Bob Seger; and I play various percussion instruments. Bob is the guy who says, "Hi ho Silver." Another portent of things to come.

## SLANG

The stars must have been lining up, because several bands were breaking up around the same time, around 1972. The MC5 had decided to do their last show at the bastion of live music in Detroit, Russ Gibb's Grande Ballroom. They invited the Contemporary Jazz Quintet, Freedom Now Singers, Bob Seger, and me to do the show with them. It was Fred "Sonic" Smith and me onstage together for the first time. I did "Part Time Love," and Bob did "Heavy Music." Mitch Ryder's Detroit was breaking up around the same time, leaving W. R. "Ron" Cooke on the loose. The Stooges weren't far behind. Scott Asheton would soon sell his drums to Dennis Thompson for a plane ticket from Hollywood back to Ann Arbor.

First, Terry Trabandt and I put something together with Bill Figg and Mike Davis. Our intent was to make a supergroup together from the Rationals and the MC5. That lasted one night. We opened for Tim Buckley at Masonic Auditorium. There was a second show at a gay festival that didn't go well. There was also a New Year's Eve gig at the Cadillac Hotel ballroom. There was a blizzard. It was starting to look like we were screwed. Terry tried one more thing. His intent was to use the two *Lightnin'* tracks we had recorded with Fred on lead guitar. He released "Take a Look" backed with "Soulmover" on Detroit Records. This was the point where we realized how extensively the music business had been incorporated. There was no way we would get airplay. Terry tried real hard but just ended up getting thrown out of Atlantic Records. That didn't bode well for our music career at all.

I had barely known Fred Smith outside of the music projects we worked together on, and the fact that he was trying to grow his hair longer than Brian Jones when I first saw him play. One night we got together and jammed on saxophones. That was just for fun. After the Rationals broke up, there was some talk of me joining MC5. We were hanging out a bit, and one night I slept on their kitchen floor at their house on the John C. Lodge Service Drive in Detroit. Fred told me his favorite album was *Meditations* by John Coltrane. I woke up the next morning and Gram Parsons was sitting in the living room. At the time, I didn't know anything about him besides being in the Byrds. We were just some musicians hanging out.

When Fred was on the last 5 tour of Europe, he called and asked me to help his wife move into their new house on Chopin Street in Detroit. I had been to the band house in Hamburg, Michigan, and later his house with Sigrid [Fred Smith's first wife] on Strawberry Lake. Chopin Street is where Sonic's Rendezvous Band began. First we tried jamming in the basement. I have to point out here that we were never a garage band. We were always a basement band. We got Miguel "Mike" Martinez to play drums, a guy Fred had found. Then we brought in W. R. "Ron" Cooke on bass. Mike Davis was now out of the question since he was heading for Lexington Federal Penitentiary in Kentucky. The place was becoming a hotbed of musical talent; probably in order to replace former inmates Billie Holiday, Gene Krupa, Chet Baker, and Red Rodney. Now they had Mike, Wayne Kramer, and Hiawatha Bailey. Fred had started a band after the 5 broke up. It included Mike Davis and Dennis Thompson and was called Ascension after a favorite Coltrane record. Ron and I had started hanging out after the Rationals broke up, and I stayed at his east-side Detroit home. I had known him from Bob Hodge's Catfish and Mitch Ryder's Detroit. Fred had a manager, Chato Hill, and he arranged a photo session and biography with the new band, Sonic's Rendezvous Band. We added a sax player and keyboard player, but that didn't work out. Next we got Fred's friend Jeff Vail on drums.

That was pretty much the lineup before Fred and I decided to try something different.

Fred and I decided to try LA, like things would be different there. Terry was already there, and we had a driveaway Cadillac so we took our time getting there. The desert was nice, so we slept in the Caddy at the Grand Canyon. Once we got to Hollywood, we checked in to Sandy Koufax's Tropicana at Scott Asheton's recommendation. Duke's coffee shop was downstairs, and they had a teardrop-shaped pool. We walked up to the Coronado, where Ron Asheton, Dennis Thompson, Jimmy Recca, James Williamson, and my friend Doug Curry lived. Terry had an apartment there and decided to go back to Ann Arbor, so now we had an apartment. We had two mattresses and that was it. Terry had left behind a few things. Not much, since he hadn't been there long. We bought a portable record player and listened to Beach Boys records all day.

No, things were not different in LA; believe it or not, they were worse. I did land a gig with Iggy Pop and Ray Manzarek at the Hollywood Palladium. That was the end of the Coronado. I locked my harmonicas in the apartment, and Iggy leapt across the third-floor balcony to get them. After the show, I broke the door down because Fred and Johnny Thunders had taken the keys. It was time to go back to the Tropicana. It looked like California was not the land of golden opportunity after all. If this was what it was like, we might as well go back to Detroit. So we did. First we went to San Francisco in another driveaway car. Then we headed for Reno. Outside of town, we got pulled over by the cops. They said if we would followed them to the first motel and checked in, we wouldn't be arrested. Those were the days of protect and serve. Then we drove all the way back to Chicago to drop off the car and fly home. We had shipped a couple cases of beer home because we thought it was illegal to bring it across the Mississippi. My girlfriend picked us up at the airport. Well, it was fun.

That winter, Fred drove a taxi, and I didn't do much of anything. In the spring, we started rehearsing in Fred and Sigrid's basement on Chopin Street again. We were still a basement band. Chato Hill agreed to manage us a second time, so we started trying to put a permanent band together. Then we moved rehearsals to my parents' basement in Ann Arbor. That's when I realized Scott Asheton was not playing with anyone, and we needed a drummer. His mom signed for a set of blue Ludwig Vistalites. Now we had a band. Fred and I did a lot of writing and rehearsing and played Second Chance a lot. It was John Carver's bar, and he liked us.

There were other places to play, so we played them, too. After about a year, Ron got so into Harley Davidsons that Fred thought we needed a new bass player. Ron didn't quit so much as we just went our separate ways; we're still friends to this day. We had a gig in a few days, so since Scott and I had been hanging around with Gary Rasmussen, we hired him. Soon we would have enough material for a set of originals. We had a set opener and closer that we decided to record with Chato Hill's help at Artie Fields's studio. The Rationals had recorded our album there, and the 5 had recorded *High Time* there, so we were familiar with the room. Artie did a great job on the session. The songs were "City Slang" and "Electrophonic Tonic." The session for "City Slang"/"Electrophonic Tonic" went well. We rehearsed for weeks as we had done with the Rationals' "Respect." That really paid off when we

actually started recording. Fred was meticulous about every aspect of the rhythm track. Other than dropping the "Sonic's" from "Electrophonic Tonic," I pretty much had reign over that side of the record. It's odd that Fred was never comfortable with his name being part of the band name. I liked it and it stuck.

We cut the band track easily. There were two takes on the solo so we spliced them together using the first half of one and the second half of the other. The lyrics were a bit trickier and controversial since Fred was still writing them when he recorded his vocal and even came back with some new lyrics for the next session. We always recorded using the Motown assembly-line method in the studio, so it was easy to punch in anything you wanted on any given overdub track. Fred had a big cardboard box full of ideas for the lyrics and was cutting and pasting what sounded best to him. You have to remember that even though the actual words are very important, the sound and rhythm of the vocals were also important. No one knows to this day what the lyrics are on the single. They seem to be almost impressionistic to me. Onstage, Fred would frequently change lyrics or just scat parts.

Once the vocals and guitar solos were on tape, we needed to put the icing on the cake. Fred wanted piano on it, so I played a Fender Rhodes all the way through. You can hear it on the breakdown after the guitar solo. Then Fred and I played four-handed grand piano all the way through, with me on the low end and Fred on the high end. The final touch was all four of us singing "oohs" and collapsing in giggle fits on each take. Finally, Artie lost his patience and made us get through it. Patti Smith says she can hear them, but for me they're subliminally lost in the mix. The mixing was pretty easy from there on out. I overdubbed the intro and end feedback, and we spent some time trying to find a percussion sound that I don't think we ever found. The only thing left was designing the label to include Fred's Orchide Records imprint. Fred's publishing would be credited to Stella's Music (later to Stratium). I always thought Stella's music was the radio Marlon Brando throws out the window in *A Streetcar Named Desire*. It was the only beautiful thing she had, and Stanley destroyed it. I think of Brando when I remember Fred. Fred wasn't afraid to push the envelope. That story would recur in Antoine de Saint-Exupery's *The Little Prince*. We only steal from the best.

Like Fred and me and all the important people I met in show business, Rock and I had a connection we didn't even know about until we ended up playing together. The first day I met Ron Asheton, some guys were messing with him. I didn't like it and let them know it. Then I took him inside for a proper introduction to Forsythe Junior High. Friends for life. I met Scott Asheton in the hallway arguing with his girlfriend. So now we all knew each other and would continue to forever. When the Stooges were inducted into the Rock and Roll Hall of Fame, Stooges drummer Scott "Rock" Asheton made it a point to mention the Dirty Shames, the band he and his brother Ron had started with Dave Alexander. I knew we all liked the same kind of music because Fred and Scott would borrow albums from me that I would never see again. Jimmie Rodgers and Hank Williams ended up in Fred's dad Dewey's collection along with my copy of Spector's *Greatest Hits in Rock*. Finally, I gave up and started giving them records as presents.

Rock and I both loved country music so we had a band within SRB called Country Action. We used to sit outside the Asheton house late at night and try to dial in WRVA in Richmond to hear truck-driving songs. Eventually, we graduated to outlaw country. Emmylou Harris, Hank Williams Jr., Roseanne Cash, Waylon and Willie, Johnny and Kristofferson, David Allan Coe, Gram Parsons, and all that stuff. Fred paid me back for ripping off my country records by teaching me "Nine Pound Hammer" by Merle Travis. Gary Rasmussen got into music listening to Homer and Jethro. Scott paid me back by teaching me to fish. We quickly graduated to walleye fishing in northern Ontario. I was sitting on Lake Prairie Bee outside Chapleau. I spent a week looking at the scenery, until the last day when I felt a snag. It was a thirty-inch pike. It became a tradition to go up every year and catch walleye. We got pretty good at it.

We met Patti Smith on her first promo tour for *Horses*. When Fred and Patti met, you could see sparks fly. I already knew Lenny Kaye, but at that moment there was no one else in the room, kind of like the scene in *West Side Story* where Tony meets Maria. It was going to change everyone's world.

At nearly the same time, Iggy was looking for a new band to back him on a European tour. Fred was reluctant to tour overseas again, but I thought it would just be only a slight delay in our schedule and then when they got back we could release the single. It turned into three months, and when they got back to the states, Iggy wanted to keep them on. Fred had the foresight to realize he had his own band with a record coming out, and that's what he was going to focus on. In the meantime, Fred and Patti were falling in love. At the time, I figured that was their thing and the bands would still exist, but that's not what happened.

First, Fred and I had an argument about some recording I had done while they were gone for three months. It got blown way out of proportion, and we ended up pulling "Tonic" off the record. I had been trying to convince Fred that we were as good as any of the bands that were touring, but he wasn't convinced. Patti wanted us to tour with her, and I thought that was a great idea. Unfortunately, I couldn't convince him of that either. In the end, they got married, both bands broke up, and they retired from show business to raise a family. That might have been the end of it, but I think show business was in their blood. They recorded an album together called *Dream of Life*. I think "People Have the Power" and "Up There Down There" are two of the finest songs they have done any way you cut it.

The single "City Slang" would remain our only release for years, but that would change. It would just take years. Outside of the single "Detroit"/"16 With a Bullet," nothing would happen until a French label called Revenge Records released an album with Destroy All Monsters on one side and Sonic's Rendezvous Band on the other. The problem was that it was a bootleg. They came here to get us to sign off on it, but that wasn't going to happen. They made us a second offer to release a new record with them. That offer we accepted, and we released *Rock Action*. We followed that with *Scots Pirates* (*Action Now* in Europe) and *Revolutionary Means*. When Fred died in 1994, Patti wanted a fitting tribute so she had a memorial commissioned at the Mariner's Church in Detroit. She also had a fitting marker for his grave, did an intimate live show at the Ark in Ann Arbor, and commissioned two album releases. That

seemed to be the end to it until Carlton Sandercock at London's Easy Action records got everyone to agree to a six-disc box set and a vinyl release of *Live, Masonic Auditorium*, with help from Bob Matheu. Their set included artwork from award-winning designer Rachel Gutek. It included liner notes by Ken Shimamoto, who, along with Geoff Ginsberg, would become one of our official archivists.

Not bad for another band that released only one song.

265

Früt in AA. © Leni Sinclair Collection.

# Strange Früt

## An East-Side Story of the Früt

*George Moseman, a.k.a. "Moseley the Punk"*

First, let me pay homage to some of the people I see appearing with the Früt in this examination of the really fun part of Detroit culture. From John Sinclair to Jarrett Koral, with Lester Bangs, Jaan Uhelszki, Barry Kramer, Cary Loren, Becky Tyner, Greil Marcus, and Jesus H. Christ, along with all of the other towering icons of our civilization thrown in for good measure.

In the beginning, the musically gifted Früt of the Loom made a name for themselves as an acid rock band. They played the Chessmate, the Crow's Nest, and later the occasional pop fest, and were managed by the irrepressible Mike Quatro. The face of the Früt of the Loom was a redheaded lead singer who left an everlasting impression on anyone who's ever seen him, Norm Liberman (a.k.a. Panama Red). As the months went by, the gigs were booked at increasingly more prestigious venues like the Atlanta Pop Festival and the IMA Auditorium in Flint, with Hendrix.

However, at the height of their popularity . . . the band broke up. The original musicians left to play the Big Daddy's club circuit, for money. Some say real (1968) money.

Norm was now the sole owner of a full stack of Marshalls (amplifiers), along with the monthly equipment payment. But he also had the gigs that were already booked by Quatro, starting with the Grand Haven roller rink on Friday night and the Saugatuck Pop Festival Saturday afternoon.

At this point, in another part of the city, three young lads were boning up on some '50s material. At 68 Union Street, Bob Holley, Neil Brenner, and George Moseman (me) were practicing harmonies for the '50s band we hoped to become.

With gigs and payments at hand, Norm approached Bob and said why don't we combine the Früt of the Loom with our '50s band and play the gigs, collect the money, and make the payments on the Marshalls. It was just perfect, except for one thing: Bob Holley, who became "Krunchy Krystals" and had played guitar in an earlier incarnation of the Früt of the Loom, was the only person in a seven-member band who had ever played an instrument. Norm, of course, was the lead singer and Bob played guitar, but David West, "Snidley Whiplash," had never played drums before and left-handed John Kosloskey, "Kozmo," who had just been elevated from roadie to bass player, had to learn to play a right-handed bass, upside down. Dennis Wild, "Wildman," another recently elevated roadie, joined me—Moseley the Punk—and Neil "Meadow Lark" Brenner as part of the "Famed Warbles," the dancing, singing trio that passed for the band's dramatic showpiece.

All of these people learned how to play instruments, sing, dance, and put on a show only days before the Saugatuck Pop Festival, which was scheduled the following Saturday. On Friday night, the show at the Grand Haven roller rink was so totally bizarre the promoter told us, "I'm not paying for that shit," whereby Norm grabbed the still-live mic and screamed to the lingering audience, "He won't give us our pay because he said we weren't a real band and we didn't play music." So Norm told the kids to scream, "Pay the Früt," and they did, long and loud. He paid us. With the help of an ounce of hash, we were totally prepared for the next day's gig. Our first pop festival, our second time in front of an audience.

To this day, none of us can imagine what we looked like to a pop festival audience.

However, we played our stoned little hearts out, and when we finished, the entire trippin' audience sat in dead silence, wondering what they had just witnessed. Then, as the veil lifted, and we were still onstage staring down the crowd, they erupted into one enormous cheer for the band that had the balls to, you know, just do it.

The saga had begun. The Früt of the Loom was signed to Westbound Records and distributed worldwide by Chess/Junus. Our albums, *Keep on Truckin* and *Spoiled Rotten*, became . . . well . . . cult classics. (Remembering, of course, that one man's cult classic is another man's terrorist.) Yes, we were musical anarchy, but we had Dave Marsh—who took heat for writing the *Creem* cover story "Will Success Spoil the Früt?" (June 1971)—Lester Bangs, Barry Kramer, and Toby Mamis (former Früt critic and now manager of Alice Cooper) defending the premise that unconscious art is still art. Or something along those lines.

The question we were asked most frequently was, "Are you guys serious?" To which we always replied, "As serious as a heart attack."

The subsequent six years were filled with more excitement than humans should be allowed to have in a hundred lifetimes. Multiple drug busts for our libertine lifestyle yielded no convictions. However, in the lobby of the federal building in downtown Detroit once stood a large display case with examples of a large variety of drugs—weed; LSD; downers; uppers; coke; green, yellow, and blue pills. And right there in the center, under a sign that read, "What people who take these drugs look like," was an eight-by-ten glossy publicity shot of the Früt. The one where we're standing around the '53 Ford with Jerry Younkins's feet sticking out from underneath.

Many years later, I met Mike Kelley through Cary Loren, in Mike's studio in Pasadena, California. Mike was probably the most prolific and internationally recognized visual artist to ever come out of Detroit. His art is in every major gallery and museum in the world. When I found out that he, Cary, and Jim Shaw were fans, we instantly became their fans back.

In the early 2000s Kelley, Loren, and Shaw created a multimedia exhibition titled "Strange Früt" as an homage to both the Billie Holiday song and to us.

In May of 2013, Kelley's "Mobile Homestead" was opening at the Museum of Modern Art Detroit (MOCAD). The Strange Früt were privileged to be able to play that opening, thanks to Marie Clair Stevens of the Mike Kelley Foundation and the wonderful people of MOCAD. Mike was spotted at the gig destroying more monsters. Mike created a hundred lifetimes of art in his too-brief visit.

# Strange Mysterious Sounds
## The Demise of Ted Lucas and the Spike-Drivers
*Mike Dutkewych*

"I'm not working for any fucking Turk."

That single sentence was one of the most damaging acts of self-sabotage in a music career of otherwise unlimited potential—the music career of Ted Lucas, Detroit's long-forgotten psychedelic folk pioneer and perhaps the most underappreciated of its countless guitar virtuosos.

Ted Lucas made records for only a decade, between 1966 and 1976. Five singles, a full-length album, and a compilation appearance—that was the sum of his musical output as a member of four bands and as a solo artist. At least one single and probably two more albums remain trapped on tapes boxed up in his son's basement, still unreleased forty years later.

The music Ted Lucas composed that did make it out into the world never really found an audience in those turbulent ten years. In the '60s and '70s, the only thing more rapid than the evolution of popular music in America was the momentum of its social and cultural growing pains. This tumult produced a ripe breeding ground for counterculture and creativity in the 1960s, and in that, Ted Lucas was intimately engaged as a Detroit music-scene trailblazer. But by the 1970s, embittered by years of watching success elude him, Ted found himself at odds with the recording industry, in a place musically that was both wholly out of touch and boldly ahead of its time.

At face value, that line about the Turk was hostile but relatively benign. When considering the context, however—it's 1967, the Turk is legendary Atlantic Records impresario Ahmet Ertegun, and the xenophobe is Ted Lucas, the leader of a band that was just offered its big break in the form of a generous recording contract—it becomes clear that the remark was anything but benign. In fact,

Ted Lucas, 1965. Photo courtesy of Robin Eichele.

it proved to be the first big tug at the loose threads dangling from Ted Lucas's promising career.

In 2008, forty-one years after Ted Lucas turned down a contract from Atlantic Records on behalf of his band, the Spike-Drivers, I received an email from an acquaintance in Los Angeles. Douglas McGowan, distinguished music collector and proprietor of reissue label Yoga Records, needed a liaison in Detroit for a project he'd finally gotten licensed after years of trying. He offered me a unique opportunity: coordinate with the family of a long-departed and longer-forgotten 1960s Detroit musician and build a digital archive of the massive horde of tapes, photos, documents, and ephemera that he left behind. In exchange, I'd receive a little money, a lot of hands-on experience exhuming important musical artifacts from an era and a city that I love, and the satisfaction of knowing I was doing a great service for fellow music enthusiasts the world over.

Here's what I didn't know at the time:

Who the hell Ted Lucas was.

How highly sought-after his music had become in record collector circles, decades later.

What kind of remarkable rollercoaster life story was buried in those dusty journals, photos, and tapes.

What a masterpiece his solitary solo album is.

I had no meaningful qualifications for a project like this, but I gladly accepted. I learned the fourth thing first and the third thing last, gradually, over the ensuing seven years. That's the story I'll attempt to detail here, for the first time.

The older of two boys born to hardworking Greek immigrants, Theodore Peter Lucas grew up on the west side of Detroit in the '40s and '50s.

Though he greatly favored the pursuit of artistic endeavors to the often-arduous long hours the rest of the Lucases spent tending the family business, Ted was nevertheless the apple of his mother's eye. His titanic personality was dwarfed only by his big Greek smile.

As a teenager in the mid-'50s, Ted was a Leiber and Stoller devotee with a particular penchant for their work with the Coasters. That songwriting duo was, as much as anyone, responsible for the early evolution of rock 'n' roll, composing a staggering number of what are now considered the greatest songs of all time. Though not always apparent in his own work, the early impact they had on Ted's musical sensibilities ran deep.

For as accomplished as he would become as a multi-instrumentalist, music performance didn't claim a place in Ted's life until his later teens. He started on the violin but ultimately gravitated to the guitar, taking lessons with renowned classical guitarist Joe Fava. Under his direction, Ted excelled. Eventually he was hired to instruct his own students at Fava Music, Joe's guitar store and studio in the Green-8 Shopping Center on Eight Mile and Greenfield.

At Fava Music, Ted taught a wide range of techniques to eager Detroit teens. From Travis picking to blues guitar, his versatility with the instrument made him a proficient teacher, and his uninhibited, charismatic approach to instruction made him a popular one. It was during his years at Fava that his natural propensities to mentor and lead—roles that he'd assume in every musical endeavor he'd ever know—really began to show.

It was also at Fava that he first encountered Sid Brown. Sid was a fellow guitarist and soon-to-be bandmate who would ultimately become the most vitriolic of Ted Lucas's detractors and among the first of his many burned bridges.

Meanwhile, in the early 1960s, as the influence of the Greenwich Village scene traveled west, a burgeoning Detroit coffeehouse circuit started to take shape, making the city a prominent destination for beatniks from all over the Midwest and Canada. Soon beat venues began welcoming acoustic musicians alongside the poets and orators that typically occupied their stages. This eventually led to a collision of beatnik aesthetics and the traditional folk music form and created a fertile environment for experimentation, both musical and otherwise.

Ted Lucas quickly became a fixture in the Detroit folk scene, frequenting spots like the Chessmate Gallery, the Unstabled Theatre, and the Retort Coffeehouse in the basement of the Mount Royal Hotel. The latter, in particular, had become a hub for traveling folk musicians like Buffy Sainte-Marie, Reverend Gary Davis, and Jose Feliciano. Even Bob Dylan made an unannounced appearance there following a sold-out performance at the Masonic Scottish Rite Cathedral. This is a noteworthy moment not only because it found the biggest folk singer in the world playing afterhours in a basement coffeehouse but also because picking onstage beside him that night was an emerging talent named Ted Lucas.

By 1964, while many of the city's folk acts were still perfectly satisfied playing sets of other people's tunes (typically traditional folk standards mixed with popular songs by big names like Joan Baez and Peter, Paul, and Mary), there was a divergent class of folk singers whose preoccupation was writing and performing original material, more for the sake of artistic expression than for the entertainment of an audience. Ted fell squarely into this category.

As his proficiency with the guitar and his stature within the Detroit folk scene rose in tandem, Ted began expanding his musical palette. His repertoire transformed and many of the more traditional arrangements soon gave way to complexities inspired by the ethnic music that permeated the city. Detroit was defined by its multiculturalism, and few knew this more intimately than the first-generation children of immigrants.

Ted was most enamored with Indian music and art, particularly sitar master composer Ravi Shankar. He studied Shankar's records closely and experimented on his guitar with modal tunings, drone strings, and picking patterns in an attempt to re-create the sitar melodies that captivated him. Ted also began exploring the boundaries of his instrument during live performances, frequently breaking into long-form guitar ragas and complex improvisations that riveted audiences. No one else in town could play guitar like Ted Lucas.

On December 7, 1964, Ted Lucas married his longtime girlfriend, Annette Abbott. Their courtship began when she was only fourteen, and in the six years that led to their wedding day, Annette was continually wowed by Ted. His growing notoriety in the music scene opened doors across the city for the couple. If there was something exciting going on in Detroit, he and Annette were surely in attendance.

Ted was plugged in all over town before long. His inventive guitar playing became his pass to the musical galaxy beyond the folk scene. It was not uncommon to see him onstage at the Minor Key opposite jazzmen like Yusef Lateef or trading tunes into the late hours with a blues giant like Mississippi John Hurt. Ted savored these opportunities and used them to further refine himself as a musician. He was a sponge soaking up moves from the masters of other genres.

The great unifier across all of these scenes was, perhaps not surprisingly, marijuana. And Ted Lucas loved to get unified. But if it was weed that had the power to unite the otherwise segregated music scenes in Detroit in 1965, it was LSD that had the power to transform them into some entirely new mutation.

Ted tripped on the first batch of Owsley acid that came to Detroit from San Francisco that year. For him and many others in the artist community, acid was the drug that changed everything. Refracting his already expansive musical palette through the prism of LSD proved powerful and inspiring. Ted Lucas experimented heavily with drugs and music throughout 1965, and by the fall, he found himself in very uncharted territory for a once simple coffeehouse singer: the trendy Roostertail supper club, leading a radical new band through an unlikely week-long engagement. The original Spike-Drivers lineup consisted of Ted Lucas, Sid and Marycarol Brown, Richard Keelan, and Steve Booker.

Ted and Sid, architects of the group, traded lead and rhythm guitar duties. Though their musical backgrounds and influences were closely mirrored, each brought a unique approach to their guitars, which, it should be noted, were now electric. Sid developed a wild frail-picking style, hijacking a technique traditionally associated with the banjo, and Ted transformed ethnic modes and melodies to match the band's brazen folk-rock sound. Their interplay was energetic, unhinged, and often bewildering to

audiences. Few in 1965 had ever witnessed a guitarist attack his strings with five picks or spindle through a searing bouzouki solo on a Les Paul. During a Spike-Drivers set, these sights were not only common, they happened at the same time.

Richard Keelan, a well-traveled folk singer and guitarist in his own right, had done time playing coffeehouses in the Village and beyond before arriving in Detroit in early 1965, a twelve-string guitar and generous songbook in tow. It took only one fateful jam session/acid trip for Richard to join the Spike-Drivers as a vocalist, guitarist, and bassist.

Sid Brown's wife, Marycarol, sang and supplied occasional auxiliary percussion. But her most essential role was, truth be told, as the band's focal point. Though she lacked the musical prowess of the other members, her voice was serviceable and sweet, and her presence onstage flitted between exotic and hypnotic.

Known around town for performing lively avant-garde percussion pieces as the house drummer at the Chessmate, Steve Booker was enlisted to provide the backbone of the band's songs. He also shared the group's affinities for exploring the music of other cultures and other states of consciousness, though he would need to be reined in regularly on both fronts.

During the nascency of the Spike-Drivers, the band worked up a short set of lighthearted songs written by their friend Joel Myerson. Originally slated for bass duties in those early months, Joel bowed out almost immediately but allowed the band to use his tunes regardless. Once the lineup was solidified, songs by Richard and Ted were placed alongside Joel's in the repertoire. Lyrics like those in Richard's "Baby Won't You Let Me Tell You How I Lost My Mind" and Ted's

"Strange Mysterious Sounds" rerouted the group away from the whimsy of the earlier material into territory that was both surreal and cerebral, much to the band's benefit. Dropping Greek, Arabic, and Indian motifs into a rock context with eccentric, acid-tinged lyrics created an aural manifestation of psychedelia.

Vocally, the Spike-Drivers leaned heavily on three- and four-part harmonies. Lead vocals were often reserved for the songwriter of a respective piece, while the other members laid lush harmonies behind them. Early on, Ted insisted the band receive formal training from Joe Fava's in-house vocal coach, Phil Holloway. He taught the group various scales, exercises, and breathing methods that greatly enhanced their performances live and on recording. This further set the Spike-Drivers apart from their contemporaries. At that time, it was uncommon to hear four-part vocal arrangements in rock music—especially moody Western harmonies atop unusual Eastern rhythms and melodies.

The physical dimension of the Spike-Drivers was also extremely important to the band's identity. Richard Keelan's wife, Connie, was a talented graphic artist who worked by day designing ads for Hudson's. She began overseeing all wardrobe, photography, and art direction for the Spike-Drivers. She helped the group hone a fresh visual aesthetic that was every bit as attention grabbing as their music. Marycarol had bountiful hair with bangs down to her eyelashes. The guys wore mop-tops and beards. The group donned matching outfits cut from material that looked like it was alive and beaming out from under a microscope. The artwork in their posters incorporated similar paramecia patterns hand drawn to frame photos of a band that looked just like it sounded: unlike anything else.

In the 1960s, the Roostertail was one of the city's preeminent nightlife destinations. Nestled on the Detroit River near the well-to-do suburb of Grosse Pointe, the upscale supper club was a far cry from the informal coffeehouse vibe of the folk scene. It's a curious and somewhat improbable setting for the debut performance by the Spike-Drivers. But leave it to fast-talkin' Ted Lucas and his unabashed belief that his band was the best in town. He bluffed owner Jerry Schoenith into booking the group to a week-long engagement without hearing so much as a single song. And the payout was a thousand dollars, which is equivalent to almost seventy-five hundred dollars in 2015. To call this an auspicious start would be a significant understatement.

The Spike-Drivers emerged from the triumphant week at the Roostertail with a glowing review in the *Detroit Free Press* and a definite buzz surrounding their band. In the following months, they performed at venues throughout Detroit, including the Midtown Theatre on Canfield and Third, the Poison Apple on East Jefferson, and the Raven Gallery on James Couzens and Outer Drive. At the latter, the band so impressed owner Herb Cohen that he offered them a weekly residency of Saturday matinees.

Attendance at the Raven Gallery shows grew steadily. The Spike-Drivers hit an early stride, though it was momentarily disrupted by the absence of percussionist Steve Booker one Saturday. Always exhausted from his Friday nights at the Chessmate, Booker struggled each weekend with the early afternoon gigs until he missed one entirely. Unfortunately for him, this was a fireable offense in the eyes of a band growing more popular and more serious. Cue Larry Cruse.

273

If Steve Booker was a wildman, speed-freak percussionist for the Spike-Drivers, Larry Cruse was his antithesis: rock solid, measured, and inconspicuous behind the kit. Several years older than the rest of the group, Larry had no connection to the folk scene that spawned his bandmates. He was a big-band drummer who'd been making his money in wedding bands and cocktail bar quartets. He just happened into the Raven one weekend, where he caught the Spike-Drivers. When he introduced himself as a fellow musician and complimented the band on their set, he had no idea he'd be hired to replace their drummer a short time later.

In the spring of 1966, thanks to the group's growing profile and Ted's wheeling and dealing about town, the Spike-Drivers landed two generous benefactors in Mort and Jackie Feigenson, owners of the Faygo soda company. Already fans of the band, the Feigensons agreed to bankroll the first Spike-Drivers single. Within weeks, the group was Chicago-bound for a late-night session at the closest facility to offer the modern wonder of an eight-track recording console, historic Chess Studios.

Chess was a factory in those days, running tape around the clock for a constant rotation of musicians and engineers. That night, following a joint session for Bo Diddley and Chuck Berry, the Spike-Drivers loaded in, set up, and cut two songs: the frenetic "High Time" and the pensive slow burner "Often I Wonder." A few hours later, the engineer boxed up the master tapes and sent the band on their way, all before the sun came up.

Back in Detroit, the Spike-Drivers continued to pack every venue they played. At one fateful Raven gig, an associate of hotshot New York manager Leonard Stogel happened to be in attendance. He

phoned in high praise of the band and urged Stogel to book the first flight to Detroit to experience the Spike-Drivers for himself. Which is precisely what he did.

Leonard Stogel signed the Spike-Drivers to a management deal just a few days later. He was a prime mover in the music biz, riding a wave of hits from a roster that included groups like Sam the Sham and the Pharaohs and Tommy James and the Shondells, and soul singer James Carr to name a few. That year, he had seen two of his artists go gold and the lot of them generate over ten million dollars in combined sales. And he was confident he'd hit another home run with the Spike-Drivers. In a release his firm sent out to announce the signing, Stogel declared, "In my opinion they will be the biggest group in this decade."

That summer, the band pressed a thousand copies of their debut 45. The single was distributed locally, stocked by Detroit record shops and bookstores, and sold at shows. The Spike-Drivers were already drawing big crowds to their gigs; now they also had a record out and a freshly inked management deal with Leonard Stogel & Associates. Momentum was building exponentially.

Stogel decided the next order of business was to bring the Spike-Drivers to New York to break them in. He arranged a number of industry showcases at venues like the Roundtable, where the group impressed label scouts, booking agents, and promoters, and Ondine, where they impressed a fellow unsigned group called the Doors. Soon word came down that the Spike-Drivers had piqued the interest of a prominent New York label, though as was usually the case with the band, it turned out to be a particularly unlikely situation. Atlantic Records, one of the world's foremost purveyors of black music—specifically jazz and rhythm and blues—invited the Spike-Drivers to an in-studio audition.

The summer of 1966 should have been an exciting time for the band, and in many ways it was. But that excitement was tempered by growing internal tension, particularly between Ted Lucas and Sid Brown. As two strong-minded artists with a lot at stake now that the Spike-Drivers were poised to make it, their contrasting visions were becoming starker. Sid believed the Spike-Drivers were all but guaranteed success if they migrated west to join the budding San Francisco scene. But Ted was more attracted to the classic Big Apple road-to-riches path that Leonard Stogel was selling them. And since that seemed to be materializing, the group ultimately agreed to stay the course in New York.

Then the audition at Atlantic Records happened.

Since the 1940s, Atlantic Records had been home to a who's who of jazz, soul, and R&B artists. In 1966, the label decided to make its first foray into white music, scouting rock bands to add to the roster. The Spike-Drivers were among the first to be considered for this new direction.

At the audition, the band recorded five songs live to tape: "Baby Won't You Let Me Tell You How I Lost My Mind," "Strange Mysterious Sounds," "Got the Goods on You," "Baby Can I Wear Your Clothes," and "Blue Law Sunday."

This was a daydream scenario for the Spike-Drivers: recording an audition tape for Atlantic Records, looking through the control room window and seeing Tom Dowd at the board, Jerry Wexler and Ahmet Ertegun conferring behind him—three legendary music men responsible for so many important records. So what broke the reverie?

The Atlantic brass was thoroughly impressed with the Spike-Drivers. So impressed that they offered the band a substantial contract on the spot. One that granted them full artistic control—which was still fairly uncommon in those days—and a generous signing bonus. If the goal of the New York trip had been to drum up label interest, mission accomplished. The group conferred among themselves while Stogel and the Atlantic business managers discussed the finer points of the offer. That's when things took a turn.

Despite the money, the artistic control, and the cachet of Atlantic Records, the band was divided on the contract. Just how divided, or over what terms, no one can recall. All anyone remembers is how the debate ended.

"I'm not working for any fucking Turk," Ted Lucas, proud son of hardworking Greek immigrants, asserted sotto voce.

Somehow, centuries-old cultural drama had been introduced, and it was now dictating his future and the futures of his four bandmates. They stood around him in the Atlantic recording studio, rightfully dumbfounded. Whatever deliberation was happening had been stopped dead by Ted's unexpected edict.

Though conflicted, it wasn't long before the other members acquiesced. After all, not only was Ted Lucas the most prominent of the band's exceptional talents, but his voice was also the loudest and his will the strongest. The Spike-Drivers declined the Atlantic Records contract at his insistence.

It's impossible to know exactly what made Ted Lucas cast the opportunity aside with such baffling prejudice, or why he waited until that second, with contract in hand, to take issue with Ahmet Ertegun's ethnicity. In the years that followed, he never discussed the Atlantic episode with anyone. In the decades that followed, Ted's bandmates have remembered it as the defining moment that set in motion the inevitable demise of the Spike-Drivers.

A few months after the group walked away from Atlantic Records, the label acquired its first white band, Cream. By the end of the decade, Atlantic would also launch Buffalo Springfield and Led Zeppelin. The label's considerable success in the rock market continues to this day. Had Ted Lucas not balked at the thought of signing with a "fucking Turk," the rock 'n' roll history books might read very differently today.

The Spike-Drivers remained in New York, dutifully playing the gigs that Leonard Stogel booked them, hoping that record deal lightning would strike twice. The Atlantic misadventure only contributed to the tension within the band. And though their showcase performances often generated enthusiasm from the industry types in attendance, that excitement hadn't translated into any more offers. Then, just as today, the recording industry was run by businessmen who much preferred safe and predictable investments to risky, unproven ones. So even though the group's unique sound won plenty of praise from the label scouts they encountered, none of the suits knew how to sell a band like the Spike-Drivers in the American marketplace. They sounded like a radio dial stuck between "Mojo Hand" and Ali Akbar Khan, and they looked like the Beatles from outer space. Not exactly a chart-topping combination in 1966. Money and morale were low until another

unusual twist of fate intervened and sent the Spike-Drivers that lightning bolt.

Leonard Stogel had worked his connections to score the band a spot at the inaugural Rheingold Central Park Music Festival. The Spike-Drivers were scheduled to play two sets leading into headliners Eric Burdon and the Animals.

On July 1, 1966, the Spike-Drivers put on a blistering performance in their opening slot, captivating the Central Park audience of ten thousand. Backstage, during a brief intermission between sets, the band received a parade of compliments from several of the festival's other acts who were similarly awestruck by the performance. Unfortunately, just before embarking on set number two, they encountered the ire of a notoriously temperamental Eric Burdon. He felt that the Spike-Drivers were purposely aiming to upstage him and insisted that organizers cut the band's remaining stage time in half. Otherwise, the Animals would not perform.

Burdon's demands were met and another triumphant moment for the group was dashed. Minutes later, insult was added to injury when the PA promptly blew up at the start of their abridged second set. Stagehands worked to restore the sound, but by the time it was repaired, the Spike-Drivers had only a few minutes of stage time remaining. Defiantly, the band broke into a rowdy, in-the-red rendition of Mose Allison's "Parchman Farm," complete with extended blues improvisations, as if to ensure that they'd be well over time by the song's chaotic conclusion.

Immediately following the set—amid thunderous applause and, it's fair to assume, a thunderous Eric Burdon tantrum—the Spike-

Drivers were approached by an impressed record producer named Jerry Ragovoy. Ragovoy's background was in R&B, so he knew a hot white blues band when he saw one. Or at least he thought he did. When he offered to bring the Spike-Drivers to Warner Brothers, neither the band nor Leonard Stogel realized that Ragovoy had arrived late to the festival and was basing his offer solely on the second set's atypical blues climax. That realization came later—after the ink was already dry on a contract with the Warner Brothers subsidiary, Reprise Records. This contract, which Stogel had adeptly negotiated to be identical to the favorable offer from Atlantic, allowed the band a chance to rectify that blown opportunity. In the end, the company agreed to the terms of the uncommonly artist-friendly contract primarily based on the strength of Ragovoy's endorsement—misguided as that proved to be once he finally got the Spike-Drivers into the studio and heard electric bouzouki licks instead of electric blues licks.

The Spike-Drivers had somehow maneuvered away from collapse after the Atlantic episode and into a promising record deal with Warner/Reprise. The label wasted no time getting them into the studio with the man who discovered them, Jerry Ragovoy, at the helm. Ragovoy's star began to rise after the Rolling Stones scored a hit with his tune "Time Is on My Side" two years earlier.

Reprise signed the Spike-Drivers for the expressed purpose of stealing away teenage-music market share from dominant British R&B cover bands like the aforementioned Rolling Stones and the Animals. To accomplish this, Ragovoy wanted to cut their best song in that first session, so the group prepped "It's Love," a rollicking, rhythmic crowd favorite written by Ted Lucas. That number, like the rest of the group's originals, was surely too far-out to contend for the top of the pop charts. This was a miscalculation on Ragovoy's part, but one he believed he could correct with a little creative studio work. Without the band's involvement, Ragovoy piled handclaps, horns, and other adornments onto "It's Love," burying the exotic string work of Ted and Sid Brown, and whitewashing the Greco–Middle Eastern rhythms that defined the song.

When the group heard this bastardized radio-ready version, it was a new low point of disillusionment. But despite their distaste for Ragovoy's adaptation of "It's Love," and the contract clause that gave them veto power, the Spike-Drivers ultimately decided not to push back. The song was submitted to the label, overdubs and all. It was mercifully shelved.

Going into the next session, Ragovoy had a better idea of what he was getting with the Spike-Drivers. The band—exceedingly cautious with this second chance at success—begrudgingly braced itself for the uncomfortable commercializing process. After all, both parties had the same objective: to score a hit. And since Ragovoy had traveled that path before, the group agreed to take his direction.

The session yielded four cuts: "Strange Mysterious Sounds," "Blue Law Sunday," "High Time," and "Baby Won't You Let Me Tell You How I Lost My Mind." Each song had its raw eccentricities dialed back in favor of cleaner pop renderings. The charisma of the Spike-Drivers, so evident in their sparky live performances, proved to be collateral damage as well. In spite of these compromises—or perhaps because of them—everyone else declared the session a success. This time, when the tapes were turned in to Reprise, the band got the green light.

The Spike-Drivers returned to Detroit battered but optimistic. Though inner tension was still prevalent and money still tight, their first single as Reprise recording artists was in the pipeline. They resumed local gigs and were encouraged to discover that their fan base had not diminished while they toiled in New York. In fact, the band's time away only seemed to bolster the buzz at home.

Meanwhile, twenty-five hundred miles away, an even bigger buzz was growing in northern California. The San Francisco sound, as it would eventually be known, swept up every fledgling band in its path in 1966. Many of the folk groups and jug bands spawned by the coffeehouse scene were dropping acid and going electric, just as the Spike-Drivers had done in Detroit a year earlier. In the Bay Area, bands like Big Brother and the Holding Company, the Grateful Dead, and Jefferson Airplane were loud, exciting, and gaining momentum.

With a major label now behind them, Sid Brown reintroduced the idea of taking the band to San Francisco. There was a lull in post-beatnik, pre-hippie Detroit, and in that moment the Spike-Drivers thrived unrivaled. But for Sid, no amount of local notoriety could match the appeal of a city full of like-minded artists out west. He made a compelling case, but once again, resistance from Ted Lucas and Leonard Stogel quashed his efforts.

Incidentally, Sid wasn't the only Detroiter captivated by the movement in San Francisco. That October, Russ Gibb opened the Fillmore-inspired Grande Ballroom on Grand River Avenue near Joy Road. And as we all know, the Detroit music scene soon took a sharp turn from there.

On November 26, 1966, the Spike-Drivers released their first single with Reprise: "Baby Won't You Let Me Tell You How I Lost My Mind" backed with "High Time." It was a commercial failure.

The band returned to New York in early 1967 to work on a follow-up. This time, Reprise tapped hit-makers Charles Koppelman and Don Rubin to produce. The pair had recently done Bobby Darin's "If I Were a Carpenter," which spent weeks climbing the Billboard charts around the same time that the Spike-Drivers single missed them completely. For Koppelman and Rubin, the mandate from Reprise was clear: polish this act up and pull a hit out of them.

The Spike-Drivers recorded just one tune with the producers—Richard Keelan's mellow, meditative "Break out the Wine." And once again, despite strong performances from the band, the final mix was milquetoast at best. This was thanks to the saccharine strings and innocuous oboe overdubs that crowded the Spike-Drivers out of their own song. Nevertheless, the Koppelman and Rubin schmaltz went unchallenged by the band, and the label scheduled it for release with Ragovoy's existing mix of "Strange Mysterious Sounds" as the flipside.

On February 25, 1967, the single for "Break out the Wine" and "Strange Mysterious Sounds" was released by Reprise. It tanked.

That was two strikes for the Spike-Drivers and Reprise; a predictable outcome considering their entire relationship was born from a misunderstanding. But even so, the failure of the second single exhausted what little positivity and patience were left in the band, and the ideological clashes between Ted Lucas and Sid Brown became even more virulent. Sid was through compromising the group's art for what he felt was a desperate grasp at the big time. Ted, equally frustrated by Reprise's mishandling of the band, thought the problem wasn't that they had sold out but that no one producing them had bought in. Like Sid, he believed the Spike-Drivers made important music. But unlike Sid, he still saw Reprise as their vehicle to break through to an audience beyond the galleries and nightclubs in Detroit.

He decided it was time to take the wheel.

One spring afternoon in 1967, Sid Brown received a call from Spike-Drivers manager Leonard Stogel. On behalf of Ted Lucas and Richard Keelan, and with the blessing of the label and management, Sid was informed that he, Marycarol, and drummer-for-hire Larry Cruse were being demoted. Though they received a halfhearted invitation to remain in the band for public appearances and live performances, it was made clear that they were no longer welcome to contribute to future songwriting or recording. Those tasks would now be done with studio musicians at the direction of Ted and Richard. Stogel went on to say that if they did not comply with these new terms, they would be fired.

Needless to say, Sid, Marycarol, and Larry were absolutely not willing to be reduced to lip-synching mannequins. And despite the take-it-or-leave-it ultimatum, they pushed back hard, invoking a fiduciary clause in the group's management contract with Stogel. In short, it stated that if any party within the Spike-Drivers or Stogel & Associates were to compromise what was in the best interests of *all* parties, the contract would become null and void. This particular clause was added during the final stages of negotiation with Stogel, after early Spike-Drivers benefactor and soda mogul Mort Feigenson insisted that his lawyers review the deal for the band. No doubt Stogel was blindsided when Sid pulled this card. And since there was no way around the airtight language of the fiduciary clause, the contract collapsed on itself. And in that moment, so did the band.

Rather than fight it out in court, Ted and Richard agreed to release Sid, Marycarol, and Larry from all debts and obligations to Reprise Records and Stogel & Associates. They also relinquished all legal rights to the Spike-Drivers name. The pair rebranded themselves the Misty Wizards, retained Leonard Stogel, and assumed the remainder of the Reprise contract.

News of the split spread fast in Detroit. The May 15, 1967, issue of *Fifth Estate* published a blow-by-blow piece on the demise of the Spike-Drivers, indicting Ted and Richard for the power play that broke up "the first psychedelic rock group that existed in Detroit."

That summer, Sid, Marycarol, and Larry carried on the Spike-Drivers with local talents Marshall Rubinoff and Ron Cobb replacing Ted and Richard. They performed often with this lineup but never released another record. The Misty Wizards, attempting to exercise the full artistic control that the Spike-Drivers seemed to surrender at every turn, ran up a massive tab with Reprise while re-recording Ted's song "It's Love" in marathon sessions throughout New York and Los Angeles. A single for the song was released on July 26, 1967. It failed to chart.

Meanwhile in San Francisco, 1967 was the year that any band with half the look or a quarter the talent of the Spike-Drivers got a record deal. Many of them became wildly successful and are celebrated to this day.

There are plenty of factors that doomed the Spike-Drivers: inner conflict, bad timing, poor judgment, questionable leadership. . . . These flaws proved fatal for the band and define their legacy.

It would be a much simpler story had they merely been marginalized by a square record exec or cheapened by a shortsighted producer. But the fact is, the Spike-Drivers were very much complicit in their own demise. By the end, they'd compromised most everything that made them vital and unique because, as artists, they felt insignificant in their own time. They made the mistake of measuring themselves by the commercial standards of an industry that couldn't comprehend them.

Of course, this is easy commentary to make half a century later. But in those mid-'60s years before the boundaries of pop music expanded radically, the Spike-Drivers had no roadmap. The band could never have known how close they were to success if not for the parade of ill-fated decisions that finally forced them apart.

But even if the Spike-Drivers failed because they were misunderstood, too far ahead of their time, desperately misguided, and ultimately divided by two supercilious, genius guitarists, there is no detracting from the real artistry and vision that they exhibited in that rocky two-year flash. The band may have imploded on takeoff, but ask any Detroit old-timer who was in the scene before the MC5 made it out of Downriver; any record collector who files

rare psych; any musician with a passing knowledge of unsung '60s rockers. They'll tell you: the Spike-Drivers were unmatched, true originals.

Detroit's forgotten psychedelic heroes.

## POSTSCRIPT

Sid and Marycarol Brown finally headed west after the second iteration of the Spike-Drivers folded in October 1967. They divorced in 1974. Sid continued writing and releasing music with groups like the Peace, Bread, and Land Band and Modality Stew. Though he eventually reconnected with Richard Keelan, he held a grudge against Ted Lucas for the rest of his life. He died in 2005.

The Misty Wizards disbanded in 1968. In January 1970, Richard Keelan left Detroit for Stratford, Ontario. There, he formed the seminal Canadian folk-rock group Perth County Conspiracy and attained the critical acclaim and commercial success that escaped him in the States. He currently lives in Toronto and still performs regularly.

Larry Cruse never played in another band. In 1973, he earned a social work degree from Wayne State University. He served as a social worker for twenty-five years before retiring in the late '90s. He currently lives in Gaylord, Michigan.

Steve Booker—who took the name Muruga in 1969—has enjoyed a long and storied music career that continues to this day. Among the highlights are stints with Merl Saunders and Jerry Garcia, Tim Hardin, Al Kooper, and a long tenure with George Clinton. He currently lives in Ann Arbor, Michigan.

In the immediate aftermath of the Spike-Drivers and the Misty Wizards, Ted Lucas studied sitar with his hero, Ravi Shankar, in California. Upon returning to Detroit, he found steady session work as the only sitar player in the musicians' union. By 1969, he was Motown's exotic instrumentalist, appearing uncredited on many of the label's later Detroit-era recordings. He performed often in the ensuing decade, both solo and with a variety of bands, including the Horny Toads, Jonathon Round's Boogie Disease, and an ill-conceived reboot of the Spike-Drivers in the mid-'70s. Through it all, lingering disillusionment and contempt for the music industry bled into his every endeavor. In 1975, after toiling away for years, he finally completed his masterpiece solo album and released it on his own dime. By then, no one was listening.

Ted Lucas battled addiction and chronic illness throughout the 1980s and until his death on September 19, 1992.

**MIKE DUTKEWYCH**

# 6 DETROIT THE '70s

# ROCKS INTO AND BEYOND

## FROM EVERYONE LOVES ALICE TO CASS CORRIDOR PUNK TO DEATH

# Alice Cooper All American
## A Horatio Alger Story for the '70s
*Lester Bangs*

*"What kinda dog is that, anyway, Mister?"*

*"It's a cross between a Manchurian yak and an Australian dingo."*

—W. C. Fields, selling a ventriloqual dog in *Poppy*

### COOPERTOWN #1

"Return of the Spiders" is playing, and here stand these two stooges in the old sense, not like guitar hoodlumps cut from Ig-patterns, but just old-time disgraced schmozoes, except that these two schmozoes are listenin' to this here rabid, highballed motherrhinofuck of a record. And one stooge looks at the other one with a pained expression on his face and sez: "Ugh, what loud unnerving shit! I couldn't stand to be around music like that for more'n a couple of minutes before my nerves 'd come unstrung! And not only that, but you actually tell me it's the first thing you like to play when you get up in the morning! You must be deranged!"

And Stooge 2, the one with the taste, why he just turns and look at the other one all sly with his eyelids half-cocked down and purrs: "I find it rather bracing myself."

And there you have it. That sense of disjuncture and harmless abrasion is what Alice Cooper's all about, I think. On the other hand, it might just be that Alice is actually conceived and founded on nothing more outre than plain or, good ol', reassuring ol' "Show Biz Entertainment." And Alice's approach to it, far from deriving from any architectonics of "Future Shock," actually draws gleefully on the most venerable, storied, sanguinely plebian of the lively

Alice Cooper in Ann Arbor, 1973. © Leni Sinclair Collection.

284

arts. It draws on vaudeville and carny and pies in the puss and the baggy pants hitting the sawdust and the bearded lady. And circuses and animal acts and all that superficially wholesome stuff stuck on independent channels that your parents while away their tube hours soaking their nerves in. Mr. Bones, the Beggar and Mrs. Davey, Honest Old Uncle Alice and his Sequin Flapping Drag Brash Cartoonoroony Whoop-up. Take the family.

So how do we resolve the contradiction? Well, for one thing, it's easy to carry garishness too far. Alice's intricate stage business and sonic assault is an exercise in tactical brinksmanship on several levels. The drag stuff carried over from being truly outrageous, with Alice looking enough like a rather reptilian Vegas hooker that a drunk businessman could've took him home for the surprise of his life, and wound through permutations of business over the years until it had petered to the spider-eye makeup and aluminum cocaine jumpsuit zipped open to the navel.

All the props and trappings and '30s horror movie settings have a specific mileage beyond which they muddle downstream into shuck-and-jive. But Alice and the crew, consummate technicians that they are, almost invariably tether the gimmickery and injection hysteria just a shadow's breadth this side of Gehenna.

On the other hand, maybe Gehenna is where it should really be their job to take us, rather than the Laugh in the Dark ride at the amusement park. I think that's something like what Iggy tried to do, and look at the Stooges era: done too soon. But just maybe there's a bit of cautionary parable lodged in that great success-and-sharp-plunge story, and that is that perhaps the only growth possible for an artist who doesn't remove himself at all from his art, so that it and his life are identical (because Iggy didn't and for a while they were), is a tailspin into welters of egocentric, relentlessly solemn self-consciousness. Especially if the artist is trying to render or conjure Gehenna, the pit, the darkness of chaos and disintegration.

The incandescent human demon personifications like Iggy, or more appropriately like the image that Iggy projected, bring to mind the old Dylan song about the house on the hill that was "brighter than any sun," and the lyric "Don't go mistaking paradise / For that home across the road." 'Cuz if you do, you'll not only wreck your health and lose your apple cheeks and vim-chocked profile but your sense of humor as well! And that's the worst fate of all. A much more sensible course, after all, than taking it upon yourself to live out all the dark impulses of the human soul, is just to pull a pretzel turnabout and become Alice Cooper instead.

And really, I don't think anybody has ever seriously invested in Alice the expectation that he should enter the flames and get seared himself just like the tortured Dwight Fryes of his songs. A good case could be made that Alice is just dallydabbling in the Deep and that his actual involvement with what he's putting forward (and not just the obvious sexual elements) is most likely about as demoniacally driven as Jim Morrison's must have been late in the years, when ol' botabelly would come lurching on to sing "Celebration of the Lizard" to an opera house full of big-eyed pubies.

Alice doesn't have a beer belly (yet), but you can bet your chrome-plated Led Zeppelin dildo he's wholesome, a contention I'll attempt to shore up with a few facts and figgers when I pass over

285

into the *Tiger Beat* meat-and-spuds of the article where you'll meet Alice and the boys in the band and even (sorry to disillusion any diehard hopes) their old ladies. Maybe. I may restrain myself from spilling too many beans since at least one member of the Cooper rancho (namely, Alice's svelte sweetie, Cindy) sort of semispecifically asked me to leave her out of it or at least (and here comes Coopertown #2) in the background.

## COOPERTOWN #2

In the kitchen, maybe, or out in the parlor washing windows with all the idiot glee befitting some TV stereotype of the unliberated drudge. Yes folks, not only does Alice Cooper dress up in women's clothes, he also exploits the woman he's got! Every night when he gets home from the concert and kicks back into his favorite overstuffed TV chair, Sandy has to approach him cross the carpet on all fours, reverent with scripted trepidation, swathed in the threads and cap of a saucy French scullery maid, and slowly and respectfully remove his red spike-heel patent leather pumps! Kneeling at his feet, she then must unsnap and peel off his pantyhose, being tactfully watchful not to cause the exhausted star the slightest discomfort, after which she worshipfully massages his shaved legs and sweaty feet for a few minutes, just to get the workaday weariness out of them, after which she serves him his pipe (pure Tangeirian kef) and beer (Blatz) and then proceeds to undo his hot pants, dig beneath the filmy black panties inside, delicately scoop the famed Al Coop porker out, and lower her ruby lips with a slowness and precision whose mastery took many, many months of schooling and unbending discipline, the cat-o-nine, the tongs, the . . . (Fade out to obscene

Burroughsian mugwump gurglings; and the most obscene thing about them, incidentally, is that they come out sounding to the attentive ear not like indescribably esoteric and squishily amphibious sex acts but the most pink-tickled geyser of gleeful and near-uncontainable laughs. What a dirty trick!)

As I was saying before the porn break, though, the fact is that Alice Cooper is really one of the wholesomest, cleanest, most upright, and well-spoken pop stars you'd ever care to meet. Just a real all-round nice guy! The perfect cherub-cheeked picture of a God-worshippin', pie-scarfin', parent-respectin' ALL AMERICAN BOY!!!!! (His parents even attended one of his shows and loved it.) And that straight-ahead lucidity can't help but carry over a bit, cross the slimy footlights into the arena of Alice the galvanic stage exorcism. It's good rock, good theater, good Alice charisma, but it's not a real nightmare. The thing about a nightmare that can really nab you by the nuts and hang you heels up in total helplessness is that usually you don't know it's not real; only at the very end maybe does the conscious mind come jimmying in and shatter the set. And Alice Cooper's nightmares—I'm thinking of *Love It to Death* in particular and the stage act in general—never take over their structures to become obsessions with dark lives and wills of their own.

What Alice's little Gothic scenarios are really is something else entirely; what they are is cartoons. And that's almost as great and important as if they were the other thing.

## COOPERTOON #3

It's 1960 or thereabouts, and the "late bloomer" Alice, who kept watching after-school cartoons all through his young manhood and still does today, is catching a Bugs Bunny sequence in his Phoenix parlor; a panorama of darkie silhouettes swinging hammers, tightening screws while singing "I've Been Workin' on de Railroad." Cut to Bugs Bunny lounging in a hollow stump munching a carrot and reading a girlie magazine. Elmer Fudd comes down the path singing "I've Been Workin' on the Railroad" in a broken voice. Bugs looks at the audience, bats the long lashes he has suddenly grown, and simpers: "Why, that sounds just like Frank Sinatra!" then disappears into the stump. Fudd sets up his surveyor's telescope right in front of the stump, looks in, and flips his lid when he sees a montage of cheesecake and black nylons from the magazine Bugs is holding in front of the lens. When Elmer leans around the telescope to get closer to the chicks, Bugs not only has long lashes but lipstick as well, and purrs: "What's up, big boy?"

"It's the wabbit!" screams Elmer in a paroxysm of rage at having his masculinity compromised by his archnemesis, then chases Bugs, who turns into a torpedo zooming through the air and straight down the nearest rabbit hole, into the mouth of which Elmer inserts the muzzle of his rifle and fires off a spasmodic volley of bullets. When he gets back to his telescope and looks in, Bugs holds one lit match in front of the lens, and Elmer sees the whole forest burning, shrieks "Fire! Fire!" Hooks and ladders erupt from Bugs's stump, Bugs climbing up in full fireman's uniform and hat, with a hose in his hand whose jet he turns on Fudd full force, blasting him back until he finally manages to grab his gun, chase the anarchic bunny back to his hole, and fill it with a few more rounds.

When he gets back to the stump, his telescope on the tripod has been replaced by a straight, rigid Bugs Bunny. Elmer peers into his eye, frowns:

"There's something awfuwwy funny going on here!" In reply, Bugs grabs him, plays his lips with the classic cartoon SMMOOOCH!! and runs off hooting like a hooligan. . . .

Not only is that what Alice Cooper at his best is all about, but it would be incredible if he were even half as subversively effective as Bugs Bunny in putting his be-Fuddled audience through the changes. They even work for the same company, though that is probably not the reason why the cartoon element has always been in the music for anyone who cared to look. Even when you couldn't understand the words, the wheedling falsetto vocals and jerky razzmatazz structures of much of the stuff on the first album's second side point to a very specific, caricatural kind of whimsy. And the very first song on *Easy Action* consolidates and confirms it—just dig the instrumental section, right after "Mr. and Misdemeanor," that romantic twosome, have finished watching the sun set together: the solos and scales are melodramatic, exaggerated, and ballooned toward precise burlesque, and you can instantly see the leering villain or be-caped Mr. Hyde slinking after Little Nell with stealthy high steps. Lucky Luciano is in there, too, and later, in "Still No Air," the whole *West Side Story* episode, complete with direct cops ("When yer a Jet yer a Jet all the way / From yer first cigarette to yer last dyin' day! Eeeasy, Action! Gotta rocket in yer pocket!!") is so blatant and hilarious that only the technical sloppiness keeps it from being a real classic.

And the interesting thing is that so many people, initially or ideally, should find these cartoons so abrasive. But then, what were all those old strips, from Bugs Bunny to Popeye, about if not pain? Not a frame passed that somebody wasn't getting conked on the bean, shot point-blank (which just singed and turned them into Niggers), or dropping off the thirtieth story. It's fun to dig the tribulations of our fellow men in that context, we eat it up. And when it's all wrapped up in a whirling storm of guitar noise, it feels even better. While I can't go as far as Dave Marsh who sez that "sometimes the tenderest thing you can do for a person is smash them right in the teeth!" I do think that we need stars and heroes able to rattle our bones and sear our brains a bit.

People who call all this darkness and negativism are merely shortsighted, if not certified candidates for white and red canes. The Stooges were the ultimate Nova blowtorch of savage nihilism, but Alice Cooper has recognized it as his function to take some of the irritation, hostility, and paranoia around us and demonstrate that it can be capitalized on and transcended with glee if we're just dementedly lucid enough. And the attendant sense of abrasiveness is nothing that'll ruin ya, Lilly Liver, but just jarring enough to be, as in the tale of two stooges bracing! I have wondered on occasion whether it might be possible to transcend the ingrained reactive recoil and get to the extraordinary musical nosh that lies somewhere inside the creaking squeak of chalk on a blackboard; I do know that for years I've found the great grindings of metal in factories or the sizzle of a welding torch an interesting and sometimes positively lulling form of Muzak.

And speaking of electric sizzles, it's also crucial to recognize that the Alice Cooper vision issues not only from cartoons but from a deep love and understanding of TV in general. We all grew up primarily on two things: rock 'n' roll and TV. Alice Cooper was the first rock group to recognize that fact and fuse the two influences in a big way, and

nobody'll be surprised if the curtains part someday on the whole band riffin' in some monster Sony. They almost made the real thing already, via an Excedrin commercial and LA kiddie show that were both axed.

But omens of future glories do appear occasionally. When I first took up residence in the Creem mansion, I was ushered to my room and: there was a TV! My very own! My first very own boob toob! My idiot box, my baby! Cute as a sow's tongue. I took to leaving it on all the time, since the steady high-pitched buzz of the TV tube is merely the most exquisitely refined electronic cousin to the hymn of feedback flowing strongly through our nervous systems, and whenever I entered the room to get something or was just wandering vaguely around I would stop and watch a short snatch of the current program. Learn a lot that way, and just like with a Burroughs cutup or Lucky Luciano bringing "a modern mosquito / To every big city," I don't mind the disjuncture at all. One Monday night I happened in on an episode of *Mayberry RFD*: it was about an amateur talent show in the quaint burg, but my ears turned backflips when I heard the yokel MCing the thing drawl brightly: "And now—our fourteenth contestant of the evening, a sweet lil' ole gal you all know from over Bear Mountain way—Miss Alice Cooper!!" And then there materialized the most sweet-temperedly purse-lipped stereotype of a Saltine States old maid you ever saw, practically falling backward behind this vast tacky gilt-flaked harp. She sanded demurely, lifted one limpid wrist, and . . .

# Twenty-Five Years of *Creem*
## Kiss and Not Tell, or Confessions of One of the Film Foxes

*Jaan Uhelszki*

Working at *Creem* was very nearly the perfect job. I say "nearly" because the pay was poor—if there was a payday that particular week. I started working for *Creem* in mid-1971 but never even received a paycheck until January 1972, on the occasion of my birthday. I'm sure it was just a coincidence that I finally got paid on that day, but then again you never knew with publisher Barry Kramer, who was very big on symbolic gestures. But if the truth be told, I would probably have paid

Kramer to let me work there. Our fearless leader counted on that kind of altruistic sentiment and gleefully paid us, in the spirit of what he saw as true egalitarianism, the modest sum of $22.75 per week. (Egalitarianism was carried to such an extreme that our staff box was alphabetically arranged, without designations or titles, until August 1975, so no one ever knew who the editor really was until then, which was actually rather useful when one needed to pass the buck.) In addition, he also provided

Jaan Uhelszki Grande Daze. © Jaan Uhelszki 2016.
Photo Courtesy of the Jaan Uhelszki's Archives.

staff members with room and board at a series of hovels in places ranging from the mean streets of Detroit to the backwoods of bucolic Walled Lake, which wasn't as bucolic as it was cheap. Why did we "Creemsters," as we were wont to call ourselves, put up with this? As Richard Siegel, Kramer's childhood pal and *Creem*'s general manager, said, "We were like the guy who shovels the shit at the circus. When asked why he didn't quit, he replied, 'What, and give up show business?'"

I know that was part of the allure for me, and it was a step up from the previous job I had held in "show business." I worked at the Grande Ballroom, a two-thousand-seat venue in the heart of Detroit, the Motor City's answer to the Fillmore East and West. It was a very hip spot, and sooner or later all the major rock acts played there. My job was dispensing sodas to a horde of drug-sloppy concertgoers. That might have seemed like a bit of a dead-end job, but for a hard-core fan like me, there were lots of fringe benefits and moments of pure luminosity that I wouldn't have traded for anything. I saw one of the very first performances of *Tommy*, was one of the handful of those who witnessed the second public performance of the Psychedelic Stooges, and saw Iggy in his "space angel" phase, performing in a long white choir robe with his face completely whitened, wearing a chrome headdress constructed from ironed and starched strips of Reynolds Wrap glued onto a bathing-cap-like form. I was on hand for the live recording of the MC5's *Kick Out the Jams*, and I watched Led Zeppelin's entire first set with my elbows propped on Jimmy Page's amp. I was a fan of the first order and soon came to realize that just seeing the bands was no longer enough—my fanaticism required expression. Maybe I needed

evidence that I was there. I remember thinking that I was probably watching musical history in the making, and I wanted to remember everything. It's currently fashionable to say, "If you remember the '60s, you weren't there," but back then I wanted both to remember and record them. I used to go home at night after I got off work at one a.m. and sit on the shag rug in my bedroom composing reviews of the bands I had just seen—Janis Joplin, Procol Harum, Creedence Clearwater Revival, the Velvet Underground—just for my own, how do you say it, edification. I don't think it was real to me until I wrote about it, and it was always better the second time around.

*Creem* used to run an ad that said:

Do it. This is just to say we want you. That should've been obvious all along, of course, but just in case it isn't here's the deal: *Nobody who writes for this rag's got anything you ain't got*, at least in the way of credentials. There's no reason why you shouldn't be sending us your stuff: fiction, reviews, features, cartoons, stuff about film, ecology, books, or whatever you have in mind that we might be able to use. Sure, we don't pay much, but then who else do ya know who'll publish you? We really will . . . ask any of our dozens of satisfied customers . . . Whaddya got to lose? Whaddya got?

As you might suppose, I took this invitation to heart, dusted off my old Sears Medalist typewriter, dashed off a review of an Elton John concert, and sent it to the publication. Much to my disappointment, my opus wasn't published, and today I can sincerely say that I am not surprised, and actually quite relieved, since I had compared John's singing to a warm bowl of oatmeal—something I had obviously meant as a compliment! I wasn't discouraged (OK, maybe a little), and I continued to keep up this one-sided relationship, next progressing to sending letters to the editor.

The Grande Ballroom's owner, Russ Gibb, was a minority stockholder in *Creem*, so I thought that it would be a natural transition for me to get a job there. I believed I had the right credentials—I knew band statistics like they were batting averages for the American League (I could tell you what band Peter Green played in before Fleetwood Mac, the original members of King Crimson, and all the neck sizes of the Beatles)—not to mention all those sodas I had distributed into the very hands of all those rock gods!

While I waited for opportunity to knock, I attended classes at Wayne State University. I was enrolled as a journalism major, with visions of Brenda Starr dancing in my head. I can see now that I was a little young for my age. One day, while waiting for a friend in the student union, I made the acquaintance of Charley Auringer, *Creem*'s art director. He was a brooding-artist type, handsome, a little remote, and if I believed in such things (and I did), he might be holding the key to my future—except it wasn't that easy. By anyone's calculation. Auringer was a difficult man to talk to, moody and taciturn. He perpetually wore a look of studied boredom, an expression that conveyed the feeling that he wanted to be anywhere but where he was.

After a few attempts at conversation, we somehow progressed past monosyllables and developed what might pass as a relationship. After a few

months of meeting for coffee, he finally took me over to the *Creem* compound. My first introduction to the clan was in the late fall of 1970. My visit coincided with the arrival of Lester Bangs, who had just come from California. He looked like some visiting professor who was assessing the advantages of relocating to this industrial wasteland. He looked so different from our indigenous population with his neatly trimmed hair and his shined shoes and his overextended mustache. When I first saw him, he was wearing a button-down shirt over a sparkling-white undershirt. During his stay, I occasionally spied him actually wearing a suit jacket—in fact, he owned one in a Prince of Wales plaid. In hindsight, I think this may have been just his way of making a good impression, because there was little evidence of his former sartorial splendor once he settled in. I remember wondering how he could look like *this* and write like *that*. I know he wondered about we midwestern denizens, too, because I overheard him telling movie editor Robbie Cruger, the most well-dressed member of the staff (she wore cashmere twin sets), that he had never seen so many ugly people gathered in one place. Maybe he just decided to emigrate to offset the averages, but whatever the enticement, he accepted Barry Kramer's offer and made plans to return after the first of the year, joining the ranks as the record review editor, a position that Dave Marsh had held but recently abandoned to become editor in chief.

Bangs was better suited to the position anyway, because he actually liked music. David always took it a little too seriously—I don't think rock music was ever just entertainment to him; instead, it had vast social and didactic powers. I think Marsh saw us as cultural arbitrators who were busy defining the

291

pop aesthetic. He brought the whiff of politics to almost everything he wrote, but then again, he came to *Creem* from the auspices of John Sinclair and his leftist White Panther Party. I think David saw us as foot soldiers in the counterculture revolution, and Lester just saw us as bozos on the bus. I remember Bangs once telling a reporter that *Creem* was "a raspberry in the face of culture, and in a sense a raspberry in the face of itself."

Not surprisingly, the two editors were perfect foils for each other, and the marriage thrived for a number of years. We used to say *Creem* was a cross between *Mad* magazine and *Esquire*, and Marsh and Bangs were largely responsible for maintaining that delicate balance between the absurd and the profane. As you might have surmised, relations began to unravel, since everything about the two of them was at odds—their sizes, their temperaments, and their work ethics. Lester was tall in the saddle, laconic, and often pharmaceutically fueled; while David was small and wiry, much-too-tightly wound, and never indulged in anything stronger than a Coca-Cola.

It all blew up about the time Lester got a cockapoo pup who was as untrained as he was. This dog, whose name was either Cookie or Susie, depending on whom you asked, took to defecating wherever she pleased, which usually turned out to be under David's desk. David complained to Lester a number of times, with Lester always assuring him that he'd take care of it. "Yeah, yeah, I'll clean it up," he promised. "It won't happen again." But it would—until one day Marsh blew up and deposited a parcel of warm dog shit directly onto Bangs's IBM Selectric, where he would be certain not to miss it. Words and fisticuffs ensued, and their growing feud polarized the staff.

David was becoming less and less enchanted with the direction *Creem* was taking and more and more embittered with members of the staff. He was becoming more well known in rock critic circles and began to receive other offers to bring truth and integrity to an often unwilling public. It seemed he wanted to become a tireless crusader, then as now, exposing injustice and moral paucity. *Creem* seemed to be on its own crusade to never take anything seriously (and certainly not David) and to deflate pomposity and solemnity wherever it was found.

David had a special knack for provoking even the most mild-mannered of souls, so when he found himself up against someone equally as contentious, sparks would fly. Barry Kramer was such a man. He, too, was small in stature, pugnacious, and had unshatterable confidence in his convictions—not an easy thing to come up against in a simple staff meeting, where one expects give-and-take to be the order of business. "There are two ways," Barry would say, "my way, and the wrong way." Comments like this only fanned the rage that lay very close to Marsh's surface, and what began as a simple discussion about cover headlines was very likely to have a violent outcome.

On many occasions, Barry would throw a typewriter through a light table or ricochet a telephone off a wall, once even overturning a full trash can on Iggy's head, who happened to be visiting during one of our confabs. Violence wasn't Kramer's first resort. Ideally he would have rather manipulated everyone's neuroses to achieve what he wanted, but if that didn't work, he was none too shy about using his fists, his feet, and once even a broomstick on the hapless members of the staff.

Much of our publisher's genius was his ability to make other people do what he wanted—and the trick was to avoid being a player in Kramer's mind games or, worse yet, being a pawn. He had the uncanny ability to sniff out personal weakness and take dead aim—wounding only the way one armed with an uncomfortable truth can.

I don't want to paint too bleak a portrait of the man. He was also gifted with great intelligence and foresight. When his demons were quelled, he was often disarming and reflective. I remember overhearing an elegant discussion he had with Jack Kronk, our circulation manager, about the difference between friendship and "being friendly," and how they were worlds apart. Late at night, one could find him in his office with a snifter of Courvoisier in hand, stabbing the air with his manicured fingers to make some usually trenchant point about the oil embargo or the latest Who album. Another evening, you could have found Barry winding mailing tape around his assistant and the receptionist while dousing a Debbie Harry cardboard stand-up in Jack Daniels before igniting it with his Dunhill lighter. He was a man of many demons and great contradictions, and one person I truly miss. Over the years I've had many dreams that Barry wasn't really gone, and my sadness is always renewed upon awakening. I believe Barry left us because, much like the lyrics to that Hendrix song say, "he wished and prayed he'd stop living, so he decided to die."

We spent a total of three years in that godforsaken enclave of alluvial mud and redneck bikers in Walled Lake, but circulation figures were up, our ad rates were climbing, and there was talk of pay raises. We were moving to new offices in the well-bred suburb of Birmingham, located down the block from Bob Seger's manager's office and above a furrier. We had really arrived! All our offices were on one floor, so we could actually look at one another when we fought, instead of shouting up two flights of stairs. Although we may have moved uptown, that didn't mean we had become civilized—that would come later at the expense of all the branch offices of the record companies who wined and dined us in such exclusive surroundings that we had to cultivate impeccable table manners.

The editorial office had high white ceilings and was painted a pale eggshell white. There were beautiful hardwood fixtures, with vast oriel windows that overlooked Woodward Avenue, and beyond that a green park. I shared the editorial space with Lester, Ben Edmonds, and John Morthland, a "professional" writer Barry brought in to teach us how to run a "real" magazine. Morthland was an extraordinarily gifted writer and editor and a gentle soul who never lost his temper. The only time you could ever tell that he was vexed was when he smoked his unfiltered cigarettes down to their nubby ends. The more he smoked, the more upset he was.

My desk was next to Lester's, a shrine to Taco Bell and *Penthouse*. His typewriter was just barely visible from underneath the rubble of food cartons, stacks of empty record jackets, and discarded press releases. There were usually a couple of unopened bottles of cough syrup around—gifts from fans that he swore he never drank anymore, or at least not if there was anything else remotely interesting and available. The drug of choice at *Creem*, 222s, were codeine-laced aspirins. About once a fortnight we would take turns driving across the Canadian border twelve miles away, where the drug was sold

293

over the counter. They were rather benign if taken in small amounts, but during an especially brutal deadline some of us had been known to gobble a couple every hour or so, around the clock. We used to tell ourselves it was for the pain, but it was more alleviate the boredom of the midwestern winters and the long, often eighteen-hour days spent putting the magazine to bed.

There was definitely more to Lester than met the eye. He was capable of great sadness and great enthusiasm, but little joy. He was a voracious writer and a voracious champion of the underdog. He despised pretension and would hold it up to the light at every turn. He was ever the knight-errant, always looking for a damsel in distress to rescue. I think that was his Achilles' heel, because he related much better to women who were damaged in some way rather than to the fully realized sort, and this predilection colored his relationships with women, which were always filled with drama and recriminations.

There may have been ambiguities surrounding Lester's personal relationships, but never about his writing. He used to write with such rapidity and grace that I used to sit at my own desk and watch in wonderment—he was like a hamster on a wheel. I measured my output unfairly against his, and I came up wanting. I acquired a phobia about my carefully and often painfully wrought prose that took me the better part of a decade to overcome. What I didn't know then was that Lester was racing against the clock—he wouldn't be with us long and had to get all that he had to say out as quickly as possible.

Bangs was a true original and had the uncanny ability to bring out the extreme in people. It really boiled down to the fact that he just liked to stir

things up to see where the shit would fall—that always made for a good story and a more amusing time, and he really enjoyed being amused at someone else's expense. I had seen him provoke Slade, a mid-'70s postglam band, to a food fight in a sumptuous Polynesian restaurant by telling them they were just over-aged Bay City Rollers, sweet-talk Grace Slick, then lead singer for Jefferson Airplane, into baring her breasts for *Creem*; and mercilessly goad Lou Reed in an especially sadomasochistic interview. That particular evening culminated in Lou Reed dedicating a song to Lester and "all you little squirts of shit at *Creem*." Lou was in rare form that night and thought himself astonishingly witty. After the show, he and Lester kept baiting each other and Lou insisted on repeatedly addressing Lester as "More Bangs" and then doubling over in rare and peculiar laughter that sounded like nothing so much as the flapping wings of some exotic tropical insect.

During this time, I had moved up the ranks from the "subscription kid" to media editor, to features editor, to the lofty heights of senior editor, a distinction I shared with Bangs. I had long gotten over my star-fright and could banter with the best of them. To keep myself humble, I kept a picture of Flo and Eddie (ex-Turtles and former members of Frank Zappa's band) above my desk. They were my very first interview subjects, whom I interrogated with my willing sidekick, Connie Kramer, Barry's wife and the true power and brains behind the throne. Connie did fine, but I fell asleep during the encounter. I woke up to the sensation of Howard Kaylan, "Eddie," roughly shaking my right shoulder. I mumbled something about being up half the night preparing for the event, but they didn't seem to believe me. It was the nadir of my budding career and, needless to say, I never wrote the story. Later in my career something like *that* would have never stopped me. I was probably inspired by Mark Farner of Grand Funk Railroad, who once told me he wrote his best songs when he was asleep. No argument there.

While I'm on the subject of confessions, I think this might be the right time to say that Lester and I stuffed the ballot box in the annual reader's poll. The first time we did it, we rolled on the floor, shrieking with laughter at our ingenious entries, wondering why we should have treated this particular event with any more reverence than anything else we did. (Could that be why both Lester and I were in the top three critics of the year for five years running?) Ben Edmonds, the managing editor, tried to stop us, but we were too far gone in our revelry, and we knew that he was more concerned that we didn't expunge his own votes than with the impropriety of it all.

Ben was more genteel than the rest of us. He hailed from Boston, spoke slowly and clearly with big, cultured vowel sounds, and gave an inordinate amount of time and energy to his wardrobe. He resembled a beached surfer but with pale skin and even paler shoulder-length blond hair. He had kind of a Samson thing going on with his coiffure, but not without cause—he really had stupendous hair. He gave a bit of class to the place and usually specialized in stories on art rock or articles on the more well-behaved members of rockdom—you know, Ian Hunter, David Bowie, Elton John, Todd Rundgren, Bryan Ferry. His stories just bordered on the fey but never really went over the edge.

He dressed in a symphony of whites and beiges, but behind his back we called him the white worm. I have an enduring affection for Edmonds, who taught me how to make an omelet and accompanied me to a Steve Miller interview. Both endeavors were pretty dicey affairs, but I think my omelet fared better.

My stories soon caught up with my cooking, and I was regularly going out on the road with bands, at the rate of about one week out of the month. This was where the best material was—catching bands in the act of being themselves—and where all the perks were, although some of them were better left unsampled. I remember once being flown in for a weekend at New York's Plaza Hotel to do a story on a very successful blue-eyed-soul duo. After an afternoon of lobster finger sandwiches and strawberries in the Palm Court, a shampoo and haircut in the salon, and shopping for sundries in the pharmacy—all financed by the band's record company—a limo was sent over to take me to the concert. After the show, I made an appointment to meet the pair the next morning to chat over coffee and croissants, but, before I left, their manager cornered me and offered me his clients for the night. I was afraid I had misunderstood him and told him I wasn't on a deadline, and an interview the next day would be soon enough. He leered at me, said that wasn't exactly what he had in mind, and then said, "Maybe I'd like to do a little undercover reporting"—*his words exactly*! If I could have thrown up the lobster on his gangster suit with some amount of decorum, I would have. Instead, I looked him straight in the eyes, politely thanked him for the rare opportunity, and told him we weren't allowed to accept gratuities—at least not that kind. These were barbaric times for women music reporters, and often the musicians you were assigned to interview just saw you as a groupie with a tape recorder. Many times I had to disabuse a cocksure lead-singer type of that notion, much to the detriment of his pride and my story.

Maybe worse than that was when a group took you out on the road and then ducked and dodged you. I was on the road with Led Zeppelin on two separate occasions. The first went off without a hitch, although I must admit I did observe some weirdness—odd dress and sexual proclivities, strange assignations with girls with poodles, and occasional bouts of overindulgence—but nothing that prevented me from reviewing the shows and filing reasonably unbiased blow-by-blow accounts of life on the road with rock's biggest bruisers. They were my favorite band and, if anything, I was hard-pressed to write anything unflattering for fear of tarnishing their reputation and bringing them down off the pedestal that I and millions like me had put them on.

But that last Led Zep excursion changed all that for me. I should have known it was an odd tour when the tour doctor accused Jimmy Page of pilfering his supply of Quaaludes. At that stage, I never even thought to ask what the doctor needed with all those pills anyway—jet lag, I told myself, as well as reminding myself that it was none of my business, not really, since I knew that *I* didn't steal them.

Anyway, I had been with the band for five days when Page finally consented to a meeting with me in his publicist's suite. However, once I got there, I could sense there was an ill wind blowing. As I

entered the room, he quaintly announced in his characteristically high-pitched voice, "Now it's time for me to cellophane my mouth." To say the least, I was a little disconcerted, and his publicist looked pale, but in retrospect I think it was probably an act. After a few awkward minutes, the publicist managed to convince Page (a little too easily, I thought) to let me ask *her* the questions, and she'd relate them to *him*. I sat there dumbfounded, and not at all invisible, as they had tried to render me. We all spoke English, right? Here these two people were trying to transmute an interview for a rock magazine into a simultaneous translation for the UN. Never one to fall down on the job (after all, it *was* a cover story), I agreed to the peculiar procedure and posed my questions to the flack; she then relayed them to Page, he answered her, and she would tell me exactly what he had just said, just as if I wasn't sitting there hearing it for myself. This went on for the better part of a half hour, without any one of us acting like there was anything out of the ordinary going on. And in Led Zeppelin-ese, maybe there wasn't. It was rather like simultaneously watching and being in a foreign movie with subtitles. It was a bizarre charade, and I had agreed to go along with it to get my story, but I wasn't exactly thrilled. It seemed to appease Page, and I had the feeling that this wasn't the first time the publicist had to devise some invention to get him to talk. As I got up to leave, he finally looked at me, in that particularly drowsy-lidded way he had, and spoke directly to me without his interpreter. He told me he intended to have a cocktail party and was going to invite everyone except the press, because they only come for the free drinks. It was a disturbing and haunting exchange, as the entire experience had been, and I wanted to tell him (but didn't) that the press certainly wouldn't have come for the company.

Not all assignments were tainted with sexual politics or star attitude, and some of the best times I ever had were when the band members treated me like one of the boys. Performing onstage with Kiss was just one of those encounters. I put on a studded dog collar, black tights, and face paint, and performed in front of five thousand people in Johnstown, Pennsylvania, for a story I had titled, "I Dreamt I Was Onstage with Kiss in My Maidenform Bra."

The groundwork for that story had been laid long before, in the spring of 1974, when Kiss came to the offices one afternoon to pose for a *Creem* profile. You remember those, don't you? They were a takeoff on the Dewar's Scotch profiles—"What kind of man drinks Dewar's?"—but in our case it was a "Boy Howdy beer" profile, a scheme we concocted to get more coverage for bands whose record companies were spending their big advertising dollars in *Creem* with minimum effort on our part. We had a profile set up for Kiss, and the four of them arrived in a rented sedan, very low-budget and unpretentious. They marched up the single flight of stairs to our offices in heavy-soled platform boots, making a somewhat less than grandiose entrance.

They were all hair, sunglasses, and bravado, trying to steal the mantle of the premier New York band from the New York Dolls. They thought "America's Only Rock 'n' Roll Magazine" was a fitting place to begin their campaign, so we, blasé observers of the rock wars, sat back and let them go into their shtick. They clomped down the hallway and took over the ladies' bathroom (when the men's would have done just as well) that *Creem* shared with the other tenants of the building. They were terrific bathroom slobs, leaving gobs of Kleenex and cotton balls in their wake, littering all the surfaces, and smearing the mirrors with petroleum jelly and lipstick.

After monopolizing the premises for quite some time, they stalked back into our editorial offices, taking up much more space than when they left. It was an amazing thing to behold—the transformation of the quartet was more than merely cosmetic; it was almost psychic. Our secretaries, who didn't give these reasonably attractive metal rocker types a second glance when they walked in the office an hour before, were transfixed and couldn't keep their eyes off them after they saw them in the makeup. Already the Gene Simmons myth was gathering steam, for he had Leslie, the publisher's assistant, on his lap while he was kissing Susie, our intern, and neither of them seemed to mind.

I didn't get it at this point, believing it was all a little too obvious and cartoonish—this was more a cinematic moment than a rock 'n' roll one, with Kiss looking more like cheap actors in a Japanese horror flick than musicians. I remember thinking, as Charley Auringer snapped their photograph in our back parking lot, that this ritualistic putting on of makeup and staging an event was very passé, kind of Warholian, but also very disturbing in a death-of-art kind of way. I hadn't yet gotten used to the idea that the '70s were about concepts and gimmicks and it would soon become the norm to create a band around a great idea, rather than the other way around. Video hadn't yet killed the radio stars.

One of the last stories I did for *Creem* while I still was on staff and living in Detroit proved to be my most unsettling, although I wasn't aware of it at the time. I had spent a few days with the band Lynyrd Skynyrd, trying to keep up with their drinking and carousing and attempting to piece together some kind of story from all the shuck and jive they insisted on heaping on me during the course of the time we spent together—you know, real riveting stuff, like they grew their hair long to cover up their red necks.

I was a little disgruntled, but I kept telling myself it was a southern thing, and if I had enough patience (a northern thing) and a strong enough constitution, I would finally come out with something to say. I wasn't wrong. On our last night together, a few nights before Christmas, Ronnie Van Zant broke down and finally had a drink. He had been on the wagon during the time I spent with the band, nursing virgin Marys and insisting that he only drank when he was working. After two Jack Daniels and Cokes, he began to unwind a little and regale me with stories of his dangerous past—like the time he got thrown out of school for attempted murder and how in 1975 alone he had been arrested for fighting five times. He evinced some regret that he couldn't be just like his father, Lacy (whose name he had tattooed on his left upper arm), saying, "I couldn't be like him. I don't even expect to live very long, because I'm living too fast . . . have the same problem Janis Joplin had but worse." There was a terrible eloquence in his words that last night, and I remember leaving the bar feeling depressed—yet nowhere as depressed as I felt eight months later, when I heard that Van Zant and other members of the band had died in a fiery plane crash returning from a job. I felt as if chilling fingers from the grave had tapped me on the shoulder and said, "See, I told you so." I was unnerved and, I guess, unprepared

to see a rock 'n' roll tragedy unfold right before my eyes. It was a sobering story, and one that would be repeated even among our own numbers—Lester and Barry both dying in the next years.

*Creem* was never the same for me after I left for Los Angeles in March of 1976 to work as a columnist on a trade publication called *Record World*. I still was on a retainer with *Creem* and functioned as an editorial consultant and columnist ("Kiss 'n' Tell") until 1986, but I missed the sense of creativity and community I had experienced in the home office. More than anything else, working there had shown me I was not alone. When I first started at *Creem*, I felt like a misfit, but I soon found out we were "all bozos on this bus." And the only thing that made us feel whole was the music. Little else was as important to us as uncovering what we thought were great works of art. There was a thrill of discovery when you played an album by a new artist for the first time and heard something so truly remarkable that you wanted to tell everyone you knew about it. It was akin to picking winners at the track. Working at *Creem* provided me with a decoder ring, a clubhouse, and my own gang—and out of that accidental mix of people, place, music, and history, something remarkable emerged.

# Who Is the Sugar Man?

*Howard A. Dewitt*

Every great man nowadays has his disciples, and it is usually Judas who writes the biography.

—Oscar Wilde

Exuberance is beauty.

—William Blake

My God, how does one write a biography?

—Virginia Woolf

When I walked into the Harkins Camelview 7 Theater to see *Searching for Sugar Man*, I had no idea who Sixto Rodriguez was or why he was important. I was in for a shock. The documentary by Swedish filmmaker Malik Bendjelloul analyzed everything that was wrong with the music business and everything that was right with Rodriguez. This documentary presented a person who is truly amazed at his success. His entire seventy-year life has been about music. Along the way, myth and reality clashed in such a way that ended up with his records, within the United States, confined to Woolworths' cut-out bin.

At the same time, his records' sales in Australia and South Africa went gold or platinum. How could a singer-songwriter who was bigger than Elvis Presley or the Rolling Stones in South Africa not make a dent in the American market? How could Rodriguez sell records in large numbers in Australia and tour the country to adoring crowds while unknown in his home country?

The *Cold Fact* album intrigued two Cape Town fans, Craig Bartholomew-Strydom and Stephen "Sugar" Segerman. They couldn't find a single word written about Rodriguez. There were rumors but few concrete cold facts. And the great Rodriguez hunt was under way.

Segerman was obsessed with Rodriguez and his music. He was determined to find every fact he could about the Sugar Man. The hunt turned up one dead end after another. None of this deterred Segerman. He knew that there was a story. He would find it.

Photo by Doug Coombe.

299

While ignored in America, Rodriguez's music was the marching tune for young, politically conscious, anti-apartheid South Africans. Rodriguez also represented the birth of the Australian counterculture. Australia's hit rock band Midnight Oil claimed Rodriguez as a mentor. In America, no one had a clue about Rodriguez's music or the man's extraordinary intellect.

Sixto Rodriguez has a family. He graduated with honors from college. He raised his daughters. He recorded two albums that failed to sell. He left the music business. He didn't receive royalties. He continued to sporadically perform. He followed *Billboard* and other music magazines. Rodriguez had a good life. He wasn't bitter. "It's the music business," Rodriguez told an interviewer when asked about lost royalties. When acclaim and financial success from *Searching for Sugar Man* provided a new life, Rodriguez didn't change. He is the same person. When *Searching for Sugar Man* won the Academy Award, he was home relaxing. He told a reporter: "It's Malik's work. Let him bask in the glory." Rodriguez continually praised and showed his appreciation for filmmaker Malik Bendjelloul.

He wrote songs. He recorded songs. He didn't agree to appear at teen dances, to lip-synch his songs on television, or to answer inane questions from DJs. He often performed with his back to the audience in order to emphasize the music over the performer. His drop-dead good looks, cool clothes, and sunglasses made him a favorite with ladies. He was bewildered by the acclaim he received after the worldwide popularity of *Searching for Sugar Man*. Rodriguez preferred to be at home with his family or hanging out at local establishments like the Motor City Brewing Company, the Cass Café, or the Old Miami Bar, all within walking distance of Rodriguez's two-story Avery Street home.

While *Searching for Sugar Man* displays his sex appeal, his songwriting genius, and his mercurial performing talent, there is more to the story. There are important women in his life: his three daughters. He also has two ex-wives with whom he remains friendly.

Rodriguez's blue-collar ethic led him to employment in home repairs, casual maintenance, heavy construction, and remodeling. He loved the work.

His first wife, Rayma, lives near the Detroit airport, and his second wife, Konny, resides in another Detroit suburb. Her given name is Constance Mary Rodriguez.

For Rodriguez, some relationships are complicated. This is the nature of the artist. During interviews, he thanks both ex-wives for helping his music evolve. There is a tranquil nature to Rodriguez that is essential to the myths surrounding his life. He is a person who is so humble that he often serves food to people who come backstage during his concerts. He thanks them for coming. The audiences and those who meet him love his gracious manner and humility.

Rayma met Sixto when they were in high school. She is part Cherokee, and her intelligence, as well as her beauty, attracted Rodriguez. When Rayma got pregnant they dropped out of school. They had two daughters, Eva and Sandra. To support the family, Sixto worked in a steel mill, an auto plant, and a linen factory. He gained diverse skills working as a bricklayer, a construction worker, and a trench digger. The Detroit housing industry offered continual employment.

He married Konny later. In 1979, they had a daughter, Regan. Somewhere along the way, they separated. Konny remains friendly with her ex-husband. "I never believed in marriage, so I sure as hell don't believe in divorce," Konny said.

Konny Rodriguez studied at Wayne State University from 1969 to 1975. There, she received a BA in psychology. When she married Sixto, Konny went to work for the Children's Hospital of Michigan. From 1984 to 2005, she worked with three different administrators and became skilled at management. She later moved to a career in senior housing and assisted living, in which she worked for the Presbyterian Villages of Michigan. There are twenty-five of these villages in Michigan, and they serve 4,300 seniors. In numerous interviews, Konny has said that Rodriguez's Detroit house is too primitive. Konny remains a bit of a mystery. She was with Rodriguez sporadically in 2012, and it appears that the financial success brought about by *Searching for Sugar Man* changed both of their lives. For some time, Konny has lived near her work in St. Claire Shores, Michigan.

Konny Rodriguez says of her husband: "He's a dyed-in-the-wool Detroiter. He's comfortable there; he's a happy camper and at peace."

She points out that the Avery Street home is lacking in key comforts. It is now being slightly renovated. Rodriguez is not spending his money making the Avery Street home look like a mansion. There is a brand-new fence that hides the side of the house from the street. There are signs of the front cement steps being improved. A large orange cone blocks a portion of the steep cement stairway leading to the front door. The homes on Avery sell from $55,000 upward. There has been an increase in young families in the area. There is slow but steady gentrification taking place. One neighbor said, "We are experiencing a flight from the suburbs to Woodbridge."

The subject of *Searching for Sugar Man*, Sixto Diaz Rodriguez, is a part Mexican, part Native American musician who grew up in the shadow of poverty. He developed an affinity for songwriting in the early 1960s. His lyrics are that of an existential poet. He listened to Bob Dylan, and, like Dylan's, his writing has an original touch. Like Dylan, he uses poetic lyrics. His subjects are the working poor, the politically disenfranchised, and those who view the system from outside the mainstream. It is the songwriting of an existential contrarian. The lyrics are beautiful. The music is soothing. In 1970, it looked like Rodriguez was destined for stardom. Then, something happened. He fell into obscurity. He raised a family. He went to work every day. He earned a college degree. He was off the music-business radar.

As he grew up in the shadow of Motown, the nascent Detroit music scene influenced his developing talent. In 1967, as Rodriguez recorded his debut single for Harry Balk, Detroit experienced a five-day riot that killed forty-three and destroyed more than two hundred buildings. He was deeply touched by the violence. Rodriguez was concerned about police brutality. School funding, community outreach, union rights, public commissions to oversee the police, and economic development were issues that brought Rodriguez support in the Cass Corridor when he ran for public office.

It is his writing about the crumbling layers of Detroit that gives Rodriguez's music its edge. He describes, in copious detail, the flourishing music scene, the lower-middle-class family problems, the decline into abject poverty, the changes in political attitudes, and the youthful rebellion of the late 1960s and early 1970s. He is a musician who writes prophetically about the Motor City. The way he perceived his surroundings and an epiphany he experienced that few people understood are integral to the Rodriguez story. What he witnessed in the world around him translates beautifully into song. No one understood it in 1970 and 1971, when his two albums were released; Rodriguez's message was lost in the shuffle. When his music finally surfaced in 2012, thanks to Malik Bendjelloul, Stephen "Sugar" Segerman, Craig Bartholomew-Strydom, and Brian Currin, the Rodriguez phenomenon burst onto the cultural scene.

When *Searching for Sugar Man* debuted on July 27, 2012, no one realized that a few weeks later Rodriguez would appear on the *Late Show with David Letterman*. It was mid-August and Rodriguez walked out on the Letterman stage with a set of symphony string musicians backing him for "Crucify Your Mind." He acquired skilled management. It is his daughter Regan who took over his career. She hired a professional road manager, she signed with various booking agencies, and she coordinates with groups around the world that back up Rodriguez. He was buried once by the industry. It won't happen again. He has a vast music-business empire in place that is well organized and looking out for his best interests.

A part of Regan's management formula is to limit interviews. This keeps the Rodriguez mystique alive. She realizes that too much press coverage generates negatives. Her skilled management has led to continual concert sellouts and a lucrative income. Rodriguez is really running the show

with his daughter's expertise. He had trouble with the industry during his first go-around. This time, Rodriguez and his family are calling the shots. It is a smart move.

He is a lyrical and musical genius and remains humble and unaffected; he wonders what all the fuss is about. He lives his life through his music. Looking back on his career, Rodriguez remarked: "I just wanted to sell some records and play bigger rooms." Once the New York premiere of *Searching for Sugar Man* hit the big screen, he was in demand.

Why write two books about Rodriguez? That is the question. The first volume runs through the *Cold Fact* LP and the second begins with Steve Rowland's *Coming from Reality* and ends with the fame and fortune resulting from the documentary. Sixto Rodriguez is articulate. He is intelligent. He is one hell of a writer. He is also a great performer. It has been a joy to interpret his journey. The Rodriguez biography is one about the phenomenon and not the man. It is also a project where more than one hundred people talked to me about the Sugar Man.

The Rodriguez story is not only heartrending, it is a look at a man who overcame adversity to record some of the best music that no one listened to in the 1970s. In 2012 through 2015, he was one of the world's best-selling artists. Rodriguez's talent needs a careful reassessment.

When Stephen "Sugar" Segerman began his search for Rodriguez on the Internet, he set up a website he titled "The Great Rodriguez Hunt." One of his coconspirators, Brian Currin, established the Climb Up on My Music website. This began the search for Rodriguez, and this incredible story took shape.

This is a tale of a humble man with a genius songwriting talent. It is a tale of humility that is second to none. As he eases into his seventies, fame and fortune have become present as talent has triumphed over adversity. The Sugar Man is back. Enjoy the ride.

Obsessive-compulsive record collectors largely fuel the Sugar Man story. The tandem of Stephen "Sugar" Segerman and Craig Bartholomew-Strydom brought him back. In Seattle, Light in the Attic, a small record label under the stewardship of Matt Sullivan, reissued the Rodriguez material. A young filmmaker from Sweden, Malik Bendjelloul, created the documentary that made America fall in love with Rodriguez. His producers Dennis Coffey, Mike Theodore, and Steve Rowland spoke of his legacy with reverence.

Sussex Record chief Clarence Avant is put through a grueling, and at times unfair, interview in *Searching for Sugar Man*. The film alleges that for years Avant collected royalties for Rodriguez's sales in Australia and South Africa. He may not have actually collected these royalties. The truth is that Avant has always been a Rodriguez supporter. In 1997 and 1998, he quietly funded what would have been a third album for the Sugar Man. Rodriguez gave up. Avant reluctantly commented that he is innocent of withholding royalties. The people who have done business with him to a person remarked that, as Mike Theodore said, "Clarence never screwed anyone." Avant's story is as interesting as Rodriguez's.

There are highs and lows in Rodriguez's career. He has recorded for some of the best producers in the game. Names such as Harry Balk, Mike Theodore, Dennis Coffey, and Steve Rowland suggest the legendary music men who have been a part of his career. There are many players, many subplots, and many main points. It is a great story of redemption and rediscovery.

The Rodriguez story does not take place in a time warp. It is part and parcel of a larger history of the music industry. His music was subject to its times and their trends. These factors didn't always help him. He lacked the business skills to prevent industry insiders from taking advantage of him. Many of the contracts were legal ones that were worded to provide songwriting and publishing royalties to the record company. The artist was billed for record storage, publicity, advertising, publishing costs, photography, graphic design, and miscellaneous expenses. The artist then received what was left. There was normally very little in the way of royalties left.

What happened to Rodriguez? The story is a familiar tale of music industry greed. When music mogul Clarence Avant appeared in *Searching for Sugar Man*, he said that he didn't know about the royalties. He had no idea what happened to the money. That appears to be the truth. When Matt Sullivan's Light in the Attic licensed Rodriguez's albums, they secured the rights from Avant. Light in the Attic said that they had good dealings with Avant and that he has paid royalties to Rodriguez since 2008.

That Rodriguez was bigger than the Rolling Stones or Elvis Presley in South Africa is an important point. His debut album, *Cold Fact*, outsold all other South African artists. But along the way, the artist known as Rodriguez got lost in myth. There was no reality. Thanks go to Stephen "Sugar" Segerman for finding Rodriguez and pitching his story to Bendjelloul.

It is as a writer that Rodriguez excels. He is primarily a singer-songwriter who is also a talented performer. The words, the images, the subtle nuances, the observations, and the humility make Rodriguez's music unique.

By 2013, the Rodriguez phenomenon was in full bloom. He was touring nonstop. The South African tours were bigger than ever, and at the eighty-fifth Oscar ceremony there was talk of a third album. The Sugar Man looked tired, but he was enjoying every minute of his improbable fame.

*Rolling Stone* reported that Rodriguez stated that "once he breaks from touring in June he will explore the possibility of recording a third album." Rodriguez mentioned *Coming from Reality* producer, Steve Rowland, as a potential partner in this endeavor. "He told me to send him along a couple of tapes, so I'm gonna do that," Rodriguez continued. "I certainly want to look him up, because he is full of ideas." *Rolling Stone* got hold of Rowland, who responded: "We both have ideas on how the album should go. . . . We both want to work together again, but it is really up to others that are involved in his future."

As I followed Rodriguez's journey, I was amazed at his resilient personality. Nothing bothers him. This stoic demeanor accentuates his existential side.

I didn't interview Sixto Rodriguez for this book. I was backstage with him for a brief moment when he appeared at California State University in the Luckman Auditorium. I was with Steve Rowland and they had a brief, but intimate, discussion. I was amazed at his kindness, his discretion, and his humble nature. He also looks healthy. There is no trace of bitterness. He has worn well considering the sheer intensity of his life. When I talked to his daughter Regan, she ducked most of my questions. It was a comfortable time backstage with Rodriguez.

He is shy and prefers to maintain his privacy. He has been ripped off by too many people and lied to by many others. His daughter, meanwhile, is smart, knowledgeable about the music industry, and knows how to hire and direct the best people for Rodriguez's concerts.

Ruben Blades, the Grammy Award–winning singer from Panama, said it best about Rodriguez when he responded to a *New York Times* review of Clive Davis's autobiography. Blades wrote: "Record executives do not discover artists, they stumble upon them." Then, as Blades suggests, the executives and the label collect more than their fair share of the royalties. Blades wrote of Janis Joplin that she probably never collected her fair share of royalties. Blades continued: "These usually go to people who can't sing, who can't write, can't perform and yet end up millionaires, while true artists, like Rodriguez, end up broke and ripped off." Thank you. Ruben Blades, for this letter to the *New York Times Book Review*.

Rodriguez is a poetic genius. He was ignored for more than four decades. His quiet gestures and discreet life obscured his talent. Then *Searching for Sugar Man* brought him the acclaim that he deserves.

When I sat down with the print interviews, the people who were central and peripheral to the story, the albums, the press material, the tapes of his concerts, the backstage stories, the Detroit neighborhood material, and the documentary there was a mountain of evidence. Much of it was conflicting, and a great deal of it was mythical. How to separate myth from reality? That was the key question.

Surprisingly, it is not music that is most important to Sixto Rodriguez. It is his humanity. It is his political activism. It is his family values. To tell the story properly, it is necessary to highlight the people around Rodriguez, the influence of Detroit, the impact of Stephen "Sugar" Segerman and Craig Bartholomew-Strydom, and the manner in which the entire music industry reacted against and then for the Sugar Man. It is a never-ending story.

This is a biography of a great American singer-songwriter who has written fewer than thirty songs. This is not a vast output. His life is partly a story about lateness, patience, fortitude, and waiting. In some ways, he is like other forgotten singer-songwriters who simply vanished into obscurity. He began as a brilliant twenty-eight-year-old recording artist. By thirty-three he was working a series of dead-end jobs that occupied his life for the next forty years.

His first album, *Cold Fact*, came out in 1970, when he was twenty-eight. He achieved stardom in 2012 when he was, as he said, "a solid seventy." That is what this story concentrates on and in this first of two volumes the Sugar Man emerges as an ethereal, mystical, almost mythical person with a talent that few possess. This perception obscures his talent as myth triumphs over reality.

His personality quirks are well known. He is drawn to lost causes and personal failures. These themes impact his songwriting. The Sugar Man's voice is exceptional when dealing with feminist issues. In telling his life story, it is important to remember that he describes hypocrisy, cruelty, dishonesty, and malevolence in his songs. These tunes argue that there is a relationship between the soul and the intellect. Rodriguez likes to deflate hypocrisy. Yet his personal beliefs are mildly stated, and he has guarded opinions. There is a sense of

control and a restraint in Rodriguez's personality. He has a lifestyle that is subtle and economical.

There is no glamour to Sixto Rodriguez and no self-advertising. He is the ultimate existentialist. He is also evasive and reserved. He writes in a quiet voice with a blend of darkness and humor.

The story of a musician who triumphed over all odds is a unique one. But he is also a person rooted in Detroit, close to his family, helped by his producers, rediscovered by Matt Sullivan and his Light in the Attic label, and then fallen in love with by the general public.

There is no adequate description of Sixto Rodriguez. We know he is humble, he has little use for money, he is an existentialist, he is a committed intellectual, he is family oriented, he is a writer, he is political, and he is a strong supporter of Detroit's culture. To understand the Sugar Man it is necessary to examine those around him, including family, musicians, producers, and industry figures; Detroit's influences; his peripatetic employment; and his education. These forces describe the Sugar Man and his strange journey to fame and fortune.

As Rodriguez's music unfolds, a line from one of his songs suggests why he is an important biographical subject. Rodriguez wrote: "Climb up on my music and my songs will set you free."

HOWARD A. DEWITT

# Dangerous Diane
## Detroit Art Rock and Punk in the Late '70s
*Diane Spodarek*

I've been around the world
You know I've seen it twice
But my own backyard
It's twice as nice

I wrote those lyrics about Detroit. My identity as an artist came out of growing up in the Motor City. From preadolescence, when I would fall asleep with a red transistor radio on my pillow and sing Motown out my bedroom window hoping Smokey Robinson would hear me; it was always about Detroit.

In 1976, everything happened fast. We lived on the Southfield Road service drive in Northwest Detroit, two blocks from Grand River Avenue. After an MFA from Eastern Michigan University and after our daughter was born, Randy Delbeke and I founded two arts organizations: the *Detroit Artists Monthly*, a visual-arts magazine, and the Alternative Space Detroit, a floating space for exhibitions and events for artists and bands. I transcribed interviews with artists on a portable typewriter in the kitchen, and Randy laid type and put together the look of the magazine in the basement. In terms of technology, it was the Stone Age; we didn't even have an answering machine on our one phone. No one did.

I was a video and performance artist experimenting with sound on a reel-to-reel Akai tape recorder. I wanted to transmute the sound into something more permanent. Vinyl was the logical step to reach a larger audience. I made my first 45 RPM record, about child abuse. As a new parent, I was consumed with what I believed was a universal truth: the most dangerous person in the room for a

Dangerous Diane.
Photo courtesy of Diane Spodarek.

306

newborn baby is its own mother. I recorded a confessional-style narrative with drums and backup singers called "Potentially Dangerous" by Dangerous Diane and the Dinettes.

> No one knows that once, just once,
> I had the urge to put my baby in
> the clothes dryer . . .
> No one knows that once, just once,
> I had the urge to leave my baby in
> the car after taking the groceries
> into the house . . .
> No one knows that once, just once,
> I had the urge to kiss my baby
> where I shouldn't.

For the B side, traditionally the throwaway side, I asked friends to play an offbeat version of Buddy Holly's "It's So Easy (to Fall in Love)." In a deadpan voice, I sang the lyrics, changing *love* to *art*:

> People tell me art is for fools
> Here I go breaking all the rules
> It's so easy . . .

We recorded at United Sound and seven hundred copies were pressed. "It'So" (instead of "It's So") was printed on the sleeve and record label, a fortuitous error by the printer, which underscored the song's irony. I took the photo for the record sleeve on the steps of the Detroit Institute of Arts. In the picture are: the late Keith Aoki (violin and guitar), Jim Hart (drums and Stroh's beer can), Tom Bloomer (piano), Dwain Bacon (bass), and the late Randy Delbeke (backup vocals). Dana, our daughter, is in

the foreground looking up at her father. Our lips look slashed because we wore white lipstick. The original record is now a collector's item that pops up on auction sites.

In 1978, I performed "It's So Easy" at the DIA for the *New Video and Performance Art* exhibition curated by John Neff and Mary Jane Jacobs. The standout performance was by Jay Yager, a sculptor and at the time a professor of art at Eastern Michigan University. He mopped the floor in the marbled North Court wearing a black graduate cap and gown. For my performance, I sang the lyrics live with the recorded music fed through tall speakers. Each time I sang "easy," I threw my record like a Frisbee into the audience.

In 1979, I sang a punk-rock song in the recital hall at the DIA as part of my acceptance speech for an award from the Michigan Foundation for the Arts. Helen Milliken, the wife of the Michigan governor, presented the awards to five artists in different disciplines. I wrote "All I Want" for Mrs. Milliken and the arts foundation patrons, many of whom were wearing pearls and furs, because they may not have another opportunity to experience a live punk-rock performance. (They were trapped.) I was standing at a podium onstage, and when I said, "To me rock and roll is art," an electric bass began its rhythmic thump from behind a curtain. As the curtain parted, I tore off my skirt and joined the punk band the Cadillac Kidz and sang a duet with Spaz:

> If you come to my bed, be creative
> Because all I want, is what you got.
> What have you said if you're dead?
> If it's in your head what have you said?

The following morning, I was on the front page of the arts section in the *Detroit Free Press*. Mike Duffy, a feature reporter, said: "Diane Spodarek . . . has taken a chance on rock and roll at the DIA . . . the award honored her for her stature as an uncompromising conceptual artist, a video poet with reputable fine arts credentials—not a rookie rock and roller. [She] . . . took a considerable gamble in trying to show that her art, her view of the world, is just as valid when you switch from video to volume." And he reviewed "Potentially Dangerous": "a . . . bizarre and terrifying monologue of a mother's fantasies about killing her baby."

The record sold in Detroit stores and played in CBGB's jukebox in New York. While Blondie, Patti Smith, Talking Heads, the Ramones, Richard Hell, and others were playing on CBGB's stage, my song about child abuse was playing the venue without me. I had reached my larger audience. The transition from performance art and rock and roll in museums to rock and roll in bars occurred quickly. Mike McDowell, editor and publisher of *Blitz*, an alternative music magazine, reviewed the record: "Dangerous Diane is a first rate musical satirist. . . . 'Potentially Dangerous' is one of the top 100 singles for 1978. . . . Dangerous Diane: Best New Solo Artist."

I also received unexpected radio play. Rockee Berlin and Skid Marx, from the Detroit band Flirt, were supporters of Detroit bands on their FM show. I listened to it every week, and one night they played Buddy Holly's and Linda Ronstadt's versions of "It's So Easy (to Fall in Love)." Skid then said, "And here is Dangerous Diane's version of 'It's So Easy.'"

I received calls to book the band—but I didn't have a band. I posted a handmade flyer in the New Miami bar: "Auditions for female musicians only.

SureShot Productions." Cameron, the manager of SureShot (and the lead guitarist in the Cadillac Kidz), was supportive of my idea to put together an all-female band. I didn't know how to audition musicians, but when Susan Clone walked in wearing four-inch heels and tight jeans and played her song "Gutter Punch," I "hired" her on the spot. Cameron was furious. He said that everyone in the music scene knew who Susan Clone was and she was no woman—she was a transsexual. I wasn't in the music scene, so I didn't know. Hell, I didn't even know what a transsexual was back then. I just thought she was a kick-ass guitar player with a voice like Lauren Bacall who was in need of a little electrolysis.

The Dangerous Diane Band was created in 1979 with Leonard Paul Johnson on drums, Marco Mealy on bass, Susan Clone on lead guitar, and me on vocals and rhythm guitar. It was not all women, but it was the only band at the time—that I was aware of—with a transsexual lead guitar player. Sometimes we wore matching dresses. I bought a 1964 cherrywood Gibson Melody Maker and learned to play guitar listening to Buddy Holly. We rehearsed in Leonard's studio on the corner of Woodward and Willis, and I was so nervous about forgetting the bar chords that I taped the chord names on the neck of my guitar. I wrote songs about Vito Acconci and Andy Warhol and about the things that drove me crazy: "Impulse Control"; "Boat People"; "Iggy's My Pop"; and "I Don't Care," a two-chord song inspired by dadaist artist Man Ray:

> What's wrong with the immediate
> Most things are
> I don't care if it's temporary
> Everything is just a memory

I don't care
I don't care
I don't care because
It takes talent to transform useful
into useless.

Our first gig was at Lili's in Hamtramck. We also played the New Miami in the Cass Corridor, the Silverbird in Pontiac, a Halloween party in a United Auto Workers' hall somewhere, and possibly other venues—I don't remember. We recorded five songs at SureShot with bass player George Poirer, who—I think—brought the Wild Turkey. The band broke up some weeks later. I performed a few special guest gigs with Flirt and the Cadillac Kidz. Randy continued to book bands under the Alternative Space name at Alvin's and the New Miami: Destroy All Monsters, Flirt, the Reruns, the Mutants, the Cubes, probably others. Randy made flyers for the gigs and these ended up being donated to the DIA along with other documents when Alternative Space Detroit and the magazine folded. Dennis Barrie from the museum came to our house and picked up boxes of cassettes, flyers, and magazines and taped interviews that are now archived at the Smithsonian Museum.

Randy and I moved to New York in 1981. He drove a cab, and I worked as a secretary. I wrote a song about it:

Each day is like another
Each day is just the same
Something is wrong here
Nothing has changed.

A live jam of "Nothing Changes" was recorded with the Ghost Band in Leonard's basement some years

back: Leonard Johnson on drums, Ron Kopack on guitar, Keith Buchannon on bass, and George Kerby on lead guitar.

There was one reunion of the Dangerous Diane Band with three of the original band members. In 2004, Leonard called me in New York and said, "Let's do a reunion gig." Leonard, Clone, and I reunited after twenty-five years, and Brian Simon played bass. We rehearsed for five days in Leonard's basement and played two gigs in the Cass Corridor, one at the Third Street Saloon and another at the Comet Bar. In 2012, we recorded four new songs with Leonard on drums, Brian Simon on guitar, and the late Steve King on bass.

In 2014, the esteemed poet M. L. Liebler invited me to perform at Wayne State University. I jammed again in Leonard's basement with Leonard on drums, Brian Simon on guitar, and Steve King played bass. It was the last time I saw Steve.

Every year, I go to Detroit to see family and hang with Leonard and his wife, Mary. I visit the DIA to see the Diego Rivera murals from the 1930s. I once read that Frida Kahlo's painting got serious when she was in Detroit with Diego—possibly because she felt isolated and neglected by him—but I like to believe it was Detroit that inspired Frida Kahlo. Detroit is like that—it brings out the creative best in everyone.

# A Band Called Death

*Ben Blackwell*

Record collectors are usually portrayed as a paramecium-like scum, petty, unshaven, unsharing, socially crippled wastes. But sometimes, when everything aligns just right, they have the ability to do something small that ultimately leads to benefiting the greater good.

In the fall of 2007, I came in for one of my infrequent shifts at Car City Records in St. Clair Shores and found an interesting CD-R behind the counter. The only person who had any info on the disc was my coworker Matt Smith. He said there was a customer, a guy he called Das (given name Don Schwenk), who had brought in the disc.

Das was friends with some guys who had a band back in the '70s. The band, Death, had released their own two-song 7-inch in 1976. But they had also recorded additional songs that had never seen the light of day. Don was in possession of a cassette copy of these seven songs, rumored to have been obtained in exchange for some weed.

As with most music played at a record store, I put it on and proceeded to immediately not pay

DEATH. Photograph by Tammy Hackney. Property and © of DL4 Musical Enterprises Inc. and DEATH®. All Rights Reserved.

attention to it. Though I wasn't listening intently, it caught my attention as not bad. As soon as it was over, I immediately played it again. "Hmm . . . this is good." I'm not sure how many more times I listened to it on that first day, but it was plenty.

The band was made up of the Hackney brothers: Bobby, David, and Dannis. I'd later come to find out they grew up on the east side, on Lillibridge Street, not too far from Belle Isle. Growing up mere miles from there myself, I felt a kinship. Knowing they were African Americans playing a form of music today dubbed protopunk, I felt impressed. This was not an everyday discovery.

It felt like this music shouldn't exist. At the time, we were erroneously told the songs were recorded in 1974 (it was later determined to have been 1975). We were also misinformed that the band members were all Jehovah's Witnesses. All of that is superfluous in the end . . . the most important part about this entire story, the thing to take away from it all, is that Death made incredibly relevant high-energy music that astonishingly had received only the bare minimum of attention.

As record collectors, history buffs, and folks without much else better to do with our time, we started digging.

Smith and fellow coworker Dion Fischer tracked down the surviving Hackney brothers through their music publishing company, and I called Bobby Hackney around Thanksgiving of that year. I didn't really have a solid angle on why I was doing so. I was writing for the *Metro Times* back then, and I guess I thought that I was pitching him on the idea that I'd write an article about the band.

One point I cannot stress enough: when I called Bobby to talk to him about his unknown band that had ceased existing thirty years prior, mentioning titles of

songs that had never been released or even known about, he was completely uninterested. The first thing he said, almost immediately, was, "I don't have any copies of the record." He'd clearly already been approached by even more hard-core collectors than myself and was hoping to end the conversation right there.

I wasn't trolling for copies of the single. I wanted context. Had they'd played any shows? (Barely.) What music had they listened to? (Hard rock, the MC5, Alice Cooper.) I asked any question that seemed even vaguely relevant, and it felt like I was bothering him the entire time. More than once, he said, "You should write an article about my new band, Lambsbread."

I had no particular interest in that endeavor and politely deflected the pitch. The conversation did not last long; Bobby told me he had business to attend to and that he would follow up and call me the following week.

I would not hear from him for almost four months.

In the meantime, I did my own thing. I posted the song "Politicians in My Eyes" on my blog and shared all seven songs from the CD-R with select friends across the country. Certain die-hard punk collectors who have very strict opinions on such things were insistent that the tracks could not have been recorded before the first Damned album was released (February 1977) and that these songs had to have been informed by that album. Real nerd shit.

I thought nothing of it and went about my business. In December, my band, the Dirtbombs, recorded a cover of "Politicians in My Eyes." Even with two drummers, the intensity of Dannis's dexterity was something we could not replicate. That shit is fast. I think our final version was passable, but it pales in comparison to the original.

311

Das, meanwhile, let folks at Car City know that he'd actually been given a twenty-five-count box of the single back in the day. The band was hoping that he'd give them to people and help spread the word. I'm not sure if any copies had even been removed from that box in the intervening thirty-two years.

Das started giving away mint-condition copies of the single to pretty much any and every employee at the store. He'd promised me one but would only give it to me in person. Given my infrequent work schedule, it would've made more sense to just leave a copy for me to pick up whenever I came in next, but he wanted to hand it to me personally.

At some point, after giving away at least five copies of the single, he handed one to Dion and asked, "Is this worth any money?" To which Dion replied, "I'd be happy to put a copy on eBay for you to find out . . . but you *have* to still give one to Ben." I did not know this conversation had taken place and thus was quite dismayed when I saw Dion's copy sell for $778. I figured Das would be wowed by his newfound winnings, and my copy would go the way of the free market.

So imagine my surprise when Das waltzes into Car City, asks if I saw the copy that sold on eBay, and then says, "Don't worry, I've still got one for you."

He walks out to his car to grab it and then makes his way toward the desk I was sitting at in the back of the store.

"So, how much are you going to give me for it?" *Ugh.*

"Well, how much do you want for it?"

"Not much."

It felt as if this interaction stretched across ten hours, each pause a lifetime, each sentence rife with implied meaning, unspoken intentions, unforeseen

context. If I had $800, I would've gladly given it to Das. That's how much this record already meant to me.

"Well," I mustered, "give me a number."

"Not much . . . I don't know . . . twenty bucks?"

It was mighty cool of Das to do that. He's forever solid in my book.

The situation would remain unchanged until March or April of 2008. At that point, I got that call back from Bobby Hackney. He relayed to me the story of how one of his sons had heard some Death songs played at a house party in San Francisco; this sudden and unexpected validation from his son was traced back to my sharing of MP3s of the music.

We got to talking more, and when I mentioned I'd worked (however briefly) at Archer Record Pressing, the vinyl manufacturer in Detroit that originally pressed the "Politicians in My Eyes" single back in 1976, I secured my brother-in-arms status with him.

My goal became to try to find someone who would release the Death material. I'd sent a copy to In the Red Records (the label that releases the Dirtbombs), left a voicemail for Jello Biafra and his Alternative Tentacles label, and I even put headphones on a rep for Sub Pop and made him listen to the songs.

Movement from any of those labels was nonexistent. I thought perhaps I'd misjudged how good the music really was. Maybe I had an undetected bias.

July came and with it, another phone call from Bobby telling me that Death had signed a recent deal with Drag City Records. Part of me was bummed out. Had the Dirtbombs not been touring our asses off at that moment, I could've been more proactive in finding a home for the album, *For the Whole World to See*. Instead, another young record collector by the name of Robert Manis had gone through many of the same steps I did (obtain record, obtain band contact info, befriend band) and ultimately placed them with a label.

I was jealous.

After the release of *For the Whole World to See*, the wonderful *New York Times* article by Mike Rubin, and the resultant universal praise, two filmmakers visited me in Nashville in October 2009 and interviewed me about my experience in the whole Death hullabaloo.

I finally met Bobby and Dannis at SXSW in Austin in March 2010. It was brief, but it felt like a culmination, finally speaking face-to-face. I ran across a massive conference hall and without pause gave Bobby a big bear hug. He was wearing a suit that reminded me of the Beatles on Ed Sullivan.

The *A Band Called Death* documentary, which included my interview, was most notable to me once it was made available on Netflix. When that happened, I received emails, texts, or high-fives a couple times a week from acquaintances who had seen the film. Bobby has repeatedly thanked me for my help getting this story out there to the wider consciousness, but I have to demur. Spreading the word is just what any true music fan would do.

Recently at a record show in Nashville, a middle-aged man and his young son came up to me. The father said, "My son is a huge fan of Death, so I just wanted to introduce him to you." When my wife and I bought a house in 2012, one of the movers asked, "Didn't you discover that Death band?" It's odd for a record collector to become even tangentially connected to a story of this import, so to be recognized in public, basically for emailing around some MP3s, is extremely unexpected. Great

music, transcendent music, ultimately conquers whatever mitigating factors are conspiring against it and rises to the top. Sometimes it just takes thirty-plus years and an old friend cracking open a dusty box before everything is in its right place at the right time. And then the greater good can be served.

**BEN BLACKWELL**

The Gories. Photo courtesy of Renate Winter.

The Gories. Photo courtesy of Doug Coombe.

# How the Gories Ruined Music

*Danny Kroha*

At first, the Gories were more purveyors of ideas and attitude rather than music. We could loosely be called musicians, but at the beginning we were more like an art project, a noise band, a cartoon of a band. We were trying to play music, and we knew we sucked at it, but sucking never stopped us, we sucked with attitude. We didn't wait till we were "good enough" to get on a stage, we just did it. We were a statement, and our statement was, "fuck you." Fuck you and your giant drum kit, fuck you and your splash cymbal, fuck you and your electronic drums, your shitty synth, your stupid hair cut, fuck you and your Les Paul, your Marshall stack, your big fucking hair and spandex, fuck you and your fucking hot licks, fuck you '80s, you fucking suck.

We looked to the '60s for inspiration. Specifically, the '60s before 1967. We were mods, not hippies. We wanted our music raw and real. Records were coming out that compiled obscure mid-'60s 45s by no-hit wonders. There were great bands who put out a 45 on a major label next to crummy inept garage bands who pressed up five hundred records and sold them at shows. We made no value judgment between bands as different in ability and talent as the Rationals and the Keggs. We devoured it all and spit it back in the faces of those who remembered and those who never knew.

Our first show was at St. Andrew's Church on the Wayne State campus. It was an open mic hosted by Rob Tyner called the Community Concert Series. To us, Rob was just some bloated old hippie playing songs about Vietnam vets on an electric autoharp. We were stupid young punks. We didn't have the foresight to realize that a Detroit music legend was giving our crappy little band a chance to play onstage at a time in our "career" when no one in Detroit would touch us with Don Rickles's dick. I wish I could thank you now, Mr. Tyner.

What follows this introduction on the Gories raison d'être is part of an interview that appeared in the March 29, 1988, issue of Tom Ness's egalitarian DIY music paper, *Jam Rag* ("New wave, heavy metal, punk, rock 'n' roll!"). I'm not sure how we rated a cover photo over Terry Bozzio (an interview with him is in the same issue), considering Tom's headline for our interview is: "Jam Rag Talks with the Gories, Possibly Detroit's Worst Band." Tom was genuinely concerned that our ineptitude was bringing down the overall quality of music in Detroit, and he also seemed to be worried about the future. He saw us as the harbingers even we didn't realize we were.

The interview:

*Mick Collins:* We were sitting around one night, listening to an album called, *Scum of the Earth,* and I said, "We can do that."

*Dan Kroha:* Yeah, and I said, "Let's do it then, Peggy can play drums."

*Peg O'Neill:* I freaked out when you guys first wanted me to play. I was like, "No way, man. No way."

*Mick:* We knew we didn't know how to play. That was the beauty of it. We said, "Well, these guys didn't know how to play, and they put out records, so why not? We'll be awful, we'll drive people out of the room screaming!"

*Dan*: It was going to be bass, drums, and guitar. Me and Mick were going to switch back and forth between guitar and bass, but—

*Mick:* We realized that neither one of us knew how to be a guitar player by himself, so—

*Dan*: Because I couldn't play leads, and Mick couldn't play full chords.

*Mick:* Still can't.

*Dan*: So we decided to go with two guitars. Our first gig was at St. Andrew's Church. That was October of '86.

*Mick:* We knew eight songs our first show, and we played all of them badly, from what I'm led to believe. I don't remember it too well.

*Peg:* I took mushrooms that night, man, and I was out. They kept turning on these lights, and I'm going, "Turn off the fucking lights!"

*Dan:* They were both drunk off their asses on Thunderbird. Mick was wasted. I stayed somewhat sober because I knew that these two were just off the nut. We were amazingly horrible.

*Mick:* It was a mess of a night.

*Dan:* And then there was the Rainbow.

*Peg*: We closed down the Rainbow.

*Dan:* It was an old warehouse/office building downtown, run by that Earth Community dude.

*Mick:* Marvin.

*Peg:* They were turning it into an art gallery, and they had bands playing upstairs.

*Mick:* We got there late and drunk again, and we got pushed to the very end. So we decided, "Hey, we're headlining!" and just kept on drinking. Peg passed out at the end of the last song—

*Dan:* On the drumset.

*Peg:* That was the night I got the bottle. We used to play this little game, whoever drank the most got the bottle, and that's the only night I got the bottle, man.

*Mick:* I got the bottle the first night.

*Dan:* It was a solid concrete room, and we were really, really loud.

*Mick:* The guy who used to do sound at the Mystery Lounge did the sound there that night, so we were super loud.

*Dan*: Apparently some guy, the landlord, he heard us and said, "Man, if you have shit like this in here again—"

*Mick:* "GET OUT!" They had to close down. We saw Marvin at St. Andrew's Church a couple of months later, and he just stared at us.

*Dan:* Then we started practicing more.

*Peg:* I play a floor tom and two ride toms. Well, mostly just one with a tambourine taped to it. I use the other one once in a while on a few of the songs.

*Dan:* There's no bass drum. No kick pedal.

*Peg*: Well, there's a bass drum. It just doesn't have a head on it. I don't use it.

*Dan:* She just uses it for a tom stand.

*Mick:* She just uses it for a leg rest. No cymbals, no high hat, no snare, and no bass. It's all rhythm section.

*Dan:* We chose the raunchiest amps we could find. I have a Vox AC30 tube amp.

*Mick:* I used to have a solid-state Silvertone. I blew out one of the speakers, and then I fried the whole thing a couple of weeks ago. So now I'm using a fifty-watt Silvertone tube amp, on loan—

*Dan:* From the Cinderella's Attic collection. I play a 1964 Fender Jaguar.

*Mick:* I busted up two guitars, and now I play a Kay. I had a Mustang copy that had no name and no brand. I pulled all the strings off it at St. Andrew's Hall, and the bridge came off with them, so we had to give it back. That was on loan, too. Then we got a Kent. Dan broke the nut when he was trying to straighten the neck, and then I pulled all the strings off it. It's sitting in Dan's room in pieces right now.

*Dan:* People are always telling us we need a bass.

*Peg:* Everyone offers to play bass for us, and we're like, "Uh, no thanks."

*Mick:* Chris from the 3-Ds offered to play bass.

*Peg:* No, he must have been kidding.

*Mick:* No, he wasn't.

*Dan:* I don't think we need one because we've kind of designed our own sound.

*Mick:* Yeah, we're so used to arranging now for two guitars and three tom-toms that we wouldn't know what to do with a bass if we had it. We kind of go for that Bo Diddley sound, where all he had was a guitar, maracas, and drums, and that would be the whole setup for the song.

*Dan:* One thing I'd like to say is that I think we've gotten a lot of good support, I mean, from the other bands around.

*Mick:* Yeah, some of the other bands like us, but club owners hate us.

*Dan:* And people who are into dance music and shit hate us.

*Peg:* It's great, because it weeds out all the assholes immediately. I mean it's like, all they have to do is listen to us, and they're out of there.

*Mick:* You're either going to go, "Oh they're horrible," or, "They're great!" People who like us tend to be rather fanatical, and sometimes I don't understand it.

*Dan:* People who like us—

*Mick:* REALLY like us, and it's genuine, and I think, "Man, what are you, nuts?" But it's cool. I like the fans we have.

*Dan:* I love the city of Detroit, man. It's a beautiful city, in its own ugly way.

*Mick:* It has its own character. There are moods that being in Detroit can evoke, that simply can't be found anywhere else. You can't stay in the suburbs and know Detroit. There aren't very many urban bands. There are very few bands that live in the city. We're influenced just by living in Detroit.

*Dan:* I work in the suburbs, and I can't even say that I love the city of Detroit there, because they'll think I'm insane. There's no use arguing with them.

*Mick:* We're as much a part of Detroit as Detroit is a part of our sound.

*Dan:* There's people all over the world who worship music from Detroit.

*Mick:* We have our sound and we're going to stick with it, rough edges and all, including the fact that we can't play worth shit, but we try to make it sound good. We don't give a fuck about being stars, we just want to crank out the tunes. They could try sticking us in a studio, but we'd still be all distorted and holler at the top of our lungs. No amount of overdubbing and multitracking and plate reverb and computerized mix-down will ever change the sound of us. As long as there's a studio on the planet without carpet on the walls, we can still get by.

Well, there you have it, a glimpse into where our little punk asses were at in the beginning of 1988. I hope you find our mix of arrogance, misanthropy, and self-deprecation charming. We really had no pretensions that we were gonna "make it," it wasn't our goal. We had nothing but disdain for bands who were trying to "get signed." All we wanted to do was fill a void. No one at that time in Detroit was making the kind of crude, primitive mix of garage rock and R&B that we wanted to hear, so we decided to do it ourselves.

We had little ambition. We were into being abstruse. We thought it would be really cool to have a record out in Switzerland. We were unapologetic when our "music" was nothing more than an out-of-tune cacophony. In spite of this, people here liked us, and they ended up being people who were movers. We caught the attention of Len "Speedcult" Puch, a maverick if there ever was one. He offered to record us and put out our first LP because we reminded him of the Cramps (whom we weren't at all trying to sound like). He put out our LP and we continued to play Hamtramck twice a month, going back and forth between Paycheck's and the Hamtramck Pub. We were filmed playing live at Len's studio (which was an annex of a giant Quonset hut behind his parents' house in new Baltimore) for a cable TV show called *Band-In*. One of the cameramen, Dan Rose, took a copy of the video with him to Tuscaloosa, Alabama, where a

record-store-owning friend of his was promoting an Alex Chilton show. After the show, Dan, his pal, and Alex were hanging out at the guy's house, and without fanfare, Dan pops in the live vid of the Gories. It catches Chilton's attention, or rather Peggy caught his attention, as the first thing he asked Dan (and me, the first time I spoke to him on the phone) was "Who's that drummer?" After he put his eyes back in his head, he told Dan that he thought this band could do well in Europe and it just happened that he was on, and had a production deal with, a label in France. He told Dan to have someone from the band give him a call because he'd like to help them out. That was the beginning of the Gories being thought of as "legit."

We drove down to Memphis. Alex had given us directions to Tav Falco's house and arranged for us to stay there while Tav was off touring with the Panther Burns in Europe. We were falling in with a very continental crowd here, you see. Tav's house was a circa 1900 one-floor, two-bedroom house in a rather déclassé neighborhood of Memphis. As we pulled up to the house, Tav's ex-girlfriend, Lorette Velvette, was climbing out of the window onto the front porch. She had broken in to retrieve her leather jacket. The next-door neighbors had an eight-foot-high fence around their dirt yard and about ten big, ugly hounds. The man of the house was confined to a wheelchair and fed the dogs pieces of rancid meat that he threw out into the dirt. When Chilton got there the next day, he pitched a tent in the backyard. While we were there, Peggy and I lived on mashed potatoes with hot sauce and macaroni and cheese; Mick, his usual potato chips and candy bars. The living room furniture consisted of a 1960s Norton motorcycle, a record player, and a box of records. We were hanging out with Alex one evening, and he pulled a record out of the box called

*Beale Street Saturday Night*, saying, "You gotta hear this." He proceeded to play us a song called "Chicken Ain't Nothin' but a Bird," the most out-of-tune track that Furry Lewis ever recorded. Alex understood.

He recorded us in a studio in a converted garage behind a house in an Eisenhower-era neighborhood. In the '70s, the mixing board had belonged to Steve Cropper. There was a two-inch, sixteen-track tape deck (by comparison, our first LP was recorded on a half-inch eight-track with a Peavey mixing board). Alex's idea was to get a high-quality recording but not to try to change our sound, or even give us any directions at all. He mostly slept on the couch in the control room while we recorded and only got up when it was time for the mix-down.

The album came out on the French label, but the promised European tour never materialized. Adding insult to injury, the cover of the record was bright pink and purple and the name of the band was written in a crappy '80s font. It was so uncool. When I complained about the cover art, the label president said to me in a thick French accent, "You are not MAH-dough-nah." Meaning, "You're not Madonna, buddy. You're not big enough to call the shots here." We went back to playing the local dives.

By the time another label asked for an LP from us and offered to bring us over the pond for a tour, we'd been a band for six years and we were pretty well burned out. We did it anyway, recording the album on a borrowed four-track cassette deck in the cinder-block woodshop behind the house I was renting on Willis Street in the Cass Corridor. It was sort of rushed and halfhearted. The label wasn't very happy with it and beefed it up with a track from one of our non-LP singles and an outtake from our first album. We finally got to do the European tour, but the band almost broke up in the middle of it. We kept it together long enough to finish the tour and broke up when we got home.

It was only in that sixth year of the band, just before we left for Europe, that people we didn't know started coming to the shows. I remember we did a show at the Old Miami and around seventy people showed up to see us. That was a big deal. Around the time we were breaking up, I got a call from a young A&R guy at Warner Brothers records asking us to do a demo. They would pay us $700 to record it and have first rights of refusal. We thought that was a joke, as we'd never spent more than like fifty bucks to record a demo. We never did it.

I had no idea that there would be so many scrappy minimalist punk bands that would come after us and claim us as an influence. I thought we were the last word in scrappy, crappy, minimalist punk bands. Nope, we were just a new beginning. There was a whole rash of kids who were inspired by us to get by on rudimentary chops, heart, and attitude. I guess if you can pull that off with aplomb, it's a feat in itself, but when I think of how good the Detroit Wheels, or the MC5, or the Rationals, or Bob Seger and the Last Heard were when they were teenagers, I'm just in awe. It's only with age that I've come to appreciate how great those guys were and have the perspective to realize just how young they were, and at the same time realize how lazy and presumptuous we were. But hey, for better or worse, we were influential, and in the years since we broke up, our music has become better known than it ever was when we were originally playing it back in the latter half of the '80s. I'm really thankful that we've all been willing and able to reunite and play shows again, and I'm proud that our songs, in their crudity and utter retardation, are truly timeless.

Photo by Doug Coombe. Courtesy of the *Detroit Free Press*.

# Kid Rock before the Fame
## The Definitive Oral History
*Brian McCollum*

> It felt like being part of this secret in Detroit that soon the whole world was going to know about.
>
> —Tommy Valentino

Why is Kid Rock so big in Detroit? Because Kid Rock got a head start in Detroit: a decade of building his name, grooming his sound, and reinventing his persona from scrappy hip-hop street kid to swaggering rock-rap showman.

In 2015, Rock's album *First Kiss* marked his departure from Atlantic Records, the company that launched him into the national spotlight with 1998's ten-million-copy-selling *Devil Without a Cause*.

Getting to that point wasn't without struggle. The teenage Kid Rock had been dropped by his first label, and he returned to Detroit in the early '90s disillusioned but determined to make it on his own terms—driven not by money but by an intense thirst for fame.

Here's a look back at those early Detroit years, 1990 through 1998, when a young Bob Ritchie hustled hard to get noticed—and molded himself into the Kid Rock the rest of the world knows today.

## CHAPTER 1: A SETBACK AND A BOUNCE BACK

Romeo-born Ritchie was a little-known seventeen-year-old rapper and DJ when he was signed by the New York hip-hop label Jive Records, which issued his 1990 debut album, *Grits Sandwiches for Breakfast*. He'd spent his teen years playing east-side house parties and making connections in Detroit's fledgling hip-hop scene, and *Grits* was his Beastie Boys–inspired record of bawdy, boasting rap.

Jive booked Kid Rock on that year's *Straight from the Underground* package tour with Too Short and others—a shot at a national audience. But his Jive stint was brief, and the young rapper was soon back in Detroit plotting his next move. It would be the key stage in Kid Rock's evolution, as his hair grew longer, his music grew louder, and his live show grew bigger.

*Mike E. Clark (Producer-mixer):* I cut his demos as a kid before he got signed in 1989. I was working with mostly young black teenagers then. I didn't know he was white—we caught each other off guard when he came in. I thought, "Yeah, sure. A white guy is going to rap." But he shut me up. He had his turntable, had his beats, his stuff already written. He had his shit together and blew me away.

He was very confident, had the high-top fade, very sharp. You could tell right away he wasn't bullshitting. He had a shitty little Casio keyboard and knew exactly how he was going to do it.

He took those demos and got a deal with Jive.

*Joe Nieporte (Manager, the Ritz and State Theatre):* I ran the original Ritz in Roseville, an 1,800-seat venue. Very large. He wanted a gig. He came in pretty cocky: "I'm going to fill this place." Every band I talk to says that. But he had a lot of wits about him. Just a strong, cool personality.

We did the gig and he put 1,200 people in there. I was blown away.

*He had a great street team, a lot of little kids helping him back then.*

*Jerry (Vile) Peterson (Publisher, Orbit magazine):* He had this giant Mount Clemens posse. The high school friends. You'd meet so many of them at once.

*Joe Nieporte:* Bob was just straight-up rap then. He didn't have a band. You've heard that early stuff—a lot of profanity, real edgy, hard-core. I wasn't a big rap fan, but I liked his stuff. But I remember telling him, "Dude, if you're going to make it to the next level, you've got to clean it up."

*Mike Himes (Owner, Record Time shop):* When *Grits Sandwiches* came out, he came in for an in-store [performance] at Ten [Mile Road] and Gratiot. He had the tall hair, spinning like he would at the bars in Mount Clemens. We had a decent turnout. Toward the end, this blond-haired skinny kid kept yelling out—"I'll battle you! I'll battle you!" Just persistently getting in Kid Rock's face. I came up to him: "Dude, this is his day, his event. Maybe one day you'll have your day, but leave the guy alone." He followed him out to the parking lot still wanting to battle.

That was Eminem. He gave him a couple of his tapes: "Check me out." At least Kid Rock was cordial about it.

*Mike E. Clark:* [In 1990] Vanilla Ice came out and stunk things up. So Jive decided they didn't want a white rapper anymore. They couldn't see the future,

and they dropped Kid Rock, which was devastating to him. He got a deal with an independent label, Continuum, and said, "[Screw] it, Clark. Let's do this record." We worked on *Polyfuze Method* at the [Ferndale studio] Tempermill in '92.

With Jive, he tried to be the rap guy, keeping it all hip-hop. But—and this is just my opinion—he got disillusioned by being dropped. So he was like, "[Screw] it, I'm going to do my own thing."

*Tommy Valentino (Music attorney):* His attitude now was, "I'm not going to count on any record company to make me a star."

*Jerry (Vile) Peterson:* The whole Vanilla Ice comparison, he dreaded so much. It was a source of shame in that whole thing. In his first interview [with *Orbit* in 1990], he was saying he's not a Vanilla Ice, that he was trying to be the real deal. And he always told me it was his parents' music that influenced him. Definitely Seger, which was like old-people music at that time.

The Polyfuze Method, *a heavy, frenetic record, was released in summer 1993.*

*Mike E. Clark:* We were adding rock guitars, sampling Pink Floyd, any crazy stuff. At one point we had a flute player come in. We just didn't care.

He liked all kinds of music. When he goes to make music, he does what he thinks sounds good. If that was mixing a flute or heavy-metal guitar on top of 808 drums—as long as it sounded good, that's what he did.

*Joe Nieporte: Polyfuze Method* had a great rap presence but also brought a strong rock feel. When I heard it, I thought, wow, this guy is on to something.

And he toned it down [lyrically]. Not a lot. But he did tone it down.

*Mike Himes:* It was his crossroads record: the hip-hop influence but starting to lean toward rock.

*David Lee (Friend):* The fact that he's now associated with so many genres of music isn't a surprise. Even though we looked at him as a hip-hop guy after the Jive thing, you could start to see those other elements—the rock 'n' roll, the country.

*Brian Pastoria (Drummer, rock band DC Drive):* I remember Bob coming to a bunch of our shows at the Ritz in the early '90s. Our singer, Joey Bowen, liked the Beastie Boys, so when we did "You Need Love," we'd have this big breakdown with Joey rapping.

Bob knew he couldn't keep going down that Vanilla Ice path. It got him attention at first, but he realized that's not where he wanted to be. He was tired of the rap thing with programmed tracks. He wanted to do the Beastie Boys thing—only in a bigger, more rock kind of way.

## CHAPTER 2: SCRAPPING FOR ATTENTION, FIDDLING WITH NEW SOUNDS

Kid Rock was fighting for a name on the scrappy Detroit hip-hop scene of the '90s, amid acts such as Insane Clown Posse, Esham, and Eminem.

In summer 1993, Rock's ex-girlfriend gave birth to his son, Robert Ritchie Jr., who became known to everyone as Junior. Later that year, Rock found his way to White Room Studios in downtown Detroit, run by brothers Michael and Andrew Nehra—rock musicians then forming the rock-soul band Robert Bradley's Blackwater Surprise.

Rock cut tracks for his second and final Continuum release, the Fire It Up EP, which featured the rock-heavy "I Am the Bullgod" and a new country twist: a gritty cover of Hank Williams Jr.'s "Country Boy Can Survive."

Rock soon launched his own label, Top Dog Records, and kept himself in local record racks with his "bootleg" cassette series featuring new tracks and reworked material.

*Bob Ebeling (Drummer, engineer):* We were living together [in Sterling Heights] at possibly his lowest point. He had lived with [girlfriend] Kelly. There were three kids; he thought two of them were his, and then he found out that one of them wasn't. He was really emotionally torn up, going through that deep heartbreak stuff.

They split up and that's when I moved in the apartment. He was also kind of disenfranchised from his dad at that point. There wasn't a lot of financial support coming from the family. So he was probably most alone at that point—being heartbroken and away from his family and being on a smaller label like Continuum, not getting as much financial support.

But the one thing that was still there: He was motivated by fame. I've worked with five or six pretty big stars—Eminem, Rufus Wainwright, Phish—and there's a certain archetype of personality that just needs to be famous. Fame is quite an ugly thing to me, and most people would be scared to death of it, but he was driven by it. He talked about it in ways that didn't even make sense to me. He relished it.

He loved when we went somewhere to eat and somebody recognized him. He had this whole reward system in his head that didn't exist in other people's heads: When people recognize you and

BRIAN MCCOLLUM

want a piece of you, it was the equivalent of being wealthy. He just ate it up.

*Al Sutton (White Room cofounder, engineer):* We were the grunge, hard-rock studio. Bands came in with amplifiers, guitars, and drums. And in walks this guy with a sampler and MPC60.

He started hanging out in the studio. We needed somebody with his skills in our camp. He could program and loop, and we needed to be a little more current in that way. We had a B-room that he basically took over, coming in midday and staying till five in the morning.

*Michael Nehra (White Room owner):* Andy [Nehra] and I were a conduit for his creativity by giving him a studio to use. We worked with him in coproduction, engineering, some writing stuff. Bob was really fun to work with back then. He was creative, and we were all really good friends. We gave him the keys to the studio after the Continuum thing, and he created a lot of cool stuff there. There was this energy between the two rooms, creating music.

*Al Sutton:* He was cleaning all the time. He's a real neat freak, had to have his place really tidy. He'd vacuum the B-room and then go to work.

We thought he was good energy to have around. If we needed something programmed, he'd be here; if he needed a guitar part or drums, we could set it up. It became this symbiotic relationship.

*Jimmie Bones (Keyboardist):* He was this guy that was always around, his Dickies and stocking cap on. He started asking me to come in: "Hey, I'm doing a track; can you throw on some piano?"

*Michael Nehra:* He was learning from my brother and me. We were there playing the guitar and bass on "Bullgod." Bob wrote the song, but my brother and I made it *sound* like "Bullgod." Bob could play some guitar, but my brother and I were rock 'n' rollers who played the groove thing with Robert Bradley, and that energy certainly rubbed off. When he first came into the studio, he didn't really sound like that.

He was starting to get more of a rock edge, and that's what we tapped into—that rock 'n' roll spirit, that Detroit soul thing.

*Mike E. Clark:* The first time I ever heard him sing, East Detroit had recently changed its name to Eastpointe. So Bob changed the lyrics to Billy Joel's "It's Still Rock and Roll to Me" to record a cover version called "It's Still East Detroit to Me." He started singing, and I was like, "Dude, you sound amazing!" He was just [messing] around, but he sounded really good. I could hear the tone. He could hit the notes.

When "Only God Knows Why" became a big hit later on [in 1999], he looked at me and said, "You know, you were the first [person] who told me I could sing."

*Jerry (Vile) Peterson:* We'd have these *Orbit* karaoke nights, and that's when I learned he could actually sing. He'd do "Stayin' Alive," all the parts. Plus, he brought the mushrooms, which made the karaoke even more fun.

*Mike Himes:* He was hustling, coming in on a regular basis to drop off his [tapes and records] on consignment. He had flyers for his shows, tickets for the DJ things he was doing. He already had a vision. He was promoting himself, trying to meet the right people. We'd sit in the store, and he'd ask me questions at length—where to get records pressed, that kind of thing. He would pick your brain, just thirsty for information.

*Al Sutton:* He was killing it on the little tapes he was releasing, selling a ton of his own cassettes out of the record stores and his car. And he was making good money playing gigs. But Bob wasn't getting a lot of credit from the hipsters and the rock scene in Detroit. It was, "Oh, he's a white rapper; no need to take him seriously."

*Mark Bass (Producer, Eminem):* He was innovative, always a few steps ahead of what hip-hop was doing. But hip-hop didn't want to hear it, because he was this white guy with the long rock hair.

*Scott Legato (Photographer):* I was a DJ, spinning rap at the Struttin' Club on Gratiot. He showed up with his records. I blew him off. Showed up again; blew him off. Third time, I owed him. So I put it on. The owner immediately ran in yelling, "Take that shit off!" I stopped the record. Kid Rock walked up and said, "You're an asshole. Give me my records back."

*Mike E. Clark:* I think ICP [Insane Clown Posse] fueled Bob a lot. He wasn't a big fan, and when he saw these guys selling out the State Theatre, it threw gas on his flame. They really didn't get along. I was the guy in the middle: friends with Bob and working with ICP.

He was tenacious: "OK, that thing didn't work; let's try this or that." And he kept gaining fans around town. He had the talent. He just needed to figure out how he could make other people realize he was a force to be reckoned with.

*Joe Nieporte:* He'd go to every high school around here and pop his trunk open when school let out, handing out free samplers. Back then, all-ages shows didn't really exist. It was eighteen and over, headliners going on at midnight. So Bob comes in, promotes his shows as all-ages with early starts, and he's getting twelve hundred kids in there.

He drew from all over [metro Detroit], but predominantly the east side. He was from Romeo, and he had cut his chops in Mount Clemens, so those were his roots.

*Uncle Kracker (Friend, DJ):* He built a following. He'd play the Majestic or the Ritz, then bounce around back to [smaller venues like] Alvin's or St. Andrew's. He would play once every six months or so—make it look like he was coming through on tour as opposed to beating everybody in Michigan over the head every weekend. He was very smart about that whole supply-and-demand thing.

You'd have nine hundred people in the room—all these little white kids who dropped acid and liked listening to gangsta rap.

*Marc Kempf (Hip-hop manager, promoter):* There were [hip-hop] scenes developing at the Hip Hop Shop and St. Andrew's Hall, the "two floors of fun." But he was a maverick. He was doing his thing. He wasn't part of another scene, coming up with other artists.

*Mark Bass:* With Bobby's thing, he didn't have to fit in the same way Marshall [Eminem] did. Marshall was on that underground-hip-hop, kind of edgy, street level. Bobby was also on the street level—just a different street with nicer lights [*laughs*]. When you saw Kid Rock onstage, it was such a show that it was more of an alternative-rock thing.

325

## CHAPTER 3: ROCK 'N' SOUL INSPIRATION AT THE BEAR'S DEN

In 1994, a festive Sunday music scene was emerging at the Bear's Den in Berkley, Michigan, led by the funky, eclectic Howling Diablos. Rock became a weekly regular, and many have cited the Diablos' rapping, fedora-topped front man Tino Gross as a big influence on Rock's onstage style.

Rock's shows to that point had been a standard rap setup—Rock rapping, Uncle Kracker or DJ Blackman on turntables—but now he was assembling a revolving group of stage musicians to join him. He adopted a band name that endures today: Twisted Brown Trucker.

*Tino Gross (Howling Diablos):* Bob's sister Carol was a cocktail waitress, and she told him about us. He told me later, "I figured if she liked you, it had to be wack, because she's my older sister. Man, was I wrong."

There was some magical energy going on in the Bear's Den. It was this real organic underground thing, all about the music. A lot of things came together there, and Bob was a big part of it. He'd come in right behind us with his turntables and record crate. He'd scratch with us, and after a while, I was giving him the mic. He'd be our toaster, rap some stuff, sing the choruses together. The Diablos' mentality was like jazz musicians'—anything can fit in.

He had been doing these all-ages shows around town, where parents dropped off their kids in the middle of the afternoon. Now he was trying to grow his brand and reach older people more into rock and blues, beyond the limited young hip-hop crowd around Detroit.

*Brad Shaw (Kid Rock photographer):* The Howling Diablos were good, and he got a lot of ideas from them. Tino is such a great showman, and the whole band are such great players. Bob was down there every Sunday night.

I'm sure he got a lot of this and that from them, there's no doubt. He put that in the back of his head. He was always about the funk and rock 'n' roll anyway. He knew his hometown stuff. He was aware of everything, from Seger to Alice Cooper.

*Jimmie Bones:* The Bear's Den thing was a real melting-pot vibe. It would start with the Diablos, then just a big jam after that, where all these players are coming up. That played a big role in making Bob known. He could get up there and freestyle and put that into a jam situation. It helped him cross over to maybe some folks who wouldn't have taken that [rap] genre very seriously or weren't all that knowledgeable about it.

*Mike E. Clark:* Bob was fascinated by all that. The fact that they could put on a live show and captivate an audience—that was inspirational.

*Tino Gross:* A lot of people will tell you he got a lot from the Howling Diablos, that's true. For me to say it, it sounds weird. But we were older, and he was a young guy soaking it in. Ideas were flowing on that scene. Our thing was probably the closest to what he ultimately ended up doing.

There were many times Bob said, "You guys are going to be the next big wave out of here." He was very much a supporter. So it wasn't like, "I'm taking their thing and running away with it." It was an overlapping, organic thing.

*Uncle Kracker:* I started DJing for him [in 1990] when I was still in high school. My first gig DJing for him, I had just gotten my license.

He figured out he could start playing bars in other cities if he had an actual backup band, too. Nobody was going to book him with just the track thing behind him. So he started putting together a group.

*Tino Gross:* I think he saw with us how it works to rap over a live band. He could see it and feel it. Sometime around the Bear's Den period, he decided to put his own thing together, similar to what we were doing, and he created a band.

*Bob Ebeling:* The first big concert with the band was at St. Andrew's, sometime in the late fall of '93. That was the first incarnation of Twisted Brown Trucker, though it wasn't called that just yet.

*Jimmie Bones:* That idea also came from Public Enemy, [rap acts] like that who were using live stuff. Chuck D had started running live bands. The Beasties, too. Those guys had a huge influence on him.

*Bob Ebeling:* He was very interactive in his show, constantly changing up the sequence. We were just blasting through all the material. He was very involved in how to manipulate the energy of the crowd—lay back for a while, then bring it up. He had the whole thing orchestrated, orchestrating the band and the background sequence.

*Michael Nehra:* He was experimenting with different musicians. There was this circle of people around Detroit. It wasn't the Jack White circle. It was this unsung, not-quite-so-hip movement that was going on.

*Bob Ebeling:* In 1994, we booked a couple of weeks on the road, odd dates in Sarnia, around Iowa and Ohio, some of the colleges. We went out and did these half-assed gigs in front of twenty people, sometimes five. If it was closer to home like Toledo,

it would be pretty packed—a couple hundred kids. And every time we were back around Detroit, it would be a full house.

You were definitely feeling the struggle of it all, unless we were home playing the Palladium or Ritz—two thousand kids, two thousand in merchandise, forty thousand dollars at the door.

It's nearly impossible to track all the early variations of Twisted Brown Trucker. There was massive turnover. That's because [band members] were saying, "OK, I'm not really getting paid from this, and he is."

*Vickie Siler (Toledo fan):* I was in my early twenties. I was mostly a rap fan, but I still loved hanging out with the drunk uncles listening to classic rock. When I saw Kid Rock, I was like, "Well, that's it!" The first time was in '93 at the Main Event in Toledo. It was five dollars or seven dollars. My friends were more excited about ICP playing in town that same night.

I could tell he had a voice like Rage Against the Machine—that harsh rocker voice—along with his rapping skills. Just this crazy dude. He had that cocky walk to him, the real pimp thing.

I worked as a stripper. I used to tell my girlfriends, "Let's go see that rapper-dude Kid Rock." He'd have the turntables going, some background beats, holding a microphone. Stripper music, I called it. That *boom-boom* bass, where you could feel it. It was dirty, dingy, nasty, just some kind of fun stuff. We'd go to the show and dance, then go back to work.

*Tino Gross:* I did an interview with Dr. John on my blues radio show, and he went on and on about the midgets who were a big part of the New Orleans rhythm-and-blues scene, the whole carnival thing down there. I gave Bob a tape of that show to listen to on a road trip.

Joe C. had already been showing up at Bob's shows as a fan. Being the guy he is, Bob doesn't miss a trick. After that, he looked out at Joe C. one night, and a lightbulb went off.

## CHAPTER 4: PARTY LIKE A ROCK STAR, WORK LIKE A SUPERSTAR

Joseph Calleja (Joe C.) was a twenty-one-year-old Taylor resident who stood three feet nine inches tall, his growth stunted by the coeliac disease that later took his life. Joe C. became an onstage staple at Rock's concerts, a dynamic, popular, dirty-mouthed presence. He was part of a live set that would eventually get honed with a light show, pyro, dancers, and a light-up "KID ROCK" backdrop.

*Joe Nieporte:* I left the Ritz in '94 to run the State Theatre [in Detroit]. I wanted to book Bob there, and there was some worry that it was too big. I really put my ass on the line. It was the first State show he did with Joe C. and Uncle Kracker, and we ended up with well over two thousand people.

*Tino Gross:* It was such a show-biz thing. Joe C. made the band more exciting. Bob was trying something new onstage, different people coming and going. But Joe C. just stuck. Onstage, it was a beautiful thing.

At the Detroit Music Awards [in 1997], we played with Bob. Ted Nugent was on the radio the next day ranting: "This Kid Rock character had a six-year-old boy up there. It's just not right!" Kid Rock just smiled and gave me a thumbs-up.

*David Lee:* There was a family atmosphere around Bob. When Junior became the same size as Joe C.,

he could never understand why Joe C. got to do stuff like run into the street, drink beer, leave with the adults. It was always hysterical.

*In 1996, still working at White Room, Kid Rock released his most rock-oriented record yet,* Early Mornin' Stoned Pimp, *on which he was joined by a host of Detroit musicians that included Gross and the Nehras. "I always wanted guitars and live stuff. And that comes with money and connections," Rock told the* Detroit Free Press *at the time. "So I've tried to surround myself with talented people that I get along with."*

*Bob Ebeling:* Bob just has this unreal constitution that can keep partying. That's the last fill-in-the-blank of "how to be a rock star." He can party for three days straight. You'll wake up that fourth day and feel like dying. He snaps out of bed ready for the party to keep going. And it's not that he's cheating—he's as drunk and stoned as anybody else. He's got something in his genes. One morning, we both woke up at the apartment after a couple hours of sleep. He was revved up and ready to continue that level of insanity. And it just came out of my mouth: "Dude, you are the early morning stoned pimp."

*Thornetta Davis (R&B singer):* He was hanging out at the White Room a lot then. I sang on a couple of things on *Early Mornin' Stoned Pimp*. He was showing us what to sing, and I said, "Wow, you've got a voice—you're not just a rapper!" And lo and behold, he's a singer now.

He wanted me to do a lyric that was pretty risqué. I'm like, "I have a little girl; can you not publicize that I'm on the album?" Sure enough, it comes out, and I'm on the credits [*laughs*].

*Bob Ebeling:* He was gaining momentum with

*Early Mornin' Stoned Pimp*, had his whole Detroit posse going, and stabilizing the band with the final lineup—Kenny Olson and Jason Krause on guitar. He had Joe C. up there, starting to get the final elements of how it was going to look. It was becoming the well-groomed show he would [later] tour with.

*Brad Shaw:* He played the Club in Toledo around that time and began the routine of changing into his pimp getup. He'd run offstage back toward us, tearing his clothes off. There wasn't much time. You've got a guy throwing on a '70s pimp outfit—it was hysterical and hard not to laugh.

He'd go back out in the pimp outfit with a gun down his pants. And it was a real gun [*laughs*]. You'd have to ask him if it was loaded. It probably was.

*Jerry (Vile) Peterson:* He was just a lot of fun to be with. If you went to the strip bar with Bob, you'd have dancers sitting all over. In those days, it was hanging out at Garfield's or strip bars. When you went out with Bob after he started getting some money, it was great. Always crazy fun.

*David Lee:* It's well known that a lot of partying was going on. We were all rolling around Detroit for a few years. Nights would turn into days pretty fast. The bars, the hundreds of beers, the chicks. He was just a cool, fun guy to be around.

But that shouldn't overshadow the fact that Bob was deadly serious about two things: raising Junior, and his career.

*Mark Bass:* The partying just added to the whole thing. Same thing that made Mick Jagger. He was never out of control. He was always a great businessman, a marketing genius.

*Brad Shaw:* It was never about laying around getting stoned, thinking he's a rock star. He was constantly asking, "What can I do to top that?" He was always going a step ahead of the last show.

He'd call at three in the morning: "Dude, I'll meet you at the White Room in an hour. I've got a stripper to help with a photo shoot."

*David Lee:* Bob and his boys dressed a little different—the windbreakers, baggy pants, high-tops. We would take them to hang out in certain rock 'n' roll establishments, and not only did they stand out, we were sometimes told they weren't welcome.

*Tino Gross:* Memphis Smoke [in Royal Oak] was really pushing the Diablos to do a show. We knew we were too wild to be in there. But we start playing, Bob shows up and gets up there rapping. Fun night. I go back in the manager's office, and he reads the riot act. "What was that blond asshole doing onstage with you guys? Don't ever bring that shit around here again. You guys don't need that!"

That sound had not been on the radio yet. And they saw rap as some garbage music that was for stupid kids. We knew it could work. To me, it was like punk rock—we were building our own scene, and not everybody was down with it.

*Al Sutton:* One of the records coming out then was Alanis Morissette's *Jagged Little Pill*. A lot of rock guys didn't like that album—it was programmed, had the drum machines. We were hanging out with a guy saying it sucked. Bob said, "You don't know what you're talking about. That record is going to be huge." Bob was totally on it. He saw the writing on the wall, where music was going, and he totally grabbed that.

*Joel Martin (Owner, 54 Sound):* This kid was doing something with the Internet that others weren't hip to yet. His small house in Royal Oak was like a crash pad and record company. When I saw the operation in his basement, it blew my mind. The mailing lists, the street teams. He had a crew of people working the computer, doing things that at the time were really foreign. He understood at the very beginning what the whole Internet thing was about.

*Al Sutton:* I was impressed. A young dude in music, already buying a house. Not too bad. He had interns that would come in from different states. It was hilarious—some kid flying in from California to make flyers for a couple of months. Bob always worked like he was a superstar.

## CHAPTER 5: A MAJOR LABEL FINALLY BITES

Alongside manager Steve Hutton, the New York music attorney Tommy Valentino was now aboard the Kid Rock team, and the pair helped foster buzz outside of Detroit, including placing key stories in the Beastie Boys' *Grand Royal* magazine and the trade publication *Hits*. In 1997, they finally snagged the attention of a big record-biz exec: Jason Flom, head of Lava Records, part of the powerhouse label Atlantic Records.

*Al Sutton:* We were at a restaurant in Royal Oak, a bunch of us hanging out, and he said, "Man, my next record . . . I've come up with this thing. I'm going to do a redneck, shit-kicking, rock 'n' roll–rap band." Everybody was laughing—"So that's it, eh?"

*Tommy Valentino:* I flew in to see him at the State Theatre [in 1996]. I was blown away by his per-

formance, how packed the place was, and the diversity of the people there—everything from bikers to strippers to in between. Younger, older, from different backgrounds, all of them into it. At one point, a woman threw a bra onstage, and I'm thinking, "This is an old-time rock 'n' roll show!"

Steve Hutton and I were shopping Kid Rock together [to record labels]. No one was interested: "White rap isn't what's in right now." They weren't getting it. It was frustrating. I kept saying, "He's not a white rapper. He's a rock star and everything in between."

I really felt that if someone just saw the live show, they were going to sign him.

*Jason Flom (Lava/Atlantic Records, [from a 2003 Detroit Free Press interview]):* Andrew Karp, an A&R guy for Lava, went to see him in Cleveland at a place called the Grog Shop. He told me, "Hey, there were only forty people there, but the guy put on a stadium show. He came out of a coffin at the beginning, he's got this vertically challenged guy, and it's a spectacle. You've got to see it."

*Tommy Valentino:* From a visual perspective, he was just starting to develop the persona that exploded, jumping up and down, hair going back and forth, no shirt. Like Anthony Kiedis of the Red Hot Chili Peppers, only dressed in hip-hop attire. He never stopped moving onstage the whole time. It was stunning to see visually.

The live show was a combination of hip-hop, rock, even some country. There was almost a Lynyrd Skynyrd thing going on. In trying to sell this [to record labels], it became clear to me that the rock angle was what really needed to be stressed.

*Jason Flom:* We went to Detroit shortly thereafter to see him at the State Theatre. And it was every bit the spectacle that we'd talked about.

*Detroit Free Press,* May 25, 1997: When Detroit hip-hop-roots-rocker Kid Rock hits the State Theatre stage Friday night, there will be some important sets of ears in the audience. It's a showcase gig, and the major-label reps are heading into the house to check out the colorful, pounding show from Rock and his crew.

*Jimmie Bones:* It was a big thing. There was a little more rehearsing that went on for that one. You could feel there was a lot at stake. But it was still a lot of fun—not like a lot of tension or anything. Something just felt like the shit was about to hit.

*Joel Martin:* I was knocked out of my seat at the State Theatre. It was like watching an explosion. Joe C. was up there. The whole presentation was so carnival-like. He's got the savvy of a P. T. Barnum. He mixed those styles, and it just worked. It seemed symbolic of changing times.

*Joe Nieporte:* Flom pulled me aside and spent half an hour drilling me with questions: *How well do you know him, does he do drugs, is his head on straight?* Bob put on a phenomenal show that day. He got signed because of that gig.

*Jason Flom:* After [the show], we arranged to meet in the basement of some disco club, some crazy place in Detroit. Rock got there about two-thirty in the morning. We sat there under the fluorescent lights, a very surreal setting, to discuss what kind of record would he make. After that meeting, he went and laid down a couple of tracks—"Somebody's Gotta Feel This" and "I Got One for Ya"—and sent them to us a few weeks later.

I was in a car in LA on Hollywood Boulevard when I put on the two tracks. I called him immediately and said, "I'll give you whatever you want." We made a deal on the phone.

## CHAPTER 6: BREAKING BIG— "DETROIT HAD IT ALL SEWED UP"

His major-label contract in hand, Rock worked on *Devil Without a Cause* through spring 1998, cutting tracks at the White Room and polishing the final versions at the Mix Room in Los Angeles. Most of the album was cowritten with Kracker.

*Tommy Valentino:* Kracker brought a different melodic sensibility. Bob could give you all the other stuff, from the beats to the arrangements to the attitude. They developed into a great songwriting team.

*Uncle Kracker:* I would help writing verses and whatnot. But more than anything else, I was his biggest cheerleader and worst critic. If something fell out of his mouth and sucked, I'd tell him. That was me being selfish: For me, Bob was probably the closest thing to the kind of music I wanted to listen to. So if he spun something that was dumb, I'd tell him.

But he's great with melodies and lyrics. And he's great under pressure.

*David Lee:* You could feel it coming, the buildup before *Devil*. When guys like [Atlantic Records founder] Ahmet Ertegun and Jason Flom are coming into town, you can tell something special is going on.

*Michael Nehra:* He took some tracks he'd previously recorded, remixed [them and] overdubbed the vocals. "Bullgod" was an older one. Others he did from scratch—"Cowboy" was a brand-new track.

It was an exciting time. We knew where Bob was heading.

*Mark Bass:* We were with Marshall [Eminem] at the Mix Room in LA [finishing *The Slim Shady LP*] at the same time Bobby was there. Marshall wanted these deep *vooka-vooka* scratches on "My Fault," so Bobby goes in and does those cuts, while Marshall goes in the other room and writes part of a song for him.

It was cool because we were both doing these records at the same time, and it was starting to feel like Detroit had it all sewed up.

Devil Without a Cause *was released in August 1998 and, after a slow initial build, exploded onto the national radar thanks to MTV appearances, the radio hits "Bawitdaba" and "Cowboy," and a milestone set at Woodstock '99 and televised to a national audience.*

*Jason Flom:* The first appearance he did on *Fashionably Loud* on MTV [in December 1998], he performed "Bawitdaba." That was one where everybody went, *"Uh oh."* The tipping point occurred at the MTV Awards [in September 1999] when he did the medley with Run-D.M.C. and Aerosmith. Watching that, I said, "Holy shit." What else could you say?

*Tommy Valentino:* When he took the stage at Woodstock, I was so nervous. I said to myself, this is going to be a really, really big moment. . . . But every minute going by he was killing it more and more. It was like an athlete in the zone. It was that powerful. He'd been playing out. But really, what he displayed in that show was the savvy of a performer who had done ten or twelve world tours.

*Mark Bass:* I'm not sure I'll be hearing [Eminem's]

"My Name Is" on a classic-rap station in twenty years. But you'll be hearing Bobby on classic rock and country. He made it work. Who thought we'd have country music with 808 kick drums.

*David Lee:* He had come back from New York after Jive with his tail between his legs. Doors were getting slammed in his face. Even around a lot of the music scene in Detroit, he was an outcast. In retrospect, that might have been the best thing to happen to him. The progress he made on his own meant they had to pay attention.

*Mike E. Clark:* That first time I saw him when he walked into the studio in 1989, nobody knew who the hell he was, and he was carrying himself with so much confidence.

When he was making *Devil Without a Cause*, he played me those first demos, and I listened to him rapping, "I'm going platinum, I'm going platinum." I said, "Come on, man. You haven't sold shit."

But he knew. He shut me up. He shut everybody up.

## STORYTELLERS

*Mark Bass:* His band Black Planet opened shows for Kid Rock in the early '90s, and Bass went on to a career producing Eminem records as part of the Bass Brothers.

*Jimmie Bones:* A veteran keyboardist on the Detroit scene who has been part of Twisted Brown Trucker for nearly two decades.

*Mike E. Clark:* The studio whiz was Kid Rock's first producer and went on to become the main collaborator with Insane Clown Posse.

*Thornetta Davis:* This longtime R&B singer did backups on early Kid Rock material and his hit "All

Summer Long." Her new album, *Honest Woman*, is due out this year.

*Bob Ebeling:* Kid Rock's onetime roommate is a drummer and Grammy-nominated studio engineer who has worked with Eminem, Phish, and others.

*Jason Flom:* Flom founded Lava Records, which signed Rock in 1998. Artists he's signed include Paramore, Lorde, and Matchbox Twenty.

*Tino Gross:* A blues, funk, and rock mainstay in Detroit for more than thirty years. Front man for the Howling Diablos.

*Mike Himes:* He opened the first Record Time shop in 1983 in Eastpointe, with eventual stores in Roseville and Ferndale.

*Marc Kempf:* Kempf was embedded in Detroit's 1990s hip-hop scene, managing Eminem and publishing *Underground Soundz* magazine.

*Uncle Kracker:* His older brother was a friend of Kid Rock; Kracker eventually became Rock's DJ and right-hand man.

*David Lee:* This Detroit attorney (who has not represented Kid Rock) was part of a rolling crew of party friends with Kid Rock and the Howling Diablos.

*Scott Legato:* Now a nationally published concert photographer, Legato was a club DJ in the 1990s.

*Joel Martin:* This local impresario and studio operator was managing Moog Stunt Team in the '90s when he met Kid Rock. He went on to work closely with Eminem, including managing the rapper's song publishing.

*Michael Nehra:* He and his brother, Andrew Nehra, founded White Room Studios, working with Big Chief and others, and they later formed Robert

Bradley's Blackwater Surprise. Today they run the music-gear company Vintage King.

*Joe Nieporte:* Managed the Ritz in Roseville, and later the State Theatre. Today he runs Funfest Productions, which manages Freedom Hill and festivals including Stars and Stripes.

*Brian Pastoria:* Long-tenured drummer with Adrenalin and DC Drive who went on to run the Harmonie Park entertainment complex.

*Jerry (Vile) Peterson:* Longtime Detroit punk and art fixture who founded *Orbit* magazine in 1990.

*Brad Shaw:* Kid Rock's go-to photographer in the 1990s, whose shots made the cover of *Early Mornin' Stoned Pimp* and *History of Rock*.

*Vickie Siler:* An early Kid Rock fan from Toledo who has attended more than seventy shows and several Kid Rock cruises.

*Al Sutton:* Sutton was White Room Studios' cofounder and engineer, and went on to start Rustbelt Studios in Royal Oak. He remains Kid Rock's go-to engineer.

*Tommy Valentino:* A veteran New York music attorney who helped land Kid Rock's deal with Lava/Atlantic in 1997.

# Kid Rock
## From Apple Orchards to the World

*Gary Graff*

Kid Rock may not have been born to perform, but he was certainly bred for it.

Growing up in Romeo, Michigan—closer to apple orchards than the trailer park of his early image—a young Bob Ritchie would often be called upon by his parents to entertain their friends at parties with a pantomime of Jim Croce's "Bad, Bad Leroy Brown." That planted a seed that later grew into hot DJ sets at basement parties in Mount Clemens and Detroit, club shows at the Ritz and the Palladium, and ultimately to festivals such as Woodstock '99 and headlining arenas and stadiums around the country.

Even after ten studio albums—six of which are certified platinum or better—Rock maintains that he and his longtime Twisted Brown Trucker (TBT) outfit are "a live band, first and foremost. That's how we've gotten everything. We've gone out and proven ourselves, whether it's been television, live onstage. . . . Everything's grown from there. We went from the bottom to the top of the touring circuit, and playing (live) is what defines us." And playing live at home has been even more crucial for Rock and company.

"Detroit's been everything to me, from the lean years to the biggest and the good years. It's where I came from," says Rock, whose 2006 *Live Trucker* album featured thirteen tracks recorded at various metro-area venues between 2000 and 2004.

It can be argued that no one, perhaps not even Rock's friend and forebear Bob Seger, has played more special-event shows than the self-proclaimed "rock 'n' roll son of Detroit." The history of Rock is dotted with guest appearances, stadium dates, oversized birthday parties, special club appearances, and even a head-scratching but galvanizing collaboration with the Detroit Symphony Orchestra. To prove that point, here's a trip through nearly two dozen of the key shows on Rock's lengthy live résumé:

May 30, 1997, State Theatre: The show that secured Rock's major-label deal with Lava/Atlantic, a blowout that lived up to all the hometown hype he poured into it and showed the rock-rap-funk fusion of the *Early Mornin' Stoned Pimp* album was just the tip of his creative iceberg.

October 23, 1999, The Palace of Auburn Hills: A year after its release, *Devil Without a Cause* was exploding with multiplatinum force, allowing Rock and his Twisted Brown Trucker band to pimp out the Palace in their biggest headline show to date. A triumph despite a few production and technical snafus.

December 31, 1999, Pontiac Silverdome: A millennium blowout with Metallica, Ted Nugent, and Sevendust. Rock was the opener but joined everyone else to usher in the twenty-first century with "Detroit Rock City."

August 31, 2000, DTE Energy Music Theatre: Rock took the party outdoors for the first time at the venue that became known as "Pine Bob" for his many guest appearances over the years—from jamming with Hank Williams Jr., Lynyrd Skynyrd, and the Zac Brown Band to presenting Lionel Richie with a sixty-fifth birthday cake in 2014.

October 27, 2001, Michigan State Fairgrounds: While the overriding purpose was to film the video for "Forever," Rock and TBT kept five thousand shivering but energetic fans entertained when the cameras were off with performances of Rolling Stones, Lynyrd Skynyrd, and Marshall Tucker songs, along with a few of his own.

March 17, 2002, The Palace: A night for hometown heroes. With Bob Seger watching from the soundboard, Ted Nugent joined Rock and company for an encore medley of Michigan rock that included the gonzo god's own "Cat Scratch Fever."

June 17, 2002, The Beach Grill: After 1.2 million fans feted the Red Wings' Stanley Cup championship, Rock and TBT entertained at a private party in St. Clair Shores, laying down a covers-heavy set and joined by Silver Bullet Band saxophonist Alto Reed and several of the more musically inclined Red Wings.

July 1, 2002, Fifth Avenue Billiards, Royal Oak: Rock gave then-fiancée Pamela Anderson a birthday gift of music, joining the Brothers Groove for renditions of Lynyrd Skynyrd's "Sweet Home Alabama," ZZ Top's "La Grange," and both the traditional and the Beatles' versions of "Happy Birthday."

September 13, 2002, DTE Energy Music Theatre: On a night off from a tour with Aerosmith, the Rock posse and Run-D.M.C. played their own show, forgoing an intermission as it morphed seamlessly from the rap trio's opening set into two hours of rock 'n' roll.

March 21, 2003, Mill Street Entry: After joining Tim McGraw onstage at the Palace earlier in the evening, Rock and several TBT members also showed up at the country star's Bread & Water benefit for the American Red Cross for a set of classic-rock and country covers. "He's a badass, isn't he?" McGraw noted as Rock left the stage. As if we didn't know.

March 27, 2004, Cobo Arena: Rock's first Cobo gig was historic enough but took on another legendary layer after Gretchen Wilson—a then-unknown who sang "Picture" with him that night—became one of country's hottest new stars.

November 4, 2004, Emerald Theatre, Mount Clemens: Rock prepared for the release of his *Kid Rock* album with this small-hall taping for VH1's *A Kid Rock Christmas*, a special that aired the following month. Uncle Kracker and the Pussycat Dolls were his special guests, and the J. Geils Band's "Detroit Breakdown" was the encore.

February 3–4, 2006, Joe Louis Arena: The Rolling Stones at halftime? Nah. The hottest concerts of the Super Bowl XL weekend featured Rock's first-ever onstage duets with Bob Seger. Hank Williams Jr. made a brief (and taciturn) appearance the second night.

February 8–9, 2007, Joe Louis Arena: Rock brought his Rock 'n' Roll Revival Tour home for a pair of revue-style shows that veered from his own material to include performances by J. Geils Band front man Peter Wolf and a dynamic Run-D.M.C. medley with Joseph "Rev. Run" Simmons, with former Allman Brothers Band guitarist Dickey Betts taking over for Wolf on the second night. "It's just a wild idea that's working really,

really well," Rock said during the tour. "There's something going on here I don't think any of us realize yet. There's something bigger than all of us that's going on, on the stage. It's crazy. It's history. It's magic. It's unbelievable."

July 17–18, 2009, Comerica Park: The proud "son of Detroit" sold out two shows at the home of the Detroit Tigers, lighting up the sky with plenty of pyrotechnics and introducing a new song, "In Times Like These," that would appear on the following year's *Born Free* album. The shows also featured plenty of covers, including the Jackson 5's "ABC," Dobie Gray's "Drift Away," and bits of the Rolling Stones' "Tumbling Dice," the Georgia Satellites' "Keep Your Hands to Yourself," Sly and the Family Stone's "Everyday People," and Guns N' Roses' "Paradise City." Opening acts included Lynyrd Skynyrd and Robert Randolph and the Family Band on the seventeenth and Alice in Chains and Cypress Hill on the eighteenth. The shows also featured the rollout of Rock's Bad Ass beer brand and a festive block party in the parking lots outside the stadium. Rock staged another two-night stand at Comerica during August of 2011, with Sammy Hagar joining him on the first night for a ramshackle romp through Grand Funk Railroad's "We're an American Band."

November 21, 2009, Renaissance Ballroom at the Detroit Marriott hotel: "My nerves are shot," Rock admitted after his guest appearance with Stevie Wonder during the $350-a-head black-tie fiftieth-anniversary celebration for Motown, which benefited the Motown Historical Museum. The Temptations and Aretha Franklin also performed at the event, but Wonder's set was the showstopper— especially when Rock joined him for a rehearsed

"Living for the City" and then, at Wonder's request, for "Superstition." A few shots of whiskey were in order in Rock's top-floor suite afterward. "I've never felt like this before," he gushed. "Forty fucking thousand people at Comerica this summer . . . Nah. Easy. But tonight it was fucking intense!"

November 25, 2010, Ford Field: As part of the campaign launching his *Born Free* album, Rock and TBT performed at halftime of the Detroit Lions' annual, nationally televised Thanksgiving day game, playing the title track amid a field full of choreographed dancers. "It's great because I'm home for Thanksgiving, number one, and it's a huge television audience," Rock said at the time. "I get to be in front of the hometown fans, and it's great to have my family down there and then go eat some turkey and watch the next football game. It's such a tradition; I used to go to these games with my dad and brother every year since I was a kid, so to be part of it now, musically, is just great." Rock made a quick return to the tradition, playing again during halftime of the 2012 Thanksgiving Day game.

January 15, 2011, Ford Field: How does one turn forty? If you're Kid Rock, you do it with sixty thousand fans at a football stadium, with a guest list that included Sheryl Crow for "Picture" and Free's "All Right Now"; Uncle Kracker on "Good to Be Me"; Peter Wolf for "Detroit Breakdown"; Rev. Run on a medley of "Rock Box," "King of Rock," and Aerosmith's "Walk This Way"; Martina McBride re-creating their then-new duet "Care"; Anita Baker leading the crowd in "The Star Spangled Banner"; and Cindy Crawford with husband Rande Gerber conducting "Happy Birthday." As if that wasn't enough, Conan O'Brien, Jay Leno, Jon Stewart,

Jimmy Kimmel, NASCAR champ Jimmie Johnson, and Beavis and Butt-Head—whose creator, Mike Judge, was in attendance—offered video tributes, and Rock received a Spirit of Detroit Award and a customized 2011 Camaro SS from Chevrolet—a provocative gift in a place called Ford Field. But Rock gave back, too, not only with music but with donations of $25,000 each to the Coalition on Temporary Shelter, the Capuchin Soup Kitchen, the Haven shelter, and the Rainbow Connection. "I don't even know what to say," Rock uncharacteristically noted at one point. "There's no place on earth I'd rather be right now than here." Ditto, sixty thousand times over.

April 16, 2011, Machine Shop, Flint: "I remember these club days," Rock told the crowd at this private event for the Jim Beam Live Music Series (Rock endorses its Red Stag brand). "I remember twelve years of doing club shit." He and the band fell back into it easily on this night, with an hour-long, thirteen-song set that provided a small-venue respite from the large halls on the *Born Free* tour. "It's fun being back in the club—for one night," Rock announced. The lucky few hundred who were there couldn't have agreed more.

May 12, 2012, Fox Theatre: Now here's one nobody saw coming—Rock and TBT with the Detroit Symphony Orchestra. It was for a good cause; with the orchestra still reeling after a musicians' strike, Rock and some corporate sponsors joined forces for a revival show that raised a cool million and found the Detroit Symphony Orchestra and conductor/musical director Leonard Slatkin (whom Rock dubbed a "badass") sporting Rock-style fedoras as they joined the rockers for a generous selection that included "Bawitdaba," "Rock N Roll Jesus," "All Summer Long," "Cowboy," and more, with special instrumental introductions for "Times Like These" and "Born Free." Rock wore a tuxedo for "Devil Without a Cause" but quickly changed to his usual black shirt, and he and TBT encored with "Son of Detroit," "Wasting Time," and "God Bless Saturday." Before the show, Rock recounted that it was Quicken Loans chairman Dan Gilbert who called him while he was backstage after a concert in Louisville, sharing a drink with one of the heirs of the Jim Beam family and perhaps a little more susceptible to outlandish suggestion: "Yeah, I had a little whiskey in me, a little bourbon," Rock recalled with a chuckle. "I said yes. I kind of committed to it that night, which I'm not sure I should've. But I'm glad I did."

August 12, 2012, DTE Energy Music Theatre: The first Palace Honors event was a bit solemn—at least until Sheryl Crow hit the stage for the feature performance of the night, and especially after Rock joined his "Picture" partner onstage for that song and a rendition of Creedence Clearwater Revival's "Up Around the Bend." "Now we got a party goin' on!" Rock proclaimed, and that was no lie.

August 20, 2013, DTE Energy Music Theatre: Rock titled his summer tour Your Best Night Ever, and it lived up to the name on the last of eight record-tying sellouts at DTE. To celebrate the achievement, as well as his "dear, sweet" mother's birthday, Rock brought Bob Seger, with whom he shared the record, onstage for a romp through "Old Time Rock and Roll." Prior to the DTE stand, Rock noted, "We probably could have done nine or ten [shows], but I was like, 'I think I'd rather be there with Kid Rock and Bob Seger together, the most sellouts.'"

# Cathouse
## The Cass Corridor's Last Great Band
*Thomas Trimble*

I got all nine emotions. Four directions.
Eighteen hells. All one Heaven.

—Cathouse, "Big Fast Out"

Like any music scene, Detroit has a long list of bands who almost made it. If you spend any time at all flipping through back issues of Detroit's alternative weekly, the *Metro Times*, you'll see profiles of long-forgotten bands described as "having what it takes." It's a familiar trope, but one that's less and less newsworthy as the whole notion of success in the music business is transformed by the collapse of the record industry and the eclipse of rock 'n' roll as pop culture's primary medium.

Every city has its own unwritten encyclopedia of genuinely gifted, exciting artists and bands who never made it but whose stories deserve to be told. Those histories are especially important for bands and artists who came of age before YouTube as fans' memories fade, cassette tapes disintegrate, and scratched CDs get thrown away or relegated to basement milk crates.

Cathouse is one of those Detroit stories worth telling. For me, and for many folks who followed Detroit rock during the 1990s, Cathouse was an extraordinary band. For readers who never saw Cathouse, that kind of claim may ring hollow. So while I'll spend the next few pages telling the Cathouse story and trying to capture the essence of their music, I'll also try to tell what's perhaps the more important and relevant story, which is the band's relationship with its fans. Indeed, one of the things that made Cathouse so special for so many people is the intense relationship they formed with the community of music lovers who called the band their own. It was a relationship that transcended the standard calculus of most rock scenes and went beyond rocking, partying, and hanging out. The diversity of Cathouse's audience is a large part of what makes their story unique. As Elizabeth Underwood, the singer of Cathouse, remembers, "At our shows, there'd be old hippies, young punks, sexy rocker chicks, greasy bad boys, men in drag, spinners in tie-dye, Rastafarians, black activists, college Greeks, and bikers in full regalia." Underwood's memories mirror my own, and, to this day, the Cathouse audience stands out from any I have ever seen during my time in Detroit.

At its most basic, Cathouse was a classic power trio fronted by an intense, dynamic female lead singer. Apart from a few early shake-ups, the consistent core of the band was singer Elizabeth Underwood, guitarist Eric Walworth, and bassist Jim Johnson. The band had a number of drummers, each of whom had a particular influence on the sound of the band during their relatively short career. Cathouse's last drummer, Patrick Pantano, also played in the late '80s Detroit postpunk band the Colors and currently plays with garage-rock stalwarts the Dirtbombs.

Drummers Aku Lahti and Tim Suliman also played stints with the group, with Lahti playing on the band's 1993 album *Falling* and Suliman on the band's locally distributed debut cassette.

Cathouse had numerous musical inspirations, from the Stones and Neil Young to the Clash, Jesus Lizard, and the Pixies. They were also associated with a strand of heavy Detroit/Ann Arbor bands beginning with the Laughing Hyenas and extending through to Wig and Mule, both of which enjoyed modest success in the rise of alternative rock during the 1990s. While the music of those bands helps explain Cathouse's musical foundations, none of their influences or inspirations adequately account for what Cathouse was able to become as a live act.

The landscape of Detroit rock and its various microscenes during the 1990s was connected to broader trends in rock and pop throughout North America and Europe, specifically the rise of grunge and garage. In my mind, Cathouse sits between those two movements on a kind of dead branch of Detroit's rock's family tree, and that partially explains why the band often falls through the cracks of Detroit rock lore. Readers might remember that Detroit garage legends the Gories released their debut LP *Houserockin'* in 1989, while the White Stripes released their self-titled debut ten years later in 1999. That record opened the door for the subsequent success of Detroit bands like the Von Bondies, the Dirtbombs, and the Go, through to current Detroit-based national acts like the Sights and Dale Earnhardt Jr. Jr.

According to Chris Varady, whose Detroit-based Nocturnal Records released records by Cathouse, 13 Engines, Wig, and the Orange Roughies, Cathouse had the potential to ride the wave created by the success of Nirvana's *Nevermind* and the rise of garage and grunge internationally. Varady's label released two records by Cathouse, 1993's *Falling* and 1996's *Sissy*, and even though the band received interest from a few major labels, the band's national break never arrived. After two records and over a hundred shows, Cathouse called it quits shortly after the release of *Sissy* in 1996.

According to Cathouse bassist Jim Johnson, the idea of Detroit's Cass Corridor had already become a bit of a myth when the band started gigging in 1988. He might be right, but as an eighteen-year-old Wayne State University undergrad from the suburbs, the "Corridor" certainly felt like a real scene when I started going to shows throughout metropolitan Detroit in the late 1980s. The "Corridor," named after the famous Michigan politician Lewis Cass and the avenue that bears his name, had long been associated with bohemian culture, fostered by the neighborhood's cultural and geographic association with Wayne State University. By the time I got to Wayne State in the fall of 1986, however, the Corridor connoted a rougher, complex mix of poverty, crime, addiction, politics, art, and—most important to the Cathouse story—rock 'n' roll.

The Corridor had a reputation distinct from Detroit's other rock scenes of the late '80s and '90s. Bands like the Layabouts and KURU didn't have good gear or good hair (if you call a mullet "good hair") like the bands from the city's northern suburbs. Bands from the Corridor tended to be more political and arty than the college-rock bands that would play nearby Hamtramck's rock clubs. Corridor bands also seemed to be less connected to Detroit's bigger venues and promoters, and as a result, they tended to stay close to home. It was rare to see them open for national acts in the city's larger, established venues. Instead, you'd be much more likely to see bands like Cathouse play at venues like Alvin's bar, located just off Wayne State's campus; the Old Miami, a homey but seedy watering hole catering to Vietnam vets; art galleries like 404 Willis; and former strip club the Gold Dollar, where the White Stripes made their now legendary debut in 1994.

In a *Detroit Metro Times* cover story on Cathouse written in April of 1994 that coincided with the release of their first album, *Falling*, music critic Thom Jurek recounted the band's origins. The group started shortly after Underwood and guitarist Walworth, who were a couple for a time, moved to Detroit from Pennsylvania and began writing songs. Bassist Jim Johnson, a friend and neighbor of Walworth's, started writing with the duo, and soon the outfit began playing local benefits, open-mic nights, and what Johnson describes as "twelve-bands-for-a-buck affairs." There were a number of drummers in those early days, but by the time the band released its first seven-song cassette in 1991, local drummer Tim Suliman had joined the group to complete the quartet. For its name, the new band took its moniker from the feline inhabitants of Underwood and Walworth's rented house, where the band practiced.

As Johnson now recounts, those early days of the band were almost exclusively focused on the art of creating music:

We got together to do something genuine without posturing or pretense. We all brought our own influences—old R&B, the Rolling Stones, '70s and '80s punk, Neil Young, Nick Cave, the Replacements—

and hoped the mix would be productive. Elizabeth had a developing poetic voice she wanted to be able to express, and Eric had already found a pretty distinctive guitar sound. Songwriting was pretty improvisational, and the mix of personalities on any given day could produce a wide variety of results, some really good, some not. If something really clicked, though, we could usually hold on to it and turn it into something credible—hopefully solid enough for it to be remembered at the next practice and ultimately worked into a set list somewhere.

While the band's early efforts focused on music, even their earliest shows demonstrated the ability to establish a connection with an audience. Much of that had to do with Underwood, who belted out her vocals from the front of the stage, usually with the microphone in her hand and the cord wrapped around her arm or neck. When she sang, she would often lock eyes with individual members of the audience. At the end of the song "Iron," for example, Underwood would repeatedly scream the question "Do you read me?" holding a person's gaze for entire phrases, simultaneously inviting and demanding connection. Underwood's lyrics were intensely personal, radiating pain, anger, and strength. Says Underwood, "I used to say I wanted to make people cry! Not by abusing them but by tapping into some shared experience of pain and grief and together, creating an outlet for it."

Underwood's charisma as a live performer was complemented by the sonic power of the musicians playing alongside her. Guitarist Eric Walworth played with his hair pulled into a long ponytail and dressed in an old white T-shirt and blue jeans. Walworth always played the same blond Telecaster through a frayed Marshall amplifier with a single distortion pedal on the floor in front of him. When Walworth played rhythm guitar, he would lean over his instrument and tap his foot while knifing his strumming arm's elbow into the air in time with the drummer's snare. When he launched into a solo, his head would tilt back or to one side. He never betrayed a rock star grimace; instead, Walworth's eyes would close as if being transported to some faraway place. Walworth's solos had a similar effect on listeners. For the solos on songs like "Oka," which closes *Sissy*, Walworth would often start slow and then build to a climax of crying bends and staccato breaks created by raking his pick across the strings of the guitar. As both bassist Jim Johnson and Nocturnal Records boss Chris Varady now attest, Walworth may have been one of the finest rock guitarists in recent Detroit history. Says Varady:

> In my studio experience, Eric was one of the easiest guitarists I've ever had the privilege of working with. As I listen back to those recordings years afterward, his contributions have become even more important in my eyes/ears. I still rewind to hear the middle-end part of "Oka" where he brings on that exhilarating guitar showcase. The song was asking for an oncoming storm, and he brought both the tornado and the quiet aftermath.

Varady also remembers bassist Jim Johnson as "one of the coolest bass players ever." Johnson's unique approach to the bass was characterized by a technique in which he would strike the strings of his guitar with the thumb of his right hand, similar to the technique of bass players like Flea from the Red Hot Chili Peppers. Instead of using his thumb to pull on the strings, however, which creates a distinctive popping sound, Johnson's adaptation of the technique produced a driving, percussive sound that was one of the hallmarks of the Cathouse sound, heard on songs like "Shot" from 1993's *Falling*.

I first saw Cathouse at a free show in the Cass Corridor sometime around 1991 at the Community Concert Series, a long-running, semimonthly event featuring music, poetry, and politics. The night I saw them play, it was obvious they had already established a sizable following among the Corridor community. Onstage, they played with a confidence and attitude that was instantly compelling. Underwood paced back and forth on the floor in front of the short stage. Her voice alternated between a defiant, raging howl and a quiet, almost pained whisper. The trio of guitarist Walworth, bassist Johnson, and drummer Suliman played a brand of punk blues that chugged behind Underwood like a gritty hybrid of the Stones and the Patti Smith Group.

Seeing a band you've never heard of for the first time is always strange; you try to make sense of what you're seeing and hearing. If the band gets your attention, you try your best just to soak up what it is you think they're trying to accomplish. It was like that for me the first time I saw Cathouse—until they played the one cover I recognized, "Bitch" from the Rolling Stones' *Sticky Fingers*. In Underwood's voice, the sexuality, aggression, and sneer of Jagger's lyrics took on an entirely new meaning. The band behind Underwood, meanwhile, played with a combination of cohesion and abandon that was simply impossible to ignore. Those in the audience, many of whom struck me as Cathouse regulars, were similarly entranced. Throughout the band's set, Underwood's gaze held both men and women under a kind of sexually and emotionally charged spell. Further back across the room, members of the audience locked into the rhythm of the band while others danced alone in the shadows.

From those earliest moments of seeing Cathouse play, I remember the audiences at Cathouse shows moving. There were many bands I saw during the '90s whose audiences hardly moved at all. Alternatively, some bands' audiences bobbed their heads or bounced one leg, and there were still others where only the girlfriends danced. But audiences at Cathouse shows vibrated, and for me that was part of the appeal of the band, their audience, and their shows. It was hard to not move at a Cathouse show, so when the rest of the world seemed frozen in a kind of slow motion, Cathouse shows guaranteed a physical and emotional release that made good on one of rock 'n' roll's most enduring promises.

Cathouse shows were passionate, often furious, ritualistic affairs. At Finney's Bar in Detroit, where bands would play with their backs to tall windows that faced Woodward Avenue, Underwood would sometimes sing to passersby through the glass or write lyrics in the condensation on the panes. Sometimes the band would argue onstage. Longtime fan Catherine Bresser remembers a Cathouse set during which Underwood laid on the stage for ten minutes or more, with audience members in varying states of confusion, worry, excitement, and empathy

for a singer—their singer—who regularly promised to crucify herself onstage. Today, Underwood says:

> The connection our fans had to us epitomized rock culture as I knew it, on the most basic level: going to see a band I loved was fun, there was an air of danger and sex to it. I never knew what was gonna happen in the grand scheme but I knew I was gonna rock, there'd be catharsis. From my perspective, that's what Cathouse fans came for—the things anyone goes to a show for. And I was aware of that from the start, mostly because even though I was onstage, I wanted the same things that I wanted when I was in an audience.

Cathouse's passionate, transformative performances inspired deep affection and loyalty among their fans, the remnants of which can still be heard in the words and voices of their most ardent admirers.

Catherine Bresser lived in Detroit for much of Cathouse's tenure. She now lives in Milwaukee and is a full-time mom, but her memories of Cathouse are still powerful touchstones for her relationship to Detroit and to music:

> The first time I saw Cathouse was in May 1991. It was the first show they played with Aku, and I was absolutely blown away by their sound and Elizabeth's intensity. I loved watching Elizabeth perform. She was mesmerizing and captivating. Her moodiness upset me at times, but her performances were so volatile, they kept me coming back. Sometimes she'd storm off in a huff or

throw things around, and other times she would send you to the moon. Some shows were awful and others sublime. Their shows were some of my favorite nights in my life.

I truly loved their music and still do. The Cathouse era was so special. The band was so important to me, and I thought their music was so powerful and excellent; I wish fervently they had caught on. Cathouse was my favorite band in an era where I thought there was a lot of outstanding music to listen to and see in Detroit. All the bands were friends with each other or related to each other in some way. I miss all that today. It was a special time for me, and Cathouse was a most special band.

Mikell Eiler is another Cathouse fan; he lived in Detroit for seven years during the 1990s and was a regular and frequent attendee of the band's shows. She first saw the band in 1991 at the annual Dally in the Alley street festival held in the neighborhood around Wayne State University, and like many Cathouse fans, her memories invoke the intoxicating draw of the group's collective persona and power:

Before the show, I saw Elizabeth intensely navigating the crowd in a bold-red velvet jumper with bright red lips, pale skin, and dark hair. She had fire in her eyes. I was very struck by her look and asked around until I found out who she was.

Soon after I saw Elizabeth for the first time, Cathouse played. I was thrilled by the music and the performance. Cathouse invoked every possible emotion in me. The music, the lyrics, and the performance were so awesome and intense. I fell in love. I was infatuated, and it didn't wear off.

Eiler established a personal relationship with the members of the band and their music. She says she saw Cathouse play over fifty times, and she credits them with having an important role in her development as a person: "The music and the way they performed was so beautiful and intense. I can't think of anything that made me more happy and inspired. I'm not a particularly emotional person, but somehow Cathouse shows never failed to bring me to the highest state of emotion and inspiration."

Cathouse's local fan base grew in both size and intensity after the release of their first album, *Falling*, and they soon began to broaden both their geographic reach and professional aspirations. Over the next five years, the band toured the well-worn trail of punk-rock bars between Detroit, Ann Arbor, Chicago, Milwaukee, Cleveland, and Pittsburgh. Touring took its toll, however, particularly on Underwood, whose singing style and persona were physically and emotionally demanding. During a grueling, six-week national tour in 1993, Underwood became seriously ill while on the road: "During the last week, I developed this weird internal bleeding that, upon coming home, I had to be hospitalized and have surgery for. My entire rib cage was full of blood, and I'd been ignoring the pain while powering through gigs, sleeping in rest-stops and eating gas-station food, just being a trooper and trying to keep everyone's morale up. The day I got home, I got myself to the hospital and was rushed into surgery that night. The whole ordeal laid me up for a month."

Touring is hard on independent bands and it took its toll on Cathouse. In addition to Underwood's harrowing illness, there is the story, which has become a local legend, of the destruction of the band's touring van. It happened just weeks after bassist Johnson had spent his entire savings to provide the band with reliable transportation for its increasingly long road trips. Johnson remembers it this way:

My GMC Sport cost me more money than any vehicle I'd ever owned—and I only had it for a few months before it went up in smoke.

We'd played a late show at Alvin's, and I was going to give Eric a ride home; we had to stop at a service station a block or so away on Woodward to get some gas. The van stalled in front of the pumps, and as I tried to restart it we heard a loud thump from the engine compartment. Smoke was quickly filling the area below the dash, a really bad sign, and when we opened the hood the whole engine compartment was blazing. The only fire extinguisher the station attendant could find didn't work, so we had to watch the fire grow. Finally, Eric said we ought to start pulling our gear out of the back, which we commenced to do as fast as we could while all the glass started exploding from the heat.

The electrical harness fused so the horn was blaring and lights flashing as we threw equipment out onto the pavement. Then we just stood and watched the whole thing

burn down to the chassis. I guess a fuel line detached or leaked onto the engine block; a spark produced somewhere must have set the whole thing burning.

The band soldiered on for a time, but after five years of shows, two albums, and a national tour, Cathouse decided to disband in 1996. Says Underwood: "We started the band because it was fun, and everything we'd done organically grew out of that. Then all of a sudden it felt like really hard work with very little reward. Resentments built, energy and passion lagged, and during that last year of Cathouse we endured a ton of physical, emotional, and economic challenges that would've killed the joy for just about anyone."

Today, the members of Cathouse live separated by thousands of miles and the varied paths their lives have taken. Shortly after the band's breakup, Elizabeth Underwood moved to New Orleans where she worked as office manager for acclaimed jazz photographer Herman Leonard. Underwood was uprooted by hurricane Katrina, and in the storm and its aftermath she lost her home and all of her personal belongings. After spending some time in Texas, she has since rebuilt her life in New Orleans and today works as a writer and artist. Underwood remembers her time in Cathouse with affection and pride: "I'm proud of what we accomplished and of our wonderful community for having been so committed and generous. We were lucky to be part of such an interesting, thriving phase of Detroit rock music. There were so many great bands around back then, each one unique and inspired, making records, touring, helping each other, hanging out— it was a creative and productive time, an amazing scene to be a part of. I'm humbled by it all and so grateful."

After Cathouse, Jim Johnson switched to guitar and played in the now defunct Detroit-based band the Come-Ons with drummer Patrick Pantano. Johnson is married to a former Cathouse fan and still lives in metropolitan Detroit where he works as an archivist. His memories of Cathouse mirror the compact, direct style of his stage persona: "For better or worse, we did what we did on our own and that seemed true to what our professional aspirations had been all along."

Eric Walworth lives with his wife in northern Michigan. He still plays guitar on a regular basis but hasn't played with a group since Cathouse. Most local bands near him are either cover bands designed to entertain tourists or metal outfits, neither of which fits Walworth's playing style or creative approach. Looking back at his time in Cathouse, he says, "For the most part, I look back on those days with fondness. We probably screwed up quite a few things along the way but at least we tried to follow those dreams for a time. All in all, it's positive memories for me."

Relistening to Cathouse's relatively small but powerful body of work brings back a flood of my own memories of one of Detroit's most underrated bands. Many of those memories are just fragments now, but in those moments of sight and sound and feeling, I trace the evolution of my personal definition of rock 'n' roll: part revival, part burlesque show, part grifter con. As a band, the members of Cathouse witnessed all of those extremes. For a moment, rock 'n' roll provided each of them with a kind of redemption, along with a glimpse of a particular sort of American dream, even as it slowly exhausted them. Like all great rock bands, their gift to their audience was letting us watch and listen to it all unfold.

# 7 HIP-HOP, DONUT TECHNO

GHETTOTECH,
S, AND
D'REAMS

# Frankly Speaking
## Awesome Dre's Outspoken Detroit
*Matt Deapo*

Hip-hop's golden age was an era of incalculable ingenuity and indeterminate length. Arguably born with Run-D.M.C.'s *Raising Hell* and buried with Biggie and 2Pac, it was broad enough to employ the entire recorded canon as its source material but petty enough to fracture in relation to substance and locality. Sticking to its guns, quite literally, California married itself to the eternal quest for "bitches and money," riding high on a wave of syrupy '70s massage-parlor funk. Alternately, New York waxed philosophical, mining jazz for its bountiful cache of sample material and incorporating Afrocentrism and absurdist humor into dexterous, grandiose rhyming patterns. On a smaller scale, Miami coasted by on speaker-blowing bass lines and the unfathomable power of a bawdy limerick, unconcerned with western animosity or northeastern intellectualism.

Initially without rap-scene representation, Detroit's late '80s renown stemmed more from reports of homicide, arson, and crack addiction than musical innovation. With the closure of city-based factories starting in the 1950s and suburban migration by corporation and private citizens alike, Detroit suffered a staggering decrease in urban population and viable employment. Left in the wake of this mass exodus was an unemployed community trapped under a pile of industrial waste and mounting debt.

Author Ze'ev Chafets surveyed the scene in his *New York Times* article "The Tragedy of Detroit": "Detroit today is a genuinely fearsome-looking place. Most of the neighborhoods appear to be the victims of bombardment—houses burned and vacant, buildings crumbling, whole city blocks overrun with weeds and the carcasses of discarded automobiles." The faintest glimmer of hope flickered with each Pistons championship and Mayor Coleman Young's integration of the Detroit Police Department, but corruption often accompanies fame and power, usually at the expense of the disenfranchised. What Detroit needed was a voice that stood in stark contrast to the status quo, one that would eloquently and forcefully expose the truth and italicize a renewed interest in education and social justice. Awesome Dre was that voice.

Leaning too close to the social consciousness of East Coast rap to ever make it as a gangster, but playing too rough to fit in with the Native Tongues posse, Andre Acker can be a bit of a paradox, one that never willingly acquiesces to the confines of hip-hop's caste system. It's through this dichotomy, this push and pull between intellect and brute force, that he generates a compelling narrative—one that investigates both sides of a significant social issue and struggles to forge a path to the solution. Taking so much to task can lead to moments of contradiction or half-formed thoughts that often result in fits of rage or bursts of obscenity, but this fiery demeanor and affront to conventional morals are what make his writing so brilliant and significant. The contrast perfectly embodies a city struggling for an identity, and his fiercely independent thinking is the spark that started a fire, resulting in a multiracial, eclectic, and outspoken hip-hop movement.

Joining the navy fresh out of high school, Acker accumulated confidence in the service, battle-rapping with his fellow recruits in their spare time and honing break-dancing moves that he'd been rehearsing since his pre-teens. With the morale of his crewmen behind him, he got the nerve to take his writing seriously, starting a collaborative known as the Hardcore Committee and signing a deal with a chic independent label known as Priority Records. His debut LP, *You Can't Hold Me Back*, boasted a tenacious demeanor and chilly aggression, ascending to number 52 on *Billboard*'s R&B/hip-hop chart and generating coverage on BET and *Yo! MTV Raps*.

Despite growing acclaim from outside the city, Dre maintained a local presence, refusing to relocate his team to Los Angeles (home base of labelmates N.W.A.) and opting instead to develop Michigan's fledgling rap culture and film the video for his LP's eponymous song at the Latin Quarters. The homegrown clip bubbles over with communal goodwill and the juiciest bits of Average White Band's "Picking Up the Pieces," generating a retro sense of enthusiasm and the buzzy euphoria of a house party. Dre even indulges in the hyperactive, choreographed dance numbers, nearly keeling over as he struggles to enunciate his methodical punchlines.

Lyrically, Awesome Dre can morph a string of insults into a deft bouquet of graceful syllables. He's tightly wound and often as gritty as the cracked Detroit pavement beneath his feet, but don't let the stern, wizened stance distract from the philological stratagem present in each stanza. Complicating each bar, either to challenge his craft or separate himself from the pack, Dre forces in supplementary units of language, mastering the art of internal rhyme and burnishing the dustiest synonyms from his vast mental thesaurus (*Stradivarius* instead of violin, *terrapin* instead of turtle).

Playing provocateur is also part of Dre's elaborate game, as best captured in *You Can't Hold Me Back*'s unsubtle sleeve art, which depicts the moments prior to Kool Moe Dee and LL Cool J's execution at the Schoolcraft Avenue railroad crossing. Though the beef is obviously for show and Dre's violent side is a mere masquerade, the vividness of the depiction allows a certain verisimilitude to seep into the writing, making passages that ruminate over removed organs and homicidal inclination seem matter-of-fact.

The song "Frankly Speaking" is the point where the purely fictional is exchanged for the literal, taking to task the "scurrilous" apathy in Detroit, the hypocrisy of the rap cognoscenti, opponents of free speech, and television's affront to human empathy. Complex issues are tackled in an even-tempered fashion resulting in a remarkable clarity of vision, one hopeful enough to envision both a compromise between Detroit's inharmonious ethnic groups and an educated-youth movement captivated by knowledge instead of passive forms of "entertainment."

Challenging the system from within, the music video for "Frankly Speaking" is audacious enough to satirize the strength of television's influence by re-creating its worst-case scenario. Brainwashed by an endless stream of potent imagery, a teen draws his father's pistol from an end table and aims the barrel at his brother's head. The video is confrontational, despite bordering on the paradoxical; it symbolically counters mindless levity with a much-needed dollop of gravity, in essence, fighting fire with fire.

The video goes on to show Dre opposing civil disobedience and invoking force in the face of adversity, fearlessly storming radio stations, newspapers, and classrooms in the name of truth and equality. It's particularly telling to see him rhyme in front of Robert Graham's *Monument to Joe Louis*, an outdoor sculpture resembling Louis's extended arm and fist, symbolically delivering a fatal blow to racial injustice and ignorance. Mirroring Joe Louis's significance is a near impossible task, but Dre aspires to make an impact, stressing a thirst for knowledge and renewed morality that answers a question posed in the video's prologue: "What does rap really stand for?"

"Committing Rhymes" further pontificates on civil concerns. Acker himself elaborated: "I was speaking for myself metaphorically about basic stereotypes, racial profiling, racism, fame, privilege, and such." As usual, he refuses to take injustice on piecemeal, hitting the mark more often than not, particularly when defining the line between "crime" and "rhyme." Dre expounds on his own experiences with authority figures and how they correlate his outspoken nature on the microphone to the potential for illicit behavior. It's this "guilty until proven innocent" attitude that fuels his venom toward the supposedly moral and logical few, those unhip to his status as a veteran, concerned citizen, and taxpayer.

Four years separate Dre's debut from its follow-up, and the frustration of wasted time and unpaid royalties are palpable on *A. D.'s Revenge*, a caustic and spiritual explication of earlier ideas but with far less patience than the artist's earlier effort. Brandishing an automatic weapon and channeling everyone from Malcolm X to Robert Mapplethorpe, Dre's presence in the title track's video screams reinvention, both politically and sonically. The music abandons funk grooves for "raggamuffin" hip-hop and the low, textural atmosphere of Jamaican dub. This expansion of horizons has coaxed out a heightened complexity, exemplified by the symbolic sample-work on "Psychological Warfare" and the astute social commentary of "What Is Legal?" and "Dis Is Babylon."

Castigating the fraudulent nature of mass media, Dre once again weaponizes art against itself, brilliantly nicking Stevie Ray Vaughan's take on Jimi Hendrix's "Voodoo Child" riff, creating a sonic parallel to his commentary on white appropriation of black culture on "Psychological Warfare."

It's a reiteration of previous notions intensified by an awakening of emotion, galvanized by a newfound affinity for the Nation of Islam and an awareness of increasingly bleak conditions in black America, which he likens to the biblical Babylon. The opening of Dre's metaphorical third eye has inspired an acute skepticism that infiltrates his writing and draws parallels between slavery, genocide at home and abroad, and a growing consumerism that only feeds into the master-slave mentality.

It's an intellectually high-minded dialogue, particularly for popular music, but one that Andre Acker was willing to initiate without the support of a scene or the comfort of commercial success. Twenty-two years after Andre began his work, Detroit's rap community is in full bloom, and Dre's fingerprints can be found on every document, his sincerity seeping into Eminem's brazen boundary pushing, Guilty Simpson's candid street commentary, and Danny Brown's loquacious lyricism. As Dre said to me, "The realness is what you feel, be it fact or fiction," and Awesome Dre's rhyming was so realistic that it made fits of reverie feel like surveillance footage.

# Eminem in 2002

*Greil Marcus*

Last year, the great basketball player and famed uncensored mouth Charles Barkley addressed himself to the Eminem question. "You know this world is fucked up when the best rapper's white and the best golfer's black," he said. Unless he said, as another of the countless printed versions of his statement had it, "America is crazy. The best . . ." You could just as well claim that if lines meant to keep certain people in their places have not only been crossed but erased, it's proof that America is anything but crazy—and it's intresting that Eminem, another famed uncensored mouth, has never made a claim like Barkley's. In *The Eminem Show*, his solipsistic extravaganza of this year, you can find him comparing himself to Elvis Presley—not to proclaim himself the new king of anything but to denigrate both Elvis and himself. He's the "fake" king, Eminem says, just like Elvis: no matter what the talent or drive, without that white skin, forget it.

Eminem may have made a fool of himself with his *Eminem Show* hit "Without Me"—the world very nearly dried up and blew away from boredom in the time between *The Marshall Mathers LP* and *The Eminem Show*, he says (as we all know, it's not as if anything else happened between the summer of 2000 and the summer of 2002)—but no one as smart as he is plays with Elvis Presley casually. Elvis is a bomb. By defusing it, Eminem gets to inhabit that fabled body without, perhaps, catching its disease.

Photo by Doug Coombe.

Much separates Eminem from Elvis. Eminem, as Charles Barkley says, can rap, and Elvis probably could not have. Elvis could sing, and Eminem, as he proves conclusively on *The Eminem Show*, cannot. Elvis was beautiful. Eminem is not. Elvis is dead, and Eminem is alive. Most of all, Eminem has the example—the disaster—of Elvis behind him, and Elvis didn't.

In her story "Nineteen Fifty-five," Alice Walker tells the tale of an Elvis-like singer and the song that made his career—the song of a black woman much like Willie Mae Thornton who first recorded a song much like Thornton's "Hound Dog." The Elvis figure's guilty knowledge that the song can never be his, and that, worse, he can never truly understand it, destroys him. Eminem's first movie, *8 Mile*, directed by Curtis Hanson—who has already made two movies, *L.A. Confidential* and *Wonder Boys*, better than the good books they were based on— opens this month, and the picture *8 Mile* is alive to Eminem's presence, and he is alive to the picture, seeming to withdraw from the camera even as he pulls its eye toward him. Taking the viewer through a few days in the life of a white Detroit rapper in a black milieu—a young man in a world where rhyming is ordinary language, the way everybody talks; a young man whose attempts to step out of oblivion are at best wary and at worst, and most believably, terrified—Eminem gives a performance that is all gravity. When the movie ends, there is a sense that it has, in fact, ended—that the movie has caught its own story. But then "Lose Yourself" begins to play under the closing credits, and in an instant it blows the film away. The music dissolves the movie, reveals it as a lie, a cheat, as if it were made not to reveal but to cover up the seemingly

bottomless pit of resentment and desire that is the story's true source. Again and again the song all but blows up in the face of the man who's chanting it, Eminem is lost in his rhymes until suddenly people are shouting at him from every direction and the music jerks him down into the chorus, where he escapes in turn. The piece builds into crescendos of power, climbing ladders of refusal and willfulness step by step, rushing nothing, never reaching the top because it is the music itself that has put the top so high. As with Jerry Lee Lewis's "Whole Lotta Shakin' Goin' On," Aretha Franklin's "I Never Loved a Man (the Way I Love You)," the Miracles' "The Love I Saw in You Was Just a Mirage," Bob Dylan's "Like a Rolling Stone," Grandmaster Flash and the Furious Five's "The Message," the Rolling Stones' "Gimmie Shelter," or Nirvana's "Smells Like Teen Spirit," it's one of those moments in pop music that throws off everything around it, offering a new challenge, proving that, now, you, whoever you are, can say anything, and with a force no one can gainsay. The cutting contest at the end of *8 Mile* is nothing compared to the cutting contest "Lose Yourself" throws down on pop music as such.

Though he may for the moment be too modest or too canny to say it, Eminem is much more like Bob Dylan than Elvis Presley. That is to say that, in "Lose Yourself" perhaps most of all but all over his career, he is in love with the momentum of language itself, that when his words are ringing, their momentum becomes his, and that when that happens he is likely to find himself at least one step ahead of anybody else.

# Eminem
## A Detroit Story
*Bill Holdship*

When it comes to Eminem, a lot of backstory probably isn't necessary, especially in Detroit. But, really, that's pretty much true anywhere in the civilized Western world (and I'd be surprised if he hasn't been used by al-Qaeda or some organization like that somewhere along the way as a symbol of Western decadence; God knows he's been used as a symbol and example of such in his *own* country enough times since he became a pop superstar and phenomenon).

But, I mean, hell, my *mom* knows who Eminem is. Five years away from the spotlight is a long time, sometimes a lifetime, in modern pop culture. And that's how long it's been since he's released an album. During that time, however, *8 Mile* seemed to be playing almost constantly on cable TV. His music was still being played everywhere. And just last year, *Vibe* magazine, in a poll, named him the "Best Rapper Alive," which was just one more accolade the Grammy and Oscar winner could place alongside *Rolling Stone*'s proclamation that Eminem is "the biggest rapper in history." Yep. Dude's a *superstar* in the truest sense of the term, a real working-class hero, as John Lennon once put it.

And he's from Detroit, something the man born Marshall Mathers thirty-six years ago never lets anybody forget—something he actually celebrates. He even appeared in a PSA about Detroit's woes and beauty during the recent network-televised Final Four basketball tournament.

Despite the media portraying him as the devil at various points in his career—just the latest in a long line of antiheroes here to steal your children's souls and minds—there always seemed to be something more just below the surface with this guy. To summarize what an anonymous poster recently wrote on a music chat board I visit, Slim Shady—Eminem's musical alter ego—is like a Shakespearean fool; there's often a lot of wisdom, even a genius, underneath his apparently mad ravings. In fact, in many ways, it could be argued that he was the first to bring a humanistic, even literary, side to hip-hop that wasn't really there before—less braggadocio and a lot more confessional technique, probably more of the latter than any rapper before him or since.

Behind all the violent talk and "offensive" humor, there was also an obvious sensitive side at play. It's very evident in his autobiographical *8 Mile* character, of course. It's also there in the way he talks about his children in interviews. There's a very poignant story in his autobiography, *What I Am*, published late last year, about how ashamed he was as a child in the lunch line at school when the other kids would overhear that he was a welfare student who got free lunches from the state. Behind the swagger and cockiness, this is someone who has obviously suffered, someone who knows what it's like to be picked on, to be the underdog. Maybe that's why he was accepted by all cultures and ethnicities in the hip-hop world (and that couldn't have been easy, particularly coming in the wake of Vanilla Ice, who almost single-handedly destroyed any inroads the Beastie Boys had made for white emcees).

In case you haven't heard yet—and you'd almost have to be a hermit with no access to the Internet or any media to have *not* heard—Slim Shady returns next Tuesday, May 19, with a new album titled *Relapse*. The record finds him working with Dr. Dre as his producer again; reports from the few people who've heard it suggest it's a return to Eminem's earlier style and form. (There's supposed to be a second album, *Relapse 2*, coming out before the end of this year as well.) Three tracks from the disc have already hit the streets—"Crack a Bottle" (featuring 50 Cent, Dre and Eminem's protégé), the grand "We Made You," and the just-released "horrorcore" tune "3 A.M."

The new tune should get the good old controversy going for the artist again, although the hilarious video for "We Made You"—which lampoons and then totally destroys modern pop culture "icons"—already achieved that when Fox News host Bill O'Reilly condemned Eminem for the video's portrayal of Sarah Palin, and then attacked the media for not taking the rapper to task for his treatment of the former Republican vice-presidential candidate. "Eminem is obviously on an obscene rant about Sarah Palin," O'Reilly said during one of his broadcasts. "Totally obscene. Totally inappropriate. Nothing good about it. The video means nothing," the old blowhard continued. "It plays before kids who are confused. But the hypocrisy and the dishonesty of the media does mean something in this country. It is out of control and is demonstrable by this." (Of course, Bill O'Reilly—or any Fox News figure, for that matter—calling the hypocrisy and dishonesty of the media into question should be an irony missed by no one.)

In Eminem's five years away from the spotlight, he suffered his fair share of tragedy and setbacks. His best friend and hip-hop mentor, Proof, was shot and killed in a senseless argument outside a Detroit nightclub. His often-volatile marriage to his wife, Kim, ended in divorce (last year's autobiography indicated that they're now on good terms, raising their daughters together). And the title of the new album refers, of course, to his recent battles with substance abuse and addiction. It took two stays in rehab for him to finally kick the habit. As he writes in a first-person narrative for *Vibe* magazine in a cover story that's also being published this week: "Now that I understand that I'm an addict, I definitely have compassion for my mother. I get it."

Truthfully, we at the *Metro Times* never seriously believed that this interview would take place. There was reportedly some bad blood between Eminem and this publication in the past, long before I got here. But as far as I'm concerned, Eminem is one of the greatest brands and exports Detroit has going for it these days. So we lobbied hard. And two weeks before the release of *Relapse*, Marshall Mathers, Slim Shady, gave us a call late one chilly Thursday afternoon.

*Metro Times*: Since I've returned to Detroit, I've become an even bigger fan of yours, especially due to your pride in the city. John Smyntek, the gossip columnist at the *Detroit Free Press*, wrote in his farewell column that no major Detroit personality had more potshots thrown at them than you did over the years. And yet, you have remained loyal and dedicated to this city. There are other hometown stars who have nothing good to say about Detroit at this point. You could live anywhere in the world. So what is it about Detroit that's so close to your heart?

*Eminem*: Oh, man. Well, I do think, one, I'm a creature of habit. You know? I'm just so comfortable here. It's where I grew up. It's where I basically spent all my teenage years. And it's just that I don't live too far from where I spent those years. I can always go back and revisit my old neighborhood any time I want. And stuff like that is very important. Even if I just want to drive by one of my old houses or something. You know? Just drive by and look at places where I came up. It brings back memories for me. And there are a lot of memories I have here in Detroit. I'm just so comfortable here, I guess.

*Metro Times*: I've read that *Relapse*, the new LP, harks back to a simpler time for you. I'm curious as to whether nostalgia played any role in the creation of the new album, particularly nostalgia for Detroit?

*Eminem*: Hmm. Nostalgia . . . [*laughs*]

*Metro Times*: In the sense of looking back at your past?

*Eminem*: In the sense of looking back at my past . . . I'm sorry. Can you repeat the question?

*Metro Times*: Sure. I've read that the new album, *Relapse* . . .

*Eminem*: Oh! OK, I get what you're saying. Yeah. Well, conceptually and musically, the new album does go back. I don't know if it's nostalgia but the record probably feels like maybe somewhere along the lines of the first two records. You know? I guess in that sense of nostalgia or whatever, it's like it's kinda going back to the feel of those two records—*The Slim Shady LP*, and *The Marshall Mathers LP*.

*Metro Times*: What are your feelings about the current plight of Detroit's auto heritage and blue-collar workers, both part of your lineage? And how do you see the city's future?

*Eminem*: Well, I don't really know how I see the future. I mean, I really wish I had an answer for what's going on here right now, you know? It really is kinda complicated for me when I look at it. But it just kinda pisses me off a little bit when people, like, I guess, refer to this city or look at this city as a whole. When you look at the crumbling auto industry . . . [*sighs*] you see and hear people blaming the auto executives and shit like that for mismanaging the companies and, you know, putting money in their own pockets and taking too big of salaries and shit like that. But I don't know if people outside of Detroit realize, OK, yeah, that *did* happen and, yeah, they made some bad decisions. But in the long run, who is it affecting? Well, the *real* people of this city who are losing their jobs. They're the ones who are being affected by this daily. It's a really complicated situation because everyone is just pointing fingers right now. But the truth is it's fucking up the lives of *real* people here. You know what I mean?

*Metro Times*: This might be too lofty of a question, but what role, if any, would you like to play in the city's future? Or do you think that's beyond your concerns?

*Eminem*: Well, I don't know that it's beyond my concerns. But I don't really know how to answer that or what role I'd like to play in this city. That, that . . . it's a little . . .

*Metro Times*: Yeah, I understand. It does seem, though, that music is still one of the few Detroit exports that people care about. And you are a Detroit institution. People can't think Eminem without thinking Detroit. So at least that's a positive.

*Eminem*: Yeah. Well, hopefully, that's a good association. I guess it is.

*Metro Times*: Even though the album harks back to your earlier stuff and maybe better times, during the last couple of years, there's been a lot of pain in your life. Proof's death. Your drug problems. There's an old cliché that says pain is the best and truest teacher. Have you learned anything important from the pain you've experienced since the last record?

*Eminem*: Well, I don't know that I've learned anything. . . . Well, you know, I guess I've actually learned quite a bit. As far as Proof passing away, I've gotten a little better at dealing with it. I guess as time goes by, you get a little better at dealing with something like that. And I've certainly learned from my own experiences with addiction. I don't know if this is gonna answer the question for you or not—but I've learned that you certainly can't get sober just because everyone else wants you to. You have to want to do it yourself. You know what I mean? When I first went into rehab, I kinda felt like I was doing it just because everyone else was ready for me to get sober. But I wasn't. And that is why I relapsed when I came out of treatment. When I came out of rehab. And it was because I just wasn't ready. I had to actually *be* ready, mentally, to say, "I'm done with this now. I've had enough."

In response to losing Proof, I've also just learned that no matter what—no matter how much I want to beat myself up over what happened, the wish that I could have done something or have been there or done something to change the course of what happened—nothing that I do or say or wish is gonna bring Proof back. So I've just kinda finally come to that realization. I don't know if I can ever totally accept his death. But I'm certainly getting better at coping with it.

You know, just a couple of days ago was pretty rough for me. When I'm doing something like getting back into performing again and shit like that—you know going onstage again and stuff like that—it just feels really empty. Those are the days when I *really* miss him. So, you know, I do still have my days with it. I have good days and bad days with it. But I'm certainly getting a little better at coping with the loss.

*Metro Times*: Some people have suggested that Proof's death was, in some ways, the end of classic Detroit hip-hop as we knew it. Or at least it shifted things into a more fragmented hip-hop scene. Do you think that's true?

*Eminem*: Well, I mean losing Proof . . . [*sighs*] Proof was so much to Detroit in so many different ways. And he meant so much to so many different people in so many different ways. Proof was like . . . I heard someone describe Proof once as like a comet. And he was like a comet because you only get to see it once in a lifetime. That made a lot of sense to me. Because it's true. You know, there will only be one Proof. And Proof was so much to this city in so many different ways. His spirit. In many ways, he just kinda *was* Detroit.

*Metro Times*: One of the things that was interesting in your autobiography is when you're discussing the topic of guns and you wrote: "Guns are bad." I'm wondering if you're happy to see hip-hop and rap in general kind of moving away from the "gangsta" element.

*Eminem*: Um, well, do you think it is moving away from that? I guess, in a sense, it does kinda feel like that, doesn't it?

*Metro Times*: Yeah. And I think you're partially responsible for that because you brought a more humanistic sense to the form.

*Eminem*: Well, that would be good. But for me, personally, I mean, I'm done with guns. You know what I mean? They certainly never ever brought anything good into my life. Especially with my own family and our history [of suicide] and shit like that. And my own personal experience with guns. And then you lose your best friend to guns. . . . No. Guns are just bad news.

*Metro Times*: I thought it was really good that you put that in the book so that kids read that. Are there any contemporary Detroit artists that you're into?

*Eminem*: Well, honestly. . . . Actually, I've been hearing a lot about . . . Black Milk.

*Metro Times*: Yeah, he's good.

*Eminem*: Yeah. I just recently heard a song . . . let me see, like last week, I think it was. But I haven't had a chance to really listen to a lot lately. It's only in the last couple of weeks that I stepped away from everything and put the pen down. So I've been like trying to get back into recent music. Because when I'm in work mode—when I'm actually writing lyrics and working on an album—I don't really listen to anybody else's records. That's just because I don't want to subconsciously take a flow or something from someone else, you know what I mean? I still want to make sure I sound like no one else when I rap. So I purposely stayed away a little bit from what's been going on in hip-hop. And I'm trying to play catch-up right now, especially with Detroit hip-hop. So it's not really fair for me to give you a good answer on that as of right now. In other words, I might need a couple of more weeks to listen and

then I'll be able to give a better answer on that.

*Metro Times*: I heard that you were in [the Eastpointe record store] Melodies & Memories a few weeks ago and that you bought a whole bunch of CDs. Someone said like $3,000 worth. I thought that was really cool when I heard that. You're giving back to the mom-and-pop stores, which is really cool, and you're supporting other people's music.

*Eminem*: Oh, yeah. Yeah, I went in there . . . let me think . . . that was really more like four or five months ago, actually.

*Metro Times*: Oh, OK.

*Eminem*: What I did was I bought a whole bunch of CDs, right? I bought like everything that was new. Everything that had just come out. And then I never got a chance to listen to it! So I've been taking like an album every day, a new CD with me every day. And then I put it in the car so I can listen to it on my ride to and from the studio. And I'm totally trying to play catch-up that way.

So it's really funny that you bring that up because all those CDs . . . well, most of them have literally been sitting inside my CD drawers unopened since then. And I'm just now taking like one out a day and trying to play catch-up.

*Metro Times*: When you say you bought all new stuff, was it just hip-hop or was it a wide variety of stuff?

*Eminem*: Uh . . . probably just hip-hop.

*Metro Times*: A lot of the early press for *Relapse* is claiming that it's "a return to form." I even recently saw a headline that read: "Can Eminem Save Hip-Hop?" How does that sit with you? Do you think that's a little bit too much pressure?

BILL HOLDSHIP

357

*Eminem*: Yeah! I'm mean, like, how can *I* save hip-hop? Hip-hop hasn't gone anywhere [*laughs*]! I mean, you know. Hip-hop is hip-hop. I don't know. I certainly wouldn't want the pressure of trying to be a hip-hop savior or anything like that. I'm just now back at a point where I'm having fun again with rap. You know what I mean? Because for a few years there, I kinda lost my way in that sense. I kinda forgot how to have fun with it. And I'm just now learning how to do that again. So I am having fun with writing songs and recording and shit like that. I'm having fun again with music so, yeah, but I'm not out to save it. . . .

*Metro Times*: Well, you know, it has been important to other artists who were at the same level of phenomenal superstardom that you achieved. Michael Jackson and Axl Rose are two of the examples where they needed to create something that's as big as what they created in the past and it drove both of them insane. Does that really matter to you at this point in time? Maintaining that same level of stardom? Or are you just in it more for your art at this point?

*Eminem*: That's exactly why I'm in it. I mean, you pretty much just answered your own question with that. I guess I'm just at a point right now where I'm content. My life is different now, as far as, like, trying to compete with anyone else or trying to be anything other than an artist. I just want to put it out there and let people hear the music.

*Metro Times*: That's great. Since I haven't heard the album yet—I guess hardly anybody's heard the album except the cuts that have been released—what are you proudest of on this new album? And was it hard to get back into the groove after five years away?

*Eminem*: Well, I'm actually proud of everything on this record, every song that's on there. Otherwise, I guess I wouldn't have put them on the record! But to answer the second question, yeah, I think that it was hard. The hardest thing for me is that I went through, like, a two-year period where I had writer's block. I literally couldn't write anything. And if I did write something and then recorded it, it was never good enough. I would sit down and listen to it over and over again, trying to find something good about it. And it just felt to me like . . . well, I always had the reaction of "Uh, this is *not* me!" I mean, it certainly wasn't up to my own standards that I had set for myself. But I started to come out of the writer's block somewhere around June and July of last year. It wasn't that it was that hard. I think I had to teach myself again. I think I had to actually relearn how to write songs again. And so I was doing little exercises to come out of that writer's block, like writing a new rhyme a day and trying to do little exercises, like mental things to just get me out of it. But right around June and July, when I started coming up with the *Relapse* concept, things started to click. I kinda knew what I was gonna talk about. I was done with the drugs and everything else, and I got to a point where I was OK with talking about that part of my life. And so I think it just kinda morphed into its own thing. I felt I could have fun with it. So from that point on, it wasn't really hard anymore. It was just fun.

*Metro Times*: That's the key. That's great. The new "We Made You" video is one of the most hilarious fucking things I've seen in a long time. The song itself is great—but the video made me laugh. It's almost like you're bringing about a rebirth of the music video. But I think there's deeper stuff there.

You tell me if I'm reading too much into it—but in the past, Eminem, especially the Slim Shady character, was always painted as this villain in pop culture. And yet in this video, you're mocking all these current iconic "heroes" in modern culture. But it's like these lame idiots are the heroes and icons of today. And it's like, "Well, who are the real villains here?" Or am I reading too much into it?

*Eminem*: Maybe you're not. Because I wanted to be like a villain in the video. Well, put it this way—the original video treatment was for me to kinda be a serial killer and just going around and knocking off all these current pop stars. But there wasn't really a way to put that into a format. I mean, Kim Kardashian does get tossed into a wood chipper, but that was pretty much as far as we could go, the most we could get away with.

But like even Portia [de Rossi], Ellen DeGeneres's wife—like charley-horsing her in the leg. You know, there's only so much you can do. So we couldn't really just paint a portrait of me being like this like pop star serial killer, which was the original concept. But, you know, for the most part, I'm probably going to go back to being the villain again.

*Metro Times*: You portray Elvis Presley in the video. It seems like he's one of the people who you're really not making fun of. And, of course, you refer to Elvis in your song "Without Me." I may be wrong about this, but it seems like you may identify with him a little bit. Is that the case? Are you an Elvis fan at all?

*Eminem*: Um, no. I never was really an Elvis fan. I'll tell you one thing, though. One respect I do have for that guy was that . . . well, obviously he was a great artist but I was just never really into his music. But

I'll tell you something—that motherfucker could dance! When I was trying to learn that "Jailhouse Rock" shit [for the video], I was like "Man, this fuckin' guy could dance!"

*Metro Times*: So who have you learned the most from in your life? And is there anybody's career that you look to for support and insight at this point in time?

*Eminem*: [*pause*] Um, well, Elton John. I talk to Elton a lot. We became friends and I talk to him about things, careerwise. And he had a substance-abuse problem in the past. So when I first wanted to get sober, I called him and spoke to him about it because, you know, he's somebody who's in the business and can identify and relate to the lifestyle and how hectic things can be. He understands like the pressure and any other reasons that you wanna come up with for doing drugs, you know.

Me and him have had similar lives and stuff. So I reached out to him and told him, "Look, I'm going through a problem and I need your advice." I also talked to T.I. a lot and, you know, we exchanged advice.

*Metro Times*: How's he handling all that's going on with him now? Going to prison for a year would be tough. Is he doing OK?

*Eminem*: Well, to be honest with you, we haven't really had an in-depth discussion about that. Just because when I was talking to him, I don't know if the conversation was—how can I say it?—I didn't know for sure if it was going to be monitored, when he first got into the legalities and everything, when he first got into the trouble he got in. But I would call him and just make sure that he was keeping his head up. But I really didn't want to say anything to him about the situation he was going through at

359

that time, just in case his calls were being monitored or anything like that. So we never really had an in-depth discussion about it, but every time I talked to him, he seemed to be taking it, I guess, as good as somebody can. For what's happened to him, I mean he's, um . . . you know he's, uh . . . Man, I'm looking for the word but I can't even find it. He's certainly being a man about it. He's being a trouper.

*Metro Times*: It's interesting that you mention Elton John because one of my favorite parts in your book is when you write about doing the duet with him at the Grammys right after the "gay" controversy. One of the best sentences in the book is: "What people do in their bedrooms is their own business." I just wish the fucking Republicans would learn that. A few years ago, right before Bush went in for the second time, you did that video with George W. Bush in it. And in the new video, you lampoon Sarah Palin. Have you ever thought about getting more political? And what did you think about that nitwit Bill O'Reilly condemning you for the Palin thing?

*Eminem*: Well, as far as getting too political, I've never really been that kind of guy. Like, I mean, I've always stood up for freedom of speech. I'm definitely a strong advocate of shit like that. But I've never really tried to get too political. I know I wrote that song—the "Mosh" song was kinda geared toward that. But that was just because I fucking hated Bush. You know? Just anything I could do to help try to get that guy out of office was a good thing. And . . . what was the second part of the question? Oh, yeah, Bill O'Reilly.

*Eminem*: Um . . . well, that guy's a turd.

*Metro Times*: [*laughs*] I hate him . . .

*Eminem*: I don't know of a better way to put it than to just say he's a turd.

*Metro Times*: It seems also in the book that we saw a more grown-up or adult element to Eminem. Controversy is still obviously going to hound you because that's just the nature of the beast. The O'Reilly thing proves that. But I'm wondering if Eminem, the father and the humanist, has finally caught up with Eminem the artist?

*Eminem*: I don't know about that. You might wanna listen to the record first [*laughs*]!

*Metro Times*: OK [*laughs*]. Well, you know, there are so many parts of the book that are just genuinely touching. They reveal you have a genuinely good heart—like when you and Proof helped that little girl who was stranded in the airport. Stuff like that. I guess what I'm wondering is if there's a change in image. I just read yesterday that you are going to be in a new movie this summer, and you can't say anything about it, but that it's a Disney movie. So, I thought, well, "That has got to be Eminem the dad coming into focus there."

*Eminem*: No, it's not a Disney movie [*laughs*]!

*Metro Times*: OK. Well, then let's forget that [*laughs*].

*Eminem:* I was just being sarcastic [*laughs*]. Yeah, I'm alongside Hannah Montana in my new short film!

*Metro Times*: Yeah, Slim Shady and Hannah Montana! You've been like the most confessional rapper in history. A lot of your real personal life has ended up in your lyrics. Now, I know Slim Shady is like an alter ego and there's definitely bits of Marshall Mathers in there. But would you agree that Slim Shady is a little bit like the hip-hop version of

Alice Cooper? And what is your relationship with the Slim Shady character now after all these years?

*Eminem*: Well, as far as him being like an Alice Cooper character or whatever like you said, well, it kinda is like that in a sense. He's this character I created through music, just like an actor or actress would create a character when they're on the screen. So it does give me the excuse and freedom to then say a lot of fucked-up shit [*laughs*]. You know what I mean?

*Metro Times*: Yeah.

*Eminem*: And at the end of the day, it's like a mix and I can certainly mix in the sense of humor that I have—the kind of warped, twisted, and distorted view that I have on things and the sense of humor I have. So it really is just a character I'm playing and I guess if you mix me and Slim Shady together . . . I mean, it's a persona. Do I really think that way in real life about everything I talk about? No, I don't. But does my mind work in a way where I can think of some fucked-up shit and just kinda blurt it out? Yes. Definitely. You know?

*Metro Times*: Right. It is interesting on that front because you got so much shit—just as most rap did—over the years. And yet some of your themes . . . like anger toward women, well, that was always part of the blues tradition. It was also evident in rock acts like the Rolling Stones, Elvis Costello. They all expressed anger at women, too. Yet you got shit for it. You also got shit over the years for "borrowing" from others. But the greatest musical artists in history have always taken from others, made a hybrid and created something greater in the process with what surrounds them. Why do you think you were picked on so much? I've noticed since I've been back here

that there's a lot of jealousy in Detroit. Do you think that that led to some of the criticism and attacks?

*Eminem*: I don't know. I really don't know. Can you repeat the first part of the question?

*Metro Times*: Yeah. Well, I was just saying, why do you . . .

*Eminem*: Why do I think I got picked on so much?

*Metro Times*: Yeah, yeah.

*Eminem*: You know something? I really don't know. I kinda think about this point every now and then and I still don't understand. There are other artists that have used the word *faggot* in their work. There are other artists who say certain things that have always been around. So why, then, when I say it is it any different?

Yeah, I have kinda always wondered that. Why is it different when I'm saying it? Let's say if I say something fucked up about Christopher Reeve, you know what I mean? Just something totally off the cuff. That's really fucked up, but how is it any different than what *South Park* is doing? Or *Family Guy*? I've always kinda felt, like, why am *I* special? Why am I that person who's always looked at and where the microscope comes out? I still, to this day, don't understand that. I guess it's just that I get a lot of attention, I don't know! It's very hard to say. I guess that maybe when I speak, I seem to draw the flies [*laughs*].

*Metro Times*: Well, again, maybe I'm reading too much into it, but it seems like you are addressing that in the new video when you're lampooning modern pop-and-rock culture. You know? As far as I'm concerned, even at your most Slim Shady worst, you were *never* as creepy as, say, Bret Michaels!

361

*Eminem*: [*laughs hard*] That's funny, man!

*Metro Times*: Thanks.

*Eminem*: You know when we were making that video there was the thing with Jessica Simpson and Tony Romo. And the Cowboys are actually my favorite team. So Tony Romo is one of my favorite quarterbacks. I don't think he's my favorite—but he's certainly one of my favorites. So I felt kinda conflicted doing the Jessica thing. Because we were gonna have a Jessica in the video. When I say, "Jessica Simpson, sing the chorus," we were gonna have a chick who looked like Jessica Simpson come out and sing the chorus. But then Jessica got fat. I mean, not really fat but she certainly got fat for . . . well, Jessica Simpson got fat for Jessica Simpson! You know what I mean? And we wanted to stay within the current of what's going on right now in pop culture. Because I think that my videos are little time capsules. Usually my first singles off of each record are little time capsules of what's going on in pop culture right at that moment.

So I've always wanted people to be able to look back at each video and go, "Oh, remember what was going on at that moment!" You know what I mean? "Oh, that's when Jessica Simpson got fat. Oh, OK!" And even if she gets thin again, that's fine. But for that moment in time, she was fat. But then I started thinking, like, "Man!" I was telling [manager and former Detroiter] Paul [Rosenberg] and everyone around me, "Man, I don't wanna piss Tony Romo off and he starts throwing games for the Cowboys!"

*Metro Times*: [*laughs*] That's great. Again, you're one of the most confessional rappers in history. In retrospect, if you had to do it over again, would you have been as confessional in your lyrics?

*Eminem*: Yeah, I definitely would because even though I've pretty much put a lot of my personal life out there, my music was always the outlet for me to get through whatever I was going through at the time. And when I put it down on paper, and when I say it in the studio, it's always been therapy for me. You know? It's like this is what I'm feeling. This is what I wanna say. And this is how I'm gonna get it out. And, you know, you put it out there to the world and whoever listens, listens. And if nobody listens, that's fine, too. But this is how I'm feeling right now. And it's like I can go back and listen to each song off of each record and remember *exactly* what I was going through at that particular moment. And exactly how I was feeling.

*Metro Times*: Do you have any relationship with any other current Detroit music stars? Have you ever talked to Kid Rock? Ever met Jack White?

*Eminem*: No, never met Jack White. But I do have a pretty good relationship with Kid Rock. I mean, you know, we hang out every now and then. We probably haven't hung out during the past year or so. Maybe two years. But, you know, I see him quite a bit. He'll come over my house, I've played basketball with him, you know? But, yeah, me and Bob are pretty good friends.

*Metro Times*: In the book, you write that you were influenced by the Beastie Boys, and I know you recently inducted Run-D.M.C. into the Rock and Roll Hall of Fame. What do you make of rappers like Asher Roth, whose sound was obviously influenced by the *Slim Shady* album? There are other current artists who've also obviously been influenced by you. Does that make you feel good? Or do you even care?

*Eminem*: Well, Asher Roth has actually said, I think, in a song that he was influenced by me. And that's fine. I feel great when other artists are influenced by me. I mean, it's certainly flattering. But as far as people saying he *sounds* like me and shit like that, well, I got his album and I don't think it sounds *anything* like me. I was just listening to it the other day, in fact. That's one of the "catch-up" music things I mentioned earlier. I really wanted to check him out because people have been telling me to check him out. And I think the kid is dope. I think he's good *and* I don't think he sounds like me. It's kinda sad that just because he's white and he raps, then he's automatically gonna get that.

*Metro Times*: Well, I think people just need labels to latch onto. You say in the book that one of your goals was to use hip-hop to bring people together and to lessen racial tension. I really think you succeeded at that in many ways. But I'm just curious: There was that piece in the *Source* all those years ago about Champtown and him accusing you of racism and all that shit. Does that still bother you? Are there any repercussions from that still? Or is that all in the past now?

*Eminem*: I just feel like I've tried to put all my beefs and all those kinda things behind me now. Everything from the *Source* beef and all that shit. I'm just trying to like move forward now. Especially, you know, with sobriety and everything. I just wanna move forward.

*Metro Times*: Cool. Last question for you. What's an average day in the life of Eminem like these days when you're not working? When you're just at home . . .

*Eminem*: Umm. An average day would be just . . . uh, when I'm not working?

*Metro Times*: Yeah. When you're just hanging at home.

*Eminem*: [*laughs*] Well, you know, I work quite a bit. But when I'm not working, I'm just hanging out with my kids and watching TV, you know? Not really anything spectacular. I get up in the mornings and I run. I run quite a bit these days.

*Metro Times*: Well, you look great. You do look like you're in great health.

*Eminem*: Oh, thanks. I just run a lot. I exercise a lot and just eat right. You know, watch what I eat and count calories and all that good, fun stuff [*laughs*].

*Metro Times*: Are you going to tour on this album?

*Eminem*: I don't know. I haven't really got that far; haven't gotten far enough to really discuss it yet. But I really don't know at this point. I guess I have to wait to see what comes up and what the demand [for the album] may be.

*Metro Times*: Right. Well, the demand will be great. Listen, Marshall, thank you so much for doing this. We really appreciate it and much good luck to you. I love the new single and I'm looking forward to the album.

*Eminem*: Alright. Thank you. I appreciate it, Bill. Bye.

## EMINEM AFTERWORD

As stated in the original introduction to this story, which was written in conjunction with Eminem's 2009 postrehab comeback, you'd really have to be a virtual hermit to be unfamiliar with the artist formally known as Marshall Mathers and his many accomplishments and achievements. *Relapse* was a modest success compared to his previous releases—it sold only five

363

million-plus copies—but it set the stage for what has followed, success that can only be labeled phenomenal.

*Recovery*, his seventh album—and his sixth consecutive number 1 (breaking the existing record for all solo artists that preceded him)—delivered a slew of hit singles, many of them revealing a new maturity of sorts, especially the anthem of hope, "Not Afraid," which probably was the class song for more graduating high-school classes than not in 2010. And one could make a case for 2013's *The Marshall Mathers LP 2* as the artist's masterpiece, topping one after another of critcs' "best of" lists that year—and in perfect Eminem fashion, creating new classics around samples from such outlandish sources as the Zombies ("Time of the Season"), Joe Walsh, and—yes!—Wayne Fontana and the Mindbenders ("Game of Love"). It was the work of pure genius, appealing equally to baby boomers and subsequent generations raised on hip-hop. The album proved there is still no better wordsmith in the game—no challengers, really—even though he has continued to court controversy every step of the way.

Howard Stern once claimed the title "King of All Media"—but Eminem could easily claim the title for himself. Since his return, he has seemingly never stopped: Record labels. Soundtrack recordings. Collaboration after collaboration. Stadium shows (perhaps the only rapper in history who can truly command and deliver in such venues; he also began using a traditional rock band to back him up, in addition to the samples, beginning in 2010 with the *Recovery* shows). He stole the stage at both Lollapalooza and Coachella, toured as a coheadliner with Rihanna (earlier selling out stadiums in record time in both NYC and Detroit as a coheadliner with Jay Z), and holds the record for best-selling digital album in history

(*Relapse*). He's contributed to numerous charities, including his foundation for Detroit's disadvantaged youth. And then there was that Super Bowl public service announcement for Detroit. And then the Chrysler commercial . . . You could fill a book on this guy, who still found time to be a model parent, which, in this writer's estimation, has always been the true measure of an individual. His daughter, valedictorian and homecoming queen of her class, is now a student at Michigan State University.

The one thing many of his fans do regret is that, much like Bruce Springsteen, he has never pursued the career he could have had on-screen. The movie *8 Mile* proved him to be a master—and he occasionally continues to display real charisma while portraying Eminem (and Slim Shady) in the visual arts, be it mugging with Sacha Baron Cohen at the MTV Awards a few years ago; cameos as himself in the James Franco vehicle *The Interview*; or the season-seven finale of HBO's *Entourage*. In July 2015, he appeared on *Only in Monroe*—a public access show out of Monroe, Michigan—when zany talk-show host and satirist Stephen Colbert, prepping for his upcoming stint as David Letterman's replacement, showed up as the program's guest host for one episode. Mathers once again proved himself to be not only funny and a true natural but also a very good sport. He remains one of Detroit's greatest goodwill ambassadors of the arts to the world at large.

# Inner-City Blues
## The Story of Detroit Techno
*Hobey Echlin*

From Motown and the MC5 to the White Stripes and Eminem, Detroit's musical exports have always been breech-birthed products of the city that inspired them. Self-made and independent, Detroit's musical legacy is a story of success in spite of—and more often than not because of—adversity. No Detroit-bred sound exemplifies this complicated love-hate relationship with its origins more than techno. A sound coldly abstract

Juan Atkins. Photo by Doug Coombe.

but somehow soulful, Detroit techno represents a convergence of the city's deteriorating economic landscape in the '80s, bored black middle-class kids looking to escape the dwindling opportunities of the auto industry, and the dawn of do-it-yourself musical software—specifically Musical Instrument Digital Interface (MIDI) technology. To understand techno—a contradictory combination of icy futurism and lush, melancholic optimism—you have to first understand the city itself.

By the '80s, the Motor City was a shadow of its former economic and cultural eminence. Rising oil prices and competition from imported cars meant the dissolution of the auto industry, which left an economic and cultural vacuum. The city's white population had long since left for the economic promise of Oakland County, to the north of Detroit's 8 Mile border, where a new freeway system complemented new suburban homebuilding and shopping mall construction. Middle-class black kids were left behind with only their imagination as a means of escape from an increasingly grim reality.

One of these kids was Juan Atkins. Raised in Northwest Detroit, as a teenager Atkins had lapsed into gang life and petty crime, prompting his family's relocation to Belleville, an innocuous suburb just west of Detroit Metropolitan Wayne

365

County Airport along the I-94 corridor to Ann Arbor. Inspired by Parliament/Funkadelic, Atkins began playing in bands and started to explore the possibilities of synthesized funk.

"[Parliament's] 'Flashlight' was the track that took me over the edge. By then, they were using synthesizers for like 70 percent of their production, and I was right along with them," states Atkins. By the early '80s, he'd teamed up with Rick Davis, a Vietnam veteran into progressive psychedelic rock and electronic music production whom he had met at a nearby community college, and formed Cybotron. The pair fit squarely into the prerap electro pantheon of acts like Egyptian Lover and Soulsonic Force. When he and Davis parted, Atkins took the Cybotron sound—hard funk with synthesizers instead of slap bass—and added, as he puts it, "a little house beat up under it."

House music—based around a straight 4/4 beat—had developed in New York and Chicago as a hangover from '70s disco, but vamped up with more aggressive sounds and new technology. Atkins's efforts resulted in Model 500, the first Detroit techno act. Their harder beat and futuristic themes were at once otherworldly but gritty, rooted in reality but packed with escapism. Taking Atkins's DIY lead, within a few years, fellow Belleville High School pals Derrick May and Kevin Saunderson launched their own labels in the form of Transmat and KMS, respectively. The three had already established themselves as promoter/DJs, helming their own party-throwing crews (Deep Space, among others) in a scene that saw sophisticated urban youth underserved by nightclubs and commercial trends renting their own spaces and throwing their own futuristic

dance parties fueled by everything from Prince to Kraftwerk and Italo-disco.

One of these crews, Sharevari, had made their own song, an eponymous Italo-disco track that received the ultimate vindication: it had been played on the local UHF dance show the *Scene* in 1982. The Belleville Three, as Juan, Derrick, and Kevin would become known, followed with their own original sounds. By 1989, all three were releasing their own records; Atkins was the electro-techno punk, May the techno-age bachelor, and Saunderson the R&B-minded wunderkind who cut his teeth playing frat parties in college.

The sound itself, however disparate among the young Belleville trio, was more expansive than that emanating from Chicago or New York in the late '80s and early '90s. Besides the early synth-funk forays of Parliament, Atkins, May, and Saunderson looked to the exotic for inspiration. Euro-disco; Giorgio Moroder's robotic, trance-inducing keyboard arpeggios; abstract composers like Manuel Gottsching and his chandelier-like soundscapes exemplified by tracks like "E2E4"; Kraftwerk and their teutonic precision; and on to the hard new wave of Cabaret Voltaire and Front 242 were all noted influences.

Techno artists received inspiration from one radio DJ in particular, the Electrifying Mojo (Charles Johnson), who played eclectic freeform sets combining Kraftwerk and P-Funk with rock icons like Peter Frampton and new-wave groups like the B-52s. Mojo's *Midnight Funk Association* radio show encouraged the inquisitive nature of techno's early producers while often giving them airplay.

Back home, built as it was on black middle-class esoteric tastes, techno remained an underground phenomenon, limited to after-hours clubs like the Music Institute, a late '80s alcohol-free black box of a room where Derrick May DJed, and to private parties frequented by mostly black, similarly minded kids. The rise of rap began driving techno further underground, but while techno defied most conventional music marketing and reflected a more abstract set of splintered tastes akin to avant-garde jazz, Detroit's pioneers began to attract a new overseas audience. Up-tempo grooves and the spiritual link to Detroit's Motown and funk legacy fired up the imagination of the United Kingdom and European audiences, inspiring the likes of the Prodigy and the Chemical Brothers, who would, ironically, resell the dance floor excitement techno inspired on European dance floors in the late '80s to American audiences as part of the electronica boom of the mid-'90s.

By the early '90s, Derrick May, who'd been fired from local clubs for attracting too black a crowd, was licensing his tunes to European labels and playing lucrative DJ gigs overseas. Kevin Saunderson's Inner City, spurred on by the success of "Good Life," a poppy track with a female singer and a solid verse-chorus-bridge arrangement, was soon touring as a live act after he hired a local rock band to whip up full-band arrangements of his MIDI-produced tracks. As Detroit's pioneers spent more time overseas, a new crop of producers sprang up, headed by militant Underground Resistance, which included Jeff Mills along with May's jazz-inspired protégé, Carl Craig, and Richie Hawtin, a white kid from Windsor, Ontario, who'd been to Detroit underground parties.

All three reflected techno's legacy in their respective ways: Craig was heir to its future-jazz aspirations, a notion he has carried out to this day with his work in electronic jazz/hip-hop projects like Innerzone Orchestra and the Detroit Experiment. Underground Resistance inherited Atkins's DIY punk-rock approach. The group's chief producer, Mike Banks—who grew up playing prog-rock guitar, boxing at Detroit's famed Kronks gym, and working as a repo man—built his own small music-industry empire. His distribution company, Submerge, was anchored by his group's mean, lean releases, most notably "Knights of the Jaguar," a track credited to Underground Resistance member DJ Rolando, which was the subject of a lawsuit with Sony in the United Kingdom when Banks refused to license the track for wider commercial release and the bigger label cut their own version. Hawtin was, for better or for worse, techno's Elvis. He saw what white suburban kids wanted from America's response to Europe's dance resurgence: conceptual techno hard enough for the dance floor but simple and loopy enough to sound good to stoned people. Streamlined and using a 909-drum-machine-fueled formula, techno's second wave launched six-figure-a-year careers and landed deals for its major players. Hawtin signed to Mute and has gone on to become something of a techno lifestyle icon, hosting his own party season every summer on the Spanish island Ibiza. Carl Craig released his 1995 Kraftwerk-inspired *Landcruising* album on Blanco Y Negro, which proved to be one step ahead of a music industry that expected more up-tempo rave anthems but that evidenced Craig's artistic integrity. He remains one of the most prolific and sought-after remixers to this day.

But by the mid-'90s, Detroit had all but forgotten about techno in its original lush form. As producers focused once again on the European market, the scene back home changed. At first dubbed "ghetto-techno," a new hybrid of techno and rap emerged as the soundtrack to black strip bars and downtown clubs. Fusing techno's fast beats with rap's call-and-response, good-time vibe, ghettotech producers like DJ Assault and Godfather built local empires by releasing ribald chant-based tunes like "Ass 'n' Titties" and "Fly Skinnies" that owe as much to Detroit techno as Miami bass, electro, and what's now called "juke." Ghettotech may have been dismissed as strictly party music, but it's telling that UK house-music duo Disclosure, the massively successful ginger-haired brothers raised on Detroit techno and '90s hip-hop, chose an obscure ghettotech track by 313 Bass Mechanics to sample for the hook for their 2015 track "Bang That."

But classic Detroit techno hasn't been forgotten. If anything, it has been elevated to a "grand old man" status with a nod to the warm summer nights and late-night shows of its late '80s and early '90s heyday. The city itself has embraced techno's origins—and its continuing relevance at the more purist forefront of electronic music—with Movement, the annual festival that began as the Detroit Electronic Music Festival in 2000. The massive party (and its after parties) held every Memorial Day in Detroit's Hart Plaza has remained committed to highlighting techno's legacy in the world while tastefully acknowledging the growing whole of electronic dance music that techno more often than not inspired. Movement showcases techno as a futuristic sound and with an eye for a good time right here, right now. In Saunderson's case, that means his sons are carrying on his legacy: they performed at Movement 2015 while dad looked on proudly.

As festival founder and original creative director Carl Craig once explained of the motivation behind what would become Movement, "I always wanted to serenade the Renaissance Center." One imagines that every Detroit techno producer felt that same wistfulness and hope when playing those first adventurous records at parties, filling in the widening social cultural and social cracks around them. Perhaps it was those feelings that inspired them to dream through their sequencers and synthesizers of a sound that could transcend their city's sophistication and decay without being bound to it, looking to the future for their sound and the entire world for their audience.

# For Dilla's Sake and the Love of Donuts

*Shane M. Liebler*

With his legacy complete, and that smile just a memory that beams from the cover of *Donuts*, we can now exhaustively examine J Dilla's catalog, attempt to categorize the rhythms, and confidently assess his value to this art form. It's not so much about what J did for hip-hop as it is what Dilla did for music—and not just modern music, I'm talking centuries' worth of sound.

You see, you only get one of each individual human being: one me, one you. There's only one of each of us, whether we seize the days of our lives or not. Nobody's normal. You only get one.

James Yancey, Dilla's real name, seized on every breath he was given in life, right up until his death in 2006 at age thirty-two—just three days after his birthday and the release of the aforementioned opus, *Donuts*.

No bloodshed, no overdoses, no shady circumstances. Instead, Dilla was sick with a rare blood disease. It was absolutely devastating to anyone who had befriended Dilla in real life or connected with him via headphones, especially considering all the incredible compositions he created in a very brief time—far too brief. He was quietly charismatic and exceptionally clever.

You only get one.

Your brain—the unique nerves, synapses, and blood swimming in your skull—processes music in measures. Dilla loved to mess with that. Using the vehicle of soulful exclamations and outbursts, Jay Dee, later known to the world as J Dilla, would unexpectedly pause and inject a drug in split-second doses—yelps, choruses, an eighth step—when your brain least suspected it.

In his own avant-hip-hop style, J sewed pieces together, ends to middles, beginnings to silence, fuzz to flourishes—no mindless looping of the chorus from an R&B chart topper for five minutes. J dug *deep*. And if he couldn't find it, he'd play it his damn self.

With musical roots that included a classical-music-inclined mother, a jazz-musician father, and a grandfather who played piano for silent films, Dilla took to music from the time he was a tot. Dilla cut his chops on piano and cello before developing a musical literacy that led him to drums, flute, and guitar. Davis Aerospace Technical High School developed his mathematical mind that would eventually make his sound so unique.

He started messing around with a neighborhood musician named Joseph "Amp" Fiddler. Eventually, he began to lock himself in the lab at Amp's house, rather than the ones at Davis HS. He discovered digital machines and manipulation.

That was it.

This kind of pissed off his beloved mother, Maureen "Ma Dukes" Yancey, but it's since been worked out. She appreciated and supported his talent and now preserves his spirit via the J Dilla Foundation, a nonprofit dedicated to music programs in inner-city schools across the nation.

After more than a decade as a fan, I still can't wrap my head around the J Dilla sound. It just

369

was—and is—so *different* in a genre that rarely surprises in the modern era, save for a few lyrical luminaries. I'm continually impressed at how fresh this stuff still sounds. His voluminous, headphone-friendly catalog remains in heavy rotation.

And then there's the man himself, James Yancey, twenty-first-century troubadour: J played pop-culture strings in a far more advanced style than traditional DJs. Hip-hop fans and hipsters alike relish the obscure sample and award it five-star ratings and coveted buzz. Jay dug deep in the crates no doubt, but the shit he came up with mesmerized. Always armed with a solid *boom-bap* backbone, his sounds exploded with calculated spontaneity.

James Yancey, composer: A simple hip-hop producer can put any random soul hook to a beat. J wove audio fabric thick with color and complexity. Some of it was just straight-up weird, but it was always wonderful. Any producer can splash paint on a canvas and make it sound beautiful. J lovingly stitched together meditative grooves, carefully selected clips, and simply shared his love of sound with the world. Live and direct. From Detroit.

James Yancey, ambassador: My first introduction to Jay Dee came by way of A Tribe Called Quest, my first and all-time favorite hip-hop band. Upon further review, I learned that many of my most beloved tunes came from the brain of some dude from Detroit. The breadcrumbs led me on a sonic journey: De La Soul, Pharcyde, Busta Ryhmes, that new single from Janet Jackson. The ear-candy expedition led me back where I started, the Motor City. On a Friday after work, I strolled into Record Time on Gratiot, fresh from a shift on the back of a garbage truck, with paycheck in hand. I plunked down something like twelve bucks for J Dilla's priceless masterwork: *Fantastic Vol. 2*.

You don't pull stuff like Slum Village out of the "local" rap section every day. No disrespect to the other Motown MCs of the day, but the first bass tickles of "Conant Gardens" induced a solid and satisfying head bob like I have never known—from any genre, place, or time. By the time James Brown was chopped up beyond recognition on "I Don't Know," I was a Jay Dee devotee. At a time when Eminem and Kid Rock were busy dissecting themselves and giving a middle finger to everyone else, this was fun and funky—and pure Detroit. Swimming in a sea of self-depreciation and noise that the rest of the nation was loving, Slum Village's slick and sometimes-silly style was refreshing. How was "Payday" not a bigger hip-hop anthem than "My Name Is"?

I was plenty puzzled and perpetually hungry for more Dilla.

The journey continues as aural treats turn up all the time—either I discover an old tune produced by Dilla or some obscure recording that's new to me.

I'm not sure the quiet Dilla said everything he needed to. He spoke through his music and there was lots of that over the course of just over a decade. He said an awful lot—to me.

James Yancey taught me how to love hip-hop. He still reminds me of why I appreciate music and, by extension, life.

You only get one.

# Ghettotech
## Detroit Is Just Here to Party
*Daniel Jones*

Smoke swirled around the small group of people at Recycle Here Detroit. The DJ had his turn after hours of hallucinatory rock and noise had finally subsided. Grinding, fast paced, and, above all, grimy, Detroit's own ghettotech assaulted our ears.

Among others, DJ Godfather and DJ Assault are the ghettotech ambassadors of the city, showing the world their unique Detroit sound. This fast and obscene movement could be nothing else and could have come from nowhere else.

Finding traction at the nexus of '80s-throwback techno and dirty club hip-hop, ghettotech flourished on the PAs of the city through the early 2000s.

## BLURRY LINES BETWEEN GENRES

In Detroit, it began with techno. After all, Detroit is where this genre was created. Broadly recognized as the originators, Juan Atkins, Derrick May, and Kevin Saunderson made up the Belleville Three as teenage friends in the early '80s and showed up to the party with their innovative new style.

The kids had started up something new. Created with new technology, like the Roland TR 808, beats changed and helped formulate the new party music. Detroit brought the new sound to the decks, and techno music caught on in the clubs and parties.

During this time, hip-hop and funk music had begun to bump uglies and the resulting sound attempted to subsume all others in the club. As these genres evolved along with techno, they all began to influence and intertwine with one another. Electronic production dominated the music scene throughout the 1980s. Melding together this sound with rhymes, New York DJs like Afrika Bambaataa successfully created their own new thing. The sound could be heard all over the hip-hop production of the time and was effectively espoused by the likes of the World Class Wreckin' Cru and, famously, Chris "The Glove" Taylor (under the raps of Ice-T) in the final battle scene of archetypal B-boy movie *Breakin'*.

Detroit techno continued to evolve over the next decade and a half. It gained wider acceptance, crossing into new markets and cultures. DJs like the Electrifying Mojo and the Wizard (musician Jeff Mills) played genre-bending sets that would schizophrenically swing between hard funk and techno, touching on mostly everything in between.

By the late '80s, the second wave of Detroit techno was well underway. Techno DJs were incorporating the battle-DJ techniques employed by hip-hop cats into their own bag of tricks. Dudes at parties and clubs were creating musical collages full of electronic breaks and impossibly fast cuts to massive effect. Ghettotech (before anyone even thought to market it, much less name it) threw techno, hip-hop, and funk into a blender. Coupled with low-down raunchy lyrics, this sound was spilled on the broad and cracked boulevards of the Motor City.

## GHETTOTECH

For ghettotech to become a thing, all it took was a spark in the late '80s. At the time, Miami bass had entered the tinder of the Detroit music scene, a club sound defined in many ways by 2 Live Crew, with its overwhelming bass, fast tempo, and furious scratching (not to mention its filthy lyrics).

The southern connection strongly influenced ghettotech's emergence. Detroit-area rappers were heavily influenced by the rise of filthy club hip-hop imported from the party going on down south and coupled it with all our unique northern electro sounds. Ghettotech was characterized by a dirty sound complete with throbbing techno bass hits and jangly hi-hats; the raunchy lyrics came off less like complete raps and more like chanted hip-hop club mantras.

With songs such as "Asses Jigglin" by DJ Assault and, later, "I Keep Banging the Beat" the fat had all been effectively trimmed from techno and hip-hop club music. In the early '90s, before ghettotech had a name, the genre was being spun on turntables and on the air everywhere, and it even had its own signature dance, the "jit." The result was an international hit.

## BACK TO THE FLOOR

The haze was clearing at Detroit Recycle Here, and the small but the enthusiastic crowd was making a showing on the poured-concrete dance floor as ghettotech was pumped out of the speakers. As a musical palate cleanser to close out the evening, there was no better genre to spin. Everyone could stop thinking for a moment before they staggered off to their homes.

The music that gets spun after hours skews toward sonic comfort food. In Philly at a similar party, their cheesesteak might tend toward their

analogous genre, "techstep." In Miami, their Cubano is Miami bass. In Detroit, the same way we might drunkenly down a Coney, ghettotech is best consumed at a breakneck pace.

And just like junk food, ghettotech loses its appeal if you put too much energy into trying to make sense of what you are confronted with. The revelers I recently watched throwing it down to some classic ghettotech tracks were in the moment. There was no question about the intent of the verses or an earnest discussion about the production. Detroit was just there to party. The following is an interview conducted with DJ Assault in May 2014:

## THE DJ ASSAULT INTERVIEW

*Dan Jones:* So, do you still live in the Detroit area?

*DJ Assault:* I'm kind of back and forth now from Detroit and Atlanta.

*Dan Jones:* Atlanta?

*DJ Assault:* Yeah, I went to school there and my mother, she's down there. It's a bit more serene than Detroit, all of the wildness. A lot of it is just working on music down there.

*Dan Jones:* Many collaborations nowadays?

*DJ Assault:* [*chuckles*] That's a funny question. I think from the past with my *career*, collaborations never worked right for me.

I don't know if I particularly like them because the majority, especially using my vocals, the majority of remixes that people do I never like.

Plus, I don't really look in terms of remixes. When I have an idea for a track that's pretty much what the track is, and I don't want a million different versions.

I think that collaborations now are because people either don't write lyrics or people don't produce tracks so they kind of try to come together as a team and do things. We're not playing classical music or composing symphonies. It's not that complicated, but it's still teams of producers. I grew out of that a long time ago.

*Dan Jones:* You feel that is part of a recent development or . . .

*DJ Assault:* Well, it's definitely with the computer age and you know, the nerds with laptops, that that came about. I get it. It's teams of people that are down for one cause, but to me it's teams of untalented people ruining music. I don't care how commercialized it becomes. It's about a career.

They are thinking more about a gimmick to capitalize on something while it's a trend, and in two years it is probably gone.

*Dan Jones:* That kind of throws me into another question: With the advent of this modern music technology has your producing methodology changed?

*DJ Assault:* Not really. It's more computer oriented now because it's faster.

*Dan Jones:* Does it make it easier?

*DJ Assault:* I don't think it makes it easier, maybe faster. You don't have to wire up different synths or samplers, different mix boards or patch bays, or MIDIing five or six different things or whatever to get the sound. Some people would say it's easier because they use a bunch of sample packs and prerecorded loop libraries and things of that nature, but I don't do that.

*Dan Jones:* I've heard you are a little conflicted about the name *ghettotech*.

*DJ Assault:* It was weird, I don't know how I got that label to my music when no one had records in like '95 doing that type of style, and then all of a sudden when more people started doing it, my music became labeled, but it was like vinyl records with that style in '95 way back then before I ever owned a record company.

I really didn't like it because I was trying to figure out what direction I was going in and I was just kind of doing something from a DJ's perspective and listening to, you know, the people that came before me and the people that I kind of looked up to.

But I didn't really know where I was going. I wasn't really a producer then. I was just kind of making beats and tracks that I thought may work in the club. I wouldn't really call that hard-core production back then but it worked.

So, I was kind of . . . I felt a bit slighted, I would say, that when I finally wrapped my head around the sound I wanted to do it was labeled, like *for me*. And if people do that style it's fine, but I never, you know, endorsed it or had any part in that labeling of the music.

*Dan Jones:* When you were first trying to figure out your sound who were you listening to?

*DJ Assault:* I mean, I look up to all the guys that are from Detroit—Juan Atkins, Kevin Saunderson, Jeff Mills, Derrick May. I mean, I'm probably skipping people. I believe in respecting and paying the proper acknowledgment to the originators of different sounds.

373

I also like a lot of bass music from the South like Atlanta and Miami bass music so it was all kind of incorporated into what I do. I didn't know what I was coming up with. I was just trying to do something that people would like, and then all of a sudden it was just labeled. I think still it's just Detroit dance music. I don't know if it's any deeper than that.

*Dan Jones:* How would you say your music has changed since when you first started?

*DJ Assault:* Well, it was really kind of sample oriented in the beginning because all I really had was a sampling workstation. It's not really dependent upon sampling now. It's all original programs and composed music, whether it's simple or complicated, whether its dance or hip-hop or R&B or whatever I decide to do.

I don't like samples. Some people say that you get ideas you would never have come up with from samples, but I say that it's a crutch.

If you can play or figure out the notes in anything you hear, you can become inspired by anything and ideas are infinite.

If you depend on samples, they can only be manipulated in so many ways. It's a limit to the quality of how they'll sound when you're altering pitch, time-stretching, and chopping them. That's why I think I will never quit making music because I'll never run out of ideas.

*Dan Jones:* How old were you when you first started making music? I mean, you are still a pretty young man.

*DJ Assault:* Yeah, I hope I never get old. I can't get old. Well, you can't get fat and Pillsbury-like 'cause that won't work.

Man, I was, shoot . . . I started collecting records on my own at like seven. I had turntables at ten, and I had Technics 1200s, some professional turntables, by the time I was fourteen.

*Dan Jones:* So you've always known this was for you. When did it become serious?

*DJ Assault:* Through some of the biggest injustices, I think it caused me to see what I really wanted to do and how it could make money. My first record, I was promised to get paid off of the music and I wasn't paid, really for doing my first couple records. But I saw, you know because I was in music retail as well, how much it was selling. My type of mind-set and mentality was, "Ok, I see it's selling at this one record store. I need to quit working this job and like put my money up to put out my own records."

If you can't see yourself succeed in something before you succeed, you'll never succeed. You have to see the finish before you start.

And I guess that's harder and harder for people because they want to see it materialize, like before their eyes, before they did all the work. It takes faith and belief in what you're doing, you know.

*Dan Jones:* For a lot of people, though, it's a tough industry.

*DJ Assault:* Well, if you play the politics of it, it's tough. "Oh, pick me, pick me! You gotta like me!" No you don't have to like me. I'm talented. I'll run my own company, do business the way I want to do business. If people don't want to do business in a way that is comfortable for me, it's no hard feelings. I'll just take it elsewhere.

That's the thing, you can't follow. People don't want to step out there and be a leader. But see, I don't care about reputation or upholding some reputation for people. I'm not saying I disrespect people, because I don't. But I don't hold like, the CEO of Sony Music Corporation as God. You know? That's not my God. I don't worship him. He doesn't have any power to me.

*Dan Jones:* What was the process of starting your record company, Jefferson Avenue?

*DJ Assault:* Man, the weird thing about it is that I was so young, like nineteen. It taught me a lot. I guess you learn in life. It wasn't really thinking, it was just doing. I would say my dream is not other people's dream. It was going well, but it got messed up with partners and stuff.

I was young, and, like I said, it's very few people that will share the same dream and vision that you have. I think things like that make it harder to succeed, because you really have to surround yourself with the right people when there's money being made.

*Dan Jones:* Like trustworthy people?

*DJ Assault:* Yeah, people who don't look at music for the money. Because I don't care about the money, believe it or not, and I'm sure I've made more money out of it than most people will ever make from music, you know. I don't chase the money. I love music. The money always came in, one way or another.

*Dan Jones:* Well, we're here talking and just downtown the Movement Electronic Music Festival is happening. How do you like it?

*DJ Assault:* Well, I don't. They changed it. Like you say, it's Movement.

*Dan Jones:* Not DEMF?

*DJ Assault:* Yeah, exactly.

*Dan Jones:* I mean, it's expensive.

*DJ Assault:* I mean, it doesn't help Detroit. It don't benefit Detroit artists. What is it? It always morphs into something. But like I said, it's people who care about the money and not the culture. They have all the fake acts and fake groups. It's like they try to rewrite history or something.

DANIEL JONES

Photo by Doug Coombe.

# Champ's Town

*Brian Smith*

It's a Tuesday night at Bev's Backstreet topless bar, a dim, living-room-warm east-side den. The handful of house girls are bored and sitting at the bar chatting up a few middle-age gents nursing sour marriages or holiday cheerlessness—the kind accustomed to walking out of places like this alone, down a C-note, and smelling like vanilla. There's a couple bikers in boots and denim.

A sylphlike white dancer in crack-revealing lavender hot pants moves across the small kidney-shaped stage slowly, languidly. She caresses the center pole with bored indifference. Taking long, self-obsessed glances at herself in the mirrored back wall, she could be Christina Applegate's porn-star kid sis. She spins slowly on her heel, bends backward, and takes a quick tally of the men in the room. It's still dead. It's still early.

James "The Blackman" Harris is DJing tonight; it's a gig he's had for three months. He's been DJing in one form or another for more than two decades. He spins Snoop, 50 Cent, Talib Kweli, Blondie, Guns N' Roses and his own custom retooling of a Doors tune. He's thin and graceful, dressed in black, a single gold chain around his neck, sports specs and a thick, sculpted Fu Manchu.

Brian "Champtown" Harmon, the brusque veteran Detroit rapper and head of his own Straight Jacket Records label, scans the room. He's looking for girls to include in a booty video he's keen on shooting for an artist on his label.

Squint your eyes, and the thickset Champ might resemble LL Cool J—block-jawed and round, dark-brown eyes, warm-up jersey.

Listen to him converse, and it's obvious he's been rapping since he was eight years old; sharp comments shoot from his lips in concise, percussive blips. Every nuance of every word designed to *hit*. His *choppity-chop* argot is constantly on, day and night—there's no off switch. He's shrewd and witty, drips the gravitas of the east-side streets he grew up on. He has a remarkable capacity for incendiary, outspoken opinionating. The braggadocio is thick, and well it should be; rap was built on hyperbole and the art of the crow. And Champ can crow.

And why not? It's said that Eminem gleaned bits of Champ early on (Eminem's music-video debut was in Champ's 1992 clip for "Do-Da-Dipity," images from which turned up in the earliest Eminem vids). There've been rumors that Insane Clown Posse nicked Champ's early jester shtick and ran with it. He influenced Kid Rock.

As 50 Cent bursts from the in-house woofers, a zaftig Nubian with an impassive expression steps onstage and soon completes a miraculous gravity-defying twirl on the pole. She slows her spin to a drop-stop on the stage floor as the music yields, finally, to its inevitable fade-out.

Champ shakes his head. Nope, not that one.

Two comely dancers take a seat at the end of the bar. Champ moves in and strikes up a conversation. "I own Straight Jacket Records," he says, offering his hand.

377

A bespectacled fortysomething white guy standing close by—who says he "works in medicine" and is here for his "chocolate fix"—overhears Champ's video rap. He chimes in. "What, you couldn't afford a business card?"

"I don't *need* no business card," Champ says in a swift quip. He leans in closer to the dancer and stays on the video tack.

The stripper nearest Champ, a wide-eyed black beauty in full-length sheer pink with a whisper of visible nipples, blinks once slowly and nods. She works her hair. She's heard lines like this before but listens attentively. Soon she asks Champ a few questions. A moment later she scribbles her phone number on a torn piece of paper and hands it to the rapper. The other dancer follows suit.

Champ can work the angles. Some local backbiters dismiss him as an audacious charlatan. Many say he's a brilliant talent scout, a gifted emcee, and a record-mogul-in-waiting. But there's something about Champ that draws people to him. It's an innate charisma, not some fabricated rap persona assembled for street cred, as would be first guess.

If anyone, this rapper/label owner and this strip-bar DJ are key figures in the early development of Detroit rap. You need a broom and dustpan to sweep up the names these guys drop. But, hey, they were there.

By his teens, Blackman was a touring DJ with major acts. He did the first Lollapalooza tour and DJed Kid Rock's first major tour. He's kicked around the city for years, worked with George Clinton, joined Enemy Squad and Soul Clique. He's currently working on a solo album, and sometimes appears with white funk-soul revivalists Detroit City Council.

Blackman's east-side house was home to an underground collective called the Beast Crew, a gaggle of kids who logged myriad hours in Blackman's basement learning rap's ropes while putting on emcee battles and working the decks.

Blackman talks about the Beast Crew's basement sessions at his house in the early '80s and how the kids did the dozens. "We ragged on each other, talked about each other's mother, dad, whatever." After a moment, in a voice barely audible above a booming drum loop, he adds, "We gave Kid Rock his ghetto pass. We're black, all about the love."

Rock and Eminem are two cultural sponges who swooped in on Detroit ghettos, appropriated black music and its aesthetic, and raced straight past "Go" to Park Place. So it is, as history has taught us, that it takes whites to popularize black music. Champ and Blackman are OK with that. They understand the playing board and know they can't change the rules. But Champ says he doesn't want to be written out of history.

Champ's self-belief is huge. He doesn't want their help or fiscal assistance. Nah, he's prideful, he can launch his label by himself.

"I know the street game, learned the beauty of patience," Champtown says in his patented style. "I'm thirty years old." He pauses, and adds before heading out of the strip bar, "I gotta make sure my shit is hittin' by the time my daughter graduates high school. I got family values. Yep."

Champ says, frequently and without prompting, that he loves his mother, his daughters, and Keasha (his twenty-nine-year-old girlfriend of twelve years) very much. He has to succeed; music is all he knows. His mother is unemployed (Pop died when he was a teenager), and he has a family to feed.

Champ's a dude driven: he wants his piece of the American dream, and he's well aware of the disparity between what he has and what he wants. He reeks of calculated self-advancement, but his motivations aren't completely tainted with self-interest. Calling him "focused" would be an understatement.

He's learned the music-biz ropes well, and understands how to slickly (re)package rebellion and humor and auction it off to the highest bidder.

His Straight Jacket "family" *is* impressive. With a bounty of local talent from various corners of Detroit, the years-in-making label roster could, overstatement aside, surpass the urban talent on many of the majors.

Champ's position over this close-knit group extends beyond the label-artist relationship into the paternal. It is a family. Think a hip-hop "Island of Misfit Toys." There's the unlikely Asian boy-band duo Yang Ku, female rapper D'Phuzion, rappers Mike Spear and Tekneek, the buff DJ/dancer/rapper Shortcut, and Champtown himself. Keasha is the label's glue, its in-house den mother and aesthetic director.

Each Straight Jacket artist shares an unwavering belief in Champ and depends on him for guidance.

What exactly does Champ bestow on these teens and twentysomethings? He teaches them performance, how the music biz turns, and "educate[s] them on how to come in and do records in twenty minutes flat, just furious. So, I put them through a major crash course on recording, muthafucking performing, learning how to respect others, and all that."

Straight Jacket works the DIY idea that owning your own music is the way to break out of the lower-middle class—financially speaking. And Champ has a keen sense of marketing and can decipher even the most gibberish-ridden publishing contract. When an artist signs to his label, they're getting his hard-won wisdom with a stop-at-nothing-to-get-his-artists-heard work ethic. Since the label has no real operating capital now—all money is on the back end, provided things go as planned—the odds are stacked high, and Champ doesn't bat an eye.

Ice-T and Public Enemy admire Champ enough to have him as a tour mate. Champ's song (with D'Phuzion), the poppy, old-school "Bang Bang Boogie," spent months quietly hovering on *Billboard*'s Hot R&B/rap singles chart, peaking at number 21 in spring 2000. The accompanying (big-money) video was a top request on The Box video network and was in regular rotation on BET and Canada's video outlet, MuchMusic. The single sold close to seventy thousand copies with no real distribution and got heavy love on radio in major markets including Atlanta, Philly, New York, and Boston, but not in Detroit.

Champ's persuasive nature got him into Prince's Paisley Park Studios before he was old enough to drive. He gave a few budding Detroit emcees, DJs, and producers (Eminem, Uncle Ill, Shortcut, Manix, Chaos Kid, the Beast Crew) their first tastes of a big-time recording facility. He befriended Prince there.

Champ is no millionaire. No, he struggles to feed his family; what money he had is now about gone. As a slew of Straight Jacket releases are readying to hit in early '05, Champ has yet to line up new national distribution for his label. No big deal, he says, adding that he thrives when the chips are down.

In fact, his career is riddled with subterfuge, local beefs, fucked-up label investors, and distribution deals gone sour. He's seen as many lows as highs.

As a rapper and producer, Champtown *is* gifted; his hyperactive rhymes on his own Straight Jacket releases have always been fizzy and shtick heavy (he simultaneously trades in *and* mocks street frenzy, but is seemingly immune to it), mixing up old school with contemporary, and propped up with burly singsong choruses.

Chic's Nile Rodgers and Public Enemy's Chuck D have been Champtown trumpeters. D and cohort Flavor Flav appeared in the "Bang Bang Boogie" video (as did hip-hop linchpin Kool Herk). D likens Champ's very-Detroit indie ideals to Berry Gordy. "Champtown is the tragic black-man story of a mind that needs his control in a business that doesn't give back," D says. "Champ gives back, and he has nurtured a nice stable of Detroit artists in recording, performance, and interview. They don't do that anymore in the music business. Finding funding should be no problem if this was a sensible industry. So from the floor up, Champtown and Straight Jacket ease the common sense back in."

East-side Detroit rap in the early to mid-'80s couldn't have been more subterranean. Kids stayed close to their neighborhoods. They had to. Few had cars, much less money. Many weren't old enough to drive. No mainstream press was documenting this splintered and neighborhood-specific scene. The crack epidemic was just kicking down east-side doors, and neighborhoods were in slow decline.

Champ came up in the Fairport neighborhood—his parents settled there from Mississippi (via Ohio) in the '70s. He hung with the notorious Detroit drug crew "Best Friends." They went to the nearby Detroit Boys and Girls Club together, where Champ would kick it on the basketball courts. Champ says he could have easily drifted down the drug-dealer route, but the "music kept me straight." Most of his friends are either dead or in jail.

"I was a pallbearer so many times before I was sixteen it wasn't even funny," Champ says.

He remembers getting called *nigger* walking to and from the Boys Club in his neighborhood, which was still predominantly white then. "We were prepared to get into it with racist muthafuckers every day."

Champ's older half brother, John, took the budding eight-year-old rapper to his first rap show, the Fresh Fest, featuring Run-D.M.C., Whodini, the Fat Boys, and Melle Mel.

Champ was kicked out of high school, spent time in youth homes for breaking and entering and stealing cars—though his mother says she had no idea the trouble her son was getting into—and eventually earned a GED.

"I'd advise everybody who's gonna do crime to give it up by the time you're fifteen," Champ says.

Herman Yancy was Champ's gym teacher at Fleming Elementary. He says:

> Brian had personality, that charisma, but he was no angel. As a fifth grader he would have been one of them guys that I would question whether or not he'd make it. A lot of these kids are dead.
>
> I still got his first tape. He brought me a tape one day a few years later and said, "I wanted to let you know that I'm doing good."

Champ loved LL Cool J and Run-D.M.C. "If Run-D.M.C wore Adidas, I had Adidas. If LL came with Kangol, I had a Kangol on. I thought that's what solo rappers wore," he says. Later on, he started wearing jester hats and dyed his hair to avoid comparisons.

But it was Run from Run-D.M.C. who cooked his head with the power of lyrical rhetoric and rapid-fire rhymes. He started rapping in fifth grade. "You can put this shit with rhymes and dog muthafuckers all day? Shit, this shit is for me," Champ says about rap's appeal.

Soon high-school kids were showing up on the Von Steuben Middle School yard to battle Champ. It's said that he never lost a round.

Champ and future acid-rapper Rashaam "Esham" Smith met in the second grade at Fleming. By middle school, Esham was Champ's human beatbox. They were performing anywhere and everywhere; rapping into the order-call mic at Seafood Bay on Gratiot, where Champ says, "customers would come just to see if the niggers are rappin'!" They were the youngest, and the preeminent, on the east side.

One drug dealer called the Hammer would force Champ and Esham to perform on command by pulling out a gun.

"Me and Esham just clicked, basically," Champ says:

Then me and him became a pair; it was like he had no choice, really. He was so good at what he do, there wasn't nobody to take him to the next level to get noticed. So us getting together was a way to make us both known. Even back then, I made sure he got his props. Made sure he got his solo. Like he'd be beatboxing, and I'd be like, "Tell 'em your name," and he'd like make a vacuum-cleaner noise and he called himself Rockbox. We always was capping on muthafuckers, too. It was like we needed each other, honestly.

As it grew, he was like, "Fuck this." Beatboxing was like playing second fiddle. People started playing him like he was a sheep. And he got really frustrated. Then he started writing his own rhymes, undercover.

Randolph Gear was an art teacher at Von Steuben. He remembers Champ and Esham well. "Champ was the class clown, and he was always interested in the music industry as a little kid. He really admired Prince. Esham was a troubled kid, always getting into fights."

The pair split up (Esham has since sold hundreds of thousands of records) their first year in high school after a beef erupted when Champ was accused of having a part in beating up Esham's brother, which Champ denies.

"I didn't even touch the motherfuckers. We actually broke up because he was telling me how he worshiped the devil. Period."

Rap for Champ was, as a street rat with a fake ID, his way into something—it gave him purpose and direction and a sense of competition. Rap kept him from sidling up to his hit-for-hire neighbors and fueled his methodology.

The Beast Crew has been described as a kind of ghetto Motown. It began around 1984. Its main purpose was to showcase neighborhood kids' skills and talents. They were a collective of DJs and emcees drawn together out of boredom, a love of music, and a desire to sidestep dope-selling clichés. The belief was if somebody would get signed to a major record deal, they could pull everybody else along. It was also a way to meet girls.

Too young to get into clubs, the only place they could convene was in the basement of Blackman's east-side house near Six Mile Road and Gratiot Avenue. Blackman describes the crew as "controlled chaos."

It was all about basement rapping, backyard parties, on-the-cheap demos and videos, and the occasional show at rental halls such as the Holiday and the Odyssey and, later, in Mount Clemens.

Detroit shows entertained crews of drug dealers, street hustlers, and local kids—boys mostly.

Blackman was a street-savvy teen then, calling himself "The Blackman from New Jersey." As a teenager, he'd done national tours with LL Cool J, Dr. Jeckyll and Mr. Hyde, MC Shan, Marley Marl, Rock Master Scott, Roxanne Shanté, and UTFO. He was the teenage godfather of the Crew. (He says he never came home with money from touring. "There wasn't any.")

Terence "T-Bone" Jones was a teen DJ in the Crew:

Black's was the only place you could go to tighten up your skills. Back then, Black was the only one that was really working with major artists. He was like maybe sixteen, seventeen, and we'd seen the future in it through him. He was trying to get people to start doing the music thing. Black would skip school. He would skip school and try to persuade you to come along with him. It'd be negative and positive at the same time. Most of all of us went to Osborn High, and skipping school was negative, but he'd be

taking you to something that's real positive. We was out gangbanging and doing all the rest of the stuff you do in the neighborhood. He was telling us, "Look, leave that alone and come do this."

We wasn't really impressed till Black started introducing us to Curtis Blow and Cool J. He knew these people. That was a big influence on us. He introduced me to Curtis Blow, Rock Master Scott, and the Dynamic Three, Real Roxanne—and that was only in the beginning. I was blown away since then. I was following him to make music.

With the ten-year-old Champ involved, the core of the Beast Crew was T-Bone, Blackman, Blackman's kid brother Mr. Glide, and Ben "Hot Mix" Koyton. Champ says there were Beast Crew hangers-on coming and going, "Thugs who'd get popped and jailed for rape or for shooting somebody. It was always the floaters that hung around us that always got into heavy street trouble. Blackman gave us all a shot."

Hot Mix, who had a job and could afford to buy records, says Champ introduced rap into the Crew's "progressive" music mix. "There was a lot of music that Champ was familiar with, different rap stuff like KRS-One and early Ice-T stuff like that that I wasn't familiar with," Hot Mix says. "We were floatin' in off the tail end of disco."

Champ, with his hyper-rhyming, freestyling mouth, was the Crew's star. Nobody could believe this kid could be so skilled at such a tender age.

Jones and Glide backed the emcee at parties and shows. "We pulled Brian in 'cause he was a spitfire, and he was young, and we'd never seen nobody that young that could rap like that," Jones says. "Like Twista do in raps; Champ raps real fast. When me and Glide would DJ, we'd have four turntables, and then we'd have little Brian in front. No backup behind him; he was just in the front by himself. It really was a little kid showcasing us. We worked with Brian, and we went into the studio and put out tapes and had a whole lot of shows, man. That was pretty much it until Kid Rock got into the picture. And that was in '87."

Blackman, Hot Mix, and KDC (a fellow member of their group) were DJing a "cabaret" party in Mount Clemens when Kid Rock appeared, wanting to spin. Blackman gave him a shot. Turns out Rock's mad DJ skills floored everybody. After that, Blackman brought Rock "down to the ghetto," put him up at his house, and used Champtown as an example of how to rap.

Jones says:

Bob [Kid Rock] got Champ in him. When we first met him, he was spinning. He wanted to get into the rap part, so he came and Black was trying to show him. By showing him it's like, "Watch Brian. You want to be an emcee? Watch Brian. Watch what Brian's doing." And that's what he would do. He would watch Brian and study Brian. Brian's a real silly kid, too. So he [Rock] became a silly person himself, you know, to put that into his act. Brian had *it*. He was a little kid, but he had it. I don't know how he got it, but he was born with it.

"Kid would get a little flustered when they would make comparisons," Hot Mix says. "I think Kid was

intimidated. He would never take the challenge to battle Champ."

Rock landed his first major-label deal with Jive, though the label had first had interest in Champ. Blackman (who was managing Champ then) says that since Rock was white, he'd get the record deal. Period. That's just how it was. (Rock romanticized his days with Blackman and the Beast Crew on "I Wanna Go Back," from 1996's *Early Mornin' Stoned Pimp*).

After squabbles and divides within the Crew, Champ split in 1990 to start Straight Jacket records. Rock later tracked Champ down at his pizza-making gig and took him on tour. On and off for three years—from 1993 to 1996—Champ, sporting a big, green 'fro, toured as Rock's hypeman, dubbed "Champtown the Incredible Green-Headed Negro." He brought Rock on at the storied 1996 State Theatre show that landed Kid his Atlantic deal.

(Kid Rock did return this writer's phone call but kept his comments brief. "I love Blackman and Champ and the Beast Crew, but I don't want to talk to *Metro Times*. They never helped me when I was coming up.")

As hip-hop's popularity rose, the shows would move to the suburbs, at high schools, where white kids were actually buying the music.

Certain radio DJs championed Detroit rap on specialty shows. Billy T was one, and he spent eleven years (between 1986 and 1997) on Detroit airwaves. His hip-hop shows such as *Billy T's Basement Tapes* and *The Rap Blast* gave budding local acts needed exposure.

Marc Kempf edited and published a rap magazine called *Underground Soundz* in the early

'90s and owns a music distributor, Long Range Distribution. He says there were just a handful of rap records that Billy T could spin in the early days.

"Billy T was a supportive DJ, and he was playing Dice, he was playing Kaos and Maestro, Kid Rock, probably did play Champtown," Kempf says. "I gotta give him his props."

"There was no payola shit then," Champ says. "Billy T was very instrumental in bringing the music out. He was all about Detroit *love*; his ears was on the street. It hasn't been right since he left. Now DJs think they're celebrities."

Radio also helped bridge the sociological line drawn between the east and west sides, that time-honored split based on class-distinction clichés.

"I think the overall Detroit rap *sound* didn't have a big difference between east side and west side," Kempf says. "But I think a lot of people were a little hesitant to venture too far off their block. I mean, everyone was hearing JLB [WJLB-FM]. I think JLB inspired the Detroit sound in '88 and '89 as much as anything. They were the only station. There was no college radio. This was '88, '89, till 105.9 [WDTJ] came around four or five years ago."

"The east side was a totally different country," says Motsi Ski from Detroit's Most Wanted, an early '90s gangsta group that transcended the east-west borders. "As far as it being divided, I don't know what it was."

"I can't put a finger on what it is," Jones says. "I can tell you this—they think they're more important on the west side because a lot of their parents come from the east side back in the early '70s. They moved to the west side to raise their kids. They were showing their kids something different. But they grew up in the Black Bottom and the rest of the spots over here on the east side. They thought they was better than we were. We're grimy, we're from the east side."

Champ is munching on a bologna sandwich in the two-bedroom east-side apartment he shares with Keasha and their two daughters—Ciara, fifteen (Keasha's before Champ), and ten-year-old Makala.

Champ talks about his days with young Eminem and the conversation is littered with phrases such as "Em should tell the truth" and "Em jus' erased these five years out of his memory like they don't exist," yet his demeanor is that of a man entirely in control of his career and life.

Is this bitterness talking, then?

"It's not bitterness," Champ says, "it's just the truth should be heard. I respect Eminem, straight up. I've never seen anybody work so hard on a single verse. But I don't like it when motherfuckers don't give me my props."

Champtown was featured in the February 2004 issue of the *Source* magazine in a heavily publicized story that attempted to tag Eminem as a racist, using old tapes and comments from Detroit hip-hop scenesters as evidence. In it, Champ accuses Eminem's manager (Paul Rosenberg) of keeping Eminem's black crew (D12) down and explains how he introduced Eminem to his side of Eight Mile Road.

Shortcut has been pals with Champ (and is signed to his label) since meeting him around 1990. A somewhat diminutive dancer/rapper who's built like a Mr. Universe competitor (and whose live persona is built on flippant, bling-bling strip-bar sleaze and old-school booty that would do Lil John proud), Shortcut was hanging with Bassmint Productions then, Eminem's crew. Shortcut says

Eminem liked what Champ was doing and "they started working together."

"Back then he [Eminem] never had a hook to a song," Shortcut says. "It would be like he was just telling a story. He never had hooks. Champ was one of the people who brought him in and showed him things, showed him hooks and humor."

Hence the "Do-Da-Dipity" single and video, and Eminem's appearance on various Champ songs.

Champ always had a video camera rolling in his posse. Early '90s video footage from a suburban high school is telling; it reveals a young Eminem finding his legs as a showman: a spindly kid immersing himself in, and wanting to be accepted by, black culture. He soaked up the transcendent force of black music from myriad sources, Champ included. Another video from a performance at 1515 Broadway (circa 1993) sees Champ standing onstage next to Eminem as protection at an all-black show.

There are videos of a Champ recording session at Paisley Park in 1992 that show Eminem as a nose-picking kid, looking no less a threat than Kid 'N Play's Kid in *House Party*, in his high-top fades and Hammer pants.

Champ lets loose a high-pitched chortle followed by rapid-fire tirade: "Can you believe how he got America fooled like he's some tough-ass motherfucker?"

Hot Mix says, "Oh, man, it's so funny that Kid never mentions him, that Em never mentions him. They would emulate things that he would say, things from his character. It's kinda sad, but you never know what goes through their heads once they hit big. Especially Em and Kid."

Jones: "But the people that are *really* major out of Detroit are Marshall [Eminem] and it's Bob

[Rock], man. And they're not telling it all. Why do these guys got all these skills?"

Detroit's Most Wanted's Motsi Ski—who's Jackie Wilson's grandson—knew Eminem and Champ then:

This isn't about fuck Kid Rock or fuck Em. It's like Em and Uncle Kracker and Rock—all these motherfuckers is on but Champ *ain't* on? *Shit*. He should've given Champ more props.

I look at all the shit my grandfather went through. Michael Jackson stole from my grandfather, ya know what I'm sayin'? Em is the biggest entertainer in the world. *The. Biggest. Star.* And I have no bitterness with Em, he deserves all the success he has. But he need to put niggers on. Just give Champ his credit.

Uncle Ill met Champ in 1990 when the two worked at Little Caesars (Champ launched Straight Jacket using profits from making pizza). They were partnered throughout the early '90s, doing recordings and shows. Among other things, they can be heard together on Champ's first solo Straight Jacket release, the EP *Call Me Joker*. Ill was Champ's hype-man, at first, and soon started rapping lines. Ill later split with Champ's on-again-off-again pal rapper Hush and formed Da Ruckus. The split was bitter on personal and business levels, and Champ felt betrayed.

"He took me to the real studio [Paisley Park] and I appreciate that," Ill says. "I kept waiting for Champ to get the big deal. Kid Rock got a deal. But not Champ. Then Uncle Kracker got a deal.

But not Champ. Em got a deal. But not Champ. Obie Trice got a deal. But not Champ. D12 got a deal. But not Champ. And Champ *knows* everybody in the business. It goes back to where the music is. Hopefully he'll get a deal soon."

"You get both sides," Shortcut says. "Like what people say about Eminem. One side says he's a hater and a racist. The next minute he's down to the end. I think it's just jealousy. I mean, Champ's had opportunities with different record labels that because of investors and poor partners, it never happened the right way. If Champ was full of it, he wouldn't have the connections that he has."

Then there's the beef. Around 1995, Eminem accused Champ of trying to get into his wife Kim's pants. Champ and others interviewed say it wasn't true. Their friendship ended.

After the *Source* piece ran, D12's Proof (another rapper who looked up to Champ) dissed Champ on a mix CD. Champ responded with a scathing rap that rips Proof up one side and down the other. The dis is available for download on the Straight Jacket website.

In the small recording studio situated in a dimly lit half of Champ's basement, D'Phuzion is putting finishing touches on her debut album *Murder Death Kill*. Keasha—who could be anyone's young mom in orange sweats and blue slippers—sits in the engineering chair. She's fiddling with sound levels on a computer screen.

Champ, who "discovered" D'Phuzion at an east-side open-mic night in 1997, stands nearby, nodding to the playback music pumping through the studio monitors.

D'Phuzion resembles a youthful Florence Ballard, beautiful with arched brows, thick lips, dark eyes. She's shy but polite; she has a habit of turning her face away when she smiles.

With lyric book in hand, she slowly pulls herself up from her chair to confront the mic that's suspended from a ceiling pipe. When the track is cued, her reticence vanishes, and a coarse, commanding rat-a-tat vocal shoots from her lips: "Cut-throat-bitch-crazy-mu-tha-fuck-a"—her rhyming and meter spot on—"Bitch-I'm-thug-I'm-thug-I'm-gutta." Her left hand slices the air on vocal accents. Sweat quickly forms on her brow. Her body sways in half time to the distorted meter thumping from her headphones. There's simmering sexuality beneath her fury. She nails the vocal in less than ten minutes.

D'Phuzion makes gangsta rap high art: Though her lyrics are crammed with spongy themes of self-assertion, street injustice, identity issues and plenty of *fuck-yous*—familiar territory certainly—in her grip, they're all her own. She takes her personal experiences and fantasies and turns them into real-life mayhem. It might not have been an overstatement when Chuck D called D'Phuzion the greatest female rapper ever.

Her forthcoming album is wildly diverse, from southern crunk to club-floor fodder, old school and contemporary, capped with a slight whiff of soul. She's tongue-in-cheek (her take on ersatz gangstas, "You Are So Gangsta") and cheeky (tackling Donna Summer on a disco remix of "Your Finger on the Trigger"). A between-song skit, "The Hater," is a brilliant piss-take on local rap beefs.

It's obvious that D'Phuzion looked up to Detroit rapper Boss (the nation's first female gangsta rapper, who had a Top 40 hit in the '90s). There's even a duet with Boss in "Street Cred."

The east-side-bred D'Phuzion started rapping at age six and says her father tipped her off to music, namely the Sugar Hill Gang, Run-D.M.C., and Kurtis Blow.

When Champ and D'Phuzion did the 1999–2000 Public Enemy tour, it was the only time Flavor Flav ever arrived on time for his own shows. He came early to see D'Phuzion perform.

Within a week, Yang Ku and Tekneek pretty much finish their respective albums.

Tekneek, a spliff-happy, sleepy-eyed nineteen-year-old, has a tattoo of himself etched into his left forearm. He has just enough arrogance to piss off teachers and parents, and it's reflected in the blips, beats, and laconic raps of *Listen to the Book I Wrote*. His mom raised him in Port Huron and he grew up on soul music, mainly because he wasn't allowed to listen to rap. Inspiration, he says, comes from the writings of James Baldwin, Poe, and Tupac. His raps *are* inspired.

Yang Ku—Bruce Kue and Downie Yang—the dancing, crooning Asian boy duo with matching streaked coifs, are first-generation Americans. The songwriters say they both adore, of all people, Richard Marx. Champ spotted them one day while shopping at the Guitar Center. Yang was just tapping on a keyboard.

"When I saw an Asian motherfucker playing urban soul music on a keyboard, I said that's it," Champ says.

Champ brought in a vocal coach for Yang Ku, who spent eight months fine-tuning their throats. They rehearse every dance move to every song before every live show, which includes a cadre of break dancers. They pipe tricky harmonies with aplomb, and sound like angels: File their brand of downy

R&B somewhere between Boys II Men, Prince, and Usher. They're calculated, sure, but completely indie in spirit; they've learned everything, they say, simply by observing American culture, particularly MTV.

"They grew up in the hood," Champ says. "They saw the struggle. They went through some of the same racial tension."

Champ and Keasha have been working these and other Straight Jacket projects for a number of years, grooming, guiding, polishing. They've enlisted ace beat-makers including Quincy "QD3" Jones III; Hank Shocklee prodigy Abnormal; and Detroiters Ghanz, Moking, and Sony Urban artist Frankie Biggz for all the new records.

Champ insists that all the Straight Jacket projects will be mixed, mastered, and ready for release "at the top of the new year." And that includes Mike Spear's *From Out of Nowhere*, Champ's own *Racial Profiling*, and Shortcut's aptly titled *Jump, Ride, Hump, Hop*.

It's a Sunday afternoon, and there's a label meeting at Champtown's place. His crew is relaxing in chairs and couches in the living room. Faygo and Pringles are set out on the dining room table for refreshments. Shortcut's kid mans the PlayStation.

Champ begins by lecturing his crew about showing up on time, then about personal presentation and marketing.

Keasha weighs in about her disappointment that the Yang Ku guys haven't completely rid themselves of their soft midriffs. She tells them that they aren't looking quite like stars yet. "If it's anything to do with Straight Jacket, you look the part." The Yang Ku guys nod in agreement.

Shortcut gets a pithy lecture about spending more time on his craft, creating raps that aren't recycled. "Everything can't be a retread here,"

Champ tells him. "It can't happen. You got to get down and put time aside to make it right."

Tekneek swears he's given up weed. Tempers flare at times; even Keasha, D'Phuzion, and Champ get into it (a row that escalated a few days later at the *Metro Times* shoot for this issue's cover; D'Phuzion stormed off before the session began).

The meeting's focus is on rapper Mike Spear. He was suspended for what Champ calls letting his ego get the best of him and for making a rude gesture toward Keasha. Spear is a lanky, high-cheekboned, and good-looking twenty-one-year-old, a guy ready for his *Total Request Live* close-up. He wants back into the label's fold.

Each Straight Jacket artist has a say about Spear. And they talk, one after the other, letting the dirty laundry air. Spear sits in a folding chair, listens quietly, often staring at his feet. When it comes time for him to speak, he does. The long apology is accepted. He's back in the crew. The two-hour meeting is over when Champ solicits twenty-five dollars from everybody for a new computer hard drive to store recordings.

Later on, a woman stops by the apartment with her thirteen-year-old daughter named Sweets in tow. Sweets is a pretty, soft-featured rapper/violinst, and she's here to audition for the label.

The Straight Jacket crew moves to the subterranean studio to hear the girl rap. She offers up a surprisingly well-constructed and droll ditty called "School Ho Rock" (after "School House Rock") that skewers playground hip sway and riffraff. The crew listens closely and politely. When the girl finishes there's resounding applause. Sweets is, of course, the next addition to Straight Jacket label. And what would Berry Gordy think?

## UPDATE ON CHAMP

Since this story ran, Champtown worked the Straight Jacket catalog for a short time. Because the high costs of keeping an indie label afloat in Detroit took its toll on his family, Champ landed a job teaching a music course at the Institute of Production and Recording in Minneapolis, Minnesota. He stayed there for three years. He's currently living in Goodyear, Arizona, where, he says, "He loves the weather but his kids hate it." He's talking to three networks about a hard-hitting TV series he has spent a few years writing and producing called *The Untold Stories of Hip-Hop*. The first episode, "Detroit," is shot, edited, and in the can. Each episode will examine a deep hip-hop story from a different major American city.

Champtown says his relationships with both Eminem and Kid Rock are up and down at best. He plans to relocate back home to Detroit in the near future.

# OF DETROIT

## COUNTRY YORK BROTHERS AND LATIN MUSICA

# Mellow Milestone

*Craig Maki*

Leslie York liked to craft songs alone with his guitar when Detroit's midnight din dropped to a hushed echo of yesterday's busy streets blended with a suggestion of tomorrow. Working in a factory imposed an unwelcome schedule, and he balanced monotonous days by performing hillbilly music most evenings with his older brother George as the York Brothers in taverns near east-side factories, in neighborhoods of people who, like George and Les, left the South for steady employment in Detroit.

York Brothers.
Photo courtesy of the Craig Maki Archives.

When the York Brothers' first record, "Hamtramck Mama," appeared in 1939, subsequent publicity, fan support, and money encouraged Les to devote more time to writing. His songs, and recordings with George, almost single-handedly built the legacy of Mellow Record Company, one of Detroit's first independent record labels.

Originally from Louisa, Kentucky, the York Brothers arrived in Detroit about 1937. George, born 1910, quit school and worked in coal mines as a teen before moving to Denver, Colorado, where he sang and picked guitar with a cowboy band on the stage and radio. In 1936, WPAY radio opened in Portsmouth, Ohio, and George took a job singing there. Leslie, born 1917, worked for the Civilian Conservation Corps and won musical talent contests in Kentucky before joining George at WPAY, playing lead guitar and singing harmony with his charismatic brother. As children, George and Les had performed with several siblings, so the debut of a York Brothers act may not have been a surprise to their family. Perhaps none suspected, however, that mild-mannered George would partner with the gregarious Leslie, who seemed on a constant hunt for good times, seeking the center of attention.

The York Brothers spent about a year in Portsmouth before they moved to Detroit, hiring into auto factories and entertaining in local cafés and bars. Between gigs, one or both would return to Portsmouth to perform on WPAY and at the Sylvan Theater in nearby Lucasville.

After more than a year of working an auto assembly line, Les completed "Hamtramck Mama," a playful blues about a lustful woman from Hamtramck, Michigan, a city incorporated within Detroit boundaries with a gangster history hidden behind the face of a Catholic culture brought by thousands of immigrant Poles.

Talk about your truckin' mamas,
boys, I've got one
She's a Hamtramck baby, and she
has her fun

She's a Hamtramck mama
And she sure does know her stuff
She's the hottest thing in town
Lordy, how she can love

You can tell her not to do it, but
she'll do it just the same
She's a Hamtramck mama that no
man can tame

The York Brothers took their guitars to Universal Recording Studios, a custom recording company on East Jefferson Avenue, and cut "Hamtramck Mama," along with "Going Home," an adaptation of Bradley Kincaid's "Little Whitewashed Chimney." Marquette Music, a decades-old Detroit vending-machine company, financed the record and placed it among pop and hillbilly titles in their jukeboxes throughout the city. But just after the recording session, Les lost his job in the factory. George, who remained employed at his workplace, told his brother he'd call him if any musical opportunities materialized in the future, and Les drove south on the "hillbilly highway," US-23.

Back in Portsmouth, Les performed solo, picking up new musicians as needed. A few weeks after his abrupt departure from Michigan, Les heard NBC radio announcer Lowell Thomas broadcast news about Detroit's district attorney seeking to ban "Hamtramck Mama" from the city's jukeboxes because public officers thought it defamatory to the good citizens of Hamtramck. The report suggested the York Brothers had done something scandalous, and possibly unlawful, which generated enough fear in Les that he swore not to return to Detroit—until a few days later, when George sent for him. The publicity sent record sales into high gear, and the York Brothers fielded invitations from bigger Detroit nightclubs, some of which began hosting hillbilly music nights in their honor.

"Hamtramck Mama" reportedly sold three hundred thousand copies in Detroit alone. George quit his day job, and the York Brothers worked lucrative, nightly bookings in Detroit. They performed their music, wrote songs, recorded, and sold records. The Yorks followed up their hit with more titillating titles, some of which included Hawaiian steel guitar, such as "Highland Park Girl" and "It Tain't No Good."

From their first recordings, the York Brothers sang loudly in studio settings, causing slight microphone distortions. In "Detroit Hulu Girl," a breakneck tempo, amplified steel guitar, and in-the-red vocals added up to a record that captured a wild performance that predicted the rough, rowdy energy of rock 'n' roll.

## ON DOWN THE LINE

The York Brothers separated from Marquette Music quickly. Their next discs, also sporting the Universal Recording Studios label, featured addresses for the studio itself and Mellow Music Shop, a few doors up Jefferson Avenue.

In 1939, Edward Kiely opened the Mellow Music Shop on East Jefferson. He soon added a second address nearby, on Dickerson. Kiely sold musical instruments, lessons, sheet music, and records. Described by singer and songwriter Jimmy Work as a nice man "up in years" when they met around 1941, Kiely also serviced jukeboxes in the vicinity. His route probably included bars and cafés that catered to a clientele that listened to country music.

In 1941, the York Brothers cut six tunes for major label Decca in a Chicago studio. Tame by comparison to their previous records, the technically superior Decca recordings revealed the Yorks' capacity for refined delivery and Leslie's talent for writing sentimental songs. To fans of the Delmore Brothers, who also recorded for Decca and who had established a reputation for singing hillbilly blues in harmony during the 1930s, the York Brothers' Decca records came across as fair imitations. However, their subsequent Detroit recordings shattered Decca's sentimental vision for them.

While the York Brothers capitalized on their Decca releases, Ed Kiely reissued "Hamtramck Mama" and "It Tain't No Good" on a label called Hot Wax, featuring twin silhouettes of shapely young ladies.

The "Hamtramck Mama" success story awakened Detroit entertainment businesses to a growing market of workers from the South. It also presented a fresh example for Detroit's country-western entertainers to follow in promoting themselves through partnering with jukebox operators, music shops, nightclubs, and radio. Other local country acts followed suit by cutting novelty songs. In 1941 and 1942, Kiely bankrolled records that wore the Universal, Hot Wax, and Mellow labels by three other local C&W groups.

Distributed in jukeboxes across the Midwest by Detroit's Buhl Sons Company, the Hot Wax label introduced "Hollywood Mama," a rewrite of "Hamtramck Mama" by Billy Casteel and the Silver Sage Buckaroos, a Detroit-based cowboy band that broadcast on WEXL radio from Royal Oak. (On the record's B side, "Wayne County Blues," Casteel wailed about corruption in local politics.) It was popular enough for Kiely to reissue on Mellow.

Rye's Red River Blue Yodlers [*sic*], led by Tennessee fiddle player Forest Rye, cut "Snake Bite Blues" backed with "Don't Come Crying Around Me Mama" (Universal), and another song with a double-entendre lyric, "On Down the Line," paired with "You Had Time to Think It Over" (Hot Wax and Mellow). Rye established himself as a musician in the Motor City in 1924, playing house parties, cafés, and radio, while working days at Ford Motor Company in Highland Park. Around 1942, Rye performed comedy as Little Willie on WSM radio's *Grand Ole Opry*, returning to Detroit during the week. He finally settled in Tennessee in 1955.

Eveline Haire and her Swingtime Cowgirls, an "all-girl" group, cut two records of western swing and blues, pressed with both Hot Wax and Mellow labels. Led by Haire, a bass player and singer, the group's performances such as "Triflin' Gal" and "Prairie Sweetheart" revealed a skilled ensemble of women that could compete with any "cowboy band." Haire sang sweetly and low-down, yodeled, and introduced three of the recordings with, "Howdy folks! This is Eveline Haire and her Swingtime Cowgirls. Take it away, gals," as if she were performing before a radio microphone. After the war, Haire and her band broadcast on WKMH radio in Dearborn.

## YORK BROTHERS BLUES

As it became clear that Decca would let their contract lapse in 1942, the York Brothers negotiated an agreement with Ed Kiely. From that point, the Mellow label—with its bold, hand-drawn "MELLOW" above the record hole; an outline of a bluebird perched atop a leafy branch originating from the second "L," the bird's body facing left and its head turned to the right, its beak spouting a stream of musical notes that drift down over its tail feathers; a draftsman's scrawl declaring, "MANUFACTURED BY MELLOW RECORD CO 965 DICKERSON AVE / DETROIT, MICH," and "MADE IN U.S.A."; and contents typeset in serif fonts listing "Hillbilly Novelty," or "Hillbilly Blues," record numbers, song titles, and authors—represented only records "By YORK BROS."

During the previous decade of economic tumult, the Great Depression forced hundreds of regional record companies out of business, leaving only the strongest labels and most popular artists opportunities to make new recordings. In historic terms, and despite concentrating on country music, Mellow emerged as Detroit's preeminent—perhaps the first—independent record company during World War II, when the federal government restricted business production by regulating

distribution of raw materials (such as shellac, the main ingredient of records at the time), gasoline, and food. Mellow's fruition also had much to do with the spending power of local country music (and York Brothers) fans. Factories in Detroit functioned at full capacity, around the clock. Detroit workers earned easy cash to spend in jukeboxes found in cafés, bars, and nightclubs. Many venues added extra shifts to entertain patrons at all hours of the day and night.

Within two years, Kiely produced fifteen new Mellow discs in quantity, featuring George's smooth vocal and old-timey rhythm guitar; Les singing high and picking wicked, as well as tender, licks through an (over-) amplified guitar; and a swinging bass by the enigmatic Jonnie Lavender, who whooped, hollered, and cackled on several recordings.

Lavender's percussive contributions turned the York Brothers' later Mellow records into a new dance music that couldn't be defined as strictly western swing, protobluegrass, or typical brothers-in-harmony fare. A frisky blues infused the music's beat, like Hank Williams's records in 1947 and Johnny Cash's in 1955. Music writers of the 1950s employed the term *rockabilly* to describe country musicians playing the hard boogie of rock 'n' roll. And during the heyday of the "arsenal of democracy," with jumping numbers such as "Going to the Shindig," "I've Got My Eyes on You," and a faster remake of "Hamtramck Mama," the York Brothers cut an early style of rockabilly music in Detroit.

Because of federal travel restrictions, the York Brothers stayed put, earning $115 a week during a time when enlisted servicemen received $30 to

$50 per month. A York Brothers engagement at the Jefferson Inn, a vaudeville nightclub on East Jefferson, drew attention from *Billboard* magazine, which also published lines from a fan letter in September 1943: "I came to Detroit in 1942 and am now in a war plant. . . . The [York Brothers] have made 135 records and are fine in their playing of old-time music. They are now broadcasting over WJLB, Detroit, four times a week," signed, "A Good Old Hillbilly from Kentucky." William Levin, owner of the Jefferson Inn, sponsored the York Brothers on WJLB radio. Also, the number of records that the letter writer stated has yet to be verified. As of 2014, researchers have identified forty-four titles, not including Decca sides, recorded by the York Brothers in Detroit before 1944.

The York Brothers explored a variety of themes on Mellow records. "New Trail to Mexico," "Rose of the Rio Grande," and "Riding and Singing My Song" could have been sung in Gene Autry movies. "If I Knew I'd Never Lose You," "Just Wanting You," and several more told stories of love and heartbreak. "Gamblers Blues," "York Brothers Blues," and "Got to Get Rid of My Worried Mind" revealed the Yorks' love for and skill in performing blues. "Hail, Hail Ol' Glory," "Hillbilly Rose," "Conscription Blues," and "A Merry Christmas to the Boys over There" acknowledged and supported American patriotism. "We're Gonna Catch That Train," "Home in Tennessee," "Mother's Sunny Smile," and "Kentucky's Calling Me" proclaimed devotion to a southern home in the distant past.

On most of their records, the York Brothers sang harmony together, but George soloed on a few sides. Les performed a talking-blues on "Not over Thirty-Five," which made light of a wartime law limiting vehicle speeds to thirty-five miles per hour. Les celebrated country folk with horses and buggies that could then get around better than "big shots in their limousines."

They also cut an instrumental called "Hula Girl Wobble," with amplified Hawaiian steel guitar (probably played by Les), bass, and acoustic guitar. This recording recently turned up in a stack of one-sided discs with titles penciled on white paper labels stamped "Mellow Record Co."—suggesting the Yorks recorded more music than Kiely could gather resources (monetarily or material) to issue. One of the white-label discs features an unknown young woman singing a novelty song accompanied by a jazz fiddle player. It appears Kiely's operations attracted more country-western artists than he was able to publish.

In July 1942, James Petrillo, president of the American Federation of Musicians, ordered a recording ban that lasted until the end of 1943. The York Brothers were making too much money to pay it attention. Dixie Music Publishing of New York City produced copies of a *York Brothers Famous Folio of Songs to Remember*, featuring transcriptions from their Mellow catalog, as well as a portrait of the York Brothers sporting dark silk cowboy shirts, white hats, and a grinning Jonnie Lavender between the brothers, holding his bass a step back.

## LONG TIME GONE

George and Les ended their party in March 1944, when they enlisted in the United States Navy. While George was assigned to entertain troops in the Pacific, the navy sent Les to fight the war in Europe. As soon as the York Brothers returned to civilian life in January 1946, they approached

WSM radio in Nashville, which found time for them on the *Grand Ole Opry*. The music they cut for Nashville's Bullet Records that year reproduced the style they'd birthed in Detroit before the war (they even remade "Hamtramck Mama"), with the additions of Warren "Swanny" Swann on bass and fiddle by Curley King. But the conservative, competitive environment of Music City, as well as personal adjustments to postwar life, led to the Yorks refining the frantic energy they displayed as young men in Detroit.

From 1947 to 1956, the York Brothers made records for Cincinnati-based King Records, which updated their sound with a full band, including piano. During the late '40s, the Yorks also played tent shows with Bill Monroe and Grandpa Jones across the South and Midwest, and continued booking weeknight gigs in Detroit nightclubs. When *Opry* management caught an inebriated Les York playing the wrong song on the Ryman Auditorium stage in 1950, he and George, who had begun experiencing trouble with nodes on his vocal cords, moved back to Detroit (by way of several weeks spent at the "Louisiana Hayride" barn dance, based in Shreveport).

Upon their return, the York Brothers cut "Motor City Boogie," a tribute to Detroit industry and workers. Besides churning out quality country music, such as "Mountain Rosa Lee," "Long Time Gone," and "My Carolina Gal," the York Brothers also made a few country-western versions of rhythm-and-blues hits for King. Detroit's Fortune Records reissued the original 1939 version of "Hamtramck Mama" on its label and kept the recording in print through the 1970s.

The York Brothers appeared regularly on WJR radio's *Big Barn Frolic* Saturday-night barn dance and scored a nationwide country-western hit with "Tennessee Tango," backed with "River of Tears," in 1953. Before winter arrived that year, the York Brothers moved their families to Dallas, Texas, where George invested in a restaurant. The brothers returned to Detroit during the next two summers for more nightclub work and radio appearances on the WJR *Goodwill Jamboree* led by Casey Clark and the Lazy Ranch Boys.

For several more summers, Les York visited Detroit on his own, playing nightclubs, Jefferson Beach Park, and WBRB radio in Mount Clemens with Danny Richards and his Gold Star Cowboys. During the final York Brothers sessions for King in late 1955 and 1956, Les sang solo or dubbed a second vocal track for his absent brother.

At the peak of rock's pressure on country music in 1957, Decca Records reunited George and Les in Nashville to cut "Everybody's Tryin' to Be My Baby," a bopping version of an old western-swing tune. Fifteen years after the York Brothers made their most rocking sides, the record went nowhere. The teenage Everly Brothers, singing with a style derived from the York Brothers and other brother acts of their generation, scored their first pop and country smashes that year. In 1958, the Everlys remade Les York's "Long Time Gone" on their album *Songs Our Daddy Taught Us*.

The York Brothers performed on country-music radio and TV shows in Dallas and Fort Worth through the '60s and produced several single records on their own. George died in Dallas in 1974. Les passed away ten years later. Best remembered for "Hamtramck Mama," "Tennessee Tango," and music they made for Mellow, Bullet, and King—all while associated with Detroit—the York Brothers left behind an admirable legacy of more than one hundred studio recordings.

## MELLOW DOWN

Detroit's Mellow Record Company never recovered its momentum after the York Brothers joined the navy in 1944. However, notes by *Billboard* in 1946, when several record companies such as Fortune emerged in Detroit, suggested Ed Kiely planned to revive his label. He was mugged while servicing his jukebox route the following year (perhaps a sign of the mob's infiltration of Detroit jukebox and vending-machine businesses). Kiely's name disappeared from the pages of *Billboard* after 1950, when he reported an uptick in jukebox revenue as Chrysler workers ended a strike at the Jefferson Avenue Assembly plant.

In 1954, *Billboard* reported that a Lula Kiely (relation to Ed Kiely wasn't specified, nor was his name mentioned) sold the Mellow Music Shop on East Jefferson. The new owners kept the name. While pushing popular records, they allowed a stock of Mellow label discs, mostly purchased by fans who remembered the York Brothers or "Hamtramck Mama," to dwindle slowly.

Forty years later, after all traces of Mellow Music, the Time Theater, and other storefronts between Drexel and Coplin streets had been demolished and removed from East Jefferson Avenue, I got to know a former Mellow customer at his own record shop on Eight Mile Road, where he introduced me to the York Brothers' music. Between puffs on cigars, the gray-bearded record hound told me what he knew and had heard about the Mellow Music Shop. His story

ended like this: One bright summer afternoon, about ten years after Lula Kiely called it quits, Mellow staff moved remaining boxes of York Brothers records—relics of Detroit's wartime environs encoded in grooves of once-precious shellac—from the shop's back room into a hot trash dumpster.

# The Big Three

## Contemporary Roots of Latin Sounds in Detroit—
## The Cruz Brothers, Ozzie Rivera, and Luis Resto

*Rhonda Welsh*

Many young people dream of having a career in music. As a teenager, Benny Cruz of Southwest Detroit was one of them. So, in 1976, he formed a band with his sister Rose and his brother Mauro. They learned a few songs, and they got their first gig at a graduation party in Detroit. Things were going well, but after a short time onstage, they found that they'd played through their entire repertoire. When they admitted this to the crowd and tried to step down, the people shouted out, "That's OK, play them again!" This led to a career for Benny and Mauro that lasted thirty years.

With Mauro on guitar and Benny on keyboard and vocals, the Cruz Brothers Band remained a family band, playing an infectious mixture of Latin rhythms and Santana-influenced guitar. Later, Benny's sister was replaced by his son Julian Cruz and his nephew Juan Patino on drums and congas, respectively. Julian and Juan grew up with music, often going on tour with Benny and working as his road crew. When they became teenagers, they made a natural transition from roadies to musicians, with some help from Benny and Mauro. Empowering others to achieve their dreams was a big part of Benny's philosophy toward music, business, and life in general. This came from an important lesson Benny learned, in part, from his own father.

The Cruz family moved from Arizona to Detroit in 1966. Benny's parents were migrant workers, laboring on farms in the West and in the steel mills of Detroit, but they wanted their children to have a different kind of life. Cruz's parents strongly emphasized the importance of education when their kids were growing up. But when Benny had reached working age, his father encouraged him to go to work in a migrant camp. So Benny worked on a farm in California for a time, just long enough to realize (as his father had known he would) that this wasn't to be the future he wanted. Shortly afterward, Benny enrolled in college, earning a bachelor's of music, teacher certification, and eventually a master's. He later pursued a doctorate of education at Wayne State University, and he became the school principal at Hope of Detroit Academy in Detroit.

Brother Mauro Cruz also took his parents' lessons to heart, and he currently supplements his career in music with a job as a school principal. The brothers both had day jobs as educators that they often combined with their love of music. They would often offer workshops to local students, trying to spread the love of the music they play. "One of my goals is to cross cultural barriers and bring this music to new cultures," Benny would explain.

Benny also tried to teach students some of the lessons he'd learned in his life and career. "Work hard to achieve your dreams," he'd say, "but always have a backup plan." He recommended that aspiring musicians educate themselves, pursuing a professional career that allows them the time and freedom to perform. This combination of the inspirational and the practical was evident in Benny's approach to music, too. He took business courses to master the art of marketing his band, developing a network of contacts, and negotiating favorable contracts—something he highly recommended to young musicians. "I've seen a lot of talented musicians go by the wayside because they didn't learn how to run a business properly," he explained.

Benny avoided this fate, achieving a successful career in music. And he did it through a mixture of talent, charisma, and business savvy. Benny tried to continually adapt to the emerging styles within Latin music, incorporating new rhythms and diverse styles into his music. "It's important to give the audience what they want. If they feel entertained, if you can make them feel like part of your music, you're guaranteed another performance." To make this connection, he said, "It helps to involve the audience from the beginning, to get them clapping and dancing, or singing a chorus. You have to touch an audience, to make them flow with the energy of your music, an energy which they give back to you. When you connect in this way, the best word to describe it is . . . magic."

Latino singer, songwriter, arranger, and producer Benny Cruz gained global recognition, having experienced tremendous regional success in the northern and midwestern United States as a solo artist and as the director of his award-winning band. Benny earned much praise as the "ambassador of Latin music" from fans and peers alike. His ability to uniquely blend many forms of music—rock, alternative, pop, salsa, merengue,

cumbia, banda, cha-cha, mambo, jazz, and heartfelt ballads that tug at human emotion—made for a breathtaking, awe-inspiring, and highly charged live performance. His uncanny ability to emote and to touch the masses with his live performance and music was a testament to his remarkable relationship with fans of all ages.

Benny Cruz was dedicated to the presentation of Latin music to the general public in an effort to maintain and enhance the knowledge of audiences the world over. Through this dedication, Benny offered various Latin music workshops, which incorporated styles and elements of music that were found in his many songs.

Over the many years of his career, Benny Cruz opened for Tito Puente, Texas Tornadoes, Ricky Smith y la Movida, and La Sombra, and he even performed with John Tesh. He has performed in Canada and Mexico. He's appeared on television, radio, and MTV. And he's performed on the stages of Detroit's Fox Theatre, State Theatre, Pontiac Silverdome, Tiger Stadium, Comerica Park, Cobo Hall, Hart Plaza, Chene Park, Majestic Theater, Masonic Temple, Cranbrook Theater, Meadowbrook Theater, Renaissance Center, Phoenix Center, Motor City Casino, Chrysler Arts, Beats & Eats Festival, Latino World Festival, Puerto Rican Festival, Fiesta Mexicana Festival, Festival Latino, Mexicantown Festival, Unity in the Community Festival, the twenty-fifth La Raza national convention, and the Detroit Institute of Arts just to name a few. The Cruz Brothers performed during the 2006 Superbowl events at the Detroit Winterblast on February 3, 2006. Unfortunately, Detroit lost one of its best, most dedicated, and most generous musicians when Benny Cruz passed away in June 2013. His passing has left a huge hole in Detroit music and Detroit Latin music, but his brother Mauro has worked tirelessly to keep the creative fires of Latino music and the memory of Benny Cruz alive.

Mauro Cruz has been playing and performing on the guitar for over thirty years. His major influence in music was the Latin music from his culture. However, growing up in what's known as both the Motor City and "Detroit rock city," Mauro, like Benny, has been influenced by Motown and Detroit rock 'n' roll. These diverse sounds opened Mauro's musical palate. His guitar influences were Carlos Santana, Jimi Hendrix, and Tony Iommi (Black Sabbath). Eventually, these musical influences spread to include Al Dimeola, Wes Montgomery, Earl Kugh, Chet Atkins, and a whole pantheon of other great guitarists. Although Mauro has been involved in music most his life, the workaday world dictated that he acquire a formal education, so Mauro applied himself to the point of getting a teaching certificate and becoming a teacher in Detroit. He didn't stop there; he went on to acquire a master's in education and then an educational specialist's degree.

## OZZIE RIVERA, BOMBARICA SHOWMAN AND ACTIVIST

Ozzie Rivera's community activism is intricately intertwined with his role as an artist. With several acts to his credit, including BombaRica and Orquesta la Inspiracion, he is a stellar percussionist and a staple on Detroit's music scene. His influences include Carlos Santana, Jose Feliciano, el Gran Combo, and Ismael Rivera.

"I took up the bongos at age sixteen, even though I was surrounded by music and musicians my entire life," he says.

Rivera deftly continues to use art and history to impact social change. He was the founding member of Casa de Unidad, which held the highly successful event Unity in the Community in Southwest Detroit's Clark Park. He follows that tradition with one of his newer undertakings, CLAVE, Community of Latino Visionaries and Artists.

Rivera sees music and community as closely related entities. "In its more fundamental stages, good music and good lyrics reflect the culture of a people. We know that culture is dynamic," Rivera says. "Even Motown, it touched a nerve that was culturally and historically important. The best music and culture has a universal appeal."

Rivera has been highly successful at tapping into the universal appeal of the music known as *bomba*. This African-influenced folk-music genre of Puerto Rico is one of the oldest, dating back to the 1600s. It was played at the sugar plantations on Saturday nights and holidays. Dance is an integral part of the music, and dancers move their bodies to every beat of the drum. For many, it was also a way to worship traditional African deities. The music has been credited with helping people deal with the hardships and oppression of slavery.

This parallel between struggle and art informs much of Rivera's work. "There is a grittiness that creates a vibrant musical culture. Detroit has that spirit. Good music comes from struggle," Rivera says.

## LUIS RESTO: FROM WAS (NOT WAS) TO EMINEM TO THE OSCARS

Pianist-keyboardist Luis Resto spent years as one of Detroit's best-kept secrets, lending his supple fingers to albums from artists as diverse as Anita Baker, Patti

Smith, and, his first big gig, Was (Not Was) and Eminem where he earned him an Oscar for his cowriting efforts of "Lose Yourself."

—Brian McCollum, *Detroit Free Press*

Luis Resto is known as one of the most creative and accomplished musicians and songwriters active in Detroit today, with a recording résumé that ranges from Patti Smith and Iggy Pop to chart-topping hip-hop artists such as Jay Z, B.o.B., 50 Cent, and, of course, Eminem.

A seminal member of the groundbreaking group Was (Not Was), Resto was highly influential in the development of that Detroit band's avant-funk ethos. As Was (Not Was) began its extended hiatus, Resto became an often-sought-after session musician, lending his talents to a wildly diverse collection of celebrated recording artists including Stevie Nicks, Mel Tormé, Anita Baker, and the legendary Highwaymen (Willie Nelson, Waylon Jennings, Kris Kristofferson, and Johnny Cash).

"My strength is to come in and channel the person I am around, I am able to interpret what the artist wants and not get in the way," Resto says.

Luis raised his profile significantly in 2001, hitting the stratosphere when he began a working collaboration with Marshall Mathers on *The Eminem Show*, a relationship that continues to this day including Mathers's newest release.

As Eminem's songwriting foil and one-time live keyboard player, Resto composed music for the hit film *8 Mile* and was cowriter of "Lose Yourself," the smash single that spent twelve weeks atop *Billboard*'s Top 100 and garnered Luis both a Grammy and an

Oscar. He continues to work with Eminem as a songwriter on recording projects.

The release of Eminem's chart-topping *Recovery* album in 2010 brought about much critical acclaim, most notably the single cowritten by Luis, "Not Afraid," which shot straight to the number 1 spot on *Billboard*'s Top 100 in its first week and received multiple Grammy nominations including one for Best Rap Song.

Luis's most recent recognizable work has been the musical arrangement and choir production for the use of "Lose Yourself" in the popular 2011 Chrysler 200 commercial featuring Eminem.

Amid all of the excitement, he has embarked on a solo career, releasing his debut album, *Combo De Momento*, in 2010 and *One Small Light* in the spring of 2012, finally stepping into the spotlight with his own compositions.

Says collaborator Don Was: "Luis Resto is the Iron Chef of music. He crosses stylistic borders with diplomatic immunity; his unique artistic vision knows no bounds. Luis has got that funky stank of genius all over him!"

# 9 DETRO
# MISCEL

IT MUSIC
LANEA

# Freeform Radio Master
## Dave Dixon on WABX
*Chris Morton*

It was 1967 and, if we were lucky, once in a great while we might hear something cool on AM radio—Buffalo Springfield's "For What It's Worth" being a harbinger of what was to come. In the autumn of that year, Detroit's WABX-FM began broadcasting *The Troubador*, an experimental show, for an hour each week.

For the first time we could listen to an eclectic mix of blues, rock, folk, and jazz all within the same program. And in stereo, no less. Within six months the X, as the station was known, was broadcasting similar programming for most of each day. For this listener, there was never any looking back at the limited, uneven, preformatted AM station offerings we had had to endure up to that point. (Remember the Zombies being followed by Percy Faith?)

As an impressionable fifteen-year-old music hound, I would frequently call and have lengthy conversations with the DJs while ostensibly doing homework. John Small, who soon moved over to WKNR-FM, was always very welcoming. Then ABX added Dave Dixon to its staff; he would go

Dave Dixon, 1969. © Leni Sinclair Collection.

on to become the esteemed leader of the legendary "Air Aces."

Dixon had a "golden ear," introducing attentive listeners to cross-cultural music on a worldwide scale. Only on his show could one be exposed to such gems as Paul Horn's "Inside the Taj Mahal," "Gandharva" from Beaver and Krause, Richard Harris singing "MacArthur Park," and Harry Nilsson's "The Point" (a complete LP side). In between, he might have mixed in a cut from John Mayall's *Blues from Laurel Canyon*, some Savoy Brown (with original vocalist Chris Youlden), Cat Mother and the All-Night Newsboys, and a track from Tim Buckley's *Happy Sad* release. Toss in some Brian Auger Trinity (featuring Julie Driscoll on vocals) and Laura Nyro singing "Eli's Coming" for good measure. Not to be overlooked, Detroit artists such as Frost (Dick Wagner), the Amboy Dukes (Ted Nugent), SRC, and the Stooges (Iggy Pop) would also be integrated into the mix.

Often, Dixon wouldn't play an entire track. Instead he would seamlessly blend portions of disparate genres into a cohesive audio excursion that might last an hour, interrupted only for an FCC-mandated station-ID break. His instrument was comprised of matching turntables, a mixing console, and a headphone set.

During his career, Dixon was fired from more than one station, being labeled as gruff and argumentative. While that very well may be true, to this listener—and frequent caller—he always had time to talk about music, share what he knew, and be an encourager. This was perhaps most important, for I had started on a voyage of musical discovery long before Dave Dixon and WABX, and I wondered why others didn't seem to find music as important to their daily existence. Instead of snuffing out that desire, his unique ability as audio interpreter, alchemist, and promoter fortified my quest to be ever on the alert for recordings of interest.

Today, the closest one can get to freeform programming in this style is college radio stations, which have limited range unless they're also streaming on the Internet like WNMC in Traverse City, Michigan. While it doesn't quite match Dixon's artistry, the Internet's Radio Paradise does a credible job of filling the void left by the demise of freeform terrestrial radio. (Albeit Dixon's shows sometimes felt extraterrestrial.)

Dixon left ABX in 1974. After ten years in the Miami/Fort Lauderdale market, he returned to Detroit, where for several years he played the same type of unique music mix on public station WDET as he had during those heady days of the "Air Aces."

After a few years doing a talk show on WXYT in Detroit, Dixon died at home in May of 1999 at age sixty. His legacy is that of programming shows in the way that a painter chooses colors and textures, painstakingly and deliberately applying them on an aural canvas to provide much more than a fleeting impression.

# The Day I Saved WABX

## Dan Carlisle

I am not sure of the date of this event, but I think it is 1968. There was so much social and personal change in my life from 1966 to 1970 that exact times are a bit gray or foggy in my memory. However, the details of the event I am going to tell you about are still sharp and clear in my mind.

I am in the little WABX production room with another staff member and I am voicing a spot for a Donovan album. At this point in the tale I need to add some background information on what was happening at this crazy little radio station located on the thirty-third floor of the David Stott Building

Dan Carlisle sitting on bench at WABX-FM. Photo Courtesy of Dan Carlisle.

in downtown Detroit: Our crappy little office space was jammed with radio equipment and record shelves piled on top of cheap royal-blue carpeting. The engineer at this time was a character named John Detz. John was also in the naval reserves and served as an assistant to a naval chaplain. His job was to accompany the chaplain when he had to visit a Detroit family and tell them their child had been killed in the Vietnam conflict. John was about to meet fate along with a small gang of hippie DJs with delusions of changing the world, one Cream, Frank Zappa, or Beatles song at a time.

John Small was the program director and general manager of WABX at this time. John was an affable, glad-handing kind of guy that was easy to like. Without any warning, he suddenly resigned and became head of WKNR-FM.

The owners of WABX also owned a small chain of FM stations in the Midwest and knew that they might have a money machine in their Detroit property. They told Detz he could be the big kahuna if he could prove he could sell commercial time to sponsors. Meanwhile, they brought in a sales guy from somewhere in Ohio who was told the same thing. At this time WABX still had some of the sponsored programs that had been the station's main money stream. We had the German hour and the Polish something-or-another plus some right-wing

Bircher crap—but they paid good money. So this other guy was going to try to sell the station as a block programmed facility.

Now back to the day in the production room doing a Donovan commercial. We knew that we were twenty-four hours away from the deadline of who could prove they had signed up more business for the station. The winner would get the prize, complete control of our beloved WABX. The little studio we were in was no more than a closet really, and opening the door with two of us in it was not possible. Suddenly, it opened just enough for me to see someone's face. It was the Ohio guy, leering at us, and he said to me, "You hippies might as well not do that commercial because tomorrow I am going to be your boss and you are all going to be fired." He laughed and shut the door.

At six p.m., I was to start my show, and on my way to the studio I glanced into the depressing and dingy office that the establishment guy was using. On the desk was a yellow legal pad and on it were his leads with names and phone numbers and how much they would pay to book time. It was a warm evening, and the building, which was a lovely old deco thing, had no air conditioning so the windows were open in the office. The windows in this building were tall and wide. They were framed by dark wood that probably was elegant in the 1920s. I remember the curtains were kind of ballooning from the kind of light breeze you get when you are thirty-three floors up. I picked up the yellow legal pad and began tearing out the sheets and reducing them to small confetti-like pieces. When I had completed the destruction, I grabbed a couple of handfuls and let them drift out into the early evening and onto the streets below. I told Dave Dixon what I did later

in the evening when he came in to do the night show. The next evening, I came in not knowing if my juvenile sabotage had worked. I sat down and started looking through my pile of albums and the door burst open and there stood Detz. John was not a warm and fuzzy person. John Detz was a Nixon kind of guy. He said to me, don't you ever tell anyone what you did. Scowling, he left the room, slamming the door behind him. I, of course, told everyone immediately. So there it is, the day I saved WABX.

# Lee Abrams and the Cold-Blooded, Calculated Assassination of Detroit Radio

## An Eyewitness Account

*Rick Allen*

In 1972 nineteen-year-old Lee Abrams was hired as program director (PD) at WRIF-FM radio in Detroit. In less than two years, he changed the sound and, most important, the face of FM rock and roll radio.

The recommendation of a friend, writer and jazz expert Geoffrey Jacques, my *Creem* credentials, and the need to meet minority-hiring requirements had gotten me a part-time on-air shift at WYSP in the fall of 1971. I went full time a few months later, working overnights (i.e., the black-guy shift). When Abrams came to WRIF I was cut back to part-time work, and all personal appearances, emceeing concerts, and the like were eliminated. So was most of my income as well as any mention of my name in any station promotion on- or off-air. I got a little satisfaction after Abrams was let go. Right around my own nineteenth birthday, I was made music director at WRIF after first turning down a shot at his old job as PD.

With Abrams in control, the focus was on courting white, male, eighteen-to-thirty-five-year-old listeners with disposable income and the big-money national advertisers that chased them. It wasn't that sinister a move from a business standpoint, but doing it meant turning away from the part of the audience that didn't fit that mold, the part of the audience that was younger, older, female, economically challenged, and, especially, nonwhite. I didn't detect any overt racism in Abrams himself, and I think it was business and profit that motivated him. But the racial tension that came to a head in 1967 had left the Motor City burning and created an atmosphere characterized by the hostile anti-integration crusade disguised as an anti-school-busing movement led by Oakland County's L. Brooks Patterson and his coalition. Abrams had found an excellent time and place for his ideas to take hold.

One of Abrams's first moves was to wrest control of the on-air content from the independent-minded jocks. If any jock could be found approximating or duplicating the tone of underground radio, control would be back in the hands of the brass, not the creative DJs like Jerry Lubin, Dan Carlisle, and Paul Greiner.

Certain types of music were restricted to specific times of the day, "day-parting" in radio Newspeak. Playlists were assembled from data gathered from surveys and focus groups made up of people with time on their hands on a weekday afternoon. The now-mandatory playlist became progressively more restrictive. My overnight shift gave me four choices an hour. It may have been even less for other shifts. Before Abrams was gone it was down to none.

All the blues, jazz, country, and most of the folk music was removed from the playlists, and the records were taken out of the studio library. Sly and the Family Stone, Rufus, and other integrated bands were gone except for War and the Allman Brothers Band. Black rock and roll was completely eliminated except for Jimi Hendrix, who was down to a cut or two. No more Little Richard, Chambers Brothers, Love, or Garland Jeffreys. Almost anything remotely outside Abrams's ethnic guidelines got the ax including Lolly Vegas's Redbone and Jorge Santana's Malo, a band that sounded a little more Latino than brother Carlos's band, which also saw its airplay reduced. Even the bluesier cuts from Led Zeppelin were kept at a minimum.

Significantly, all Detroit and regional music was pulled except for Alice Cooper's hits, Grand Funk's "Closer to Home," and occasionally the Amboy Dukes' "Journey to the Center of the Mind." In the days before the *Beautiful Loser* and *Night Moves* albums put him on the national scene, Bob Seger got "Ramblin' Gamblin' Man" but that was about it. "Heavy Music" might have gotten a play or two but "East Side Story," "Persecution Smith," and other regional hits were out, taking with them Dick Wagner's the Frost, The Teegarden and Van Winkle, Savage Grace, and even the Stooges and the MC5. Losing Michigan- and Detroit-area acts, especially the soul-heavy acts like the Rationals and Mitch Ryder and spectacularly creative groups like Parliament/Funkadelic, felt like a deliberate attack on Detroit's rich music history.

Motown was gone, too, except for Rare Earth's abominable take on the Temptations' "Get Ready." Abrams banned Stevie Wonder just as his career was about to enter a second, even-bigger phase. His 1972 tour with the Rolling Stones brought him before many who missed or overlooked his earlier work or had yet to pick up on black music or Motown in general. Stones fans were, or became, Stevie Wonder

fans. But that didn't matter much, either. There was only a smattering of Stones left, too.

Detroit has always had radio stations and nightspots aimed at particular groups: country stations and bars that catered mostly to whites and R&B stations and bars and clubs catering to blacks. But the town that produced the world's preeminent white rapper also nurtured black artists like Hank Ballard and the Midnighters, whose R&B was very close to country. And who, black or white, didn't listen to Motown, Johnny Cash, Ray Charles, and Elvis Presley even if they didn't necessarily buy their records or go to their shows?

My family's Pinkston Music Co. owned and operated jukeboxes in some of the restaurants and nightspots in Detroit's black neighborhoods. A record didn't keep its slot long if it didn't bring in the coins. It meant something that singles from Frank Sinatra, Barbra Streisand, Tony Bennett, the Righteous Brothers, and Mitch Ryder were almost automatic buys when my dad and I bought the latest sides at Consolidated One-Stop, the record wholesaler on Linwood Avenue near Davison not far from my house, the Reverend C. L. Franklin's New Bethel Baptist Church, and Motown's Hitsville U.S.A.

Detroit has always had its ears open.

While the Abrams playlist emphasized acts that seemed to have little noticeable influence from black music, women had been given short shrift even before Abrams, and precious few, none of them black, survived the cut. The revamped Fleetwood Mac hadn't hit yet so we got mostly Janis Joplin and a sprinkling of Joni Mitchell and Grace Slick.

In the two or so years I was there, the station went from "underground" to "progressive" to AOR

(Album Oriented Rock). Most important, it no longer played rock and roll. It was now *rock* and we were indoctrinated in using the term exclusively. I couldn't stand the term and never used it except as a verb or when mouthing official station slogans. Rock music is something lesser, something that came after rock and roll had done the grunt work and made it safe for any square to mousse their hair and shred empty notes on a pointy guitar. Rock is plastic cool. Rock is gutless. Rock is rock and roll with the blood and soul drained out of it.

In the twenty-first century, a lot of artists are exploding racial stereotypes in music. Taylor Swift, Bruno Mars, and Janelle Monae share radio space, and hip-hop culture may have done more racial outreach than rock and roll and maybe even jazz, though they're still working at it. Outlets that play the hits serve slices of the multicultural pie as they did before and during the FM explosion that began in the late 1960s. But at rock stations, particularly classic-rock stations, the Abrams legacy still holds sway: Playlists are rigid and mind-numbingly repetitive and unadventurous. Anything tinged with the remotest hint of funk is ignored. You'll hear few female-driven acts outside of Fleetwood Mac and Heart. Local artists have to follow the Beatles' example and hit big out of town before they get airplay at home.

But Abrams's legacy of racially Balkanizing radio and its audience is his most enduring contribution to American radio. You'll get Hendrix or Thin Lizzy now and then and that's about it for black or integrated classic-rock acts unless you count Lenny Kravitz and that's a low-down dirty shame.

# Gary Grimshaw
## Poster Child

*L. E. Grimshaw*

If there ever was a synchronistic circumstance of vocation paired with innate talent, appropriate personality, and work ethic, it was the career that began when Gary Grimshaw was first handed over the phone call from Russ Gibb asking for "some of those posters like they have in San Francisco." The call had come in to Rob Tyner, artist in his own right and lead singer of the newly organized band the MC5. Tyner's band had been asked to open the club that Russ Gibb wanted to operate in Detroit fashioned after those he saw on a visit to the West Coast. The club was called the Grande Ballroom.

The MC5 would become the house band for the Grande Ballroom. It was the autumn of 1966, a seminal year for Gary Grimshaw and many other young adults. Gary was twenty years old.

Grimshaw, as Rob used to call him, was staying at Rob's home because he had recently returned from San Francisco, having been stationed on nearby Treasure Island. While still in the United States Navy, he'd seen his first Fillmore Auditorium poster on a public bus, on the privacy panel behind the driver. After finding some street clothes, he went to the Fillmore more than once, and he witnessed some awesome early acts there. He went to the Avalon Ballroom, saw the scene, and admired the artwork on those posters, too. As he came into San Francisco often, over a period of many weeks, he saw new posters all around town each week. He said they were everywhere. In his career he would

do some Fillmore posters himself: for Spinal Tap, Buddy Guy, Patti Smith, the B-52s; but that won't happen until the 1990s.

In 1966, Gary also participated in the second-ever Berkeley Peace March. The dynamic speakers at that early march would influence him and solidify his political ideals. He would partner with others of like mind to mirror the work for the benefit of

Gary Grimshaw. © Leni Sinclair Collection.

413

community and peace back in Michigan. Gary would also produce an astounding amount of graphic work for a number of causes and clients: to assist in the legalization of marijuana up through the 1990s; for the release of unjustly incarcerated prisoners; to end the war in Vietnam (where he served his country as a communications officer in the United States Navy); for *Creem* magazine; for blues societies; for underground newspapers the *San Francisco Oracle*, the *Sun*, the *Fifth Estate*; for musical events, universities, and community organizations. It was all graphic work of hand lettering, illustrating, typesetting, and crafting posters, ads, and articles. Custom work would fill his board later in his career, when he'd take on projects such as guitars and wedding invitations. He would never do work simply for the fee, and he undervalued his worth in monetary terms, famously.

It was, after all, Rob Tyner who received the fateful phone call from Russ Gibb with a request to do the artwork for the first-ever Grande Ballroom event. Inclusive by nature, Rob simply told Russ, "Hold on," turned to Gary, and said, "It's for you, Grimshaw."

Gary Grimshaw had a family history rich with artistic talent in a production setting, including a grandfather who was a designer at GM. Gary was born in Detroit in 1946 and raised in the downriver community of Lincoln Park, Michigan. He graduated from Lincoln Park High. His classmates were future members of the MC5: his best friend was Robert Derminer, a fellow artist and music lover. Gary's mom used to drive Rob and Gary into Detroit to attend jazz concerts and other cultural events when they were in high school together. Rob and Gary were both prodigious producers of model

414

cars (painted, of course) and drawings of cars. When Gary had a paper route as a young man, one of his customers was the family of Wayne Kramer. He liked Wayne's mom. He admired Fred Smith from the moment he met him.

## *MAD* MAGAZINE, MOTOWN, AND JAZZ

Rob Derminer changed his name when he went into music professionally; to reflect his admiration for McCoy Tyner, a jazz pianist, he dubbed himself Rob Tyner. Rob passed into spirit in 1991, and Gary designed his circular grave marker at Becky Tyner's request. Rob's widow remained a dear friend to Gary and was with Gary when he passed away. Rob was a huge influence on Gary, and Gary dedicated one of his last published books, called *Detroit Rocks*, to Rob.

At Gary's own memorial on January 19, 2014, many people spoke of remembering Gary best quietly at work at his drawing table, in the middle of producing a light show, at work at a mimeograph machine, or assisting others in his large network of friends and associates. Always at work.

Deadlines were a natural part of Gary's schedule; he was comfortable doing artwork on a tight schedule. Gary's board—the setup of his drawing table and the surrounding area—was always of major importance no matter where he lived, and it was a focus through his entire life each time he moved. Each new home was scrutinized first for the prime location of his board. He had a definite way of creating an environment, his "control tower," with his drawing board, his library of reference and art books, media and stereo components, television (more than one in his later years), recording and listening devices, flat files, and the like. His studio. A very consistent aspect of Gary's adulthood was his studio, and he spent the majority of his time there. In later years, each move came with a custom, scale, hand drawing of the layout of the new studio area on par with a professional CAD sketch.

Gary lived in communal situations in early adulthood, and many times his control tower was in a living room, a basement, or another shared space. It was during his working hours at the board, while being observed by all, that he became a deep and personal influence on a great many people, without directly speaking to them on the subject of art. He walked the walk and let others talk the talk. His mentorship of others was so profound that even he never fully realized in his lifetime the full effect he had and how it created ripple effects. Gary's work and Gary's life were one and the same. He was simply being himself.

A detail of a Leni Sinclair 1967 photo of Gary and others sitting in the official MC5 van shows a poster taped to the outside of the vehicle. That poster was for a venue Gary and his friends and colleagues started as an "anti-Grande" venture. They felt that being the house band, the light-show operators, and the marketing for the Grande was benefiting Russ first and foremost, and therefore not their collective. The group found a better location; they called it The See. They booked their first weekend and created the advertising for the events. The venue did not live past its first evening, however. The poster on the van is for a show that never happened; it would have been the second show, but the landlord cleared out the box office, so the bands did not get paid. In later years, Gary

would say he considered that poster some of his best work. After that one night, the group returned to Russ and the Grande.

## LATER YEARS

Gary would go on to create over forty-five images for the Grande Ballroom, not including Russ Gibb productions at sister venues and events and ads for print. Many of the images were only produced in the postcard format because Russ soon discovered his target audience of high-school students could more easily distribute handbills, rather than posters. Handbills are so much less expensive than large posters. That fact is part of what brings such a high price for vintage Grimshaw posters to collectors in this day; there are simply not that many left.

Gary did not end up having a collection of his own vintage posters in later years. When his artwork was rediscovered, after the publication of the poster "bible" called *The Art of Rock Posters from Presley to Punk* by Paul Grushkin, Gary immediately liquidated his collection of vintage posters for what turned out to be pennies on the dollar. That was in 1986. Gary probably was never paid more than seventy-five dollars to create an artwork for the Grande, or any artwork from that era. Earnings generally went to the fund of the collective he was a part of. For the most part, he did want for anything in his life. He remained working class, always connected to the community in some way. He was definitely an artist of the people, and they adored him and his art. They felt it was their own, like Gary visually expressed their feelings as well as his own.

He developed a unique style that stands next to the famous "big five" of the West Coast, who made

415

the posters that first inspired Gary's own work. He began to trade off Grande poster jobs with other artists. He shared many of the assignments that he was given with Robin Sommers, Carl Lundgren, Donny Dope, and others. When he and his then-sweetheart Judy Janis went to Boston for a year to study macrobiotics with Michio Kushi, Gary left his Grande poster work to others with whom he had trained and collaborated. But Gary never left the music business. His entire life's work would become music related from the moment of that fateful phone call from Russ Gibb. In a handful of years, Gary Grimshaw was wildly successful in creating what would have been a profound body of work all on its own, had he not produced any additional art. Only he never stopped working.

When computers came, he slowly but fully embraced new processes to create art with quality almost equal to his handwork. He became famous for his lettering styles very early on. His overall style over the whole of his career could not be easily characterized by any one look, however, such as a psychedelic look. He was much more prolific, imaginative, talented, and versatile than one look or category could describe. He was much more than a commercial or a fine artist; he was an artist, period.

What was consistent in Gary's work was his use of creative imagination, a high quality of draftsmanship, his technique, and his pure talent as an artist as well as his dedication to and work for community. He was and is respected for his art and his ethics, his humble ways, and his quiet manner. He would consistently be associated with musicians, the music industry, poets, poetry, authors, and intellectuals as well as other artists in his life and work for the entire forty-seven years of his career.

You are invited to continue to discover more about Gary and his fine work at garygrimshaw.org. Gary was a surprising individual and a great artist.

Gary Grimshaw's online signature was a simple wish for all people on earth: Peace & Power.

# Grande Daze, Bubble Puppies, and Suburban Hippie Rock

*Dr. Herman Daldin*

The 1960s was a magical and hope-filled era, especially for an adolescent. Adolescents are dreamers, and the dream that the world was becoming more accepting of creativity and individuality seemed almost tangible. In Detroit, we had Plum Street, love-ins, protests, and music. Music, especially, was changing and growing, allowing for more freedom and accessibility. Creative groups were forming, and the demand for venues in which to share and demonstrate the new sounds, sights, and ideas of the period was growing as well. I was enamored and seduced by the music and the scene that surrounded the art that was ushering in a fresh generation of thinkers and music lovers. I knew that I wanted to be a part of this world and to experience the creativity and beauty with others who shared my desires.

When I was fifteen years old, I became part of a band that we ultimately named Train. We had ties to the local music scene and to the Artist Workshop on the Wayne State University campus. We sculpted a new sound, attempting to capture and combine components of rock, jazz, folk, and electronic music of the time in an attempt to carve out our own niche in the Detroit music scene. Our goal was not to be a dance band but to produce music meant to be heard and felt—music that would feed the soul. Soon, Dick Crockett, a DJ from WABX, asked if he could manage us. We felt that we were on the verge of something momentous, and it was only the beginning! Suddenly, I found myself living in

two worlds: high school and the world of music. In the music scene, I met people who would become lifelong friends. We met in dressing rooms, on stages, in band-related activities, and at parties and we had a mutual passion: the music.

Our first big experience as Train was at the Grande Ballroom. I wasn't even old enough to get in as a customer, but this was my other world, and I felt accepted here as a musician. It was Christmas Eve 1968 when I received a call at my home from

Herman Daldin. Photo courtesy of Herman Daldin.

417

"Uncle Russ" Gibb, the man who had created the Grande Ballroom. He said that the New York Rock and Roll Ensemble were snowed in and would be unable to play that night. He asked if we would open for someone whom I considered to be one of the best singers in rock music, Arthur Brown and his act, the Crazy World of Arthur Brown. I was astounded and excited. After explaining to my mother that Uncle Russ was not a relative but was a responsible, influential man in the performing-arts field, I was ready to debut with my band at this world-renowned venue. We arrived, set up our equipment, did a sound check, and went backstage to wait for the show to begin. The atmosphere backstage was similar to that of Plum Street, charged with anticipation and excitement. There was incense burning, and music playing, and in the dim lighting people roamed around or sat on the floor against the walls. There was a large wooden dance floor with a raised walkway around its perimeter, separated only by pillars. I recall meeting Arthur Brown, Vincent Crane, and Carl Palmer that night before we performed. What a thrill for a teenage rock musician. Truly a dream come true.

Soon, it was our time to play. The Grande's MC, Dave Miller, came back to get us. He and I were surprised to see each other. We attended the same high school but moved in different circles, of course, since he was as a senior and I was a sophomore. In high school, our slight age difference was insurmountable, but, in this place, in this time, it was inconsequential; we have remained dear friends ever since. It could never have happened in the high-school world; it was the music that bridged that gap.

Dave gave our introduction to the audience, and we went onstage. I had never been so nervous.

It seemed such a surreal experience: a huge ballroom with a light show, strobe lights, and fog machines all running simultaneously combined to make a huge echo off the back wall. It was challenging to keep the beat and concentrate on our sound so that the audience at the Grande that night might feel our music the way we wanted it to be felt. I felt strong and totally immersed in my music; it was a dynamic feeling. Sitting onstage later, watching the Crazy World of Arthur Brown, was—to use the parlance of the time—mind-blowing. I had never before seen such theatrics in conjunction with such dynamic music. It was a glorious, orgasmic assault on the senses. Later, during the 1970s, I was to play with a band that Arthur Brown created, Kingdom Come. That night at the Grande was one I will never forget and it served to further ignite the flame in me to pursue my dreams. We played at the Grande Ballroom a total of seven times, and I am proud to be a part of that quintessential facet in Detroit's rock 'n' roll history.

We continued to grow, playing many local clubs and on bills with several international and local greats of the time including Johnny Winter, Sly and the Family Stone, Dr. John, James Gang, Bob Seger, Bubble Puppy, and, of course, the MC5. I met music legends most teenagers only dreamed of meeting. Many of these would become friends; we hung out, went to movies, traveled together, ate meals together; they became my second family. As I was still in high school, I again divided my world in two and lived what I considered my real life after school with these people who understood me and my passion for music. In school, I was reserved and quiet; I worked hard in my classes, but my true self was revealed only to my music friends—it was with them that I felt connections.

In the spring of 1969, two landmark festivals took place that were arguably the most spectacular concerts in the history of Detroit rock 'n' roll. On April 7 of that year, a show was to take place at the Olympia Stadium, just down the road from the Grande Ballroom. It was a huge venue with a capacity for 15,000 people; it had previously been used for the Beatles' two Detroit appearances and Red Wing hockey games. For this show, the arena was arranged with two stages next to each other. The stage lighting was blindingly bright, which allowed only vague visuals of the audience from the stages. Twenty bands were scheduled for the show, mostly local. When I learned that our set was to be between those of Bob Seger and the MC5, I was ecstatic; I couldn't believe that we were given such a terrific time slot. The show went from two p.m. until midnight or so, with twenty bands in the lineup; each band was allotted thirty minutes. In a way, it was optimal because, of course, each band wanted to captivate the audience with a memorable set, to play their best and most popular songs, and to epitomize the experience with spectacular visuals. The show was fast-paced and high intensity with no downtime between sets. The enthusiasm of the audience grew and snowballed with energy generated by musicians and spectators alike. By late evening, the capacity crowd was completely immersed in the music and the dynamic atmosphere. The organizers had done their jobs well; each band knew the time restrictions and, for the most part, adhered to them. There were no dressing rooms backstage, no frills; we came in, went onstage, performed, packed up quickly, and exited through the back door. There were postconcert parties hosted by various bands that continued all night and well into the next day. The

MC5 had asked us to use their equipment in order to save them set-up time. Their amplification system transformed our more hybrid, spacier music into an enormously powerful sound that could be felt as well as heard. As I walked off the stage after our set, John Sinclair, manager of the MC5, hugged me and complimented my playing. I received glowing comments from musicians in fellow bands as well, and, especially because I was one of the youngest performers there, I was very excited and pleased.

Only several weeks later, one of the largest outdoor rock 'n' roll festivals in Michigan was organized by the founder of the Grande Ballroom, the man who had helped launch our band, Russ Gibb. For the last weekend in May 1969, the Detroit Rock and Roll Revival festival, held at the Michigan State Fairgrounds, had a lineup of twenty-seven bands, ranging from local favorites to internationally renowned bands, with a few historic icons as well, like Chuck Berry. Many were also regulars from the Grande Ballroom, but there were introductory tours on the bill as well, such as Johnny Winter. As with the Detroit Pop Festival, there were two stages built next to each other, but they were further apart this time, leaving more room for the thousands of fans and giving them the option of moving around.

It was risky to plan such a venture in the month of May in Michigan. The weather is capricious; it can be rainy and cool, but it can also be unseasonably hot. Fortunately, the weather that weekend was perfect, with sunny days and warm evenings. In fact, on the stage, during the daytime performances, it was beastly hot and extraordinarily sunny. The grounds had a large, dusty dirt area in front of the stages with bleachers arranged at the back. This design was perfect for the car and horse races that often took place there. But die-hard music lovers don't care where they hear the music; they just want to be there. For most of the two-day (twelve hours a day) festival, the space was relatively packed, and, as with the April concert, there was little downtime between acts; the music was continuous.

I recall that the Bonzo Dog Band ended up playing, and I believe that Terry Reid canceled his appearance. Bonzo Dog Band was a fun and playful group of British musicians who later had success in other groups.

Most of the bands that performed were reflective of the kind of music presented by Russ Gibb at the Grande Ballroom: heavier rock bands, new rock, and old rock alongside jazz and folk-rock bands. Before it even happened, all the musicians knew what a monumental festival this was going to be and, consequently, performed at their best in order to boost their popularity and sell albums. It was all about pleasing the fans.

My band, Train, performed late on the first afternoon on the left stage. The sun, low in the sky, beat directly upon us, unrelentingly. Rather than making everyone lethargic, the heat seemed to energize everyone and intensify the atmosphere. The audience members were dancing, and the electricity was onstage as well. I was young and daring then, wearing my shirt open and neglecting to wear sunglasses. I came away enthralled and euphoric but with a severe sunburn on my chest. Ah, youth! Our one-hour performance was well received and it was gratifying to have other musicians come to talk to us and congratulate us on our set.

There were continuous parties behind the stages, and people came and went, talking with each other, sharing stories, food, drink, and friendship. I think

that everyone there knew that this was a significant moment in time, that it would become a concert to remember for years to come for everyone who attended and, especially, for those of us who had performed; we were forever pieces of Detroit's rock 'n' roll history.

# Random Thoughts

## A Brief History of WSU's Legendary Zoot's Coffee

*Aaron Anderson*

From the first time I stepped into Zoot's I knew it was a special place. Tired of the downtown bar scene, a friend of mine had convinced me to check out the new coffeehouse a few blocks from our place on Alexandrine. Coffeehouses were a rare sight in the '90s and even more uncommon in the Cass Corridor. But there it was, brightly lit and welcoming in the bleak landscape of after-dark Corridor life. Located in the first floor of a Victorian home and sandwiched in between a transient hotel and a locals-only dive bar, it was a strange and beautiful sight. At the time, Zoot's was still trying to be a traditional coffeehouse with jazz music, potluck dinners, and loners striking intellectual poses while chain-smoking cigarettes. It was warm and welcoming. They served only one type of coffee, which was spiced, and, if you ever had a cup, I'm sure you can still recall that distinctive flavor to this day. It was full of vintage furniture, had a lending library, and, if you hung out long enough, a bottle of wine might be shared. There was a certain DIY sophistication, an almost European vibe, that stood out like a sore thumb in the gritty Cass Corridor of that time. And there was Zoot herself, a majestic and loving chocolate Doberman. I knew almost immediately I wanted to be a part of this. Maybe I knew that it would become the epicenter for underground music in Detroit. Maybe I knew it would be the future gathering place of all those tired of the most recent corporate "broternative" takeover of youth culture. Maybe I knew it would become a space where the next new things could not only be attempted but be supported. Most likely I didn't; but I knew something good was going to happen at 4470 Second Avenue.

You can't stop the underground. By the time I got hired in at Zoot's, there had already been a trickle of rock and avant-jazz shows. It was not quite a venue yet, and shows were still treated as special events. It was most likely in this time that one of the more important things about Zoot's booking came about, the fifteen-dollar PA fee. I'm not sure where the number came from, but for fifteen dollars you got an all-ages space that held roughly 150 people, with no strings attached. That allowed a person booking a show to not only keep the door price low but also pay the bands, both touring and local, well. It's hard to imagine a fan-driven and ethically motivated booking policy, but that's what it became. If you loved a band and wanted to bring them to Detroit, here was the place. If you wanted to do a show with your favorite local band that could not get booked anywhere else, here was your chance. All you needed was an employee to sign off on the date and it was yours.

As the shows ramped up and more people got involved in the booking process, a scene started to evolve. It was a scene of music lovers and underdog supporters that now had a space free of bar politics and typical venue hassles. Zoot's started to become the spot to see something new, something exciting, something fresh. There was an emphasis on bringing in the unusual, the sincere, the band that deserved a break. And the place filled up. It swelled with all the outsiders of current "alternative" culture, with all those dedicated to the underground, with all those bored of closed-minded rock clubs, and all those who knew we could build something better in Detroit. Somehow in the middle of all this, another employee and I bought Zoot's from the original owner.

For a few years we did it. Zoot's became the spot other bands told each other about. The place you had to play in Detroit. Where the kids showed up and went nuts, you were treated well, and the bands got paid. It became the place you took your friend to when you wanted to show them something cool. It became the place to meet your new best friend or fall in love. Zoot's would become the incubator for the next wave of underground Detroit rock. It was all of that and then some. And no single person can take credit for it. Zoot's was not the product of a single person or vision but the sum of all its visitors and the music that filled it every night. A real live scene. A time and place that could only happen then and with all involved, never to be reproduced. Half of what we did right was by accident, and for the other half we were just guessing.

We were all just kids. But we did it. We filled the air in there with the sounds of the Silver Apples; Eggs; Rodan; Blonde Redhead; Medeski, Martin, and Wood; Eugene Chadbourne; Songs; Ohia; the Dirty Three; Low; Cat Power; Bardo Pond; God Speed! You Black Emperor; Smog; Roy Brooks; Dub Narcotic Sound System; Run On; To Live and Shave in L.A.; and the Apples in Stereo. We sweated and went crazy for Quintron; the Make-Up; Braid; Sleater-Kinney; Hot Water Music; Harry Pussy; Cold Cold Hearts; Henry's Dress; Ultra Bide; the Get Up Kids; Braniac; Melt Banana; Boy Sets Fire; and the infamous A.C.

show. We supported and loved Outrageous Cherry; Tiger 100; Demolition Doll Rods; Windy & Carl; the Snitches; Godzuki; MacPherson; the Witches; Gravitar; Galen; Monaural; King for a Day; Jaks; Thoughts of Ionesco; Immigrant Suns; Fuxa; the Detroit Cobras; Sawdust; Chore; Roosevelt's Inaugural Parade; Asha Vida; and every single Time Stereo project. We had film showings, science lectures, soul dance parties, book fairs, art openings, "battle of the bands" competitions, benefits, festivals, and Noise Camp. It seemed like every night there was something fresh and different going on. We were one step ahead of the squares and always would be. We made it happen with our combined passion, dedication, and belief that Detroit not only could have a special place like Zoot's but deserved it.

And then it all stopped. Through financial mismanagement and personal issues, Zoot's fell apart. On November 2, 1997, we had our final show. After four short years, the doors closed. It seems like such a small amount of time, but it left an impression on all those who passed through those giant front doors. It left a lasting mark of empowerment and creative action in all of us. The foundation and network of the next wave of underground music from Detroit was set in motion. Friendships and partnerships as close as family were made that still exist today. The inspiration we felt then still burns in us all and motivates us to make new spaces, make better music, and be anything but ordinary. The people who came to Zoot's went on to open their own businesses in the city, book their own shows, start their own record labels, form their own bands, believe that whatever it is they wanted to do it could be done in Detroit. We were all just kids, but Zoot's is where we saw something special happen and the memories of those magic nights beam out of our hearts and into everything we do. A real live scene.

# Rarities of the Revolution
## Archie Shepp, the MC5, and John Sinclair
*Pat Thomas*

Saxophonist Archie Shepp got his start playing with avant-garde pianist Cecil Taylor. He participated in the 1965 sessions for John Coltrane's seminal album *A Love Supreme*, but his contributions were left off of the original release—later appearing as bonus tracks on the 2002 expanded edition.

Also in 1965, Shepp released *Fire Music* for Impulse!, which included a spoken elegy called "Malcolm, Malcolm Semper Malcolm." The MC5 adapted "Hambone" from *Fire Music* with words by Rob Tyner, retitled it "Ice Pick Slim," and added it to their repertoire. Tyner's lyrics were a nod to author Robert Beck, aka Iceberg Slim—known for his street novels including *Pimp*, *Trick Baby*, and others. Shepp's album also inspired MC5 manager (and founder of the White Panther Party) John Sinclair to use *Fire Music* as the title for a 1966 collection of his own revolutionary poems.

For years, John Sinclair played an essential part in spreading awareness of jazz and black culture in the Detroit area. He organized concerts and workshops, taught classes in jazz and poetry, and covered the regional music scene for *DownBeat*. Besides the aforementioned *Fire Music* poetry collection, Sinclair published two books between 1965 and 1967 that honored Ornette Coleman (*This Is Our Music*) and John Coltrane (*Meditations*). These two volumes also celebrated Elvin Jones, Miles Davis, Marion Brown, Andrew Hill, and Albert Ayler. These tributes came in the shape of poems that were essentially record reviews, capturing the essence of their music. In 1968, in the ultimate (if naïve) white tribute to Black Power, Sinclair would form the infamous White Panther Party, which he anticipated would become the "voice of the lumpen hippie, just like the Black Panther Party was the voice of the lumpen proletariat."

## OTHER RARE MOTOWN RELEASES CONNECTED TO THE SOCIOPOLITICAL LANDSCAPE OF DETROIT

Motown stepped up to the task to musically speak out against Detroit's summer of '67. In early 1968, the Federal Department of Housing and Urban Development (HUD) gave $60,000 to the Detroit Youth Opportunity Program. The money was earmarked for jobs, education, and recreation to keep the summer of '68 cool for Detroit-area youth.

Motown produced two theme songs in support of the social-economic program. The first, "Detroit Is Happening" was a variation of the Supremes' "The Happening," with words of encouragement spoken by local celebrity Willie Horton of the Detroit Tigers.

The second release, "I Care about Detroit," was written specifically for the occasion by Jack Combs and Jimmy Clark. Performed by Smokey Robinson and the Miracles, it's too bad they didn't ask Smokey to write it, as the music is flat and the lyrics are cornball:

I'm proud to call this city my

hometown

It's been good to you and me

Let's learn to work and live in

harmony

As I care about Detroit.

It sounds more like a greeting card from the chamber of commerce than a deflection to chill out pissed-off urban rioters.

Songwriter Jimmy Clark specialized in insipid message songs. Two years earlier he penned "Play It Cool, Stay in School," a one-sided promotional single by Brenda Holloway, released on the Tamla label in cooperation with the Detroit Women's Ad Club. Record collectors should note that the 1968 singles weren't released on Motown, but on logo-free labels that stated: "This special record by permission and cooperation of Motown Record Corporation and Stein & Van Stock, Inc."

## THE TRIBE

In Detroit, musicians Wendell Harrison, Phil Ranelin, and others formed a collective known as the Tribe, who saw themselves as "an extension of the tribes in the villages of Africa, our mother country. In Africa everyone had a talent to display. There were no superstars: just people, and collectively all the people of the village played a vital role in shaping that culture. We see all black communities within this country as villages and the tribes are the people residing within them. Pure music must reflect the environment that we live in if it is to be educational and beneficial to our culture. It must portray our way of life."

The 1973 *A Message from the Tribe* featured Wendell Harrison, Jeamel Lee, and Phillip Ranelin on sax, vocals, and trombone, respectively—all members of the Detroit-based collective. The Tribe was a band, record label, production company, and publishing house—all brought together under the umbrella of musical, political, and intellectual freedom. Their slogan was, "A new dimension in cultural awareness."

*A Message from the Tribe* contained both an instrumental and a vocal version of Ranelin's composition, "Angela's Dilemma." The septet provides a relaxed, progressive backing to Jeamel Lee's melodic vocals:

Angela is a sister with much pride

Who has long seen too many

greats die

Imprisoned and far from the

freedom

Her power is still felt from within

She must be free.

A year later, Ranelin and the Tribe would record *The Time is Now!* Their second release replaced lyrical statements with a harder-edged instrumental direction. Compositions like the title track "The Time is Now!" and "Black Destiny" recall the free jazz of Archie Shepp, the electric-keyboard punctuation of early-'70s Miles Davis, and a soulful groove reminiscent of Hank Mobley. This time, Ranelin didn't use vocals, but, in case listeners were unsure of the Tribe's message, the album jacket declared, "The time is NOW!! The time is now, for unity among the people! The time is now, for all men to be able to control their own destinies! The time is now, for oppression, racism, greed, hate and poverty to end! The time is now, for revolution!"

# Detroit's Historical Archer Records from the Inside-Outside

*Ben Blackwell*

Records have been pressed in Detroit and the southeastern Michigan area by numerous outfits for quite some time. Sav-Way Industries churned out untold quantities of Vogue picture discs from 1946 through 1947, all of which are still collected and sought out today. Vargo started out pressing 78s in Detroit in 1950 and later ended up as American Record Pressing in Owosso, handling the earliest Motown pressings as well as work for Vee Jay, Cameo-Parkway, and countless other small local outfits. While that plant burned down in 1972, its memory still lives on in the fanciful "ARP" script pressed into the dead wax (old vinyl records that have been melted down to be reused) of records manufactured there. Falcon (Detroit, then Royal Oak), Sound Inc. (New Haven), and Trinity (Ecorse) were all smaller local pressing concerns with small, brief footprints that were still vital and important to local music.

The end-all and be-all of vinyl manufacturing in Detroit is inarguably Archer Record Pressing. Started by Norm Archer in late 1965 and pressing their first 45, "That's Alright" by Ed Crook, in 1966, the plant still runs smoothly today, a family business run by Norm's son Joe through the mid-'90s and currently helmed by third-generation record presser Mike Archer.

The inauspicious building on East Davidson, just off of Van Dyke, blends in well with its machine-shop neighbors, and only the primitive mural depiction of an Arthurian archer on an exterior wall gives any clue as to what happens inside. Day in and day out, Archer continues to supply quality LPs and singles not only for the niche local market but for folks all across the country as well as overseas.

While huge, multiplatinum-selling releases have never come through Archer's door, the number of important, seminal, and influential records that have come off those presses is incalculable.

In line with the dominant musical form when the plant opened, Archer pressed many of the most prized titles in the northern-soul genre. Small, local, obscure hobby record labels like Demoristic, Mandingo, Magic City, and Mutt may be unknown to the general public, but releases on these labels are widely considered the gold standard among the fanatic all-night dance crowds. Each of these labels was hoping for just a little slice of Motown's market share, and while they failed to capitalize in their initial offerings, titles from Dusty Wilson, the Versatones, and the Four Tracks on these labels consistently sell for hundreds of dollars and have been known as "rent payers" among local used record shops.

One of the most compelling things about a plant like Archer is that these titles, which pretty much walked in off the street, would share space with work being done by the "big" independent labels in town. While Archer handled jobs for both Fortune and

Hideout Records, pure Detroit titles like the Faygo promotion "Remember When You Were a Kid?"; Curtis Gadson's ode to the 1984 world-champion Detroit Tigers, "Bless You Boys"; and promotional/instructional singles pressed on behalf of all the auto companies proved to be some of the bigger press runs that Archer has seen over the years.

Mike Archer speaks wistfully about having to work overnight to press copies of Gadson's hot single in the height of demand for "Bless You Boys." He was still only a teenager, but the demands of a family-run business forced such situations. Having worked at the plant in the summer of 2007, if only for three days, I can assure you that they have much more stringent oversight of employees currently and rarely, if ever, have to pull all-nighters.

Without a doubt, the best thing done by any member of the MC5 after the breakup of that band was Fred Smith's Sonic's Rendezvous Band, and their untouchable "City Slang" single was pressed at Archer, via Freddy Brooks's Orchide imprint, back in 1978. While it would be the only song the band would ever release while they were active, it still carries the immediacy and bluster of a finely tuned muscle car growling down the avenue.

Recently, a troll through old customer invoices at Archer helped solve a question that had arisen about the "first" Detroit techno record. While hunting down such designations is usually a fool's errand, the question has always centered around A Number of Names's "Sharevari" and Cybotron's "Alleys of Your Mind." Arguments arise about either record being released no more than a week or two prior to the other.

The invoice for "Sharevari" dates the order at October 9, 1981. Cybotron's first appearance on an invoice is October 29, 1981. *But* Cybotron's record was initially pressed at QCA Record Pressing in Cincinnati and was supplied a catalog number there of 107034. That code translates thus: the first digit is the last digit of the year (1981) the next two are the month of mastering (07, so July) and the next three indicate how many orders had been placed prior to that job that month (so there were thirty-three previous orders taken in July 1981).

It appears that what was pressed at Archer (likely just white-label copies of the "Alleys" single) was a one-time rush job because QCA couldn't press their red-white-and-black labels, or even labels that were just red and black, fast enough. Lore has it that Cybotron (Rick Davis and Juan Atkins) moved twenty-five thousand copies of the single from the trunk of their car, a massive amount, and, if true, surely would explain the enlistment of multiple factories across the Midwest to keep up with demand. Archer would also go on to manufacture the rare brown-label first pressing of Atkins's seminal Model 500 single "No UFOs" in 1985. This would be the best-known release on Atkins's Metroplex imprint, which was, along with Derrick May's Transmat and Kevin Saunderson's KMS, one of the most important and influential labels not only for Detroit techno but for the genre worldwide.

At the same time early techno shows up on the presses at Archer, so does what's come to be considered the earliest Detroit rap record. Credited to Paris (in actuality a teenage McDonald's employee named Darryl Nicholson), "Rock Down Parts 1 & 2 (Schoolboy Rap)" was pressed in a quantity of five hundred copies and promptly forgotten. Nicholson would continue his Blue Rose Records imprint through his aliases the Breeze and BMW at other plants, but he clearly paved the way for the bulk of impressive local rap and hip-hop releases pressed at Archer to this day.

B-Boyz, A-tack, Critics Choice, the Eveready Crew, Twice as Nice, Rough and Ready, Worthy D and the Boys, Ill Chief Rockers, K Stony Jam, MC Jam, Get Flesh Crew, Fresh Boys, and Girli Girl, as well as the first vinyl appearance of Insane Clown Posse (Carnival of Carnage) and countless other one-offs and never-heard-ofs, were all pressed at Archer, and all share in a similar, simple, Archer-printed label layout. The number of rap 12-inch records that show up in Archer logs in the late '80s and early '90s is staggering, and tracking them all of them down would be impossible in a lifetime.

On the complete opposite end of the spectrum, Archer pressed boatloads of records for local schools and churches. The Church of God in Christ at 3458 Buchanan in Detroit pressed a handful of well-respected singles under the C.O.G.I.C. banner throughout the '70s, featuring the likes of Rev. Drayton and Barbara Jean Mayes. Drayton's "By and By" cooks on a weird bongo groove that no other gospel recording before or since manages to attain. R. S. Records and Sacred Sounds both pressed multiple releases at the plant, while projects like the University of Michigan Men's Glee Club, the Crary Elementary School Chorus, and Strum from the Monroe County Community College Modern Music Workshop all pressed at the humble little building on Davidson.

Through Polish polka records pressed for Polonia Records in Hamtramck; to Mexican tunes emanating from Del Rey Records in Southwest Detroit; to the futuristic jazz of Tribe Records titles; to the outsider artists like Richard Ristagno,

Tulsa City Truckers, and Rip Schredder; through the downriver teenage rock 'n' roll of Dwarf; to the otherworldliness of Poncho C. Saint Fingers; on to the dulcet country sounds of Clio, Michigan's Ranger Records, and Jackon's Jessup Records, Archer Record Pressing truly has had its tendrils through all of the important, unimportant, lauded, and forgotten music through Michigan and Detroit for fifty years. They continue strongly today with supply not even close to keeping up with demand as the vinyl industry has experienced unexpected and unprecedented growth in the past five years. No matter what trends or styles come and go, through it all, Archer manages to press on.

# Majesty Crush Lurking in the Shadows of Motown and Detroit Techno

*Hobey Echlin*

Not so much standing, more like lurking in the shadows of Detroit's more heralded musical legacies of Motown, techno, garage rock, and hip-hop was a band conceived in the city's bored middle-class suburbs, birthed in its inner city, and doomed to a quasi-cult status as an unlikely footnote to the British shoegazer subgenre of grunge-era alternative rock.

Joshua Glazer, writing for the acclaimed and respected music website allmusic.com, offered this wistful eulogy:

> Detroit's only contenders in the UK's shoegazer scene, Majesty Crush combined the effects-laden guitar work and dreamy vocals of British groups like My Bloody Valentine, the Verve, and Lush with a strong hometown-influenced rhythm section. The group's only full-length album, released with zero promotional support by the ill-fated Warner Music Group subsidiary Dali Records, is a testament to what might have been, if only the band's four members lived in Manchester, England instead of Detroit. Hobey Echlin's impossibly catchy basslines on "No. 1 Fan" and "Pennies for Love" meld with Odell Nails's creative, yet rock-solid drums and Michael Segal's single-note guitar washes, laying the base for David Strougther's uniquely sinister vocals about love, obsession, and … obsession. Two songs, "Uma" and "Seles" are straight-faced odes to the actress and tennis player, respectively. Tragically, Dali folded almost immediately after the album's release, making Majesty Crush the little lost American cousin of the UK dream-pop scene.

Majesty Crush were Detroit's guiltiest pleasure during their brief life as the Motor City's lone Afro-punk shoegazers of the early '90s. Drawing as equally from Joy Division as Motown and too musically naïve to get too far away from writing perfectly sinister pop songs, the four piece, led by a crazy lead singer (Dave Strougther), and including a dreadlocked drummer who hosted a children's show on local cable (Odell Nails III), an area record-store clerk (Michael Segal) who played a three-string guitar (two of which were tuned to the same note), and a music journalist-cum-bassist (Hobey Echlin), was a stunning if outgunned anathema to the neogrunge-indie and cold techno scenes of the city at the time.

Coming together in Strougther's inner-city basement in 1990, the band jelled around a love of minimalist and droning sounds (which was about all they could play) but were pushed further by the singer's Motown obsessions and inspired by similar sounds from England.

Nails and Echlin were veterans of Spahn Ranch, a short-lived but influential group from the late '80s Detroit postpunk scene that also included His Name is Alive, a band from Livonia led by producer Warren Defever that had the distinction of being the lone Michigan band to release records on the United Kingdom's 4 A.D. label, home to angelic goth bands like Cocteau Twins and Dead Can Dance. But if His Name is Alive were signed to 4 A.D., it was Spahn Ranch, led by singer Bob Sterner, who sounded more like Detroit heirs to the 4 A.D. sound. Sterner's vocal acrobatics and choirboy crescendos made the dark, shimmering sounds of Spahn Ranch resonate like some hopeful, slightly brighter hue of blues amid the glorious din of the band's tribal, psychedelic backbeat. As fanzine *Motorbooty* put it, Spahn Ranch sounded like "new-age music for people with black leather jackets." Sterner's previous band, Grief Factory, which featured writer Peter Markus on bass, hinted at the more straightforward roots of what would become Detroit's shoegaze sound: the refined directness of the MC5 and the Stooges distilled into a mantra-like repetition of vocal gymnastics and blissed-out epiphanies. If Spahn Ranch took this to dark, psychedelic depths, Majesty Crush brought it back into a seemingly brighter light that had more to do with Smokey Robinson than Jane's Addiction.

Strougther and Nails had grown up in Southfield, a Detroit suburb not known for its multiculturalism. Strougther's mother was German (his parents met when his father was stationed overseas in the army), while Nails's family were proud Oklahoma transplants—and pioneering ones: Nails's father was the first black superintendent of the Pontiac public school system. Strougther and Nails palled around with the extended families of Motown royalty (their Southfield neighbors) while being drawn to the excitement and otherworldliness of Detroit's postpunk scene, with its goth clubs like Todd's and its steady roster of touring acts from the vibrant if obscure postpunk scenes around the world.

Following the demise of Spahn Ranch, Nails and Strougther reenlisted Echlin on bass and conscripted Segal, an influential record-store clerk with an encyclopedic knowledge of obscure vinyl that more than made up for the fact that he could only play a handful of songs on a guitar with two notes. Early songs like "Sunny Pie," a kind of darker, doomed dream-pop take on the same kind of workplace crush (no pun intended) Prince talked about in "Raspberry Beret," and "Cicciolina," a churning thumper about the Italian porn-star-turned-politician, had narratives sung by an engaging front man. This distinguished the band from other shoegaze acts like Dusk, Spectacle, Thirsty Forest Animals, Ethos, and Asha Vida, who all boasted better musicianship than showmanship. Other acts sounded like their British counterparts. Majesty Crush sounded like Majesty Crush, because they weren't good enough to sound like anyone else.

Majesty Crush also had a unique cultural relevance that shared techno's taste for transcendence. The group thrived amid the despondence of Detroit. Strougther, once jailed for looking like a breaking-and-entering suspect in his Indian Village neighborhood, came out of a weekend in the clink to write "Pennies for Love." Gangsta bliss anyone?

Their exotic look (black guys who sound British!) and easily digestible sound made Majesty Crush scene darlings, landing them opening slots for every band with an early '90s alternative-rock-radio hit, from Mazzy Star to Jesus Jones.

Though they released only a handful of singles and EPs and one major album—1994's lost classic *Love 15* on the ill-fated Dali label (home to the Queens of the Stone Age forerunner Kyuss and Nashville legend Lucinda Williams)—Majesty Crush inspired a fandom that was as obsessive and swooning as their music. Catholic high-school girls would mail Strougther heart-shaped boxes, burly bedroom producers would get all tingly right next to the goth chicks at shows, and usually smug scenesters would admit to using Crush's ghetto-shoegaze sighs to make out to. Alas, as Dr. Tyrrell told the replicant in *Blade Runner*, "The star that burns twice as fast burns half as long," and Majesty Crush disbanded in the mid-'90s, only to be resurrected by an all-female tribute band (2001's Majesty Blush). The cult of Crush lives on, though: Full Effect Records released *I Love You in Other Cities: The Best of Majesty Crush 1990–1995*, compiling the band's history with extensive liner notes for a new generation of "number-one fans" to get in their heads and hearts and obsess over.

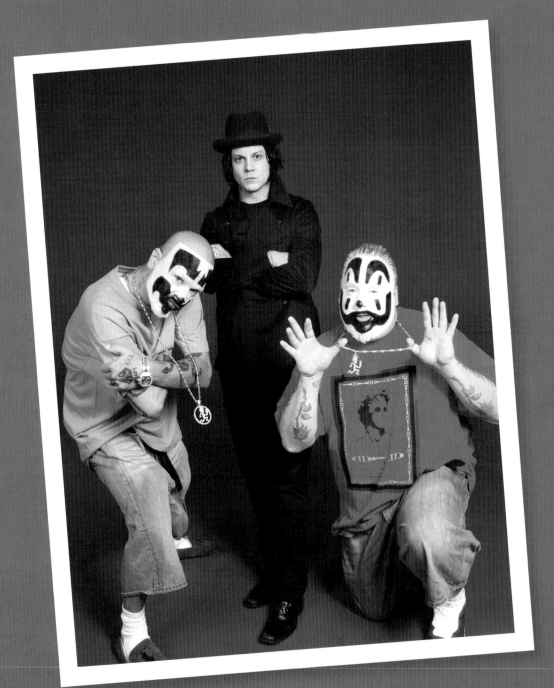

Jack with Insane Clown Posse. © Leni Sinclair Collection.

# A View of Third Man Records from the Inside

*Ben Blackwell*

Third Man Records is an anomaly. When it started in 2001, it existed solely on paper, as a sort of insurance policy for the White Stripes. When the band began signing deals with larger record labels like V2 and XL, the idea was that the larger record labels would license albums from the Third Man Records entity, and, once the licensing period was up, the rights of the material would revert to the band through Third Man.

Come 2008, those deals were mostly expired and the rights to the vinyl catalog remained solely with the phantom entity of Third Man Records. At that same time, White Stripes singer/guitarist/songwriter Jack White had just purchased a building near downtown Nashville with the intent of storing his musical equipment there. With a surfeit of offices in the building, Jack turned to the idea of making Third Man an actual business.

I got the phone call on Halloween 2008. I was standing outside Arthur Bryant's Barbeque in Kansas City. Jack said he wanted to make Third Man a functioning record label that would just reissue the White Stripes back catalog on vinyl. I'd spent the previous five years running my own Cass Records label out of my high-school bedroom, and I had been working for the White Stripes since their inception. "I can't do this without you" was all he had to tell me. I had nothing much going on in Detroit at that point anyway.

Jack's reasoning that the White Stripes catalog should be enough to keep a record label functioning

and busy was totally sound and accurate, but we hadn't anticipated that in the interim he would form a new band, the Dead Weather, and write and record an entire album with that outfit. So when we opened the doors on March 11, 2009, it wasn't to unveil to the world a mess of White Stripes vinyl reissues, it was to introduce a brand-new band with a full-length album in the can.

The opening took place within a week of the Dow Jones Industrial Average hitting its true market bottom in the height of the recession. By all signs, it was not a time to be opening a record label, and certainly not the time to be opening a vinyl-focused record label.

But the collapse of the financial industry timed well with the collapse of digitally based music purchases. Folks were less and less inclined to pay for digital content. A younger generation, one that had grown up with only a faint idea of tangible music, saw records with canvas-worthy album jackets and the oft-romanticized crackly, warm-fidelity vinyl as intriguing.

The Third Man offices in Nashville are also located less than two miles away from United Record Pressing, the biggest vinyl-pressing plant in the country and, quite possibly, the world. Everything lined up perfectly for the label, but there were still ideas to shake up.

For a medium that's over one hundred years old, there proved to be lots of compelling innovations and tricks that we could employ on vinyl records. Ideas like hiding grooves underneath the paper center label of an LP (the Dead Weather's *Sea of Cowards*), dual-groove records (Jerry King on *The Auctioneer*), records with grooves that played from the inside out (Edgar Oliver on *In the Park*), and records that played at unusual speeds (a 3-RPM compilation LP for our third anniversary, a 78-RPM single as part of our Paramount Records reissues).

For Jack's *Lazaretto* LP we put every crazy idea we could muster all into one package. In addition to what I've already listed, we also included a hologram in the vinyl and, depending on where you drop your needle, the song "Just One Drink" begins with either an acoustic or electric intro, while the rest of the song is the same.

*Lazaretto* sold over forty thousand copies on vinyl in its first week of release, setting the record for most single-week sales of a piece of vinyl since SoundScan started tracking music sales in 1991.

Big-selling records are nice every once in a while, but we also do things without worrying too much about how much they'll sell. When Rivers Cuomo of Weezer asked me what Third Man's mission statement was, I realized I didn't specifically know. When I asked Jack, he replied without hesitation, "To make things that don't exist."

That includes our direct-to-vinyl recording setup. In our live performance space (dubbed the Blue Room after an activities room at Holy Redeemer Church in Southwest Detroit, where White attended grade school) we are able to record bands in a way that has been obsolete since the late 1940s. That means no overdubs, no redos, no starting and stopping. What happens onstage is *exactly* what makes it onto the record. We've done records using this process with the Shins, Mudhoney, and Jack Johnson, and we even recorded, pressed, and released

a Jack White single all in the span of three and a half hours in April 2014.

Third Man has focused intently on 7-inch 45-RPM singles, primarily through our Blue Series. Intended as one-off releases by artists who may be contracted elsewhere, may be just passing through town, or don't want to commit to a full-length LP, the Blue Series singles all follow a simple process: the artist records at Jack's studio (located just down the road from Third Man, right behind his house) for a day or two at most and then takes cover photos in the previously mentioned Blue Room to give it all a noticeably unified look.

We've done Blue Series records with folks as varied as Tom Jones, Beck, and Stephen Colbert. I'm more proud of how many Detroit artists we've been able to feature in these singles, though, artists like Black Milk, the Thornbills, Duane, and Insane Clown Posse.

In over five years of confounding and confusing press and fans alike, the ICP single is still the most polarizing thing we've ever done at Third Man. We received all sorts of hate short of death threats. Folks vowing to never buy any of our music ever again. For what? Putting out a record by rappers that have been maligned and made fun of for decades.

For me, the idea that resonates about those guys is that they are entirely self-made. Not since the Grateful Dead has a musical group straight up *created* their own recognizable subculture from nothing. Sure, lots of bands have fans with clever names, but Juggalos are so omnipresent that no less than the FBI has labeled them as a gang and a criminal organization.

Beyond that, ICP releases their own music, produces their own radio show, controls all of their own merchandising and direct-to-customer sales (spanning everything from toddler wear to skateboards and energy drinks), puts on the massive Gathering of the Juggalos festival . . . all to their fans' delight and a bottom line of a multimillion-dollar operation. That's where my interest came from, the fact that ICP was doing the music-fan interaction their own way, knowing exactly what their audience wants, without the involvement of any corporate suits. That impressed me. They are shrewd businessmen. Jack was impressed by the fact that Insane Clown Posse was the only act in the world that he could say he was working with and folks genuinely would not believe him. It became an artistic challenge. Having Jack and ICP collaborate on a song originally written by Mozart (the title of which translates to "Lick My Ass") was something that could only ever happen at Third Man.

Recording Neil Young in the world's only Voice-o-Graph booth open to the public was another happening that could only take place at Third Man. These booths used to be a common sight at arcades, USO bases, and even the top of the Empire State Building. They were billed as places where folks could literally "hear yourself as others hear you" for the first time in history.

While the booths were primarily used for audio postcards for family and friends, Young decided to use the medium to record a collection of covers of songs he was influenced by when he was an up-and-coming songwriter. With the fidelity of a beat-to-hell 78, full of crackles and distortion, the end result brims with ambiance and emotion. The fact that Young timed the record to coincide with his unveiling of his high-definition-audio system

PONO was the kinda queer juxtaposition that we absolutely love here at Third Man.

We're proud to house no shortage of other artistic amenities: 16-mm film projectors for a once-monthly avant-garde cinema series, a fully functional photo-developing dark room, an amply stocked video-editing suite, climate-controlled master-tape storage, a whimsical storefront open to the public selling all sorts of sundry goods, parking space for our Rolling Record Store (basically the storefront in a converted DHL truck), massive warehouse space, direct-to-customer mail order, fan-club fulfillment. What we have here is not too different in vision from what Insane Clown Posse and Psychopathic Records have. We are both valiant supporters of DIY; we're just selling to different customers.

I usually find myself telling folks that coming here every morning is kinda like going to the circus. While for me it's definitely a nine-to-five job, it encompasses so much more than that. It really feels like Jack has created an environment that truly causes artistic ideas to bloom. There are looks of inspiration on any number of the faces of folks who've passed through the building, from T-Bone Burnett, Radiohead, Bob Dylan, Willie Nelson, Justin Timberlake, Aziz Ansari, Dave Buick—these people all get it.

The fact that Jack didn't start this label until he'd been a working performer for over a decade was the true secret. He was able to focus on the White Stripes and the Raconteurs with all of his vision without being distracted by the label side of things. With the briefest pause in those bands' worlds, with ownership of a catalog that'd be the envy of any label, *that* was the precise time to strike. Sometimes people ask, "How can I start my own Third Man

Records?" I tell them that the first thing they need to do is be Jack White. Second, they need to have eight monster albums under their belts before even thinking of starting the label. From there, everything else is easy.

Seven years after opening, across 350 releases with over 2 million pieces of vinyl pressed, I feel like we're just now hitting our stride. We've just added a publishing division and we're chomping at the bit to take some of our left-field approaches to the record business and apply them to books. If there's one thing I've learned here, it's the fact that if you let art lead, the possibilities and end results are unfathomable.

# Future Now
## Detroit's Twenty-First-Century Record Label Jett Plastic
*Jarrett Koral*

Having collected records for as long as I can remember, it only seemed like a logical next step to form my own record label. Sure, there were risks involved, one of which was losing thousands upon thousands of dollars in initial-investment cash (something that I, luckily, was able to avoid), but Detroit has an enormous share of musical talent, most of which is going unheard. Is it because of the public's unwillingness to listen?—er, no. Working musicians are trying every day to get their music to new and welcoming audiences, but, as usual, there's a hitch. I like to believe that there are two kinds of musicians. One being the self-sufficient musician who's able to work by himself, with little help, to formulate a career. They're able to promote themselves, and they always seem to be one step ahead. Jack White is certainly one of these people, along with Ty Segall, a guy who seems to have a new record out every week.

These are musicians who never rest, and through doing so, they're able to have flourishing careers. However, there's also another type of musician. Musicians who make extremely poetic and amazing music but are unable to see how to promote it. When founding my label, it was my intent to focus on these "little guys" and to get their music heard in Detroit and beyond.

To help me focus on building a new label, I looked up past emails that I had received from rock 'n' roll troubadour and LA legend Kim Fowley, one of which, dated January 8, 2013, consists of me sending him MP3s of the Bootsey X album that I released in late 2013. In it, Fowley stated, "Of course you have good ears. Do it, what's there to lose?"

Running a record label out of my parents' basement isn't abnormal; in fact, it's how many punk labels started in the 1970s. When told that running a record label wasn't a very rock 'n' roll thing to do, I replied, "It might not be very rock 'n' roll, but it sure as hell is punk rock!"

I identify myself as a music lover first and a businessman second. If somebody comes along with a record I like, and I'm asked to release it, I do it. I'm not afraid, like major record labels, of not making thousands of dollars on a record, and that's why independent labels are so important. We're able to focus on the details, while major labels are only concerned with how much product they can get out and how much of it can get played on the radio. I'm running a label out of my parents' basement, for Pete's sake.

I have a room in the basement, the door of which is adorned with a red plastic faceplate that reads "OFFICE." The inside is filled with inventory and personal artifacts, including a wall signed by those who have visited JPR headquarters, from John Sinclair to M. L. Liebler. In any other setting, this would make no sense. Why does it make sense for me to be devoting this much time and energy into a vinyl-only record label that doesn't make any money? It's all for the love of music, the business, and the overall game.

Before pressing a first record, I knew I had to come up for a name for the label, but, as the runout groove on the first 7-inch states, "all the good names were taken." My childhood nickname, Jett, from the McCartney and Wings tune "Jet," surely had to be a factor. I took out index cards and began to skim through the dictionary. *Jett Waxx?*—nope. *Jett Plastic* came up. Makes sense. Records, plastic. Check! I went for *Recordings* to both sound fancier and more sophisticated and also to sound like Infinity Cat Recordings, an indie label from Nashville that I greatly admire.

Without any prior knowledge of record manufacturing, I decided to dive headfirst, and I approached a local band who was looking to release a 7-inch. This only goes to show how fast the process went. A few days later, I hopped on down to Archer Record Pressing, a plant in Detroit—whose story as told by Ben Blackwell is included in this very anthology—and dropped off the masters for the record. I scoured White Stripes fan forums and record blogs searching for listeners, and, after a few months, there were no more records left to sell. When putting out a 7-inch single, most are lucky to make their money back, let alone make a profit. At this point, after the release of several 7-inch singles, every dollar I've made back has gone back into the business. I'd rather have something better to show for my hard work and dedication than a load of expensive tchotchkes on a dusty shelf. I was honored to have been able to work with the Necros, a legendary hardcore-punk band and one of the first acts on Touch and Go Records, on a live album. I knew member Todd Swalla for a good deal of time

before the Necros release, as he was in a blues-rock outfit named Boogaloosa Prayer, a group that I went to see every time they played in Detroit. After a Boogaloosa release on the label never materialized, I approached Todd, asking if there was any Necros material he wanted to issue on vinyl. Turns out, someone found a quarter-inch reel-to-reel in their attic from a show they recorded in Lawrence, Kansas, so we had it transferred and prepped for vinyl.

Luck like that rarely happens; however, it struck again in late 2014. I released a 7-inch single for a local band named the ILL Itches, and the guitarist of the group, Josh Woodcock, had started his own budding label named GranDetroit Records. We were joking around one day, trying to come up with a new release concept that we could work on together, as he had just wrapped up the *Pathetic Sounds of Detroit* compilation, a sort of sequel to Jack White's 2000 *Sympathetic Sounds of Detroit* comp. One of us jokingly said, "The Pizza Underground!" We thought it was funny because it would absolutely never be possible to release a record by them. We sent them an email on a whim, and they were excited to be approached for a vinyl release. We had the release out for Record Store Day 2014, an event where exclusive vinyl is released to independent record stores all over the world. Given the short amount of time we had, we were only able to produce six hundred copies. It came as a surprise that record stores had preordered nearly two thousand copies. It felt strange having to turn some stores down and to tell them we didn't have any copies due to the instant sellout, but, it was, of course, ultimately rewarding. If you told me a year ago that I would be releasing a record by Macaulay Culkin's Velvet Underground–themed parody band, I would think that you were insane.

It didn't make sense at the time, but it somehow all comes together. At this point, I've listened to the Pizza Underground more than the real VU, which might be a small problem.

I'm not in this business to make money; I just want to keep releasing music I love that other people normally wouldn't have a chance to hear, and, by doing so, I'm helping the music industry. I'm not selling millions of records, but credit is due to small labels like my own that keep pushing on for the vinyl revolution. Detroit is special, especially because the music community is such a close-knit group of people who all know each other. Musicians are able to support each other through and through, but of course we're always waiting for the "next big thing." The White Stripes had that in the mid-2000s, and I see loads of people saying that the scene is over and we'll never have another music scene explosion like the one in the late '90s and early 2000s. Anybody who attends shows in the area knows that the music here is special and it's on the rise in public reception. New bands are emerging, and the future of Detroit rock 'n' roll lies in our hands, truly.

JARRETT KORAL

# ACKNOWLEDGMENTS

There are many kind, generous, and wonderful friends to thank for making this incredible life-long dream of mine to forever preserve in a book some important Detroit music history. I think it is only proper to thank my beloved late grandmother, who raised me, for giving me my first Elvis Presley album at age four. Grandma continued to nurture me on the Ink Spots, Sophie Tucker, and Pearl Bailey in my early elementary school years, and she later weaned me on Dion's "Ruby Baby," which was the first 45 rpm record I ever bought with my own pennies at S. S. Kresge's. So, Grandma—this is for you with love for a great education, childhood, and life from your grateful grandson. "When I get to heaven, gonna look for grandma's hand."

Thanks to my pals and longtime heroes ("I'm not worthy!") who stood by me for a couple of years in the making of this book: Dave Marsh and Peter Benjaminson, who led me to my hero Greil Marcus, who then led me to the supportive and kind John Morthland, who granted me safe passage into Lester Bangs's archives. Of course, I am always indebted to my good friend Ben Edmonds as well as the great music journalists and Detroit music scholars Susan Whitall, Jaan Uhelszki, Bill Holdship, Gary Graff, John Sinclair, Jim Gallert, Lars Bjorn, Michael Hurtt, S. R. Boland, Brian Smith, Larry Gabriel, W. Kim Heron, Hobey Echlin, Herb Jordan, Howard Dewitt, Brian McCollum, Pat Thomas, Marsha Music, Chris Morton, and Gary Carner. Thanks to the many young up-and-coming music journalists Matt Deapo, Daniel Jones, my cool son Shane M. Liebler, and Mike Dutkewych, and to my good poetry and musician friends who, upon my request, became first-rate music essayists: Bill Harris, Melba Joyce Boyd, Rev. Robert Jones, Scott Morgan, Aaron Anderson, Cary Loren, Diane Spodarek, John Rodwan, Jr., Matthew Smith, George Moseman (a.k.a. Moseley the Punk), Willy Wilson, Ben Blackwell, Jarrett Koral, Danny Kroha, Rhonda Welsh, Thomas Trimble, and Dr. Herman Daldin.

A special musical shout-out to the folks who taught me more than any school ever could, my beloved heroes and Air Aces for eternity: Dave Dixon, Jerry Lubin, Dan Carlisle, Dennis Frawley (I still keep my WABX decoder ring under my pillow just in case . . .), and of course sweet Judy Adams—Morphogenesis lives!!!

The cherry on the top of this musical delight is Detroit Eminent Artist for 2016 Leni Sinclair, who kindly allowed us to use her photos. Thank you my dearest for capturing all the magical, musical moments of our lives in your expert lens.

Thank you Kathy Wildfong, my wise editor, longtime friend, and wonderful consultant. I am also grateful to editorial, design, and production manager Kristin Harpster, great book designer Bryce Schimanski, and my ace publicist team, Emily Nowak, Jamie Jones, and Kristina Stonehill. Thanks also to Jane Ferreyra and the lovely Annie Martin for just being there for me. And to Anthony Ringuette for all his excellent assistance.

I must also thank greatly my student, friend, and Beatles and Detroit Music brother Eddie Baranek who helped me much in compiling the permissions and gathering these essays from some of the authors. I am honored to have such a good friend and a trustworthy assistant. Thanks and gratitude to my wonderful WSU English Department intern Kendyl J. Layne, and my student assistant Aaron James Proudfoot for helping greatly with the Further Reading List and the authors' bios. You

# ACKNOWLEDGMENTS

three helped make this process run smoothly and on time. Thank you!

I must thank my colleagues Dr. Caroline Maun, Dr. Gloria Heppner, Ms. Sarah James, and Dr. Ellen Barton, former chair of the English Department, for supporting and helping me apply for the President's Research Enhancement Program Arts & Humanities Grant for 2014–2015. This grant was a great aid to supporting this project and my forthcoming memoir, *Hound Dog: A Poet's Life of Rock, Revolution, and Redemption*.

I want to thank my longtime friend and colleague Dr. Walter Edwards, director of the Humanities Center, for allowing me to once again be a 2015–2016 Resident Scholar at the WSU Humanities Center.

Finally, my wife, Pam Liebler, who gets special love for just putting up with all of my insane projects, extensive global travels, and a poetry life since we were very young teens at Lake Shore High School in our beloved St. Clair Shores. Thanks me luv for all these years of kindness and support!

# FURTHER READING

## DETROIT JAZZ

Bjorn, Lars, and Jim Gallert. *Before Motown: A History of Jazz in Detroit, 1920–60*. University of Michigan Press, 2001.

Borden, Ernest H. *Detroit's Paradise Valley*. Arcadia Publishing, 2003.

Bowles, Dennis. *Dr. Beans Bowles "Fingertips" the Untold Story*. Amazon Digital Services, 2012.

DeVaeaux, Scott. *The Birth of Bebop: A Social and Musical History*. University of California Press, 1999.

Milan, Jon. *Detroit: Ragtime and the Jazz Age*. Arcadia Publishing, 2009.

Williams, Jeremy. *Detroit: The Black Bottom Community*. Arcadia Publishing, 2012.

## DETROIT BLUES

Hooker, John Lee. *John Lee Hooker—A Blues Legend*. Hal Leonard Corporation, 1991.

## EARLY DETROIT SOUL: THE PRE-MOTOWN SOUNDS

Boland, S. R., and Marilyn Bond. *The Birth of the Detroit Sound: 1940–1964*. Arcadia Publishing, 2002.

Douglas, Tony. *Jackie Wilson: The Man, the Music, the Mob*. Mainstream Publishing, 2001.

Whitall, Susan. *Fever: Little Willie John's Fast Life, Mysterious Death, and the Birth of Soul*. Titan Books, 2011.

## MOTOWN: THE SOUND OF YOUNG AMERICA

Benjaminson, Peter. *Mary Wells: The Tumultuous Life of Motown's First Superstar*. Chicago Review Press, 2012.

Benjaminson, Peter. *The Lost Supreme: The Life of Dreamgirl Florence Ballard*. Lawrence Hill Books, 2008.

Benjaminson, Peter. *The Story of Motown*. Grove Press, 1979.

Betts, Graham. *The Motown Encyclopedia*. AC Publishing, 2014.

Edmonds, Ben. *Marvin Gaye: What's Going On and the Last Days of the Motown Sound*. Canongate Books, 2002.

Gaye, Jan, and David Ritz. *After the Dance: My Life with Marvin Gaye*. Harper Collins, 2015.

Jordan, Herb, ed. *Motown in Love: Lyrics from the Golden Era*. Pantheon Books, 2006.

Morgan, Pat. *Motown Artist by Artist: A Compilation of the Top 100 Motown Artists*. G2 Entertainment, 2014.

Posner, Gerald. *Motown: Music, Money, Sex, and Power*. Random House, 2005.

Ribowsky, Mark. *Signed, Sealed, and Delivered: The Soulful Journey of Stevie Wonder*. Wiley, 2010.

Ross, Diana. *Secrets of a Sparrow*. Random House Value Publishing, 1993.

Ryan, Jack. *Recollections, the Detroit Years: The Motown Sound by the People Who Made It*. Ed. Thomas J. Saunders. Glendower Media, 2012.

Smith, Suzanne E. *Dancing in the Street: Motown and the Cultural Politics of Detroit*. Harvard University Press, 1999.

Stevenson, William Mickey. *Motown's First A&R Man Presents the A&R Man*. Stevenson International Entertainment, 2015.

Whitall, Susan. *Women of Motown: An Oral History*. Harper Perennial, 1998.

Wilson, Mary. *Dreamgirl: My Life as a Supreme.* St. Martin's Press, 1986.

## DETROIT ROCKS: THE '60S

Bartkowiak, Matthew J. *The MC5 and Social Change: A Study in Rock and Revolution.* McFarland, 2009.

Callwood, Brett. *The Stooges: Head On, A Journey through the Michigan Underground.* Wayne State University Press, 2011.

Carson, David A. *Grit, Noise, and Revolution: The Birth of Detroit Rock 'n' Roll.* University of Michigan Press, 2006.

Cosgrove, Stuart. *Detroit 67: The Year that Changed Soul.* Clayton Publishing, 2015.

McLeese, Don. *The MC5's Kick Out the Jams.* Continuum, 2005.

Miller, Steve. *Detroit Rock City: The Uncensored History of Rock 'n' Roll in America's Loudest City.* Da Capo Press, 2013.

Simmons, Michael, and Cletus Nelson. *MC5: The Future Is Now!* Creation, 2004.

Sinclair, John. *Guitar Army: Rock and Revolution with the MC5 and the White Panther Party.* Process, 2007.

Sinclair, John. *It's All Good: A John Sinclair Reader.* Headpress, 2009.

## DETROIT ROCKS INTO THE '70S AND BEYOND: FROM EVERYONE LOVES ALICE TO CASS CORRIDOR PUNK TO DEATH

Bangs, Lester. *Psychotic Reactions and Carburetor Dung.* Anchor Books, 1987.

Delicato, Armando, and Elias Khalil. *Detroit's Cass Corridor.* Arcadia Publishing, 2012.

Derogatis, Jim. *Let It Blurt: The Life and Times of Lester Bangs, America's Greatest Rock Critic.* Broadway Books, 2000.

DeWitt, Howard A. *Searching for Sugar Man: Sixto Rodriguez' Mythical Climb to Rock N Roll Fame and Fortune.* CreateSpace, 2015.

Dunaway, Dennis, and Chris Hodenfield. *Snakes! Guillotines! Electric Chairs!: My Adventures in The Alice Cooper Group.* Thomas Dunne, 2015.

Graff, Gary. *Travelin' Man: On the Road and Behind the Scenes with Bob Seger.* Wayne State University Press, 2010.

Hackney, Bobby Dean. *Rock 'N' Roll Victims, the Story of a Band Called Death: My Story of Growing up in Detroit, My Family, and Rock 'N' Roll.* BookBaby, 2015.

Matheu, Robert, and Brian J. Bowe. *Creem: America's Only Rock 'N' Roll Magazine.* Harper Collins, 2007.

Rettman, Tony. *Why Be Something That You're Not: Detroit Hardcore, 1979–1985.* Revelation Records, 2010.

Rudick, Nicole. *Return of the Repressed: Destroy All Monsters, 1973–1977.* Ed. Mike Kelley and Dan Nadel. PictureBox, 2011.

Strydom, Craig Bartholomew, and Stephen "Sugar" Segerman. *Sugar Man: The Life, Death and Resurrection of Sixto Rodriguez.* Bantam Press, 2015.

## HIP HOP, GHETTOTECH, DONUTS, AND TECHNO DREAMS

Dawkins, Marcia Alesan. *Eminem: The Real Slim Shady.* Praeger, 2013.

Eminem. *The Way I Am.* Plume, 2009.

Ferguson, Jordan. *Donuts*. Bloomsbury Academic, 2014.

Hanf, Mathias Kilian. *Detroit Techno: Transfer of the Soul through the Machine*. VDM Publishing, 2010.

Hasted, Nick. *The Dark Story of Eminem*. Omnibus Press, 2011.

J, Violent, and Hobey Echlin. *ICP: Behind the Paint*. Psychopathic Records, 2003.

Matos, Michaelangelo. *The Underground Is Massive: How Electronic Dance Music Conquered America*. Harper Collins, 2015.

Needs, Kris. *George Clinton & the Cosmic Odyssey of the P-Funk Empire*. Omnibus Press, 2014.

Reynolds, Simon. *Energy Flash: A Journey through Rave Music and Dance Culture*. Faber & Faber, 2012.

## SOUNDS OF DETROIT: COUNTRY YORK BROTHERS AND LATIN MUSICA

Maki, Craig, and Keith Cady. *Detroit Country Music: Mountaineers, Cowboys, and Rockabillies*. University of Michigan Press, 2013.

## DETROIT MUSIC MISCELLANEA

Carson, David. *Rockin' Down the Dial: The Detroit Sound of Radio from Jack the Bellboy to the Big 8*. Momentum Press, 2000.

Keith, Michael C. *Voices in the Purple Haze: Underground Radio and the Sixties*. Praeger, 1997.

Thomas, Pat. *Listen Whitey!: The Sounds of Black Power, 1965–1967*. Fantagraphics, 2012.

# CONTRIBUTORS

Rick Allen, a.k.a. R. A. Pinkston IV, was born and raised in Detroit. He graduated from Cass Tech in 1971. Rick became a staff writer for *Creem*, *Harp*, *Blurt*, and *Vintage Guitar Magazine*. In addition, he worked as a broadcaster on FM radio at WRIF in Detroit and WYSP in Philadelphia. He is now fronting his own band, Rick Allen and the Upsetters, as the guitarist and lead singer. Rick lives happily in Philadelphia with his wife, Diane Lucas.

Aaron Anderson manages a record store in Metro Detroit and is still searching for the ultimate musical truth.

Lester Bangs (who died in 1982 at age thirty-three) was a rock journalist for *Creem*, *Rolling Stone*, *Village Voice*, and countless other magazines. And while his critical acumen, perspicacity, and acerbic wit were his most important contributions to rock and roll, Bangs's brief musical career, which debuted with the release of the single "Let It Blurt" in 1979, is worth considering if only because he was a creditable songwriter. As his longtime friend Greil Marcus aptly put it, "Bangs's work amounted to 'one man's attempt to confront his loathing of the world, his love for it, and to make sense of what he found in the world and within himself.'" Marcus edited Bangs' posthumous anthology of writing, *Psychotic Reactions and Carburetor Dung*.

Peter Benjaminson was a former reporter for the *Detroit Free Press*. He is the author of *The Story of Motown* (Grove Press, 1979), the first book ever published in this country about the Motown Record Company; *The Lost Supreme: The Life of Dreamgirl Florence Ballard* (Lawrence Hill Books, 2008); *Mary Wells: The Tumultuous Life of Motown's First Superstar* (Chicago Review Press, 2012), the only book ever published about Mary "My Guy" Wells; and *Super Freak: The Life of Rick James* (to be published by Chicago Review Press in 2016). For more, visit http://www.peterbenjaminson.com.

Lars Bjorn is a Professor Emeritus of Sociology at the University of Michigan-Dearborn and the coauthor of *Before Motown: A History of Jazz in Detroit, 1920–60* with Jim Gallert (University of Michigan Press, 2001). He is also the editor of the *SEMJA Update*, the monthly jazz newsletter of the Southeastern Michigan Jazz Association. SEMJA is dedicated to jazz education and organizes jazz clinics at the Ford Detroit International Jazz Festival every year. In the late 1970s, Bjorn was a board member of the Detroit Jazz Center and took part in publishing *Detroit Jazz Who's Who* with Herb Boyd and Leni Sinclair in 1984. He has also published articles on jazz in sociological research journals.

Ben Blackwell is the creator and director of Cass Records, one of two drummers in the Detroit-based rock band the Dirtbombs, a music writer, and a vinyl record collector. He runs Third Man Records in Nashville, and he is the official archivist of the White Stripes.

S. R. Boland is a well-known and respected Detroit music historian and promoter, and he is the co-author of *The Birth of the Detroit Sound: 1940–1964*. In addition, S. R. has written for the *Detroit News* and other local papers and magazines as a music/radio/pop culture writer. He is a drummer who heads up the local R&B band the Party Stompers.

CONTRIBUTORS

Melba Joyce Boyd is a Distinguished University Professor and Chair of the Department of Africana Studies at Wayne State University in Detroit. She is a biographer, editor, and author of nine books of poetry. She is the author of *Wrestling with the Muse: Dudley Randall and the Broadside Press*, which received the 2004 Honor Award for Nonfiction from the Black Caucus of the American Library Association; *Discarded Legacy: Politics and Poetics in the Life of Frances E. W. Harper, 1825–1911*, which was widely acclaimed and reviewed; and *Roses and Revolutions: The Selected Writings of Dudley Randall*, which won the 2010 Independent Publishers Award, the 2010 Library of Michigan Notable Books Award, and was a finalist for the NAACP Image Award and the Foreword Book Award for Poetry. Her last collection of poetry, *Death Dance of a Butterfly*, received the 2013 Library of Michigan Notable Book Award for Poetry.

Dan Carlisle worked at California radio stations KSAN, KKCY, and KOFY. He then relocated to New York where he worked for Sirius Satellite Broadcasting in NYC. He recently moved back to San Francisco with his partner. He is currently working at KCBS as a tech producer on the overnights. He flies to L.A. now and then to do weekends on KCBS-FM.

Gary Carner is the author of *Pepper Adams' Joy Road: An Annotated Discography*, *The Miles Davis Companion: Four Decades of Commentary*, and *Jazz Performers: An Annotated Bibliography of Biographical Materials*. From 1984 until Pepper Adams's death in 1986, Carner collaborated with him on his memoirs. Carner's research on Adams's career (collected at

pepperadams.com) spans four decades. Carner blogs about Adams at gc-pepperadamsblog.blogspot.com and has produced all forty-two of Adams's compositions for Motéma Music.

Dr. Herman Daldin was a suburban teenage garage rocker who became a true renaissance man. He ended up playing in front of tens of thousands in his band Train. Daldin's band played the Grande Ballroom, and the First Annual Detroit Rock 'N' Roll Revival at the State Fair Grounds in 1970, and he played the Saugatuck Pop Festival. He has recorded on many sessions at Motown in their famous "Snake Pit" and at United Sound. He holds graduate degrees from Wayne State University, and he is currently a practicing psychologist in Metro Detroit who has published in many professional journals on psychology, psychoanalysis, and social trends.

Matt Deapo is a Philadelphia-based arts blogger, presently scrutinizing the recorded history of rap music for Hip Hop Top 50 (hiphoptop50.blogspot.com). He was born in Syracuse, New York, in 1981 and graduated from St. Bonaventure University with an MA in English literature in 2005, spending a majority of his collegiate career locked in the DJ booth at the campus radio station. His next writing project will take a thematic approach to film criticism. His personal obsessions include popular culture, tall pints of beer, and his beautiful, supportive wife.

Rebecca "Tyner" Derminer is the wife of the late Rob Tyner, lead singer and founding member of the MC5. Becky is a businesswoman, clothing designer, caterer, and longtime social activist. She still resides near her alma mater, Wayne State University in

450

Detroit, where she and Rob first met and where she majored in English. Becky makes occasional appearances to speak in Professor M. L. Liebler's Motown/Detroit Learning Community class at Wayne State University.

Howard A. DeWitt received his PhD from the University of Arizona and taught at Ohlone College in the San Francisco area for thirty-five years. He is the author of biographies of Chuck Berry, Van Morrison, Paul McCartney, Elvis Presley, and Del Shannon, as well as *Searching for Sugar Man: Sixto Rodriguez' Mythical Climb to Rock N Roll Fame and Fortune*. For more, visit www.facebook.com/howard.a.dewitt.

Mike Dutkewych is a writer and archivist from Detroit. In 2010, he collaborated with Yoga Records to reissue the Ted Lucas album. He is currently at work on a biography of the late musician. For more, visit www.mikedet.com.

Hobey Echlin was the founding bass player for Majesty Crush and is a former Detroit-based music journalist. He considers himself lucky to have lived in downtown Detroit in the early '90s, going to clubs like Todd's, the Music Institute, and Warehouse. As a contributor to the *Detroit Metro Times*, he won an AAN award in 1994 for his article "Mixing the Body Electric," an early history of Detroit techno. His work has appeared in *Village Voice*, *Rolling Stone*, *MOJO*, and *Paper Magazine*, where he is currently a West Coast contributing editor. He lives in Long Beach, California, where he teaches yoga and deejays #spanningtime.

Ben Edmonds, former editor of *Creem* magazine and longtime contributor to *Rolling Stone* and other US publications, is the coauthor of *Backstage Passes* with Al Kooper and a former US correspondent for *MOJO*. He is currently researching a biography of Tim Hardin.

Larry Gabriel, journalist, poet, and musician, is a columnist for the *Detroit Metro Times*. He was the former editor of the *Detroit Metro Times* and the UAW's *Solidarity Magazine*, and was a feature writer and editor for the *Detroit Free Press*. Gabriel has won awards for column writing, editorial writing, and feature story writing and editing from the Michigan Press Association, and was named Best Columnist in 2012 by the Association for Alternative Newsmedia. He studied poetry writing with Anselm Hollo and Diane Wakoski at Michigan State University. Gabriel's book, *Daddy Plays Old-Time New Orleans Jazz*, is a history of six generations of musicians in his family. Gabriel holds a bachelor's degree in human communication from Michigan State University and a master's degree in speech communication from Pennsylvania State University.

Jim Gallert is a veteran jazz broadcaster, researcher, and writer. He produced and hosted jazz programs on WDET-FM ("Jazz Yesterday," "Detroit Jazz Alive") and WEMU-FM ("Swing City") for twenty-five years. He later co-hosted "Detroit JazzStage," a locally produced podcast focused on Detroit musicians. Gallert has participated in every Detroit Jazz Festival as a staff writer, emcee, broadcaster, artist selection committee member, or host of "Meet the Artist" sessions. Jim with Lars Bjorn produce and host presentations, panel discussions, interviews, and music performances

CONTRIBUTORS

in the Jazz Talk Tent at the Detroit Jazz Festival (www.detroitjazzfest.com). Gallert and Bjorn were recipients of the Detroit Jazz Festival Jazz Guardian award in 2010 for their research, education, and advocacy of Detroit's amazing jazz history. As a writer, Jim coauthored the "Blues and Jazz" chapter in the *African American Almanac, Ninth Edition* with Joseph Guy. He's authored detailed biographies of Detroit jazz musicians including Phil Lasley, Alma Smith, Todd Rhodes, George Benson, and Willie Anderson. His writings have appeared in local, national, and international publications and have been used as CD liner notes. Some of his research, photographs from his extensive collection, and writing were included in *Before Motown: A History of Jazz in Detroit, 1920–60.*

Gary Graff is an award-winning music journalist and author in Detroit, reporting for a variety of local and national print, online, and radio outlets. He is a music journalist with the *Oakland Press* and *Billboard Magazine*, and on Detroit radio's WCSX-FM Classic Rock News. He has authored many books including *Neil Young: Long May You Run: The Illustrated History, Rock 'n' Roll Myths: The True Stories Behind the Most Infamous Legends*, and *The Ties that Bind: Bruce Springsteen A to Z.*

L. E. Grimshaw is the wife of the late great Detroit '60s poster artist Gary Grimshaw. She worked closely with Gary and his poster art business. She now proudly carries Gary's bright flame forward into the new century. For more info on how to purchase Grimshaw posters and merchandise, visit www.garygrimshaw.org.

452

Bill Harris is an Emeritus Professor of English at Wayne State University. He is a playwright, poet, and arts critic. He formerly served as artistic coordinator at JazzMobile and the New Federal Theatre in New York. His plays have been produced nationwide, and he has published books of plays, poetry, and reappraisals of American history. *Booker T. & Them: A Blues* is his latest publication. He received the Kresge Foundation Eminent Artist award for 2011.

W. Kim Heron spent thirteen years as managing editor of the *Detroit Metro Times*, following stints at *Detroit Sunday Journal*, *Detroit Free Press*, and *Lansing State Journal*. He was also the decade-plus host of the jazz shows "Destination Out" and "The Kim Heron Program" at WDET-FM, where he was proud to have Faruq Z. Bey as a guest. Heron is currently a senior communications officer for the Kresge Foundation. He was inducted into the Michigan Journalism Hall of Fame in 2013.

Bill Holdship is a former editor of *Creem, BAM Magazine, Variety, Radio & Records, New Times LA*, and *Detroit Metro Times*, among other publications. A longtime contributing editor to *SPIN*, his work has appeared in *MOJO, Los Angeles Times, NME*, and nearly every publication that has featured music coverage during the years since he started writing about it.

Michael Hurtt, a native of South Bend, Indiana, is a musical archaeologist of both the performing and writing variety. Having lived in New Orleans for the better part of two decades, his arrival in Detroit was precipitated by the federal levee failures of 2005. A longstanding fascination with the city's culture, music, and history has kept him there. A founding member of the Ponderosa Stomp and a 2012 Kresge fellow in the literary arts, he is currently at work on a book about Detroit's Fortune Records with fellow motor city music maniac, Billy Miller.

Daniel Jones lives, writes, eats, parties, and keeps his bike on Detroit's East Side. You can catch his byline on several local arts and culture outlets both electronic and in glossy RL.

Rev. Robert Jones Sr. is an inspirational storyteller and musician celebrating the history, humor, and power of American roots music. An award-winning multi-instrumentalist, he plays the guitar, harmonica, mandolin, banjo, and fiddle. His deep love for traditional African American and American traditional music is shared in live performances that interweave timeless stories with original and traditional songs. For more than twenty-five years Robert has entertained and educated audiences of all ages in schools, colleges, libraries, union halls, prisons, churches, and civil rights organizations. At the heart of his message is the belief that our cultural diversity tells a story that we should celebrate, not just tolerate. Acclaimed photographer James Fraher writes about Robert: "Perhaps the world's most highly educated blues musician, an ordained minister, a longtime DJ, and a living encyclopedia of blues history, the Reverend Robert Jones is comfortable among juke joint loud talkers, fancy-hatted church ladies, and PhDs alike."

Herb Jordan is a songwriter, music producer, and commentator on American culture. He grew up in Detroit and was an auto worker before attending law school. He taught at the University of Michigan Law School where he received the L. Hart Wright Outstanding Faculty Member Award. Jordan is a recipient of the Thomas M. Cooley Distinguished Brief Award for scholarly writing. He has composed for Count Basie, received numerous songwriting awards, and produced a Grammy-nominated album, *American Song* by Andy Bey, and a Soul Train Award-winning album, *21*, by pianist Geri Allen. Jordan is the co-owner of the 1963 Beatles music publishing catalog. His book, *Motown in Love: Lyrics from the Golden Era*, was published by Pantheon books in 2006. Other writings by Herb Jordan can be found at www.adagegroup.net.

Jarrett Koral developed an interest in music from a young age. He plays in local rock groups the Barking Irons and the Früt, in addition to writing freelance articles for the *Detroit Metro Times*. He lives in Saint Clair Shores, Michigan, where he runs Jett Plastic Recordings (www.jettplasticrecordings.com).

Danny Kroha is the one of the founding members, with Mick Collins and Peggy O'Neill, of Detroit's legendary, minimalist, post-punk band the Gories. He was also part of the popular bands Rocket 455 and the Demolition Doll Rods. Currently he has launched a solo career channeling the Delta Blues spirit of Son House on a piece of wood, a nail, and some strings. His new album, *Angels Watching Over Me*, is his highly acclaimed album release on Jack White's Third Man Records. He also leads the R&B, early-garage inspired Danny & the Darleans.

M. L. Liebler is an internationally known and widely published Detroit poet, university professor, literary arts activist, and arts organizer. He is the author and editor of more than sixteen books and chapbooks including the award-winning *Wide Awake in Someone Else's Dream* (Wayne State University Press, 2008), which won both the Paterson Poetry Prize for Literary Excellence and the American Indie Book Award for 2009. Liebler has taught at Wayne State University in Detroit since 1980, and he is the founding director of both the National Writer's Voice Project in Detroit and the Springfed Arts: Metro Detroit Writers Literary Arts Organization. Liebler is the coeditor of the acclaimed Made in Michigan Series from Wayne State University Press. In 2011, his groundbreaking anthology *Working Words: Punching the Clock & Kicking Out the Jams* (Coffee House Press) was given a Library of Michigan Notable Book Award. In 2016, he will release a new collection of poems titled *I Want to Be Once* (Wayne State University Press) and an anthology titled *Bob Seger's House and Other Stories* (coedited with Mike Delp). For more, visit www.mlliebler.com.

Shane M. Liebler is a music blogger, music lover, and devotee of J Dilla. He was raised in St. Clair Shores, and he graduated with a degree in journalism from St. Bonaventure University in upstate New York where he hosted a weekly hipster college radio music show titled *The Take Ove*r. He has loved music since he was quite young; his father heard him strumming obscure Dylan songs on the guitar from his bedroom where he studied under Robert Jones. "Sad Eyes Lady" anybody? He currently lives and works as a "creative" in Syracuse, New York, with his son Kass.

Craig Maki is a writer, musician, researcher, and record collector of American roots music, particularly concerning Detroit and Southeast Michigan. With research assistance from Keith Cady, Maki wrote *Detroit Country Music: Mountaineers, Cowboys, and Rockabillies*, published by the University of Michigan Press in 2013. See the book for a detailed overview of the York Brothers' career. Visit Maki's website at www.carcitycountry.com to explore more stories about early country music in Detroit.

Greil Marcus is the author of *Mystery Train* (1975, 2015), *Lipstick Traces* (1989, 2009), and most recently, *The History of Rock 'n' Roll in Ten Songs* (2014), *Three Songs, Three Singers, Three Nations* (2015), and *Real Life Rock: The Complete Top Ten Columns, 1986–2014* (2015). He is also the coeditor of *A New Literary History of America* with Werner Sollors. He lives in Oakland, California. His website is www.greilmarcus.net.

Dave Marsh, Pontiac native, left Wayne State after his freshman year to write for and edit *Green Magazine*. He later worked at *Rolling Stone*, *Playboy*, *Newsday*, and many other magazines and newspapers. He has written and edited more than twenty-five books, including two best-selling biographies of Bruce Springsteen (available together as *Two Hearts*), *Before I Get Old: The Story of the Who*, books about "Louie Louie" (the first history of a single rock song), and *The Beatles Second Album*. He is now heard regularly on Sirius XM and can be found online at the rockrap.com website and his own davemarsh.us.

Joel Martin is a well-known, longtime Detroit producer who learned his craft from both Artie Fields and Harry Balk. He is the publisher of

Eminem's music, and he has also produced The Romantics, Sponge, Sean Forbes, and many others at his 54 Sound Recording Studio. He makes good dawgs too at the Atomic Dawg in Berkley (www.atomicdawg.com).

Brian McCollum is a longtime, award-winning music journalist for the *Detroit Free Press*.

Scott Morgan has been belting out rock and soul tunes since he was a pre-teenager in the early '60s. One of the true legends of the Detroit rock music scene, Scott first attracted local attention as the soulful front man for Ann Arbor's garage heroes the Rationals. After the Rationals broke up, Scott joined ex-MC5 guitarist Fred "Sonic" Smith, former Stooges drummer Scott Asheton, and onetime-Up bassist Gary Rasmussen to form the near-mythical Sonic's Rendezvous Band. The band released just one single, the classic "City Slang," before Smith left the band in 1980. The remaining band members added Kathy Deschaine to their lineup and continued on as the Scott Morgan Band, releasing the album *Rock Action* in 1990. Re-christened Scots Pirates, they issued a pair of albums: a self-titled effort in 1994 followed by *Revolutionary Means* in 1995. In the late 1990s Morgan teamed with ex-MC5 guitarist Wayne Kramer and Radio Birdman front man Deniz Tek in the band Dodge Main, issuing a self-titled album on Total Energy. In 2000, Scott joined forces with members of two of Europe's hottest bands, the Hellacopters and Nitwitz, to form the Hydromatics. The band released *Parts Unknown*, featuring many of the tunes Scott wrote during his period with the Sonic's Rendezvous Band that were never recorded. In 2001, Scott issued *Medium Rare*, a compilation of unreleased tracks from 1970 through 2000 on Real O Mind. He has toured Europe extensively, both with the Hydromatics and Radio Birdman's Deniz Tek, plus an Italian backing band. The Hydromatics also recorded a second record, *Powerglide*, which was released in early 2002 on Italian label Freakshow. In 2001 Scott formed a new band called Powertrane with Mitch Ryder guitarist Robert Gillespie, bassist Chris Taylor, and drummer Andy Frost. They have issued a live album, *Ann Arbor Revival Meeting*, on Real O Mind. Scott is working on a new full-length studio CD of original material due in 2016 or 2017 with Eddie Baranek & the Sights. For more, visit www.scottmorganmusic.com.

Chris Morton is a freelance B2B communications whiz who lives in the Upper Hudson Valley region. He remembers the '60s and *was* there. In his teens, he presented a "shadow show" alongside the MC5 at a Cranbrook School be-in. In those days, a few very late nights/early morning hours were spent visiting the psycho tropics. Chris enjoyed listening to Dave Dixon and other Air Aces as they carried him away into the ether. 1969 being OK (*all across the USA*), a year later he found himself on the Goose Lake International Pop Festival film crew. His one-off Grande Ballroom handbill appeared in a B. B. King exhibit at the Rock and Roll Hall of Fame and Museum; it was immortalized once again in the Grande documentary, *Louder than Love*.

George "Moseley the Punk" Moseman was in the popular, beloved, outside-the-box band the Frües (a.k.a. Früt of the Loom) from Mt. Clemens, Michigan. Moseley the Punk was one of the famous backup singers in the Frües named "The

Famed Warbles." The Früt released two albums on Westbound Records: *Keep On Truckin'* and *Spoiled Früt.* They have recently released a new 45 rpm on the growingly famous Jett Plastic Recordings of St. Clair Shores. For more, visit www.motorcitymusicarchives.com/frutoftheloom.html.

Marsha Music was born in Detroit and grew up in Highland Park, Michigan—a city within the city of Detroit. She is the eldest daughter of seminal pre-Motown record producer Joe Von Battle and his second wife, Detroit beauty and music lover Shirley Baker. He opened his blues and gospel record shop in 1945. Marsha is a self-described "primordial Detroiter" and "Detroitist"; she is a former labor leader and activist and has written acclaimed essays, stories, and poems about the city's music, and its past and future. She is a noted presenter and speaker, and has contributed to important anthologies, narratives, documentary films, oral histories, an HBO movie, and a much-heralded reading with the Detroit Symphony. Marsha Music was awarded a 2012 Kresge Literary Arts Fellowship and a 2015 Knight Arts Challenge. She has received accolades for her one-woman show, *Marsha Music, Live on Hastings Street!* She is developing important projects in literature, film, recordings, and spoken performances. She resides in Detroit and is married to artist David Philpot. She writes on her blog, Marsha Music—A Grown Woman's Tales from Detroit (marshamusic.wordpress.com).

John G. Rodwan Jr. is the author of *Holidays & Other Disasters* (Humanist Press, 2013) and *Fighters & Writers* (Mongrel Empire Press, 2010), and co-author of *Detroit Is: An Essay in Photographs* (KMW

Studio, 2015). His writing on music has appeared in *Jazz Research Journal*, *American Interest*, *Palimpsest*, and elsewhere. He lives in Detroit.

John Sinclair, author, poet, and activist (born October 2, 1941, in Flint, Michigan), mutated from small-town rock 'n' roll fanatic and teenage disc jockey to cultural revolutionary, pioneer of marijuana activism. In 1966–67, the jazz poet, downbeat correspondent, founder of the Detroit Artists Workshop, and underground journalist joined the front ranks of the hippie revolution, managing the "avant-rock" MC5 and organizing countless free concerts in the parks, White Panther rallies, and radical benefits. Sinclair is now performing throughout Europe solo and in duet with guitarist Mark Ritsema, in Detroit with the Motor City Blues Scholars, and around the United States with a wide variety of collaborators. The poet was recently honored as the international recipient of the prestigious Targa Matteo Salvatore in Foggia, Italy. For more, visit www.johnsinclair.us.

Brian Smith has written for many magazines and alt-weeklies, and his fiction has appeared in a variety of literary journals. He's an award-winning journalist, first as a staff writer and columnist at the *Phoenix New Times* and then as an editor at the *Detroit Metro Times*. Before writing full time, Smith was a songwriter who fronted rock 'n' roll bands. He has penned tunes with lots of folks, including Alice Cooper. His debut collection of short stories, *Spent Saints*, is out in 2016 on Ridgeway Press. For more, visit www.briansmithwriter.com.

Matthew Smith is a musician, producer, and writer. He plays in the bands Outrageous Cherry, the

Volebeats, and Chatoyant. He has worked with a wide variety of artists, including the Go, Crime and the City Solution, and Rodriguez, and has produced albums by Andre Williams and Nathaniel Mayer.

RJ Spangler is a Detroit drummer, producer, manager, and journeyman musician. As a band leader, RJ's main focus is the nine-piece Planet D Nonet, which has garnered four Detroit Music Awards since its inception in 2007. This group is also known as the PD9. RJ leads a strong organ trio (with two EPs out), a soulful blues band (RJ's Gang), and RJ's KC6, where they investigate the blues and jazz of Kansas City. Other important credits include artistic director of Jazzin' on Jefferson, an event he co-founded eleven years ago, and twenty-two years as co-founder/co-artistic director of the AntiFreeze Blues Festival at the Magic Bag Theater. RJ has been chairman of the Detroit Blues Society for over ten years and served as VP for another ten years. He curates at the Detroit Blues Heritage Series for the DBS in cooperation with the Scarab Club, which he has been involved with since its inception eighteen years ago. He was introduced to jazz and blues by his uncle, drummer Bud Spangler, who played with Detroit jazz legends the Tribe and co-founded Strata Records. By the early '80s Spangler had formed his own jazz band, the Sun Messengers, who earned over ten Motor City Music Awards. He left the band in 1992 to devote himself to working with blues artists. For more, visit www.rjspangler.com.

Diane Spodarek is a Canadian-American artist and writer with a background in the visual and performing arts. Her awards include artist's fellowships from the NEA, the New York Foundation for the Arts, Creative New Zealand, and the Michigan Council for the Arts. Her creative work appears in various literary anthologies, including *Dumped: Women Unfriending Women*, in the journal *Limestone*, and others. She performed her one-person show, *The Drunk Monologues*, in New York City, Michigan, Japan, and New Zealand. She was a featured reader of her work at the 92nd Street Y Tribeca and is a member of PEN. Diane lives in Westbeth Artists' Housing in the West Village, NYC. (http://tinyurl.com/dspodarek and www.dangerousdiane.blogspot.com.)

Pat Thomas is the author of *Listen, Whitey!: The Sights and Sounds of Black Power, 1965–1975* and the forthcoming *Did It!: From Yippie to Yuppie, Jerry Rubin: An American Revolutionary* (both published by Fantagraphics). He serves as an A&R consultant to various record labels and has produced reissues of vintage music by Sly Stone, Gene McDaniels, Allen Ginsberg, the Dream Syndicate, Public Image Limited, Carole King, and more. He served as a consultant to the new PBS documentary, *The Black Panthers: Vanguard of the Revolution*. He can be reached at www.facebook.com/pat.thomas.18.

Thomas Trimble teaches English and writing at Wayne State University in Detroit, and he is the founding member of American Mars (www.americanmars.com).

Jaan Uhelszki was one of the founding editors at Detroit's legendary *Creem*, where she helped pioneer a new form of rock journalism that combined critical analysis with a fan's love of music. Since that time her work—characterized by a keen observational eye and an ability to draw out previously unheard confessions—has appeared in *USA Today, Rolling Stone, Spin, NME,* and *Guitar World.* Currently the editor at large at *Relix* and *Uncut*'s American correspondent, she is the only journalist to have ever performed in full makeup with Kiss. Luckily, now she only wears Nars eyeliner.

Rhonda Welsh is a poet, writer, performer, and educator. She is the author of *Red Clay Legacy* and the curator of Wayne State University's "The Business of Art." She also writes about music and popular culture when the spirit moves her. (www.rhondawelsh.com.)

Susan Whitall was born in Philadelphia and has lived in Metro Detroit since she was ten. After earning a BA in English, she translated an article about heavy metal from French to English and parlayed that into a job at *Creem* in 1975. She left as editor in 1983, and has been a music and feature writer at the *Detroit News* since then. She is the author of *Women of Motown* (Avon, 1998) and *Fever: Little Willie John's Fast Life, Mysterious Death and the Birth of Soul* (Titan Books, 2011). Visit her website at www.susanwhitall.com.

Willy Wilson is a well-known Detroit broadcaster. He has hosted programs on WDET-FM Public Radio in Detroit over the years. Currently he hosts the acclaimed weekly radio show *The Motor City's Burning* on CJAM-FM radio broadcasting to the US from its base in Windsor, Ontario. In addition, Willy is a programmer and publicist at the popular Magic Bag Theater in Ferndale, Michigan. Keep up with Willy at www.facebook.com/willy.wilson1.

Al Young is the former California poet laureate and the author of many books, including collections of poetry, novels, and memoirs. "The Drummer Omar: Poet of Percussion," his tribute to jazz great Omar Clay, will appear in *Best American Poetry 2016.* A memoir of his decades-long friendship with poet Denise Levertov is featured in biographer Donna Hollenberg's forthcoming *Denise Levertov in Company* (University of South Carolina Press). Forthcoming from Al Young include: *22 Moon Poems, October Variations,* and *Love Offline.* He is a Distinguished Professor in California College of the Arts' MFA in Writing program in San Francisco. (www.alyoung.org.)

# CREDITS

# CREDITS

Mike Dutkewych: "Strange Mysterious Sounds: The Demise of Ted Lucas and the Spike-Drivers." Printed with the kind permission of the author. © Mike Dutkewych. 2015.

Hobey Echlin: "Inner-City Blues: The Story of Detroit Techno." Reprinted with the kind permission of the author. © Hobey Echlin. 2015.

Hobey Echlin: "Majesty Crush Lurking in the Shadows of Motown and Detroit Techno." Reprinted with the kind permission of the author. © Hobey Echlin. 2015.

Ben Edmonds. "What's Going On? Marvin Gaye and the Final Days of Motown." Reprinted with the kind permission of the author. © Ben Edmonds. 2001.

Larry Gabriel: "Rebirth of Tribe." Printed with the kind permission of the author. © Larry Gabriel. 2015.

Jim Gallert: "Bebop in Detroit: Nights at the Blue Bird Inn." Printed with the kind permission of the author. © Jim Gallert. 2015.

Jim Gallert: "Teddy Harris: A Jazz Man in Motown." Printed with the kind permission of the author. © Jim Gallert. 2015.

Gary Graff. "The Story of Hitsville: Motown Days," "Amboy Duke," "Bob Seger: The Early Days," and "Kid Rock: From Apple Orchards to the World." All appeared in slightly different form in various publications. Printed with the kind permission of the author. © Gary Graff. 2015.

L. E. Grimshaw: "Gary Grimshaw: Poster Child." Printed with the kind permission of the author. © L. E. Grimshaw. 2015.

Bill Harris: "For Beans" and "Roy Brooks: Detroit Downbeat." Printed with the kind permission of the author. © Peter Bill Harris. 2015.

W. Kim Heron: "Musician Interrupted: Faruq Z. Bey." This essay appeared in slightly different form in the *Metro Times*. Printed with the kind permission of the author and the *Metro Times*. © W. Kim Heron. 2003.

Bill Holdship: "Eminem: A Detroit Story." This essay appeared in slightly different form in the *Metro Times*. Printed with the kind permission of the author and the *Metro Times*. © Bill Holdship. 2009 & 2015.

Michael Hurtt: "Nine Times Out of Ten: The Clix Records Story." Printed with the kind permission of the author. © Michael Hurtt. 2015.

Daniel Jones: "Ghettotech: Detroit Is Just Here to Party." Printed with the kind permission of the author. © Daniel Jones. 2015.

Rev. Robert B. Jones Sr.: "Searching for the Son: Delta Blues Legend Son House in Detroit." Printed with the kind permission of the author. © Rev. Robert Jones Sr. 2015.

Herb Jordan: "An Elegant Equation: Changing World, Changing Motown." A version of this originally appeared in Liner Notes of the Universal Music Box of 1967 Motown Singles. Printed with the kind permission of the author. © Herb Jordan. 2015.

Herb Jordan: "Half a Mile from Heaven: The Love Songs of Motown." A version of this originally appeared in *Motown in Love: Songs of the Golden Era*. Printed with the kind permission of the author and Pantheon Books. © Herb Jordan. 2015.

Jarrett Koral: "Future Now: Detroit's Twenty-First-Century Record Label Jett Plastic." Printed with the kind permission of the author. © Jarrett Koral. 2015.

**CREDITS**

Jaan Uhelszki. "Twenty-Five Years of *Creem*: Kiss and Not Tell, or Confessions of One of the Film Foxes." A version of this appeared in *Creem* magazine. Printed with the kind permission of the author. © Jaan Uhelszki. 2015.

Rhonda Welsh: "The Big Three: Contemporary Roots of Latin Sounds in Detroit: The Cruz Brothers, Ozzie Rivera, and Luis Resto." Printed with the kind permission of the author. © Rhonda Welsh. 2015.

Susan Whitall: "Detroit, My Detroit." Printed with the kind permission of the author. © Susan Whitall. 2015.

Willy Wilson: "The Story of Detroit's Third Power Band." Printed with the kind permission of the author. © Willy Wilson. 2015.

Al Young: "A Top-Down Motown Bebop Pubescence." Printed with the kind permission of the author. © Al Young. 2015.

# INDEX

# INDEX

486

HEAVEN WAS DETROIT

HEAVEN WA